A TEXTBOOK OF QUANTITATIVE TECHNIQUES

A TEXTBOOK OF QUANTITATIVE TECHNIQUES

By

N.P. BALI
Formerly, Principal
S.B. College, Gurgaon
Haryana

P.N. GUPTA
B.Sc.(Hons.),M.Sc.(Delhi)
M.Phil (KU),Pre.Ph.D.(IIT Delhi)
Head, Deptt. of Mathematics
Indira Gandhi National College, Ladwa
Kurukshetra University
Haryana

Dr C.P. GANDHI
Ph.D, U.G.C.-NET
Associate Professor, Deptt. of Mathematics
Rayat & Bahra Institute of Engineering & Bio-technology, Kharar
Chandigarh

UNIVERSITY SCIENCE PRESS

(An Imprint of Laxmi Publications Pvt. Ltd.)

An ISO 9001:2015 Company

BENGALURU • CHENNAI • GUWAHATI • HYDERABAD
KOCHI • KOLKATA • LUCKNOW • RANCHI
NEW DELHI

Printed and bound in India

First Edition : 2008; *Second Edition* : 2015, *Edition* : 2025

ISBN **:** 978-81-318-0778-1

Branches

✆	Bengaluru	080-26 75 69 30
✆	Chennai	044-24 34 47 26
✆	Guwahati	0361-254 36 69
✆	Hyderabad	040-27 55 53 83
✆	Kochi	0484-405 13 03
✆	Kolkata	033-40 04 77 79
✆	Lucknow	0522-430 36 13
✆	Ranchi	0651-224 24 64

PUBLISHED IN INDIA BY

(An Imprint of Laxmi Publications Pvt. Ltd.)

An ISO 9001:2015 Company
113, GOLDEN HOUSE, GURUDWARA ROAD, DARYAGANJ,
NEW DELHI - 110002, INDIA

Corporate Office : B-33, Sector-5, Noida,
Gautambuddha Nagar (U.P.) - 201 301, INDIA
Telephone : +91-120-44 46 900
www.laxmipublications.com
info@laxmipublications.com

PREFACE TO THE SECOND EDITION

A Textbook of Quantitative Techniques has been written according to the latest syllabus of **Quantitative Techniques (MBA-104)** *of Punjab Technical University, Jalandhar*. The main objective of this book is to acquaint the MBA students with various statistical and mathematical tools which are widely used in decision making for various business activities. This book has been prepared by keeping in mind the student's capability of solving the mathematical as well as statistical problems so that MBA graduates can understand, analyze and interpret their knowledge in the promotion of their business skills.

The subject matter of this book has been presented in a comprehensive and lucid way and the relevant case study has also been discussed in the concerned chapter.

Errors or misprints, if any, are unintentional and regretted. Any suggestion/ recommendation for improvement of this book are always invited.

We hope that this book will prove to be an asset to the students.

—Authors

PREFACE TO THE FIRST EDITION

A Textbook of Quantitative Techniques has been written strictly according to the latest syllabus of **Quantitative Techniques (MBA-104)** *of Punjab Technical University, Jalandhar and various other universities.* The above cited book has been prepared by keeping in mind the students' capability of solving the mathematical as well as statistical problems. The subject matter has been presented in a comprehensive and lucid way.

Errors or misprints, if any, are unintentional and regretted. Any suggestion/ recommendation for improvement of the book, are invited.

We hope that this book will prove to be an asset to the students.

—Authors

FOREWORD

There is a dire necessity to find solutions to the mathematical/statistical problems faced by the M.B.A. students with different graduation background. Especially students with non mathematical background come across great difficulties. There is a lack of troubleshooting instinct in the students as they feel certain hesitations and lack of confidence to solve curriculum problems.

I have taken the deeper view into the contents of the book '**A Textbook of Quantitative Techniques**' by N.P.Bali and C.P Gandhi. I feel at last there is a ray of hope for the students pursuing M.B.A. degrees to understand basics of the subject.

I strongly recommend this book for the sure shot success. It is a key to all the mathematical as well as statistical problems. The focus of the book is specifically on the students who are reluctant to take up the basics of the mathematical issues. The book unfolds the intricacies of the basics of mathematical solutions and forms the correlation of the mathematics with the other subjects.

I applaud the efforts of the authors who have put forth a solution to all the intricacies of the subject in a very comprehensive manner. The authors can be approached for any recommendations regarding the contents and subject matter.

With Best Regards

Dr. D.S. Randhawa

Director, Rayat Institute of Management, Railmajra, Nawanshahar, Punjab

Unit-I
Introduction to Statistics

1 Introduction to Statistics

1.1. INTRODUCTION

The word '**Statistics**' has been derived from an Italian word 'statista' which means 'State' or 'Province'. Most of the researchers also believe that the word 'Statistics' comes from the German word 'Statistik' which means 'Political State'. The word 'Statistics' was first appeared in the famous book entitled, **"Elements of Universal Erudition"** written by a famous author **'J.F. Baran'.**

1.2. MEANING OF STATISTICS

The word 'statistics' may be defined as *"the science of collection, organisation, presentation, analysis and interpretation of numerical data."*

According to **Prof. Bowley,** *"Statistics may be called the science of counting."*

But this definition covers only one aspect of science, namely the collection of data. It ignores other important aspects like organization, presentation, analysis and interpretation.

According to **Prof. Boddington**, *"Statistics is the science of estimates and probabilities."* This definition is also not complete as it does not cover all the aspects of statistics.

According to **Berenson** and **Levin**, *"Statistics, as a science, can be viewed as the application of the scientific method in the analysis of numerical data for the purpose of making rational decisions."*

Croxton and **Cowden** has defined 'Statistics' as below:

"Statistics may be defined as the collection, presentation, analysis and interpretation of numerical data".

This definition covers almost all the important aspects of "Statistics" but ignores one aspect, that is *"organization of numerical data"*

Hence, based upon the above discussion, we can conclude that the word, "Statistics" satisfies the five characteristics, which are given below:

***(i)* Collection:** It is the first step in the investigation of any statistical data and it forms the foundation of any statistical analysis. A faulty data cannot be reliable. The data can be collected from the existing published or unpublished sources or it can be collected by the researcher himself.

***(ii)* Organization:** It is the second step in the investigation of any statistical data. The data collected from the published sources are generally in an organized form. But, the data collected from unpublished sources need to be organized as it may contain the irrelevant data. The collected data must be edited carefully so that any inconsistency, irrelevancy and wrong computations may be corrected or removed. Once the data have been edited, the next step is to classify it.

Here, the classification of data means to arrange the data according to some common characteristics possessed by the individuals forming the data. After classification, the next step in organization is tabulation of data. Here, the tabulation of data means to arrange the data in rows and columns. The purpose of tabulation of data is to have clarity in the data presentation.

***(iii)* Presentation:** We have collected and organized the data. Now, it is ready for presentation. There are two different modes in which we can present the collected data.

(*a*) Graphs

(*b*) Diagrams.

***(iv)* Analysis:** This is the fourth step of the statistical investigation. The 'analysis' means to get important information useful for decision-making. We can analyse the collected, organized and presented data by using statistical methods such as *measures* of *central tendency, measures of dispersion, moments, skewness* and *kurtosis,* etc.

***(v)* Interpretation:** This is the last stage of any statistical investigation. The word 'interpretation' means drawing conclusions from the collected, organized, presented and analysed data. It is a difficult job and needs a high-degree skill. If the data has not been properly interpretated, the conclusions obtained may be faulty. Properly interpretated data will give valid conclusions which will help the researchers in suitable decisions.

Lastly us, **Prof. Ya-Lun-Chou**, has defined 'statistics' as:

"Statistics is a method of decision-making in the face of uncertainty on the basis of numerical data and calculated risks."

1.3. SCOPE OF STATISTICS

We are familiar by the statistical methods *i.e.,* the methods which can be used to analyse the statistical data are known as *statistical methods*. These statistical methods can be applied to a very number of fields such as, Economics, Sociology, Anthropology, Management, Phychology, Education, Agriculture, etc. But Economics and Business are the two major areas where statistical methods can play a vital role. Also, the government agencies, private business firms and research organizations use statistical methods in the forecasting, controlling and exploring their potentials.

Statistics can become the most important tool for taking decisions in the midst of uncertainty. There is hardly any branch of science today that does not make use of statistics. We now discuss its scope as below:

I. In Business

(*i*) Due to growing size and increasing competition, the problems of the business firms are becoming more complex. Most of the problems are being resolved in the light of factual information. Therefore, statistical methods can be used in finding the solutions of these problems in a systematic way.

(*ii*) With the growth in the size of business firms, it has now become impossible for the owners to maintain personal contact with the thousands and lakhs of customers. Hence, the big firms are facing a great degree of uncertainty concerning future operations. Due to this, the firms may not be able to make profits. Statistics tools can be used to deal systematically the uncertainty. The higher the degree of accuracy, of a busines's man estimates, the greater is the success, attending on his business.

(*iii*) The business activities consists of mainly, production, sale, purchase, finance, accounting, market and production research and quality control. By using statistical methods, we can obtain abundant quantitative information, which can be used in formulating suitable policies.

(*iv*) By using the techniques of time series, the businessman can predict the effect of a large number of variables with a fair degree of accuracy.

II. In Economics

(*i*) Economics is concerned with the production and distribution of wealth, consumption, saving and investment of income. For the proper understanding of the economic problems and in the formation of economic policies, statistical methods can be effectively used.

(*ii*) In production, statistics can help us in adjusting the supply and demand management.

(*iii*) In consumption, statistics can enable us to find out the way in which people of different starta of society spend their income. This will help us in knowing the standard of living and paying capacity of the people.

(*iv*) In stock exchange, statistics can be used to make laws of prices based on supply and demand.

(*v*) Financial statistics can be used in banking, short-term credit, consumer finance, public finance, etc.

(*vi*) Statistics can be used for comparison of market prices, cost and profits of individual firms.

(*vii*) By using statistical land legal tools, we can analyse operational studies of public utilities.

(*viii*) Analysis of population, land economics and economic geography can be done by solving using statistical approach.

(*ix*) Statistical data and statistical methods can play a vital role insolving various problems such as poverty, unemployment, etc.

III. In Testing of Hypothesis: Statistical methods can be helpful in formulating and testing of a hypothesis. For example, the hypothesis, like whether it would rain or not, whether a certain drug is effective in curing swine flu, whether the credit squeeze is effective in checking price increases, etc., can be tested by appropriate statistical tools.

IV. In Prediction Theory: Statistics tools can be used in framing suitable policies and plans well in advance of the time of their implementation. This would help us in knowing the expected demand for the coming years.

V. In Formulating Suitable policies: Statistics can provide us the basic material for framing suitable policies. For example, by using statistics, we can obtain the data about population, its distribution by age and sex, the rate of growth of population, etc. This data can be used in determining the future needs such as food, clothing, housing, education, water, electricity, transport, etc. Similarly, detailed information on the unemployed persons, their skills, experiences, etc. can be helpful for framing suitable policies to tackle the problems in future.

1.4. IMPORTANCE OF STATISTICS

The importance of statistics in the recent years cannot be over emphasized. The growing size and increasing competition in the business has increased its importance. Statistics is now regarded as one of the most important tools for taking decision in the midst of uncertainty. In fact, there is hardly any branch of science today that does not make use of statistics. The following are the main factors which are responsible for its importance.

I. In Planning: Planning is necessary for formulating future policies. Plans and policies of an organization are to be formulated well in advance of the time of their implementation. A knowledge of future trends is very helpful in framing suitable policies and plans. Statistical methods provide the necessary tools for forecasting the future. Hence, statistics is indispensable in planning.

II. In Business (*P.T.U. M.B.A. Dec., 2012*): Statistical knowledge is very helpful to the businessman. Using statistics, he formulates different policies and plans, which further helps him in forecasting the future trends. With the help of statistical techniques, he estimates the market fluctuations, changes in the demand conditions, etc. Hence, statistics can help a businessman for becoming a successful businessman.

III. In Economics: There is a variety of economics problems such as consumption, production, distribution of income and assets, poverty, unemployment, etc. These problems are being solved by using and analysing the statistical data. Also, these problems are described, compared and correlated using statistics. Using statistics in Economics, many economic laws such as **Engel's law of consumption, Pareto's law of distribution of income**, etc., have formulated. Similarly, statistical tools like **index numbers** have become barometers of Economics.

IV. In Politics: By sampling a few voters prior to the election, observers work out the percentage of the votes the candidate will receive in the election. The estimated percentage is used to decide whether a greater campaigning effort is required to assure success.

V. In Natural Science: Statistical techniques are being used in the natural sciences like Astronomy, Biology, Medicine, Meteorology, Zoology, Botany, etc. In diagosing the correct disease, doctors rely heavily on actual data like temperature of the body, pulse rate, blood pressure, etc. In judging the efficiency of a particular drug for curing a certain disease, doctors conduct experiments upon the number of people who are cured after using the drug. In fact, it is difficult to find any scientific activity where statistical data and statistical methods are not used.

VI. In Banking: Almost all the banks use various statistical tools to make a very careful study of the cash requirements without which they may find short of cash and their existence is at sake.

VII. In Computers: The modern computers are capable of performing millions of calculations in mere seconds. This is of great benefit to business and other organizations for maintaing records of their operations.

VIII. In Administration: In ancient times, statistics was used to collect data relating to manpower, crimes, income, etc., for formulating different policies. Now its role has became mainfold. It has become indispensable for the administrators. It is being widely used for the formulation and forecasting different policies and plans of the state administration.

IX. In Business Management: Management has become a specialised job and a manager is called upon to plan, organize supervise and control the operations of the business. Statistical tools like collection, classification, analysis and interpretation of data are essential in business management. The success of modern business primarily depends on accurate forecasting of the future demand and trends. For this, statistics is essential.

X. In Research: Statistics is indispensable in research work. One cannot think of undertaking any research activities without using statistics. Most of the advancement in knowledge has taken place because of experiments conducted with the help of statistical methods. For example, statistical methods are being used to design and analyse the experiments on different type of fertilizers, different types of soils, growth of animals under different diets etc. Statistical methods also affect research in medicine and public health.

In fact, statistics of today has risen from the science of statecraft to the science of universal applicability.

1.5. LIMITATIONS OF STATISTICS

Although statistics has many applications in almost all sciences like physical, social, natural, etc. But it has some limitations, which restricts its scope and importance. The following are the important limitations of **statistics.**

I. It does not study qualitative phenomenon: As statistics deals with numerical data, we can not apply it for the study of those problems which can be stated and expressed qualitatively. As an example, honesty, efficiency, intelligency, blindness, deafness, beauty etc., can not be studied directly. Another example, "Export volume of Punjab has increased considerably during the last five years", cannot be analysed statistically. However, it is possible to analyse such problems statistically by expressing them numerically. As an example, the intelligence level in a class of students can be studied on the basis of their IQ (intelligence quotients).

II. It does not study individual measurements: A single or isolated figure cannot be a part of statistics, unless, it is a part of the aggregate of facts relating to any particular field of enquiry. As an example, price of a single item, increase in the share price of a particular bond, the wages earned by a individual worker, the marks obtained by one student of a class etc., does not constitute statistics. However, the wages of all workers in a factory, average marks obtained by the students in a class, etc., can be analysed statistically.

III. Statistical results are not universal: The conclusions obtained from various statistical methods and tools are true only under some conditions. In other words, statistical results are true only on an average.

IV. It can be misused: The greatest limitation of statistics is that statistics is liable to be misused. For proper use of statistics, we should have enough skill and experience to draw accurate conclusions. It is a great danger for those who do not possess sufficient experience and ability to analyse and interpret statistical data and draw accurate conclusions. As an example, "*The conclusion that the smoking causes cancer because 90% of people who smoke die before the age of 72 years.*", is statistically invalid. Because, the above example does not mention the percentage of those people who do not smoke and die before reaching the age of 72.

Hence, "Statistics are like clay of which you can make a God or Devil as you please."

1.6. APPLICATIONS OF INFERENTIAL STATISTICS IN MANAGERIAL DECISION-MAKING

The 'statistics' can be divided into the following two categories:

I. Descriptive statistics

II. Inferential statistics.

By **Descriptive statistics** we mean those statistical methods which are used in the collection, organization, presentation, analysis and interpretation of data. The most commonly used methods of statistical analysis include, measures of central tendency, measures of dispersion, skewness, moments, kurtosis, correlation and regression etc. **Descriptive statistics** also involve various statistical tools such as Bar charts, Pie charts, Pictographs, Cartograms, line graphs, range chart, band graph, ratio charts, histograms, frequency curve, ogives etc. On the other hand, **Inferential statistics** include those statistical methods which faciliate the estimation of various characteristics of a population or making decisions concerning a population on the basis of sample results. **Sample** and **Population** are relative terms.

An aggregate of items under study is called **population** or **universe**. A finite subset of a population or universe is called a **sample.** The number of individuals in a sample is called the **sample size**.

Inferential statistics mainly work on two factors: **statistical estimation** and **hypothesis testing.**

In statistical estimation, we estimate the value of the population parameter from sample statistics. **In hypothesis testing**, we test some hypothesis about the parent population from which the sample is drawn.

In many situation, we collect data for a large group of elements such as companies, households, products, customers, voters, etc. But, it is not possible to draw conclusion based upon the information obtained from the large population. Therefore, we study a group of individuals, called **sample** and draw a conclusion about a population on the basis of information contained in a sample drawn from that population.

This helps the decision-maker to draw conclusions about the characteristic of a large population under study.

With the growth in the size of business firms, it is quite impossible for the decision-makers to maintain personal contact with the thousands of customers. A manager has to plan, organize, supervise and control the whole operations of any business activity. But due to little contact with the customers, he faces a great degree of uncertainty regarding future policies. Also, most of the production, now-a-days, is in anticipation of demand and therefore, unless he makes a careful study of the market, he may not be able to make profits.

Statistical reports provide a summary of business activities which improve the capability of making more effective decisions regarding future activities. Below are some major areas where a businessman can make use of statistics for making good decisions.

I. In Marketing: Before a product is launched, the manager of a firm, along with his team, makes a pilot survey. For this, he makes use of various statistical techniques to analyse data on various factors such as purchasing power of customers, habits of the customers, number of competitors, pricing of other products, etc. Such studies help the manager in knowing the possible market potential for the product. Therefore, by using the concerned statistical techniques, he can make advertising strategies, routing of salesman, establish sales territories and hence improve the sales of his products.

II. In Production: By using statistical methods, a manager can carry research and development programmes for improving the quality of existing products and set quality control standards for the coming products. This will help him in taking the decisions about the quantity and time of either self-manufacturing or buying from outside.

III. In Finance: By studying the correlation analysis of profits and dividends, a firm manager can predict and decide probable dividends for the coming years. Similarly, the analysis of data on assets and liabilities, income and expenditure, sales and purchase, etc., can help the manager to ascertain the financial results of various operations.

IV. In Manpower Planning: For the smooth functioning of big organizations, a proper manpower planning is essential. A manager can make use of statistical studies of wages, incentive plans, cost of living, labour turnover rates, employment trends, accident rates, training and development programmes, Employer-employee relationships, etc. This will help him in formulating future policies and plans for the overall success of on **organization**.

Hence, statistics and statistical methods can provide the businessman with one of his most valuable tools for decision-making.

TEST YOUR KNOWLEDGE 1.1

1. What is statistics? How do you think that the knowledge of statistics is essential in management decisions? Give examples.
2. Write a brief note on the application of statistics in business and industry.
3. Discuss the meaning and scope of statistics.
4. Define 'statistics' and give its main limitations.
5. Explain how statistics plays an important role in management planning and decision-making?
6. What role does business statistics play in the management of a business enterprise? Examine its scope and limitations.
7. With the help of few examples, explain the role of statistics as a managerial tool.
8. 'Statistics is a method of decision-making in the face of uncertainty on the basis of numerical data and calculated risks'. Comment and explain with suitable illustrations.
9. 'Modern statistical tools and techniques are important for improving the quality of managerial decisions.' Explain this statement and discuss the role of statistics in the planning and control of business.
10. Bring out the applications of statistics in economics and business administration as a scientific tool. Also point out any two limitations of statistics.
11. Give an example of the use of descriptive statistics and inferential statistics in each of the following areas of application in a business firm.
    (*a*) Production management
    (*b*) Financial management
    (*c*) Marketing management
    (*d*) Personnel management.

2

Source and Collection of Data

2.1. INTRODUCTION

Data may be collected either from the primary source or the secondary source. By **Primary source,** we mean a source which collects the data itself.

And a secondary source is one that makes available data collected by some other agency. Thus, *"primary sources are the first hand evidence left behind by the observers of the time of events."*

Examples of primary sources are:

Autobiographies, diaries, emails, letters, correspondences, eyewitnesses, opinion polls, transcripts, cartoons, postcards, posters, photographs, films etc.

"Secondary sources are materials that digest, analyse, evaluate and interpret information contained within the primary sources."

Examples of secondary sources are:

Biographies, textbooks, encyclopaedias, dictionaries, handbooks, commentaries, art, music, research articles of any disciplines, etc.

2.2. WHICH SOURCE OF DATA IS BETTER?

Whenever possible, we should prefer to make use of primary source because of the following reasons:

(*i*) Primacy source contains data in greater details as compared to secondary source.

(*ii*) The primary source includes the schedule and procedure used in collecting the data.

(*iii*) The secondary source may contain mistakes due to errors in the transcription made when the figures were copied from the primary source.

2.3. CLASSIFICATION OF DATA SOURCES

Data sources can be classified into two main categories:

I. Primary data

II. Secondary data

I. Primary Data: It is a data obtained by a study specifically designed to fulfil the needs of the problem at hand. Primary data is original in character and is generated from a large number of surveys conducted by some individuals, institutions, research bodies and mostly by Government. For example, the data obtained by the Census Department of India, Ministry of Home Affairs, etc., are *primary data*.

II. Secondary Data: Data which are not originally collected but rather obtained from some sources, either published or unpublished, are known as *secondary data*.

For example, for the Census Department of India and Ministry of Home Affairs, the Census Data is primary whereas for all others, who use the Census Data, is secondary.

2.4. DIFFERENCE BETWEEN PRIMARY AND SECONDARY DATA

The following points will justify the difference between primary data and secondary data.

(*i*) The data which is primary in the hands of one become secondary in the hands of other.

(*ii*) The data which is primary for the individuals is secondary for the rest of the world.

2.5. ADVANTAGES OF SECONDARY DATA

(*i*) In some cases, it is not possible to collect primary data, then, secondary data becomes the important source for our investigation.

(*ii*) Secondary data can be made available faster than primary data.

For an investigator, it is his choice either to use primary data or secondary data. But the choice between the two data, mainly depends on the following:

(*i*) The collecting agency like individual, organization or Government body.

(*ii*) Financial resource (*P.T.U. M.B.A. Dec., 2012*)

(*iii*) Time

(*iv*) Degree of accuracy.

But most of the statistical surveys depend upon secondary data. Primary data is mainly used in those cases where the secondary data does not provide an adequate basis for analysis. In some cases, both, primary as well as secondary data may be used.

2.6. METHODS OF COLLECTING PRIMARY DATA OR SOURCES OF PRIMARY DATA

The various methods of collecting primary data are shown in the following diagram (Fig. 2.1). We now discuss these methods in details. Their merits, demerits and suitability have also been discussed briefly.

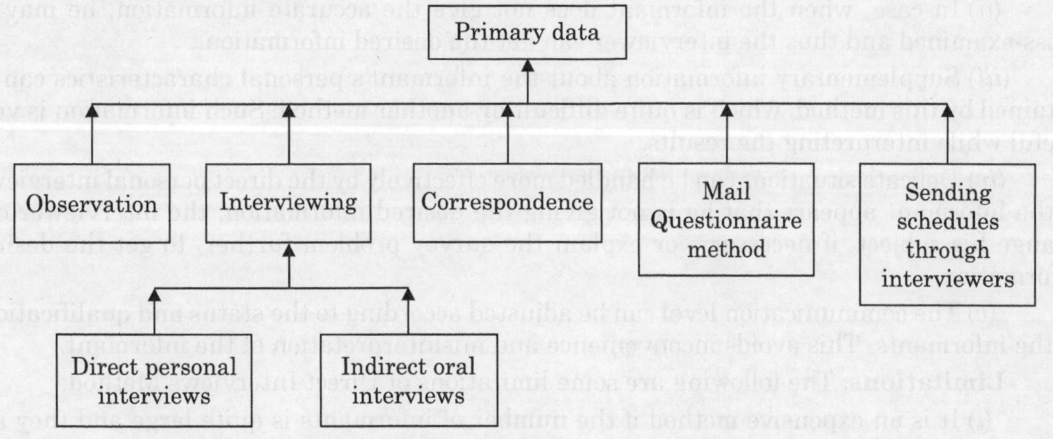

Fig. 2.1. Collection of primary data

I. Observation: In this method, the investigator does not ask the questions directly. He observes and records the behaviour of the informants about the event in which he is interested. He can also use mechanical devices like voice recorder, mobiles, tape recorder, etc., to record the desired data.

Merits: The advantage of this method is:

This method is the best in those cases when the respondent is not in a position to speak or express his feelings or ideas about a particular event. For example, in diagnosis of a particular disease, the diverse opinions of a patient can be studied by observing his behaviour.

Limitations: Some of the limitations of this method are:

(*i*) It is a difficult task to collect the data on account of one's observation. The various factors like observer's training, his opinions, and expectations may not meet the required information.

(*ii*) Observations and inferences may be interdependent.

(*iii*) There may be inadequacy of the sense organs which may reflect significant variations in the observation of the same phenomenon.

Suitability: This method is best suitable for researchers requiring non-self report descriptive data.

II. Interviewing: Interveiws can be conducted either face-to-face or over telephone. Interviews provide an opportunity to establish a report with the interviewer and help to get the valuable information.

***(a)* Direct Personal Interviews:** In this method, there is a face-to-face contact with the informants. The interviewer asks them questions based upon the undergoing survey and collects the desired information. For example, suppose, an investigator wants to know the working conditions of staff nurses at PGI, Chandigarh, he would go to the concerned departments, contact the staff nurses and get the desired information. The information, thus obtained would be original.

Merits: The following are some advantages of direct personal interviews:

(*i*) This method gives accurate information because the interviewer can clear up the doubts of the informants about doubty questions and thus obtain correct information.

(*ii*) In case, when the informant does not give the accurate information, he may be cross-examined and thus the interviewer can get the desired information.

(*iii*) Supplementary information about the informant's personal characteristics can be obtained by this method, which is quite difficult by another method. Such information is very useful while interpreting the results.

(*iv*) Delicate situations can be handled more effectively by the direct personal interviews. If the informant appears that he is not giving the desired information, the interviewer can change his subject, if necessary, or explain the survey problem further, to get the desired information.

(*v*) The communication level can be adjusted according to the status and qualifications of the informants. This avoids inconvenience and misinterpretation of the informant.

Limitations: The following are some limitations of Direct Interviews Method:

(*i*) It is an expensive method if the number of informants is quite large and they are spread over a wide area.

(*ii*) The chance of bias is more under this method as compared to any other methods.

(*iii*) The interviewer needs to be trained and supervised thoroughly. Otherwise, untrained and poorly skilled interviewer may not able to obtain the desired information.

(*iv*) This is a time-consuming method because direct personal interviews can be held only at the convenience of the informants. For example, working women at Rayat Bahra Group can be interviewed either in the evening or on weekends. Since, only one hour or two can be used for interviews in the evening, the work may have to be continued for a long time.

Suitability: This method is best suitable for intensive field surveys.

Note: It may be noted that instead of conducting a face-to-face contact, the interviewer may also obtain the desired information on telephone. For example, the television viewers may be asked to comment on New Education Policy on phone. This method is less expensive than the personal interviews. But there are some serious defects in this method, such as,

(*i*) A limited group of individuals can be interviewed because everyone may not be having phone.

(*ii*) A limited number of questions can be asked on phone.

(*iii*) The informant on telephone may give vague and reckless answers.

(*iv*) There may be a communication error on telephone.

Hence, telephone interviews are not very commonly used.

(*b*) Indirect Oral Interviews: This method of data collection can be applied in those cases when the informants do not incline to respond, if approached directly or the desired information to be obtained is of a complex nature.

For instance, an investigator wants to collect information regarding addiction to drugs, alcohol etc., people may not be ready to supply correct information about their own habits. Then, the investigator contacts third parties called **witnesses**, which are capable of supplying the correct information. The witnesses may be friends, neighbours, etc., or close relatives. **Another example**, if a fire has broken out at a certain place, the cause of the fire may be traced by contacting the nearby people living in that area. Similarly, clues about thefts or murders are being obtained by the police officials by interrogating the third parties who are supposed to have knowledge about the case under investigation.

Enquiry commissions and committees appointed by the State Head, generally, adopt this method to get peoples' views and possible details of facts relating to the enquiry.

Merits: The following are some merits of this method:

(*i*) This method is effective at the exploratory stage of research work.

(*ii*) Time consumed is less as compared to personal interviews.

Limitations: Some of limitations of Indirect Oral Interviews Method are:

(*i*) It may not be possible to arrive at correct conclusions if the people involved do not know the full facts of the problem.

(*ii*) The correctness of the information also depends upon the ability and skill of the interviewers.

(*iii*) It also depends upon the honesty of the interviewers. It might happen that because of bribery, nepotism, or certain other reasons, the interviewers may not reveal the actual facts and supply the wrong information.

Suitability: This method is best suitable in those cases where Indirect Sources of Information are not available.

III. Correspondence: In this method, the investigator appoints some mediators or correspondents at different places to collect the desired information. These correspondents collect and transmit the concerned information to the data processing unit. Newspaper agencies usually adopt this method. Information relating to many events such as accidents, riots, strikes delay time in flights, arrival and departure of trains in busy period, etc., may be supplied to the central office by the various correspondents. Many departments of Government also adopt this method to collect regular information which is to be collected from a wide area. For example, in the construction of consumer price index, wholesale price index, living price index, etc., regular information is obtained from the various correspondents appointed in different places.

Merits: Some of the merits of this method are:

(*i*) It is a cheap and suitable method.

(*ii*) It is the only method for appropriate extensive investigation.

Limitations: Sometimes, due to lack of personal prejudice and bias of the correspondents, this method may not ensure accurate results.

Suitability: The method is best suitable in those cases where the regular information is required from a wide area. As an example, this method is best suitable in case of **crop estimates**.

IV. Mail Questionnaire Method: A questionnaire is a set of questions, specially prepared, for extracting information from the target respondents. In this method, a list of questions relating to the desired information is prepared and sent to the various informants by post or mail. A request is made to the informants through a covering letter to fill up the questionnaire and send it back within a specified time. After receiving the questionnaire from the various respondents, the interviewers analyse it and extract the desired information.

Merits: The main advantages of this method are:

(*i*) It is an efficient method of collecting data when the interviewer knows exactly what is required.

(*ii*) It is easily adaptable in those cases where the field of investigation is quite large and the respondents are spread over a wide area.

Limitations: Some of the limitations of this method are:

(*i*) This method is not effective in those cases when the respondents are illiterate and they cannot understand the written questions and send the answers in writing.

(*ii*) There may be some uncertainty about the responses.

(*iii*) The informants may not supply the correct information and thus the degree of accuracy may not be high.

Suitability: This method is best suitable in those cases where the informants are spread over a wide geographical area.

V. Sending Schedules Through Interviewers: It is a method of sending schedules through the interviewers. Here the term, '*schedule*' is quite different from the term, '*questionnaire*'. "*Questionnaire refers to a device for securing answers to questions by using a format which the informant fills in him/her self. On the other hand, schedule is the name applied to a set of questions which are asked and filled in a face-to-face situation with another respondent.*" Thus, the interviewers contact the informants, get answers to the questions contained in the schedule. He himself fills in the schedule in his own hand writing. It may be noted that the main difference between the "Mail questionnaire Method" and "Sending Schedules Through Interviewers" is that, in the former method, the questionnaire is sent to the informants by post or mail whereas in the latter, the interviewer delivers the schedule personally to the informants.

Merits: Some of the merits of this method are:

(*i*) This method is much better than that of Mail Questionnaire Method.

(*ii*) There is very big response as the interviewers contact the informants personally.

(*iii*) The information is more reliable as the accuracy can be checked on the spot.

Limitations: Some of its limitations are:

(*i*) It is quite expensive method since the interviewers are generally paid workers.

(*ii*) It require a lot of skill, experience and training.

(*iii*) The data collected may contain variation when questions are asked by a number of different interviewers, it is possible that different personalities of different interviewers will cause variation in the answers obtained.

Suitability: This method is best suitable in those cases which demand high role of response from the informants.

2.7. DESIGNING THE QUESTIONNAIRE

As such, there are no set principles that must be used to design a questionnaire. A systematic diagram of designing a questionnaire is shown below. (Fig. 2.2)

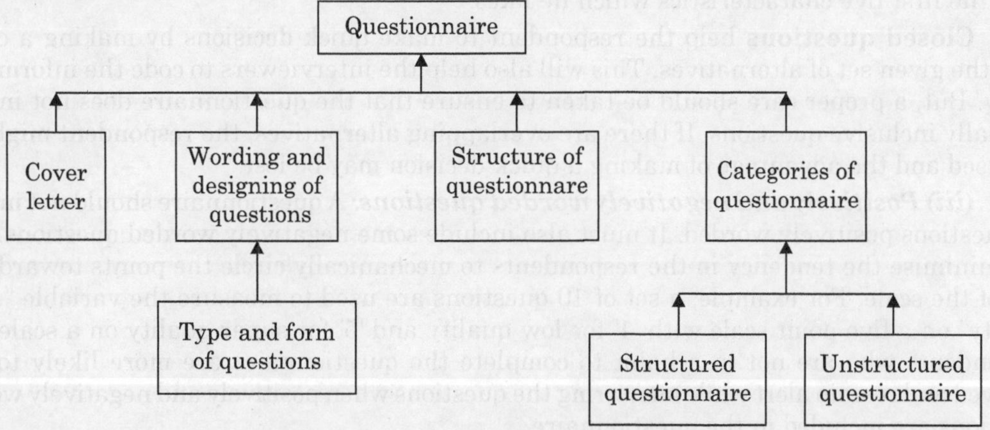

Fig. 2.2. Designing The Questionnaire

The success of the questionnaire method of collecting information depends on the proper designing of the questionnaire. It is a highly skilled job and requires a great deal of specialization and experience. We now discuss in details how to design a questionnaire.

I. Cover Letter: In the first step, the interviewer has to introduce himself and then state the objective of the survey. While drafting a cover letter. The following points may be kept in mind.

(*i*) A brief note about the purpose of the survey and how the respondent would tend to benefit from it, should be enclosed.

(*ii*) A self-address stamped envelope should be enclosed for returning the questionnaire.

(*iii*) The respondent should be assured that his answers will be kept confidential.

(*iv*) If possible, he should be given special offer like free gifts, lunch coupons, etc., on returning the filled in questionnaire.

II. Wording and Designing of Questions: The writing of good questions is an art. For valid and reliable responses, the interviewer needs to design well-worded questions, which are being discussed below:

Type and Form of questions:

(i) Open ended questions: These type of questions allow the respondents to answer them in any way they choose. Some examples of open-ended questions are:

• State five things that are challenging in the job

• Why do you use oral-B toothbrush.

• What do you think about your boss?

• Why do you want to joint Royat Bahra Group?

A proper care should be taken to use this type of questions only where the respondent can answer them correctly. The open-end questions leave the respondent free to give any answer he likes. However, open-end questions are difficult to tabulate as there is no restriction placed upon the variety of answers. Hence, effort should be to minimise the number of open end questions in the questionnaire.

(ii) Closed questions: A closed question is that question in which the respondent is asked to make choices from a given set of alternatives. *For example*, instead of asking the respondent to "state any five things that are challenging in the job", the interviewer may list ten or twelve characteristics that might seem challenging in jobs and ask the respondent to rank the first five characteristics which he likes.

Closed questions help the respondent to make quick decisions by making a choice from the given set of alternatives. This will also help the interviewers to code the information easily. But, a proper care should be taken to ensure that the questionnaire does not involve mutually inclusive questions. If there are overlapping alternatives, the respondent might get confused and the advantage of making a quick decision may be lost.

(iii) Positively and negatively worded questions: A questionnaire should not include all questions positively worded. It must also include some negatively worded questions. This will minimise the tendency in the respondents to mechanically circle the points towards one end of the scale. For example, a set of 10 questions are used to measure the variable "super quality" on a five point scale with '1' for low quality and '5' for super quality on a scale. The respondents who are not in a habit to complete the questionnaire are more likely to stay involved and remain alert while answering the questions when positively and negatively worded questions are included in the questionnaire.

For example, if the respondent had circled ⑤ for a given positively worded question, "I feel I am very effective in my job", he cannot circle ⑤ again to the negatively worded question "I do not feel I am very effective in my job". Also, the use of double negatively worded questions tends to confuse the respondents. For example, the negatively worded questions such as "the healthy people need no tonics" and "only the healthy people should be given no tonics" create a confusing situation in the minds of the respondents.

(iv) Double-Barreled questions: Double barreled questions are those questions which include different possible answers. For example, the question "Do you think that there is a big demand of the item and it will sell well?", is a double-barreled question. Such questions should be avoided and two or more questions should be asked. In the above question, one could answer 'YES' to the first part (*i.e.,* there is a big demand of the item) and a 'No' response to the last part (*i.e.* it will sell well). In this case, two questions: Q.1. "Do you think that there is a big demand of the item" and Q.2. "Do you think that the item will sell well?", should be asked.

(v) Ambiguous questions: An ambiguous question is one where the meaning of the question or the intended answer is not clear. For example, the question such as, "Did you see the girl with the telescope?", the respondent might not be sure whether the question refers to the "the girl who is holding the telescope" or "the girl by using the telescope". Such questions should be avoided in the questionnaire.

(vi) Biased and leading questions: The wording of the question should not lead the respondents to feel committed to answer in a certain way. The question such as "How do you often go to Gurudwara?", may lead the respondent in a falsy way if he, infact, never goes to the Gurudwara. A biased question is one worded in such a way that a particular answer is favoured over others. For example, the question such as "Do you want to eat a hamburger or the usual vegetable sandwich?", is a biased question as it favours hamburger over vegetable sandwich. Hence, in the questionnaire, biased and leading questions should be avoided.

III. Structure of Questionnaire: A questionnaire may include the following components:

(i) Introductory statement: It describes the purpose of the questionnaire, the information required, and how it is to be used. It also introduces the researchers and explains whether the information given by the respondents would be confidential or anonymous.

(ii) Demographic questions: A question used to gather data about specific attributes of the respondent is called *demographic question*. For example, the questions such as "Do you own a bike?", "Are you male?", "Did you vote in the last election?", etc. are demographic questions *Demographic questions* should be positioned first as they can be answered easily and will serve as a "warming" to what follows.

Factual and opinion questions: A question that can be answered only in one way based on the text is known as factual question. On the other hand, a question that requires reflection on the part of the respondent is known as opinion question. In the questionnaire, factual questions should be positioned early whereas opinion questions should be positioned after the demographic and factual questions.

IV. Categories of Questionnaire: A questionnaire can be categorized into two ways:

(*i*) Structured questionnaire

(*ii*) Unstructed questionnaire.

Structured questionnaire is a formal list of questions to be posed to the informants in a pre-determined order. The responses are also completely predetermined. Further a structured questionnaire can be *disguised* and *non-disguised*. If the objectives are not clear, the questionnaire is said to be disguised. If the objectives are clear, the questionnnaire is said to be *non-disguised*. Further, a *structured undisguised questionnaire* is one where the objectives of the study and the particulars of the sponsor are disclosed to the respondents.

A structured disguised questionnaire is one where the objectives of the study and its sponser are not disclosed to the respondents.

Unstructured Questionnaire: In this case, the interviewer does not offer a limited set of responses, but provides only a frame of response within which the informants are expected to answer.

The *unstructured questionnaire* is used in exploratory research studies or when the interviewer is dealing with a complex phenomenon which does not lend itself to structured questioning. Such questionnaires are also useful when the interviewer requires to know the respondent's needs, attitude and motivation level. But this method is time consuming and costly. Editing and tabulation of unstructed questionnaire also impose practical difficulties.

A sample of a questionnaire is given below:

Specimen of a Questionnaire

Consumer's Satisfaction Performa

Name: Mr/Ms/Mrs: ______________________________ Age (Years): ________

Address: ____

City/State: ____________________ Pin Code: ______________Mobile: ____________

Email: ____

Marital status:	☐ Married	☐ Single	Occupation: ________
Family type:	☐ Joint	☐ Nuclear	
Family members:	☐ Adults	☐ Children	
Family income	☐ Less than 10,000	☐ 10,000 to 15,000	
Per month	☐ 15,000 to 20,000	☐ More than 20,000	

Q.1. Which type of food do you normally eat at home?

☐ North Indian ☐ South Indian ☐ Mughlai ☐ Chinese
☐ Continental ☐ Italian ☐ Fast food ☐ Others ______

Q.2. How frequently do you eat out?

In a Week ☐ Once ☐ Twice ☐ Thrice ☐ More than thrice
In a Fortnight ☐ Once ☐ Twice ☐ Thrice ☐ More than thrice
In a Month ☐ Once ☐ Twice ☐ Thrice ☐ More than thrice

Q.3. You usually go out with your

☐ Family ☐ Friends ☐ Colleagues ☐ Others ______

Q.4. Any specific days when you go out:

☐ Weekdays ☐ Weekends ☐ Holidays
☐ Special Occasions ☐ No specific days

Q.5. You generally go out for:

☐ Lunch ☐ Snacks ☐ Dinner ☐ Party/Picnics
☐ Brunch ______

Q.6. Where do you usually go?

☐ Pizza hut ☐ Dominno's ☐ Restaurant ☐ Others ______

Q.7. Who decides on the place to go?

☐ Husband ☐ Wife ☐ Children ☐ Yourself

Q.8. How much do you spend on eating out (one time)?

☐ Below ₹ 200 ☐ ₹ 200–500 ☐ ₹ 500–800
☐ More than ₹ 800 ______

Q.9. What are the factors that determine your choice for the restaurant?
Rank the following from 1–9 (9–highest score):

☐ Pizza hut ☐ Domino's ☐ Restaurant ☐ Others ______

Q.10. Name the fast food giants that you are aware of (in Chandigarh).

☐ Chawla's ☐ KFC ☐ McDonalds ☐ Pizza Hut
☐ Domino's ☐ Slice of Italy ☐ Pizza Express ☐ Others ______

Q.11. How frequently do you go out/order for fast food?

☐ Very frequently ☐ Often ☐ Sometimes ☐ Never ______

Q.12. What do you prefer?

☐ Going Out ☐ Home delivery ☐ Take away ______________

Q.13. Which of the places mentioned above in Q.10 are visited by you (any why):

(*i*) Most frequently ____
(*ii*) Sometimes ____
(*iii*) Never ____

Q.14. What are the distinguishing factors you look for in fast food service? (Rank from 1 to 8, 8–highest score)

☐ Quality ☐ Service ☐ Location ☐ Wide Menu Range

☐ Price ☐ Taste ☐ Home Delivery ☐ Others ________

Q.15. What your order normally consists of?

☐ Pizza ☐ Burgers ☐ Footlong ☐ Curries and Breads

☐ Soups ☐ Pasta ☐ Desert ☐ Others ________

Q.16. The price paid by you for the above is:

Outlets	***Little High***	***Very High***	***Just Right***
Chawla's			
KFC			
Mcdonalds			
Domino's			
Slice of Italy			
Pizza Express			
Others			

Remarks (if any): Date and Place:

2.8. METHODS OF COLLECTING SECONDARY DATA OR SOURCES OF SECONDARY DATA

We have studied in our previous discussions that the primary data can be collected from many sources such as "observation", "interviewing", "correspondence", "questionnaire," and "scheduling" etc. We now discuss those sources from where we can collect the secondary data. The secondary data can be collected through two main sources which are:

I. Published sources (or External sources) of secondary data

II. Unpublished (or Internal) sources of secondary data.

I. External Sources of Secondary Data: External sources are those sources which exist outside the organization. Collecting external data is a difficult task. Besides newspapers and business magazines, the following are the external data sources.

(a) Government publications: These publications are very rich in data and many of these, are freely available on the concerned departmental website. These include:

***(i)* CSO: It is Central Statistical Organization:** This organization publishes the national accounts statistics. It contains estimates of national income for several years, growth rate etc. It also contains the records of various major activities such as agriculture, industry, trade, transport, etc. Annual surveys of industries is published by the CSO. It gives information about the total number of employes, units of production, materials used, etc.

***(ii)* Register General of India:** This office includes details of males, females, births and deaths details etc.

***(iii)* Ministry of Commerce and Industry:** Thus, office provides information on wholesale price index relating to food, fuel, power, grains, etc. It also generates consumer price index for industrial workers, cultural workers, urban and rural workers, etc.

***(iv)* Department of Economic Affairs:** This office conducts economic surveys and generates information on income, consumption, expenditure, investment, savings, foreign trade etc.

(*v*) National Sample Survey: This office works under the ministry of planning and it provides social, economical, industrial, agricultural related data.

(*vi*) Planning Commission: This office provides data related to Indian Economy.

(*vii*) Reverse Bank of India Bulletins: This office provides information on Banking, savings and investments. It also prepares currency and finance reports.

(*viii*) Labour Bureau: This office provides information on skilled, unskilled, technical, non-technical jobs etc.

(*ix*) State Statistical Abstract: This office provides data related to various activities like commercial, education, occupation, etc.

(*x*) Director General of Commercial Intelligence: This office provides information about foreign trade, import and export related data.

(*b*) *Non Government Publications:* These includes various industrial and trade associations such as:

(*i*) The Indian Cotton Mills Association
(*ii*) The Chambers of Commerce Association
(*iii*) The Bombay Stock Exchange—It provides data related to financial accounts
(*iv*) Associations of Press Media
(*v*) Export Formation Council
(*vi*) Confederation of Indian Industries (CII)
(*vii*) Woollen Mills and Textile Mills etc.

(*c*) *Syndicate Services:* These include

(*i*) ORG (Operations Research Group)
(*ii*) IMRB (Indian Market Research Bureau)

These offices collect and tabulate the market information regularly for their subscribers. The main advantages of *syndicate services* are that these services are becoming popular since the constraints of decision-making are changing and we need to take new decisions in the light of changing environment.

(*d*) *International Organizations:* These include:

(*i*) ILO (International Labour Organization). This offices publishes data on total and active population, employment and unemployment, wages and consumer prices etc.

(*ii*) OECD (Organization for Economic Cooperation and Development). This office publishes data on foreign trade, industry, food, transport, science, etc.

(*iii*) IMA (International Monetary Fund). This office publishes data on national and international foreign exchange regulations, foreign trade, economic developments, etc.

II. Internal (Unpublished) Sources of Data: The data generated within an organization in the process of routine business activities are termed as **internal secondary data**. For example, financial accounts, production, quality central, etc., are internal sources of data.

The various internal sources of data are:

(*i*) Sales force report: It gives information about the sales of products.

(*ii*) Accounting resources: It gives information about internal factors.

(*iii*) Internal experts: These people give information about how a particular thing is working.

2.9. ADVANTAGES OF SECONDARY DATA

Secondary data are easy to collect and involve less time and cost. We can identify deficiencies and gaps easily in the collected data and take steps to overcome the same.

2.10. DISADVANTAGES OF SECONDARY DATA

The unit of measurement may not be same as required by the subscribers.

TEST YOUR KNOWLEDGE

True or False Questions (1–10):

1. The statistical method used to summarize data depends upon whether the data are qualitative or quantitative. (T/F)
2. All facts numerically stated are not statistics. (T/F)
3. Statistical thinking focuses on ways to understand, manage, and reduce variation. (T/F)
4. An average value computed from the set of all observations in the population is called a statistic. (T/F)
5. Descriptive statistical methods are used for presenting and characterising data. (T/F)
6. A statistic is a summary measure that describes the characteristics of a population. (T/F)
7. A descriptive measure computed from a sample of the population is called a parameter. (T/F)
8. Enumerative studies involves decision-making regarding a population and/or its characteristics. (T/F)
9. A continuous variable can also be used for quantitative data when every value within some interval is a possible result. (T/F)
10. The summary numbers for either a population or a sample are called descriptive statistics. (T/F)
11. In a recent study of causes of death in males aged 60 years and older, a sample of 120 males indicated that 48 died as a result of some form of heart disease.
    (*a*) Develope a statistic that can be used as an estimate of the percentage of males aged 60 years or older who die from some form of heart disease
    (*b*) Are the data on the causes of death qualitative or quantitative?
    (*c*) Discuss the role of statistical inference in this type of medical research.
12. Determine whether each of the following random variables is categorical or numerical. If it is numerical, determine whether the phenomenon of interest is discrete or continuous.
    (*a*) Amount of time the personal computer is used per week
    (*b*) Number of persons in the household who use the personal computer
    (*c*) Amount of money spent on clothing in the last month
    (*d*) Favourite shopping centre
    (*e*) Amount of time spent on shopping for clothing in the last month.
13. State whether each of the following variables is qualitative or quantitative and indicate the measurement scale that is appropriate for each.
    (*a*) Age
    (*b*) Gender
    (*c*) Class rank
    (*d*) Mode of automobile
    (*e*) Annual sales
    (*f*) Soft-drink size (small, medium or large)
    (*g*) Earnings per share
    (*h*) Method of payment (cash, check, credit card)

14. Suppose the following information is obtained from a person on his application for a car loan from a bank:

(*a*) Place of residence: sec-35, CHD
(*b*) Type of residence: Single-family home
(*c*) Date of birth: 24 August 1998
(*d*) Monthly income: ₹ 50,000
(*e*) Occupation: Software engineer
(*f*) Employer: I.T. company
(*g*) Number of years at job: 07
(*h*) Other income ₹ 20,000 per year
(*i*) Marital status: Married
(*j*) Number of children: 2
(*k*) Loan requested: ₹ 1,00,000
(*l*) Term of loan 20 years
(*m*) Other loan: Study
(*n*) Amount of other loan: ₹ 1,00,00

Classify each of the 14 responses by type of data and level of measurement.

Answers

1. True **2.** True **3.** True
4. False **5.** True **6.** False
7. False **8.** True **9.** True
10. True

3

Classification and Tabulation of Data

3.1. INTRODUCTION

In previous chapter, we have learnt how to collect data. Data may be collected from primary sources as well as secondary sources. The collected data, usually contains schedules and question naire, and it does not give any idea about the salient features of the problem under study. Such data cannot be suitable for presentation, analysis and interpretation. For this reason, the collected data is organized and summarised in such a way that patterns may be easily revealed and interpreted. Classification and tabulation of data gives such a clear picture of the problem under study that no further analysis is required. Classification, infact, is the first step in tabulation. Items of common characteristics are to be brought together before the data can be displayed together.

3.2. MEANING OF CLASSIFICATION

Classification of data is the process of arranging data into groups or classes on the basis of certain properties. Classification of data is an activity very similar to sorting of letters in a post office. Sorting facts on one basis of classification and then on another basis is called cross-classification.

3.3. OBJECTIVES OF CLASSIFICATION

The classification of statistical data serves the following purposes:

(*i*) It condenses the raw data into a suitable form which can be analysed statistically.

(*ii*) From classified data, comparisons and inferences can be drawn easily. For example, university students in M.B.A. course are divided according to sex and then, their results can be compared easily.

(*iii*) Classified data is free from complexities.

(*iv*) It highlights the salient features of the data.

(*v*) It provides information about the mutual relationship among different elements of a data set. For example, we have collected data based on literacy and criminal tendency of a group of people. After classifying, it can be established whether there is any relation between literacy and criminal tendency.

3.4. REQUISITES OF AN IDEAL CLASSIFICATION

An ideal classification satisfies the following characteristics:

(*i*) **Unambiguouty:** The classified data should be unambiguous. Various classes should be defined in such a way that there should be no room for confusion. Only one class for each element should be there in the data set.

(*ii*) **Exhaustive and Mutually Exclusive Classes.** Each element of the data set must belong to a class. Each class should be mutually exclusive so that each element must belong to only one class. For example, classification of illiterate people according to the age: "Below 45 years and above 60 years" is not a correct class because people of age 45 to 60 may belong to both the classes.

(*iii*) **Stability.** The classification of a data set into various classes should remain unchanged.

(*iv*) **Flexibility.** A classified data should be flexible so that suitable adjustments can be made easily in new situations and circumstances. Here, the term **'flexibility'** does not mean instability. It also does not mean rigidity of classes. The term is used in a relative sense. One time classification cannot remain stable forever. With the passage of time, some classes may became obsolete and hence have to be dropped and new classes have to be added. The classified data should be able to adjust itself and yet retain its stability.

3.5. TYPES OF CLASSIFICATION

Statistical data are classified after taking into account the nature, scope and objective of an investigation. The data can be classified into the following four categories (Fig. 3.1).

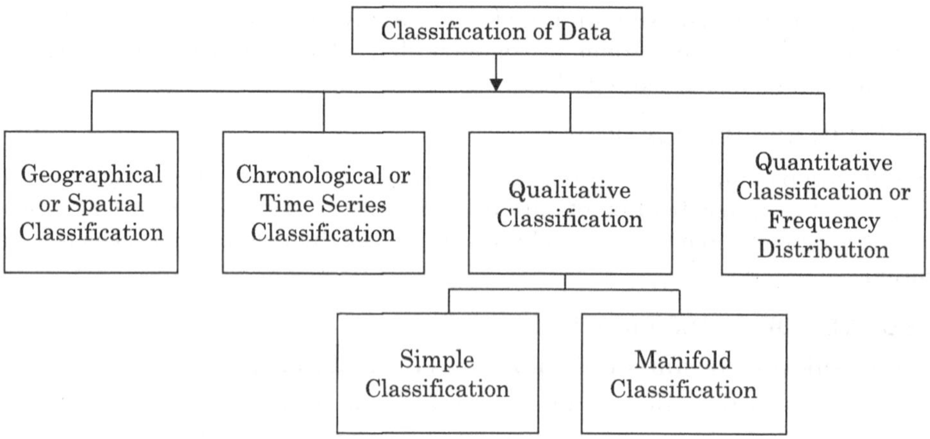

Fig. 3.1 Classification of data.

(*i*) **Geographical or Spatial Classification.** In this type of classification, data are classified on the basis of geographical or locational differences such as cities-wise, districts-wise or villages-wise. The following is an example of a geographical classification (Fig. 3.2).

		2011 Census		
State:	Chandigarh	Delhi	Punjab	Haryana
Density/sq. km	9252	11297	550	573

Fig. 3.2 Geographical or Spatial Classification.

Geographical Classification is also known as **Spatial Classification.** Such classification is generally listed in alphabetical order for easy reference. This approach is followed in the case of reference tables. Elements in the data set are also listed by the frequency size to emphasize the importance of various geographical regions. This approach is followed in the case of summary tables.

(*ii*) **Chronological Classification.** When the data is classified on the basis of time, the classification is known as **Chronological** or **Time Series Classification**. In such classifications, data are usually listed in chronological order starting with the earliest period. The following is an example of chronological classification (Fig. 3.3).

	Chandigarh Population					
Year	1961	1971	1981	1991	2001	2011
Population in (lakhs)	1.19	2.57	4.51	6.42	9.01	10.54

Fig. 3.3 Chronological or Time Series Classification.

(*iii*) **Qualitative Classification.** In this type of classification, data are classified on the basis of attributes such as sex, literacy, region, caste, education etc. It can be done into two ways.

(*a*) ***Simple Classification.*** In this classification, each class is subdivided into two sub-classes. One such example of a sample classification is given below (Fig. 3.4).

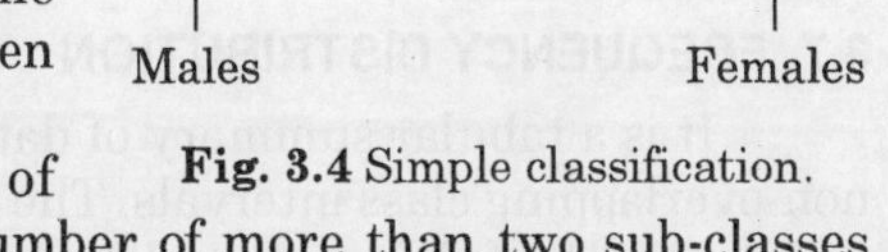

Fig. 3.4 Simple classification.

(*b*) ***Manifold Classification.*** In this type of classification, a class is sub divided into a number of more than two sub-classes which may be sub-divided further. One such example of this type of classification is give below: (Fig. 3.5)

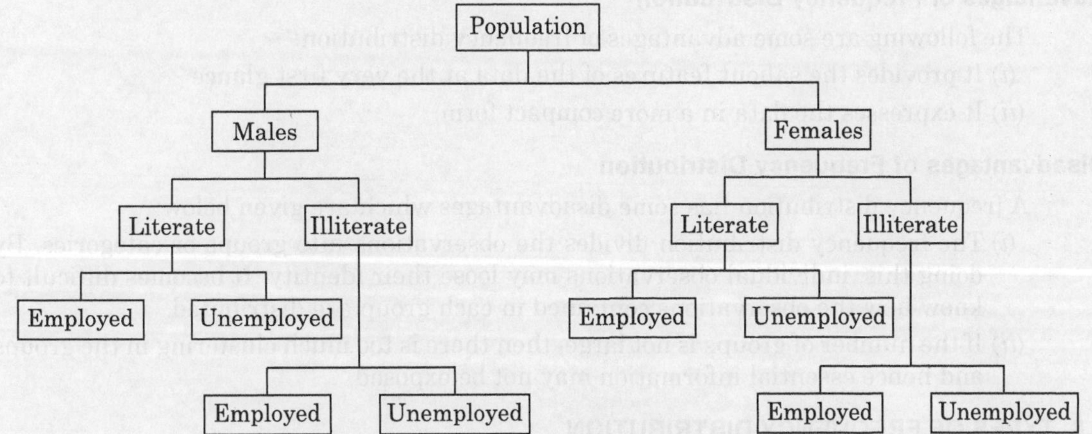

Fig. 3.5 Manifold Classification.

(*iv*) **Quantitative Classification.** In this type of classification, data are classified on the basis of some characteristics which can be measured such as height, weight, income, age, expenditure, production, sales, purchases etc. A quantitative classification is also known as **frequency distribution.** As example of a quantitative classification is given below: (Fig. 3.6)

Age (in years)	*Number of students in a school*
5–10	40
10–15	60
15–20	80
20–25	70

Fig. 3.6 Quantitative Classification.

3.6. ORGANIZING DATA USING DATA ARRAY

When a raw data is arranged in rank order, from smallest to the largest or from largest to the smallest the ordered sequence, thus obtained is called an ordered array.

Advantages of an Ordered Array

The following are some advantages of an ordered array.

(*i*) Data can be divided into various sections.

(*ii*) If any values appear more than once in the array, it can be identified.

(*iii*) Highest and lowest observations in the data can be easily identified.

Disadvantages of an Ordered Array

The following are some disadvantages of an ordered array:

(*i*) It is a time-consuming job to prepare an ordered array of large data

(*ii*) It does not summarize and organizes the data

(*iii*) It does not provide the salient features of the data.

3.7. FREQUENCY DISTRIBUTION

It is a tabular summary of data showing the number of observations in each of several non-overlapping class intervals. The number of observations in each class is called **frequency** and denoted by *f*. A frequency distribution is also known as **grouped data** and *non-overlapping classes* are also known as **groups** or **categories.**

Advantages of Frequency Distribution

The following are some advantages of frequency distribution:

(*i*) It provides the salient features of the data at the very first glance.

(*ii*) It expresses the data in a more compact form.

Disadvantages of Frequency Distribution

A frequency distribution has some disadvantages which are given below:

(*i*) The frequency distribution divides the observations into groups or categories. By doing this, individual observations may loose their identity. It becomes difficult to know how the observations contained in each group are distributed.

(*ii*) If the number of groups is not large, then there is too much clustering in the groups and hence essential information may not be exposed.

3.8. TYPES OF FREQUENCY DISTRIBUTION

By **variable**, we mean a quantity which can vary from one individual to another, *e.g.*, height, weight, age, wage, are variables. A variable is of two types, namely, discrete and continuous.

Discrete (or Discontinuous) Variable. It is that variable whose value changes by steps or jumps and cannot assume a fractional value. In such a case, data are obtained by counting *e.g.*, the number of children a man can have.

Continuous Variable. A variable which can take any numerical value within a certain range is called a continuous variable. In such a case, data are obtained by measurement *e.g.*, the heights or weights of the individuals.

A frequency distribution along with discrete variable is called a **discrete frequency distribution**.

As an example, Consider the number of children in 20 families:

1, 1, 2, 3, 4, 3, 2, 1, 1, 4, 5, 2, 4, 2, 2, 1, 3, 3, 2, 5

The above data may be put in the form given below:

No. of children (x_i)	1	2	3	4	5
Frequency (f_i)	5	6	4	3	2

The above distribution is called **discrete frequency distribution.**

Further, A frequency distribution along with a continuous variable is known as **continuous frequency distribution**.

Consider another example, as shown below:

Marks	0–10	10–20	20–30	30–40	40–50
No. of students	6	11	5	4	4

This distribution is called **continuous frequency distribution.**

Remark. The class 0–10 means the marks obtained between 0 and 10, including 0 and excluding 10.

3.9. THREE TYPES OF SERIES

In this chapter, we will come across the following three types of series :

(*a*) **Individual Observations.** (*i.e.*, when frequencies are not given)

It is a series of observations of the form

$$x_1, \quad x_2, \quad x_3, \quad ......, \quad x_n$$

(*b*) **Discrete Series.** It is a series of observations of the form

x	x_1	x_2	x_3	......	x_n
f	f_1	f_2	f_3	......	f_n

(*c*) **Continuous Series.** It is a series of observations of the form

Class Interval	a_1–a_2	a_2–a_3	......	a_n–a_{n+1}
f	f_1	f_2	......	f_n

For the purpose of further calculations in statistical work, the mid-point of each class is taken to represent the class.

Thus, if m_i is the mid-point of a class, then $m_i = \dfrac{a_i + a_{i+1}}{2}$ and the above series (*c*) takes the form :

Mid-value (m_i)	m_1	m_2	......	m_n
Frequency (f_i)	f_1	f_2	......	f_n

The mid-value of a class may also be denoted by x_i.

3.10. CONSTRUCTION OF A FREQUENCY DISTRIBUTION

The process of constructing a frequency distribution can be divided into two parts.

I. Construction of a discrete frequency distribution

II. Construction of a continuous frequency distribution.

I. Construction of a Discrete Frequency Distribution. The process of constructing a discrete frequency distribution is very simple. Just count the number of times an observation is repeated which is called the frequency of that class. Prepare a column of 'tallies'. In another column, place all possible values of the variable from the lowest to the highest. A **block** containing five **bars** is prepared and leave some space in between each block. Finally, count the number of **bars** and write the frequency. The process is more clear in the following example.

Example 1. *In a survey of 35 families in rural area, the number of children per family gave the following data:*

1, 0, 2, 3, 4, 5, 6, 7, 2, 3, 4, 0, 2, 5, 8, 4, 5, 12, 6, 3, 2, 7, 6, 5, 3, 3, 7, 8, 9, 7, 9, 4, 5, 4, 3.

Construct a discrete frequency distribution.

Sol. Take each item from the data at a time, and place a tally mark (|) opposite to the number of children it belongs. Tally marks are recorded in **bunch of five.** Having occurred four times, the fifth occurrence is represented by putting a cross tally (~~||||~~). The count of tally marks gives us the frequency. Thus, the required discrete frequency distribution of the given data is shown below.

No. of children	*Tally marks*	*Frequency*
0	||	2
1	|	1
2	||||	4
3	~~||||~~ |	6
4	~~||||~~	5
5	~~||||~~	5
6	|||	3
7	||||	4
8	||	2
9	||	2
10	–	0
11	–	0
12	|	1
	Total	35

II. Construction of a Continuous Frequency Distribution

To condense the raw data into a continuous frequency distribution the following steps should be taken.

Step I. Deciding The Number of Classes

Rule I. Let K represents the number of classes and N, the total number of observations, then the value of K satisfying $2^K \geq N$ will be the required number of classes. Here K should be the smallest positive integer.

Consider the example I. Here, the total number of observations is 35. *i.e.,* N = 35, then by rule I.

$$2^3 = 8 < 35,\ 2^4 = 16 < 35,\ 2^5 = 32 < 35.$$

$$2^6 = 64 > 35$$

∴ We choose K = 6 as the number of classes or groups.

Rule II. Strug's Rule of Calculating Number of Classes

According to this rule,

$$K = 1 + 3.222 \log_{10} N, \text{ where}$$

K = number of classes,

N = Total number of observations

In example I, above, we have

$$K = 1 + 3.222 \log_{10} 35 = 1 + 3.222\ (1.5441)$$
$$= 1 + 4.975 = 5.975 \cong 6$$

i.e., we choose K = 6 as the number of classes.

Step II. Determining the Width of Class Intervals

In the construction of a continuous frequency distribution, it is desirable that the width of each class interval should be of same size. The size or width of each class interval (denoted by *h*) can be determined by using the following formula.

Width of class interval (*h*)

$$= \frac{\text{Largest numerical value} - \text{Smallest numerical value}}{\text{Number of classes}}$$

or
$$= \frac{\text{Range}}{\text{Number of classes}}$$

In example I, we have

$$h = \frac{12 - 0}{6} = 2$$

∴ In example 1, the width of each class interval = 2.

Step III. Determining the Class Limits (Boundaries)

The limits of each class interval should be defined clearly so that each observation of the data set belongs to one and only one class. Further, each class has two limits:

(*i*) Lower limit (*ii*) Upper limit.

The **lower limit** of the first class is usually a number ≤ lowest value of the data. The **upper limit** of the last class is usually a number ≥ the largest value of the data.

In example I, the first class is 0–2. Similarly, the other classes are 2–4, 4–6, 6–8, 8–10 and 10–12. The continuous frequency distribution of the data given in example 1 (above) in shown below.

Class intervals	*Tally marks*	*Frequency*
0–2	|||	3
2–4	~~||||~~ ~~||||~~	10
4–6	~~||||~~ ~~||||~~	10
6–8	~~||||~~ ||	7
8–10	||||	4
10–12	|	1
	Total	35

Fig. 3.6 Continuous Frequency Distribution.

3.11. MID-POINT OF CLASS INTERVALS OR CLASS MARK

The mid-value of a class is called **class mark,** *e.g.*, the class mark of the class 1000–1100 is $\frac{1000+1100}{2} = 1050$

Further, $\text{Class mark} = \frac{\text{lower limit} + \text{upper limit}}{2}$

$$= \frac{2\text{ lower limit} + \text{upper limit} - \text{lower limit}}{2}$$

$$= \text{lower limit} + \frac{1}{2}\text{ (Difference of upper limit and lower limit)}$$

Example 2. *Consider the marks obtained by 60 students of M.B.A in final examination in quantitative techniques according to their roll numbers.*

38, 41, 40, 0, 26, 15, 5, 45, 7, 32, 2, 18, 42, 8, 31, 27, 4, 12, 35, 15, 0, 7, 28, 46, 9, 16, 29, 34, 10, 7, 5, 1, 17, 22, 35, 8, 36, 47, 11, 30, 19, 0, 16, 14, 16, 18, 41, 38, 2, 17, 42, 45, 48, 28, 7, 21, 8, 28, 5, 20.

Make an array of the above data and construct a continuous frequency table.

Sol. The given data is raw data or ungrouped data. We arrange them as a grouped frequency distribution. We condense the given data into classes or groups as below:

Step I. Determine the range of the data, *i.e.,* difference in the largest and the smallest numbers occurring in the data.

Here range = 48 – 0 = 48

Step II. Decide the number of classes or groups into which raw data is to be grouped.

Using Strug's rule of calculating the number of classes, we have

$$K = 1 + 3.222 \log_{10} 60 = 1 + 3.222\ (1.77815) = 6.729 \cong 7$$

Let us take the number of classes = 7 (No. of classes should not be less than 5 and more than 30).

Step III. Divide the range by the number of classes to determine the width or size of class interval.

Here size of class interval $= \frac{48}{7} = 6.8 \cong 7$ (integer)

As far as possible, classes should be of the same size.

Step IV. The observations corresponding to the common point of two classes should always be included in the higher class *e.g.,* if 20 is an element of the given data and 10–20 and 20–30 are two classes, then 20 is to be put in the class 20–30 and not in 10–20. That is, every class should be regarded as open to the right.

Step V. Take each item from the data one at a time, and place a tally mark (|) opposite to the class to which it belongs. Tally marks are recorded in bunches of five. Having occurred four times, the fifth occurrence is represented by putting a cross tally (卌).

Step VI. The count of tally marks in a particular class provides us with the frequency in that class.

Step VII. Marks are called the variable (x) and the number of students in a class is known as the frequency (f) or class frequency of the variable.

Step VIII. The total of all frequencies must be equal to the number of observations in the raw data.

Using the above steps, we have the following continuous frequency table.

Class interval (marks x)	*Tally marks (number of students)*	*Frequency f*	*Cumulative frequency c.f.*
0–7	𝍸 𝍸	10	10
7–14	𝍸 𝍸 ‖	12	22
14–21	𝍸 𝍸 ‖	12	34
21–28	||||	4	38
28–35	𝍸 |||	8	46
35–42	𝍸 ‖	7	53
42–49	𝍸 ‖	7	60
		Total = 60	

Fig. 3.7 Continuous Frequency Table.

Example 3. *The following data gives the number of children in 20 families 5, 2, 3, 3, 1, 2, 2, 4, 2, 5, 4, 1, 1, 2, 3, 4, 1, 1, 2, 3.*

Make an array of the above data and construct a continous frequency table.

Sol. The given data is raw data or ungrouped data. We arrange them as a grouped frequency distribution. We condense the given data into classes or groups as below.

(*i*) Here range = Difference in the largest and the smallest numbers occurring in the data = 5 – 1 = 4

(*ii*) Using Strug's rule, the number of classes is given as

$$K = 1 + 3.222 \log 10^{20} = 1 + 4.1919 = 5.1919 \cong 5$$

| Number of classes should not be less than 5 and more than 30

(*iii*) Size of the class interval = $\frac{4}{5} = 0.8 \cong 1$ (integer)

(*iv*) Using the above steps, we have the following continuous frequency table

Class interval (marks x)	*Tally marks (number of students)*	*Frequency f*	*Cumulative frequency c.f.*
0–1	—	0	0
1–2	𝍸	5	5
2–3	𝍸 |	6	11
3–4	||||	4	15
4–5	|||	3	18
5 and above	‖	2	20
		Total = 20	

Fig. 3.8 Continuous Frequency Table.

Example 4. *Present the following as an ordinary grouped frequency table*

Marks below	*No. of students*
10	*5*
20	*12*
30	*32*
40	*40*
50	*45*
60	*48*

Sol. Given is the cumulative frequency distribution.

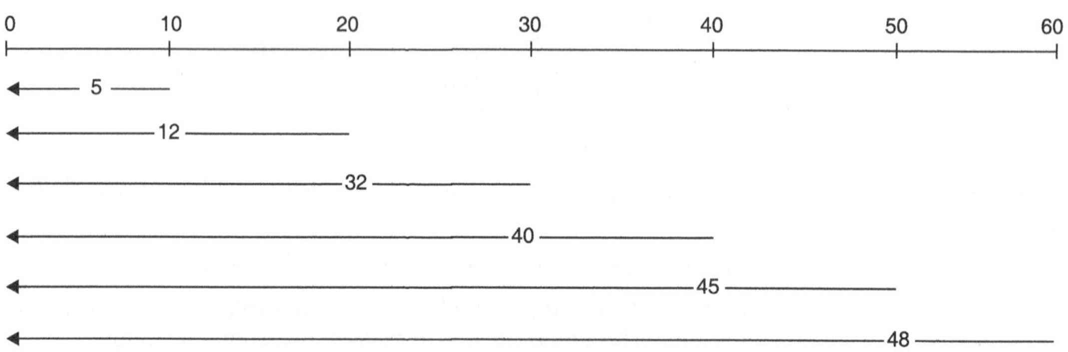

The required grouped frequency table is shown below.

Marks (*x*)	*No. of students* (*f*)
0–10	5
10–20	12 – 5 = 7
20–30	32 – 12 = 20
30–40	40 – 32 = 8
40–50	45 – 40 = 5
50–60	48 – 45 = 3

Fig. 3.9 Grouped Frequency Table.

3.12. CLASSIFICATION OF DATA ACCORDING TO THE CLASS INTERVALS

The data can be classified into two ways :

(*a*) Exclusive Method

(*b*) Inclusive Method.

(*a*) Exclusive Method. When the class intervals are so fixed that the upper limit of one class is the lower limit of the next class, it is known as **Exclusive Method of Classification** of data. That is to say, in this method, the upper limit of a class is not included in the class, *e.g.*, in the class 0–10, of marks obtained by a student, a student who has obtained 10 marks is not included in the class 0–10, he is counted in the next class 10–20.

***(b)* Inclusive Method.** In this method, the classes are so formed that the upper limit of a class is also included in that class, *e.g.* :

Wages	*No. of workers*
1000–1099	125
1100–1199	150
1200–1299	200

Here the upper limit of a class is not the lower limit of the next class. Therefore, the data is classified inclusively.

Consider the following data :

I		II	
Wages	*No. of workers*	*Wages*	*No. of workers*
1000–1100	125	1000–1099	125
1100–1200	150	1100–1199	150
1200–1300	200	1200–1299	200
Exclusive Classification		Inclusive Classification	

Both the exclusive and inclusive classification, give the same class frequency, but different class intervals. In exclusive classification, the class interval is 100 where as in inclusive classification, the class interval is 99. We now discuss a method to convert inclusive classification of data into exclusive classification.

3.13 METHOD : OF CONVERTING INCLUSIVE CLASSIFICATION INTO EXCLUSIVE CLASSIFICATION

Let a–b is a class in inclusive classification. Take $\left(a-\frac{h}{2}, b+\frac{h}{2}\right)$ as a class in exclusive classification, where

h = (lower limit of a class) – (upper limit of the previous class). Consider the following example.

Example 5. *Convert the following data classification :*

Wages	*No. of workers*
1000–1099	*125*
1100–1199	*150*
1200–1299	*200*

into exclusive classification.

Sol. Here $h = 1100 - 1099 = 1200 - 1199 = 1$

$$\Rightarrow \quad \frac{h}{2} = \frac{1}{2} = 0.5$$

The exclusive classification is

Wages	*No. of workers*
999.5–1099.5	125
1099.5–1199.5	150
1199.5–1299.5	200

Example 6. *The following set of numbers represents the total number of transactions at the end of a day in 40 ATMs.*

10	*17*	*15*	*22*	*11*	*16*	*19*	*24*	*29*	*18*
25	*26*	*32*	*14*	*17*	*20*	*23*	*27*	*30*	*12*
15	*18*	*24*	*36*	*18*	*15*	*21*	*28*	*33*	*38*
34	*13*	*10*	*16*	*20*	*22*	*29*	*29*	*23*	*31*

Arrange these into a frequency distribution having a suitable number of classes.

Sol. Here N = 40, choose K such that $2^K \geq 40$

Here, $2^5 = 32, \quad 2^6 = 64$

$\therefore$ $2^6 \geq 40$

Hence K = 6

Also, By Strug's rule, $K = 1 + 3.222 \log_{10} 40 = 6.1618 \cong 6$

Also the smallest value is 10 and the largest 38, therefore the class interval is given by

$$h = \frac{\text{Range}}{\text{Number of classes}} = \frac{38 - 10}{6} = \frac{28}{6} = 4.66 \cong 5$$

Now performing the actual tally and counting the number of values in each class, we get the frequency distribution by exclusive method as shown below.

Class interval	*Tally*	*Frequency*
10–15	𝍸 I	6
15–20	𝍸 𝍸 I	11
20–25	𝍸 IIII	9
25–30	𝍸 II	7
30–35	𝍸	5
35–40	II	2
	Total	40

Fig. 3.10 Exclusive classification.

Example 7. *The take-home salary (in ₹) of 30 unskilled women workers from a company for a particular month are:*

2482	*2392*	*2499*	*2412*	*2440*	*2444*
2446	*2540*	*2394*	*2365*	*2412*	*2458*
2482	*2394*	*2450*	*2444*	*2440*	*2494*
2460	*2425*	*2500*	*2390*	*2414*	*2365*
2390	*2460*	*2422*	*2500*	*2470*	*2428*

Arrange these into a frequency distribution having a suitable number of classes.

Sol. Here N = 30, choose K such that $2^K \geq 30$

Here, $2^4 = 16 < 30, \; 2^5 = 32 \geq 30$

$\therefore$ K = 5

Also, by Strug's rule, $K = 1 + 3.222 \log_{10} 30 = 5.7592$

$\therefore$ We can also take K = 6

In the data set, the smallest value is 2365 and the largest is 2540, so the width of each class interval will be

$$h = \frac{\text{Range}}{\text{Number of classes}} = \frac{2540 - 2365}{5} = \frac{175}{5} = 35$$

Sorting the data values into classes and counting the number of values in each class, we get the frequency distribution by exclusive method as given below:

Class interval (Salary ₹)	*Tally*	*Frequency (Number of female workers)*
2365–2400	卌 I	6
2400–2435	卌 II	7
2435–2470	卌 卌	10
2470–2505	卌 I	6
2505–2540	I	1
	Total	30

Fig. 3.11 Exclusive Classification.

Example 8. *Consider the following increase in D.A. (Daily Allowances) in the salaries of employees of a company at the following rates.*

₹ 250 for the salary range up to ₹ 4749
₹ 260 for the salary range up to ₹ 4750
₹ 270 for the salary range up to ₹ 4950
₹ 280 for the salary range up to ₹ 5150
₹ 290 for the salary range up to ₹ 5350

There is no increase of D.A. for salary ₹ 5500 or more. What will be the additional amount required to be paid by the company in a year which has 32 employees with the following salaries (in ₹)

5422	*4714*	*5182*	*5342*	*4835*	*4719*	*5234*	*5035*
5085	*5482*	*4673*	*5335*	*4888*	*4769*	*5092*	*4735*
5542	*5058*	*4730*	*4930*	*4978*	*4822*	*4686*	*4730*
5429	*5545*	*5345*	*5250*	*5375*	*5542*	*5585*	*4749*

Sol. Sorting the data values into classes and counting the number of values in each class, the exclusive classification of the frequency distribution is given below.

Class interval (Pay Range)	*Tally*	*Frequency (Number of Employees) (f)*	*Rate of D.A. (x)*	*Total Amount Paid (fx)*
upto 4749	卌 III	8	250	2000
Between 4750–4949	卌	5	260	1300
Between 4950–5149	卌	5	270	1350
Between 5150–5349	卌 I	6	280	1680
Between 5350–5549	卌 III	8	290	2320
	Total	32		8650

Fig. 3.12 Frequency distribution.

Hence addition amount required by the company for payment of D.A. is ₹ 8650.

Example 9. *The number of items of similar type produced in a factory during the last 50 days are as under:*

21	*22*	*17*	*23*	*27*	*15*	*16*	*22*	*15*	*23*
24	*25*	*36*	*19*	*14*	*21*	*24*	*25*	*14*	*18*
20	*31*	*22*	*19*	*18*	*20*	*21*	*20*	*36*	*18*
21	*20*	*31*	*22*	*19*	*18*	*20*	*20*	*24*	*35*
25	*26*	*19*	*32*	*22*	*26*	*25*	*26*	*27*	*22*

Arrange these observations into a frequency distribution with both inclusive and exclusive class intervals by choosing a suitable number of classes.

Sol. Here N = Total number of observations = 50

$\therefore$ $2^K \geq 50$ is true if K = 6.

Also
$$h = \frac{\text{Largest numerical value} - \text{Smallest numerical value}}{\text{Number of classes}}$$

$$= \frac{36 - 14}{6} = 3.66 \cong 4$$

Performing the actual tally and counting the number of observation is each class, we get the following frequency distribution with inclusive class intervals as shown in Fig. 3.13.

Class interval	*Tally*	*Frequency*
14–17	𝍸 I	6
18–21	𝍸 𝍸 𝍸 III	18
22–25	𝍸 𝍸 𝍸	15
26–29	𝍸	5
30–33	III	3
34–33	III	3
	Total	50

Fig. 3.13 Inclusive Classification.

Further, Converting the class intervals shown in Fig. 3.13 into exclusive class intervals is shown in Fig. 3.14.

Here, $h = 18 - 17 = 22 - 21 = 1$

$\therefore \quad \frac{h}{2} = \frac{1}{2} = 0.5$

Class interval	*Mid-value*	*Frequency*
13.5–17.5	15.5	6
17.5–21.5	19.5	18
21.5–25.5	23.5	15
25.5–29.5	27.5	5
29.5–33.5	31.5	3
33.5–37.5	35.5	3
	Total	50

Fig. 3.14 Exclusive classification.

3.14. BIVARIATE FREQUENCY DISTRIBUTION

If the data involves only one variable, then the frequency distribution so obtained is called a *univariate frequency distribution.* (see examples 2, 3, 4 above). When the data involves two variables (such as profit (x) and expenditure (y), Income (x) and loss (y), supply (x) and demand (y) of a group of individuals etc., then the frequency distribution so obtained is called a **bivariate frequency distribution** or **two-way frequency distribution**. It one variable, say, x is grouped in m classes and the other variable, say y is grouped into n classes. Then total number of cells in the bivariate frequency table will be $m \times n$. The frequencies of the values of the variable x for a given values of the variable y and vice-versa are called **conditional frequencies**. The frequencies of the values of the variables x and y together with their frequency totals are called the **marginal frequencies.**

Example 10. *Consider the following data on income and expenditure on food of a group of 25 families. Construct a bivariate frequency distribution by classifying the income into class intervals as 200–300, 300–400, 400–500, ... and so on, and the expenditure into class-intervals as 10–15, 15–20, 20–25,... and so on.*

Also write the marginal distribution of the variables income and expenditure and the conditional distribution of income when the expenditure lies between 15 and 20.

Income	*Expenditure*	*Income*	*Expenditure*	*Income*	*Expenditure*	*Income*	*Expenditure*	*Income*	*Expenditure*
550	*12*	*225*	*25*	*680*	*13*	*202*	*29*	*689*	*11*
623	*14*	*310*	*26*	*300*	*25*	*255*	*27*	*523*	*12*
310	*18*	*640*	*20*	*425*	*16*	*492*	*18*	*317*	*18*
420	*16*	*512*	*18*	*555*	*15*	*587*	*21*	*384*	*17*
600	*15*	*690*	*12*	*325*	*23*	*643*	*19*	*400*	*19*

Sol. Denote the income variable by x and the expenditure variable by. The class 200–300 includes the number of those people whose income lies in 200–300, excluding 300. The number of such people is zero. The class 600–700 includes the income such as 600, 623, 640, 643, 680, 689, 690. Therefore the number of people whose income lies in the class 600–700, excluding 700 is 7.

The bivariate frequency distribution showing income and expenditure on food of 25 families is shown below.

Income (x) / *Expenditure (y)*	*200–300*	*300–400*	*400–500*	*500–600*	*600–700*	*Marginal frequency* (f_y)
10–15	–	–	–	||	||||	6
15–20	–	|||	||||	||	||	11
20–25	–	|	–	|	|	3
25–30	|||	||	–	–	–	5
Marginal frequency (f_x)	3	6	4	5	7	25

Fig. 3.15 Bivariate Frequency Distribution for Income (x) and Expenditure (y).

Now, the conditional distribution of x when y lies between 15–20 is given below:

Income (x)	200–300	300–400	400–500	500–600	600–700
15–20	0	3	4	2	2

Example 11. *The following data give the points scored in a lawn tennis match by two players A and B at the end of 20 games.*

(10, 12) (7, 11) (7, 9) (15, 19) (17, 21) (12, 8) (16, 10) (14, 14) (22, 18) (16, 7)

(15, 16) (22, 20) (19, 15) (7, 18) (11, 11) (12, 18) (10, 10) (5, 13) (11, 7) and (10, 10)

Assuming class intervals as: 5 – 9, 10 – 14, 15 – 19 ..., for both A and B, prepare.

(i) Bivariate frequency table

(ii) Conditional frequency distribution of B given A > 15.

Sol. The ordered pair (10, 12) indicates that the points scored by the player A is 10 and of B is 12. We calculate the frequencies of various cells. We have considered some cells and obtained the frequencies of these cells as below.

Player A / *Player B*	*5–9*	*10–14*	*15–19*	*20–24*
5–9	C_{11}	C_{12}	C_{13}	C_{14}

To calculate the frequency of the cell C_{11}. For player A, the points scored by him are lying in the class 5–9. The points scored by the player B are lying in the class 5–9. Number of such ordered pairs is 1. (*i.e.*, (7, 9))

To calculate the frequency of the cell C_{12}. For player A, the points scored by the player A are lying in the class 10 – 14. For player B, the points scored by him are lying in the class 5–9. Number of such ordered pairs are 2 (*i.e.*, (12, 8) and (11, 7)).

Similarly, the frequencies of other various cells can be calculated.

The bivariate frequency table for the two players A and B is shown below:

Player A scores → / *Player B scores* ↓	*5–9*	*10–14*	*15–19*	*20–24*	*Marginal frequency* (f_y)
5–9	|	||	|	–	4
10–14	||	~~||||~~	|	–	8
15–19	|	|	|||	|	6
20–24	–	–	|	|	2
Marginal frequency (f_x)	4	8	6	2	20

Fig. 3.16 Bivariate Frequency Table.

The conditional distribution for the player B given A > 15 is given below:

Player A → / *Player B* ↓	*15–19*	*20–24*
5–9	|	–
10–14	|	–
15–19	|||	|
20–24	|	|
	6	2

Fig. 3.17 Conditional Frequency Table.

3.15. TYPES OF FREQUENCY DISTRIBUTION

A frequency distribution can be divided into three types:

I. Cumulative frequency distribution

II. Percentage frequency distribution

III. Relative frequency distribution.

We now discuss these types of frequency distributions in details. (Fig. 3.18)

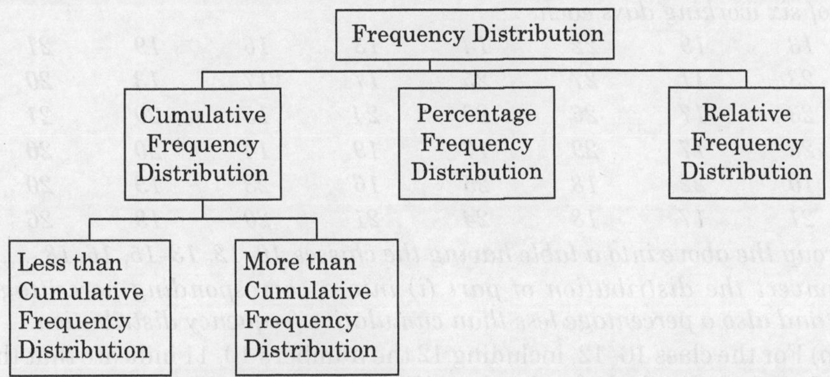

Fig. 3.18 Types of Frequency Distribution.

I. Cumulative Frequency Distribution. In this type of cumulative frequency distribution, the frequencies of each class interval are added successively from top to bottom or from bottom to top. A cumulative frequency distribution is of two types.

(*i*) Less than cumulative frequency distribution

(*ii*) More than cumulative frequency distribution.

(*i*) **In less than cumulative frequency distribution**, the frequencies of each class interval are added successively from top to bottom and we represent the cumulative number of observation less than or equal to the class frequency to which it relates.

(*ii*) **In more than cumulative frequency distribution**. The frequencies of each class interval are added successively from bottom to top and we represent the cumulative number of observations greater than or equal to the class frequency to which it relates. Consider the following example.

Example 12. *Consider the marks distribution in a class.*

Marks	*No. of students*
0–10	*4*
10–20	*6*
20–30	*9*
30–40	*6*
40–50	*2*

Prepare the "cumulative frequency less than" and "cumulative frequency greater than".

Sol.

Marks	*Frequency*	*c.f. less than*	*c.f. greater than*
0–10	4	4 ↓	27 ↑
10–20	6	10	23
20–30	9	19	17
30–40	6	25	8
40–50	2	27	2

Fig. 3.19 Cumulative Frequency Table.

II. Percentage Frequency Distribution. In this type of frequency distribution, the number of observations for each class interval is converted into a percentage frequency by dividing it by the total number of observations in the entire distribution. Multiply the quotient so obtained by 100 to get the percentage frequency distribution.

Consider the following example

Example 13. *Consider the following number of two wheelers sold by a dealer during eight weeks of six working days each.*

13	*19*	*22*	*14*	*13*	*16*	*19*	*21*
23	*11*	*27*	*25*	*17*	*17*	*13*	*20*
23	*17*	*26*	*20*	*24*	*15*	*20*	*21*
23	*17*	*29*	*17*	*19*	*14*	*20*	*20*
10	*22*	*18*	*25*	*16*	*23*	*19*	*20*
21	*17*	*18*	*24*	*21*	*20*	*19*	*26*

(a) Group the above into a table having the classes 10–12, 13–15, 16–18, ..., and so on

(b) Convert the distribution of part (i) into a corresponding percentage frequency distribution and also a percentage less than cumulative frequency distribution.

Sol. (*a*) For the class 10–12, including 12 the numbers 10, 11 indicate that the frequency of the class 10–12 is 2. Similarly for the class 13–15, (including 15) the numbers 13, 14, 13, 13, 15, 14 indicate that the frequency of the class is 6. Thus, the following distribution is obtained.

Number of two wheelers sold (Class intervals)	*Tally*	*Number of Days (Frequency)*
10–12	||	2
13–15	~~||||~~ |	6
16–18	~~||||~~ ~~||||~~	10
19–21	~~||||~~ ~~||||~~ ~~||||~~ |	16
22–24	~~||||~~ |||	8
25–27	~~||||~~	5
28–30	|	1
	Total	48

Fig. 3.20 Frequency Table.

(*b*) The percentage frequency distribution and percentage less than cumulative frequency distribution are obtained below.

Number of two wheelers sold (Class intervals)	*Number of Days (Frequency)*	*Cumulative Frequency (less than)*	*Percentage Frequency*	*Percentage less than cumulative frequency*
10–12	2	2	$\frac{2}{48} \times 100 = 4.1666 \cong 4.17$	4.17
13–15	6	8	$\frac{6}{48} \times 100 = 12.5 = 12.50$	16.67
16–18	10	18	20.83	37.50
19–21	16	34	33.34	70.84
22–24	8	42	16.67	87.51
25–27	5	47	10.41	97.92
28–30	1	48	2.08	100.00
Total	48		100.00	

Fig. 3.21 Percentage and Less Than Cumulative Percentage Table.

III. Relative Frequency Distribution: To convert a frequency distribution into a corresponding **relative frequency distribution,** we divide each class frequency by the total number of observations in the entire distribution. One such frequency distribution is shown below: (Fig. 3.22)

Number of Accidents	*No. of Weeks (Frequency)*	*Relative Frequency*	*Percentage Frequency*
0–4	5	$\frac{5}{50} = 0.10$	$\frac{5}{50} \times 100 = 10$
5–9	22	$\frac{22}{50} = 0.44$	$\frac{22}{50} \times 100 = 44$
10–14	13	$\frac{13}{50} = 0.26$	$\frac{13}{50} \times 100 = 26$
15–19	8	$\frac{8}{50} = 0.16$	$\frac{8}{50} \times 100 = 16$
20–24	2	$\frac{2}{50} = 0.04$	$\frac{2}{50} \times 100 = 4$
	50	1.00	100

Fig. 3.22 Relative and Percentage Frequency Table

Example 14. *The frequency distribution of the ages of the inhabitants of two villages are given below :*

Age group	*No. of inhabitants*	
	Village A	*Village B*
0–5	*18*	*35*
5–10	*26*	*38*
10–20	*25*	*40*
20–30	*29*	*32*
30–40	*21*	*27*
40–50	*14*	*23*
50–60	*6*	*18*
60–80	*4*	*15*

Prepare the relative frequency table.

Sol.

Age Group	*No. of inhabitants*		*Relative frequency*	
	Village A	*Village B*	*Village A*	*Village B*
0–5	18	35	$\frac{18}{143} \times 100 = 12.6$	$\frac{35}{228} \times 100 = 15.3$
5–10	26	38	$\frac{26}{143} \times 100 = 18.2$	$\frac{38}{228} \times 100 = 16.6$
10–20	25	40	17.4	17.5
20–30	29	32	20.2	14.03
30–40	21	27	14.6	11.84
40–50	14	23	9.79	10.08
50–60	6	18	4.19	7.89
60–80	4	15	2.79	6.57
Total	143	228		

Fig. 3.23 Relative Frequency Table.

TEST YOUR KNOWLEDGE 3.1

1. Explain the characteristics and objectives of a frequency distribution.
2. Discuss two methods of classifying data in class-intervals.
3. Distinguish clearly between a continuous variable and a discrete variable. Give two examples of continuous variables and two examples of discrete variables that might be used by a statistician.
4. What are the advantages of using a frequency distribution to describe a body of raw data? What are the disadvantages?
5. When constructing a grouped frequency distribution, should equal intervals always be used? Under what circumstance should unequal intervals be used instead?
6. What are the advantages and disadvantages of using open-end intervals when constructing a group frequency distribution?
7. Why is it necessary to summarize data? Explain the approaches available summarize data distributions.
8. Discuss various types of frequency distribution.
9. How can you construct a frequency distribution? Discuss with examples.
10. What do you understand by bivariate or two-way frequency distribution?
11. The weights in grams of 50 apples picked at random from a consignment are as follows:

    106, 107, 76, 82, 109, 107, 115, 93, 187, 195, 123, 125, 111, 92, 86, 70, 126, 68, 130, 129, 139, 119, 115, 128, 100, 186, 84, 99, 113, 204, 111, 141, 136, 123, 90, 115, 98, 110, 78, 90, 107, 81, 131, 75, 84, 104, 110, 80, 118, 82.

    Form the grouped frequency table by dividing the various range into intervals of equal width, each correspond to 20 gms in such a way that the mid-value of the first class corresponds to 70 gms.
12. Form an ordinary frequency table from the following table:

Marks	*No. of students*
above 0	40
above 10	30
above 20	25
above 30	18
above 40	12
above 50	0

13. Form an ordinary frequency table from the following data:

Marks	*No. of students*
below 10	5
below 20	7
below 30	13
below 40	20
below 50	30
below 60	38

14. If class mid-points in a frequency distribution of the ages of a group of persons are : 25, 32, 39, 46, 53, and 60, find:

    (*a*) the size of the class-interval (*d*) the class boundaries

    (*c*) the class limits, assuming that the age quoted is the age completed on the last birthdays

15. A wholesaler's daily shipments of a particular item varied from 1,152 to 9,888 units per day. Indicate the limits of nine classes into which these shipments might be grouped.

Answers

11. Ground frequency table

Weight in grams	*No. of apples*	*Frequency*
60–80	𝍸	5
80–100	𝍸 𝍸 |||	13
100–120	𝍸 𝍸 𝍸 ||	17
120–140	𝍸 𝍸	10
140–160	|	1
160–180	—	0
180–200	|||	3
200–220	|	1
	Total	50

12.

Marks	*No. of students*
0–10	10
10–20	5
20–30	7
30–40	6
40–50	12

13.

Marks	*No. of students*
0–10	5
10–20	2
20–30	6
30–40	9
40–50	8
50–60	8

14. (*a*) Size of the class interval = Difference between the mid-values of any two consecutive classes $= 32 - 25 = 39 - 32 = 7$

(*b*) The class boundaries for different classes are obtained by adding (for upper class boundaries or limits) and subtracting (for lower class boundaries or limits) half the magnitude of the class interval from the mid-values. The class boundaries for the class mid-point 25 is

$$\left(25 - \frac{7}{2}, 25 + \frac{7}{2}\right) = (21.5, 28.5)$$

Class-intervals:	21.5 – 28.5	28.5 – 35.5	35.5 – 42.5	42.5 – 49.5	49.5 – 56.5	56.5 – 63.5
Mid values:	25	32	39	46	53	60

(*c*) The distribution can be expressed in inclusive class intervals with width of 7 as: 22 – 28, 29 – 35, ..., 56 – 63.

3.16. TABULATION OF DATA

A table in statistics is a systematic arrangement of statistical data in rows and columns. Rows are horizontal arrangements of data where as columns are vertical arrangements of data. The purpose of a table is to present the statistical data in a simpler form which is suitable for comparison so that the investigator can easily get the desired information.

Meaning of Tabulation

Tabulation is a way of summarizing and presenting the statistical data in rows and columns.

According to Prof. Tuttle: *The logical listing of related quantitative data in vertical columns and horizontal rows of numbers with sufficient explanatory and qualifying words, phrases and statements in the form of titles, headings and explanatory notes to make clear the full meaning, context and the origin of the data.*

From this definition, we get an idea of the structure of a statistical table which helps us in organizing a given set of data.

According to Prof. D.Gregory and H.Word,

- Tabulation is the process of condensing classified data in the form of a table so that it may be more easily understood, and so that any comparison involved may be more readily made.

According to Prof. D.W. Paden and E.F.Lindquist

- It is a medium of communication of great economy and effectiveness for which ordinary prose is inadequate. In addition to its formation in simple presentation, the statistical table is also a useful tool of analysis.

According to Prof. Karmel

Tabulation summarizes the data by using columns and rows and entering figures in the body of the table.

According to Prof. Secrist

- Tables are means of recording, in permanent form, the analysis that is made through classification and by placing in a position just the things that are similar and should be compared.

From this definition, we find that tabulation is a process of classifying the statistical data in a systematic way so that comparisons can be made easily.

Difference Between Tabulation and Classification

Broadly speaking, tabulation and classification are not two different processes. In fact, these two phrases go together. Classification is the first step for tabulation. Before a statistical data is tabulised, it has to be classified.

3.17. OBJECTIVES OF TABULATION

The main objectives of tabulation are discussed as under:

(i) **It Reduces the Complexity.** Tabulation of a statistical data reduces the bulk of information into a simplified and meaningful form. When a data is tabulated, unwanted and unnecessary repetitions are avoided. Data is represented in rows and columns in a systematic way. Hence an investigator can get a very clear picture of data what he desires.

(ii) **It Saves Space.** Tabulation condenses the statistical data into a meaningful form and hence a large amount of space is saved because of non-duplicating of its heading and sub-headings.

(iii) **It Faciliates Comparison.** Data presented in a table faciliates quick comparison. Since a table is divided into various parts, rows and columns etc. data can be studied more quickly than without it.

***(iv)* It Reveals Pattern.** A condensed data in the form of a table reveals the pattern of data which otherwise cannot be studied in a descriptive form of it.

***(v)* It Helps as a Reference.** When the data are arranged in rows and columns they can be easily used as a reference for future needs.

3.18. PARTS OF A TABLE

The following systematic diagram will help us in understanding the various parts of a statistical table.

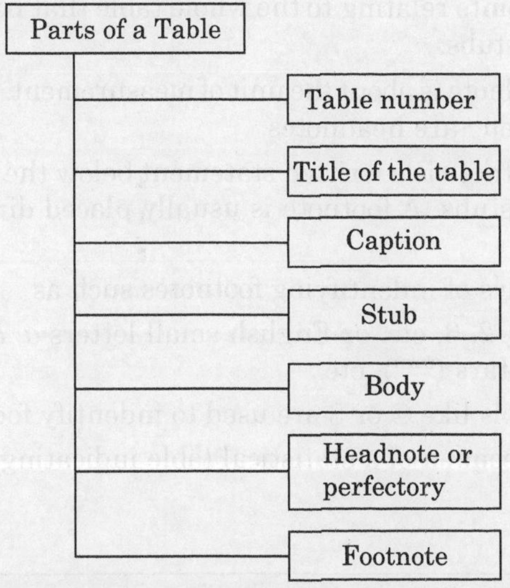

Fig. 3.24 Construction of a Statistical Table.

Tabulation is an art of presenting the statistical data. A statistical table should contain all the requisite information in a limited space but without any loss of clarity. The main parts of a statistical table are being discussed below.

I. Table Number. Each table should be given a number. The table number may be given either in the centre at the top above the title or inside the title at the top.

The table number may also be given in the bottom of the table on the left-hand side. However, if space permits, the table number should be given in the centre.

II. Title of the Table. Each table must be given a brief, self-explanatory complete title. A complete title can answer the questions what, where and when in that sequence. The following main points are required to title a table.

(*i*) It should express the nature of data contained

(*ii*) It should indicate the time period of data obtained

(*iii*) It should explain geographical or physical aspects of data covered

(*iv*) It should show the categories of data contained.

III. Caption. The heading for columns are called **captions.** Captions explain what the columns represent. A **caption** may contain one or more column headings. Under a column heading, there may be sub-headings. The caption should be clearly defined and placed at the middle of the column. If different columns are expressed in different units, the units should be mentioned with the captions. A caption should be shown in small letters as compared with the main part of the title. This would save the space.

IV. Stub. The heading for row is called stub. It must be clear and concise. Two or more rows with similar headings may be grouped under a common heading to avoid repetition. The stubs are usually wider than column headings but must be kept narrow. When a stub occupies more than one line, the figures of the table should be written in the last line.

V. Body. This part of the table contains the numerical information. This numerical information is arranged according to the descriptions given for each column and each row.

VI. Perfectory (or Headnote). A headnote, also called perfectory, is a brief statement applying to all or a major part of the material in the table. It is usually enclosed in brackets. It is used to explain certain points relating to the whole table that have not been included in the title nor in the captions or stubs.

In other words, a headnote is about the unit of measurement. For example "In thousands", "in million tonnes", "in kg" etc. are headnotes.

VII. Footnote. A footnote is a written statement below the table. It is written to clarify either the title captions or stubs. A footnote is usually placed directly below the body of the table.

There are various ways of indentifying footnotes such as

(*i*) Small numbers 1, 2, 3, etc. or English small letters *a, b, c,* etc. or one star (*), two stars (**), three stars (***), etc.

(*ii*) Sometimes symbols like @ or $ are used to indentify footnotes.

The following is a specimen of a statistical table indicating the above discussed parts.

Table No.:

Title: **Headnote:**

Stub heading	*Caption heading*				*Rows total*
	Subhead		*Subhead*		
	Column head	*Column head*	*Column head*	*Column head*	
Sub entries					
Columns total					

Footnotes

Fig. 3.25 Format of a Statistical Table

It may be further noted that the information which is not available should be indicated by writing N.A. or by dash (–) in the body of the table. Also use of ditto marks ("), 'etc.' and use of abbreviated words should also be avoided in the table.

3.19. REQUISITES OF A GOOD STATISTICAL TABLE AS GIVEN BY VARIOUS AUTHORS ARE GIVEN BELOW

(*i*) *In the final analysis, there are only two rules in tabular presentation that should be applied rigidly. First, the use of common sense when planning a table, and second the viewing of the proposed table from the stand point of user. The details of mechanical arrangement must be governed by a single objective, that is to make the statistical table as easy to read and to understand as the nature of the material will permit.* **—J.C. Capt**

(ii) A good statistical table is not a mere careless grouping of columns and rows of figures, it is a triumph of ingenuity and technique, a master-piece of economy of space combined with a maximum of clearly presented information. To prepare a first class table, one must have a clear idea of the facts to be presented, the contrasts to be stressed, the points upon which emphasis is to be placed and lastly a familiarity with the technique of preparation.

—Harry Jerome

3.20. TYPES OF TABLES

The different types of tables used in statistical investigations are as below:

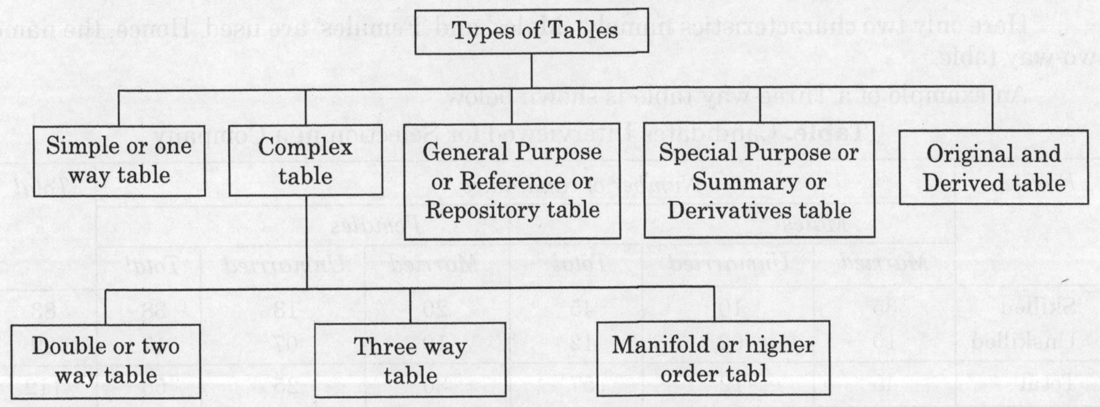

Fig. 3.26. Types of Tables.

We now discuss the various types of tables in details.

I. Simple or One-Way Table. In a simple table, only one characteristic is shown. This is the simple type of table. One such table is shown below.

Table. Number of Employees in a Bank According to Age Group

Age (in years)	*No. of employees*
Below 25	8
Between 25–30	12
Between 30–35	16
Between 35–40	18
Between 40–45	15
Between 45–50	13
Between 50–55	8
Above 55	4

II. Complex Table. In a complex table, more than are characteristics are shown. These tables are more popular in practice because they enable full information of all related facts.

(*i*) A complex table with two characteristics is known as **two-way table.**

(*ii*) A complex table with three characteristics is known as **three way table** and such type of tabulation is called **Treble Tabulation**.

(*iii*) A complex tabulation with four or more characteristics is known as **manifold tabulation.**

An example of a two-way table is shown below:

Table. Candidates Interviewed for Selection in a Company

Profile	*Number of candidates*		*Total*
	Males	*Females*	
Skilled	45	38	83
Unskilled	12	17	29
Total	57	55	112

Here only two characteristics namely, 'Males' and 'Females' are used. Hence, the name two-way table.

An example of a Three-way table is shown below

Table. Candidates Interviewed for Selection in a Company

Profile	*Number of candidates*						*Total*
	Males			*Females*			
	Married	*Unmarried*	*Total*	*Married*	*Unmarried*	*Total*	
Skilled	35	10	45	20	18	38	83
Unskilled	10	02	12	10	07	17	29
Total	45	12	57	30	25	55	112

Note that here the three characteristics like "Males", "Females" and their "Marital Status" are given in the above table. Hence the name **three-way table.**

(*iv*) **Manifold or Higher Order Table.** When three or more characteristics are represented in the same table, such a table is called higher order table or manifold table. The need of such tables arise when we wish to present a number of characteristics in one table simultaneously. As the number of characteristics increases, the table would become more and more confusing and hence upto four characteristics should be used in the same table. For example, if the data given in table. A is also available for other companies, then this table would became a manifold table.

III. General Purpose Table. A general purpose table is also called *reference table* or *repository table.* In such tables, data are presented in details so that it can be used for general or reference use on the same subject. In other words, these tables serve as repository of information and are arranged for easy reference. For example, tables contained in the census reports, tables published by government agencies etc. are general tables.

IV. Special Purpose Table. These tables are also known as *summary tables* and provide information for particular discussion. These tables are also called *derivatives tables.*

Many authors have indentified the purpose of general and special purpose tables, which are given below:

(*i*) *Primary and usually the sole purpose of a reference table is to present data in such a manner that individual items may be found readily by a reader.*

—Croxton and Cowden

(*ii*) *These tables are those in which data are recorded not the detailed data which have been analysed but rather the results of the analysis.* **—John I. Griffin**

(iii) Reference tables contain ungrouped data basic for a particular report, usually containing a large amount of data and frequently selected to tabular appendix.

—Horace Secrist

(iv) **Original and Derived Tables.** Original tables are also known as classification tables. Such a table contains data collected from a primary source. If the information contained in the table has been derived from the general table then such a table is known as **derived table**.

Example 15. *In a sample study about coffee-drinking habits in two town, the following information was received.*

Town X: Females were 40 percent. Total coffee drinkers were 45 percent and male non-coffee drinkers were 20 percent.

Town Y: Males were 55 percent. Male non-coffee drinkers were 30 percent and female coffee drinkers were 15 percent.

Represent this data in a tabular form.

Sol. We first present the given data in the following table:

Let the total number of males and females in both towns X and Y be 100 each. The missing entries have been marked by *1, *2, *3, and so on.

Table. Drinking habits (in percentage)

Attributes	*Town X*			*Town Y*			*Total*
	Males	*Females*	*Total*	*Males*	*Females*	*Total*	
Coffee drinkers	40	–(*1)	45	–(*2)	15	–(*3)	–(*10)
Non-coffee drinkers	20	–(*4)	–(*5)	30	–(*6)	–(*7)	–(*11)
Total	–(*8)	40	100	55	–(*9)	100	–(*12)

Town X. Total number of coffee drinkers = 45

Total number of males coffee drinkers = 40

∴ Total number of females coffee drinkers = 45 – 40 = 5, which is the missing entry represented by (*1)

Total number of females non-coffee drinkers = Total number of females – total number of females coffee drinkers

= 40 – 5 = 35, which is the missing entry represented by (*4)

∴ Total number of non-coffee drinkers

= Total number of males non-coffee drinkers + total number of females non-coffee drinkers

= 20 + 35 = 55, which is the missing entry represented by (*5)

Town Y. Total number of males coffee drinkers

= Total number of males – Total number of males non-coffee drinkers

= 55 – 30 = 25, which is the missing entry represented by (*2)

Total number of coffee drinkers

= Total number of males coffee drinkers + Total number of females coffee drinkers

= 25 + 15 = 40, which is the missing entry represented by (*3)

Similarly, we can calculate others missing entries as explained below

Here $*7 = 100 - *3 = 100 - 40 = 60$

$*6 = *7 - 30 = 60 - 30 = 30$

Also $*9 = 15 + *6 = 15 + 30 = 45$

$*10 = 45 + *3 = 45 + 40 = 85$

$*11 = *5 + *7 = 55 + 60 = 115$

$*12 = 100 + 100 = 200$

∴ The required information is summarised in the following table.

Table. Drinking Habits (in Percentage)

Attributes	*Town X*			*Town Y*			*Total*
	Males	*Females*	*Total*	*Males*	*Females*	*Total*	
Coffee drinkers	40	**5**	45	**25**	15	**40**	**85**
Non-Coffee drinkers	20	**35**	**55**	30	**30**	**60**	**115**
Total	**60**	40	100	55	**45**	100	**200**

The missing entries are shown in bold fonts.

Example 16. *Industrial finance in India has showed great variation in respect of sources of funds during the first, second, and third five-year plans. There were two main sources–internal and external. The internal sources of funds are–depreciation, free reserve and surplus. The external sources of funds are–capital issues, borrowings.*

During the first plan, internal and external sources accounted for 62 % and 38% of the total, and of the depreciation, fresh capital, and other sources formed 29%, 7% and 10.6% respectively.

During the second plan, internal sources decreased by 17.3% compared to the first plan, and depreciation was 24.5%. The external finance during the same period consisted of 10.9% fresh capital and 28.9% percent borrowings.

Compared to the second plan, external finance during the third plan decreased by 4.4% and borrowings and 'other sources' were 29.4% and 14.9% respectively. During the third plan, internal finance increased by 4.4% and free reserves and surplus formed 18.6%.

Tabulate this information with the above details as clearly as possible observing the rules of tabulation.

Sol. We first present the given data in the following table. The missing entries have been marked by *1, *2, *3, and so on.

Table. Industrial Finance Report (in Percentage)

Sources of Funds							
Year	*Internal Sources*			*External Sources*			
	Depreciation	*Free reserve and surplus*	*Total*	*Fresh capital*	*Borrowings*	*Other sources*	*Total*
First year	29	–(*1)	62	7	–(*6)	10.6	38
Second year	24.5	–(*2)	–(*3)	10.9	28.9	–(*7)	–(*8)
Third year	–(*4)	18.6	–(*5)	–(*10)	29.4	14.9	–(*9)

Internal Sources:

(*i*) **In First Year Plan.**

% of free reserve and surplus sources + % of depreciation sources = 62

⇒ *1 + 29 = 62 ⇒ *1 = 62 – 29 = 33

∴ The missing entry represented by *1 is 33.

(*ii*) **In Second Year Plan.** It is given that internal sources decreased by 17.3% compared to the first year

∴ *3 = 62 – 17.3 = 44.7

Also 24.5 + *2 = *3

⇒ *2 = 44.7 – 24.5 = 20.2

(*iii*) **In Third Year Plan.** It is given that internal sources increased by 4.4% compared to second year plan

∴ *5 = *3 + 4.4 = 44.7 + 4.4 = 49.1

Also *4 + 18.6 = *5

⇒ *4 = *5 – 18.6 = 49.1 – 18.6 = 30.5

External sources. Proceeding similarly, we can get

*6 = 38 – 7 – 10.6 = 20.4

*8 = 100 – 44.7 = 55.3

*7 = 55.3 – 10.9 – 28.9 = 15.5

*9 = 55.3 – 4.4 = 50.9

*10 = 50.9 – 29.4 – 14.9 = 6.6

The given information is summarized in the following table.

Table. Industrial Finance Report (in Percentage)

	Sources of Funds						
Year	*Internal Sources*			*External Sources*			
	Depreciation	*Free reserve and surplus*	*Total*	*Fresh capital*	*Borrowings*	*Other sources*	*Total*
First year	29	**33**	62	7	**20.4**	10.6	38
Second year	24.5	**20.2**	**44.7**	10.9	28.9	**15.5**	**55.3**
Third year	**30.5**	18.6	**49.1**	**6.6**	29.4	14.9	**50.9**

The missing entries are marked in bold fonts.

3.21. CASE STUDIES

Case Study I. *Public works department (P.W.D.*) of a state government has taken up a scheme of providing drinking water to every village. During the first four years of a five-year plan, the department has installed 39,664 tubewells. Out of the funds earmarked for natural calamities, the department sunk 14,072 tubewells during the first four years of the plan. Thus, out of the plan fund, 9245 and 8630 tubewells were sunk in 2005–2006 and 2006–2007 respectively. Out of the natural calamities fund, the number of tubewells sunk in 2005–2006*

*Source-Internet

and 2006–2007 were 4511 and 637, respectively. The expenditure for 2005–2006 and 2006–2007 was ₹ 863.41 lac and ₹ 1185.65 lac respectively.

The number of tubewells installed in 2007–2008 was, 16,740 out of which 4800 were installed out of the natural calamites fund and the expenditure of sinking of tubewells during 2007–2008 was ₹ 1411.17 lac.

The number of tubewells installed in 2008–2009 was 13,973, out of which 9849 tubewells were sunk out of the fund for the plan and the expenditure during the first four years was ₹ 5543.05 lac.

Questions for discussions.

Assuming that you are a data analyst in P.W.D. You are required to

(i) Present the data in a tabular form

(ii) Point out the year in which the expenditure was highest.

Sol. We first present the given data in the following table. The missing entries are marked by *1, *2, *3 etc.

Table. Number of Tubewells and Their Expenditure

Plan year	*Number of tubewells*		*Total expenditure (in ₹ lac)*
	Out of funds plan	*Out of natural calamities funds*	
2005–2006	9245	4511	863.41
2006–2007	8630	637	1185.65
2007–2008	–(*1)	4800	1411.17
2008–2009	9849	–(*2)	–(*3)
Total	39664	14072	5443.05

We need to find

(*i*) The total number of tubewells sunk in the year 2007–2008 in **out of funds plan**.

(*ii*) The total number of tubewells sunk in the year 2008–2009 in **out of natural calamities** funds.

(*iii*) The total expenditure during the year 2008–2009

(*iv*) The year for which the expenditure was highest.

We proceed as below:

(*i*) In the year 2007–2008,

Total number of tubewells sunk = 16740

out of 16740, total number of tubewells sunk from *out of natural calamities funds* = 4800

∴ Required number of tubewells sunk in *out of funds plan*

= 16740 – 4800 = 11940, which is the missing entry represented by (*1)

(*ii*) In the year 2008–2009, total number of tubewells sunk = 13973

Out of 13973, total number of tubewells sunk from *out of funds plan* = 9849

∴ Required number of tubewells sunk from *out of natural calamities funds*

= 13973 – 9849 = 4124, which is the missing entry represented by (*2)

(*iii*) Total expenditure during the first four years of a **five-year plan** = ₹ 5443.05 lac

It is given that the total expenditure for the years 2005–2006, 2006–2007, 2007–2008 are ₹ 863.41 lac, ₹ 1185.65 lac, and ₹ 1411.17 lac respectively.

∴ Required total expenditure for the year 2008–2009 is

= 5443.05 – (863.41 + 1185.65 + 1411.17)

= ₹ 1982.82 lac which is the missing entry represented by (*3)

(*iv*) The year for which the expenditure was highest (₹ 1982.82 lac) was 2008–2009.

Hence the data of the given problem is summarized in the following table.

Table. Number of Tubewells and Their Expenditure

Plan year	*Number of tubewells*		*Total expenditure (in ₹ lac)*
	Out of funds plan	*Out of natural calamities funds*	
2005–2006	9245	4511	863.41
2006–2007	8630	637	1185.65
2007–2008	**11940**	4800	1411.7
2008–2009	**9849**	**4124**	**1982.82**
Total	39664	14072	5443.05

The missing entries have been marked in bold fonts

Case Study II. *The annual report of a* ***Public library*** *reveals the following information regarding the reading habits of its members.*

Out of the total of 3718 books issued to the members in the month of June, 2100 were fiction books. There were 467 members of the library during the period and they were classified into five classes–A, B, C, D and E. The number of members belonging to the first four classes were respectively 15, 176, 98 and 129 and the number of fiction books issued to them were 103, 1187, 647 and 58 respectively. The number of books other than text books and fiction books issued to these four classes of members were respectively 4, 390, 217 and 341. Text books were issued only to members belonging to classes C, D and E and the number of text books issued to them were respectively 8, 317 and 160.

During the same period, 1246 periodicals were issued. These include 396 technical journals of which 36 were issued to member of class B, 45 to class D, and 315 to class E.

To members of classes B, C, D and E, the number of other journals issued were 419, 26, 231 and 99 respectively.

The report however, showed an increase of 4.1 percent in the number of books issued in the month of May, though there was a corresponding decrease of 6.1 percent in the number of periodicals and journals issued to members.

Questions for discussion:

As a library head, you are supposed to

(*i*) *Present the data in a tabular form*

(*ii*) *Find the number of technical journals issued in the month of May,*

(*iii*) *Find the number of text books issued in the month of May.*

(*iv*) *Find the total number of books issued in the month of May.*

Sol. We first present the given data in the following table. The missing entries are denoted by star symbol *1, *2, *3 and so on. Also the entry, which is not required, has been marked by the cross symbol (×).

Table. Public Library's Annual Report on Reading Habits of Its Members

		Classes					*Total*	
		A	*B*	*C*	*D*	*E*	*June*	*May*
Total number of members		15	176	98	129	–(*1)	467	×
Books	Fiction Books	103	1187	647	58	–(*2)	2100	(*14)
	Text Books	×	×	8	317	160	–(*3)	–(*15)
	Other Books	4	390	217	341	–(*5)	–(*4)	–(*16)
	Total	–(*6)	–(*7)	872	716	–(*8)	3718	–(*13)
Periodicals and journals	Technical journals	×	36	×	45	315	396	–(*18)
	Other journals	–(*10)	419	26	231	99	–(*9)	–(*19)
	Total	–(*11)	455	–(*12)	276	414	1246	–(*17)

We are required to find out the missing information in the month of June and May.

I. Missing Information for the Month of June.

Total number of members in the month of June = 2100

(*i*) Number of members belonging to class E in the month of June

= 467 – (15 + 176 + 98 + 129)

= 49, which is the missing information represented by (*1)

(*ii*) Total number of **fiction books issued** in the month of June = 2100

∴ Total number of **fictions books issued** to class E in the month of June

= 2100 – (103 + 1187 + 647 + 58)

= 105, which is the missing information represented by (*2)

(*iii*) Total number of books (Friction, text and other books) = 3718

Total number of text books issued = 8 + 317 + 160

= 485, which is the missing information represented by (*3)

Total number of **fiction books** issued = 2100

∴ Total number of **other books** issued = 3718 – (485 + 2100)

= 1133, which is the missing information represented by (*4)

(*iv*) Total number of **other books** issued to class E = 1133 – (4 + 390 + 217 + 341)

= 181, which is the missing information represented by (*5)

(*v*) Since no text books were issued to class A and class B.

∴ Total number of books (fiction, text and other books) to class A and class B are 103 + 4 = 107 (*6) and 1187 + 390 = 1577 (*7) respectively.

(*vi*) Also total number of books (fiction, text and other books) to class E

= 105 + 160 + 181 = 446 (*8)

(*vii*) Total number of **periodicals** issued = 1246

Total number of **technical journals** issued = 396

∴ Total number of **other journals** issued = 1246 – 396

= 850, which is the missing information represented by (*9)

(*viii*) Number of other **journals issued** to class A

= 850 – (419 + 26 + 231 + 99)

= 75, which is the missing information represented by (*10)

(*ix*) No **technical journals** were issued to class A and C.

∴ Total number of periodicals (technical and other journal) issued to class A and C are 75 (*11) and 26 (*12) respectively.

Missing Information for the Month of May

(*a*) Books

(*i*) From the given report, an increase of 4.1% in the number of books was made in the month of May. (Fiction, text and other books)

∴ Total number of books issued in the month of May

$$= 3718 \times \left(\frac{100}{100 + 4.1}\right) = 3571.56$$

≅ 3572, which is the missing information represented by (*13)

(*ii*) Total number of **fiction books** issued in the month of May

$$= 2100 \times \frac{100}{100 + 4.1} = 2017.29$$

≅ 2017, which is the missing information represented by (*14)

(*iii*) Total number of text books issued in the month of May

$$= 485 \times \left(\frac{100}{100 + 4.1}\right) = 465.89$$

≅ 466, which is the missing information represented by (*15)

(*iv*) Total number of **other books** issued for the month of May

$$= 1133 \times \left(\frac{100}{100 + 4.1}\right) = 1088.37$$

≅ 1088, which is the missing information represented by (*16)

(*b*) Periodicals

(*i*) A decrease of 6.1% is reported in the issue of **periodicals and journals** in the month of May, therefore,

Total number of **periodicals and Journals** issued in the month of May

$$= 1246 \times \left(\frac{100}{100 - 6.1}\right) = 1326.94$$

≅ 1327, which is the missing information represented by (*17)

(*ii*) Total number of **technical Journals** issued in the month of May

$$= 396 \times \left(\frac{100}{100 - 6.1}\right) = 421.72$$

$\cong$ 422, which is the missing information represented by (*18)

(*iii*) Total number of **other Journals** issued in the month of May

$$= 850 \times \left(\frac{100}{100 - 6.1}\right) = 905.21$$

$\cong$ 905, which is the missing information represented by (*19)

The required data is summarized in the following table.

Table. Public Library's Annual Report on Reading Habits of its Members

		Classes					*Total*	
		A	*B*	*C*	*D*	*E*	*June*	*May*
Total number of members		15	176	98	129	**49**	467	×
Books	Fiction Books	103	1187	647	58	**105**	2100	**2017**
	Text Books	×	×	8	317	160	**485**	**466**
	Other Books	4	390	217	341	**181**	**1133**	**1088**
	Total	**107**	**1577**	872	716	**446**	3718	**3571**
Periodicals and journals	Technical journals	×	36	×	45	315	396	**422**
	Other journals	**75**	419	26	231	99	**850**	**905**
	Total	**75**	455	**26**	276	414	1246	**1327**

The missing entries are shown in bold fonts.

TEST YOUR KNOWLEDGE 3.2

1. What is statistical table? Explain clearly the essentials of a good table.
2. What are the different components of a table?
3. What are the characteristics of a good table?
4. Explain the role of tabulation in presenting business data, and discuss briefly the different methods of presentation.
5. Explain the terms 'classification' and 'tabulation'. Point out their importance in a statistical investigation. What precautions would you take in tabulating statistical data?
6. What are the requisites of a good table? State the rules that serve as a guide in tabulating statistical data.
7. The following information about weather conditions at different stations were recorded at 8.30 a.m. on Thursday, 29 September 2011.

   At Jalandhar station, the maximum and minimum temperatures in 24 hrs were 28°C and 20°C respectively. The rainfall in the past 24 hrs at Jalandhar was nil. Since First June, the rainfall was 185 mm which is 105 mm below normal.

Amritsar's minimum and maximum temperatures in 24 hrs for the day were 19°C and 23°C respectively. It had no rainfall in the past 24 hrs and since First June, the rainfall was 252 mm which is 54 mm below normal.

The minimum temperature at Pathankot was 21°C and the rainfall in the past 24 hrs was nil. Since First June, it experienced 434 mm of rainfall which is 24 mm below normal.

Mohali's maximum temperature in 24 hrs was 28°C. It had 4 mm of rain in the past 24 hrs and since First June, it had 955 mm of rain.

Chandigarh's maximum and minimum day temperature were 30°C and 26°C respectively. It had 3 mm of rainfall in the past 24 hrs. Since First June, it experienced a rainfall of 1079 mm which is 154 mm above normal.

Present the above data in a tabular form.

8. Present the following data in a tabular form:

A certain manufacturer produces three different products 1, 2 and 3. Product 1 can be manufactured in one of the three plants A, B or C. However, product 2 can be manufactured in either plant B or C, whereas plant A or B can manufacture product 3. Plant A can manufacture in an hour 10 pieces of 1 or 20 pieces of 3, 20 pieces of 2, 15 pieces of 1, or 16 pieces of 3 can be manufactured per hour in plant B. C can produce 20 pieces of 1 or 18 pieces of 2 per hour.

Wage rates per hour ₹ 20 at A, ₹ 40 at B and ₹ 25 at C. The costs of running plants A, B and C are respectively ₹ 1000, 500 and 1250 per hour. Materials and other costs directly related to the production of one piece of the product are respectively ₹ 10 for 1, ₹ 12 for 2, and ₹ 15 for 3. The company plans to market product 1 at ₹ 15 per piece, product 2 at ₹ 18 per piece and product 3 at ₹ 20 per piece.

9. Transforming the ratios into corresponding numbers, prepare a complete table for the following information. Give a suitable title to the table.

In the year 2009, the total strength of students of three colleges X, Y and Z in a city were in the ratio 4 : 2 : 5. The strength of college Y was 2000. The proportion of girls and boys in all colleges was in the ratio 2 : 3. The faculty-wise distribution of boys and girls in the faculties of Arts, Science and Commerce was in the ratio 1 : 2 : 2 in all the three colleges.

10. Let the national income of a country for the years 2000–01 and 2001–02 at current prices be ₹ 80,650, ₹ 90,010 and ₹ 90,530 crore respectively, and per capita income for these years be ₹ 1050, ₹ 1056 and ₹ 1067 respectively. The corresponding figures of national income and per capita income at 1999–2000 prices for the above years were ₹ 80,650; ₹ 80,820 and ₹ 80,850 crore and ₹ 1050, ₹ 1051 and ₹ 1048 respectively. Present this data in a table.

11. Present the following information in a suitable form supplying the figure not directly given. In 2011 out of a total of 4000 workers in a factory, 3300 were members of a trade union. The number of women workers employed was 500 out of which 400 did not belong to any union.

In 2010, the number of workers in the union was 3450 of which 3200 were men. The number of non-union workers was 760 of which 330 were women.

12. A survey of 370 students from the Commerce faculty and 130 students from the Science Faculty revealed that 180 students were studying for only C.A. Examinations, 140 for only Costing Examinations, and 80 for both C.A. and Costing Examinations. The rest had opted for part-time Management courses. Of those studying for costing only, 13 were girls and 90 boys belonged to the Commerce Faculty. Out of the 80 studying for both C.A. and Costing, 72 were from the Commerce faculty amongst whom 70 were boys. Amongst those who opted for part-time Management Courses, 50 boys were from the Science Faculty and 30 boys and 10 girls from the Commerce faculty. In all, there were 110 boys in the Science Faculty.

Present this information in a tabular form. Find the number of students from the Science faculty studying for part-time Management Courses.

13. An Aluminium Company is in possession of certain scrap materials with known chemical composition. Scrap 1 contains 65% aluminium, 20% iron, 2% copper, 2% manganese, 3% magnesium and 8% silicon. The aluminium content of scrap 2, scrap 3, and scrap 4 are 70%, 80% and 75% respectively. Scrap 2 contains 15% iron, 3% copper. 2% manganese, 4% magnesium and the rest silicon. Scrap 3 contains 5% iron. The iron content of scrap 4 is the same as that of scarp 3, scrap 4 contains twice as much percentage of copper as scrap 3, scrap 3 contains 1% copper. Scrap 3 contains manganese which is 3 times as much as copper it contains. The percentage of magnesium and silicon in scrap 3 are 3% and 8% respectively. The magnesium and silicon contents of scrap 4 are respectively 2 times and 3 times its manganese contents. The company also purchase some aluminium and silicon as needed. The aluminium purchased contains 96% pure aluminium, 2% iron, 1% copper and 1% silicon respectively, whereas the purchased silicon contains 98% silicon and 2% iron respectively. Present the above data in a table.

14. The 'Financial Highlights' of a public limited company in recent years were as follow:

In the year ending on 31 March, 2008 the turnover of the company, including other income, was ₹ 157 million. The profit of the company in the same year before tax, investment allowance, reverse, and prior year's adjustment was ₹ 19 million, and the profit after tax, investment allowance, reserve and prior year's adjustment was ₹ 8 million. The divided declared by the company in the same year was 20%. The turnover, including other income, for the years ending on 31 March, 2009, 2010 and 2011 were ₹ 169, ₹ 191, and ₹ 197 million respectively. For the year ending on 31 March, 2009, the profit before tax, investment allowance, reverse and prior year's adjustment was ₹ 192 million and the profit after tax, and so on ₹ 7.5 million, while the dividend declared for the same year was 17%. For the year ending on 31 March, 2010, 2011 and 2012, the profits before tax, investment allowance, reserve, and prior year's adjustment were ₹ 21, 12, 13 million respectively, while the profits after tax, and so on, of the above three years were ₹ 9.5, 4, and 9 million respectively. The turnover, including other income, for the year ending on 31 March, 2012 was ₹ 243 million. The dividend declared for the year ending on 31 March, 2010, 2011 and 2012 was 17%, 10% and 20% respectively. Present the above data in a table.

15. In a trip organised by a college, there were 50 persons, each of whom paid ₹ 2500 on an average. There were 40 students each of whom paid ₹ 2700. Members of the teaching staff were charged at a higher rate. The number of servants was 5 and they were not charged any amount. The number of ladies was 20% of the total and one was a lady teacher. Tabulate the above information. Also,

(*i*) Find the total contribution

(*ii*) Find the per head contribution of each teaching staff.

Answers

7. **Table.** Weather conditions at different stations (at 8.30 A.M 29–09–2012)

Stations	*In 24 hours*		*Ranifall (mm)*			
	Temperature (°C)		*Past 24 hrs*	*Since First June*	*Above Normal*	*Below Normal*
	Minimum	*Maximum*				
Jalandhar	20	28	0	185	–	105
Amritsar	19	23	0	252	–	54
Pathankot	21	–	0	434	–	24
Mohali	–	28	4	955	–	–
Chandigarh	26	30	3	1079	154	–

8. **Table.** Production schedule of a manufacture

Plant	*Rate of manufacturing per hour (pieces)*			*Wage rates per hour (₹)*	*Cost of running Per hour (₹)*
	1	*2*	*3*		
A	10	–	20	20	1000
B	15	20	16	40	500
C	20	12	15	25	1250
Material and other direct cost per piece (₹)	10	12	15	–	–
Product price per piece (₹)	15	18	20	–	–

9. **Table.** Distribution of students according to Faculty and Colleges in the year 2009

Colleges	*Faculty*									*Total*
	Art			*Science*			*Commerce*			*(1) + (2) + (3)*
	Boys	*Girls*	*Total (1)*	*Boys*	*Girls*	*Total (2)*	*Boys*	*Girls*	*Total (3)*	–
X	480	320	800	960	640	1600	960	640	1600	4000
Y	240	160	400	480	320	800	480	320	800	2000
Z	600	400	1000	1200	800	2000	1200	800	2000	5000
Total	1320	880	2200	2640	1760	4400	2640	1760	4400	11,000

10. **Table.** National income and per capita income of the country

Year	*National Income*		*Per capita income*	
	At current prices (₹ in crore)	*At 1999–2000 prices (₹ in crore)*	*At Current Prices*	*At 1999–2000 Prices*
1999–2000	80,650	80,650	1050	1050
2000–2001	90,010	80,820	1056	1051
2001–2002	90,530	80,850	1067	1048

11. **Table.** Members of union by sex

Year	*2010*			*2011*		
	Males	*Females*	*Total*	*Males*	*Females*	*Total*
Member	3300	250	3450	3200	100	3300
Non-member	430	330	760	300	400	700
Total	3630	580	4210	3500	500	4000

12. **Table.** Distribution of students according to Faculty and Professional Courses

Faculty courses	*Commerce*			*Science*			*Total*		
	Boys	*Girls*	*Total*	*Boys*	*Girls*	*Total*	*Boys*	*Girls*	*Total*
Part-time management	30	10	40	50	10	60	80	20	100
C.A. only	150	8	158	16	6	22	166	14	180
Costing only	90	10	100	37	3	40	127	13	140
C.A. and Costing	70	2	72	7	1	8	77	3	80
Total	340	30	370	110	20	130	450	50	500

13. **Table.** The chemical composition of scraps and purchased minerals

Materials	*Chemical composition (in percentage)*					
	Aluminium	*Iron*	*Copper*	*Manganese*	*Magnesium*	*Silicon*
Scrap 1	65	20	2	2	3	8
Scrap 2	70	15	3	2	4	6
Scrap 3	80	5	1	3	3	8
Scrap 4	75	5	2	3	6	9
Aluminium	96	2	1	–	–	1
Silicon	–	2	–	–	–	98

14. **Table.** Financial highlights of the public Ltd. Company.

Year Ended 31 March	*Turnover including Other Income (in Million of (₹)*	*Profit before tax Investment Allowance Reserve and Prior Year Adjustment (in Million of ₹)*	*Profit after tax Investment Allowance Reserve and Prior Year Adjustment (in Million of ₹)*	*Percent*
2008	157	19	8	20
2009	169	18	7.5	17
2010	191	21	9.5	17
2011	197	12	4	10
2012	243	13	9	20

15.

Type of participants	*Sex*			*Contribution*	*Total*
	Males	*Females*	*Total*	*Per member (₹)*	*Contribution (₹)*
Students	31	9	40	2700	1,08,000
Teaching staff	4	1	5	3400	17,000
Servant	5	–	5	–	–
Total	40	10	50	–	1,25,000

(*i*) Total contribution = Average contribution × Number of persons in the group

$$= 2500 \times 50 = ₹\ 1,25,000$$

(*ii*) Per head contribution of teaching staff $= \dfrac{\text{Total contribution} - \text{Contribution of students}}{\text{Numbers of teaching staff}}$

$$= \frac{1,25,000 - (40 \times 2700)}{5} = ₹\ 3400.$$

4

Depiction (Graphical and Diagramatical) of Data

4.1. INTRODUCTION

The term "depiction of data" means diagrammatical and graphical representation of statistical data. A frequency distribution when represented by means of a diagram or graph makes the unwieldy data intelligible. A better prospective can be had by representing the frequency distribution diagrammatically since graphs or diagrams, if drawn attractively, are eye-catching and leave a more lasting impression on the mind of the observer. Diagrams and graphs are a good visual aid. But they do not give accurate measurements of the variable as are given by the tables.

Another disadvantage is that by taking different scales, the facts may be miss represented.

4.2. OBJECTIVES OF DIAGRAMMATICAL AND GRAPHICAL REPRESENTATION OF DATA

(*a*) To compare two or more variables in a small time.

(*b*) To read and understand a complex data.

(*c*) To get a clear-cut idea about the variations in the values of the variables.

4.3. UTILITY OF DIAGRAMMATICAL AND GRAPHICAL REPRESENTATION OF DATA

(*a*) The diagrammatical or graphical representation of data give bird's eye-view of the whole collection of statistical data collected for statistical computation.

(*b*) They can easily attract and draw the attention of the observer.

(*c*) They are capable of leaving long lasting impression of the numerical values which cannot be easily remembered.

(*d*) They are time-saving.

4.4. LIMITATIONS OF DIAGRAMMATICAL AND GRAPHICAL REPRESENTATION OF DATA

(*a*) The representation of data through diagrams or graphs is not able to show the minor differences between two or more series.

(*b*) The diagrams or graphs cannot reveal the same facts as a statistical table can do.

(*c*) 2-dimensional and 3-dimensional diagrams are not easy to understand the facts of a given data.

(*d*) Diagrams and graphs provide only an approximate idea, where a greater accuracy is needed, they are not suitable.

4.5. GENERAL RULES FOR DRAWING DIAGRAMS

Below are some general guidlines which should be taken into consideration while preparing diagrams.

1. Title. Each diagram should have a suitable title. The title may be given either at the top of the diagram or below it.

2. Proportion of Length and Breadth. A proper proportion between the height and width of the diagram should be maintained. If either the height and the width is too short or too long in proportion, the diagram would look ugly. However, ratio of $\sqrt{2}$: 1 or 1.414 (for long side) : 1 (for short side) may be made as suggested by **Lutz** in his famous book entitled "Graphical Presentation".

3. Size. The size of a diagram should be such that all the relevant characteristics of the data are properly displayed and can be easily understood.

4. Proper Scale. The scale showing the given values, if possible, should be in even numbers (2, 4, 6 etc.) or in multiples of 5, 10 or 20. Odd values like 1, 3, 5, 7 should be avoided. The scale should also specify the size of the unit and what it represents. For example, "millions of tonnes", "number of individual in thousands", "units produced in lacs" etc. The scale adopted should be indicated on both the axes (horizontal and vertical) if different scales are used. All lettering should be easily readable without turning the chart up and down.

5. Footnotes and Source Notes. In order to clarify certain points about the diagram, footnotes and sources notes may be given at the bottom of the diagram.

6. Index. An index illustrating different types of lines, shades, designs or colours used in the construction of the diagram should be given to understand the contents of the diagram.

7. Simplicity. Diagrams should be as simple as possible so that the reader can understand the diagram's meaning clearly and easily. Too much information should not be loaded in a single diagram as it may create confusion.

4.6. TYPES OF DIAGRAMS

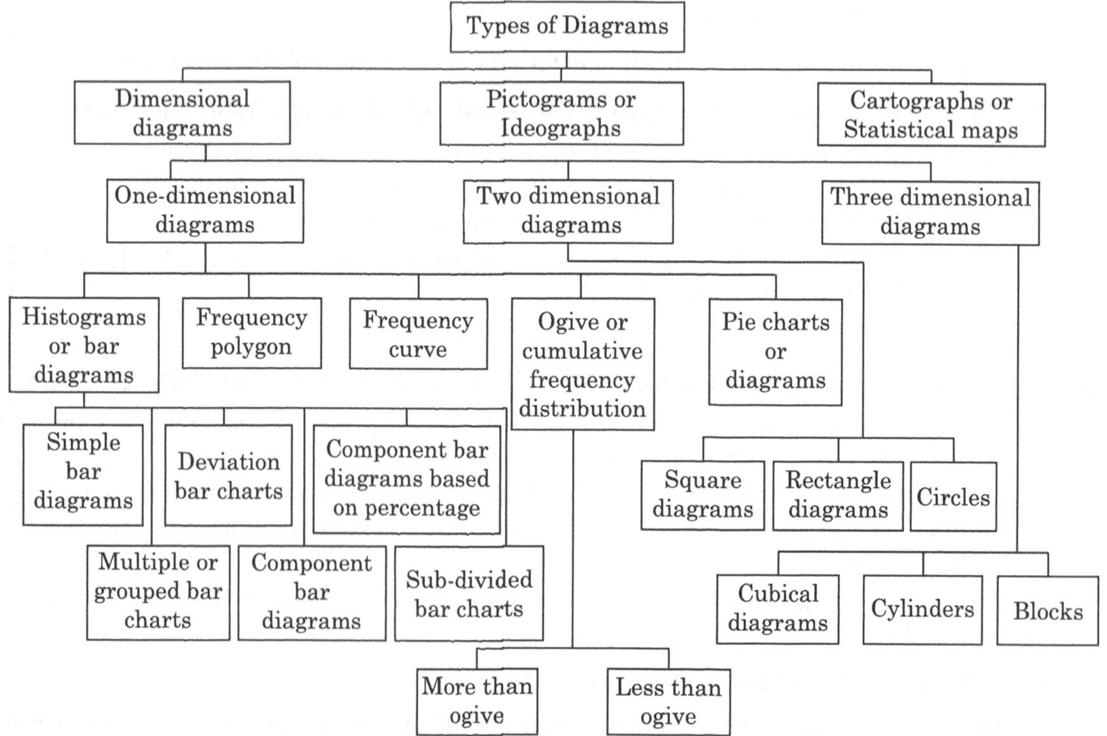

Fig. 4.1 Different types of diagrams

There are a variety of diagrams used to represent statistical data. Different types of diagrams can be used to describe a set of data, which can be divided into the following categories.

I. Dimensional diagrams

II. Pictograms or ideographs

III. Cartographs or statistical maps.

A systematic diagram of various types of diagrams is shown in previous page. (Fig. 4.1)

We now discuss various types of diagrams in details.

4.7 DIMENSIONAL DIAGRAMS

4.7. (*a*) One Dimensional Diagrams

These types of diagrams are in the shape of horizontal or vertical lines of bars. The length of the bars or the lines are in the proportion to the different figures. The width of the bar is chosen accordingly as the number of bars and the space available.

I. Histograms (Bar diagrams). These diagrams are used to graph both types of data (grouped and ungrouped data). In case of an ungrouped data, values of the variables are scaled along the horizontal axis and the number of observations (frequencies) along the vertical axis of the graph. The plotted points are connected by straight lines to get the final shape of the distribution. The height of boxes (or rectangles) measure the number of observations in each of the classes.

Method to Draw Histogram (or Bar Diagrams).

In drawing the histogram of a given grouped frequency distribution :

(*i*) Mark off along the x-axis all the class intervals on a suitable scale. (If class-intervals are equal, then each = 1 cm is quite suitable).

(*ii*) Mark frequencies along y-axis on a suitable scale.

(*iii*) It must not be assumed that scale for both the axes will be same. We can have different scales for the two axes. The determination of scale depends upon our convenience and the type and nature of data. The scale or scales should be so chosen as to fit the size of graph-paper and to hold all the figures of the data.

(*iv*) Construct rectangles with the class-intervals as bases and heights proportional (if the class intervals are equal) to frequencies.

A diagram with all these rectangles is called a **histogram.**

Example 1. *The weights (in grams) of 40 oranges picked at random from a basket are as follows* :

45, 49, 55, 30, 110, 75, 100, 40, 60, 65, 40, 100, 75, 70, 60, 70, 95, 85, 80, 35, 45, 40, 50, 60, 65, 55, 45, 90, 85, 75, 85, 75, 70, 110, 100, 80, 70, 55, 30, 70.

Represent the data by means of a histogram.

Sol. Range = Largest numerical value in the data–Smallest numerical value in the data = 110 – 30 = 80

Using Strug's rule, the number of classes is given as

$$K = 1 + 3.222 \log_{10} 80$$
$$= 1 + 3.222\ (1.903089987)$$
$$= 7.131755938 \cong 7$$

Also, width of the class interval $= \dfrac{\text{Range}}{\text{K}}$

$$= \frac{8}{7} = 11.42 \cong 12$$

The given data can be summerized in the following table.

Weights of oranges (in gms.)	*No. of oranges*	*Frequency*
30–42	𝍸 II	7
42–54	IIII	4
54–66	𝍸 III	8
66–78	𝍸 IIII	9
78–90	𝍸	5
90–102	𝍸	5
102–114	II	2
Total		40

The histogram of the above frequency distribution is given below :

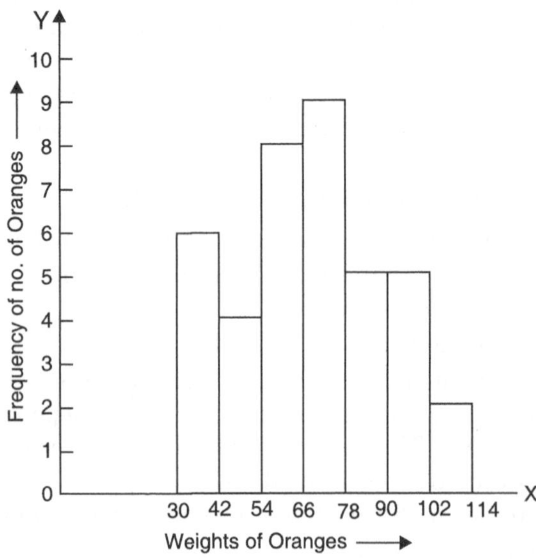

Fig. 4.2. Histogram

Types of Histograms or Bar Diagrams. The various types of histograms or bar diagrams are as under:

(*a*) Simple bar diagrams

(*b*) Multiple or grouped bar charts

(*c*) Deviation bar charts

(*d*) Sub-divided bar charts

(*e*) Component bar diagrams

(*f*) Component bar diagrams based on percentage.

We now illustrate the various types of **histograms or bar diagrams** by suitable examples.

(*a*) **Simple Bar Diagrams.** In this type of diagram, there are as many bars as the number of figure, *i.e.,* one bar represents only one figure. Simple bar diagrams are used to compare the values of a single variable with respect to time or geographical locations.

Example 2. *The strength of a college in different years, is given below*

Years :	*2003*	*2004*	*2005*	*2006*	*2007*	*2008*	*2009*	*2010*
Strength of college :	*700*	*900*	*800*	*875*	*950*	*1000*	*1100*	*1100*

Present the information in the form of a simple bar diagram.

Sol.

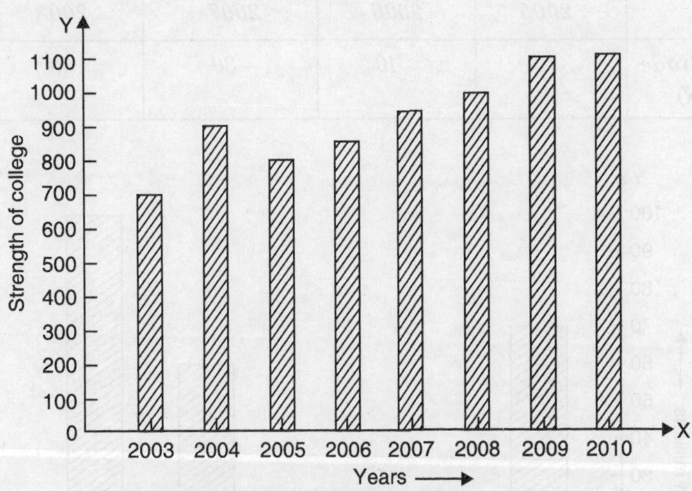

Fig. 4.3. Simple Bar Diagram

(*b*) **Multiple Bar Charts.** A multiple bar chart is also known as grouped (or compound) bar chart. These diagrams are those diagrams which are used to compare two or more related variables with respect to some characteristics of the data. Draw bars for one set of values and for the second set of values, draw bars adjacent to the first one. These bars are shaded differentially to distinguish between various variables.

Example 3. *Draw a multiple bar diagram to show the following data :*

Country	*A*	*B*	*C*	*D*
Export (million ₹)	*14*	*16*	*20*	*15*
Import (million ₹)	*10*	*12*	*10*	*16*

Sol.

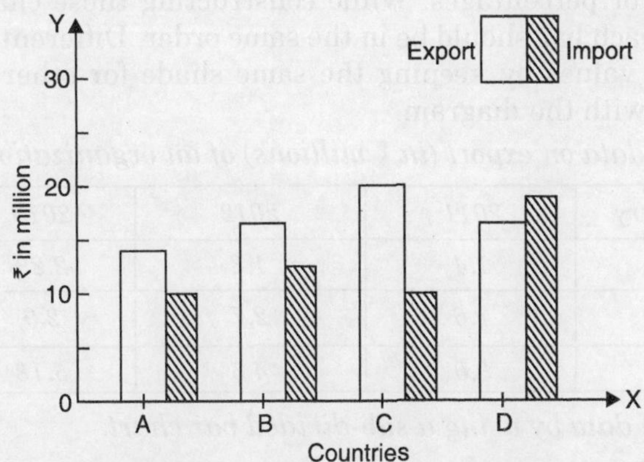

Fig. 4.4. Multiple Bar Diagram

(*c*) **Deviation Bar Diagrams.** These diagrams are those diagrams which are used to compare the net deviation of related variables with respect to some characteristics of the data. Bars representing positive deviation are shown above the base line, while representing negative deviations are shown below the base line. Such types of diagrams represent the deviations in magnitudes as well as in directions.

Example 4. *Represent the following data by using a suitable diagram :*

Years	*2005*	*2006*	*2007*	*2008*	*2009*
Balance of trade (in million ₹)	*70*	*– 40*	*– 30*	*60*	*100*

Sol.

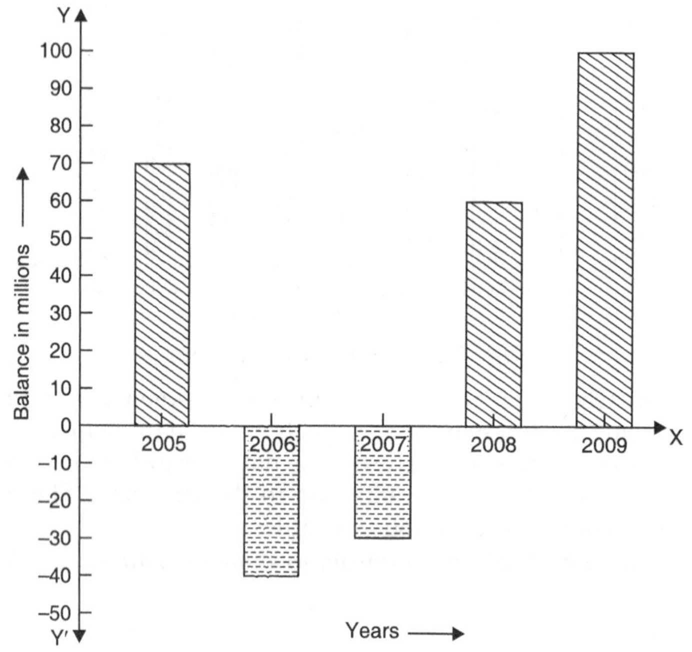

Fig. 4.5. Deviation bar diagram

(*d*) **Sub-divided Bar Charts.** Sub-divided bar charts are best suitable for presenting data in terms of ratios or percentages. While constructing these charts (or diagrams), the various components in each bar should be in the same order. Different shades may be used to represent various ratio values by keeping the same shade for other bars. An index of the shades should be given with the diagram.

Example 5. *The data on export (in ₹ millions) of an organization are given below:*

Country	*2011*	*2012*	*2013*
U.S.A.	*1.4*	*1.8*	*2.29*
U.K.	*1.6*	*2.7*	*2.9*
Total	*3.0*	*4.5*	*5.18*

Express the above data by using a sub-divided bar chart.

Sol. The required sub-divided bar chart of the given data is shown below:

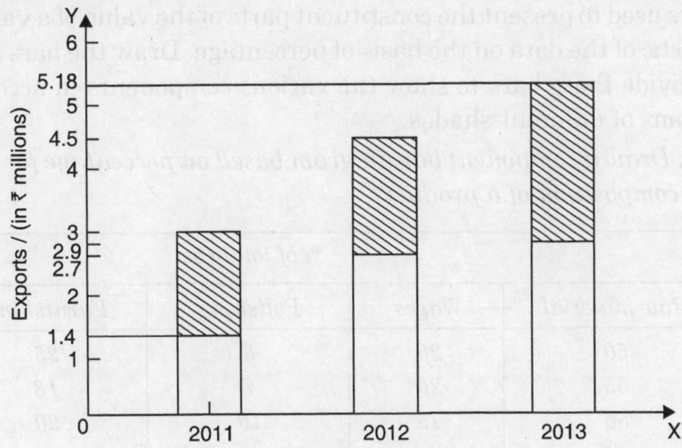

Fig. 4.6. Sub-divided bar chart

(*e*) **Component Bar Diagrams.** These types of diagrams are used to present the constituent part of the value of a variable with respect to some characteristics of the data. Draw the bars for the total sum of the values of different variables and then divide these bars to show the various components of the variable, by means of different shades.

Example 6. *Represent the following data by using component bar diagram :*

Years	*Number of students*			
	B. Pharma	*B. Tech*	*B.E*	*Total*
1999	*200*	*100*	*50*	*350*
2000	*250*	*100*	*70*	*420*
2001	*300*	*150*	*100*	*550*
2002	*300*	*150*	*100*	*550*
2003	*400*	*100*	*100*	*600*

Sol.

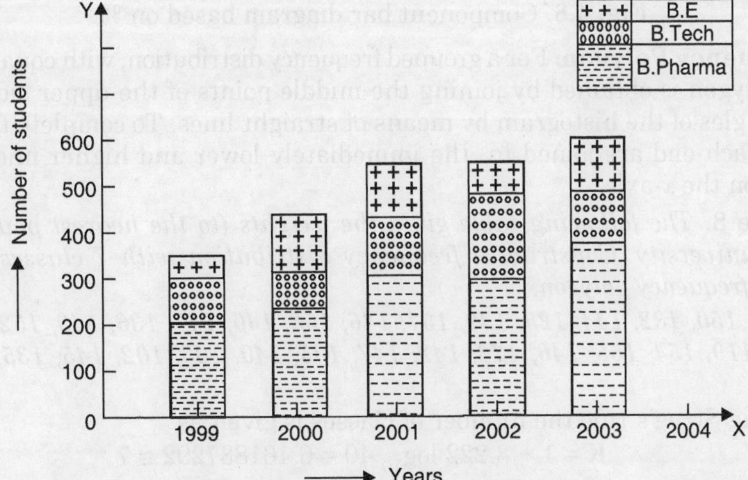

Fig. 4.7. Component bar diagram

(*f*) **Component Bar Diagram Based on Percentage.** These diagrams are those diagrams which are used to present the constituent parts of the value of a variable with respect to some characteristic of the data on the basis of percentage. Draw the bars for total aggregate (100%) and then divide these bars to show the various components in accordance with their percentage, by means of different shades.

Example 7. *Draw a component bar diagram based on percentage for the following data regarding the cost composition of a product :*

Years	*% of total cost*				
	Raw material	*Wages*	*Polishing*	*Furnishing*	*Total*
2001	*50*	*20*	*5*	*25*	*100*
2002	*55*	*20*	*7*	*18*	*100*
2003	*55*	*15*	*10*	*20*	*100*
2004	*50*	*15*	*15*	*20*	*100*

Sol.

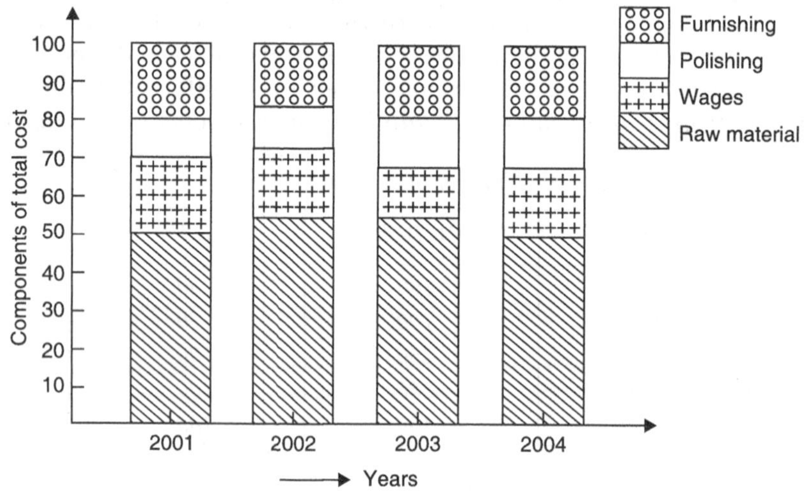

Fig. 4.8. Component bar diagram based on %

II. Frequency Polygon. For a grouped frequency distribution, with equal class-intervals, a frequency polygon is obtained by joining the middle points of the upper sides (tops) of the adjacent rectangles of the histogram by means of straight lines. To complete the polygon, the mid-points at each end are joined to the immediately lower and higher mid-points at zero frequency, *i.e.* on the *x*-axis.

Example 8. *The following table gives the weights (to the nearest pound) of 40 male students at a university. Construct a frequency distribution with 7 classes and draw the histogram and frequency polygon.*

138, 164, 150, 132, 144, 125, 149, 157, 146, 158, 140, 147, 136, 148, 152, 144, 168, 126, 138, 176, 163, 119, 154, 165, 146, 173, 142, 147, 135, 140, 135, 102, 145, 135, 142, 150, 156, 145, 128.

Sol. Using Strug's rule the number of classes is given as

$$K = 1 + 3.222 \log_{10} 40 = 6.161837292 \cong 7$$

Also, width of the class interval

$$= \frac{\text{Largest numerical value} - \text{Smallest numerical value}}{\text{Number of classes}}$$

$$= \frac{176 - 102}{7} = \frac{74}{7} = 10.5714 \cong 11$$

Weight (*to the nearest pound*)	*Tally marks*	*Frequency*
102—113	|	1
113—124	|	1
124—135	||||	4
135—146	~~||||~~ ~~||||~~ ||||	14
146—157	~~||||~~ ~~||||~~ ||	12
157—168	~~||||~~	5
168—179	|||	3
Total		40

The histogram and frequency polygon are shown below :

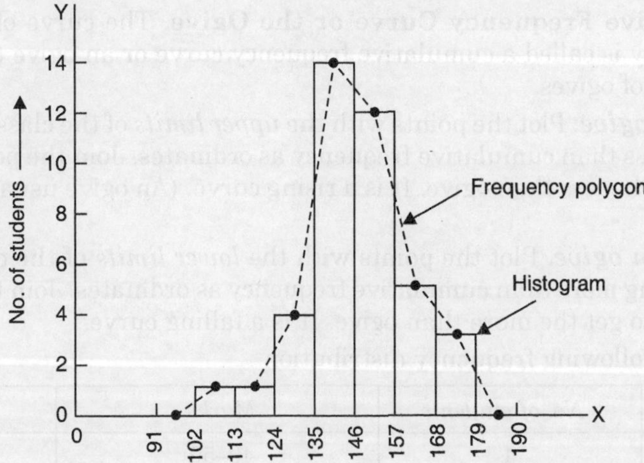

Fig. 4.9. (*Histogram :* rectangles ; *Frequency polygon :* shown dotted)

III. Frequency Curve. It is a curve which is plotted by joining the points of a frequency polygon through free hand smooth curves and not through straight lines.

Example 9. *Represent the following data in the form of a frequency curve, frequency polygon and histogram :*

Marks	*10 – 20*	*20 – 30*	*30 – 40*	*40 – 50*	*50 – 60*	*60 – 70*	*70 – 80*	*80 – 90*
No. of students	*10*	*15*	*25*	*30*	*20*	*20*	*15*	*5*

Sol.

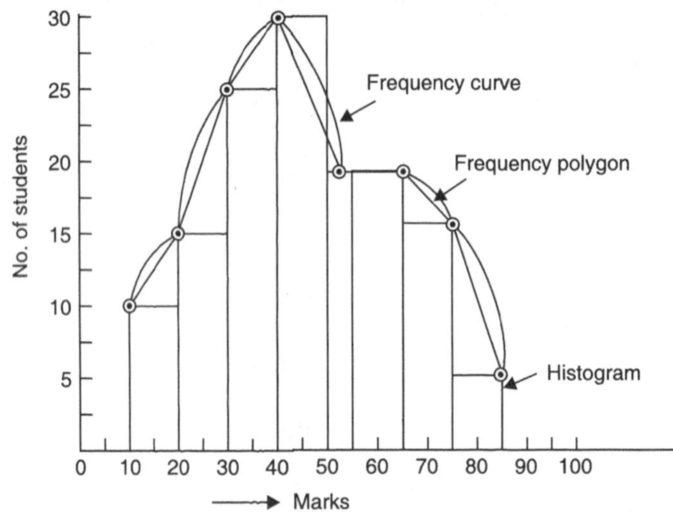

Fig. 4.10. (*Histogram :* Rectangles, Frequency polygon: Straight lines, Frequency curve: Free hand smooth curve)

IV. Cumulative Frequency Curve or the Ogive. The curve obtained by plotting cumulative frequency is called a cumulative frequency curve or an ogive (pronounced ogive). There are two types of ogives.

(*i*) ***Less than ogive.*** Plot the points with the *upper limits* of the classes as abscissae and the corresponding less than cumulative frequency as ordinates. Join the points by a free hand smooth curve to get the less than ogive. It is a rising curve. (An ogive usually means less than ogive).

(*ii*) ***More than ogive.*** Plot the points with the *lower limits* of the classes as abscissae and the corresponding more than cumulative frequency as ordinates. Join the points by a free-hand smooth curve to get the more than ogive. It is a falling curve.

Consider the following frequency distribution :

Marks	*No. of students*	*Marks*	*No. of students*
10–20	4	40–50	20
20–30	6	50–60	18
30–40	10	60–70	2

Let us convert it first into a 'less than cumulative frequency distribution and then into a 'more than cumulative frequency distribution.

Marks less than	*No. of students*	*Marks more than*	*No. of students*
20	4	10	60
30	(+ 6 =) 10	20	(– 4 =) 56
40	(+ 10 =) 20	30	(– 6 =) 50
50	(+ 20 =) 40	40	(– 10 =) 40
60	(+ 18 =) 58	50	(– 20 =) 20
70	(+ 2 =) 60	60	(– 18 =) 2
		70	(– 2 =) 0

Example 10. *Draw the two ogives for the following distribution showing the number of marks of 59 students :*

Marks	*No. of students*	*Marks*	*No. of students*
0–10	*4*	*40–50*	*12*
10–20	*8*	*50–60*	*6*
20–30	*11*	*60–70*	*3*
30–40	*15*		

Sol.

Marks	*No. of students*	*Less than c.f.*	*More than c.f.*
0–10	4	4	59
10–20	8	12	55
20–30	11	23	47
30–40	15	38	36
40–50	12	50	21
50–60	6	56	9
60–70	3	59	3

Plotting the points (10, 4), (20, 12), (30, 23), (40, 38), (50, 50), (60, 56), (70, 59) and joining them by free-hand, the smooth rising curve so obtained is less than ogive.

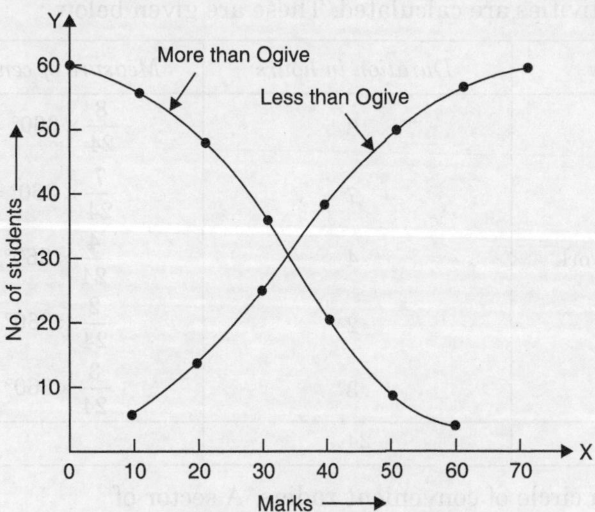

Fig. 4.11. Ogives

Plotting the points (0, 59), (10, 55), (20, 47), (30, 36), (40, 21), (50, 9), (60, 3) and joining them by free-hand, the smooth falling curve so obtained is more than ogive.

V. Pie-charts or Pie-diagrams. These types of diagrams are used to show the component parts of a total. For example, it is used to represent the division of a total amount into its different components. The Pie-chart is so called because it resembles with the Greek letter π (pie) and the components resemble slices cut from pie (π).

Working Method to Draw Pie-charts or Diagrams

(1) Draw a circle of proper size. The radius of the drawn circle is proportional to the space available and the factors for presentation.

(2) Divide the circle into sectors such that sum of the angles of each sector is equal to 360°.

We illustrate by examples.

Example 11. *The number of hours, spent by a school boy on different activities in a working day, is given below :*

Activity	*Number of hours*
Sleep	*8*
School	*7*
Homework	*4*
Play	*2*
Others	*3*
Total	*24*

Present the information in the form of a pie-chart.

Sol. Number of hours spent on different activities in a day of 24 hours are converted into component parts of 360°. Since the duration of sleep is 8 hours, hence, it should represent $\frac{8}{24} \times 360° = 120°$. Therefore, the sector of the circle representing sleep hours should have a central angle of 120°. Similarly, the degree measures of angles subtended by sectors representing other activities are calculated. These are given below :

Activity	*Duration in hours*	*Measure of central angle*
Sleep	8	$\frac{8}{24} \times 360° = 120°$
School	7	$\frac{7}{24} \times 360° = 105°$
Homework	4	$\frac{4}{24} \times 360° = 60°$
Play	2	$\frac{2}{24} \times 360° = 30°$
Others	3	$\frac{3}{24} \times 360° = 45°$
Total	24	360°

Now we draw a circle of convenient radius. A sector of central angle 120° is fixed to show the time spent in hours on sleep. Similarly, sectors representing time spent on other activities are marked, say, clockwise. Protractors are used for correct markings of the different sectors. Different sectors of the circle are shaded with different designs as shown in figure. Given hours of different activities are provided close to the side of the pie-chart.

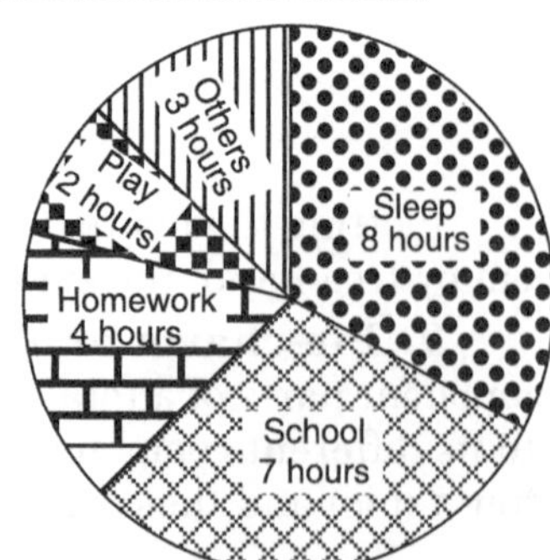

Fig. 4.12. Pie-diagram

Example 12. *The number of students in a hostel speaking different languages is given below. Present the data in a pie-chart.*

Languages	*Hindi*	*English*	*Marathi*	*Tamil*	*Bengali*	*Total*
Number of Students	*40*	*12*	*9*	*7*	*4*	*72*

Sol. Number of students speaking different languages in a total of 72 students are converted in component parts of 360°. Now we find angle of sectors.

Languages	*Number of students*	*Measure of central angle*
Hindi	40	$\frac{40}{72} \times 360° = 200°$
English	12	$\frac{12}{72} \times 360° = 60°$
Marathi	9	$\frac{9}{72} \times 360° = 45°$
Tamil	7	$\frac{7}{72} \times 360° = 35°$
Bengali	4	$\frac{4}{72} \times 360° = 20°$
Total	72	360°

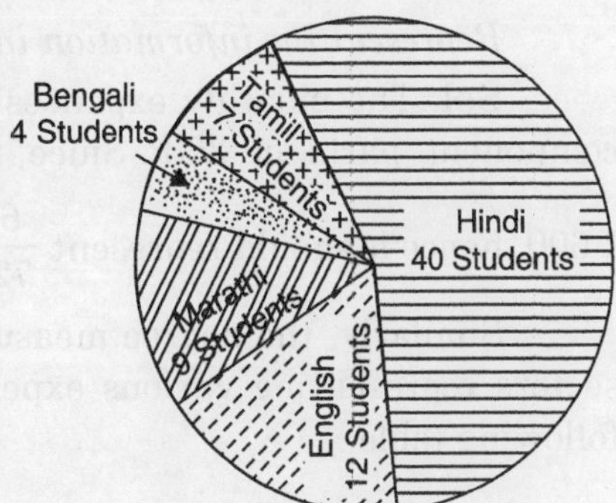

Fig. 4.13. Pie-diagram

A circle of convenient radius is now drawn and the above angles are marked at the centre of the circle, 5 radii will then divide the whole circle into five required sectors. The different sectors are shaded with different designs. Figure gives the required pie-chart.

Example 13. *The following pie-chart (figure) represents the number of valid votes obtained by four students who contested for school leadership. The total number of valid votes polled was 720. Answer the following questions by reading the pie- chart :*

(*i*) *Who has won the election ?*

(*ii*) *What is the minimum number of votes obtained by any candidate ?*

(*iii*) *By how many votes did the winner defeat the nearest contestant ?*

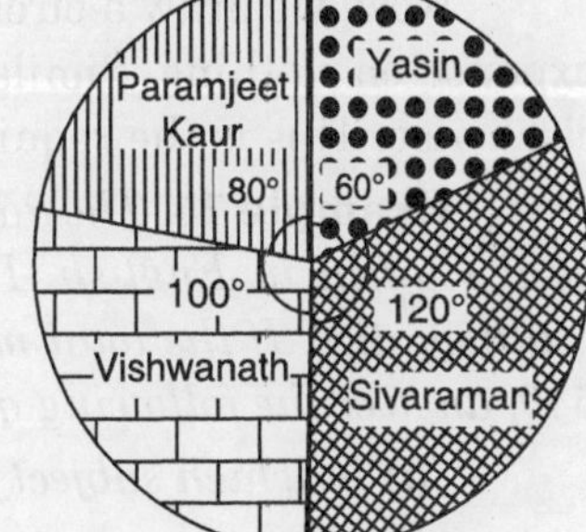

Fig. 4.14. Pie-diagram

Sol. (*i*) Sivaraman is represented by a sector of greatest central angle, *i.e.*, 120°. Therefore, Sivaraman has won the election.

(*ii*) Yasin is represented by a sector of least central angle, *i.e.*, 60°.

Therefore, minimum votes obtained by Yasin = $\frac{60}{360} \times 720 = 120$ votes.

(*iii*) The nearest contestent of Sivaraman is Vishwanath.

Votes obtained by Sivaraman = $\frac{120}{360} \times 720 = 240$

Votes obtained by Vishwanath $= \frac{100}{360} \times 720 = 200$

$\therefore$ Shivaraman defeated Vishwanath by 240 – 200 = 40 votes.

Example 14. *In the month of July 2002, a householder spent his monthly salary amounting to ₹ 7200 on different items as given below :*

Items	*Clothing*	*Food*	*House Rent*	*Education*	*Miscellaneous*
Amount spent (in ₹)	*600*	*4000*	*1200*	*400*	*1000*

Represent the information in the form of a pie-chart.

Sol. The monthly expenses ₹ 7200 are converted into component parts of 360°. Since, the expenses on clothing is ₹ 600, hence it should represent $\frac{600}{7200} \times 360° = 30°$.

Similarly, the degree measure of angles subtended by sectors representing various expenses are calculated in the following table :

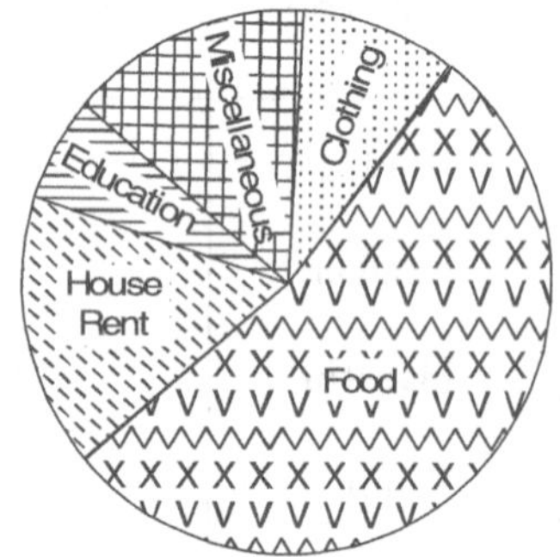

Fig. 4.15. Pie-chart

Items	*Clothing*	*Food*	*House Rent*	*Education*	*Miscellaneous*	*Total*
Spent (in ₹)	600	4000	1200	400	1000	7200
Measure of central angle	$\frac{600 \times 360°}{7200}$ = 30°	$\frac{4000 \times 360°}{7200}$ = 200°	$\frac{1200 \times 360°}{7200}$ = 60°	$\frac{400 \times 360°}{7200}$ = 20°	$\frac{1000 \times 360°}{7200}$ = 50°	360°

Now, we draw a circle of convenient radius. A sector of central angle 30° will show the expense on clothing. Similarly, sectors representing the different expenses are marked, say, clockwise. This is the required pie-diagram.

Example 15. *The adjoining pie-chart (figure) gives the marks scored in an examination by a student in English, Hindi, Science, Social Science and Mathematics. If the total marks obtained by the student were 540, answer the following questions:*

(*i*) *In which subject the student scored 105 marks ?*

(*ii*) *How many more marks were obtained by the student in Mathematics than in Hindi ?*

(*iii*) *Examine whether the sum of marks obtained in Social Science and Mathematics is more than that in Science and Hindi.*

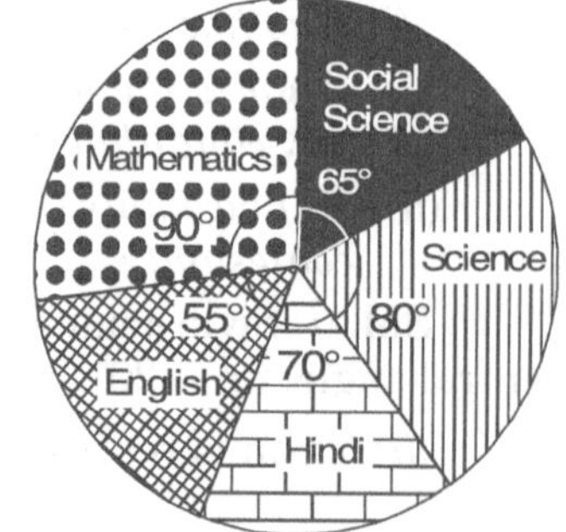

Fig. 4.16. Pie-chart

Sol. (*i*) For the total marks 540, central angle = 360°

$\therefore$ For 105 marks, central angle $= \frac{105}{540} \times 360° = 70°$

Since, central angle of the sector representing Hindi is 70°, hence, the student scored 105 marks in Hindi.

(*ii*) The difference of central angles of the sectors representing Mathematics and Hindi

$$= 90° - 70° = 20°$$

∴ Corresponding difference of marks

$$= \frac{20}{360} \times 540 = 30$$

Hence, the student scored 30 marks more in Mathematics than that in Hindi.

(*iii*) The sum of central angle of the sectors representing Social Science and Mathematics

$$= 65° + 90° = 155°$$

Similarly, the sum of central angles of the sectors representing Science and Hindi

$$= 80° + 70° = 150°.$$

Since, 155° > 150°, so the sum of marks obtained in Social Science and Mathematics is more than that in Science and Hindi.

Example 16. *Percentage of the different products of a village in a particular district are given below. Draw a pie-chart representing this information.*

Items	*Wheat*	*Pulses*	*Jwar*	*Groundnuts*	*Vegetables*	*Total*
%	$\frac{125}{3}$	$\frac{125}{6}$	$\frac{25}{2}$	$\frac{50}{3}$	$\frac{25}{3}$	*100*

Sol. The products (100) of the village are converted into component parts of 360°. Since the production of wheat $= \frac{125}{3}$ %, hence, it should represent $\frac{125}{3} \times \frac{360°}{100} = 150°$.

Therefore, the sector of the circle representing production of wheat should have a central angle of 150°. Similarly, the degree measure of angles subtended by sectors representing other products are calculated in the following table :

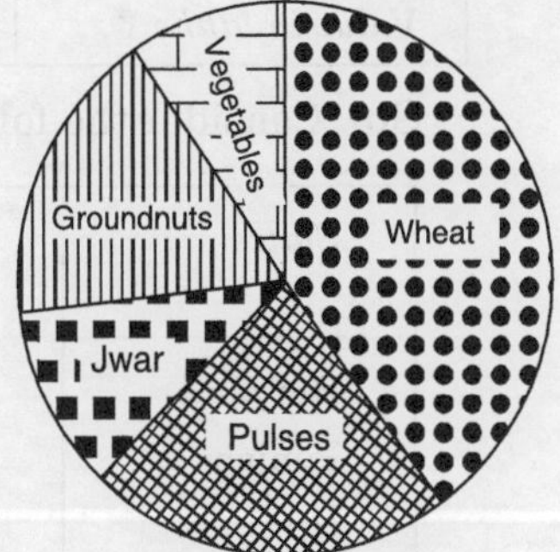

Fig. 4.17.

Items	Wheat	Pulses	Jwar	Groundnuts	Vegetables	Total
%	$\frac{125}{3}$	$\frac{125}{6}$	$\frac{25}{2}$	$\frac{50}{3}$	$\frac{25}{3}$	100
Measure of central angle	$\frac{125}{3} \times \frac{360°}{100}$ = 150°	$\frac{125}{6} \times \frac{360°}{100}$ = 75°	$\frac{25}{2} \times \frac{360°}{100}$ = 45°	$\frac{50}{3} \times \frac{360°}{100}$ = 60°	$\frac{25}{3} \times \frac{360°}{100}$ = 30°	360°

Now, we draw a circle of convenient radius. A sector of central angle 150° will show the wheat production of the village. Similarly, sectors representing the different products are marked, say, clockwise. Different sectors of the circle are shaded with different designs.

Limitations of Pie Diagrams (or Charts). As compared to bar diagrams, pie diagrams or charts are less effective for accurate reading. When the given series are divided into a large number of components or the difference between the components is very small, Pie charts are not suitable to represent such data. For example, if a series has 6, 7, 8 or 10 components, it will be very confusing to differentiate the relative values portrayed specially when the several small sectors are of almost equal size.

4.7(b). TWO-DIMENSIONAL DIAGRAMS

The diagrams in the shapes of squares, rectangles and circles, are known as two dimensional diagrams. We take the areas in the proportion to the size of items which they represent. The following are the three types of two-dimensional diagrams :

(*a*) Square diagrams

(*b*) Rectangular diagrams

(*c*) Circular diagrams.

We now illustrate the various types of 2-D diagrams by suitable examples.

(*a*) **Square Diagrams.** Sometimes, we deal with such data in which we come across many variables having the values which are very high and vary widely in magnitude. In such types of representation, we use square diagrams. The square diagrams are used to compare the values of variable which vary widely in magnitude. In these diagrams, we draw squares in such a way that their areas are in proportion with the values of the variables.

Example 17. *Represent the following figures relating the values of sugar manufactured in various states of India by making square diagrams :*

States	*Haryana*	*Punjab*	*H.P.*	*U.P.*
Value in lakhs ₹	*2500*	*3600*	*400*	*4900*

Sol. Consider the following table :

States	*Values in lakhs* x	$\sqrt{x}$	*Ratio in* $\sqrt{x}$
Haryana	2500	50	5
Punjab	3600	60	6
H.P.	400	20	2
U.P.	4900	70	7

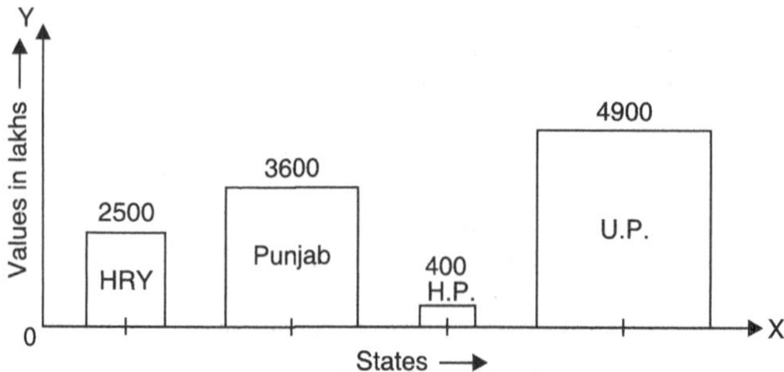

Fig. 4.18. Square diagrams

(*b*) **Rectangular diagrams.** The data in which the two variables are related with respect to some characteristic, can be easily shown by rectangular diagrams. When the variables of a data are composed of various components, we use rectangular diagrams to represent the such data.

Example 18. *Represent the following data using rectangular diagrams :*

Years	*2001*	*2002*	*2003*
Cost per unit (₹)	*15*	*20*	*25*
No. of units sold	*300*	*500*	*400*

Sol.

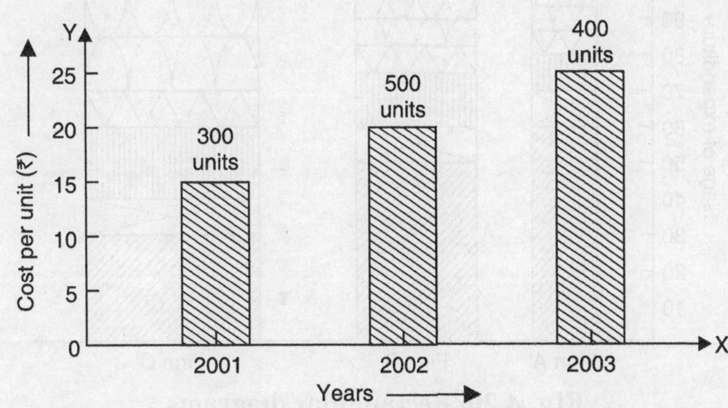

Fig. 4.19. Rectangular diagrams

Example 19. *Represent the following data by a suitable diagram :*

Items of expenditure	*Firm A*	*Firm B*	*Firm C*
Food	*20*	*60*	*120*
Clothing	*4*	*15*	*70*
House rent	*3*	*20*	*80*
Education	*2*	*6*	*25*
Petrol	*2*	*10*	*70*
Others	*2*	*8*	*50*

Sol. We firstly find the percentage of expenditure on each item for each firm.

Items	*Firm A*		*Firm B*		*Firm C*	
	₹	*%age*	₹	*%age*	₹	*%age*
Food	20	$\frac{20}{33} \times 100 = 60.6$	60	$\frac{60}{119} \times 100 = 50$	120	28.91
Clothing	4	12.2	15	12.50	70	16.86
House rent	3	9.10	20	16.70	80	19.27
Education	2	6.06	6	5.00	25	6.0
Petrol	2	6.06	10	8.30	70	16.86
Others	2	6.06	8	7.50	50	12.04
Total	33	100.08	119	100.00	415	99.94

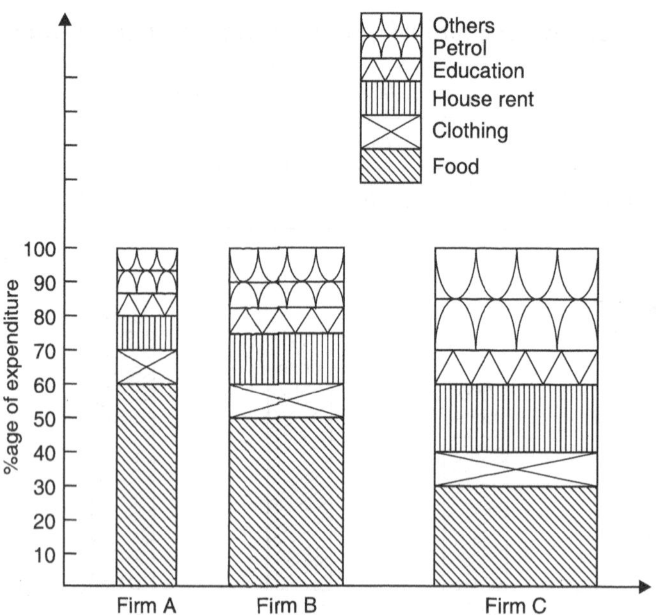

Fig. 4.20. Rectangular diagrams

(*c*) **Circular Diagrams.** These diagrams are used to show the various components of the variables under consideration. Draw circles such that their areas are in proportion with the values of the variable under consideration. The radii of these circles are proportional to the square roots of the values of the variables.

Example 20. *Represent the following data by circular diagrams :*

Years	*2001*	*2002*	*2003*	*2004*
Population (in crores)	*64*	*81*	*100*	*121*

Sol. Since, the values of the variables increasing very rapidly, we can use circular diagrams.

Years	2001	2002	2003	2004
Population X	64	81	100	121
$\sqrt{X}$	8	9	10	11
Ratio in $\sqrt{X}$	$\frac{8}{8} = 1$	$\frac{9}{8} = 1.125$	$\frac{10}{8} = 1.25$	$\frac{11}{8} = 1.375$

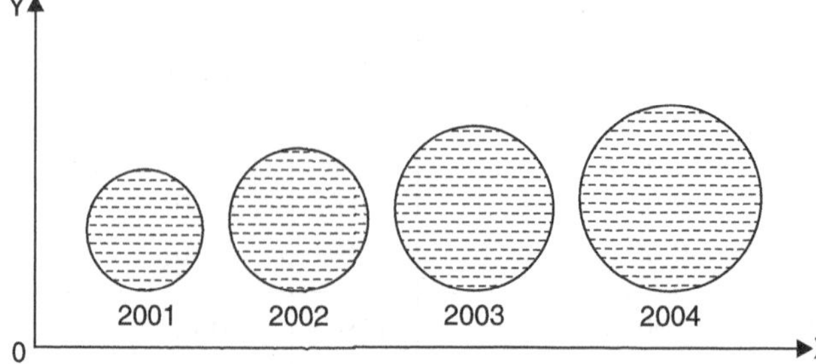

Fig. 4.21. Circular diagrams

Limitations of Two Dimensional Diagrams

In drawing a square, one has to take the square root of the values of various items that are to be shown in the diagrams. Similarly, in drawing a circle, one has to take the area of the circle proportional to the square of its radius. And the radius of the circle can be obtained by dividing the value of π and taking square root of this value.

These methods of drawing squares and circles are difficult and are not very popular in statistical work.

4.7(c). THREE-DIMENSIONAL DIAGRAMS

The diagrams in the shapes of cubes, cylinders and blocks, are known as three dimensional diagrams. The various types of 3-D diagrams are :

(*a*) Cubical diagrams

(*b*) Cylinders

(*c*) Blocks.

In two-dimensional diagrams, when the two values of the variable vary widely in magnitude, we use square diagrams. But in the cases, when the square roots of the values of the variable may also vary widely in magnitude, then we use cubical diagrams. Draw cubes such that their sides are proportional to the cube roots of the corresponding value of the variable.

Example 21. *Represent the following data diagrammatically by using cubical diagram :*

Factory	*A*	*B*	*C*
No. of items sold	*8000*	*27000*	*64000*

Sol.

Factory	*Itmes X*	$X^{1/3}$	*Ratio in* $X^{1/3}$
I	8000	20	2
II	27000	30	3
III	64000	40	4

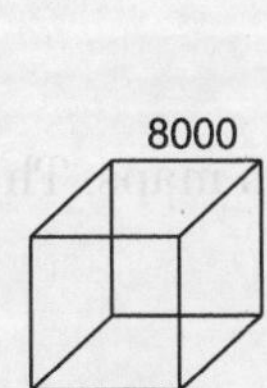

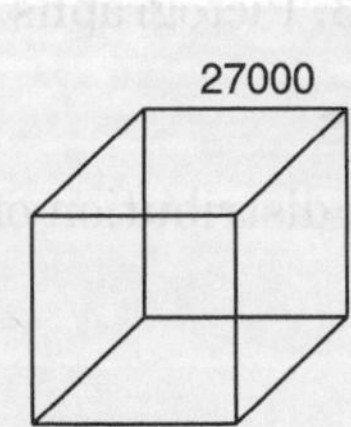

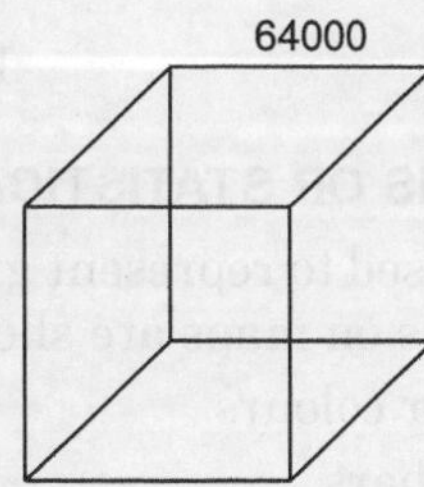

Fig. 4.22. Cubical diagrams

Limitations of Three Dimensional Diagrams

In drawing a cube, one has to take the side of a cube proportional to the cube-root of the side. It is very difficult for the eye to read such diagrams and hence they are not recommended for statistical presentation.

4.8. PICTOGRAMS OR IDEOGRAPHS

A pictogram is a special type of pictorial bar chart. These diagrams are useful for those people who cannot understand the charts or diagrams. Small symbols or simple pictures can be used to represent the size of the data.

Construction of Pictograms. In constructing pictograms or ideographs, the following points should be kept in mind:

(*i*) Use simple, clear concise and interesting symbols

(*ii*) A symbol should be neither large nor small

(*iii*) Larger quantities are shown by increasing the number of symbols and not by increasing the size of the symbols.

Example 22. *Make a pictographic or ideographic presentation of the number of mobiles phones during a week by Nokia.*

Day	*Monday*	*Wednesday*	*Friday*	*Sunday*
No. of mobile phones	*2004*	*2996*	*4219*	*5324*

Sol. Dividing the given number of mobiles phones by 1000, we get

Number of mobiles phones on Monday $= \frac{2004}{1000} = 2.004 \cong 2$

Number of mobiles phones on Wednesday $= 2.996 \cong 3$

Number of mobiles phones on Friday $= 4.219 \cong 4$

Number of mobiles phones on Sunday $= 5.324 \cong 5$

Representing the above information in the following pictograph:

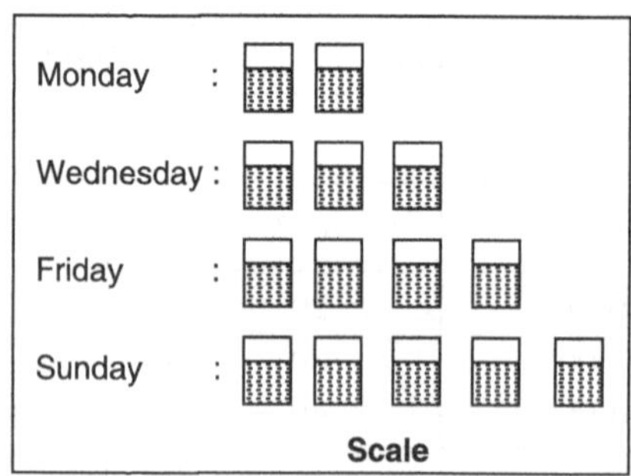

Fig. 4.23. Pictographs

4.9. CARTOGRAMS OR STATISTICAL MAPS

These are used to represent graphical distribution of data on maps. The various figures in different regions on maps are shown by

(*i*) Shades or colours

(*ii*) Dots or bars

(*iii*) Diagrams or pictures

(*iv*) Numerical figures.

4.10. GRAPHICAL REPRESENTATION OF DATA

A frequency distribution when represented by means of a graph makes the unwidely data intelligible. A better perspective can be held by representing the frequency distribution graphically, since graphs, if drawn neatly, are eye catching and leave a more lasting impression on the mind of the observer. Graphs are a good visual aid. But graphs do not give accurate measurements of the variable as are given by the tables. Another disadvantage is that by taking different scales, the facts may be misrepresented.

4.11. CLASSIFICATION OF DIFFERENT TYPES OF GRAPHS

The graphs can be classified into various categories as shown by the following diagram :

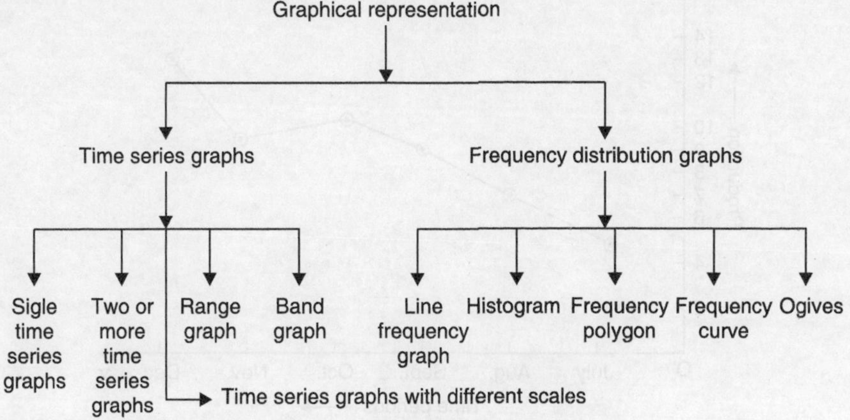

Fig. 4.24. Classification of graphs

We now discuss in details the various types of graphs.

Time series graphs

If in the given data, the values of the variables are based on time, then the graph of this type of series is known as time series graphs. The time variable is taken along horizontal axis (x-axis) and the second variable along vertical axis (y-axis). The x-axis, in this type of graph as also called base line.

4.12. TYPES OF TIME SERIES GRAPHS

The following are the various type of time series graphs :

(*a*) Single time series graphs.

(*b*) Two or more time series graphs.

(c) Two time series graphs with different scales.

(*d*) Range graph.

(*e*) Band graph.

We now illustrate the various time series graphs by suitable examples.

(*a*) **Single Time Series Graphs.** These graphs are those graphs in which value of only one variable is shown with respect to time periods.

Example 23. *Represent the following data graphically :*

Months	*July*	*Aug.*	*Sept.*	*Oct.*	*Nov.*	*Dec.*
Production in tonnes	*5*	*7*	*8*	*10*	*9*	*13*

Sol.

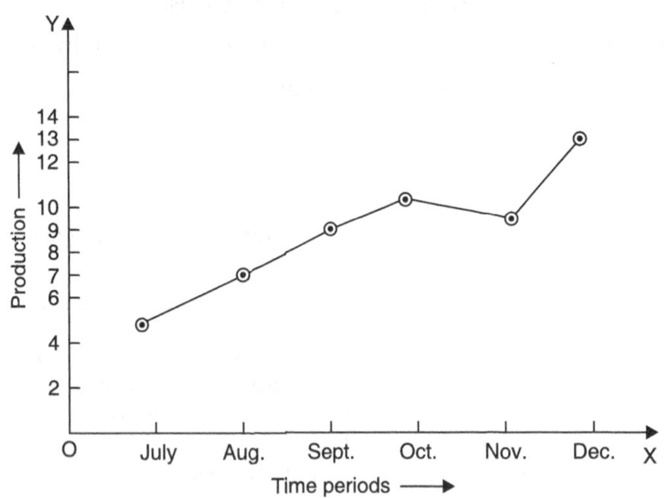

Fig. 4.25. Single time series graph

(*b*) **Two or More Time Series Graphs.** In this type of graphs, the values of two or more than two variables are simultaneously shown with respect to time. Different variables can be shown by different lines.

Example 24. *Represent the following data graphically :*

Years	*2001*	*2002*	*2003*	*2004*	*2005*	*2006*
Marks in Pharma. Maths	*90*	*95*	*80*	*85*	*90*	*95*
Marks in Pharma. Chem.	*70*	*80*	*70*	*70*	*75*	*85*

Sol. From the given data, we observe that the minimum value of the marks obtained in mathematics as well as in chemistry are quite high, therefore, we make use of false base line. Break the vertical scale and neglect the portion between zero and the minimum value as shown by dotted lines in the figure.

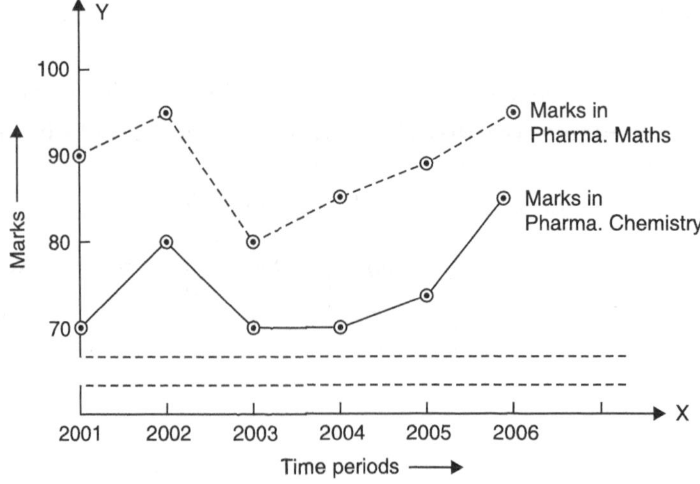

Fig. 4.26. Two time series graphs

(*c*) **Two Time Series with Different Scales.** This type of graphs are used when the value of two variables are expressed in two different units. Along *y*-axis, one variable is taken on the left of the base line and another is taken on the right of the base line. The average value of both the variables are kept in the middle of the graph.

Example 25. *The following are the figures on the production of items in quintals and the values of that items in rupees between January to July, 2005. Represent the following data graphically :*

Months	*January*	*February*	*March*	*April*	*May*	*June*	*July*
Production (in thousand quintals)	*15*	*25*	*20*	*20*	*25*	*30*	*35*
Values (in thousand ₹)	*230*	*350*	*250*	*300*	*425*	*650*	*750*

Sol.

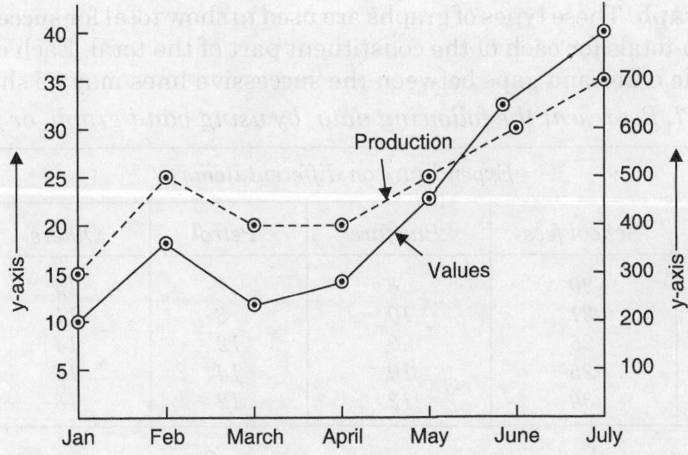

Fig. 4.27. Two time series graphs with different scales

(*d*) **Range Graph.** The maximum and minimum values of the variables can be determined by range graphs. For example, the maximum and minimum values of the temperature distribution for different time periods, can be well-determined by using range graph. Take time along horizontal axis and the given variable along *y*-axis.

Example 26. *The average maximum and minimum prices of shares of a mutual equality fund of a company X are given below.*

Years	*2001*	*2002*	*2003*	*2004*	*2005*	*2006*	*2007*
Max. value	*2000*	*2100*	*2050*	*2300*	*2100*	*2400*	*2500*
Min. value	*1800*	*1850*	*1850*	*1900*	*1700*	*2000*	*2100*

Represent the data graphically, by using range graph.

Sol. From the given data, we observe that the maximum and minimum value of the shares is quite high. Therefore, we make use of false base line. Break the vertical scale and neglect the portion between zero and the minimum value as shown by the dotted lines in the figure.

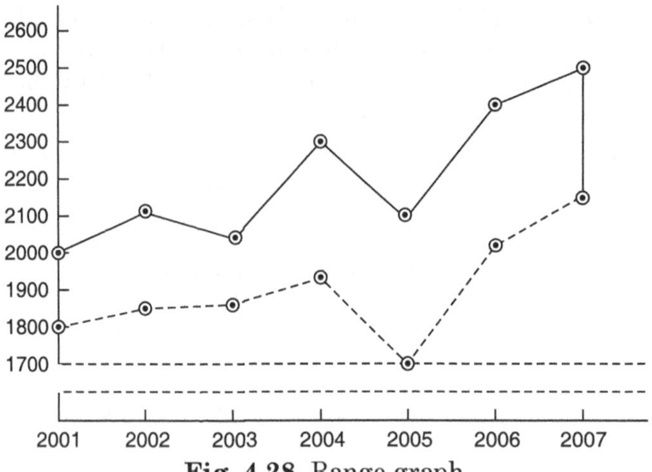

Fig. 4.28. Range graph

(*e*) **Band Graph.** These types of graphs are used to show total for successive time periods broken up into sub-totals for each of the constituent part of the total. Each constituent part is plotted are over the other and gaps between the successive lines may be shaded.

Example 27. *Represent the following data, by using band graph, or graphically :*

Expenditure on different items					
Years	*School fees*	*Bus fare*	*Petrol*	*Others*	*Total*
2001	*20*	*8*	*7*	*15*	*50*
2002	*21*	*10*	*8*	*11*	*50*
2003	*25*	*9*	*12*	*14*	*60*
2004	*25*	*10*	*14*	*16*	*68*
2005	*30*	*12*	*12*	*18*	*72*

Sol.

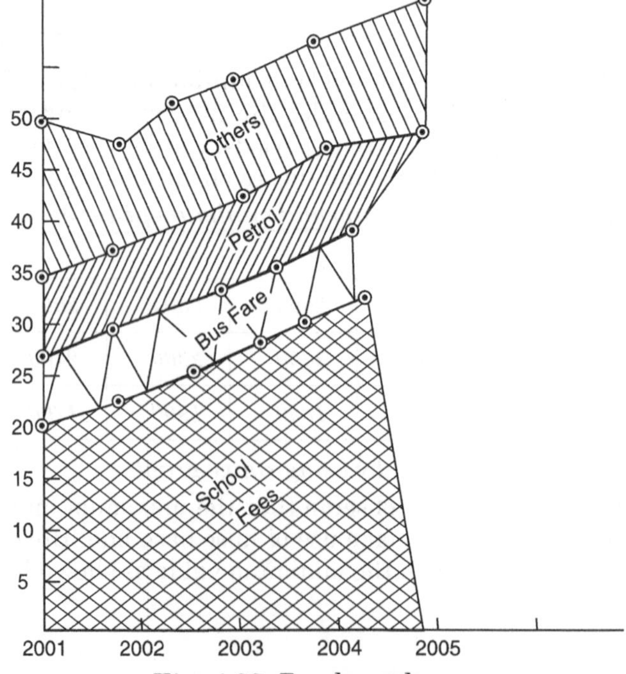

Fig. 4.29. Band graph

4.13. FREQUENCY DISTRIBUTION GRAPHS

These graphs represent the frequency distribution of a given data on graph papers. The number of times a different value of the repeated variables is known as frequency of the variable. The following are its various types :

(*a*) Line frequency graph
(*b*) Histogram
(*c*) Frequency polygon
(*d*) Frequency curve
(*e*) Cumulative frequency curve or ogive.

We now illustrate the various types of frequency distribution graphs by suitable examples.

(*a*) **Line Frequency Graph.** It is the graph presenting a discrete frequency distribution of a given data on a graph paper. The frequency of the variable is shown in the form of a straight line or dotted lines either along *x*-axis or *y*-axis.

Example 28. *Represent the following data graphically:*

No. of students	*5*	*10*	*10*	*15*	*12*
Weight in kg	*30*	*35*	*40*	*45*	*50*

Sol.

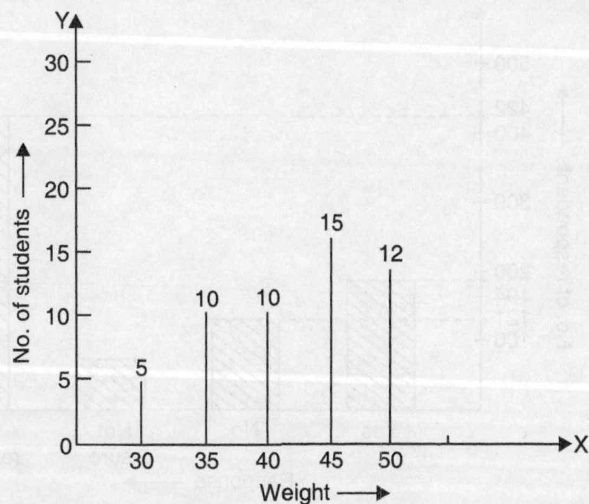

Fig. 4.30. Line frequency graph

The various graphslike Histograms, frequency, polygon, frequency curve, ogive etc. have been explained in previous sections.

4.14. CASE STUDIES

Housing complex. The welfare committee of a large housing complex wants to understand the possibility of appointing private security guards at the entrance gate of the complex for 24-hour duty. There are 810 flats in the housing complex, and the owners were asked to vote for or against the proposal. The following data were collected.

Response	*No. of Respondents*
Yes	194
No	121
Not sure	73
No response	422

Questions For Discussions:

(a) Convert the data to percentages and construct (i) a bar char and (ii) a pie chart. Which of these charts do you prefer to use? Why?

(b) Eliminating the 'no response' group, convert the remaining 388 responses to percentages and again construct bar and pie charts.

Suppose you have been designated as poll officer, based on your analysis of the data, what would you like to suggest to the president of the welfare committee?

Sol. (*a*) Given data, after converting to percentages, is given below.

Response	*No. of respondents*	*%*	*App. %*
Yes	194	$\frac{194 \times 100}{810} = 23.95$	24
No	121	14.93	15
Not sure	73	9.01	9
No response	422	52.09	52
Total	810		100

(*i*) The bar diagram (or chart) of the above data is shown below:

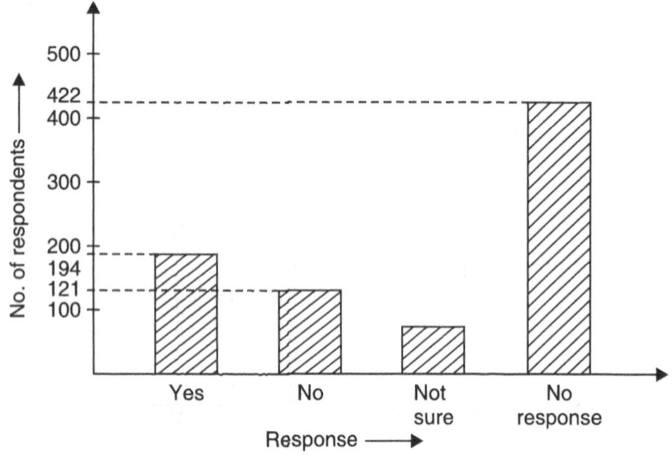

Fig. 4.31. Bar diagram

(*ii*) We now convert the given data in Pie-chart. The no. of respondents can be converted into component parts of 360° as shown in the following table.

Response	*No. of respondents*	*%*	*App. Central angle*
Yes	194	$\left(\frac{194 \times 360°}{810}\right) = 86.22°$	86°
No	121	53.77°	54°
Not sure	73	32.44°	33°
No response	422	187.55°	187°
Total	810		360°

Draw a circle of convenient radius. A central angle of 86° shows the 'yes' response. Similarly, sectors representing the different responses are marked, say, clockwise. The pie-diagram is shown below.

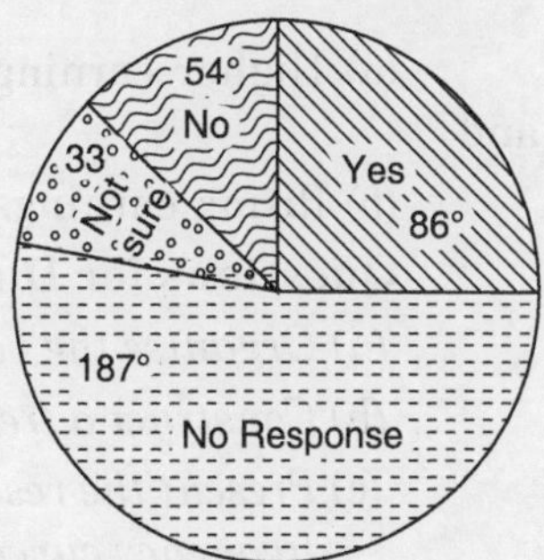

Fig. 4.32. Pie-chart

Since, there are only four components, momely, 'Yes', 'No', 'No sure' and 'No response', any one diagram, either the bar diagram or pie-chart can be used to represent the given data.

(*b*) Now, eliminating the 'No response', we convert the remaining 388 responses to % and construct the bar chart as well as pie-chart.

(*i*)

Response	*No. of respondents*	*%*	*App.%*	*Central angle*
Yes	194	$\frac{194 \times 100}{388} = 50$	50	$\left(\frac{194 \times 360}{388}\right) = 180°$
No	121	31.18	31	= 112.26° ≅ 112°
Not sure	73	18.81	19	67.73° ≅ 68°
Total	388		100	

The bar diagram and pie-chart of the above data are shown below

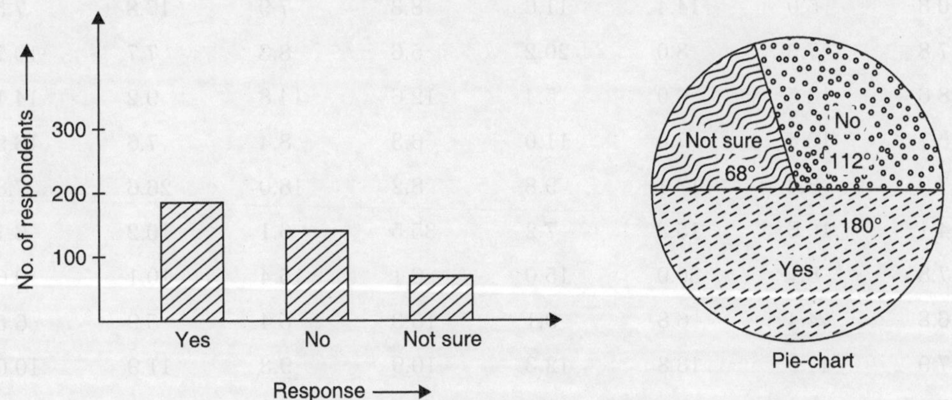

Fig. 4.33.

Suggestion. The sector corresponding to 'yes response' is large as compared to other sectors. Therefore, as a poll officer, I would like to suggest the president of the welfare society to hire security guards at the entrance gate of the complex for 24 hour duty.

Case Study II: Portfolio Management. A portfolio manager keeps a close watch on price-earnings ratios (defined as current market price divided by earnings for the most recent four quarters) of 200 common stocks. He reasons that, when the majority of stocks in a representative sample have low price-earnings (P-E) ratios by historical standards, it is time to become an aggressive buyer. Low P-E ratios may mean that investors in general are unrealistically pessimistic. Moreover stocks with low P-E ratios can benefit in a two-fold way when earnings increase.

(*a*) Higher earnings multiplied by a constant P-E ratio means a higher market price and

(*b*) Rising earnings are usually accompanied by rising P-E ratios.

Questions for Discussion:

(a) Organise the values of the variable into an array.

(b) Construct a frequency distribution table.

(c) Present the resulting frequency distribution as a histogram or frequency polygon or frequency curve and comment on the pattern.

(d) Construct a cumulative frequency distribution and ogive.

Price-Earnings Ratios for 200 common stocks							
11.1	12.6	26.7	5.2	8.3	5.5	6.8	7.6
7.3	18.1	14.6	10.9	7.2	9.5	9.2	11.8
12.0	16.9	10.1	14.6	5.2	7.5	11.1	19.9
14.9	7.4	6.0	39.9	29.3	35.1	6.8	39.0
6.1	6.2	26.8	33.7	9.6	16.6	10.9	11.2
22.6	46.0	7.3	29.7	10.3	6.4	9.6	7.6
10.3	5.0	14.4	11.6	8.3	7.9	17.8	7.5
7.8	7.3	8.0	20.2	5.6	8.3	7.7	10.7
8.6	14.5	6.0	5.4	12.6	14.8	9.2	14.1
15.7	10.4	7.0	11.0	6.3	8.4	7.6	16.9
7.9	8.3	13.1	9.8	8.2	18.0	26.6	7.8
4.1	10.6	15.3	7.2	35.5	6.1	10.2	6.1
7.8	8.1	30.0	15.0	6.1	15.4	10.1	9.6
6.8	4.4	6.8	9.1	16.3	5.4	5.9	6.5
7.9	44.9	13.8	12.3	10.9	9.3	11.9	10.0
7.6	17.9	7.1	8.4	35.5	7.4	7.7	8.3
15.8	8.3	23.1	8.4	12.4	7.8	8.2	9.8
13.7	15.8	4.7	7.9	26.4	6.2	11.4	13.2
8.6	11.7	8.6	13.7	9.3	16.6	8.7	39.7
14.0	9.1	7.1	10.9	23.4	13.3	10.9	24.0
11.9	8.7	15.6	27.7	10.4	16.9	6.9	5.5
22.8	8.5	22.2	5.8	14.7	8.0	7.5	10.5
4.4	7.1	63.8	12.5	13.3	10.5	5.5	16.0
53.1	7.4	24.1	15.3	29.1	11.0	9.9	36.3
9.6	6.6	5.1	7.8	8.4	38.3	20.4	9.1

Table A

Sr.no.	Given data	Sorted data	Sr.no.	Given data	Sorted data	Sr.no.	Given data	Sorted data	Sr.no.	Given data	Sorted data
1	11.1	4.1	51	26.7	7.6	101	8.3	10.1	151	6.8	15.3
2	7.3	4.4	52	14.6	7.6	102	7.2	10.2	152	9.2	15.3
3	12	4.4	53	10.1	7.7	103	5.2	10.3	153	11.1	15.4
4	14.9	4.7	54	6	7.7	104	29.3	10.3	154	6.8	15.6
5	6.1	5	55	26.8	7.8	105	9.6	10.4	155	10.9	15.7
6	22.6	5.1	56	7.3	7.8	106	10.3	10.4	156	9.6	15.8
7	10.3	5.2	57	14.4	7.8	107	8.3	10.5	157	17.8	15.8
8	7.8	5.2	58	8	7.8	108	5.6	10.5	158	7.7	16
9	8.6	5.4	59	6	7.8	109	12.6	10.6	159	9.2	16.3
10	15.7	5.4	60	7	7.9	110	6.3	10.6	160	7.6	16.6
11	7.9	5.5	61	13.1	7.9	111	8.2	10.7	161	26.6	16.6
12	4.1	5.5	62	15.3	7.9	112	35.5	10.9	162	10.2	16.9
13	7.8	5.5	63	30	7.9	113	6.1	10.9	163	10.1	16.9
14	6.8	5.6	64	6.8	8	114	16.3	10.9	164	5.9	16.9
15	7.9	5.8	65	13.8	8	115	10.9	10.9	165	11.9	17.8
16	7.6	5.9	66	7.1	8.1	116	35.5	10.9	166	7.7	17.9
17	15.8	6	67	23.1	8.2	117	12.4	11	167	8.2	18
18	13.7	6	68	4.7	8.2	118	26.4	11	168	11.4	18.1
19	8.6	6.1	69	8.6	8.3	119	9.3	11	169	8.7	19.9
20	14	6.1	70	7.1	8.3	120	23.4	11.1	170	10.9	20.2
21	11	6.1	71	15.6	8.3	121	10.4	11.1	171	6.9	20.4
22	22.8	6.1	72	22.2	8.3	122	14.7	11.2	172	7.5	22.2
23	4.4	6.2	73	63.8	8.3	123	13.3	11.4	173	5.5	22.6
24	53.1	6.2	74	24.1	8.3	124	29.1	11.6	174	9.9	22.8
25	9.6	6.3	75	5.1	8.4	125	8.4	11.7	175	20.4	23.1
26	12.6	6.4	76	5.2	8.4	126	5.5	11.8	176	7.6	23.4
27	18.1	6.5	77	10.9	8.4	127	9.5	11.9	177	11.8	24
28	16.9	6.6	78	14.6	8.4	128	7.5	12	178	19.9	24.1
29	7.4	6.8	79	39.9	8.5	129	35.1	12.3	179	39	26.4
30	6.2	6.8	80	33.7	8.6	130	16.6	12.4	180	11.2	26.6
31	46	6.8	81	29.7	8.6	131	6.4	12.5	181	7.6	26.7
32	5	6.8	82	11.6	8.6	132	7.9	12.6	182	7.5	26.8
33	7.3	6.9	83	20.2	8.7	133	8.3	12.6	183	10.7	27.7
34	14.5	7	84	5.4	8.7	134	14.8	13.1	184	14.1	29.1
35	10.4	7.1	85	11	9.1	135	8.4	13.2	185	16.9	29.3
36	8.3	7.1	86	9.8	9.1	136	18	13.3	186	7.8	29.7
37	10.6	7.1	87	7.2	9.1	137	6.1	13.3	187	6.1	30
38	8.1	7.2	88	15	9.2	138	15.4	13.7	188	9.6	33.7
39	4.4	7.2	89	9.1	9.2	139	5.4	13.7	189	6.5	35.1
40	44.9	7.3	90	12.3	9.3	140	9.3	13.8	190	10.6	35.5
41	17.9	7.3	91	8.4	9.3	141	7.4	14	191	8.3	35.5
42	8.3	7.3	92	8.4	9.5	142	7.8	14.1	192	9.8	36.3
43	15.8	7.4	93	7.9	9.6	143	6.2	14.4	193	13.2	38.3
44	11.7	7.4	94	13.7	9.6	144	16.6	14.5	194	39.7	39
45	9.1	7.4	95	10.9	9.6	145	13.3	14.6	195	24	39.7
46	8.7	7.5	96	27.7	9.6	146	16.9	14.6	196	5.5	39.9
47	8.5	7.5	97	5.8	9.8	147	8	14.7	197	10.5	44.9
48	7.1	7.5	98	12.5	9.8	148	10.5	14.8	198	16	46
49	7.4	7.6	99	15.3	9.9	149	11	14.9	199	36.3	53.1
50	6.6	7.6	100	7.8	10.1	150	38.3	15	200	9.1	63.8

Sol. The given data and the sorted data are given in the above table A. From the table A we observe that there are 127 items falling in the class 4–12, 42 items in the class 12–20, 14 items in the class 20–28, 8 items in the class 28–36, 5 items in the class 36–44, 2 items in the class 44–52 and 1 item in each class 52–60 and 60–68 respectively.

(*a*) and (*b*). The given data is raw data or ungrouped data. We arrange them as a grouped frequency distribution. We condense the given data into classes or groups as below.

The largest element = 63.8, smallest element = 4.1. If K denotes the number of classes and N the total number of observations, them the value of K will be the smallest +ve exponent of 2 such that $2^K \geq 200$ (since N = 200)

Clearly $2^8 = 256 > 200 \quad \therefore \quad K = 8$

Hence, there are 8 classes or groups.

$$\text{Also, width of each class} = \frac{\text{Range}}{\text{Total number of classes}}$$

$$= \frac{63.8 - 4.1}{8} = \frac{59.7}{8} = 7.46 \cong 8, \text{ say,}$$

Using the above data, we have the following frequency table.

Classes	*Tally marks*	*Frequency (Less than)*	*Cumulative frequency (Less than)*	*Cumulative frequency (more than)*
4–12	25(卌) ||	127	127	200
12–20	8(卌) ||	42	169	73
20–28	2(卌) ||||	14	183	31
28–36	卌 |||	8	191	17
36–44	卌	5	196	9
44–52	||	2	198	4
52–60	|	1	199	2
60–68	|	1	200	1
Total		200		

(*c*) The histogram, the frequency polygon and the frequency curve of the given data is shown below (Fig. 4.34).

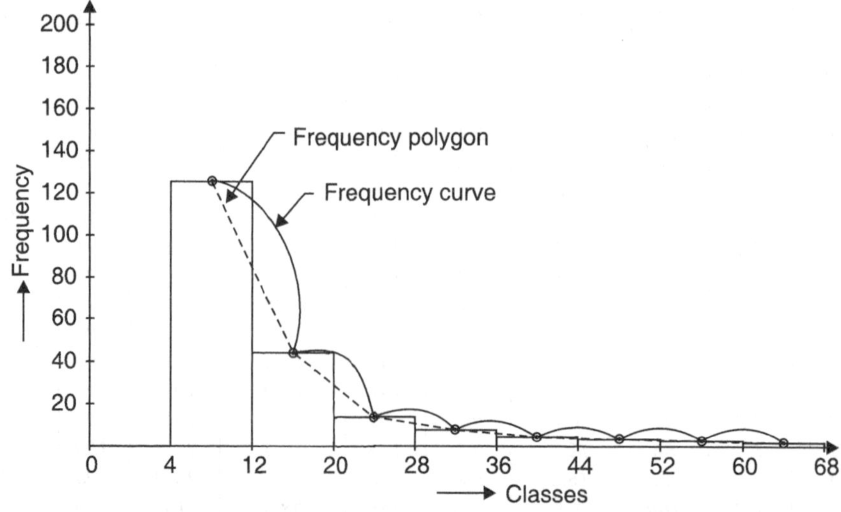

Fig. 4.34. Histogram, frequency polygon and frequency curve

Comment. From the Fig. 4.34, we conclude that when the price earning ratio lies in the class 4–12, the number of buyers is 127, which is **maximum** and when the price earning ratio lies in the class 52–60 or 60–68, the number of buyers is 1 (**minimum**).

(*d*) To construct a cumulative frequency distribution, plot the following points (12, 127), (20, 169), (28, 183), (36, 191), (44, 196), (52, 198), (60, 199) and (68, 200) on the graph paper and join them by free hand. The smooth rising curve so obtained is "less than ogive" curve.

Similarly, plot the points (4, 200), (12, 73), (20, 31), (28, 17), (36, 9), (44, 4), (52, 2) and (60, 1) on the graph paper and join with a free hand. The smooth falling curve so obtained is "more than ogive" curve.

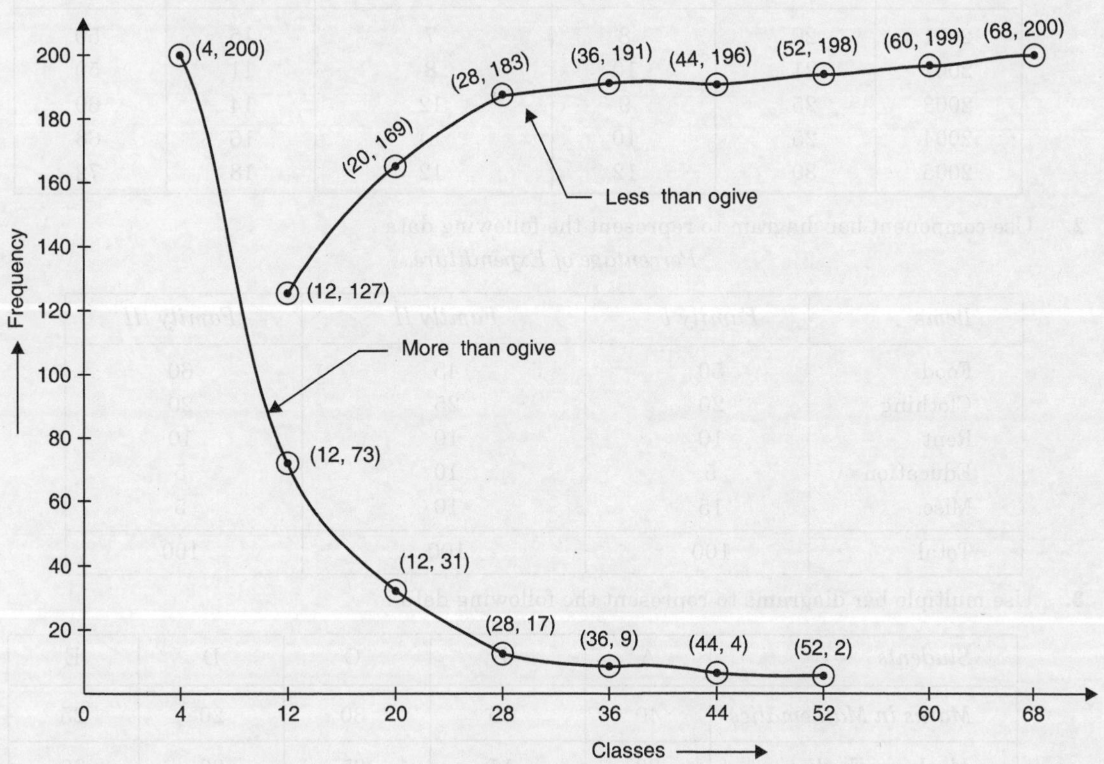

Fig. 4.35. Ogives

TEST YOUR KNOWLEDGE

1. (*a*) Present the following data diagrammatically by using simple bar diagram :

Years	2001	2002	2003	2004	2005	2006
No. of doctors	400	500	700	400	6500	750

(*b*) Represent the following data diagrammatically :

Expenditure on different items

Years	*Food*	*Clothing*	*Fuel and lighting*	*Misc.*	*Total*
2001	20	8	7	15	50
2002	21	10	8	11	50
2003	25	9	12	14	60
2004	25	10	14	16	68
2005	30	12	12	18	72

2. Use component bar diagram to represent the following data :

Percentage of Expenditure

Items	*Family I*	*Family II*	*Family III*
Food	50	45	60
Clothing	20	25	20
Rent	10	10	10
Education	5	10	5
Misc.	15	10	5
Total	100	100	100

3. Use multiple bar diagrams to represent the following data :

Students	A	B	C	D	E
Marks in Mathematics	40	35	30	20	25
Marks in English	30	15	25	20	30

4. Using deviation bar diagram, represent the following data :

Years	2000	2001	2002	2003	2004	2005
Savings/Deficit (In thousand ₹)	30	– 20	10	15	– 25	20

5. Construct a pie-diagram to represent the following expenditure of five year plan :

Government	Central Government	Part A state	Part B state	Part C state	Total
Expenditure in crores of rupees	1400	350	175	175	2100

6. Construct a pie-diagram for the following data in which student population of the university A is given :

University A	Arts	Science	Commerce	Law	Medicine
Population	800	500	300	100	100

7. Draw a pie-chart diagram for the following data of investment :

Ministry	Community development	Agriculture	Industries	Transport and communication	Social services
Investment of rupees in crores	1100	900	700	600	300

8. Draw a pie-diagram to represent the following data on money spent (in crores of rupees) on various items during the Eighth Five Year Plan :

Items	*Money spent (in crores of ₹)*
Agriculture	12500
Energy	15000
Industry	10000
Rural development	20000
Social service	21250
Miscellaneous	11250
Total	90000

9. Read the following pie-diagram and find out the amount spent on education :

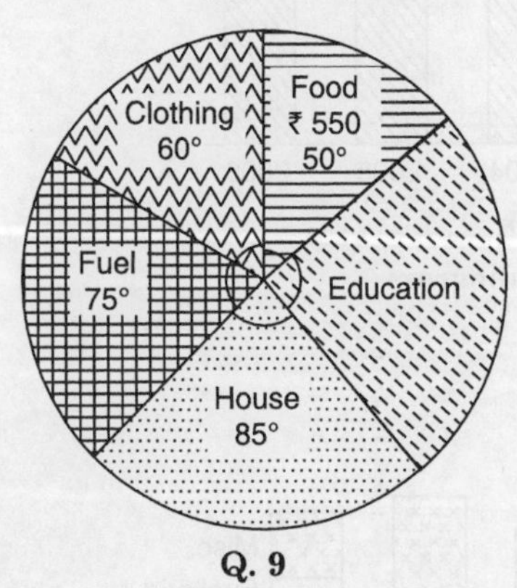

Q. 9

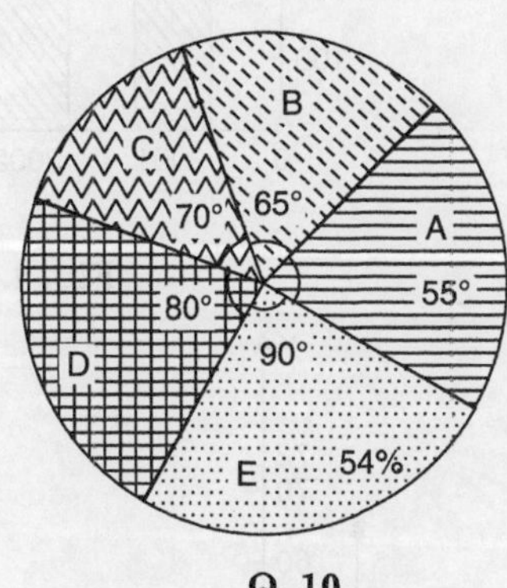

Q. 10

10. A pie-diagram of literacy of five cities is given above. From the pie-diagram, find the percentage of literacy in city A.

11. The pie-chart shown below shows the monthly expenditure of a family on food, clothing, rent, miscellaneous expenses and savings.

Read the pie-chart carefully and answer the following questions :

(*i*) What is the central angle for savings ?

(*ii*) What is the ratio of expenditure on food to that on rent ?

(*iii*) If the family spends ₹ 825 on clothing, what is its total monthly income ?

(*iv*) What per cent of the total income does the family save ?

[Hint. (*i*) Central angle for savings

$= 360° - (108° + 90° + 36° + 72°) = 54°.$

(*ii*) Ratio of expenditure on food to that on rent

= ratio of their central angles = 108 : 90 = 6 : 5.

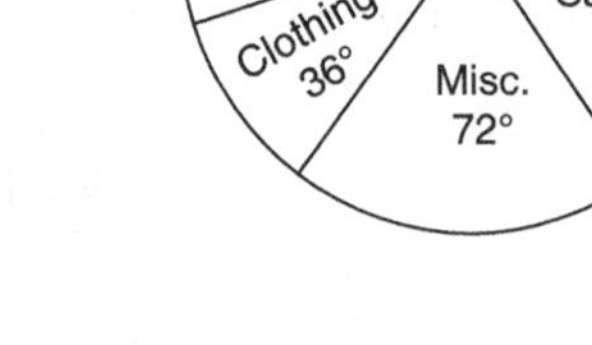

(*iii*) Central angle for clothing

$$= \left(\frac{\text{money spent on clothing}}{\text{total value}} \times 360\right)^{\circ}$$

$$\Rightarrow \quad 36 = \frac{825}{\text{(total value)}} \times 360$$

$$\Rightarrow \quad \text{total value} = \left(\frac{825}{36} \times 360\right) = 8250.$$

∴ In that case, the total monthly income is ₹ 8250.

(*iv*) Savings % $= \left(\frac{\text{central angle for savings}}{360^{\circ}} \times 100\right)\% = \left(\frac{54^{\circ}}{360} \times 100\right)\% = 15\%.$

Answers

1. (*a*)

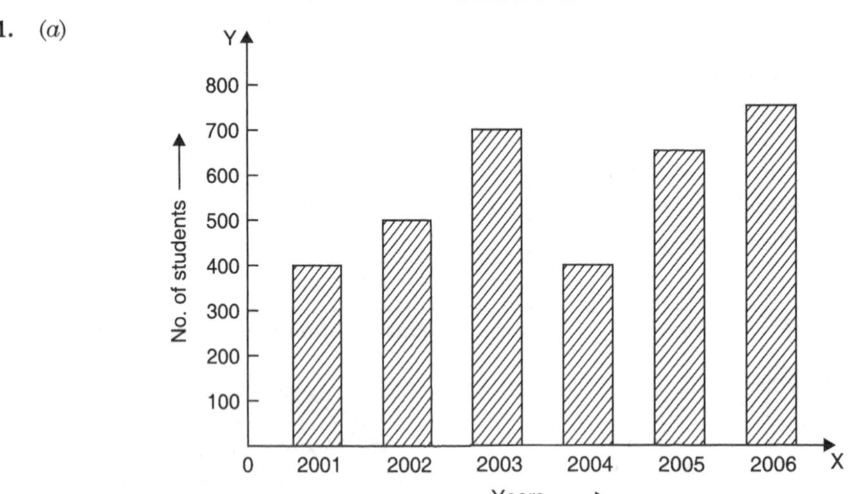

Fig. 4.36. Simple bar diagram

(*b*)

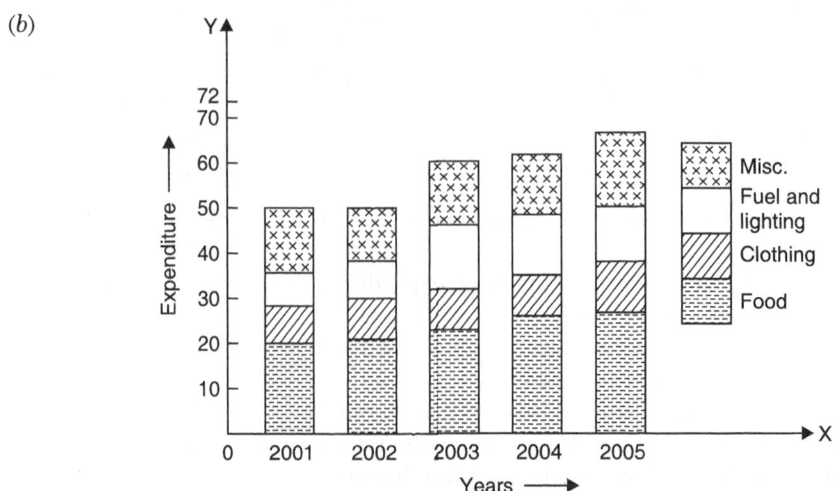

Fig. 4.37. Component bar diagram

2.

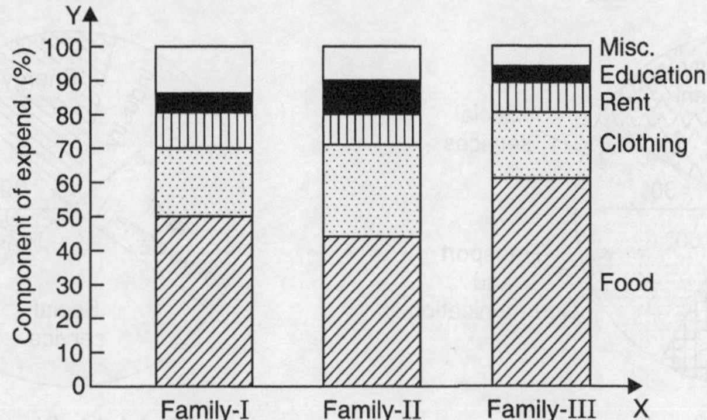

Fig. 4.38. Component bar diagram based on %

3.

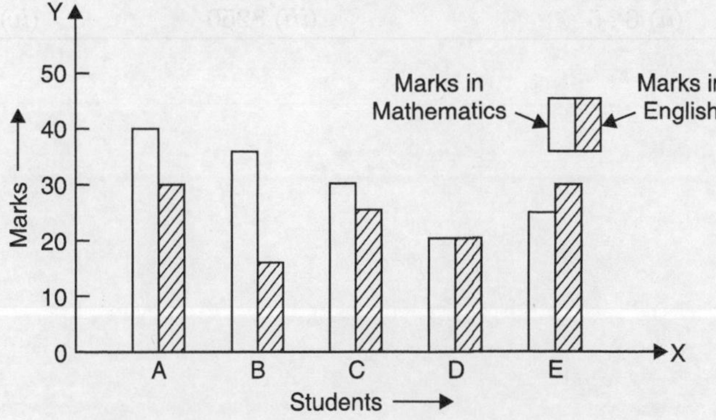

Fig. 4.39. Multiple bar diagram

4.

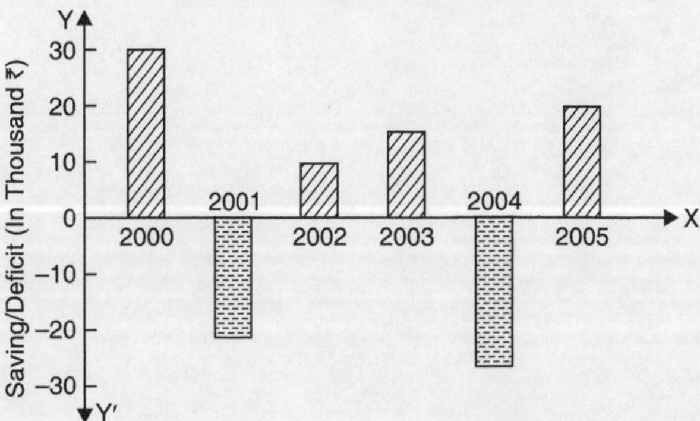

Fig. 4.40. Deviation bar diagram

5.

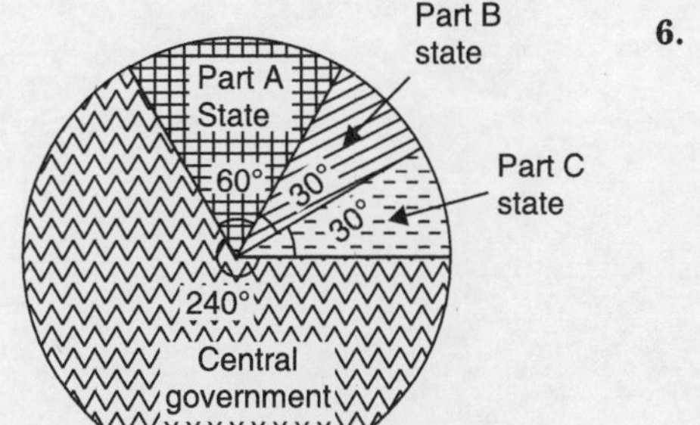

Fig. 4.41. Pie-diagram

6.

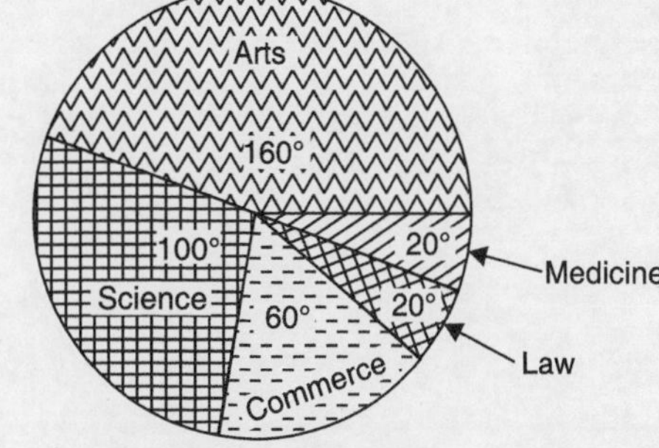

Fig. 4.42. Pie-diagram

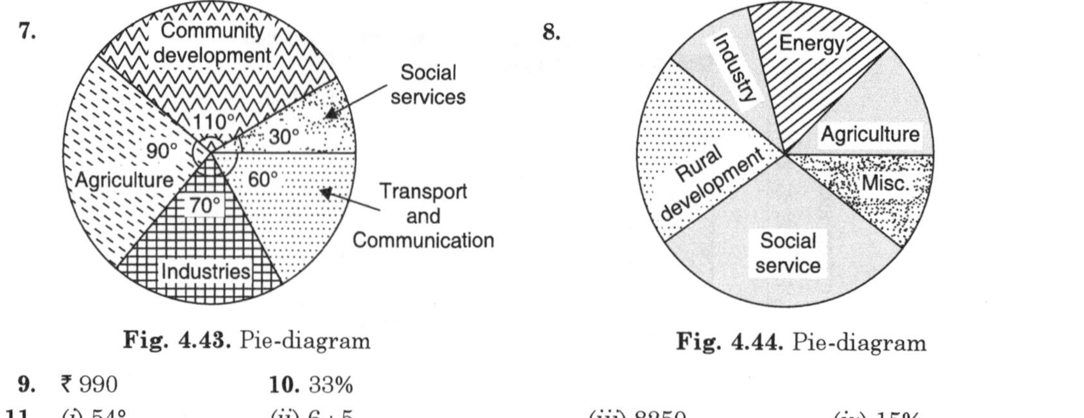

Fig. 4.43. Pie-diagram

Fig. 4.44. Pie-diagram

9. ₹ 990 **10.** 33%

11. (*i*) 54° (*ii*) 6 : 5 (*iii*) 8250 (*iv*) 15%.

5

Measures of Central Tendency

MEAN

5.1. AVERAGES OR MEASURES OF CENTRAL TENDENCY OR MEASURES OF LOCATION

(P.T.U., M.B.A. Dec. 2005, May 2010)

An average or a central value of a data or of a statistical series is the value of the variate which describes the characteristic of the entire data or associated frequency distribution. In other words, an average of a distribution is the value of the variable which is representative of the entire distribution. Since an average represents the entire data, therefore, its values lie somewhere in between two extremes *i.e.,* the largest and the smallest items. For this reason, an average is called a measure of location or a measure of central tendency.

There are five measures of central tendency :

(*a*) A. M. or mean (*b*) Median (*c*) Mode

(*d*) Geometric mean (*e*) Harmonic mean.

5.2. REQUISITES FOR AN IDEAL MEASURE

According to Prof. Yule, the following are the characteristic to be satisfied for an ideal measure for central tendency.

(*a*) It should be rigidly defined

(*b*) It should be easily calculated

(*c*) It should be based on all observations

(*d*) It should be suitable for further mathematical treatment. It means, if we are given the averages and sizes of a number of series, we should be able to calculate the averages of the composite series obtained on combining the given series.

(*e*) It should be affected as little as possible by fluctuations of sampling. In addition to above, we may add the following which is not due to Prof. Yule.

(*f*) It should not be affected much by extreme values.

5.3. ARITHMETIC MEAN (A.M.) *(P.T.U., M.B.A. Dec. 2009)*

I. In the case of Individual observations (when frequency is not given)

(*a*) Direct Method. If $x_1, x_2, ..., x_n$ are the given observations, then A.M. $\overline{x}$ is given by

$$\overline{x} = \frac{x_1 + x_2 + ... + x_n}{n} = \frac{1}{n}\sum_{i=1}^{n} x_i$$

(b) Short-Cut Method (Shift of origin). Shifting the origin to an *arbitrary point a,* the formula

$$\bar{x} = \frac{1}{n}\Sigma x \quad \text{becomes} \quad \bar{x} - a = \frac{1}{n}\Sigma(x - a)$$

$$\bar{x} = a + \frac{1}{n}\Sigma d_x, \text{ where} \quad d_x = x - a$$

Thus, $$\bar{x} = a + \frac{1}{n}\Sigma d_x,$$

where a = arbitrary number, called *Assumed Mean*

$$\Sigma d_x = \Sigma(x - a) = (x_1 - a) + (x_2 - a) + \ldots\ldots + (x_n - a)$$

= sum of the deviations of the variate x from a

n = number of observations.

II. In the case of Discrete Series :

(a) Direct Method. If the frequency distribution is

$x : x_1, x_2, x_3, \ldots\ldots, x_n.$

$f : f_1, f_2, f_3, \ldots\ldots, f_n$, then

$$\bar{x} = \frac{f_1x_1 + f_2x_2 + \ldots\ldots + f_nx_n}{f_1 + f_2 + \ldots\ldots + f_n} = \frac{\Sigma fx}{N}, \quad \text{where } N = f_1 + f_2 + \ldots\ldots + f_n = \Sigma f$$

(b) Short-Cut Method (Shift of origin). Shifting the origin to an arbitrary point 'a', the formula

$$\bar{x} = \frac{1}{N}\Sigma fx \quad \text{becomes} \quad \bar{x} - a = \frac{1}{N}\Sigma f(x - a)$$

$$\bar{x} = a + \frac{1}{N}\Sigma fd_x, \quad \text{where } d_x = x - a$$

Thus, $$\bar{x} = a + \frac{1}{N}\Sigma fd_x, \quad \text{where } a = \text{Assumed mean}$$

$$\Sigma fd_x = \Sigma f(x - a) = f_1(x_1 - a) + f_2(x_2 - a) + \ldots\ldots + f_n(x_n - a)$$

$$N = f_1 + f_2 + \ldots\ldots + f_n = \Sigma f.$$

Note. If the frequencies are given in terms of class intervals, the mid-values of class intervals are considered as x and then the above formulae are applied.

Step Deviation Method

III. In the case of continuous series having equal class intervals, say of width h, we use a different formula shift of origin and change of scale

Let $$u = \frac{x - a}{h} \text{ then } x = a + hu$$

∴ $$\Sigma fx = \Sigma f(a + hu) = a\,\Sigma f + h\Sigma fu$$

Dividing both sides by $N = \Sigma f$, we get

$$\frac{\Sigma fx}{N} = a + \frac{h\Sigma fu}{N} \quad \text{or} \quad \bar{x} = a + h\frac{\Sigma fu}{N}, \text{ where } u = \frac{x - a}{h}.$$

ILLUSTRATIVE EXAMPLES

Example 1. *By using short cut method, find the A.M. of the following observations,*
15, 20, 25, 19, 12, 11, 13, 17, 18, 20.

Sol. Calculation of A.M. here $n = 10$ and take $a = 12$

x_i	$d_x = x_i - a$
15	– 3
20	8
25	13
19	7
12 (= a)	0
11	– 1
13	1
17	5
18	6
20	8
	Total = 44

$$\therefore \text{ A.M. } \bar{x} = a + \frac{1}{n}\Sigma dx$$
$$= 12 + \frac{44}{10}$$
$$= 12 + 4.4$$
$$= 16.4.$$

Example 2. *The postage expenses on the letters dispatched from an office on a day resulted in the following frequency distribution. Find the mean postage per letter.*

Postage (in ₹)	*15*	*10*	*18*	*45*	*70*
No. of letters	*47*	*25*	*56*	*40*	*22*

Sol. Calculation of mean

x_i *(postage in ₹)*	f_i *(no. of letters)*	f_ix_i
15	47	705
10	25	250
18	56	1008
45	40	1800
70	22	1540
Total	$\Sigma f_i = 190$	$\Sigma f_ix_i = 5303$

Here mean postage is given by

$$\bar{x} = \frac{\Sigma f_ix_i}{\Sigma f_i}$$
$$= \frac{5303}{190} = ₹\ 27.91$$

Example 3. *Find the mean from the following data* :

Marks	*No. of students*	*Marks*	*No. of students*
Below 10	*5*	*Below 60*	*60*
Below 20	*9*	*Below 70*	*70*
Below 30	*17*	*Below 80*	*78*
Below 40	*29*	*Below 90*	*83*
Below 50	*45*	*Below 100*	*85*

Sol. The frequency distribution table can be written as (Assumed Mean = 55)

Marks	*Mid-values (x)*	*f*	*x – 55*	$u = \frac{x-55}{10}$	*fu*
0–10	5	5	– 50	– 5	– 25
10–20	15	4	– 40	– 4	– 16
20–30	25	8	– 30	– 3	– 24
30–40	35	12	– 20	– 2	– 24
40–50	45	16	– 10	– 1	– 16
50–60	55 (= A)	15	0	0	0
60–70	65	10	10	1	10
70–80	75	8	20	2	16
80–90	85	5	30	3	15
90–100	95	2	40	4	8
		$N = \Sigma f = 85$			$\Sigma fu = -56$

$$\text{Mean } \bar{x} = a + h\frac{\Sigma fu}{N} = 55 + 10 \times \left(\frac{-56}{86}\right) \qquad [\text{Here } a = 55,\ h = 10]$$

$$= 55 - \frac{112}{17} = 48.41 \text{ marks.}$$

Example 4. *Find the mean wage from the following data :*

Wages	*800*	*820*	*860*	*900*	*920*	*980*	*1000*
No. of workers	*7*	*14*	*19*	*25*	*20*	*10*	*5*

Sol. Applying Step Deviation Method, since h = common magnitude of the class interval is not known. So, divide the range by the number of classes. The nearest integer to the value obtained gives the magnitude of the class interval.

Here range = 1000 – 800 = 200

No. of classes = 7

$$\therefore \qquad h = \frac{200}{7} = 28.57 \equiv 29$$

Also the deviations (d_i) should be divisible by h. So we take h = 20 (The nearest value to 29). Take assumed mean A = 900. We consider the following table :

Wages x_i	*Frequency* f_i	$d_i = x_i - A$	$u_i = \frac{x_i - A}{h}$	$f_i\mu_i$
800	7	– 100	– 5	– 35
820	14	– 80	–4	– 56
860	19	– 40	– 2	– 38
900 (= A)	25	0	0	0

920	20	20	1	20
980	10	80	4	40
1000	5	100	5	25
	N = 100			Total = – 44

Required mean $\bar{x} = A + h \dfrac{\sum_{i=1}^{n} f_i u_i}{N} = 900 + 20\left(-\dfrac{44}{100}\right)$

$$= 900 - \frac{880}{100} = 891.2.$$

Example 5. *Find the A.M. for the following frequency distribution.*

Daily wages (₹)	*13–17*	*18–20*	*23–27*	*28–32*	*33–37*	*38–42*	*48–52*	*53–57*
No. of workers	*2*	*22*	*19*	*14*	*3*	*4*	*1*	*1*

Sol. Calculation of A.M. Take Assumed mean A = 35, $h = 5$

Classes	*Mid-values* (x_i)	*Frequency* (f_i)	$d_i = x_i - A$	$u_i = \dfrac{x_i - A}{h}$	$f_i u_i$
13–17	15	2	– 20	– 4	– 8
18–20	19	22	– 16	– 3.2	– 70.4
23–27	25	19	– 10	– 2	– 38
28–32	30	14	– 5	– 1	– 14
33–37	35 (= A)	3	0	0	0
38–42	40	4	5	1	4
48–52	50	1	15	3	3
53–57	55	1	20	4	4
		Total = 66			– 119.4

To find h, here range = 57 – 13 = 44

No. of classes = 8

$$\therefore \quad h = \frac{44}{8} = 5.5 \cong 5 \text{ (nearest integer)}$$

Required A.M. $= A + h \dfrac{\Sigma f_i u_i}{\Sigma f_i} = 35 + 5 \times \dfrac{-119.4}{66}$

$$= 35 - \frac{597}{66} = 35 - 9.45 = 25.95.$$

Example 6. *Find the mean for the following frequency distribution by*
(a) Direct Method *(b) Short-Cut Method* *(c) Step-Deviation Method*

Class interval	*84–90*	*90–96*	*96–102*	*102–108*	*108–114*
Frequency	*8*	*12*	*15*	*10*	*5*

Sol. (*a*) **Direct Method.** Consider the following table

Class interval	*Mid-values* (x_i)	*Frequency* (f_i)	f_ix_i
84–90	87	8	696
90–96	93	12	1116
96–102	99	15	1485
102–108	105	10	1050
108 –114	111	5	555
		$\Sigma f_i = 50$	$\Sigma f_ix_i = 4902$

Required mean $= \dfrac{\Sigma f_i x_i}{\Sigma f_i} = \dfrac{4902}{50} = 98.04$

(*b*) **Short-Cut Method.** Consider the following table. Take Assumed mean A = 99

Class interval	*Mid-values* (x_i)	*Frequency* (f_i)	$d_i = x_i - A$	f_id_i
84–90	87	8	– 12	– 96
90–96	93	12	– 6	– 72
96–102	99 (= A)	15	0	0
102–108	105	10	6	60
108–114	111	5	12	60
	Total	50		– 48

∴ Required mean $\overline{x} = A + \dfrac{\Sigma f_i d_i}{\Sigma f_i} = 99 + \left(\dfrac{-48}{50}\right)$

$= 99 - 0.96 = 98.04.$

(*c*) **Step-Deviation Method.** Take Assumed mean $A = 99$

Here, range $= 114 - 84 = 30$

No. of classes $= 5$

∴ $h = \dfrac{30}{5} = 6$

Class interval	*Mid-values* (x_i)	*Frequency* (f_i)	$d_i = x_i - A$	$u_i = \dfrac{x_i - A}{h}$	$f_i u_i$
84–90	87	8	– 12	– 2	– 16
90–96	93	12	–6	– 1	– 12
96–102	99	15	0	0	0
102–108	105	10	6	1	10
108–114	111	5	12	2	10
	Total	50			– 8

Required mean $\quad \bar{x} = \text{A} + h\dfrac{\Sigma f_i u_i}{\Sigma f_i} = 99 + 6 \times \left(\dfrac{-8}{50}\right)$

$$= 99 - \frac{48}{50} = 99 - 0.96 = 98.04.$$

Example 7. *The weekly observations on cost of living index in a certain city for a particular year are given below. Find the average weekly cost of living index.*

Cost of living index	*below 150*	*150–160*	*160–170*	*170–180*	*180–190*	*190 above*
No. of weeks	*5*	*10*	*20*	*9*	*6*	*2*

Sol. Here the lower limit of the first class and the upper limit of the last class are not known. Also the size of the remaining classes is 10. Therefore we can assume the first class as 140–150 and the last class at 190–200.

Consider the following table. Take Assumed mean $A = 165$

Class interval	*Mid-values* (x_i)	*Frequency* (f_i)	$d_i = x_i - A$	$u_i = \dfrac{x_i - A}{h}$	$f_i u_i$
140–150	145	5	– 20	– 2	– 10
150–160	155	10	– 10	– 1	– 10
160–170	(A =)165	20	0	0	0
170–180	175	9	10	1	9
180–190	185	6	20	2	12
190–200	195	2	30	3	6
	Total	$\Sigma f_i = 52$			$\Sigma f_i u_i = 7$

$\therefore$ Required average weakly cost $\quad = A + h\dfrac{\Sigma f_i u_i}{\Sigma f_i} = 165 + 10\left(\dfrac{7}{52}\right)$

$$= 165 + 1.34 = 166.34.$$

Example 8. *Find the missing frequency in the following frequency distribution if the mean of the distribution is 1.46.*

No. of accidents	*0*	*1*	*2*	*3*	*4*	*5*	*Total*
Frequency	*46*	–	–	*25*	*10*	*5*	*200*

Sol. Let f_1, f_2 be the required frequencies. Since sum of all frequencies = 200 (given)

$\therefore \quad 46 + f_1 + f_2 + 25 + 10 + 5 = 200$

$\Rightarrow \quad f_1 + f_2 = 200 - 86 = 114$ ...(1)

Also, mean of the distribution $= \dfrac{\sum_{i=1}^{n} f_i x_i}{\sum_{i=1}^{n} f_i} = 1.46$

$$\Rightarrow \quad \frac{0 \times 46 + 1 \times f_1 + 2 \times f_2 + 3 \times 25 + 4 \times 10 + 5 \times 5}{200} = 1.46$$

$\Rightarrow \quad f_1 + 2f_2 + 75 + 40 + 25 = 292$

$\Rightarrow \quad f_1 + 2f_2 = 292 - 140 = 152$ ...(2)

Solving (1) and (2), $\quad f_1 = 76, \quad f_2 = 38.$

Example 9. *The mean of 200 items was 50. Later on it was discovered that two items were misread as 92 and 8 instead of 192 and 88. Find out the correct mean.*

Sol. Given incorrected value of $\bar{x} = 50$, $n = 200$. Using $\bar{x} = \dfrac{\Sigma x}{n}$, we have

Incorrected value of $\quad \Sigma x = n\bar{x} = 50 \times 200 = 10000$

$\therefore$ Corrected value of Σx = Incorrected value of Σx – (Incorrected items) + (Corrected items)

$= 10000 - (92 + 8) + (192 + 88)$

$= 10000 - 100 + 280 = 10180$

Hence corrected mean $= \dfrac{\text{Corrected } \Sigma x}{n} = \dfrac{10180}{200} = 50.9.$

Example 10. *The purchase department of a company XYZ has obtained samples of tube lights from the well known brands A and B. Following is record of length of life on the basis of tests conducted on these samples.*

Length of life (hrs)	*XYZ*	
	Company A	*Company B*
less than 1000	2	6
1000–3000	20	10
3000–5000	4	10
5000–7000	12	17
7000–9000	15	10
> 9000	7	7

Which company's tube lights are more consistent ? (P.T.U., M.B.A. May 2000)

Sol. The tube light having greater average life will be more consistent.

Calculation of A.M. for company A

Since the lower limit of the first class and the upper limit of the last class is not known and since the width of other class is 2000. Therefore we take the first class as – 1000 to 1000 and the last class as 9000 – 11000. Take assumed mean A = 6000. Consider the following Table.

Classes	*Mid point* x_i	*Frequencies* (f_i)	$d_i = x_i - A$	$u_i = \frac{x_i - A}{h}$	$f_i u_i$
– 1000–1000	0	2	– 6000	– 3	– 6
1000–3000	2000	20	– 4000	– 2	– 40
3000–5000	4000	4	– 2000	– 1	– 4
5000–7000	6000	12	0	0	0
7000–9000	8000	15	2000	1	15
9000–11000	10000	7	4000	2	14
		$\Sigma f_i = 60$			$\Sigma f_i u_i = -21$

Required mean $\quad \bar{x}_A = A + \frac{\Sigma f_i\, u_i}{\Sigma f_i} \times h$

$$= 6000 + \left(\frac{-21}{60}\right) \times 2000$$

$$= 6000 - 700 = 5300 \text{ hrs.}$$

Calculation for A.M. for company B. Take assumed mean A = 6000, h = 2000

Classes	*Mid point* x_i	*Frequencies* f_i	$d_i = x_i - A$	$u_i = \frac{x_i - A}{h}$	$f_i u_i$
– 1000–1000	0	6	– 6000	– 3	– 18
1000–3000	2000	10	– 4000	– 2	– 20
3000–5000	4000	10	– 2000	– 1	– 10
5000–7000	6000	17	0	0	0
7000–9000	8000	10	2000	1	10
9000–11000	10000	7	4000	2	14
		$\Sigma f_i = 60$			$\Sigma f_i u_i = -24$

$\therefore$ Required mean $\quad \bar{x}_B = A + \frac{\Sigma f_i\, u_i}{\Sigma f_i} \times h$

$$= 6000 + \left(\frac{-24}{60}\right) \times 2000$$

$$= 6000 - 800 = 5200 \text{ hrs.}$$

Hence we observe that the average tube's life $\bar{x}_A$ of company A is grater than the average tube's life $\bar{x}_B$ of company B. $\therefore$ The tube lights of company A are more consistent.

Example 11. *The A.M., median and mode of a group of 75 observations, were calculated as 27, 29 and 34 respectively. It was later discovered that one of the observation was wrongly read as 43 instead of 53. Find the corrected value of mean, median and mode.*

Sol. (*a*) **Calculation of corrected mean. Given**

$$\bar{x} = 27 \Rightarrow \frac{\sum_{i=1}^{n} x_i}{75} = 27$$

$$\Rightarrow \qquad \sum_{i=1}^{n} x_i = 75 \times 27 = 2025$$

i.e., Incorrected value of $\sum_{i=1}^{n} x_i = 2025$

$\because$ Corrected value of $\sum_{i=1}^{n} x_i = \left(\text{Incorrected value of } \sum_{i=1}^{n} x_i\right)$

– (Incorrected item) + (Corrected item)

$= 2025 - 43 + 53 = 2035.$

$$\therefore \quad \text{Corrected mean} = \frac{\text{Corrected } \sum_{i=1}^{n} x_i}{75} = \frac{2035}{75} = 27.13.$$

(*b*) **Calculation of corrected median and corrected mode.**

The value of the median will not be affected by this error because median is a positional average and the median value is 29, which is for away from the value 43.

Similarly, the value of the mode will also not be affected by this error because mode is also a positional average and the mode value is 34, which is far away from the value 43.

5.4. PROPERTIES OF ARITHMETIC MEAN

Property I. *The algebraic sum of the deviations of all the variates from their arithmetic mean is zero.*

Proof. Let d_x be the deviation of the variate x from the mean $\bar{x}$, then $d_x = x - \bar{x}$

$$\therefore \quad \Sigma f d_x = \Sigma f (x - \bar{x}) = \Sigma fx - \bar{x}\,\Sigma f$$

$$= N\bar{x} - N\bar{x} = 0 \qquad \Big| \because \bar{x} = \frac{\Sigma fx}{N}, \text{ where } N = \Sigma f$$

Property II. *The sum of the squares of the deviations of a set of values is minimum when taken about mean.*

Proof. Let the frequency distribution be x_i/f_i, $i = 1, 2, \ldots, n$. Let z be the sum of the squares of the deviations of the given values from an arbitrary point a (say).

$$\therefore \quad z = \sum_{i=1}^{n} f(x - a)^2.$$

We have to show that z is minimum when $a = \bar{x}$. Now z will be minimum when $\frac{dz}{da} = 0$

and $\frac{d^2z}{da^2} > 0$

$$\frac{dz}{da} = \sum_{i=1}^{n} 2f(x-a).(-1) = 2\sum_{i=1}^{n} f(x-a)$$

$$\therefore \quad \frac{dz}{da} = 0 \text{ gives} \qquad -2\Sigma f(x-a) = 0$$

$$\Rightarrow \qquad \Sigma fx - a\Sigma f = 0$$

$$\Rightarrow \qquad N\bar{x} - aN = 0 \qquad \left[\because \bar{x} = \frac{\Sigma fx}{N}, \Sigma f = N\right]$$

$$\Rightarrow \qquad \bar{x} - a = 0 \qquad (\because \; N = \Sigma f \neq 0)$$

$$\Rightarrow \qquad a = \bar{x}$$

Also, $$\frac{d^2z}{da^2} = -2\sum_{i=1}^{n} f(-1) = 2\Sigma f = 2N > 0$$

Hence z is minimum when $a = \bar{x}$.

Property III. (*Mean of the composite series*)

If $\bar{x}_i$ $(i = 1, 2, \ldots\ldots, k)$ be the arithmetic means of k distributions with respective frequencies n_i $(i = 1, 2, \ldots\ldots, k)$, then mean $\bar{x}$ of the whole distribution obtained by combining the k distributions is given by

$$\bar{x} = \frac{n_1\bar{x}_1 + n_2\bar{x}_2 + \ldots + n_k\bar{x}_k}{n_1 + n_2 + \ldots + n_k} = \frac{\sum_{i=1}^{k} n_i\bar{x}_i}{\sum_{i=1}^{k} n_i}$$

Proof. Let $x_{11}, x_{12}, x_{13}, \ldots\ldots, x_{1n_1}$ be the variables of the first distribution, $x_{21}, x_{22}, \ldots\ldots, x_{2n_2}$ be the variables of the second distribution, and so on. Then by definition

$$\left.\begin{aligned} \bar{x}_1 &= \frac{1}{n_1}(x_{11} + x_{12} + \ldots\ldots + x_{1n_1}) \\ \bar{x}_2 &= \frac{1}{n_2}(x_{21} + x_{22} + \ldots\ldots + x_{2n_2}) \\ &\ldots\ldots\ldots\ldots\ldots\ldots\ldots\ldots\ldots\ldots \\ \bar{x}_k &= \frac{1}{n_k}(x_{k1} + x_{k2} + \ldots\ldots + x_{kn_k}) \end{aligned}\right\} \quad \ldots(A)$$

The mean $\bar{x}$ of the whole distribution of size $(n_1 + n_2 + \ldots\ldots + n_k)$ is given by

$$\bar{x} = \frac{(x_{11} + x_{12} + \ldots\ldots + x_{1n_1}) + (x_{21} + x_{22} + \ldots\ldots + x_{2n_2}) + \ldots\ldots + (x_{k1} + x_{k2} + \ldots\ldots + x_{kn_k})}{n_1 + n_2 + \ldots\ldots + n_k}$$

$$= \frac{n_1\bar{x}_1 + n_2\bar{x}_2 + \ldots\ldots + n_k\bar{x}_k}{n_1 + n_2 + \ldots\ldots + n_k} = \frac{\sum_{i=1}^{k} n_i\bar{x}_i}{\sum_{i=1}^{k} n_i}.$$

Example 12. *The mean annual salary paid to all employees of a company was ₹ 5000. The mean annual salaries paid to male and female employees were ₹ 5200 and ₹ 4200 respectively. Determine the percentage of males and females employed by the company.*

Sol. Let p_1 and p_2 represent percentage of males and females respectively.

Then $p_1 + p_2 = 100$ ...(1)

Mean annual salary of all employees ($\bar{x}$) = ₹ 5000

Mean annual salary of all males ($\bar{x}_1$) = ₹ 5200

Mean annual salary of all females ($\bar{x}_2$) = ₹ 4200

Using $\bar{x} = \dfrac{p_1\bar{x}_1 + p_2\bar{x}_2}{p_1 + p_2}$, we get $5000 = \dfrac{5200p_1 + 4200p_2}{100}$

or $52p_1 + 42p_2 = 5000$ or $26p_1 + 21p_2 = 2500$ or $26p_1 + 21(100 - p_1) = 2500$ [Using (1)]

or $5p_1 = 2500 - 2100 = 400$ $\therefore$ $p_1 = 80$ and $p_2 = 100 - 80 = 20$

Hence the percentage of males and females is 80 and 20 respectively.

5.5. MERITS OF ARITHMETIC MEAN

The following are the merits of arithmetic mean :

(*i*) It is the simplest measure to understand and easiest to compute. Grouping of data is not required while calculating mean where as it is necessary in calculating mode. Similarly, arraying of data is not required where as it is necessary in case of median.

(*ii*) It is affected by the value of every item in the series.

(*iii*) It is rigidly defined *i.e.* everyone who computes the A.M. gets the same answer while applying its formula. Also, it is suitable for further algebraic treatment.

(*iv*) It does not vary too much when repeated samples are taken from the same population.

(*v*) It is not based on the position in the series and hence it is a calculated value.

5.6. DEMERITS OF ARITHMETIC MEAN

(*i*) It cannot be determined graphically or by inspection.

(*ii*) It cannot be determined if a single observation is missing.

(*iii*) A.M. is affected very much by extreme values. In case of extreme values A.M. gives a disorted picture of the distribution and hence no longer remains the representative of the distribution.

(*iv*) In extremely asymmetrical distribution, A.M. is not a suitable measure of location.

(*v*) A.M. cannot be used if we are dealing with qualitative characteristic such as intelligence, honesty, beauty, etc.

(*vi*) A.M. cannot be calculated if the extreme class is open *i.e.,* if below 10 or above 90 is given in a frequency distribution.

5.7. WEIGHTED MEAN

Let $w_1, w_2, \ldots\ldots, w_n$, are the weights attached to the observations $x_1, x_2, \ldots\ldots, x_n$, then

weighted A.M. $= \dfrac{\Sigma w_i x_i}{\Sigma w_i}$

Weighted mean gives the result equal to the simple mean if the weights assigned to each of the variate values are equal. It results in higher value than the simple mean if the smaller weights are given to smaller observations and larger weights to larger observations.

If the weights attached to larger observations are small and those attached to smaller observations are large, then the weighted mean results in smaller value than the simple mean.

Example 13. *Find the weighted mean of first n natural number, the weights being the corresponding number.*

Sol. Given

x_i	1	2	3	......	n
w_i	1	2	3	......	n

Required weighted mean $= \dfrac{\Sigma w_i x_i}{\Sigma w_i} = \dfrac{1^2 + 2^2 + 3^2 + \ldots + n^2}{1 + 2 + 3 + \ldots + n}$

$$= \frac{\Sigma n^2}{\Sigma n} = \frac{\frac{n(n+1)(2n+1)}{6}}{\frac{n(n+1)}{2}} = \frac{2n+1}{3}$$

5.8. PROPERTIES OF WEIGHTED MEAN

(*i*) Weighted mean is useful in problems relating to

(*a*) Construction of index numbers

(*b*) Standardised birth and death rates

(*ii*) The simple A.M. is equal to the weighted mean if the weights are equal.

(*iii*) The simple A.M. is less than the weighted mean if greater weights are assigned to greater values and smaller weights are assigned to small values.

(*iv*) The simple A.M. is greater than the weighted mean if the smaller weights are attached to greater values and greater weights to smaller values.

Example 14. *A train runs 25 miles at a speed of 30 m.p.h. Another 50 miles at a speed of 40 m.p.h. then due to repair of tracks, for 6 minutes at a speed of 10 m.p.h. and finally covers the remaining distance of 24 miles at a speed of 24 m.p.h. What is the average speed in m.p.h ?*

Sol. Take the time as weights, we consider the following table :

Speed (m.p.h.) x_i	*time* w_i	$w_i x_i$
30	50	1500
40	85	3000
10	6	60
24	60	1440
	191	6000

As the first train, covers 30 miles in 60 minute

$\Rightarrow$ 1 mile will be covered in $\frac{60}{30}$ minutes

$\Rightarrow$ 25 mile will be covered in $\frac{60}{30} \times 25 = 50$ minute

Average speed $= \frac{\Sigma w_i x_i}{\Sigma w_i} = \frac{6000}{191} = 31.47$ m.p.h.

TEST YOUR KNOWLEDGE 5.1

1. If $\bar{x}_1 = 50$, $\bar{x}_2 = 27$, $n_1 = 9$, $n_2 = 5$, find the combined mean. *(P.T.U., M.B.A. May 2008)*
2. The weight of 15 students are given below :

Weights (in kg)	50	52	54	55	57
No. of students	4	5	2	3	1

Find the mean weight.

3. The mean of 5 observations is 7. Later on, it was found that two observations 4 and 8 were wrongly taken instead of 5 and 9. Find the correct mean.
4. The mean weight of 150 students in a certain class is 60 kg. The mean weight of the boys in the class is 70 kg and that of the girls is 55 kg. Find the number of boys and number of girls in the class.
5. The mean marks obtained by 300 students in the subject of advanced mathematics are 45. The mean of the top 100 of them was found to be 70 and the mean of the last 100 was known to be 20. What is the mean of the remaining 100 students.
6. Obtain the mean wages from the following data :

Wages (₹)	900	950	1000	1100	1260	1140	1500
No. of workers	26	22	18	19	15	3	2

7. Using step-deviation method, find the A.M. of the wages given as below data

Wages (₹)	2000	2100	2200	2300	2400	2500	2600
No. of workers	5	15	32	42	15	12	4

8. Using direct method, find the mean head diameter per screw, where the measurement (in mm) of the diameters of the heads of 107 screws gave the following frequency distribution.

Diameter (mm)	33–45	36–38	39–41	42–44	45–47
Frequency	17	19	23	21	27

9. In a certain examination, the average grade of all students in class A is 68.4 and students in class B is 71.2. If the average of both classes combined is 70, find the ratio of the number of students in class A to the number of students in class B.

10. Find the A.M. for the following data.

Income (₹)	below 300	300–350	350–400	400–500	500–600	600 and above
Frequency	66	78	85	41	36	24

11. Following table gives 'less than commulative frequencies' of 199 men, each of age 20 years or more of a group. Find the mean age of the group.

Age below (in years)	25	30	35	40	45	50	55	60	65	70
Frequency	21	40	90	130	146	166	176	186	195	199

12. The following is the data to the marks of 70 students in physical chemistry.

Marks (more than)	20	30	40	50	60	70
No. of students	70	63	40	30	18	7

Find the mean marks.

13. Find the missing frequency from the following data:

Marks	0–10	10–20	20–30	30–40	40–50	50–60
No. of Students	5	15	20	—	20	10

The arithmetic mean is 34 marks. (*P.T.U., M.B.A. Dec. 2010*)

Answers

1. 41.78 **2.** 46 kg **3.** 7.4 **4.** Boys 50, Girls 100
5. 45 **6.** ₹ 1042.10 **7.** ₹ 2279 **8.** 40.61 mm
9. 30 : 40 **10.** ₹ 391.59 **11.** 38.7 years **12.** 47.57
13. 180

MEDIAN

5.9. MEDIAN (*P.T.U., M.B.A. Dec. 2006*)

The **median** of a statistical series is defined as the size of the middle most item (or the A.M. of two middle most items), provided the items are in order of magnitude.

For example, the median for the series 4, 6, 10, 12, 18 is 10 and for the series 4, 6, 10, 12, 18, 22, median is $\frac{10+12}{2} = 11$.

It can be observed that 50% items in the series would have value less than or equal to median and 50% items would be with values greater than or equal to the value of the median.

For an individual series, the median is given by :

$$\textbf{Median} = \textbf{Size of } \frac{n+1}{2} \textbf{ th item,}$$

where $x_1, x_2, ..., x_n$ are the values of the variable under consideration. The values $x_1, x_2, ..., x_n$ are supposed to have been arranged in order of magnitude.

If $\frac{n+1}{2}$ comes out to be in decimal, then we take median as the A.M. of size of $\frac{n}{2}$th and $\left(\frac{n}{2}+1\right)$th items.

5.10. WORKING RULES FOR FINDING MEDIAN FOR AN INDIVIDUAL SERIES

I. Arrange the given items in order of magnitude.

II. Find the total number 'n' of items.

III. Write : median = size of $\left(\frac{n+1}{2}\right)$ th item.

IV. (*i*) If $\frac{n+1}{2}$ is a whole number, then $\frac{n+1}{2}$ th item gives the value of median.

(*ii*) If $\frac{n+1}{2}$ is in fraction, then the A.M. of $\frac{n}{2}$th and $\left(\frac{n}{2}+1\right)$th items gives the value of median.

For a frequency distribution, in which frequency (*f*) of different values (*x*) of the variable are given, we have

$$\textbf{Median = Size of } \frac{\mathbf{N+1}}{\mathbf{2}} \textbf{th item.}$$

The values of the variable are supposed to have been arranged in order of magnitude.

5.11. WORKING RULES FOR FINDING MEDIAN FOR A FREQUENCY DISTRIBUTION

I. Arrange the values of the variable in order of magnitude and find the cumulative frequencies (*c.f.*).

II. Find the total 'N' of all frequencies and check that it is equal to the last *c.f.*

III. Write : median = size of $\left(\frac{N+1}{2}\right)$th item.

IV. (*a*) If $\frac{N+1}{2}$ is a whole number, then $\left(\frac{N+1}{2}\right)$ th item gives the value of median. For this, look at the cumulative frequency column and find that total which is either equal to $\left(\frac{N+1}{2}\right)$ or the next higher than $\left(\frac{N+1}{2}\right)$ and determine the value of the variable corresponding to this. That gives the value of median.

(*b*) If $\frac{N+1}{2}$ is in fraction, then the A.M. of $\frac{N}{2}$th and $\left(\frac{N}{2}+1\right)$ th items gives the value of median.

In case, the values of the variable are given in the form of classes, we shall assume that items in the classes are uniformly distributed in the corresponding classes. We define :

$$\textbf{Median = Size of } \frac{\mathbf{N}}{\mathbf{2}} \textbf{th item.}$$

Here we shall get the class in which $\left(\frac{N}{2}\right)$th item is present. This is called the **median class.** To ascertain the value of median in the median class, the following formula is used.

$$\textbf{Median} = \mathbf{L} + \left(\frac{\mathbf{N/2 - C}}{\mathbf{f}}\right)\mathbf{h},$$

where L = Lower limit of the median class

C = Cumulative frequency of the class preceding the median class

f = Simple frequency of the median class

h = Width of the median class.

The following points must be taken care of while calculating median :

1. The values of the variable must be in order of magnitude. In case of classes of values of the variable, the classes must be strictly in *ascending order* of magnitude.

2. If the classes are in *inclusive form*, then the actual limits of the *median class* are to be taken for finding L and h.

3. The classes may not be of equal width.

4. In case of open end classes, it is advisable to find average by using median.

5.12. WORKING RULES FOR FINDING MEDIAN FOR A FREQUENCY DISTRIBUTION WITH CLASS INTERVALS

I. Arrange the classes in the ascending order of magnitude. The classes must be in 'exclusive form'. The widths of classes may not be equal. Find the cumulative frequencies (*c.f.*).

II. Find the total 'N' of all frequencies and check that it is equal to the last *c.f.*

III. Write : median = size of $\left(\frac{N}{2}\right)$ th item.

IV. Look at the cumulative frequency column and find that total which is either equal to $\frac{N}{2}$ or the next higher than $\frac{N}{2}$ and determine the class corresponding to this. That gives the 'median class'.

V. Write : median $= L + \left(\frac{N/2 - C}{f}\right) h.$

Put the values of L, N/2, C, f, h and calculate the value of median.

ILLUSTRATIVE EXAMPLES

Example 1. *Find the median for the series : 4, 6, 9, 4, 2, 8, 10.*

Sol. The values of the variable arranged in ascending order are x : 2, 4, 4, 6, 8, 9, 10.

Here $n = 7$. $\therefore \quad \frac{n+1}{2} = \frac{7+1}{2} = 4$

$\therefore$ Median = Size of 4th item = 6.

Example 2. *Find the median for the series : 205, 170, 131, 174, 153, 142, 147, 157, 196, 148.*

Sol. The values of the variable arranged in ascending order x : 131, 142, 147, 148, 153, 157, 170, 174, 196, 205.

Here $n = 10$. $\therefore \frac{n+1}{2} = \frac{10+1}{2} = 5.5$

$\therefore$ Median = Size of 5.5th item

$= \frac{\text{size of 5th item + size of 6th item}}{2} = \frac{153+157}{2} = 155.$

Example 3. *The following are the marks obtained by a batch of 10 students in a certain class test in Statistics and Accountancy :*

Roll No.	*1*	*2*	*3*	*4*	*5*	*6*	*7*	*8*	*9*	*10*
Marks in Statistics	*63*	*64*	*62*	*32*	*30*	*60*	*47*	*46*	*35*	*28*
Marks in Accountancy	*68*	*65*	*35*	*42*	*26*	*85*	*44*	*80*	*33*	*72*

In which subject is the level of knowledge of students higher ?

Sol. In this problem, median would be the most suitable average.

Marks in Statistics arranged in ascending order are : 28, 30, 32, 35, 46, 47, 60, 62, 63, 64.

Here $n = 10$. $\therefore \frac{n+1}{2} = \frac{10+1}{2} = 5.5$

$\therefore$ Median = size of 5.5th item

$= \frac{\text{size of 5th item + size of 6th item}}{2} = \frac{46+47}{2} = 46.5$ marks.

Marks in Accountancy arranged in ascending order are : 26, 33, 35, 42, 44, 65, 68, 72, 80, 85.

Here, $n = 10$. $\therefore \frac{n+1}{2} = \frac{10+1}{2} = 5.5$

$\therefore$ Median = size of 5.5th item

$= \frac{\text{size of 5th item + size of 6th item}}{2} = \frac{44+65}{2} = 54.5$ marks.

$\therefore$ Level of knowledge of students is higher in Accountancy.

Example 4. *Find the median for the following frequency distribution :*

x	*10*	*12*	*14*	*16*	*18*	*20*	*22*
f	*2*	*5*	*12*	*20*	*10*	*7*	*3*

Sol. **Calculation of Median**

x	*f*	*c.f.*
10	2	2
12	5	7
14	12	19
16	20	39
18	10	49
20	7	56
22	3	59 = N
	N = 59	

$\frac{N+1}{2} = \frac{59+1}{2} = 30$

$\therefore$ Median = size of 30th item = 16.

Example 5. *The number of students absenting from schools were recorded for 100 days as below. Find the median number of students absenting per day.*

No. of students who absented	*5*	*6*	*7*	*8*	*9*	*10*	*11*	*12*	*13*
No. of days	*12*	*14*	*16*	*25*	*9*	*8*	*7*	*5*	*4*

Sol. **Calculation of Median**

No. of students who absented x	*No. of days* f	*c.f.*
5	12	12
6	14	26
7	16	42
8	25	67
9	9	76
10	8	84
11	7	91
12	5	96
13	4	100
	N = 100	

$$\frac{N+1}{2} = \frac{100+1}{2} = 50.5$$

$\therefore$ Median = size of 50.5th item

$$= \frac{8+8}{2} = 8 \text{ students.}$$

Example 6. *Find the median for the following wage distribution for a certain factory :*

Monthly wage (₹)	*50–80*	*80–100*	*100–110*	*110–120*	*120–130*	*130–150*	*150–180*	*180–200*
No. of workers	*30*	*127*	*140*	*240*	*176*	*135*	*20*	*3*

Sol. **Calculation of Median**

Monthly wage (₹)	*No. of workers* f	*c.f.*
50–80	30	30
80–100	127	157
100–110	140	C = 297
L = 110–120	f = 240	537
120–130	176	713
130–150	135	848
150–180	20	868
180–200	3	871 = N
	N = 871	

$$\frac{N}{2} = \frac{871}{2} = 435.5$$

Here Median = size of 435.5th item

$\therefore$ Median class is 110–120.

$$\therefore \text{ Median } = L + \left(\frac{N/2 - C}{f}\right)h$$

$$= 110 + \left(\frac{435.5 - 297}{240}\right)10$$

$$= 110 + 5.77 = ₹\ 115.77.$$

Example 7. *Find the median score of the scores on Reading Comprehension Test (Age 12+) of 1000 students which are given below :*

Score (out of 75)	*Frequency*	*Score (out of 75)*	*Frequency*
0–5	*6*	*25–30*	*250*
5–10	*12*	*30–35*	*185*
10–15	*50*	*35–40*	*110*
15–20	*120*	*40–45*	*32*
20–25	*225*	*45–50*	*10*

Sol. **Calculation of Median**

Score (out of 75)	*f*	*c.f.*
0–5	6	6
5–10	12	18
10–15	50	68
15–20	120	188
20–25	225	C = 413
L = 25–30	*f* = 250	663
30–35	185	848
35–40	110	958
40–45	32	990
45–50	10	1000 = N
	N = 1000	

$$\frac{N}{2} = \frac{1000}{2} = 500$$

Here Median = size of 500th item

∴ Median class is 25 – 30.

$$\therefore \quad \text{Median} = L + \left(\frac{N/2 - C}{f}\right)h$$

$$= 25 + \left(\frac{500 - 413}{250}\right)5$$

$$= 25 + 1.74 = 26.74 \text{ marks.}$$

Example 8. *Find the median for the following data :*

Weekly wage (in ₹)	*60–69*	*70–79*	*80–89*	*90–99*	*100–109*	*110–119*
No. of workers	*5*	*15*	*20*	*30*	*20*	*8*

Sol. Here the classes are given in the 'inclusive form'. To find median, we shall have to convert, these classes in the 'exclusive form'.

Consider 70 – 69 = 1 and $\frac{1}{2}$ of '1' = 0.5.

Also, 60 – 0.5 = 59.5 and 69 + 0.5 = 69.5.

∴ Actual limits of the class 60–69 are 59.5 and 69.5.

Hence 60–69 in the exclusive form is 59.5–69.5. Similarly, we write all classes in the 'exclusive form'.

Calculation of Median

Weekly wage (in ₹)	*No. of workers f*	*c.f.*
59.5–69.5	5	5
69.5–79.5	15	20
79.5–89.5	20	C = 40
L = 89.5–99.5	*f* = 30	70
99.5–109.5	20	90
109.5–119.5	8	98 = N
	N = 98	

$$\frac{N}{2} = \frac{98}{2} = 49$$

Here Median = size of 49th item

∴ Median class is 89.5 – 99.5.

$$\therefore \quad \text{Median} = L + \left(\frac{N/2 - C}{f}\right)h$$

$$= 89.5 + \left(\frac{49 - 40}{30}\right)10$$

$$= 89.5 + 3 = ₹\ 92.5.$$

Example 9. *The following table gives the distribution of marks secured by some students in a certain examination :*

Marks	*0–20*	*21–30*	*31–40*	*41–50*	*51–60*	*61–70*	*71–80*
No. of students	*42*	*38*	*120*	*84*	*48*	*36*	*31*

Find the median marks.

Sol. Calculation of Median

Marks	*No. of students* f	*c.f.*
0–20	42	42
21–30	38	C = 80
31–40	f = 120	200
41–50	84	284
51–60	48	332
61–70	36	368
71–80	31	399 = N
	N = 399	

$$\frac{N}{2} = \frac{399}{2} = 199.5$$

Here Median = size of 199.5th item

∴ Median class is 31–40.

Median class in the 'exclusive form' is 30.5–40.5.

$$\therefore \quad \text{Median} = L + \left(\frac{N/2 - C}{f}\right)h$$

$$= 30.5 + \left(\frac{199.5 - 80}{120}\right)10$$

$$= 30.5 + 9.96 = 40.46 \text{ Marks.}$$

Example 10. *Find the median for the following frequency distribution :*

Height (above) (in inches)	*60*	*62*	*64*	*66*	*68*	*70*	*72*	*74*
No. of students	*793*	*712*	*687*	*530*	*465*	*387*	*142*	*0*

Sol. Calculation of Median

Height (in inches)	f	*c.f.*
60–62	793 – 712 = 81	81
62–64	712 – 687 = 25	81 + 25 = 106
64–66	687 – 530 = 157	106 + 157 = 263
66–68	530 – 465 = 65	C = 263 + 65 = 328
68–70	f = 465 – 387 = 78	328 + 78 = 406
70–72	387 – 142 = 245	406 + 245 = 651
72–74	142 – 0 = 142	651 + 142 = 793
	N = 793	

$$\frac{N}{2} = \frac{793}{2} = 396.5$$

Here Median = size of 396.5th item

∴ Median class is 68–70.

$$\therefore \quad \text{Median} = L + \left(\frac{N/2 - C}{f}\right)h$$

$$= 68 + \left(\frac{396.5 - 328}{78}\right)2$$

$$= 68 + 1.76 = 69.76 \text{ inches.}$$

Example 11. *You are given the following incomplete frequency distribution. It is known that the total frequency is 1000 and that the median is 413.11. Estimate the missing frequencies.*

Value	*Frequency*	*Value*	*Frequency*
300–325	*5*	*400–425*	*326*
325–350	*17*	*425–450*	–
350–375	*80*	*450–475*	*88*
375–400	–	*475–500*	*9*

Sol. Let the missing frequencies of the classes 375–400 and 425–450 be a and b respectively. Median is given to be 413.11.

Value	*Frequency* f	*c.f.*
300–325	5	5
325–350	17	22
350–375	80	102
375–400	a	$102 + a = c$
400–425	$326 = f$	$428 + a$
425–450	b	$428 + a + b$
450–475	88	$516 + a + b$
475–500	9	$525 + a + b = 1000$
	N = 1000	

∴ Median class is 400–425.

Now, median $= \text{L} + \left(\dfrac{\text{N}/2 - \text{C}}{f}\right)h$

Here, $\text{L} = 400,\ \dfrac{\text{N}}{2} = 500,\ f = 326,$

$\text{C} = 102 + a,\ h = 25.$

$$\therefore\ 413.11 = 400 + \left(\frac{500 - (102 + a)}{326}\right)25$$

$$\Rightarrow\ (13.11)326 = (500 - 102 - a)\ 25$$

or $\quad 4273.86 = (398 - a)\ 25 \quad \text{or} \quad 398 - a = 170.95$

or $\quad a = 227.05 = 227$ (nearly)

Also, $\quad 525 + a + b = 1000 \quad \therefore \quad b = 1000 - 525 - 227 = 248$

∴ The missing frequencies are 227 and 248.

Example 12. *An incomplete distribution is given below :*

Variable	*Frequency*
0–10	*10*
10–20	*20*
20–30	–
30–40	*40*
40–50	–
50–60	*25*
60–70	*15*

(*i*) *You are given the median value is 35. Find out missing frequency (given total frequency 170).*

(*ii*) *Calculate the arithmetic mean of the complete table.*

Sol. Let f_1 and f_2 be the required missing frequencies.

Given $10 + 20 + f_1 + 40 + f_2 + 25 + 15 = 170$

$$\Rightarrow\ f_1 + f_2 = 170 - 110 = 60$$

Calculation of median.

Variable	*Frequency* (f)	*Comulative frequency* (*c.f.*)
0–10	10	10
10–20	20	30
20–30	f_1	$C = 30 + f_1$
30–40	$f = 40$	$70 + f_1$
40–50	f_2	$70 + f_1 + f_2 = 130$
50–60	25	155
60–70	15	170
	N = 170	

Consider $\frac{N}{2} = \frac{170}{2} = 85$

Here Median = size of 85th item and median class is 30–40

Now, $$\text{median} = L + \left(\frac{\frac{N}{2} - C}{f}\right) \times h$$

$$\Rightarrow \quad 35 = 30 + \left(\frac{85 - 30 - f_1}{40}\right) \times 10 = 30 + \frac{55 - f_1}{4}$$

$$\Rightarrow \quad 5 = \frac{55 - f_1}{4} \quad \Rightarrow \quad 55 - f_1 = 20$$

$$\Rightarrow \quad f_1 = 55 - 20 = 35$$

Also $\quad f_1 + f_2 = 60 \quad \Rightarrow \quad f_2 = 60 - 35 = 25$

Calculation of A.M. Take assumed mean A = 35

Variable	*Mid value* (x_i)	*Frequency* (f_i)	$d_i = x_i - A$	$f_i d_i$
0–10	5	10	– 30	– 300
10–20	15	20	– 20	– 400
20–30	25	35	– 10	– 350
30–40	35 (= A)	40	0	0
40–50	45	25	10	250
50–60	55	25	20	500
60–70	65	15	30	450
	Total	160		150

$$\therefore \quad \text{Required mean} = A + \frac{\Sigma f_i\, d_i}{\Sigma f_i} = 35 + \frac{150}{170}$$

$$= 35 + 0.88 = 35.88.$$

Example 13. *10% of the workers in a firm employing a total of 11000 workers earn less than ₹ 5 per day, 200 earn between ₹ 5 and 9.99, 30% between ₹ 10 and 14.99, 250 workers between ₹ 15 and 19.99 and the rest ₹ 20 and above. Find the median wage.*

Sol. Converting the given data in the form of a frequency distribution, we have the following table :

Wages	*Number of workers (f)*	*c.f.*
Below 5	$1000 \times \frac{10}{100} = 100$	100
5–9.99	200	300
10–14.99	$1000 \times \frac{30}{100} = 300$	600
15–19.99	250	850
20 and above	150	1000
	$\Sigma f = 1000$	

Here $\frac{N}{2} = \frac{1000}{2} = 500$

$\therefore$ Median = size of $\frac{N}{2}$th item = size of 500th item.

i.e., Median class is 10 – 14.99. But the actual limits of this class is 9.99 – 14.99.

$\therefore$ $L = 9.99,\ C = 300,\ f = 300,\ h = 5$

Hence $$\text{Median} = L + \left(\frac{\frac{N}{2} - C}{f}\right) \times h = 9.99 + \frac{500 - 300}{300} \times 5$$

$$= 9.99 + 3.33 = ₹\ 13.32$$

5.13. MATHEMATICAL PROPERTY OF MEDIAN

In a statistical data, the sum of numerical values of deviation of items from median is always least, *i.e.,* $\sum_{i=1}^{n} f_i \,|x_i - \text{Median}|$ is always least, where f_i is the frequency of x_i $(1 \le i \le n)$.

5.14. MERITS OF MEDIAN

1. It is rigidly defined.
2. It is well defined.
3. It is not affected by the presence of extreme items.
4. It is best suited in the presence of open end classes.
5. It can also be located graphically.

5.15. DEMERITS OF MEDIAN

1. It is not based on all the observations *e.g.*, the median of 10, 25, 50, 60 and 65, is 50. We can replace the observation 10 and 25 by any two values which are smaller than 50% without affecting the value of the median. This property is called – **median is insensitive.** Due to this property, median is also called a **positional average.**

2. As compared to mean, it is affected much by fluctuation of sampling.

3.It is not capable of further algebric treatment.

4. It can only be calculated when the data is in order of magnitude.

Uses. Median is the only average to be used while dealing with qualitative data, *i.e.*, to find average intelligence, or average honesty etc.

TEST YOUR KNOWLEDGE 5.2

1. Find the median for the series : 20, 18, 22, 27, 25, 12, 15. *(P.T.U. M.B.A. Dec., 2008)*
2. The runs scored by 11 members of a cricket team are 34, 27, 15, 29, 31, 50, 13, 43, 56, 0, 2. Find the median score
3. The marks obtained by 12 students are : 25, 20, 32, 23, 40, 27, 30, 25, 20, 10, 15, 41. Find the median.
4. Find the median of the following observations : 46, 64, 87, 41, 58, 77, 35, 90, 55, 92, 33. If 92 is replaced by 99 and 41 by 43 in the above data, find the new median.
5. Find the value of median for the following data :

x	1	2	3	4	5	6	7	8	9
f	5	6	7	2	2	1	2	1	1

6. The number of students absent in a school was recorded every day for 147 days and the raw data was presented in the form of frequency distribution given below :

No. of students absent	5	6	7	8	9	10	11	12	13	15	18	20
No. of days	1	5	11	14	16	13	10	70	4	1	1	1

Find the median and describe what information it conveys ?

7. In a survey of 304 families, the following frequency distribution of the number of children was obtained :

No. of children	0	1	2	3	4	5
No. of families	43	55	60	64	48	34

Find the median for this distribution.

8. Calculate the median for the following data :

Class	*Frequency*	*Class*	*Frequency*	*Class*	*Frequency*
10–20	6	40–50	2	70–80	9
20–30	8	50–60	4	80–90	4
30–40	10	60–70	7	90–100	6

9. Find the value of median for the following series :

Class	1–10	11–20	21–30	31–40	41–50
No. of items	10	21	51	45	26

10. Find the value of median for the following data :

Weight (in kg)	60–64	65–74	75–79	80–84	85–94	95–99	100–104
No. of items	10	39	35	20	26	9	6

11. Calculate median and arithmetic average for the following data :

Class interval	10–20	10–30	10–40	10–50	10–60	10–70	10–80	10–90
Frequency	4	6	56	97	124	137	146	150

12. Calculate median for the following data :

Mid-value	115	125	135	145	155	165	175	185	195
Frequency	6	25	48	72	116	60	38	22	3

13. Find the median marks :

Marks less than	10	20	30	40	50	60
No. of students	4	10	30	40	47	50

14. An incomplete frequency distribution is given below :

Variable	10–20	20–30	30–40	40–50	50–60	60–70	70–80
Frequency	12	30	?	65	?	25	18

It is given that median value is 46 and the total number of items is 229. You are required to find the missing frequencies.

15. The median for the following data is 525.

Class interval	0–100	100–200	200–300	300–400	400–500	500–600	600–700	700–800	800–900	900–1000
Frequency	2	5	x	12	17	20	y	9	7	4

Find the values of x and y if the total frequency is 100.

Answers

1. 20 **2.** 29 **3.** 25 **4.** 58, 58

5. 3

6. 12 students ; For about half the number of days, 12 or less students were absent.

7. 2 children **8.** 55 **9.** 29.42 **10.** 77.86 kg

11. 44.63, 47 **12.** 153.79 **13.** 27.5 marks **14.** 34, 45

15. 9, 15.

MODE

5.16. MODE

(P.T.U., M.B.A. Dec., 2009, 2010, May 2006)

The **mode** of a statistical series is defined as that value of the variable around which the values of the variable tend to be most heavily concentrated. It can also be defined as that value of the variable whose own frequency is dominating and at the same time, the frequencies of its neighbouring items are also dominating. Thus, we see that mode is that value of the variable around which the items of the series cluster densely. Let us consider the data regarding the sale of readymade shirts.

Size (in inches)	30	32	34	36	38	40	42
No. of shirts sold	5	22	24	38	16	8	2

Here we see that the frequency of 36 is highest and the frequencies of its neighbouring items (34, 38) are also dominating. Here the most fashionable, modal size is 36 inches. Technically, we shall say that the mode of the distribution is 36 inches.

In case of mode, we are to deal with the frequencies of values of the items. Thus, if we are to find the value of mode for an individual series, we will have to see the repetition of different items, *i.e.*, we would be in a way expressing it in the form of frequency distribution. Thus, we start our discussion for evaluating mode for frequency distributions. There are two methods of finding mode of a frequency distribution.

5.17. MODE BY INSPECTION

Sometimes the frequencies in a frequency distribution are so distributed that we would be able to find the value of mode just by inspection. For example, let us consider the frequency distribution :

x	4	5	6	7	8	9	10	11	12
f	1	2	1	5	12	4	2	2	1

Here we can say, at once, that mode is 8.

5.18. MODE BY GROUPING

Let us consider the distribution :

x	4	5	6	7	8	9	10	11	12
f	4	5	7	14	8	15	2	2	1

Here the frequency of 9 is more than the frequency of 7, whereas the frequencies of neighbouring items of 7 are more than that for 9. In such a case, we would not be able to judge the value of mode just by inspecting the data. In case there is even slight doubt as to which is the value of mode. We discuss the method of finding mode by grouping. In this method, two tables are drawn. These tables are called 'Grouping Table' and 'Analysis Table'. In the **grouping table**, six columns are drawn. The column of frequencies is taken as the column I. In the column II, the sum of two frequencies are taken at a time. In the column III, we exclude the first frequency and take the sum of two frequencies at a time. In the column IV, we take the sum of three frequencies at a time. In the column V, we exclude the first frequency and take the sum of frequencies, taking three at a time. In the last column, we exclude the first two frequencies and take the sum of three frequencies at a time. The next step is to mark the maximum sums in each of the six columns.

In the **analysis table**, six rows are drawn corresponding to each column in the grouping table. In this table, columns are made for those values of the variable whose frequencies accounts for giving maximum totals in the columns of the grouping table. In this table, marks are given to the values of the variable as often as their frequencies are added to make the total maximum in the columns of the grouping table. The value of the variable which get the maximum marks is declared to be the mode of the distribution..

In case, the values of the variable are given in the form of classes, we shall assume that the items in the classes are uniformly distributed in the corresponding classes. Here we shall get a 'class' either by the *method of inspection* or the *method of grouping*. This class is called the **modal class.** To ascertain the value of mode in the modal class, the following formula is used :

$$\textbf{Mode} = \textbf{L} + \left(\frac{\Delta_1}{\Delta_1 + \Delta_2}\right)\textbf{h},$$

where L = Lower limit of the modal class

Δ_1 = Difference of frequencies of modal class and pre-modal class

Δ_2 = Difference of frequencies of modal class and post-modal class

h = Width of the modal class.

The following points must be taken care of while calculating mode :

1. The values (or classes of values) of the variable must be in ascending order of magnitude.

2. If the classes are in inclusive form, then the actual limits of the modal class are to be taken for finding L and h.

3. The classes must be of equal width.

It may be noted that while analysing the analysis table, we may find two or more values (or classes of values) of the variable getting equal marks. In such a case, the grouping method fails. Such a distribution is called a **multi-modal distribution.**

5.19. EMPIRICAL MODE

In case of a multi-modal distribution, we find the value of mode by using the relation :

Mode = 3 Median – 2 A.M.

This mode is called **empirical mode** in the sense that this relation can not be established algebraically. But it is generally observed that in distributions, the value of mode is approximately equal to 3 median – 2 A.M. That is why, this mode is called *empirical mode*.

5.20. WORKING RULES FOR FINDING MODE

I. If mode is not evident by the 'method of inspection', then the 'method of grouping' should be used.

II. In case, the values of variable are given in terms of classes of equal width, then step I, will give the 'modal class'.

III. To find value of the mode, use the formula : mode $= \text{L} + \left(\frac{\Delta_1}{\Delta_1 + \Delta_2}\right) h$.

IV. In case, the distribution is multi-modal, then find the value of mode by using the formula : 'mode = 3 median – 2 A.M'.

ILLUSTRATIVE EXAMPLES

Example 1. *Find the mode for the following individual series :*

x	5	7	3	5	2	1	5	8	5

Sol. **Calculation of mode**

x	Tally bars	f
5	||||	4
7	|	1
3	|	1
2	|	1
1	|	1
8	|	1

x (in ascending order)	f
1	1
2	1
3	1
5	**4**
7	1
8	1

By inspection, mode = **5.** (Max. frequency is 4 which corresponds to 5)

Example 2. (*i*) *Find the mode for the following data :*

25, 16, 19, 48, 19, 20, 34, 15, 19, 20, 21, 24, 19, 16, 22, 16, 18, 20, 16, 19.

(*ii*) *If one of the 19's is changed to 16 in the above data, find the new mode.*

Sol. (*i*) **Calculation of mode**

x	Tally bars	f
25	|	1
16	||||	4
19	||||| (crossed)	5
48	|	1
20	|||	3
34	|	1
15	|	1
21	|	1
24	|	1
22	|	1
18	|	1

x (in ascending order)	f
15	1
16	4
18	1
19	**5**
20	3
21	1
22	1
24	1
25	1
34	1
48	1

By inspection, mode = 19. This is so because the frequency of 19 is maximum and the frequencies of the neighbouring items are also dominating.

(*ii*) Here one of the 19's is changed to 16.

∴ The new frequency distribution is as follows :

x	15	16	18	19	20	21	22	24	25	34	48
f	1	4 + 1 = 5	1	5 − 1 = 4	3	1	1	1	1	1	1

Here the frequency of 16 is maximum but the frequencies of neighbouring items of 4 are more dominating. In this case, use apply the method of grouping to find the value of mode.

Grouping Table

x	*I* *f*	*II*	*III*	*IV*	*V*	*VI*
15	1					
		6				
16	**5**					
18	1		6	7		
		5			**10**	
19	4					
20	3		**7**			**8**
		4		**8**		
21	1					
					5	
22	1		2			3
		2				
24	1					
25	1		2	3		
		2				
34	1				3	3
			2			
48	1					

Analysis Table

Column	15	16	19	20	21	18
I	1					
II	1	1				
III			1	1		
IV			1	1	1	
V		1	1			1
VI			1	1		1
	2	2	4	3	1	2

∴ Mode = 19.

Example 3. *Find the mode for the following distribution :*

Profit ('000 ₹)	*28*	*29*	*30*	*31*	*32*	*33*
No. of firms	*4*	*7*	*10*	*6*	*2*	*1*

Sol. **Calculation of Mode**

Profit ('000 ₹) x	*No. of firms* f
28	4
29	7
30	10
31	6
32	2
33	1

By inspection, mode is ₹ 30,000. This is so because the frequency of 30,000 is very high as compared with the frequencies of other values of x. Moreover, the frequencies of the neighbouring items are also dominating.

Example 4. *Find the value of mode for the following distribution :*

x	4	5	6	7	8	9	10	11	12
f	15	18	12	30	27	40	20	20	12

Sol. For the given distribution, we cannot judge the value of mode, just by inspection. In this case, we shall apply the method of grouping. The values of the variable are already in order of magnitude.

Method of Grouping

Size (x)	Frequency					
	I	II	III	IV	V	VI
4	2	7				
5	5		13	15		
6	8	17			22	
7	9		21			29
8	12	26		35		
9	14		**28**		**40**	
10	14	**29**				**43**
11	15		26	**40**		
12	11	24			39	
13	13					

Explanation :

In column I, *original* frequencies are written.

In column II, frequencies of column I are combined *two by two.*

In column III, *leave the first frequency of column I* and combine the others *two by two.*

In column IV, frequencies of column I are combined *three by three.*

In column V, *leave the first frequency of column I* and combine the others *three by three.*

In column VI, *leave the first two frequencies in column I* and combine the others *three by three.*

In all these columns, the maximum frequency is written in bold black type.

Note. All operations are done on column I.

Now we frame another table in which against every maximum item of columns I to VI, we write down the corresponding size or sizes. The size (x) which occurs maximum number of times is the mode.

Columns	*Size of item having max. frequency*
I	11
II	10, 11
III	9, 10
IV	10, 11, 12
V	8, 9, 10
VI	9, 10, 11

Since the item 10 occurs maximum number of times (*i.e.*, 5 times), hence the mode is 10.

Example 5. *Calculate the mode from the following data*

Class	*20–24*	*25–29*	*30–34*	*35–39*	*40–44*	*45–49*	*50–54*	*55–59*
F	*3*	*5*	*10*	*20*	*12*	*6*	*3*	*1*

Sol. Here the greatest frequency 20 lies in the class 35 – 39. Hence modal class is 35 – 39. But the actual limits of this class are 34.5 – 39.5.

i.e., $l = 34.5, f_m = 20, f_1 = 10, f_2 = 12, h = 4$

$$\therefore \quad \text{Mode} = l + \frac{f_m - f_1}{2f_m - f_1 - f_2} \times h = 34.5 + \frac{20 - 10}{40 - 10 - 12} \times 4$$

$$= 34.5 + \frac{10}{18} \times 4 = 34.5 + \frac{20}{9} = 36.7.$$

Example 6. *Find the mode for the following frequency distribution :*

Class	*10–20*	*20–30*	*30–40*	*40–50*	*50–60*	*60–70*
f	*10*	*15*	*30*	*12*	*8*	*6*

Sol. By 'inspection', modal class is 30–40.

Now, $\text{mode} = L + \left(\dfrac{\Delta_1}{\Delta_1 + \Delta_2}\right) h$

Here $L = 30$, $\Delta_1 = 30 - 15 = 15$, $\Delta_2 = 30 - 12 = 18$, $h = 10$

$\therefore$ $\text{Mode} = 30 + \left(\dfrac{15}{15+18}\right) 10 = 30 + 4.545 = 34.545.$

Example 7. *Find the mode for the following frequency distribution :*

Class	*0–5*	*5–10*	*10–15*	*15–20*	*20–25*	*25–30*	*30–35*	*35–40*	*40–45*	*45–50*
f	*6*	*9*	*4*	*2*	*10*	*8*	*7*	*5*	*1*	*3*

Sol. We find the 'modal class' by using the 'method of grouping'.

Grouping Table

Class	*f* *I*	*II*	*III*	*IV*	*V*	*VI*
0–5	6	15				
5–10	9		13	19		
10–15	4	6			15	
15–20	2		12			16
20–25	**10**	**18**		**20**		
25–30	8		**15**		**25**	
30–35	7	12				**20**
35–40	5		6	13		
40–45	1	4			9	
45–50	3					

Analysis Table

Column	*20–25*	*25–30*	*30–35*	*15–20*	*35–40*
I	1				
II	1	1			
III		1	1		
IV	1	1		1	
V	1	1	1		
VI		1	1		1
Total	4	5	3	1	1

Since the total is maximum for the class 25–30, the modal class is 25–30.

Now $\text{mode} = L + \left(\dfrac{\Delta_1}{\Delta_1 + \Delta_2}\right) h$

Here $L = 25$, $\Delta_1 = 8 - 10 = -2$, $\Delta_2 = 8 - 7 = 1$, $h = 5$.

$\therefore$ $\text{Mode} = 25 + \left(\dfrac{-2}{-2+1}\right) 5 = 25 + 2 = 27.$

Example 8. *If the mode and mean of a moderately asymmetrical series are 16″ and 15.6″ respectively, what would be its most probable median ?*

Sol. We have mode = 16″ and mean = 15.6″.

The formulae is mode = 3 median – 2 A.M.

$\therefore \quad 16 = 3 \text{ median} - 2(15.6)$

$\Rightarrow \quad 3 \text{ median} = 16 + 31.2 = 47.2$

$\therefore \quad \text{median} = \dfrac{47.2}{3} = 15.73''.$

Example 9. *Calculate the mean and mode (by grouping method) from the following data.*

Central size	*15*	*25*	*35*	*45*	*55*	*65*	*75*	*85*
Frequencies	*5*	*9*	*13*	*21*	*20*	*15*	*8*	*3*

(P.T.U., M.B.A. Dec. 2005)

Sol. We first determine the lower and upper limits of each class. Here the class interval is 10 and hence the first class should be 10 – 20 (as mid-point is 15)

Calculation of mean. Take assumed mean A = 55, h = 10

Classes	*Mid values* (x_i)	*Frequency* f_i	*c.f.*	$d_i = x_i - A$	$u_i = \dfrac{x_i - A}{h}$	f_iu_i
10–20	15	5	5	– 40	– 4	– 20
20–30	25	9	14	– 30	– 3	– 27
30–40	35	13	27	– 20	– 2	– 26
40–50	45	21	48	– 10	– 1	– 21
50–60	55	20	68	0	0	0
60–70	65	15	83	10	1	15
70–80	75	8	91	20	2	16
80–90	85	3	94	30	3	9
		$\Sigma f_i = 94$				$\Sigma f_iu_i = -54$

$\therefore \quad$ Required mean $\bar{x} = A + h\dfrac{\Sigma f_iu_i}{\Sigma f_i} = 55 + 10 \times \left(\dfrac{-54}{94}\right) = 55 - 5.744 = 49.25.$

Calculation of Mode (by grouping method)

In column I, write the original frequencies.

Column II is obtained by combining the frequencies two by two *i.e.* 5 + 9 = 14 etc.

In column III, leave the first frequency of column I, then combine the frequencies two by two *i.e.* 9 + 13 = 22 etc.

In column IV, combine the frequencies, three by three *i.e.* 5 + 9 + 13 = 27 etc.

In column V, leave the first frequency of column I, then combine the frequencies three by three *i.e.* 9 + 13 + 21 = 43 etc.

In column VI, leave the first two frequencies, then combine the frequencies three by three *i.e.* 13 + 21 + 20 = 54 etc.

Classes	*Columns*					
	I	II	III	IV	V	VI
10–20	5					
		14		27		
20–30	9					
30–40	13		22		**43**	
		34				
40–50	21					
			41			**54**
50–60	20					
		35		**56**		
60–70	15					
			23		**43**	
70–80	8					
		11				
80–90	3					

The maximum frequency in each column is written in bold black type.

To find mode, consider the following table :

Analysis Table

Column No.	*Classes*		
	40–50	*50–60*	*60–70*
I	1		
II		1	1
III	1	1	
IV	1	1	1
V	1	1	
VI	1	1	1
Total	5	5	3

Here the series is bi-modal and hence we shall use the empirical formula *i.e.*

Mode = 3 Median – 2 Mean.

Calculation of Median

Here $\frac{N}{2} = \frac{94}{2} = 47$

The cumulative frequency just greater than 47 is 48. ∴ Median class is 40–50.

i.e. $L = 40, C = 27, f = 21, h = 10$

$$\therefore \quad \text{Median} = L + \frac{\frac{N}{2} - C}{f} \times h = 40 + \frac{47 - 27}{21} \times 10$$

$$= 40 + 9.524 = 49.524$$

Hence $\text{Mode} = 3 \times (49.524) - 2 \times (49.25)$

$$= 148.572 - 98.51 = 50.062.$$

5.21. MODE IN CASE OF CLASSES OF UNEQUAL WIDTHS

When the values of the variable are given in the form of classes and the classes are not of equal width, then we would not be able to proceed directly to find the modal class either by the method of inspection or by the method of grouping. In fact, we are to compare the frequencies of different classes in order to observe the concentration of items about some item. If the classes happen to be of unequal width, then we would not be able to compare the frequencies in different classes. To make the comparison meaningful, we will first make classes of equal width by grouping two or more classes or by breaking classes, as per the need.

Example 10. *Calculate mode for the following distribution :*

Marks	*No. of students*	*Marks*	*No. of students*
0–2	*8*	*25–30*	*45*
2–4	*12*	*30–40*	*60*
4–10	*20*	*40–50*	*20*
10–15	*10*	*50–60*	*13*
15–20	*16*	*60–80*	*15*
20–25	*25*	*80–100*	*4*

Sol. In this frequency distribution, the classes are not of equal width. Before ascertaining the modal class, we shall make the widths of classes equal.

Marks	*No. of students*
0–20	8 + 12 + 20 + 10 + 16 = 66
20–40	25 + 45 + 60 = 130
40–60	20 + 13 = 33
60–80	15
80–100	4

By inspection, modal class is 20–40.

Now $$\text{mode} = L + \left(\frac{\Delta_1}{\Delta_1 + \Delta_2}\right) h$$

Here $L = 20$, $\Delta_1 = 130 - 66 = 64$, $\Delta_2 = 130 - 33 = 97$, $h = 20$

$$\therefore \quad \text{Mode} = 20 + \left(\frac{64}{64 + 97}\right) 20 = 20 + 7.9503 = 27.9503.$$

Example 11. *Calculate median and mode for the following data :*

Class	*2*	*3*	*4*	*5–7*	*7–10*	*10–15*	*15–20*	*20–25*
Frequency	*1*	*2*	*2*	*3*	*5*	*10*	*8*	*4*

Sol. We make classes as 0–5, 5–10, 10–15, 15–20 and 20–25.

Class	*Frequency* f		*c.f.*
0–5	1 + 2 + 2 = 5		5
5–10	3 + 5 = 8		13
10–15	10		23
15–20	8		31
20–25	4		35 = N
	N = 35		

Calculation of Median

$$\frac{N}{2} = \frac{35}{2} = 17.5$$

$\therefore$ Median = size of 17.5th item

$\therefore$ Median class is 10–15.

$$\therefore \quad \text{Median} = L + \left(\frac{N/2 - C}{f}\right)h = 10 + \left(\frac{17.5 - 13}{10}\right)5 = 10 + 2.25 = 12.25.$$

Calculation of Mode

By inspection, modal class is 10–15.

Now $$\text{mode} = L + \left(\frac{\Delta_1}{\Delta_1 + \Delta_2}\right)h$$

Here $L = 10$, $\Delta_1 = 10 - 8 = 2$, $\Delta_2 = 10 - 8$, $h = 5$.

$$\therefore \quad \text{Mode} = 10 + \left(\frac{2}{2+2}\right)5 = 10 + 2.5 = 12.5.$$

5.22. LOCATING MODE GRAPHICALLY

In a frequency distribution, the value of mode can also be determined graphically.

Method :

Step I. Draw a histogram of the given data

Step II. Draw two lines diagonally in the inside of the modal class bar, starting from each upper corner of the bar to the upper corner of the adjacent bar.

Step III. Draw a perpendicular line from the intersection of the two diagonal lines to x-axis, which will give the modal value.

Example 12. *Find the mode of the following frequency distribution, graphically. Also verify the result by direct method.*

Class	*0–100*	*100–200*	*200–300*	*300–400*	*400–500*	*500–600*
f_i	*12*	*18*	*27*	*20*	*17*	*6*

Sol. Here maximum frequency = 27

∴ Modal class : 200–300. Draw the histogram of the given following distribution, which is shown in the figure.

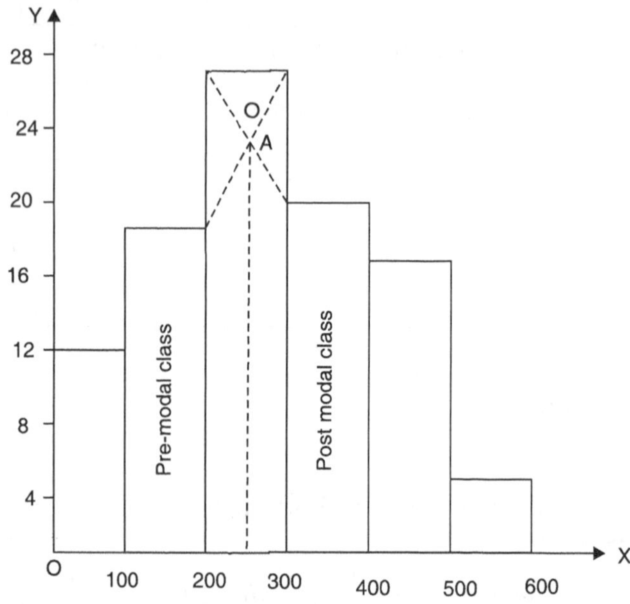

The perpendicular line drawn from A, meets the x-axis at 256.

∴ mode = 256.

By **direct method,**

Here modal class is 200–300

$$\therefore \quad L = 200, \quad \Delta_1 = 27 - 18 = 9$$

$$\Delta_2 = 27 - 20 = 7,$$

$$h = 100$$

$$\therefore \quad \text{Mode} = L + \left(\frac{\Delta_1}{\Delta_1 + \Delta_2}\right) h = 200 + \frac{9}{9+7} \times 100$$

$$= 200 + \frac{9}{16} \times 100 = 200 + \frac{225}{4} = 200 + 56.25$$

$$= 256.25 \cong 256.$$

Remarks :

(*i*) Mode can also be determined from a frequency polygon, in which a perpendicular is drawn on the base from the apex of the polygon and the point where it meets the base, gives the modal value.

(*ii*) Graphical method of determining mode can be used only where there is one class containing the highest frequency. If two or more classes have the same highest frequency, mode cannot be determined graphically.

Example 13. *10% of the workers in a firm employing a total of 1000 workers earn less than ₹ 5, 200 earn between ₹ 5 – 9.99, 30% between 10 and 14.99, 250 workers between 15 and 19.99 and the rest 20 and above. What is the median ?*

Sol. Arrange the given data in tabular form, we get

Earnings	*No. of workers*	*c.f.*
Below	$\frac{10}{100} \times 1000 = 100$	100
5–9.99	200	300
10–14.99	$\frac{30}{100} \times 1000 = 300$	600
15–19.99	250	850
20 above	150	1000

Here $\frac{N}{2} = \frac{1000}{2} = 500$, median class = 9.99 – 14.99

$$L = 9.99,\ h = \frac{10 - 9.99}{2} = 0.005$$

$$\therefore \quad \text{Required median} = L + \frac{\frac{N}{2} - C}{f} \times h = 9.99 + \frac{500 - 300}{300} \times 0.005$$

$$= 9.99 + 0.0033 = 9.993.$$

Example 14. *The A.M. mode and median of a group of 75 observations were 27, 34, 29. It was later discovered that one observation was wrongly read as 43, instead of the correct value 53. Find the correct mean, mode and median.*

Sol. Let $x_1, x_2, \ldots\ldots x_n$, be the given observations. Then as given, mean $\bar{x} = 27$

$$\Rightarrow \quad \frac{\sum_{i=1}^{n} x_i}{75} = 27 \quad \Rightarrow \quad \sum_{i=1}^{n} x_i = 75 \times 27 = 2025$$

$$\text{Corrected value of } \sum_{i=1}^{n} x_i = 2025 - (\text{Incorrected item}) + (\text{corrected item})$$

$$= 2025 - 43 + 53 = 2035$$

$$\therefore \quad \text{Corrected mean} = \frac{\text{corrected} \sum_{i=1}^{n} x_i}{75} = \frac{2035}{75} = 27.13$$

Further, the values of median and mode will not be affected by this error because the median and mode are positional averages. Also the median is 29, which is far away from 43 and 53. Similarly the value of mode is 34.

Hence the corrected mode = 34, and the corrected median = 29.

5.23. MERITS OF MODE

(*i*) It is the most typical or representative value of a distribution.

(*ii*) It is not affected by extreme values for example the mode of 10, 2, 80, 12, 120, 60, 10, 3, 10 is 10 as 10 has repeated thrice.

(*iii*) It can be calculated in case of open-end distributions without any adjustment.

(*iv*) It can be determined graphically whereas mean cannot be determined.

(*v*) It can also be used to describe qualitative phenomenon, for example to compare the customers preferences for different types of soap, tooth paste etc., mode is the best measure.

5.24. DEMERITS OF MODE

1. It is not simple to understand.

2. It is not well defined. There are number of formulae to calculate mode, not necessarily giving the same answer.

3. It is not capable of further algebraic treatment.

Uses. Mode is the only average to be used to find an ideal size, *i.e.,* in business forecasting, in the manufacturing in ready-made garments.

5.25. RELATION BETWEEN MEAN, MEDIAN AND MODE

(*a*) In case of symmetrical distribution, the value of mean, median and mode coincide.

(*b*) In case of asymmetrical distribution or skewed distribution, the values of mean, median and mode are not equal. In such cases, a very important relation due to karl pearson, is given by

$$\text{Mode} = 3 \text{ Median} - 2 \text{ Mean}$$

or

$$\text{Mode} - \text{Mean} = 3 \text{ (Median} - \text{Mean)}$$

i.e., the distance between mean and mode is 3 times the distance between mean and median.

Example. *In a moderately asymmetrical distribution the mode and mean are 32.1 and 35.4 respectively. Find the median.*

Sol. In a moderately asymmetrical distribution, we know that

$$\text{mode} = 3 \text{ median} - 2 \text{ mean} \quad \text{...(1)}$$

Given mode = 32.1, mean 35.4

$\therefore$ (1) gives $\quad 32.1 = 3 \text{ median} - 2(35.4)$

$\Rightarrow \quad 3 \text{ median} = 32.1 + 70.8 = 102.9$

$\Rightarrow \quad \text{Median} = \dfrac{102.9}{3} = 34.3$

TEST YOUR KNOWLEDGE 5.3

1. Find the value of mode for the following series :

10, 12, 17, 12, 10, 12, 16, 11.

2. Find the mode for the following series :

0, 1, 6, 7, 2, 3, 7, 6, 6, 2, 6, 0, 5, 6, 0 (*P.T.U., M.B.A. May, 2009*)

3. Find the value of mode for the following frequency distribution :

x	10	11	12	13	14	15	16	17	18
f	2	4	6	8	10	9	6	2	1

4. Calculate the mode for the following frequency distribution :

x	4	5	6	7	8	9	10	11	12	13
f	2	5	8	9	12	14	14	15	11	13

5. Find the median and mode for the following frequency distribution :

x	4	5	6	7	8	9	10
f	10	11	10	30	28	7	3

6. The number of fully formed apples on 100 plants were counted with the following results :

2	plants	had	0	apples
5	,,	,,	1	,,
7	,,	,,	2	,,
11	,,	,,	3	,,
18	,,	,,	4	,,
24	,,	,,	5	,,
12	,,	,,	6	,,
8	,,	,,	7	,,
6	,,	,,	8	,,
4	,,	,,	9	,,
3	,,	,,	10	,,

(*i*) How many apples are there ?

(*ii*) What is the average number of apples per plant ?

(*iii*) What is the modal number of apples ?

7. Find the mode for the following frequency distribution :

Class	0–4	4–8	8–12	12–16
f	4	8	5	6

8. Find the mode for the following frequency distribution :

Marks	0–5	5–10	10–15	15–20	20–25	25–30	30–35
No. of students	11	20	31	45	30	12	6

9. The following table gives the weight of 50 students of a class. Find the modal weight :

Weight (in kg)	37–41	42–46	47–51	52–56	57–61	62–66	67–71
No. of students	3	7	11	14	7	6	2

10. Calculate the modal value for the following frequency distribution :

Marks	*No. of candidates*	*Marks*	*No. of candidates*
0–9	6	50–59	263
10–19	29	60–69	133
20–29	87	70–79	43
30–39	181	80–89	9
40–49	247	90–99	2

11. Following table shows the marks obtained by 60 students. Calculate (*i*) median (*ii*) mode.

Marks		*No. of students*
More than	70%	8
,,	60%	18
,,	50%	40
,,	40%	40
,,	30%	55
,,	20%	60

12. Obtain the median and mode for the following series :

Marks	10–25	25–40	40–55	55–70	70–85	85–100
Frequency	6	20	44	26	3	1

13. Calculate median and arithmetic average for the following data. Also calculate mode with the help of median and A.M.

Variable	100–110	110–120	120–130	130–140	150–160	160–170	170–180
Frequency	4	6	20	32	33	8	2

14. Find out the median and mode for the following :

Wage (in ₹)	5–15	15–25	25–35	35–45	45–55	55–65
No. of employees	4	6	10	5	3	2

15. The following table shows the distribution of 100 families according to their expenditure per week. Number of families corresponding to the groups ₹ 1,000–2,000 and ₹ 3,000–4,000 are missing. The mode is given to be ₹ 2,400. Calculate the missing frequencies :

Expenditure (₹)	0–1,000	1,000–2,000	2,000–3,000	3,000–4,000	4,000–5,000
No. of families	14	?	27	?	15

16. Calculate mode for the following distribution :

Class	0–4	4–6	6–8	8–12	12–18	18–20
Frequency	4	6	8	12	7	2

17. Find the mode for the following data :

Size of items	*Frequency*	*Size of items*	*Frequency*
0–4	5	20–24	14
4–8	7	24–28	6
8–12	9	28–32	3
12–16	17	32–36	1
16–20	15	36–40	0

18. Calculate the median and mode for the following :

Class	*Frequency*	*Class*	*Frequency*
10-20	4	10–60	124
10–30	16	10–70	137
10–40	56	10–80	146
10–50	97	10–90	150

19. The ages of employees in two factories A and B are given below :

Age of employees (in years)	*Number of employees*	
	Factory A	*Factory B*
20–30	5	8
30–40	26	40
40–50	78	58
50–60	104	90
60–70	98	83

Find the modal age of employees in Factory A and Factory B.

20. In a moderately asymmetrical distribution, the value of median and mode are 20.6 and 26 respectively. Find the mean.

Answers

1. 12 **2.** 6 **3.** 15.733 **4.** 10

5. median = 30 mode = 9

6. (*i*) 486 (*ii*) 4.86 (*iii*) 5 **7.** 6.286 **8.** 17.414

9. 53 **10.** 47.5488 **11.** (*i*) 54.54% marks (*ii*) 56.67% marks

12. 48.18 marks, 48.57 marks **13.** 137.03, 140.14, 130.81

14. ₹ 30, ₹ 29.44 **15.** 23, 21 **16.** 7

17. 18.67 **18.** 44.63, 40.67 **19.** 58.12 years, 58.2 years

20. Mean = 17.9.

Hint

15. Let the frequencies of the classes 1000–2000 and 3000–4000 be a and b respectively.

$$\therefore \quad 2400 = 2000 + \left(\frac{27-9}{(27-a)+(27-b)}\right) \times 1000 \quad i.e., \quad 400 = \frac{(27-a)100}{54-a-b}$$

Also, $a + b = 44$.

PARTITION VALUES

5.26. DEFINITION OF PARTITION VALUES

We have already seen that the median divide the items in a series into two equal parts. On the same lines, we can think of those values of the variable which may partition the series into four equal parts or ten equal parts or hundred equal parts. The values of the variable which partition a statistical series into equal parts, are called **partition values.**

Quartiles. The values of the variable which partition the series into four equal parts are called **quartiles** denoted by Q_1, Q_2, Q_3. In the distribution, 25% items would have value less than or equal to Q_1 and 75% items would be having value greater than or equal to Q_1. Similarly, this can interpret Q_2 and Q_3. It may be noted that Q_2 would be same as the median.

(P.T.U., M.B.A. May 2006)

Deciles. The values of the variable which partition the series into ten equal parts, are called **deciles** denoted by $D_1, D_2, \ldots, D_9$. In the distribution, 10 K% items would be less than or equal to D_K and (100–10 K)% items would be having value greater than or equal to D_K, $(1 \le K \le 9)$.

Percentiles. The values of the variable which partition the series into 100 equal parts, are called **percentiles** denoted by $P_1, P_2, \ldots, P_{99}$. In the distribution, K% items would be less than or equal to P_K and (100–K)% items would be having value greater than or equal to P_K, $(1 \le K \le 99)$.

For an individual series, the quartile values are given by

$$Q_K = \text{size of } K\left(\frac{n+1}{4}\right)\text{th item}, \quad K = 1, 2, 3\ ;$$

where $x_1, x_2, \ldots, x_n$ are the values of the variable under consideration. The values $x_1, x_2, \ldots, x_n$ are supposed to have been arranged strictly in *ascending* order of magnitude. If $K\left(\frac{n+1}{4}\right)$ comes out to be in decimal, then Q_K is found by the *method of interpolation*.

Similarly, $$D_K = \text{size of } K\left(\frac{n+1}{10}\right)\text{th item}, \quad K = 1, 2, \ldots, 9.$$

$$P_K = \text{size of } K\left(\frac{n+1}{100}\right)\text{th item}, \quad K = 1, 2, \ldots, 99.$$

5.27. WORKING RULES FOR FINDING POSITIONAL MEASURES FOR AN INDIVIDUAL SERIES

I. Arrange the given items in the ascending order of magnitude.

II. Find the total number 'n' of items.

III. Write : (*i*) $Q_K = \text{size of } K\left(\frac{n+1}{4}\right)\text{th item}, K = 1, 2, 3.$

(*ii*) $D_K = \text{size of } K\left(\frac{n+1}{10}\right)\text{th item}, K = 1, 2, \ldots, 9.$

(*iii*) $P_K = \text{size of } K\left(\frac{n+1}{100}\right)\text{th item}, K = 1, 2, \ldots, 99.$

IV. If $K\left(\frac{n+1}{4}\right)\left(\text{or } K\left(\frac{n+1}{10}\right) \text{or } K\left(\frac{n+1}{100}\right)\right)$ is in fraction, then the corresponding positional measure is found by the method of interpolation.

For a frequency distribution, we define :

$$Q_K = \text{size of } K\left(\frac{N+1}{4}\right)\text{th item}, \quad K = 1, 2, 3.$$

$$D_K = \text{size of } K\left(\frac{N+1}{10}\right)\text{th item,} \quad K = 1, 2, ..., 9.$$

$$P_K = \text{size of } K\left(\frac{N+1}{100}\right)\text{th item,} \quad K = 1, 2, ..., 99.$$

Here also the values of the variable are supposed to have been arranged in the ascending order of magnitude.

5.28. WORKING RULES FOR FINDING POSITIONAL MEASURES FOR A FREQUENCY DISTRIBUTION

I. Arrange the values of the variable in the ascending order of magnitude and find the cumulative frequencies (*c.f.*).

II. Find the total 'N' of all frequencies and check that it is equal to the last *c.f.*

III. Write : (*i*) $Q_K = \text{size of } K\left(\frac{N+1}{4}\right)\text{th item, } K = 1, 2, 3.$

(*ii*) $D_K = \text{size of } K\left(\frac{N+1}{10}\right)\text{th item, } K = 1, 2, ..., 9.$

(*iii*) $P_K = \text{size of } K\left(\frac{N+1}{100}\right)\text{th item, } K = 1, 2, ..., 99.$

IV. We have $Q_1 = \text{size of} \frac{N+1}{4}\text{th item.}$

(*a*) If $\frac{N+1}{4}$ is a whole number, then $\frac{N+1}{4}$th item gives the value of Q_1. For this, look at the cumulative frequency column and find that total which is either equal to $\frac{N+1}{4}$ or the next higher than $\frac{N+1}{4}$ and determine the value of the variable corresponding to this. That gives the value of Q_1.

(*b*) If $\frac{N+1}{4}$ is in fraction, then Q_1 is found by the method of interpolation.

Same procedure is followed for finding other positional measures.

In case, the values of the variable are given in the form of classes, then we shall assume that the items in the classes are uniformly distributed in the corresponding classes. Here we define

$$Q_K = \text{size of } K\left(\frac{N}{4}\right)\text{th item,} \quad K = 1, 2, 3.$$

$$D_K = \text{size of } K\left(\frac{N}{10}\right)\text{th item,} \quad K = 1, 2, ..., 9.$$

$$P_K = \text{size of } K\left(\frac{N}{100}\right)\text{th item,} \quad K = 1, 2, ..., 99.$$

By using these formulae, we shall get the class in which the corresponding partition value would lie. This class is called the corresponding **partition value class.** To ascertain the partition value, we shall use the required formula from the list given below :

$$Q_K = L + \left(\frac{K\left(\frac{N}{4}\right) - C}{f} \right) h, \quad K = 1, 2, 3.$$

$$D_K = L + \left(\frac{K\left(\frac{N}{10}\right) - C}{f} \right) h, \quad K = 1, 2, ..., 9.$$

$$P_K = L + \left(\frac{K\left(\frac{N}{100}\right) - C}{f} \right) h, \quad K = 1, 2, ..., 99.$$

where L = lower limit of the corresponding partition value class

C = cumulative frequency of the class preceding the corresponding partition value class

f = simple frequency of the corresponding partition value class

h = width of the corresponding partition value class.

The following points must be taken care of while calculating partition values :

1. The values (classes of values) of the variable must be strictly in the ascending order of magnitude.

2. If the classes are in inclusive form, then actual limits of the partition value class are to be taken for finding L and h.

3. The classes may not be of equal width.

5.29. WORKING RULES FOR FINDING POSITIONAL MEASURES FOR A FREQUENCY DISTRIBUTION WITH CLASS INTERVALS

I. Arrange the classes in the ascending order of magnitude. The classes must be in exclusive form. The width of the classes may not be equal. Find the cumulative frequencies (*c.f.*).

II. Find the total 'N' of all frequencies and check that it is equal to the last *c.f.*

III. Write : (*i*) Q_K = size of $K\left(\frac{N}{4}\right)$th item, K = 1, 2, 3.

(*ii*) D_K = size of $K\left(\frac{N}{10}\right)$th item, K = 1, 2, ..., 9.

(*iii*) P_K = size of $K\left(\frac{N}{100}\right)$th item, K = 1, 2, ..., 99.

IV. We have Q_1 = size of $\frac{N}{4}$th item. Look at the cumulative frequency column and find that total which is either equal to $\frac{N}{4}$ or the next higher than $\frac{N}{4}$ and determine the class corresponding to this. That gives the 'Q_1-class'.

V. Write : $Q_1 = L + \left(\frac{N/4 - C}{f}\right)h$. Put the values of L, N/4, C, f, h and calculate the value of Q_1. Same procedure is followed for finding other positional measures.

ILLUSTRATIVE EXAMPLES

Example 1. *Calculate the partition values Q_1, Q_3, D_2, D_7, P_{22}, P_{38}, P_{80} for the following data:*

4, 7, 3, 9, 4, 12, 7, 12, 6, 18, 19, 20, 4, 7, 6, 5, 17, 16, 19.

Sol. The values of the variable arranged in ascending order of magnitude are :

3, 4, 4, 4, 5, 6, 6, 7, 7, 7, 9, 12, 12, 16, 17, 18, 19, 19, 20.

Here $n = 19$.

Q_1 : $1\left(\frac{N+1}{4}\right) = \frac{19+1}{4} = 5$

$\therefore$ Q_1 = size of 5th item = 5.

Q_3 : $3\left(\frac{N+1}{4}\right) = 3\left(\frac{19+1}{4}\right) = 15$

$\therefore$ Q_3 = size of 15th item = 17.

D_2 : $2\left(\frac{N+1}{10}\right) = 2\left(\frac{19+1}{10}\right) = 4$

$\therefore$ D_2 = size of 4th item = 4.

D_7 : $7\left(\frac{N+1}{10}\right) = 7\left(\frac{19+1}{10}\right) = 14$

$\therefore$ D_7 = size of 14th item = 16.

P_{22} : $22\left(\frac{N+1}{100}\right) = 22\left(\frac{19+1}{100}\right) = 4.4$

$\therefore$ P_{22} = size of 4.4th item

= size of 4th item + (0.4)(size of 5th item – size of 4th item)

= 4 + (0.4)(5 – 4) = 4.4

P_{38} : $38\left(\frac{N+1}{100}\right) = 38\left(\frac{19+1}{100}\right) = 7.6$

$\therefore$ P_{38} = size of 7.6th item

= size of 7th item + 0.6 (size of 8th item – size of 7th item)

= 6 + (0.6)(7 – 6) = 6.6

P_{80} : $80\left(\frac{N+1}{100}\right) = 80\left(\frac{19+1}{100}\right) = 16.$

$\therefore$ P_{80} = size of 16th item = 18.

Example 2. *The following data relates to the sizes of shoes sold at a store during a given week. Find* Q_1, Q_3, D_1, P_{98} :

Size of shoes	*5*	*6*	*7*	*8*	*9*	*10*	*11*
Frequency	*120*	*137*	*330*	*400*	*312*	*81*	*17*

Sol. **Calculation of Partition Values**

Size of shoes x	*Frequency* f	*c.f.*
5	120	120
6	137	257
7	330	587
8	400	987
9	312	1299
10	81	1380
11	17	1397 = N
	N = 1397	

$\mathbf{Q_1}$: $$1\left(\frac{N+1}{4}\right) = \frac{1397+1}{4} = 349.5$$

∴ Q_1 = size of 349.5th item

= size of 349th item + (0.5)(size of 350th item – size of 349th item)

= 7 + (0.5)(7 – 7) = 7.

$\mathbf{Q_3}$: $$3\left(\frac{N+1}{4}\right) = 3\left(\frac{1397+1}{4}\right) = 1048.5$$

∴ Q_3 = size of 1048.5th item

= size of 1048th item + (0.5)(size of 1049th item – size of 1048th item)

= 9 + (0.5)(9 – 9) = 9.

$\mathbf{D_1}$: $$1\left(\frac{N+1}{10}\right) = \frac{1397+1}{10} = 139.8$$

∴ D_1 = size of 139.8th item

= size of 139th item + (0.8)(size of 140th item – size of 139th item)

= 6 + (0.8)(6 – 6) = 6.

$\mathbf{P_{98}}$: $$98\left(\frac{N+1}{100}\right) = 98\left(\frac{1397+1}{100}\right) = 1370.04$$

∴ P_{98} = size of 1370.04th item

= size of 1370th item + (0.04)(size of 1371th item – size of 1370th item)

= 10 + (0.04)(10 – 10) = 10.

Example 3. *Find out Q_1, Q_3, D_2, D_9, P_5, P_{30}, P_{83} for the following data :*

Monthly Rent (in ₹)	*200–400*	*400–600*	*600–800*	*800–1000*	*1000–1200*
No. of families	*6*	*9*	*11*	*14*	*20*
Monthly Rent (in ₹)	*1200–1400*	*1400–1600*	*1600–1800*	*1800–2000*	
No. of families	*15*	*10*	*8*	*7*	

Sol. Calculation of Partition Values

Monthly Rent (in ₹)	*No. of families* *f*	*c.f.*
200–400	6	6
400–600	9	15
600–800	11	26
800–1000	14	40
1000–1200	20	60
1200–1400	15	75
1400–1600	10	85
1600–1800	8	93
1800–2000	7	100 = N
	N = 100	

Q_1 : $\frac{N}{4} = \frac{100}{4} = 25$

∴ Q_1 = 25th item. ∴ Q_1 class is 600–800.

∴ $$Q_1 = L + \left(\frac{\frac{N}{4} - C}{f}\right)h = 600 + \left(\frac{25 - 15}{11}\right) 200 = ₹\ 781.82.$$

Q_3 : $3\left(\frac{N}{4}\right) = 3\left(\frac{100}{4}\right) = 75$

∴ Q_3 = 75th item. ∴ Q_3 class is 1200–1400.

∴ $$Q_3 = L + \left(\frac{3\left(\frac{N}{4}\right) - C}{f}\right)h = 1200 + \left(\frac{75 - 60}{15}\right) 200 = ₹\ 1400.$$

D_2 : $2\left(\frac{N}{10}\right) = 2\left(\frac{100}{10}\right) = 20.$

∴ D_2 = size of 20th item. ∴ D_2 class is 600–800.

$\therefore \quad D_2 = L + \left(\dfrac{2\left(\dfrac{N}{10}\right) - C}{f} \right) h = 600 + \left(\dfrac{20-15}{11} \right) 200 = ₹\ 690.91.$

D_9 : $\quad 9\left(\dfrac{N}{10}\right) = 9\left(\dfrac{100}{10}\right) = 90$

$\therefore \quad D_9$ = size of 90th item. $\therefore$ D_9 class is 1600–1800.

$\therefore \quad D_9 = L + \left(\dfrac{9\left(\dfrac{N}{10}\right) - C}{f} \right) h = 1600 + \left(\dfrac{90-85}{8} \right) 200 = ₹\ 1725.$

P_5 : $\quad 5\left(\dfrac{N}{100}\right) = 5\left(\dfrac{100}{100}\right) = 5$

$\therefore \quad P_5$ = size of 5th item. $\therefore$ P_5 class is 200–400.

$\therefore \quad P_5 = L + \left(\dfrac{5\left(\dfrac{N}{100}\right) - C}{f} \right) h = 200 + \left(\dfrac{5-0}{6} \right) 200 = ₹\ 366.67.$

P_{30} : $\quad 30\left(\dfrac{N}{100}\right) = 30\left(\dfrac{100}{100}\right) = 30$

$\therefore \quad P_{30}$ = size of 30th item. $\therefore$ P_{30} class is 800–1000.

$\therefore \quad P_{30} = L + \left(\dfrac{30\left(\dfrac{N}{100}\right) - C}{f} \right) h = 800 + \left(\dfrac{30-26}{14} \right) 200 = ₹\ 857.14.$

P_{83} : $\quad 83\left(\dfrac{N}{100}\right) = 83\left(\dfrac{100}{100}\right) = 83.$

P_{83} = size of 83th item. $\therefore$ P_{83} class is 1400–1600.

$\therefore \quad P_{83} = L + \left(\dfrac{83\left(\dfrac{N}{100}\right) - C}{f} \right) h = 1400 + \left(\dfrac{83-75}{10} \right) 200 = ₹\ 1560.$

Example 4. *Calculate the quartiles, 6th decile, 9th decile, 47th percentage, 70th percentile from the following data :*

Marks	*Less than 80*	*Less than 70*	*Less than 60*	*Less than 50*	*Less than 40*	*Less than 30*	*Less than 20*	*Less than 10*
No. of students	*100*	*90*	*80*	*60*	*32*	*20*	*13*	*5*

Sol. **Calculation of Partition Values**

Marks	*Classes in exclusive form*	*No. of students f*	*c.f.*
0–9	0–9.5	5	5
10–19	9.5–19.5	13 – 5 = 8	5 + 8 = 13
20–29	19.5–29.5	20 – 13 = 7	13 + 7 = 20
30–39	29.5–39.5	32 – 20 = 12	20 + 12 = 32
40–49	39.5–49.5	60 – 32 = 28	32 + 28 = 60
50–59	49.5–59.5	80 – 60 = 20	60 + 20 = 80
60–69	59.5–69.5	90 – 80 = 10	80 + 10 = 90
70–79	69.5–79.5	100 – 90 = 10	90 + 10 = 100 = N
		N = 100	

Q_1 : $\frac{N}{4} = \frac{100}{4} = 25$

∴ Q_1 = size of 25th item. ∴ Q_1 class is 29.5–39.5.

∴ $$Q_1 = L + \left(\frac{\frac{N}{4} - C}{f}\right) h = 29.5 + \left(\frac{25 - 20}{12}\right) 10 = 33.67 \text{ marks.}$$

Q_3 : $3\left(\frac{N}{4}\right) = 3\left(\frac{100}{4}\right) = 75$

∴ Q_3 = size of 75th item. ∴ Q_3 class is 49.5–59.5.

∴ $$Q_3 = L + \left(\frac{3\left(\frac{N}{4}\right) - C}{f}\right) h = 49.5 + \left(\frac{75 - 60}{20}\right) 10 = 57 \text{ marks.}$$

D_6 : $6\left(\frac{N}{10}\right) = 6\left(\frac{100}{10}\right) = 60$

∴ D_6 = size of 60th item. ∴ D_6 class is 39.5–49.5.

∴ $$D_6 = L + \left(\frac{6\left(\frac{N}{10}\right) - C}{f}\right) h = 39.5 + \left(\frac{60 - 32}{28}\right) 10 = 49.5 \text{ marks.}$$

D_9 : $9\left(\frac{N}{10}\right) = 9\left(\frac{100}{10}\right) = 90$

∴ D_9 = size of 90th item. ∴ D_9 class is 59.5–69.5.

$$D_9 = L + \left(\frac{9\left(\frac{N}{10}\right) - C}{f}\right) h = 59.5 + \left(\frac{90 - 80}{10}\right) 10 = 69.5 \text{ marks.}$$

P_{47} : $47\left(\frac{N}{100}\right) = 47\left(\frac{100}{100}\right) = 47$

$\therefore$ P_{47} = size of 47th item. $\therefore$ P_{47} class is 39.5–49.5.

$$\therefore \quad P_{47} = L + \left(\frac{47\left(\frac{N}{100}\right) - C}{f}\right)h = 39.5 + \left(\frac{47 - 32}{28}\right)10 = 44.86 \text{ marks.}$$

P_{70} : $70\left(\frac{N}{100}\right) = 70\left(\frac{100}{100}\right) = 70$

$\therefore$ P_{70} = size of 70th item. $\therefore$ P_{70} class 49.5–59.5.

$$\therefore \quad P_{70} = L + \left(\frac{70\left(\frac{N}{100}\right) - C}{f}\right)h = 49.5 + \left(\frac{70 - 60}{20}\right)10 = 54.5 \text{ marks.}$$

Example 5. *Given below is the distribution of marks obtained by 50 students in a class test :*

Marks	*0–10*	*10–20*	*20–30*	*30–40*	*40–50*	*50–60*
No. of students	*3*	*5*	*9*	*12*	*18*	*3*

If 70% students pass the test, find the minimum marks needed by a student to pass the examination.

Sol. Since 70% students passed the test, the percentage of failed students is 30%. Let minimum pass marks be K.

$\therefore$ 30% students have got marks less than K.

$\therefore$ $P_{30} = K$.

Marks x	*No. of students* f	*c.f.*
0–10	3	3
10–20	5	8
20–30	9	17
30–40	12	29
40–50	18	47
50–60	3	50 = N
	N = 50	

$30\left(\frac{N}{100}\right) = 30\left(\frac{50}{100}\right) = 15$

$\therefore$ P_{30} = size of 15th item. $\therefore$ P_{30} class is 20–30

$$\therefore \quad P_{30} = L + \left(\frac{30\left(\frac{N}{100}\right) - C}{f}\right) h = 20 + \left(\frac{15-8}{9}\right) 10 = 27.78 = 28 \text{ (nearly)}$$

$\therefore$ K = 28, *i.e.*, the minimum pass marks are 28.

Example 6. *Find the percentage of workers who earned more than ₹ 840.*

Income (in ₹)	*500–600*	*600–700*	*700–800*	*800–900*	*900–1000*	*1000–1100*
No. of workers	*12*	*17*	*22*	*29*	*12*	*6*

Sol.

Income (in ₹)	*No. of workers f*	*c.f.*
500–600	12	12
600–700	17	29
700–800	22	51
800–900	29	80
900–1000	12	92
1000–1100	6	98 = N
	N = 98	

Let K% workers get less than ₹ 840 $\therefore$ $P_K = 840$

$\therefore$ P_K class is 800–900.

Now $$P_K = L + \left(\frac{K\left(\frac{N}{100}\right) - C}{f}\right) h \text{ implies } 840 = 800 + \left(\frac{K\left(\frac{98}{100}\right) - 51}{29}\right) 100$$

$$\Rightarrow \quad 40 = \left(\frac{0.98K - 51}{29}\right) 100 \quad \Rightarrow \quad 1160 = 98K - 5100$$

$$\Rightarrow \quad K = \frac{6260}{98} = 63.88.$$

$\therefore$ % of workers getting less than ₹ 840 = 63.88%

$\therefore$ % of workers getting more than ₹ 840 = 100% – 63.88% = 36.12%

$\therefore$ 36.12% workers are getting more than ₹ 840.

TEST YOUR KNOWLEDGE 5.4

1. Find the value of Q_1 and Q_3 for the series :

7, 6, 9, 4, 8, 7, 5.

2. Find the values of Q_1, Q_3, D_2, D_7, P_{21}, P_{37} for the following individual series :

6, 9, 3, 11, 18, 5, 17, 36, 45.

3. Find the values of Q_1, Q_3, P_{19}, P_{51}, P_{90} for the following individual series :

21, 17, 16, 31, 32, 39, 16, 31, 14, 19.

4. Find quartiles for the following series :

Size	*Frequency*	*Size*	*Frequency*
4	40	12	50
5	48	13	52
6	52	14	41
7	56	15	57
8	60	16	63
9	63	17	52
10	57	18	48
11	55	19	40

5. From the figures given below, find Q_1, Q_3, D_2, D_9, P_{36}, P_{57} :

Age (in years)	20–25	25–30	30–35	35–40	40–45	45–50	50–55	55–60
No. of Persons	50	70	100	180	150	120	70	59

6. The following table gives the age in years of 800 persons. Find Q_1, D_9, P_{35}, P_{92} :

Age (in years)	20–60	20–55	20–40	20–30	20–50	20–45	20–25	20–35
No. of persons	800	740	400	120	670	550	50	220

7. From the following data, find the values of Q_1, Q_3, D_1, D_3, P_{47} :

Size of item	0–10	10–20	20–30	30–40	40–50	50–60	60–70	70–80
Frequency	2	18	30	45	35	20	6	3

8. The following series relates to the marks obtained by students, in a class test :

Marks	0–10	10–20	20–30	30–40	40–50	50–60	60–70	70–80	80–90	90–100
No. of students	11	18	25	28	30	33	22	15	12	10

Find the median, the quartiles and the first and the ninth deciles.

9. Find the values of Q_1, Q_3, D_2, D_7, P_{12}, P_{39} for the following distribution :

Income (in ₹)	Below 30	30–40	40–50	50–60	60–70	70–80	80 and above
No. of Persons	69	167	207	65	58	27	10

10. Find the median, lower and upper quartiles from the following table :

Marks below	10	20	30	40	50	60	70	80
No. of students	15	35	60	84	94	127	198	249

11. Following is the distribution of marks in Accountancy obtained by 50 students :

Marks (more than)	0	10	20	30	40	50
No. of students	50	46	40	20	10	3

If 60% of the students pass this test, find the minimum marks obtained by a pass candidate.

12. Find the percentage of workers who earned more than ₹ 10200 for the following data.

Income (in ₹)	7000–8000	8000–9000	9000–10000	10000–11000	11000–12000
No. of workers	4	8	9	6	3

13. The following table gives the weekly wages in rupees in a certain commercial organisation :

Wage (in ₹)	30–32	32–34	34–36	36–38	38–40	40–42	42–44	44–46	46–48	48–50
No. of workers	3	8	24	31	50	61	38	21	12	2

Find the number of wage earners receiving between ₹ 37 and ₹ 47.

Answers

1. $Q_1 = 5, Q_3 = 8$ **2.** $Q_1 = 5.5, Q_3 = 27, D_2 = 5, D_7 = 18, P_{21} = 5.1, P_{37} = 8.1$

3. $Q_1 = 16, Q_3 = 31.25, P_{19} = 16, P_{51} = 20.22, P_{90} = 38.3$ **4.** $Q_1 = 8, Q_3 = 15$

5. Q_1 = 33.99 years, Q_3 = 47.05 years, D_2 = 31.99 years, D_9 = 53.51 years, P_{36} = 36.88 years, P_{57} = 41.85 years

6. Q_1 = 34 years, D_9 = 53.57 years, P_{35} = 35.67 years, P_{92} = 54.71 years

7. $Q_1 = 26.58, Q_3 = 46.93, D_1 = 17.72, D_3 = 29.23, P_{47} = 35.5$

8. Median = 46.67 marks, Q_1 = 28.8 years, Q_3 = 63.64 years, D_9 = 81.33 years

9. Q_1 = ₹ 34.9, Q_3 = ₹ 51.42, D_2 = ₹ 33.09, D_7 = ₹ 48.99, P_{12} = ₹ 30.20, P_{39} = ₹ 39.95

10. Median = 59.24 marks, Q_1 = 30.94 marks, Q_3 = 68.42 marks **11.** 25 marks

12. 74% **13.** ₹ 191.

5.30. GEOMETRIC MEAN (G.M.) (*P.T.U., M.B.A. Dec. 2010*)

(*a*) **For individual observations,** (*i.e.,* when frequencies are not given). The G.M. of n individual observations $x_1, x_2, \ldots\ldots, x_n, x_i$ $(i = 1, 2, 3, \ldots n) \neq 0$ is nth root of their product. Thus

$$G = (x_1, x_2, x_3, \ldots\ldots, x_n)^{1/n}$$

Taking logarithm both sides

$$\log_{10} G = \frac{1}{n}(\log_{10} x_1 + \log_{10} x_2 + \ldots\ldots + \log_{10} x_n)$$

$$= \frac{1}{n}\sum_{i=1}^{n} \log_{10} x_i \quad \Rightarrow \quad G = \text{antilog}\left[\frac{1}{n}\sum_{i=1}^{n} \log_{10} x_i\right]$$

(*b*) **In case of frequency distribution,**

x :	x_1	x_2	......	x_n
f :	f_1	f_2	......	f_n

The G.M. is defined by

$$G = \left(x_1^{f_1}, x_2^{f_2}, x_3^{f_3} \ldots\ldots, x_n^{f_n}\right)^{1/N}$$

$$N = \Sigma f_i$$

or Taking logarithm both sides,

$$\log_{10} G = \frac{1}{N}(f_1 \log_{10} x_1 + f_2 \log_{10} x_2 + \ldots\ldots + f_n \log_{10} x_n)$$

$$= \frac{1}{N}\sum_{i=1}^{n} f_i \log_{10} x_i$$

$$\Rightarrow \qquad G = \text{antilog}\left[\frac{1}{N}\sum_{i=1}^{n} f_i \log_{10} x_i\right]$$

(c) **In case of continuous distribution,** x is taken to be the value corresponding to the mid-points of the class interval.

ILLUSTRATIVE EXAMPLES

Example 1. *Compute the geometric mean from the following data :*

Marks	*No. of students*
0–10	*10*
10–20	*5*
20–30	*8*
30–40	*7*
40–50	*20*

Sol. Consider the following table :

Marks	*Mid-values (x)*	*No. of students (f)*	$\log_{10} x$	$f \log_{10} x$
0–10	5	10	0.6990	6.9900
10–20	15	5	1.1761	5.8805
20–30	25	8	1.3979	11.1832
30–40	35	7	1.5441	10.8087
40–50	45	20	1.6532	33.0640
		50		67.9264

Here
$$\log_{10} G = \frac{1}{N}\sum_{i=1}^{n} f_i \log_{10} x_i$$

$$= \frac{1}{50} \times 67.9264 = 1.3585$$

$$= G = \text{antilog}\ (1.3585) = 22.83$$

Example 2. *The daily income of 10 workers in a factory are given below :*

85 70 15 75 500 8 45 250 40 36

Find the G.M.

Sol. Calculation of G.M.

x	$log_{10}\, x$
85	1.9294
70	1.8451
15	1.1761
75	1.8751
500	2.6990
8	0.9031
45	1.6532
250	2.3979
40	1.6021
36	1.5563
	$\Sigma \log_{10} x = 17.6373$

$\therefore$ **Required geometric mean**

$$G = \text{antilog}\left[\frac{1}{N}\sum_{i=1}^{10} \log_{10} x_i\right]$$

$$= \text{antilog}\left(\frac{17.6373}{10}\right)$$

$$= \text{antilog}\ (1.7637) = 58.03.$$

Example 3. *Find the average rate of increase in population which in the first decade has increased by 20%, in the second decade by 30% and in the third decade by 40%.*

Sol. Let x = The population at the end of the decade, taking population of the previous decade as 100.

Consider the following table.

Decade	*% increase*	x	$log_{10}\, x$
Ist	20	120	2.0792
2nd	30	130	2.1139
3rd	40	140	2.1461
			$\Sigma \log_{10} x = 6.3392$

$$\text{G.M.} = \text{antilog} \sum_{i=1}^{3}\left(\frac{\log_{10} x_i}{3}\right) = \text{antilog}\left(\frac{6.3392}{3}\right) = \text{antilog}\ (2.113) = 129.7$$

$\therefore$ Required rate of increase in population = 129.7 – 100 = 29.7% per decade.

Example 4. *A machinery depreciated by 40% in the first year, 25% in the second year and 10% p.a. during the next three years. Find the average rate of depreciation during the whole period.*

Sol. The average rate of depreciation can be calculated by using G.M. Consider the following table :

Year	*Diminishing value taking 100 as base (x)*	$log_{10}\, x$
1st	100–40 = 60	1.7782
2nd	100–25 = 75	1.8751
3rd	100–10 = 90	1.9542
4th	100–10 = 90	1.9542
5th	100–10 = 90	1.9542
		$\Sigma \log_{10} x = 9.5159$

$$\therefore \quad \text{G.M.} = \text{antilog}\left(\frac{\Sigma \log_{10} x}{n}\right) = \text{antilog}\left(\frac{9.5159}{5}\right) = \text{antilog}\ (1.9032) = 80$$

i.e., the diminishing value is ₹ 80 and hence the depreciation will be 100 – 80 = 20%. Thus the average rate of depreciation during the whole period = 20%.

Example 5. *The G.M. of 10 observations was calculated as 28.6. It was later discovered that one of the observations was taken as 23.4 instead of 32.4. Calculate the correct G.M.*

Sol. The G.M. of n observations $x_1, x_2, ..., x_n$, is given by

$$\text{G.M.} = (x_1 . x_2 . x_3 ... x_n)^{1/n} \quad ...(1)$$

Here $n = 10$, and G.M. = 28.6

$\therefore$ (1) gives $\quad 28.6 = (x_1 . x_2 . x_3 ... x_{10})^{1/10}$

$\Rightarrow \quad x_1 . x_2 . x_3 ... x_n = (28.6)^{10}$

i.e., Incorrected value of $x_1 . x_2 ... x_n = (28.6)^{10}$

Now one of the observation was taken as 23.4 instead of 32.4.

$\therefore$ Corrected value of $x_1 . x_2 . x_3 ... x_n$

$$= \frac{(\text{Incorrected value of } x_1.x_2 ... x_n) \times 32.4}{23.4}$$

$$\therefore \quad \text{Corrected G.M.} = (\text{Corrected } x_1 . x_2 . x_3 ... x_n)^{1/10}$$

$$= \left(\frac{(28.6)^{10} \times 32.4}{23.4}\right)^{1/10} \quad ...(2)$$

Consider $$y = \left(\frac{(28.6)^{10} \times 32.4}{23.4}\right)^{1/10}$$

$$\Rightarrow \quad \log_{10} y = \frac{10 \log_{10} 28.6 + \log_{10} 32.4 - \log_{10} 23.4}{10}$$

$$= \frac{10 \times 1.4564 + 1.5105 - 1.3692}{10} = \frac{14.7053}{10} = 1.47053$$

$\Rightarrow \quad y = \text{antilog}\ (1.47053) = 29.54$

From (2), $\quad$ G.M. = 29.54.

Example 6. *Find the missing information in the following table.*

	I	*II*	*III*	*Combined*
Number	*10*	*8*	–	*24*
A.M.	*20*	–	*6*	*15*
G.M.	*10*	*7*	–	*8.397*

Sol. Calculation of missing number (c) in the first row.

Since combined sum of numbers = 24

$\Rightarrow \quad 10 + 8 + c = 24$

$\Rightarrow \quad c = 6.$

Calculation of missing mean $\bar{x}_2$ in the second row. Let x be the combined mean. Then,

$$\bar{x} = \frac{n_1\bar{x}_1 + n_2\bar{x}_2 + n_3\bar{x}_3}{n_1 + n_2 + n_3} \qquad \text{...(1)}$$

Here $\bar{x} = 15$, $\bar{x}_1 = 20$, $\bar{x}_2 =$ To find, $\bar{x}_3 = 6$, $n_1 = 10$, $n_2 = 8$, $n_3 = 6$

$\therefore$ (1) gives $$15 = \frac{10 \times 20 + 8 \times \bar{x}_2 + 6 \times 6}{10 + 8 + 6}$$

$$\Rightarrow \quad 15 \times 24 = 200 + 8\bar{x}_2 + 36$$

$$\Rightarrow \quad 8\bar{x}_2 = 360 - 200 - 36 = 124$$

$$\Rightarrow \quad \bar{x}_2 = \frac{124}{8} = 15.5$$

Calculation of missing G.M. g in 3rd row.

Let g be the required G.M., then

$$10^{10} \times 7^8 \times g^6 = (8.397)^{24}$$

Taking logarithm both sides,

$$\log_{10} 10^{10} \times 7^8 \times g^6 = \log_{10} (8.397)^{24}$$

$$\Rightarrow \quad 10 \log_{10} 10 + 8 \log_{10} 7 + 6 \log_{10} g = 24 \log_{10} (8.397)$$

$$\Rightarrow \quad 10 + 8 \times (0.8451) + 6 \log_{10} g = 24\ (0.9241)$$

$$\Rightarrow \quad 6 \log_{10} g = 22.1784 - 10 - 6.7608 = 5.4176$$

$$\Rightarrow \quad \log_{10} g = \frac{5.4176}{6} = 0.9029 \quad \Rightarrow \quad g = \text{antilog}\ (0.9029) = 7.997.$$

Example 7. *Show that in finding the A.M. of a set of readings on thermometre, it does not matter whether we measure temperature in centigrade or Farhenite, but in finding the G.M. it does matter which scale we use.*

Sol. Let $C_1, C_2, ..., C_n$ be the n readings on the Centigrade thermometre. The A.M. of $C_1, C_2, ..., C_n$ is given by

$$\overline{C} = \frac{C_1 + C_2 + ... + C_n}{n}$$

But $$F = 32 + \frac{9}{5}C$$

$\therefore$ The Farhenite readings of $C_1, C_2, ..., C_n$ are $32 + \frac{9}{5}C_1,\ 32 + \frac{9}{5}C_2,\ ......,\ 32 + \frac{9}{5}C_n$.

Let $\overline{F}$ be the A.M. of these observations. Then

$$\overline{F} = \frac{\left(32 + \frac{9}{5}C_1\right) + \left(32 + \frac{9}{5}C_2\right) + ... + \left(32 + \frac{9}{5}C_n\right)}{n}$$

$$= \frac{32n + \frac{9}{5}(C_1 + C_2 + ... + C_n)}{n}$$

$$\Rightarrow \quad \overline{F} = 32 + \frac{9}{5}\overline{C}$$

Hence, in finding the A.M. of a set of n readings on a thermometre, it does not matter, whether we measure temperature in F° or C°.

Further, the G.M. of n readings in centigrade is

$$G = (C_1 . C_2 . C_3 \ldots\ldots C_n)^{1/n}$$

and the G.M. of n readings in Farhenite scale is

$$G_1 = \left[\left(32 + \frac{9}{5}C_1\right)\left(32 + \frac{9}{5}C_2\right)\ldots\ldots\left(32 + \frac{9}{5}C_n\right)\right]^{\frac{1}{n}}$$

$$\neq 32 + \frac{9}{5}(C_1, C_2 \ldots\ldots C_n)^{\frac{1}{n}}.$$

Hence, in finding the G.M. of n readings on a thermometre, the scale centigrade or Fahrenheit is **Important.**

5.31. MERITS OF G.M.

(*a*) It is based upon all observations

(*b*) It is not affected much by fluctuations of sampling.

(*c*) It gives more weights to small items.

Demerits of G.M. If any one of the observation is zero, G.M. becomes zero and if any one of the observation is negative, G.M. becomes imaginary.

Uses. It is used to find the rate of population of growth (*b*) the rate of interest (*c*) in the construction of index numbers.

5.32. GEOMETRIC MEAN OF COMPOSITE SERIES

If G_1, G_2, ..., G_k are the geometric means of k-distributions with frequencies n_1, n_2, ..., n_k, respectively, then the combined geometric mean $\overline{G}$ of the whole distribution obtained by combining the k distributions is given by

$$\overline{G} = \text{antilog}\left(\frac{n_1 \log G_1 + n_2 \log G_2 + \ldots + n_k \log G_k}{n_1 + n_2 + \ldots + n_k}\right)$$

Example 8. *Three sets of data contain 8, 7 and 5 observations and their geometric means are 8.52, 10.12 and 7.75, respectively. Find the combined geometric mean of 20 observations.* (P.T.U., M.B.A. May 2010)

Sol. Given $n_1 = 8, n_2 = 7, n_3 = 5$

$$G.M_1 = 8.52,\ G.M_2 = 10.12,\ G.M_3 = 7.75$$

The combined G.M. of the given observations is given by

$$G.M_{123} = \text{antilog}\left[\frac{n_1 . \log G.M_1 + n_2 . \log G.M_2 + n_3 . \log G.M_3}{n_1 + n_2 + n_3}\right]$$

$$= \text{antilog}\left[\frac{8 \times \log 8.52 + 7 \times \log 10.12 + 5 \times \log 7.75}{20}\right]$$

$$= \text{antilog}\left[\frac{7.44 + 7.03 + 4.44}{20}\right] = \text{antilog}\left[\frac{18.91}{20}\right] = \text{atilog } 0.9455 = 8.82$$

5.33. HARMONIC MEAN (H.M.)

The H.M. of a number of observations is the reciprocal of the A.M. of the reciprocal of the given values, *i.e.*, the H.M. of n observations x_1, x_2, ..., x_n. is

$$H = \frac{1}{\frac{1}{x_1} + \frac{1}{x_2} + \ldots\ldots + \frac{1}{x_n}} = \frac{1}{\frac{1}{n}\sum_{i=1}^{n} x_i}$$

In case of frequency distribution, If $x_1, x_2, \ldots\ldots, x_n$ (none of them being zero) have the frequencies $f_1, f_2, \ldots\ldots, f_n$ respectively, then the harmonic mean is given by :

$$H = \frac{1}{\frac{f_1}{x_1} + \frac{f_2}{x_2} + \ldots\ldots + \frac{f_n}{x_n}} = \frac{1}{\frac{1}{N}\sum_{i=1}^{n} \frac{f_i}{x_i}}, \text{ where } N = \sum_{i=1}^{n} f_i$$

In case of class intervals x is taken to be the mid-value of the class interval.

Remark. In equal distances are covered per unit of time with speeds $V_1, V_2, \ldots\ldots, V_n$ then the average speed is given by the H.M. of $V_1, V_2, \ldots\ldots, V_n$, *i.e.*,

$$\text{Average speed} = \frac{n}{\sum_{i=1}^{n} \frac{1}{V_i}}$$

Example 9. *Find out the harmonic mean of the following data :*

Marks (out of 150)	*No. of students*
10	*2*
20	*3*
40	*6*
60	*5*
120	*4*

Sol.

x	f	$\frac{1}{x}$	$\frac{f}{x}$
10	2	0.100	0.200
20	3	0.050	0.150
40	6	0.025	0.150
60	5	0.017	0.085
120	4	0.008	0.032
	20		0.617

$$\text{H.M.} = \frac{N}{\sum_{i=1}^{n} \frac{f_i}{x_i}} = \frac{20}{0.617} = 32.4$$

Example 10. *A cyclist pedals from his house to his college at a speed of 10 m.p.h. and back from the college to his house at 15 m.p.h. Find the average speed. When equal distances are covered with unequal speeds, the H.M. is the proper average.*

Sol. Here $V_1 = 10, V_2 = 15, n = 2$

$$\therefore \text{ Average speed} = \frac{2}{\frac{1}{15} + \frac{1}{10}} = \frac{2}{\frac{10+15}{150}} = \frac{300}{25} = 12 \text{ m.p.h.}$$

Example 11. *An aeroplane flies along the four sides of a square at the speeds of 100, 200, 300 and 400 km/hr. What is the average speed of the aeroplane in its flight around the square.*

Sol. Here $V_1 = 100$, $V_2 = 200$, $V_3 = 300$, $V_4 = 400$, $n = 4$.

$$\therefore \text{ Average speed } = \frac{4}{\frac{1}{100}+\frac{1}{200}+\frac{1}{300}+\frac{1}{400}} = \frac{4\times 1200}{12+6+4+3} = \frac{4800}{25} = 192 \text{ km/hr.}$$

Example 12. *Find the harmonic mean from the following data.*

2574, 475, 75, 5, 0.8, 0.08, 0.005, 0.0009.

Sol. Calculation of Harmonic mean

x	$1/x$
2574	0.0004
475	0.0021
75	0.0133
5	0.2
0.8	1.2500
0.08	12.500
0.005	200.00
0.0009	1111.1111
	$\Sigma\, 1/x = 1325.0769$

$\therefore$ The required harmonic mean is given by

$$\text{H.M.} = \frac{n}{\sum_{i=1}^{8} \frac{1}{x_i}} = \frac{8}{1325.0769} = 0.006.$$

5.34. MERITS OF HARMONIC MEAN

(*a*) It is based upon all observations

(*b*) It is not affected much by fluctuations of sampling.

Demerits of H.M. :

(*a*) It is difficult to compute as compared to A.M.

(*b*) It has very limited applications.

Uses. It is used when small items have to be given greater weightage.

5.35. RELATION BETWEEN A.M., G.M. AND H.M.

For any series, A.M. $\geq$ G.M. $\geq$ H.M. and equality occurs if each individuals are indentical, *i.e.*, A.M. is the maximum for a series and H.M. is the least. G.M. would be less than the A.M., but greater than the H.M.

5.36. CASE STUDIES

Case Study I: Kanta Bread

'Kanta Bread' company is manufacturing bread. The selling price of bread is fixed by the government. In view of increasing raw material prices, the only way to sustain the profit level is by efficient control over the production process to reduce the cost of production. A large quantity of production shows small savings per unit of production and results in a significant amount cumulatively. Among various factors affecting the cost of production, the yield of the finished product obtained from a given quantity of raw materials is of considerable significance.

The process of manufacturing bread involves mixing of wheat flour (maida) with the required quantity of water and other ingredients as per the standard formula. The mixed bulk dough is subjected to yeast fermentation for a given period. Then this bulk quantity of dough is transferred to a machine called Divider, which divides the dough mechanically into small pieces of required weight, which are individually further processed and baked to get the finished product called bread.

For manufacturing a 800g loaf of bread the required weight of dough piece coming from the Divider should be between 880g and 885g. This weight is termed as *dividing weight.* There is provision on the Divider machine to set the required dough piece weight. The smallest division (or increment) in weight that can be set on this machine is 5g. As a measure of safety, 885g is the weight that is usually set on the machine.

The performance of the machine, with respect to the accuracy of the weight of dough pieces delivered by it, is dependent on various factors such as the level of lubrication and the consistency of the dough. But these variations are less and the weight variation would be within ± 30g of the set weight for a good Divider. Larger variations than this in weight occur only if the dough dividing mechanism (called Divider Head) has undergone considerable wear and tear.

The weight variation in the dough pieces from the Divider results in weight variation in the final product (bread). But the Bread weight, which is declared as 800g is covered by the Weights and Measures (Packaged Commodities) Act, 1976. As per the rules of this Act, the average net weight of a random sample (Sample size is 20 bread) should not be less than the declared weight. The maximum permissible error in relation to the quantity contained in the individual package is 6 percent of the declared weight. Also, it is stipulated that the number of individual packages showing an error in deficiency of weight greater than the maximum permissible error (*i.e.*, 6%) should not be more than 5 percent of the packages drawn as samples. The sample size as per the rule as applicable to bread is 20 individual packages. If the product does not confirm to the rules, then punitive action can be taken against the manufacturer.

In order to ensure that the rules under this Act are not violated, the rules are applied to the weights of the divided dough piece itself. Thus in terms of these rules, it is required:

(*i*) That the average weight of a random sample of 20 divided dough pieces should be 880g to 885g.

(*ii*) That the weight of an individual dough piece should not be less than 832g (*i.e.*, 885g – 6% = 832g)

(*iii*) That not more than one piece out of 20 (*i.e.*, 5%) should have a weight less than 832g.

Thus the performance of the Divider should confirm these standards. However, it was complained by the production department that the weight variation at the Divider is very large and hence in order that the law is not violated, they are forced to set the Divider at a higher dividing weight than the normally required weight setting dividing, resulting in less on yield of the products.

Questions for Discussion: *What is the average weight of dough pieces delivered by the Divider with the weight setting at 885g?*

2. What is the percentage of dough pieces with weight less than 832g, if any?

3. What should be the lowest dividing weight setting on the Divider, so that the number of dough pieces with weight less than 832g are less than 5 per cent, as stipulated by the law, (if already not so)?

4. The monetary loss to the company on account of setting the higher dividing weight as decided in Q.3 above could be calculated, which would help in deciding whether the Divider head should be replaced or not.

***Data:** The output of the Divider is 1000 pieces per hour. The weight of 20 dough pieces per hour were taken using an accurate weighing scale. (Recording this weight is a routine quality control check). Ten sets of such dough weight on the machine were taken at different times. All the individual observations on these ten sets were pooled together to get the population of data with total 200 observations, given below:*

S.No.	Dividing Weight	SNo.	Dividing Weight	S.No.	Dividing Weight	S.No.	Dividing Weight	S.No.	Dividing Weight
1.	875	41.	895	81.	836	121.	912	161.	870
2.	870	42.	910	82.	823	122.	912	162.	895
3.	852	43.	907	83.	910	123.	885	163.	870
4.	880	44.	912	84.	889	124.	895	164.	910
5.	909	45.	890	85.	897	125.	840	165.	910
6.	909	46.	895	86.	885	126.	860	166.	885
7.	893	47.	862	87.	892	127.	866	167.	920
8.	875	48.	875	88.	886	128.	875	168.	877
9.	830	49.	895	89.	886	129.	868	169.	909
10.	859	50.	867	90.	897	130.	861	170.	915
11.	827	51.	910	91.	897	131.	873	171.	920
12.	907	52.	900	92.	880	132.	893	172.	884
13.	909	53.	880	93.	870	133.	883	173.	910
14.	910	54.	900	94.	920	134.	878	174.	925
15.	915	55.	910	95.	927	135.	873	175.	900
16.	920	56.	897	96.	930	136.	893	176.	875
17.	905	57.	875	97.	925	137.	825	177.	895
18.	890	58.	905	98.	915	138.	830	178.	930
19.	925	59.	975	99.	875	139.	845	179.	863
20.	900	60.	909	100.	890	140.	830	180.	913
21.	895	61.	890	101.	890	141.	840	181.	903
22.	875	62.	880	102.	923	142.	835	182.	843
23.	903	63.	890	103.	828	143.	830	183.	878
24.	863	64.	825	104.	825	144.	860	184.	883
25.	913	65.	845	105.	910	145.	855	185.	878
26.	903	66.	875	106.	866	146.	860	186.	897
27.	893	67.	890	107.	825	147.	835	187.	916
28.	878	68.	892	108.	830	148.	886	188.	907
29.	878	69.	821	109.	845	149.	888	189.	912
30.	883	70.	826	110.	830	150.	890	190.	895
31.	897	71.	904	111.	855	151.	878	191.	885
32.	916	72.	915	112.	835	152.	858	192.	862
33.	813	73.	900	113.	855	153.	875	193.	879

Contd....

34.	*863*	*74.*	*900*	*114.*	*836*	*154.*	*858*	*194.*	*900*
35.	*900*	*75.*	*905*	*115.*	*860*	*155.*	*865*	*195.*	*872*
36.	*905*	*76.*	*885*	*116.*	*835*	*156.*	*888*	*196.*	*900*
37.	*898*	*77.*	*890*	*117.*	*865*	*157.*	*868*	*197.*	*905*
38.	*878*	*78.*	*889*	*118.*	*915*	*158.*	*865*	*198.*	*885*
39.	*878*	*79.*	*865*	*119.*	*930*	*159.*	*880*	*199.*	*895*
40.	*898*	*80.*	*845*	*120.*	*865*	*160.*	*905*	*200.*	*902*

Sol. We first sort the given data in ascending order in the following table. Take assumed mean A = 885g. The different values of the deviations d_i and d_i^2 have been calculated in the following table.

S.No.	*dividing weight*	d_i	d_i^2	S.No.	*dividing weight*	d_i	d_i^2	S.No.	*dividing weight*	d_i	d_i^2	S.No.	*dividing weight*	d_i	d_i^2
1.	813	–72	5184	51.	866	–19	361	101.	886	1	1	151.	904	19	361
2.	821	–64	4096	52.	866	–19	361	102.	888	3	9	152.	905	20	400
3.	823	–62	3844	53.	867	–18	324	103.	888	3	9	153.	905	20	400
4.	825	–60	3600	54.	868	–17	289	104.	889	4	16	154.	905	20	400
5.	825	–60	3600	55.	868	–17	289	105.	889	4	16	155.	905	20	400
6.	825	–60	3600	56.	868	–17	289	106.	890	5	25	156.	905	20	400
7.	825	–60	3600	57.	870	–15	225	107.	890	5	25	157.	905	20	400
8.	826	–59	3481	58.	870	–15	225	108.	890	5	25	158.	907	22	484
9.	827	–58	3364	59.	870	–15	225	109.	890	5	25	159.	907	22	484
10.	828	–57	3249	60.	870	–15	225	110.	890	5	25	160.	907	22	484
11.	830	–55	3025	61.	872	–13	169	111.	890	5	25	161.	909	24	576
12.	830	–55	3025	62.	873	–12	144	112.	890	5	25	162.	909	24	576
13.	830	–55	3025	63.	873	–12	144	113.	890	5	25	163.	909	24	576
14.	830	–55	3025	64.	875	–10	100	114.	890	5	25	164.	909	24	576
15.	830	–55	3025	65.	875	–10	100	115.	892	7	49	165.	909	24	576
16.	830	–55	3025	66.	875	–10	100	116.	892	7	49	166.	910	25	625
17.	835	–50	2500	67.	875	–10	100	117.	893	8	64	167.	910	25	625
18.	835	–50	2500	68.	875	–10	100	118.	893	8	64	168.	910	25	625
19.	835	–50	2500	69.	875	–10	100	119.	893	8	64	169.	910	25	625
20.	835	–50	2500	70.	875	–10	100	120.	893	8	64	170.	910	25	625
21.	836	–49	2401	71.	875	–10	100	121.	895	10	100	171.	910	25	625
22.	836	–49	2401	72.	875	–10	100	122.	895	10	100	172.	910	25	625
23.	840	–45	2025	73.	875	–10	100	123.	895	10	100	173.	910	25	625
24.	840	–45	2025	74.	877	–8	64	124.	895	10	100	174.	910	25	625
25.	843	–42	1764	75.	878	–7	49	125.	895	10	100	175.	912	27	729
26.	845	–40	1600	76.	878	–7	49	126.	895	10	100	176.	912	27	729
27.	845	–40	1600	77.	878	–7	49	127.	895	10	100	177.	912	27	729

28.	845	–40	1600	78.	878	–7	49	128.	895	10	100	178.	912	27	729
29.	845	–40	1600	79.	878	–7	49	129.	895	10	100	179.	913	28	784
30.	852	–33	1089	80.	878	–7	49	130.	897	12	144	180.	913	28	784
31.	855	–30	900	81.	878	–7	49	131.	897	12	144	181.	915	30	900
32.	855	–30	900	82.	878	–7	49	132.	897	12	144	182.	915	30	900
33.	855	–30	900	83.	879	–6	36	133.	897	12	144	183.	915	30	900
34.	858	–27	729	84.	880	–5	25	134.	897	12	144	184.	915	30	900
35.	858	–27	729	85.	880	–5	25	135.	897	12	144	185.	915	30	900
36.	859	–26	676	86.	880	–5	25	136.	898	13	169	186.	916	31	961
37.	860	–25	625	87.	880	–5	25	137.	898	13	169	187.	916	31	961
38.	860	–25	625	88.	880	–5	25	138.	900	15	225	188.	920	35	1225
39.	860	–25	625	89.	883	–2	4	139.	900	15	225	189.	920	35	1225
40.	860	–25	625	90.	883	–2	4	140.	900	15	225	190.	920	35	1225
41.	861	–24	576	91.	883	–2	4	141.	900	15	225	191.	920	35	1225
42.	862	–23	529	92.	884	–1	1	142.	900	15	225	192.	923	38	1444
43.	862	–23	529	93.	885	0	0	143.	900	15	225	193.	925	40	1600
44.	863	–22	484	94.	885	0	0	144.	900	15	225	194.	925	40	1600
45.	863	–22	484	95.	885	0	0	145.	900	15	225	195.	925	40	1600
46.	863	–22	484	96.	885	0	0	146.	900	15	225	196.	927	42	1764
47.	865	–20	400	97.	885	0	0	147.	902	17	289	197.	930	45	2025
48.	865	–20	400	98.	885	0	0	148.	903	18	324	198.	930	45	2025
49.	865	–20	400	99.	886	1	1	149.	903	18	324	199.	930	45	2025
50.	865	–20	400	100.	886	1	1	150.	903	18	324	200.	975	90	8100

From the above table, $\Sigma d_i = -464$, $\Sigma d_i^2 = 157520$

Given, total number of observations (n) = 200

Since the weight set by the divider = 8859g,

We take deviations $d_i = x_i - A = x_i - 885$.

(1) Average weight of dough pieces delivered by the divider with the weight setting at 885g

$$= A + \frac{\Sigma d_i}{n} = 885 + \left(\frac{-464}{200}\right) = 885 - 2.32 = 882.68\text{g}$$

(2) Required percentage of dough pieces with weight less than 832g is given by the percentile value of $\left(\frac{P_6 + P_7}{2}\right)$

$$885\text{g} - 6\% \text{ of } 885\text{g} = 885\text{g} - 6 \times \frac{885\text{g}}{100} = 885\text{g} - 53.1\text{g} = 831.9 \cong 832\text{g}$$

Now, using $P_K = K\left(\frac{N}{100}\right)^{th}$ observation,

we have $$P_6 = 6 \times \left(\frac{200}{100}\right)^{th} \text{ item} = 12^{th} \text{ item} = 830$$

Similarly $P_7 = 7 \times \left(\frac{200}{100}\right)^{th}$ item = 14th item = 830

$$\therefore \quad \frac{P_6 + P_7}{2} = \frac{830 + 830}{2} = 830$$

Let the required percentage be x. Then we should have

$$885\text{ g} - x = 830\text{g}$$

$$\Rightarrow \quad x = 885\text{g} - 830\text{g} = 55\text{g}$$

$\therefore$ required % = 5.5%

(3) We first find the standard deviation of the given data, here

$$\text{s.d.} = \sqrt{\frac{\Sigma d_i^2}{n}} = \sqrt{\frac{157520}{200}} = 28.06\text{g}$$

We know that $\mu \pm 2\sigma$ covers ≅ 95% of the observations *i.e.*, only 5% of the observations do not fall in the range $\mu \pm 2\sigma$

But $\mu \pm 2\sigma = 882.68 \pm 56.12 = (826.56, 938.8)$

The lowest dividing weight setting on the divider so that the number of dough pieces with weight less than 832g are less than 5% is **826.56g ≅ 827g.**

(4) In part (3), the lowest weight for 5% of the total number of dough pieces is 827g, which is slightly less than 832g.

Hence the divider head should not be replaced and it does not violate the standards.

Case Study II: Factory Wages: A factory pays workers on piece rate basis and also a bonus to each worker on the basis of individual output in each quarter. The rate of bonus payable is as follows:

Output (in unit)	*Bonus (₹)*
70–74	40
75–79	45
80–84	50
85–89	60
90–94	70
95–99	80
100–104	100

The individual output of a batch of 50 workers is given below

94, 83, 78, 76, 88, 86, 93, 80, 91, 82, 89, 97, 92, 84, 92, 80, 85, 83, 98, 103, 87, 88, 88, 81, 95, 86, 99, 81, 87, 90, 84, 97, 80, 75, 93, 101, 82, 82, 89, 72, 85, 83, 75, 72, 83, 98, 77, 87, 71, 80

Questions for Discussion

By suitable classification you are required to find:

(a) Average bonus per worker for the quarter

(b) Average output per worker.

Sol. (*a*) **Hint:** Average bonus = A.M. of all 50 observations = ₹ 59.7

(*b*) Total quarterly bonus paid = 59.7 × 50 = ₹ 2985

Average output per worker = x = 86.1 units.

TEST YOUR KNOWLEDGE 5.5

1. (*a*) Calculate geometric mean of the following data :

125 1462 38 7 0.22 0.08 12.75 0.5

(*b*) Compute the geometric mean of the following data :

x :	10	15	18	20	25
f :	2	3	5	6	4

2. If n_1 and n_2 are the sizes, G_1 and G_2 the geometric means of two series respectively, then the geometric mean G of the combined series is given by $\log G = \dfrac{n_1 \log G_1 + n_2 \log G_2}{n_1 + n_2}$.

3. The marks obtained by 25 students in a test are given below :

Marks :	11	12	13	14	15
No. of students :	3	7	8	5	2

Find the harmonic mean.

4. (*a*) Compute the harmonic mean of the following data :

Class	*Frequency*
0–10	4
10–20	6
20–30	10
30–40	7
40–50	3

(*b*) Find out the geometric mean for the following data :

Marks	*Frequency*
4–8	6
8–12	10
12–16	18
16–20	30
20–24	15
24–28	12
28–32	10
32–36	6
36–40	2

5. Three cities A, B, C are equidistant from each other. A motorist travels from A to B at 30 km/hr, from B to C at 40 km/hr and from C to A at 50 km/hr. Determine the average speed.

6. Show that in finding the arithmetic mean of a set of readings on a thermometer, it does not matter whether we measure temperature in Centigrade or Fahrenheit, but that in finding the geometric mean, it does matter which scale we use.

7. Calculate the harmonic mean of the following data :

3834 382 63 8 0.4 0.03 0.009 0.005

8. An automobile driver travels from plain to hill station 100 km. distance at an average speed of 30 km. per hour. He then makes the return trip at average speed of 20 km per hour. What is the average speed over the entire distance of 200 km ?

9. The rate of a certain commodity in the first month is 0.4 kg per rupee, it is 0.6 kg per rupee in the second month and 0.5 kg per rupee in the third week. Find the average price.

Answers

1. (*a*) 18.20 (*b*) 6.952 **3.** 12.7 marks

4. (*a*) 16.03 (*b*) 18.14 **5.** 38.3 km/hr **7.** 0.003726

8. 24 km per hour **9.** 0.486 kg per rupee

6

Measures of Dispersion

6.1. MEANING OF MEASURES OF DISPERSION *(P.T.U., M.B.A. Dec., 2003 May 2002)*

Suppose there are two classes of students with average percentage of marks 56% each, it would not be justified to take for guaranteed that the students of both classes are approximately of same level of intelligence. It may be just possible that the students of first class are getting marks between 50% and 59% and the students of the second class getting between 8% and 90%. Thus, we see that even if the average value of two series are same, the items may be of quite different in nature, in the two series. The measures of central tendency are inadequate to give the complete idea about the items in the series. We would be very much helped, if we are also given some idea about the *scatter* of items about some average value.

6.2. MEASURE OF DISPERSION

A measure of scatteredness of items about some average is also called a **measure of dispersion.** We may define a **measure of dispersion** or a measure of variation of a statistical data as the measurement of the spread of the items about an average value.

6.3 (a). REQUISITES OF A GOOD MEASURE OF DISPERSION

The requisites of a good measure of a dispersion are same as those for a good measure of central tendency. For the sake of completeness, we list the requisites as under :

1. It should be simple to understand.
2. It should be easy to compute.
3. It should be well defined.
4. It should be based on all the items.
5. It should not be unduly affected by the extreme items.
6. It should be capable of further algebraic treatment.
7. It should have sampling stability.

Dispersion is the measure of variation. It measures the degree of scatterdness of the observations in a distribution around the central value.

6.3 (b). SIGNIFICANCE OF MEASURES OF DISPERSION OR VARIATION

(P.T.U., M.B.A. Dec., 2012)

The measures of dispersion have a significant role in statistics because of the following :

1. They are helpful in determining the reliability of an average.
2. They serve as a basis for the control of the variability.
3. They are useful in comparing two or more series with regard to their variability. A high degree of variation means little uniformity or consistency where as a low degree of variation means great uniformity or consistency..

The various measures of dispersion are :

1. Range
2. Quartile Deviation
3. Mean Deviation
4. Standard Deviation.

6.4. RANGE

This is the simplest measure of dispersion and is given by the difference between the greatest and least values of the distribution *i.e.*, R = L – S, where L = Largest item, S = smallest item

For example, if the marks of 5 students are 45, 92, 26, 81 and 72. Then the range R = 92 – 26 = 66.

Coefficient of range. It is given by coefficient of Range = $\dfrac{L-S}{L+S}$

Significance of range. If the averages of two distribution are almost same, a comparison of range indicates that the distribution with the smaller range has less dispersion and the average of that distribution is more typical of the group.

Example 1. *The following are the prices of shares of a company from Monday to Saturday. Find the range and its coefficient.*

Day	*M*	*T*	*W*	*Th*	*F*	*S*
Prices	*200*	*210*	*218*	*260*	*220*	*250*

Sol. Here largest item L = 2 60

Smallest item S = 200

∴ Range = 260 – 200 = ₹ 60

$$\text{Also coefficient of range} = \frac{L-S}{L+S} = \frac{260-200}{260+200} = \frac{60}{460} = 0.13.$$

Range for continuous series. To determine range for a continuous series,

(*a*) Find the difference between the upper limit of the highest class and the lower limit of the lowest class.

Or

(*b*) Find the difference of the mid-point of the highest class and the mid-point of the lowest class.

In practice, both methods are used.

Example 2. *Find the range and its co-efficient from the following data :*

Marks	*10–20*	*20–30*	*30–40*	*40–50*	*50–60*
No. of students	*8*	*10*	*13*	*8*	*5*

Sol. Here the highest class is 50–60 and the lowest class is 10–20

i.e., upper limit of the upper class = 60

lower limit of the lower class = 10

∴ Range = 60 – 10 = 50

$$\text{Also coefficient of range} = \frac{60-10}{60+10} = \frac{50}{70} = \frac{5}{7} = 0.714$$

6.5. MERITS

1. Range is the simplest method to study dispersion as compared to all other methods of studying dispersion.

2. It takes minimum time to calculate the value of range.

6.6. LIMITATIONS

1. Range is not based on each and every item of the distribution.

2. It cannot say anything about the character of the distribution with less in the two extreme observations.

6.7. USES

The following are the uses of range.

1. In quality control. In checking the quality of a product, control charts are prepared and in preparing these charts, range plays a very important role. If the range increases beyond a certain point, it means there is a time to check the production by machines.

2. In share market. To study the variations in shares and stocks prices, range is very useful.

3. In weather forecasting. The meterological department finds the difference between the minimum temperature and maximum temperature. This type of information is of great use to the general public.

6.8. QUARTILE DEVIATION

Quartile measure is a better measure than the range, as it makes use of 50% of the data. But since it ignores the 50% data. It can't be regarded as a reliable measure.

It is defined by $Q.D. = \frac{Q_3 - Q_1}{2}$, where Q_3 = The upper quartile, Q_1 = The lower quartile.

Also the difference $Q_3 - Q_1$ is known as **interquartile range.**

6.9. COEFFICIENT OF QUARTILE DEVIATION

The Q.D. is an absolute measure. And absolute measure cannot be used for comparison purposes if they are expressed in different units.

For example, variation in heights and weights of a set of students cannot be compared with the help of Q.D., since they are in terms of cms and kgs. Therefore, we define the relative measure of dispersion (which is independent of units) as follows :

$$\text{Coefficient of quartile deviation} = \frac{Q_3 - Q_1}{Q_3 + Q_1}$$

ILLUSTRATIVE EXAMPLES

Example 1. *Find the quartile deviation of the data : 39, 75, 73, 63, 50, 51, 57, 60, 58, 62, 51, 61. Also find the co-efficient of quartile deviation.*

Sol. Arranging the data in ascending order, we get

39, 50, 51, 51, 57, 58, 60, 61, 62, 63, 63, 75.

Here, $Q_1 = \text{Value of } \left(\frac{12+1}{4}\right)^{th} \text{ term}$

$= \text{Value of } (3.25)^{th} \text{ term} = 51 + 0.25(51 - 51) = 51$

$$Q_3 = \text{Value of } \left[3\left(\frac{12+1}{4}\right)^{th}\right] \text{ term}$$

$$= \text{Value of } [3 \times 3.25]\text{th term} = \text{Value of } 9.75\text{th term}$$

$$= 62 + 0.75\ (63 - 62) = 62.75$$

$\therefore$ $$\text{Q.D.} = \frac{Q_3 - Q_1}{2} = \frac{62.75 - 51}{2} = 5.875. \text{ Further coefficient of}$$

$$\text{Q.D.} = \frac{Q_3 - Q_1}{Q_3 + Q_1} = \frac{62.75 - 51}{62.75 + 51} = \frac{11.75}{113.75} = 0.1032.$$

Example 2. *Find the interquartile range from the data :*

28, 18, 20, 24, 27, 30, 15.

Sol. Arranging the data in ascending order, we get

15, 18, 20, 24, 27, 28, 30

Here $Q_1 = \text{Value of } \left(\frac{7+1}{4}\right)^{th}$ item = Value of 2nd item = 18

Also $Q_3 = \text{Value of } \left(3 \cdot \left(\frac{7+1}{4}\right)\right)^{th}$ item = Value of 6th item = 28

$\therefore$ Interquartile range = $Q_3 - Q_1$ = 28 – 18 = 10.

Example 3. *Calculate the quartile deviation and its coefficient from the following data*

Marks	*0–10*	*10–20*	*20–30*	*30–40*	*40–50*
No. of students	4	15	28	16	7

Sol. The quartile deviation is given by $\text{Q.D.} = \dfrac{Q_3 - Q_1}{2}$.

Calculation of Q_3 :

Marks	*Frequencies* f_i	*Cumulative frequencies* *c.f.*
0–10	4	4
10–20	15	19
20–30	28	47
30–40	16	63
40–50	7	70
	$\Sigma f_i = 70 = N$	

Here $$\frac{3N}{4} = \frac{3 \times 70}{4} = 52.5$$

The cumulative frequency just greater than 52.5 is 63 and the corresponding quartile class is 30–40.

Also $L = 30,\ h = 10,\ f = 16,\ C = 47$

$$\therefore \quad Q_3 = L + \frac{\frac{3N}{4} - C}{f} \times h = 30 + \frac{52.5 - 47}{16} \times 10 = 30 + 3.43 = 33.43.$$

Calculation of Q_1

Here $\frac{N}{4} = \frac{70}{4} = 17.5$ | $N = \Sigma f_i$

The cumulative frequency just greater than 17.5 is 19 and the corresponding quartile class is 10–20.

Also $L = 10, h = 10, f = 15, C = 4$

$$\therefore \quad Q_1 = L + \frac{\frac{N}{4} - C}{f} \times h = 10 + \frac{17.5 - 4}{15} \times 10 = 10 + 9 = 19$$

Hence $Q.D. = \frac{Q_3 - Q_1}{2} = \frac{33.43 - 19}{2} = 7.215$

The coefficient of quartile deviation $= \frac{Q_3 - Q_1}{Q_3 + Q_1} = \frac{33.43 - 19}{33.43 + 19} = \frac{14.43}{52.43} = 0.2752.$

Example 4. Find *quartile deviation and its coefficient from the following data :*

Marks	*less than 35*	*35–37*	*38–40*	*41–43*	*above 43*
No. of students	*14*	*62*	*99*	*18*	*7*

Sol. Calculation of quartile deviation. Consider the following table :

Marks	*Frequency* f	*Cumulative frequency*
less than 35	14	14
35–37	62	76
38–40	99	175
41–43	18	193
above 43	7	200
	$\Sigma f = 200 = N$	

To find Q_1. Here $\frac{N}{4} = \frac{200}{4} = 50$ *i.e.* Q_1 lies in 35–37

$L = 35, C = 14, f = 62, h = 2$

$$Q_1 = L + \frac{\frac{N}{4} - C}{f} \times h = 35 + \frac{50 - 14}{62} \times 2 = 35 + 1.16 = 36.16$$

To Find Q_3. Here $\frac{3N}{4} = \frac{3 \times 200}{4} = 150$ *i.e.,* Q_3 lies in 38–40

$L = 38, C = 76, f = 99, h = 2$

$$\therefore \quad Q_3 = L + \frac{\frac{3N}{4} - C}{f} \times h = 38 + \frac{150 - 76}{99} \times 2 = 38 + 1.49 = 39.49$$

The quartile deviation is given by

$$\text{Q.D.} = \frac{Q_3 - Q_1}{2} = \frac{39.49 - 36.16}{2} = 1.67$$

Further, the coefficient of quartile deviation is given by

$$\text{Coefficient of Q.D.} = \frac{Q_3 - Q_1}{Q_3 + Q_1} = \frac{39.49 - 36.16}{39.49 + 36.16} = \frac{3.33}{75.65} = 0.044.$$

Merits of Q.D.

(1) It is the best measure of dispersion in measuring variation in open end distributions.

(2) It is not affected by the extreme values.

Demerits of Q.D.

(1) It is not suitable for further algebraic treatment

(2) It is too much affected by fluctuations of sampling.

(3) It is not useful for statistical inference.

Uses of Q.D. This measure gives test view in small samples.

MEAN DEVIATION (M.D.)

6.10. MEAN DEVIATION (M.D.)

Mean deviation is also called **average deviation.**

The **mean deviation** of a statistical data is defined as the arithmetic mean of the numerical values of the deviations of items from some average.

Generally, mean and median are used in calculating mean deviation. Here we shall be calculating M.D. by using A.M. only. Mean deviation using A.M. is denoted as M.D.$(\bar{x})$.

6.11. COEFFICIENT OF MEAN DEVIATION (M.D.)

For comparing two or more series for variability, the corresponding relative measure, 'Coefficient of M.D.', is used. This is defined as :

$$\textbf{Coefficient of M.D.(A.M.)} = \frac{\textbf{M.D. (A.M.)}}{\textbf{A.M.}}.$$

6.12. MEAN DEVIATION FOR INDIVIDUAL SERIES

Let $x_1, x_2, \ldots\ldots, x_n$ be an individual series *i.e.,* these are n given values of the variable x.

The mean deviation (M.D.$(\bar{x})$) of this individual series from mean is defined as

$$\mathbf{M.D.}(\bar{\mathbf{x}}) = \frac{|\mathbf{x}_1 - \bar{\mathbf{x}}| + |\mathbf{x}_2 - \bar{\mathbf{x}}| + \ldots\ldots + |\mathbf{x}_n - \bar{\mathbf{x}}|}{\mathbf{n}},$$

where $\bar{x}$ is the A.M. of the given series.

In short, we write :

$$\mathbf{M.D.}(\bar{\mathbf{x}}) = \frac{\sum_{i=1}^{n} |\mathbf{x}_i - \bar{\mathbf{x}}|}{\mathbf{n}} \quad \text{or simply as} \quad \mathbf{M.D.}(\bar{\mathbf{x}}) = \frac{\Sigma|\mathbf{x} - \bar{\mathbf{x}}|}{\mathbf{n}}.$$

6.13. WORKING RULES TO FIND M.D.($\bar{x}$) FOR INDIVIDUAL SERIES

Let $x_1, x_2, \ldots\ldots, x_n$ be the given individual series.

I. Find $\bar{x}$ by using the formula $\bar{x} = \frac{\Sigma x}{n}$.

II. Find deviations $x_1 - \bar{x}, x_2 - \bar{x}, \ldots\ldots, x_n - \bar{x}$ of the items $x_1, x_2, \ldots\ldots, x_n$ from $\bar{x}$.

III. Find the numerical values of $x_1 - \bar{x}, x_2 - \bar{x}, \ldots\ldots, x_n - \bar{x}$ and write these as $|x_1 - \bar{x}|$, $|x_2 - \bar{x}|, \ldots\ldots, |x_n - \bar{x}|$.

IV. Find the sum of these numerical values and write this sum as $\Sigma|x - \bar{x}|$.

V. Divide the sum $\Sigma|x - \bar{x}|$ by n. This gives the value of M.D.($\bar{x}$).
To find the value of coefficient of M.D. ($\bar{x}$), divide M.D. ($\bar{x}$) by A.M., *i.e.*, $\bar{x}$.

ILLUSTRATIVE EXAMPLES

Example 1. *Find the mean deviation from the mean for the following data :*

12, 3, 18, 17, 4, 9, 17, 19, 20, 15, 8, 17, 2, 3, 16, 11, 3, 1, 0, 5.

Also find the number of items between $\bar{x}$ – M.D.($\bar{x}$) and $\bar{x}$ + M.D.($\bar{x}$).

Sol. **Calculation of M.D. ($\bar{x}$)**

x	$x - \bar{x}$ ($\bar{x} = 10$)	$\|x - \bar{x}\|$
12	2	2
3	– 7	7
18	8	8
17	7	7
4	– 6	6
9	– 1	1
17	7	7
19	9	9
20	10	10
15	5	5
8	– 2	2
17	7	7
2	– 8	8
3	– 7	7
16	6	6
11	1	1
3	– 7	7
1	– 9	9
0	– 10	10
5	– 5	5
$\Sigma x = 200$		$\Sigma\|x - \bar{x}\| = 124$

$$\bar{x} = \frac{\Sigma x}{n} = \frac{200}{20} = 10.$$

$$\therefore \qquad \text{M.D.}\ (\bar{x}) = \frac{\Sigma |x - \bar{x}|}{n} = \frac{124}{20} = 6.2.$$

Now $\bar{x} - \text{M.D.}(\bar{x}) = 10 - 6.2 = 3.8$ and $\bar{x} + \text{M.D.}(\bar{x}) = 10 + 6.2 = 16.2$.

Items lying between 3.8 and 16.2 are 12, 4, 9, 15, 8, 16, 11, 5 and these are 8 in numbers.

$\therefore$ 8 items lie between $\bar{x} - \text{M.D.}(\bar{x})$ and $\bar{x} + \text{M.D.}(\bar{x})$.

TEST YOUR KNOWLEDGE 6.1

Find the M.D. ($\bar{x}$) for the following individual series (Q. No. 1–3) :

1. 6, 7, 10, 12, 13, 4, 8, 12.

2. 4, 7, 8, 9, 10, 12, 13, 17.

3. 6.5, 5, 5.25, 5.5, 4.75, 4.5, 6.25, 7.75, 8.5.

Find the M.D.($\bar{x}$) and coefficient of M.D.($\bar{x}$) for the following individual series. Also find the number of items between $\bar{x}$ – M.D.($\bar{x}$) and $\bar{x}$ + M.D.($\bar{x}$) (Q. No. 4–6) :

4. 3,000, 4,000, 4,200, 4,400, 4,600, 4,800, 5,800.

5. 21, 23, 25, 28, 30, 32, 38, 39, 46, 48.

6.

Daily wage (in ₹)	130	160	150	150	180	150	140	180	160	100

7. Find the quartile deviation and its coefficient for the data given below :

Marks	*No. of students*
35–36	14
36–37	20
37–38	42
38–39	54
40–41	45
41–42	21
42–43	8

8. Find the coefficient of quartile deviation and co-efficient of variation for the data :

Wages	*No. of workers*
Below 20	8
Below 40	20
Below 60	50
Below 80	70
Below 100	80

Answers

1. 2.75	**2.** 3	**3.** 1.1	**4.** 571.43, 0.13, 5
5. 7.8, 0.24, 5	**6.** ₹ 16, 0.11, 5	**7.** 1.553, 0.019	**8.** 42.65%, 0.273.

6.14. MEAN DEVIATION FOR FREQUENCY DISTRIBUTION

In a frequency distribution, let $f_1, f_2, \ldots\ldots, f_n$ be the respective frequencies for the values $x_1, x_2, \ldots\ldots, x_n$ of the variable x.

The mean deviation (M.D.($\bar{x}$)) of this frequency distribution from mean is defined as

$$\text{M.D.}(\bar{x}) = \frac{f_1|x_1 - \bar{x}| + f_2|x_2 - \bar{x}| + \ldots\ldots + f_n|x_n - \bar{x}|}{f_1 + f_2 + \ldots\ldots + f_n},$$

where $\bar{x}$ is the A.M. of the given frequency distribution.

In short, $\text{M.D.}(\bar{x}) = \dfrac{\sum_{i=1}^{n} f_i|x_i - \bar{x}|}{\sum_{i=1}^{n} f}$ or simply as $\text{M.D.}(\bar{x}) = \dfrac{\Sigma f|x - \bar{x}|}{N}$.

Here $N = \Sigma f$, *i.e.*, the sum of all frequencies.

When the values of the variable are given in the form of classes, then their respective mid-points are taken as the values of the variable.

6.15. WORKING RULES TO FIND M.D.($\bar{x}$) FOR FREQUENCY DISTRIBUTION

I. If the values of the variable are given in the form of classes, then their respective mid-points are taken as the values of the variable. Let $f_1, f_2, \ldots\ldots, f_n$ be the respective frequencies for the values $x_1, x_2, \ldots\ldots, x_n$ of the variable x.

II. In the table, find the products of 'f' and 'x'.

III. Find the sums Σfx and N and divide Σfx by N to get the value of $\bar{x}$.

IV. Find deviations $x_1 - \bar{x}, x_2 - \bar{x}, \ldots\ldots, x_n - \bar{x}$ of the items $x_1, x_2, \ldots\ldots, x_n$ from $\bar{x}$.

V. Find the numerical values of $x_1 - \bar{x}, x_2 - \bar{x}, \ldots\ldots, x_n - \bar{x}$ and write these as $|x_1 - \bar{x}|, |x_2 - \bar{x}|, \ldots\ldots, |x_n - \bar{x}|$.

VI. In the next column, find $f|x - \bar{x}|$ and find the sum of these values and write this sum as $\Sigma f|x - \bar{x}|$.

VII. Divide the sum $\Sigma f|x - \bar{x}|$ by N. This gives the value of M.D.($\bar{x}$).
To find the value of coefficient of M.D.($\bar{x}$), divide M.D.($\bar{x}$) by A.M., *i.e.*, $\bar{x}$.

ILLUSTRATIVE EXAMPLES

Example 1. *Find the mean deviation from mean and its coefficient for the following frequency distribution :*

x	5	7	9	10	12	15
f	8	6	2	2	2	6

Sol. **Calculation of M.D.($\bar{x}$)**

x	f	fx	$x - \bar{x}$ ($\bar{x} = 9$)	$\lvert x - \bar{x} \rvert$	$f\lvert x - \bar{x} \rvert$
5	8	40	− 4	4	32
7	6	42	− 2	2	12
9	2	18	0	0	0
10	2	20	1	1	2
12	2	24	3	3	6
15	6	90	6	6	36
	$N = 26$	$\Sigma fx = 234$			$\Sigma f\lvert x - \bar{x} \rvert = 88$

$$\bar{x} = \frac{\Sigma fx}{N} = \frac{234}{26} = 9.$$

$$\text{Now, M.D.}(\bar{x}) = \frac{\Sigma f\,|x - \bar{x}|}{N} = \frac{88}{26} = 3.38$$

and $$\text{coefficient of M.D.}(\bar{x}) = \frac{\text{M.D.}(\bar{x})}{\bar{x}} = \frac{3.38}{9} = 0.38.$$

Example 2. *Find the M.D. from A.M. for the following data :*

x	3	5	7	9	11	13
f	2	7	10	9	5	2

Sol. **Calculation of M.D.($\bar{x}$)**

x	f	fx	$x - \bar{x}$ ($\bar{x} = 7.8$)	$\lvert x - \bar{x} \rvert$	$f\lvert x - \bar{x} \rvert$
3	2	6	− 4.8	4.8	9.6
5	7	35	− 2.8	2.8	19.6
7	10	70	− 0.8	0.8	8.0
9	9	81	1.2	1.2	10.8
11	5	55	3.2	3.2	16.0
13	2	26	5.2	5.2	10.4
	$N = 35$	$\Sigma fx = 273$			$\Sigma f\lvert x - \bar{x} \rvert = 74.4$

$\therefore \quad \bar{x} = \frac{\Sigma fx}{N} = \frac{273}{35} = 7.8.$

Now, $\quad \text{M.D.}(\bar{x}) = \frac{\Sigma f\,|x - \bar{x}|}{N} = \frac{74.4}{35} = 2.13.$

Example 3. *Find the mean deviation from the mean for the following data :*

Class	*95–105*	*105–115*	*115–125*	*125–135*	*135–145*	*145–155*
Frequency	*9*	*13*	*26*	*30*	*12*	*10*

Sol. **Calculation of M.D.($\bar{x}$)**

Class	*f*	*Mid-point of class x*	*fx*	$x - \bar{x}$ ($\bar{x}$ = 125.3)	$\|x - \bar{x}\|$	$f\|x - \bar{x}\|$
95–105	9	100	900	– 25.3	25.3	227.7
105–115	13	110	1430	– 15.3	15.3	198.9
115–125	26	120	3120	– 5.3	5.3	137.8
125–135	30	130	3900	4.7	4.7	141.0
135–145	12	140	1680	14.7	14.7	176.4
145–155	10	150	1500	24.7	24.7	247.0
	$N = 100$		$\Sigma fx = 12530$			$\Sigma f\|x - \bar{x}\|$ = 1128.8

$\therefore \quad \bar{x} = \frac{\Sigma fx}{N} = \frac{12530}{100} = 125.3.$

Now, $\quad \text{M.D.}(\bar{x}) = \frac{\Sigma f\,|x - \bar{x}|}{N} = \frac{1128.8}{100} = 11.288.$

6.16. MERITS OF M.D

1. It is simple to understand.
2. It is easy to compute.
3. It is well defined.
4. It is based on all the items.
5. It is not unduly affected by the presence of extreme items.
6. It can be calculated by using any average.

6.17. DEMERITS OF M.D.

1. It is not capable of further algebraic treatment.
2. It does not take into account the signs of the deviations of items from the average value.

TEST YOUR KNOWLEDGE 6.2

1. Find M.D.($\overline{x}$) for the following data :

x	10	30	50	70	90
f	4	24	28	16	8

2. Find M.D.($\overline{x}$) and its coefficient for the following data :

x	2	5	6	8	10	12
f	2	8	10	7	8	5

3. Compute M.D. from mean for the following data :

Marks	10	15	20	25	30
No. of students	2	4	6	8	5

4. Calculate mean deviation from mean and its coefficient for the following frequency distribution :

Size	2	4	6	8	10	12	14	16
Frequency	2	2	4	5	3	2	1	1

5. Find the mean deviation from the mean for the following data :

Class	10–20	20–30	30–40	40–50	50–60	60–70	70–80
Frequency	2	3	8	14	8	3	2

6. Calculate M.D. from mean for the following data regarding the difference of age between husbands and wives :

Difference in age (in years)	0–5	5–10	10–15	15–20	20–25	25–30	30–35	35–40
No. of couples	449	705	507	281	109	52	16	4

7. Calculate coefficient of mean deviation from mean for the following data :

Marks	140–150	150–160	160–170	170–180	180–190	190–200
No. of students	4	6	10	18	9	3

8. Find M.D. from mean for the following distribution :

Class	15–24	25–34	35–44	45–54	55–64
Frequency	4000	16000	28000	33000	28000

9. Calculate M.D. from mean and its coefficient for the following frequency distribution :

Marks less than	80	70	60	50	40	30	20	10
No. of students	100	90	80	60	32	20	13	5

Answers

1. 16 **2.** 2.3, 0.31 **3.** 5.12 marks **4.** 2.8, 0.35
5. 10 **6.** 5.34 years **7.** 0.062 **8.** 9.66
9. 14 marks, 0.31.

STANDARD DEVIATION (S.D.)

6.18. DEFINITION OF STANDARD DEVIATION (S.D.)

(P.T.U., M.B.A. Dec. 2006)

It is the most important measure of dispersions. It finds indispensable place in advanced statistical methods.

The **standard deviation** of a statistical data is defined as the positive square root of the A.M. of the squared deviations of items from the A.M. of the series under consideration.

The S.D. is often denoted by the Greek letter 'σ'.

6.19. COEFFICIENT OF S.D., C.V., VARIANCE

For comparing two or more series for variability, the corresponding relative measure, called **coefficient of S.D.** is used. This measure is defined as :

$$\textbf{Coefficient of S.D.} = \frac{\textbf{S.D.}}{\bar{x}}.$$

The product of coefficient of S.D. and 100 is defined as the **coefficient of variation.**

$$\therefore \qquad \textbf{Coefficient of variation} = \left(\frac{\textbf{S.D.}}{\bar{x}}\right) 100.$$

This measure is denoted as C.V.

$$\therefore \qquad \textbf{C.V.} = \left(\frac{\textbf{S.D.}}{\bar{x}}\right) 100.$$

In practical problems, we prefer comparing C.V. instead of comparing coefficient of S.D. The coefficient of variation is also represented as percentage.

The square of S.D. is called the **variance** of the distribution.

6.20. STANDARD DEVIATION FOR INDIVIDUAL SERIES

Let $x_1, x_2, \ldots\ldots, x_n$ be an individual series *i.e.*, these are n given values of the variable x. The standard deviation of this individual series is defind as

$$\text{S.D.} = \sqrt{\frac{(x_1 - \bar{x})^2 + (x_2 - \bar{x})^2 + \ldots\ldots + (x_n - \bar{x})^2}{n}},$$

where $\bar{x}$ is the A.M. of the given series.

In short, $\text{S.D.} = \sqrt{\dfrac{\sum_{i=1}^{n} (x_i - \bar{x})^2}{n}}$ or simply as $\text{S.D.} = \sqrt{\dfrac{\Sigma (x - \bar{x})^2}{n}}$.

6.21. WORKING RULES TO FIND S.D. FOR INDIVIDUAL SERIES

Let $x_1, x_2, \ldots\ldots, x_n$ be the given individual series.

I. Find $\bar{x}$ by using the formula $\bar{x} = \dfrac{\Sigma x}{n}$.

II. Find deviations $x_1 - \bar{x}, x_2 - \bar{x}, \ldots\ldots, x_n - \bar{x}$ of the items $x_1, x_2, \ldots\ldots, x_n$ from $\bar{x}$.

III. Find the squares of $x_1 - \bar{x}, x_2 - \bar{x}, \ldots\ldots, x_n - \bar{x}$.

IV. Find the sum of these squares and write this sum as $\Sigma(x-\bar{x})^2$.

V. Divide the sum $\Sigma(x-\bar{x})^2$ by n and then take its positive square root. This gives the value of S.D.

ILLUSTRATIVE EXAMPLES

Example 1. *Find the S.D. and C.V. for the following data : 4, 6, 10, 12, 18.*

Sol. **Calculation of S.D, C.V.**

x	$x-\bar{x}$ $(\bar{x}=10)$	$(x-\bar{x})^2$
4	– 6	36
6	– 4	16
10	0	0
12	2	4
18	8	64
$\Sigma x = 50$		$\Sigma(x-\bar{x})^2 = 120$

$$\bar{x} = \frac{\Sigma x}{n} = \frac{50}{5} = 10.$$

$$\therefore \text{S.D} = \sqrt{\frac{\Sigma(x-\bar{x})^2}{n}} = \sqrt{\frac{120}{5}} = \sqrt{24} = 4.899.$$

$$\text{C.V.} = \left(\frac{\text{S.D.}}{\bar{x}}\right)100 = \left(\frac{4.899}{10}\right)100 = 48.99\%.$$

Example 2. *The scores of a batsman 38, 70, 48, 34, 42, 55, 63, 46, 54, 44. Find the standard deviation.*

Sol. Calculation of standard deviation :

x	$x-\bar{x}$ $(\bar{x}=49.4)$	$(x-\bar{x})^2$
38	– 11.4	129.96
70	20.6	424.36
48	– 1.4	1.96
34	– 15.4	237.16
42	– 7.4	54.76
55	5.6	31.36
63	13.6	184.96
46	– 3.4	11.56
54	4.6	21.16
44	–5.4	29.16
$\Sigma x = 494$		$\Sigma(x-\bar{x})^2 = 1126.4$

Here $$\bar{x} = \frac{\Sigma x}{n} = \frac{494}{10} = 49.4$$

$$\therefore \quad \text{S.D.} = \sqrt{\frac{\Sigma(x-\bar{x})^2}{n}} = \sqrt{\frac{1126.4}{10}} = \sqrt{112.64} = 10.61$$

Example 3. *Find mean and variance for the following data : 2, 4, 5, 6, 8, 17.*

Sol. **Calculation of mean and variance**

x	$x - \bar{x}$ $(\bar{x} = 7)$	$(x - \bar{x})^2$
2	– 5	25
4	– 3	9
5	– 2	4
6	– 1	1
8	1	1
17	10	100
$\Sigma x = 42$		$\Sigma(x - \bar{x})^2 = 140$

$$\text{Mean } \bar{x} = \frac{\Sigma x}{n} = \frac{42}{6} = 7$$

$$\text{Variance} = \frac{\Sigma (x - \bar{x})^2}{n} = \frac{140}{6} = 23.33.$$

Example 4. *The variance of 20 observations is 5. If each observation is multiplied by 2, find the new variance of the resulting observations.*

Sol. Let the observations be $x_1, x_2, \ldots\ldots, x_{20}$.

$$\therefore \quad \text{Variance} = (\text{S.D.})^2 = \frac{\sum_{i=1}^{20} (x_i - \bar{x})^2}{20}$$

$$\therefore \quad \frac{\sum_{i=1}^{20} (x_i - \bar{x})^2}{20} = 5 \quad \text{or} \quad \sum_{i=1}^{20} (x_i - \bar{x})^2 = 100 \qquad \ldots(1)$$

New observations are $2x_1, 2x_2, \ldots\ldots, 2x_{20}$.

Let $\bar{y}$ and $\bar{x}$ be respectively the A.M. of new and given observations.

$$\therefore \quad \bar{y} = \frac{2x_1 + 2x_2 + \ldots\ldots + 2x_{20}}{20} = 2\left(\frac{x_1 + x_2 + \ldots\ldots + x_{20}}{20}\right) = 2\bar{x}.$$

$$\text{Now} \quad \text{variance} = \frac{\sum_{i=1}^{20} (2x_i - \bar{y})^2}{20} = \frac{\sum_{i=1}^{20} (2x_i - 2\bar{x})^2}{20} = \frac{\sum_{i=1}^{20} 4(x_i - \bar{x})^2}{20}$$

$$= 4 \times \frac{\sum_{i=1}^{20} (x_i - \bar{x})^2}{20} = 4\left[\frac{100}{20}\right] = 20. \qquad \text{(Using (1))}$$

Theorem. *For the individual series $x_1, x_2, \ldots\ldots, x_n$, prove that S.D.* $= \sqrt{\frac{\Sigma x^2}{n} - \bar{x}^2}$. *Also,*

$$\textit{variance} = \frac{\Sigma x^2}{x} - (\bar{x})^2.$$

Proof. We have S.D. $= \sqrt{\dfrac{\sum_{i=1}^{n}(x_i - \bar{x})^2}{n}}$.

Now $\quad \sum_{i=1}^{n}(x_i - \bar{x})^2 = \sum_{i=1}^{n}(x_i^2 + \bar{x}^2 - 2x_i\bar{x}) = \sum_{i=1}^{n} x_i^2 + n\bar{x}^2 - 2\bar{x}\sum_{i=1}^{n} x_i$

$$= \sum_{i=1}^{n} x_i^2 + n\bar{x}^2 - 2\bar{x}(n\bar{x}) = \sum_{i=1}^{n} x_i^2 - n\bar{x}^2. \qquad \left(\because \bar{x} = \frac{1}{n}\sum_{i=1}^{n} x_i\right)$$

$$\therefore \qquad \text{S.D.} = \sqrt{\frac{\sum_{i=1}^{n}(x_i - \bar{x})^2}{n}} = \sqrt{\frac{\sum_{i=1}^{n} x_i^2 - n\bar{x}^2}{n}} = \sqrt{\frac{\sum_{i=1}^{n} x_i^2}{n} - \bar{x}^2}.$$

$$\text{Further variance} = (\text{S.D})^2 = \frac{\sum_{i=1}^{n} x_i^2}{n} - (\bar{x})^2.$$

Example 5. *Calculate the mean and variance of the first n natural numbers.*

Sol. Here the values of the variable x are $1, 2, 3, \ldots\ldots, n$.

$$\therefore \qquad \bar{x} = \frac{\Sigma x}{n} = \frac{1 + 2 + 3 + \ldots\ldots + n}{n} = \frac{\frac{n(n+1)}{2}}{n} = \frac{\mathbf{n+1}}{\mathbf{2}}.$$

$$\text{Variance} = \frac{\Sigma x^2}{n} - \bar{x}^2 = \frac{1^2 + 2^2 + 3^2 + \ldots\ldots + n^2}{n} - \left(\frac{n+1}{2}\right)^2$$

$$= \frac{\frac{n(n+1)(2n+1)}{6}}{n} - \left(\frac{n+1}{2}\right)^2 = \frac{(n+1)(2n+1)}{6} - \frac{(n+1)^2}{4}$$

$$= \frac{n+1}{2}\left[\frac{2n+1}{3} - \frac{n+1}{2}\right] = \frac{n+1}{2} \cdot \frac{n-1}{6} = \frac{n^2-1}{12}.$$

Example 6. *The mean of 8 observations is 9 and their variance is 9.25. If six of the observations are 6, 7, 10, 12, 12 and 13, find the remaining two observations.*

Sol. Given observations are 6, 7, 10, 12, 12, 13.

Let the other two observations be x_7 and x_8, where $x_7 \geq x_8$. We have $\bar{x} = 9$.

$\Rightarrow \quad \dfrac{\Sigma x}{8} = 9 \quad \Rightarrow \Sigma x = 72 \quad \Rightarrow \quad 6 + 7 + 10 + 12 + 12 + 13 + x_7 + x_8 = 72$

$\Rightarrow \quad x_7 + x_8 = 12$ ...(1)

Also variance = 9.25

$$\Rightarrow \quad \frac{\Sigma x^2}{8} - \bar{x}^2 = 9.25 \Rightarrow \frac{\Sigma x^2}{8} - (9)^2 = 9.25$$

$$\Rightarrow \quad \Sigma x^2 = 8(9.25 + 81) = 722$$

$$\Rightarrow \quad (6)^2 + (7)^2 + (10)^2 + (12)^2 + (12)^2 + (13)^2 + x_7^2 + x_8^2 = 722$$

$$\Rightarrow \quad 36 + 49 + 100 + 144 + 144 + 169 + x_7^2 + x_8^2 = 722$$

$$\Rightarrow \quad x_7^2 + x_8^2 = 80 \qquad \ldots(2)$$

Solving (1) and (2), we get $x_7 = 8$, $x_8 = 4$.

Example 7. A *student obtained the A.M. and S.D. of 100 observations as 40 and 5.1 respectively. Later on, it was discovered that he had wrongly copied down an observation as 50 instead of 40. Calculate the correct value of S.D.*

Sol. No. of items = 100

Incorrect $\bar{x} = 40$, Incorrect S.D. = 5.1

Correct item = 40, Incorrect item = 50

Now $\bar{x} = \frac{\Sigma x}{n}$ implies $40 = \frac{\text{Incorrect } \Sigma x}{100}$.

$\Rightarrow$ Incorrect $\Sigma x = 4000$

Now, Correct Σx = Incorrect Σx – (Incorrected items) + (Corrected items)

$= 4000 - 50 + 40 = 3990$

$$\therefore \quad \text{Correct } \bar{x} = \frac{3990}{100} = 39.9.$$

$$\text{Now} \quad \text{S.D.} = \sqrt{\frac{\Sigma x^2}{n} - (\bar{x})^2}.$$

$$\Rightarrow \quad 5.1 = \sqrt{\frac{\text{Incorrect } \Sigma x^2}{100} - (40)^2}$$

$$\text{or} \quad 26.01 = \frac{\text{Incorrect } \Sigma x^2}{100} - 1600$$

$$\text{or} \quad \text{Incorrect } \Sigma x^2 = (1626.01)\, 100 = 162601$$

$$\therefore \quad \text{Correct } \Sigma x^2 = 162601 - (50)^2 + (40)^2 = 161701$$

$$\text{Hence} \quad \text{Correct S.D.} = \sqrt{\frac{\text{Corrected } \Sigma x^2}{n} - (\text{Corrected } \bar{x})^2}$$

$$= \sqrt{\frac{161701}{100} - (39.9)^2} = \sqrt{1617.01 - 1592.1} = 5.$$

6.22. SHORT-CUT METHOD FOR S.D. FOR INDIVIDUAL SERIES

We have seen that the calculation of S.D. involves lot of computation work. Even if the value of A.M. is a whole number, the calculations are not so simple. In case, A.M. is in decimal, then the calculation work would become more tedious. In problems, where A.M. is expected to be in decimal, we shall use this method, which is based on deviations (or step deviations) of items in the series.

Let $x_1, x_2, ..., x_n$ be an individual series.

Let $$u_i = \frac{x_i - A}{h},\ 1 \le i \le n, \text{ where } A \text{ and } h \text{ are arbitrary but fixed constants.}$$

$$\therefore \quad x_i = A + hu_i$$

Now, $$\bar{x} = \frac{1}{n}\sum_{i=1}^{n} x_i = \frac{1}{n}\sum_{i=1}^{n}[A + hu_i] = \frac{1}{n}\left[nA + h\sum_{i=1}^{n} u_i\right]$$

$$= A + h\,.\,\frac{1}{n}\sum_{i=1}^{n} u_i = A + h\bar{u}, \quad \text{where } \bar{u} = \frac{1}{n}\sum_{i=1}^{n} u_i.$$

We have $$\text{S.D.} = \sqrt{\frac{\sum_{i=1}^{n}(x_i - \bar{x})^2}{n}}.$$

Now $$\sum_{i=1}^{n}(x_i - \bar{x})^2 = \sum_{i=1}^{n}[(A + hu_i) - (A + h\bar{u})]^2$$

$$= \sum_{i=1}^{n}(hu_i - h\bar{u})^2 = h^2\sum_{i=1}^{n}(u_i - \bar{u})^2 = h^2\sum_{i=1}^{n}(u_i^{\ 2} + \bar{u}^{\ 2} - 2u_i\,\bar{u})$$

$$= h^2\left[\sum_{i=1}^{n} u_i^{\ 2} + n\bar{u}^{\ 2} - 2\,\bar{u}\sum_{i=1}^{n} u_i\right]$$

$$= h^2\left[\sum_{i=1}^{n} u_i^{\ 2} + n\left(\frac{\sum_{i=1}^{n} u_i}{n}\right)^2 - 2\left(\frac{\sum_{i=1}^{n} u_i}{n}\right)\sum_{i=1}^{n} u_i\right]$$

$$= h^2\left[\sum_{i=1}^{n} u_i^{\ 2} + \frac{1}{n}\left(\sum_{i=1}^{n} u_i\right)^2 - \frac{2}{n}\left(\sum_{i=1}^{n} u_i\right)^2\right]$$

$$= h^2\left[\sum_{i=1}^{n} u_i^{\ 2} - \frac{1}{n}\left(\sum_{i=1}^{n} u_i\right)^2\right].$$

$$\therefore \quad \text{S.D.} = \sqrt{\frac{\sum_{i=1}^{n}(x_i - \bar{x})^2}{n}} = \sqrt{\frac{\sum_{i=1}^{n} u_i^{\ 2}}{n} - \left(\frac{\sum_{i=1}^{n} u_i}{n}\right)^2} \times h.$$

More briefly,

$$\textbf{S.D.} = \sqrt{\frac{\Sigma u^2}{n} - \left(\frac{\Sigma u}{n}\right)^2} \times h, \quad \textbf{where } u = \frac{x - A}{h}.$$

Note. From the above result, we can say that the standard deviation is independent of change of origin, but not of scale:

Corollary 1. In particular, let $h = 1$.

$$\therefore \qquad u = \frac{x - A}{1} = x - A = d, \text{ say.}$$

$$\therefore \qquad \textbf{S.D.} = \sqrt{\frac{\Sigma d^2}{n} - \left(\frac{\Sigma d}{n}\right)^2}, \textbf{ where } d = x - A.$$

Corollary 2. In particular, let $A = 0$ and $h = 1$.

$$\therefore \qquad u = \frac{x - 0}{1} = x$$

$$\therefore \qquad \text{S.D.} = \sqrt{\frac{\Sigma x^2}{n} - \left(\frac{\Sigma x}{n}\right)^2}$$

or

$$\textbf{S.D.} = \sqrt{\frac{\Sigma x^2}{n} - \bar{x}^2}.$$

Remark. In practical problems, it is advisable to first find deviations 'd' of the values of the variable (x) from some suitable numbers 'A'. Then we see, if there is any common factor (h) greater than one, in the values of the deviations. If there is no common factor greater than one, then we use the formula :

$$\text{S.D.} = \sqrt{\frac{\Sigma d^2}{n} - \left(\frac{\Sigma d}{n}\right)^2}.$$

In case, there is a common factor h (> 1), then we calculate $u = \frac{x - A}{h}$ *i.e.*, $u = \frac{d}{h}$ and use the formula :

$$\text{S.D.} = \sqrt{\frac{\Sigma x^2}{n} - \left(\frac{\Sigma x}{n}\right)^2} \times h.$$

6.23. WORKING RULES TO USE THE FORMULA : S.D. = $\sqrt{\frac{\Sigma d^2}{n} - \left(\frac{\Sigma d}{n}\right)^2}$

I. Choose the constant 'A' and find deviations (d) of items from A.

II. Find squares of deviation (d^2).

III. Find sums Σd and Σd^2.

IV. Calculate S.D. = $\sqrt{\frac{\Sigma d^2}{n} - \left(\frac{\Sigma d}{n}\right)^2}$.

Example 8. (*a*) *The scores of 10 students in a test, out of maximum marks 50, were as follows : 28, 36, 34, 28, 48, 22, 35, 27, 19, 41. Find the variance.*

(*b*) *Later on the maximum marks were increased to 100 and accordingly each student's score was double. Find the variance of the new scores.*

Sol. (*a*) **Calculation of variance**

x	$d = x - A$ $(A = 30)$	d^2
28	– 2	4
36	6	36
34	4	16
28	– 2	4
48	18	324
22	– 8	64
35	5	25
27	– 3	9
19	– 11	121
41	11	121
	$\Sigma d = 18$	$\Sigma d^2 = 724$

$$\text{Variance} = (\text{S.D.})^2 = \frac{\Sigma d^2}{n} - \left(\frac{\Sigma d}{n}\right)^2 = \frac{724}{10} - \left(\frac{18}{10}\right)^2 = 69.16.$$

(*b*) In this case, the new scores are : 56, 72, 68, 56, 96, 44, 70, 54, 38, 82.

Calculation of new variance

x	$d = x - A$ $(A = 60)$	d^2
56	– 4	16
72	12	144
68	8	64
56	– 4	16
96	36	1296
44	– 16	256
70	10	100
54	– 6	36
38	– 22	484
82	22	484
	$\Sigma d = 36$	$\Sigma d^2 = 2896$

$$\therefore \quad \text{Variance} = \frac{\Sigma d^2}{n} - \left(\frac{\Sigma d}{n}\right)^2 = \frac{2896}{10} - \left(\frac{36}{10}\right)^2 = 276.64.$$

$\therefore$ The variance of new scores is four times the variance of old scores.

6.24. WORKING RULES TO USE THE FORMULA : S.D. = $\sqrt{\frac{\Sigma u^2}{n} - \left(\frac{\Sigma u}{n}\right)^2} \times h$

I. Choose the constant 'A' and find deviations (d) of items from A.

II. Find common factor (h) of deviations (d) and find u which is equal to d/h.

III. Find squares of step deviations (u^2).

IV. Find sums Σu and Σu^2.

V. Calculate S.D. = $\sqrt{\frac{\Sigma u^2}{n} - \left(\frac{\Sigma u}{n}\right)^2} \times h$.

Example 9. *The following are scores made by two batsmen Dhoni and Yuvi in a series of innings :*

Dhoni	*12*	*115*	*6*	*73*	*7*	*19*	*119*	*36*	*84*	*29*
Yuvi	*47*	*12*	*76*	*42*	*4*	*51*	*37*	*48*	*13*	*0*

(*i*) *Who is the better run getter ?*

(*ii*) *Who is more consistent ?*

Sol. Calculation of C.V. for Dhoni

Score x	x^2
12	144
115	13225
6	36
73	5329
7	49
19	361
119	14161
36	1296
84	7056
29	841
$\Sigma x = 500$	$\Sigma x^2 = 42498$

$$\bar{x} = \frac{\Sigma x}{n} = \frac{500}{10} = 50 \text{ runs}$$

and
$$\text{S.D.} = \sqrt{\frac{\Sigma x^2}{n} - (\bar{x})^2} = \sqrt{\frac{42498}{10} - (50)^2} = 41.83 \text{ runs.}$$

$$\therefore \quad \text{C.V.} = \frac{\text{S.D.}}{\bar{x}} \times 100 = \frac{41.83}{50} \times 100 = 83.66\%.$$

Calculation of C.V. for Yuvi

Score x	x^2
47	2209
12	144
76	5776
42	1764
4	16
51	2601
37	1369
48	2304
13	169
0	0
$\Sigma x = 330$	$\Sigma x^2 = 16352$

$$\bar{x} = \frac{\Sigma x}{n} = \frac{330}{10} = 33 \text{ runs}$$

and
$$\text{S.D.} = \sqrt{\frac{\Sigma x^2}{n} - (\bar{x})^2} = \sqrt{\frac{16352}{10} - (33)^2} = 23.37 \text{ runs.}$$

$$\therefore \quad \text{C.V.} = \frac{\text{S.D.}}{\bar{x}} \times 100 = \frac{23.37}{33} \times 100 = 70.82\%.$$

(*i*) A.M. for Dhoni = 50 runs and A.M. for Yuvi = 33 runs

∴ **Dhoni is better run getter.**

(*ii*) C.V. for Dhoni = 83.66% C.V. for Yuvi = 70.82%.

∴ **Yuvi is more consistent.**

Remark. In the above example, we have used the formula S.D. = $\sqrt{\frac{\Sigma x^2}{n} - (\bar{x})^2}$ to find the value of S.D., because in this data, it is not convenient to take deviations.

Example 10. *Goals scored by two teams in a football session were as follow.*

No. of goals scored	*No. of matches played*	
	Team A	*Team B*
0	*15*	*20*
1	*10*	*10*
2	*7*	*5*
3	*5*	*4*
4	*3*	*2*
5	*2*	*1*
Total	*42*	*42*

Calculate the coefficient of variation and state which team is more consistent.

Sol. To find which team is more consistent, we find coefficient of variation of both the teams.

Team A. The coefficient of variation is given by C.V. = $\frac{\sigma}{\bar{x}} \times 100$

x	$d = x - \bar{x}$	$d^2 = (x - \bar{x})^2$
15	8	64
10	3	9
7	0	0
5	– 2	4
3	– 4	16
2	– 5	25
$\Sigma x = 42$	$\Sigma d = 0$	$\Sigma(x - \bar{x})^2 = 118$

Here $\bar{x} = \frac{1}{n}\ \Sigma x = \frac{1}{6}\ (42) = 7$

$$\sigma = \sqrt{\frac{\Sigma d^2}{n} - \left(\frac{\Sigma d}{n}\right)^2}$$

$$= \sqrt{\frac{118}{6} - 0} = 4.43$$

∴ $\text{C.V.} = \frac{4.43}{7} \times 100 = 63.29$

Team B. The coefficient of variation is given by

$$\text{C.V.} = \frac{\sigma}{\bar{y}} \times 100$$

Here $\bar{y} = \frac{1}{n}\Sigma y = \frac{1}{6} \times 42 = 7$

$$\sigma = \sqrt{\frac{\Sigma d^2}{n} - \left(\frac{\Sigma d}{n}\right)^2}$$

$$= \sqrt{\frac{252}{6} - 0}$$

$$= \sqrt{42} = 6.48$$

y	$d = y - \bar{y}$	$d^2 = (y - \bar{y})^2$
20	13	169
10	3	9
5	– 2	4
4	– 3	9
2	– 5	25
1	– 6	36
$\Sigma y = 42$	$\Sigma d = 0$	$\Sigma d^2 = 252$

$\therefore$ $$\text{C.V.} = \frac{6.48}{7} \times 100 = 92.57.$$

Conclusion. As the co-efficient of variation for the team A is less than the coefficient of variation for the team B.

$\therefore$ Team A is more consistent

Example 11. *An analysis of monthly wages of workers of two organizations C and D yielded the following details.*

Organizations	*C*	*D*
No. of workers	*50*	*60*
Average monthly wages	*₹ 60*	*₹ 48*
Variance	*100*	*144*

Obtain the overall average monthly wages of all the 110 workers,. Also determine which organization is more equitable in regard to wages.

Sol. Let n_1 and n_2 be the number of workers, $\bar{x}_1, \bar{x}_2$ be their average monthly wages, σ_1^2, σ_2^2, be their variances of the organizations C and D respectively.

Given, $n_1 = 50,\ n_2 = 60$

$\bar{x}_1 = 60,\ \bar{x}_2 = 48$

$\sigma_1^2 = 100,\ \sigma_2^2 = 144$

Let $\bar{x}$ be the average monthly wages of all the workers, then

$$\bar{x} = \frac{n_1\bar{x}_1 + n_2\bar{x}_2}{n_1 + n_2} = \frac{50 \times 60 + 60 \times 48}{50 + 60} = \frac{3000 + 2880}{110}$$

$$= \frac{5880}{110} = ₹\ 53.45$$

We now find coefficients of variations for both organizations C and D.

C.V. for organization C

$$\text{C.V.} = \frac{\sigma_1}{\bar{x}_1} \times 100 = \frac{10}{60} \times 100 = 16.67$$

C.V. for organization D

$$\text{C.V.} = \frac{\sigma_2}{\bar{x}_2} \times 100 = \frac{12}{48} \times 100 = 25$$

Since the co-efficient of variation in organization C is less than the coefficient of variance in organization D. ∴ The organization C is more equitable.

TEST YOUR KNOWLEDGE 6.3

1. What is the difference between mean deviation and standard deviation ?

   (*P.T.U., M.B.A. May 2003*)

2. For a frequency distribution, the value of variance is 12. Find its standard deviation.
3. For a frequency distribution, we have S.D. = 2, A.M. = 15. Find the value of the coefficient of variation.
4. For a frequency distribution, we have C.V. = 26.73% and A.M. = ₹ 39.5. Find the value of its S.D.
5. A group of 100 selected students is with average height 168.8 cm and coefficient of variation 3.2%. What is the S.D. of their height ?
6. For a frequency distribution, we have S.D. = 9.56, A.M. = 32.82. Find the values of the variance and the coefficient of variation.
7. In a cricket season, batsman *A* gets an average score of 64 runs per inning with a S.D. of 18 runs, while batsman *B* gets an average score of 43 runs with a S.D. of 9 runs in about an equal number of innings. Discuss the efficiency and consistency of both the batsmen.
8. Find the S.D. and C.V. for the following individual series : 12, 6, 7, 3, 15, 10, 18, 5.
9. Find the mean and variance for the following data : 6, 7, 10, 12, 13, 4, 8, 12.
10. Find the variance and standard deviation for the following data : 65, 58, 68, 44, 48, 45, 60, 62, 60, 50.
11. The mean and standard deviation of 6 observations are 8 and 4, respectively. If each observation is multiplied by 3, find the new mean and new standard deviation of the resulting observations.
12. Given that $\bar{x}$ is the mean and σ^2 is the variance of n observations $x_1, x_2, x_3, \ldots\ldots\ldots, x_n$. Prove that the mean and variance of the observations $ax_1, ax_2, ax_3, \ldots\ldots\ldots ax_n$ are $a\bar{x}$ and $a^2\sigma^2$ respectively $(a \neq 0)$.
13. The mean of 5 observations is 4.4 and their variance is 8.24. If three of the observations are 1, 2, and 6, find the other two observations.
14. The analysis of the results of a budget survey of 150 families gave an average monthly expenditure of ₹ 120 on food items with a S.D. of ₹ 15. After the analysis was completed it was noticed that the figure recorded for one household was wrongly taken as ₹ 15 instead of ₹ 105. Determine the correct value of the average expenditure and its S.D.
15. The mean and standard deviation of 20 observations are found to be 10 and 2 respectively. On rechecking, it was found that an observation 8 was incorrect. Calculate the correct mean and standard deviation in each of the following cases :

    (*i*) If the wrong item is omitted.

    (*ii*) If it is replaced by 12.

16. Find which of the following batsmen is more consistent in scoring :

Batsman A's score	5	7	16	27	39	53	56	61	80	101	105
Batsman B's score	0	4	16	21	41	43	57	78	83	90	95

Answers

2. 3.46 **3.** 13.33% **4.** ₹ 10.56

5. 5.40 c.m. **6.** 91.39, 29.13 **7.** *A* is efficient and *B* is more consistent.

8. 4.87, 51.26%. **9.** 9, 9.25 **10.** 66.2, 8.14 **11.** 24, 12

13. 4, 9 **14.** 10.2, 1.99 **15.** (*i*) 10.11, 1.997 (*ii*) 10.2, 1.99

16. 67.07%, 69.51%, Batsman *A* is more consistent.

Hints

7. Batsman with higher average is more efficient and batsman with lower C.V. is more efficient.

12. Let $\bar{x}$ be the A.M. of given observations.

$$\therefore \qquad \text{New A.M.} = \frac{ax_1 + ax_2 + \ldots\ldots + ax_n}{n} = a\left(\frac{x_1 + x_2 + \ldots\ldots + x_n}{n}\right) = a\bar{x}$$

and
$$\text{new variance} = \frac{\Sigma\,(ax_i - a\bar{x})^2}{n} = \frac{a^2\,\Sigma\,(x_i - \bar{x})^2}{n} = a^2\sigma^2.$$

6.25. STANDARD DEVIATION FOR FREQUENCY DISTRIBUTION

Let $f_1, f_2, \ldots\ldots, f_n$ be the respective frequencies for the values $x_1, x_2, \ldots\ldots, x_n$ of the variable x.

The standard deviation (S.D.) for this frequency distribution is defined as

$$\textbf{S.D.} = \sqrt{\frac{f_1(x_1 - \bar{x})^2 + f_2(x_2 - \bar{x})^2 + \ldots\ldots + f_n(x_n - \bar{x})^2}{f_1 + f_2 + \ldots\ldots + f_n}},$$

where $\bar{x}$ is the A.M. of the given frequency distribution.

In short, we write

$$\textbf{S.D.} = \sqrt{\frac{\sum_{i=1}^{n} f_i(x_i - \bar{x})^2}{\sum_{i=1}^{n} f_i}} \quad \text{or simply as} \quad \textbf{S.D.} = \sqrt{\frac{\Sigma f(x - \bar{x})^2}{\text{N}}}.$$

Here $N = \Sigma f$, *i.e.*, the sum of all frequencies.

When the values of the variable are given in the form of classes, then their respective mid-points are taken as the values of the variable.

6.26. WORKING RULES TO FIND S.D. FOR FREQUENCY DISTRIBUTION

I. If the values of the variable are given in the form of classes then their respective mid-points are taken as the values of the variable.

Let $f_1, f_2, \ldots\ldots, f_n$ be the respective frequencies for the values $x_1, x_2, \ldots\ldots, x_n$ of the variable x.

II. In the table, find the product of 'f' and 'x'.

III. Find the sums Σfx and N and find $\bar{x}$ by using the formula $\bar{x} = \dfrac{\Sigma fx}{N}$.

IV. Find deviations $x_1 - \bar{x}, x_2 - \bar{x}, \ldots\ldots, x_n - \bar{x}$ of the items $x_1, x_2, \ldots\ldots, x_n$ from $\bar{x}$.

V. Find the squares of $x_1 - \bar{x}, x_2 - \bar{x}, \ldots\ldots, x_n - \bar{x}$.

VI. In the next column, find $f(x - \bar{x})^2$ and find the sum of these values and write this sum as $\Sigma f(x - \bar{x})^2$.

VII. Divide the sum $\Sigma f(x - \bar{x})^2$ by N and then take its positive square root. This gives the value of S.D.

ILLUSTRATIVE EXAMPLES

Example 1. *Calculate S.D. and C.V. for the following data :*

x	5	15	25	35	45	55
f	12	18	27	20	17	6

Sol. **Calculation of S.D. and C.V.**

x	f	fx	$x-\bar{x}$	$(x-\bar{x})^2$	$f(x-\bar{x})^2$
5	12	60	– 23	529	6348
15	18	270	– 13	169	3042
25	27	675	– 3	9	243
35	20	700	7	49	980
45	17	765	17	289	4913
55	6	330	27	729	4374
	$N = 100$	$\Sigma fx = 2800$			$\Sigma f(x-\bar{x})^2 = 19900$

$$\bar{x} = \frac{\Sigma fx}{N} = \frac{2800}{100} = 28$$

$$\text{S.D.} = \sqrt{\frac{\Sigma f(x-\bar{x})^2}{N}} = \sqrt{\frac{19900}{100}} = \sqrt{199} = 14.11.$$

$$\therefore \quad \text{C.V.} = \left(\frac{\text{S.D.}}{\bar{x}}\right) 100 = \left(\frac{14.11}{28}\right) 100 = 50.39\%.$$

Example 2. *Calculate S.D. and C.V. for the following frequency distribution :*

Class	4—8	8—12	12—16	16—20	20—24	24—28	28—32	32—36	36—40
Frequency	11	13	16	14	14	9	17	6	4

Sol. **Calculation of S.D. and C.V.**

Class	x	f	fx	$x-\bar{x}$	$(x-\bar{x})^2$	$f(x-\bar{x})^2$
4—8	6	11	66	– 14	196	2156
8—12	10	13	130	– 10	100	1300
12—16	14	16	224	– 6	36	576
16—20	18	14	252	– 2	4	56
20—24	22	14	308	2	4	56
24—28	26	9	234	6	36	324
28—32	30	17	510	10	100	1700
32—36	34	6	204	14	196	1176
36—40	38	4	152	18	324	1296
		N = 104	$\Sigma fx = 2080$			$\Sigma f(x-\bar{x})^2 = 8640$

$$\bar{x} = \frac{\Sigma fx}{N} = \frac{2080}{104} = 20.$$

Now,
$$\text{S.D.} = \sqrt{\frac{\Sigma f(x-\bar{x})^2}{N}} = \sqrt{\frac{8640}{104}} = \sqrt{83.08} = 9.11$$

and
$$\text{C.V.} = \left(\frac{\text{S.D.}}{\bar{x}}\right) 100 = \left(\frac{9.11}{20}\right) 100 = 45.55\%.$$

6.27. SHORT-CUT METHOD FOR S.D. FOR FREQUENCY DISTRIBUTION

We have seen that the calculation of S.D. involves lot of computation work. Even if the value of A.M. is a whole number, the calculations are not so simple. In case, A.M. is in decimal, then the calculation work would become more tedious. In problems, where A.M. is expected to be in decimal, we shall use this method, which is based on deviations (or step deviations) of items in the series.

In a frequency distribution, let $f_1, f_2, \ldots\ldots, f_n$ be the respective frequencies for the values $x_1, x_2, \ldots\ldots, x_n$ of the variable x.

Let $u_i = \dfrac{x_i - A}{h}$, $1 \le i \le n$, where A and h are arbitrary but fixed constants.

$\therefore$ $x_i = A + hu_i$

Now
$$\bar{x} = \frac{1}{N}\sum_{i=1}^{n} f_i x_i = \frac{1}{N}\sum_{i=1}^{n} f_i\,[A + h\,u_i] = \frac{1}{N}\left[A\sum_{i=1}^{n} f_i + h\sum_{i=1}^{n} f_i u_i\right]$$

$$= A + h\,.\,\frac{1}{N}\sum_{i=1}^{n} f_i\,u_i = A + h\bar{u}\,, \text{ where } \bar{u} = \frac{1}{N}\sum_{i=1}^{n} f_i u_i.$$

We have
$$\text{S.D.} = \sqrt{\frac{\sum_{i=1}^{n} f(x_i - \bar{x})^2}{N}}.$$

$$\text{Now, } \sum_{i=1}^{n} f_i(x_i - \overline{x})^2 = \sum_{i=1}^{n} f_i\,[(A + hu_i) - (A + h\overline{u})]^2 = \sum_{i=1}^{n} f_i(hu_i - h\overline{u})^2$$

$$= h^2 \sum_{i=1}^{n} f_i(u_i - \overline{u})^2 = h^2 \sum_{i=1}^{n} (f_i {u_i}^2 + f_i\overline{u}^2 - 2f_i\, u_i\overline{u})$$

$$= h^2 \left[\sum_{i=1}^{n} f_i {u_i}^2 + \overline{u}^2 \sum_{i=1}^{n} f_i - 2\overline{u} \sum_{i=1}^{n} f_i u_i \right]$$

$$= h^2 \left[\sum_{i=1}^{n} f_i {u_i}^2 + \left(\frac{\sum_{i=1}^{n} f_i u_i}{N} \right)^2 N - 2 \left(\frac{\sum_{i=1}^{n} f_i u_i}{N} \right)^n \sum_{i=1}^{n} f_i u_i \right]$$

$$= h^2 \left[\sum_{i=1}^{n} f_i {u_i}^2 + \frac{1}{N} \left(\sum_{i=1}^{n} f_i u_i \right)^2 - \frac{2}{N} \left(\sum_{i=1}^{n} f_i u_i \right)^2 \right]$$

$$= h^2 \left[\sum_{i=1}^{n} f_i {u_i}^2 - \frac{1}{N} \left(\sum_{i=1}^{n} f_i u_i \right)^2 \right].$$

$$\therefore \qquad \text{S.D.} = \sqrt{\frac{\sum_{i=1}^{n} f_i\,(x_i - \overline{x})^2}{N}} = \sqrt{\frac{\sum_{i=1}^{n} f_i {u_i}^2}{N} - \left(\frac{\sum_{i=1}^{n} f_i u_i}{N} \right)^2} \times h.$$

More briefly,

$$\textbf{S.D.} = \sqrt{\frac{\Sigma f u^2}{N} - \left(\frac{\Sigma f u}{N} \right)^2} \times h, \quad \textbf{where } u = \frac{x - A}{h}.$$

Corollary 1. In particular, let $h = 1$.

$$\therefore \qquad u = \frac{x - A}{1} = x - A = d, \text{ say.}$$

$$\therefore \qquad \textbf{S.D.} = \sqrt{\frac{\Sigma f d^2}{N} - \left(\frac{\Sigma f d}{N} \right)^2}, \quad \textbf{where } d = x - A.$$

Corollary 2. In particular, let $A = 0$ and $h = 1$.

$$\therefore \qquad u = \frac{x - 0}{1} = x$$

$$\therefore \qquad \text{S.D.} = \sqrt{\frac{\Sigma f x^2}{N} - \left(\frac{\Sigma f x}{N} \right)^2}$$

$$\therefore \qquad \text{S.D.} = \sqrt{\frac{\Sigma fx^2}{N} - (\bar{x})^2}\,.$$

Remark. In practical problems, it is advisable to first find deviations 'd' of the values of the variable (x) from some suitable number 'A'. Then we see, if there is any common factor (h) greater than one, in the values of the deviations. If there is no common factor greater than one, then we use the formula :

$$\text{S.D.} = \sqrt{\frac{\Sigma fd^2}{N} - \left(\frac{\Sigma fd}{N}\right)^2}\,.$$

In case, there is a common factor h (> 1), then we calculate $u = \frac{x - A}{h}$ *i.e.*, $u = \frac{d}{h}$ and use the formula :

$$\text{S.D.} = \sqrt{\frac{\Sigma fu^2}{N} - \left(\frac{\Sigma fu}{N}\right)^2} \times h.$$

6.28. WORKING RULES TO USE THE FORMULA : S.D. = $\sqrt{\frac{\Sigma fd^2}{N} - \left(\frac{\Sigma fd}{N}\right)^2}$

I. Choose the constant 'A' and find deviations (d) of items from A.
II. Find the products 'fd' of f and d.
III. Find the products 'fd^2' of fd and d.
IV. Find sums Σfd and Σfd^2.

V. Calculate $\qquad \text{S.D.} = \sqrt{\frac{\Sigma fd^2}{\text{N}} - \left(\frac{\Sigma fd}{\text{N}}\right)^2}\,.$

Example 3. *Find mean and standard deviation for the following data :*

x	*92*	*93*	*97*	*98*	*102*	*104*	*109*
f	*3*	*2*	*3*	*2*	*6*	*3*	*3*

Sol. **Calculation of $\bar{x}$ and S.D.**

x	f	$d = x - A$ ($A = 100$)	fd	fd^2
92	3	– 8	– 24	192
93	2	– 7	– 14	98
97	3	– 3	– 9	27
98	2	– 2	– 4	8
102	6	2	12	24
104	3	4	12	48
109	3	9	27	243
	N = 22		$\Sigma fd = 0$	$\Sigma fd^2 = 640$

$$\overline{x} = A + \frac{\Sigma fd}{N} = 100 + \frac{0}{22} = 100.$$

$$\text{S.D.} = \sqrt{\frac{\Sigma fd^2}{N} - \left(\frac{\Sigma fd}{N}\right)^2} = \sqrt{\frac{640}{22} - \left(\frac{0}{22}\right)^2} = 5.39.$$

Example 4. *The scores of two batsmen A and B for 20 innings are tabulated below. Which of the two may be regarded as the more consistent batsman ?*

Score		*50*	*51*	*52*	*53*	*54*	*55*	*56*	*57*
No. of innings	*A*	*1*	*0*	*0*	*4*	*3*	*6*	*3*	*3*
	B	*1*	*2*	*2*	*6*	*3*	*4*	*2*	*0*

Sol. **Calculation of C.V. for Batsman A**

Score x	*No. of innings* f	$d = x - A$ $(A = 53)$	fd	fd^2
50	1	– 3	– 3	9
51	0	– 2	0	0
52	0	– 1	0	0
53	4	0	0	0
54	3	1	3	3
55	6	2	12	24
56	3	3	9	27
57	3	4	12	48
	N = 20		$\Sigma fd = 33$	$\Sigma fd^2 = 111$

$$\overline{x} = \text{A} + \frac{\Sigma fd}{N} = 53 + \frac{33}{20} = 54.65$$

$$\text{S.D.} = \sqrt{\frac{\Sigma fd^2}{N} - \left(\frac{\Sigma fd}{N}\right)^2} = \sqrt{\frac{111}{20} - \left(\frac{33}{20}\right)^2} = 1.68$$

$$\therefore \quad \text{C.V. for A} = \left(\frac{\text{S.D.}}{\overline{x}}\right) 100 = \left(\frac{168}{54.65}\right) 100 = 3.07\%.$$

Calculation of C.V. for Batsman B

Score x	*No. of innings* f	$d = x - A$ $(A = 53)$	fd	fd^2
50	1	– 3	– 3	9
51	2	– 2	– 4	8
52	2	– 1	– 2	2
53	6	0	0	0
54	3	1	3	3
55	4	2	8	16
56	2	3	6	18
57	0	4	0	0
	N = 20		$\Sigma fd = 8$	$\Sigma fd^2 = 56$

$$\bar{x} = \text{A} + \frac{\Sigma fd}{\text{N}} = 53 + \frac{8}{20} = 53.4$$

$$\text{S.D.} = \sqrt{\frac{\Sigma fd^2}{\text{N}} - \left(\frac{\Sigma fd}{\text{N}}\right)^2} = \sqrt{\frac{56}{20} - \left(\frac{8}{20}\right)^2} = 1.62$$

$$\therefore \quad \text{C.V. for B} = \left(\frac{\text{S.D.}}{\bar{x}}\right) 100 = \left(\frac{1.62}{53.4}\right) 100 = 3.03\%.$$

$\therefore$ C.V. for B < C.V. for A. $\therefore$ Batsman B is more consistent.

Example 5. *Find the mean and variance for the following frequency distribution :*

Class	*0–10*	*10–20*	*20–30*	*30–40*	*40–50*
Frequency	*5*	*8*	*15*	*16*	*6*

Sol. **Calculation of $\bar{x}$ and variance**

Class	*f*	*x*	*d = x – A* *A = 25*	*fd*	*fd²*
0–10	5	5	– 20	– 100	2000
10–20	8	15	– 10	– 80	800
20– 30	15	25	0	0	0
30–40	16	35	10	160	1600
40–50	6	45	20	120	2400
	N = 50			$\Sigma fd = 100$	$\Sigma fd^2 = 6800$

$$\bar{x} = \text{A} + \frac{\Sigma fd}{N} = 25 + \frac{100}{50} = 27$$

$$\text{Variance} = \frac{\Sigma fd^2}{N} - \left(\frac{\Sigma fd}{N}\right)^2 = \frac{6800}{50} - \left(\frac{100}{50}\right)^2 = 132.$$

6.29. WORKING RULES TO USE THE FORMULA : S.D. = $\sqrt{\frac{\Sigma fu^2}{N} - \left(\frac{\Sigma fu}{N}\right)^2} \times h$

I. Choose the constant 'A' and find deviations (*d*) of items from A.

II. Find common factor (*h*) of deviations (*d*) and find *u* which is equal to *d*/*h*.

III. Find the products '*fu*' of *f* and *u*.

IV. Find the products 'fu^2' of *fu* and *u*.

V. Find sums Σfu and Σfu^2.

VI. Calculate S.D. = $\sqrt{\frac{\Sigma fu^2}{\text{N}} - \left(\frac{\Sigma fu}{\text{N}}\right)^2} \times h.$

Example 6. *Find the mean and standard deviation for the following frequency distribution :*

x	*6*	*10*	*14*	*18*	*24*	*28*	*30*
f	*2*	*4*	*7*	*12*	*8*	*4*	*3*

Sol. **Calculation of $\overline{x}$ and S.D.**

x	f	$d = x - A$ ($A = 18$)	$u = \frac{d}{h}$ ($h = 2$)	fu	fu^2
6	2	– 12	– 6	– 12	72
10	4	– 8	– 4	– 16	64
14	7	– 4	– 2	– 14	28
18	12	0	0	0	0
24	8	6	3	24	72
28	4	10	5	20	100
30	3	12	6	18	108
	N = 40			$\Sigma fu = 20$	$\Sigma fu^2 = 444$

$$\overline{x} = A + \left(\frac{\Sigma fu}{N}\right) h = 18 + \left(\frac{20}{40}\right) 2 = 19$$

$$\text{S.D.} = \sqrt{\frac{\Sigma fu^2}{N} - \left(\frac{\Sigma fu}{N}\right)^2} \times h = \sqrt{\frac{444}{40} - \left(\frac{20}{40}\right)^2} \times 2 = 6.59.$$

Example 7. *Find the value of coefficient of variation for the following frequency distribution :*

Class	*0–5*	*5–10*	*10–15*	*15–20*	*20–25*	*25–30*	*30–35*	*35–40*	*40–45*
No. of items	*20*	*24*	*32*	*28*	*20*	*16*	*34*	*10*	*16*

Sol. **Calculation of C.V.**

Class	f	x	$d = x - A$ ($A = 22.5$)	$u = d/h$ ($h = 5$)	fu	fu^2
0–5	20	2.5	– 20	– 4	– 80	320
5–10	24	7.5	– 15	– 3	– 72	216
10–15	32	12.7	– 10	–2	– 64	128
15–20	28	17.5	– 5	– 1	– 28	28
20–25	20	22.5	0	0	0	0
25–30	16	27.5	5	1	16	16
30–35	34	32.5	10	2	68	136
35–40	10	37.5	15	3	30	90
40–45	16	42.5	20	4	64	256
	N = 200				$\Sigma fu = -66$	$\Sigma fu^2 = 1190$

Now, $$\overline{x} = A + \left(\frac{\Sigma fu}{N}\right) h = 22.5 + \left(\frac{-66}{200}\right) 5 = 20.85$$

$$\text{S.D.} = \sqrt{\frac{\Sigma fu^2}{N} - \left(\frac{\Sigma fu}{N}\right)^2} \times h = \sqrt{\frac{1190}{200} - \left(\frac{-66}{200}\right)^2} \times 5 = \sqrt{5.84} \times 5 = 12.1.$$

$\therefore$ $$\text{C.V.} = \left(\frac{\text{S.D.}}{\bar{x}}\right) 100 = \left(\frac{12.1}{20.85}\right) 100 = \mathbf{58.03\%}.$$

6.30. S.D. OF COMBINED GROUP

Let σ_1 and σ_2 be the S.D. of two groups containing n_1 and n_2 items respectively. Let $\bar{x}_1$ and $\bar{x}_2$ be their respective A.M. Let $\bar{x}$ and σ be the A.M. and S.D. of the **combined group** respectively.

$\therefore$ $$\bar{x} = \frac{n_1\bar{x}_1 + n_2\bar{x}_2}{n_1 + n_2}$$

We define $d_1 = \bar{x}_1 - \bar{x}$ and $d_2 = \bar{x}_2 - \bar{x}$.

The S.D. of the combined group is given by the formula,

$$\sigma = \sqrt{\frac{\boldsymbol{n_1\sigma_1^2 + n_2\sigma_2^2 + n_1d_1^2 + n_2d_2^2}}{\boldsymbol{n_1 + n_2}}}.$$

This result can be extended to even more than two groups.

Example 8. *The following data gives the A.M. and S.D. of three sub-groups. Calculate the A.M. and S.D. of the combined group.*

Sub-group	*No. of men*	*Average wage (in ₹)*	*S.D. (in ₹)*
A	*50*	*61*	*8*
B	*100*	*70*	*9*
C	*120*	*80.5*	*10*

Sol. Let suffixes 1, 2, 3 be referred to information regarding groups *A, B, C* respectively.

$\therefore$ $n_1 = 50$ $\quad \bar{x}_1 = 61$ $\quad \sigma_1 = 8$

$n_2 = 100$ $\quad \bar{x}_2 = 70$ $\quad \sigma_2 = 9$

$n_3 = 120$ $\quad \bar{x}_3 = 80.5$ $\quad \sigma_3 = 10.$

Let $\bar{x}$ and σ be the A.M. and S.D. of the combined group respectively.

Now, $$\bar{x} = \frac{n_1\bar{x}_1 + n_2\bar{x}_2 + n_3\bar{x}_3}{n_1 + n_2 + n_3} = \frac{50(61) + 100(70) + 120(80.5)}{50 + 100 + 120} = \frac{19710}{270} = ₹\ 73.$$

$\therefore$ $d_1 = \bar{x}_1 - \bar{x} = 61 - 73 = -12$, $d_2 = \bar{x}_2 - \bar{x} = 70 - 73 = -3$, $d_3 = \bar{x}_3 - \bar{x} = 80.5 - 73 = 7.5$.

Now $$\sigma = \sqrt{\frac{n_1\sigma_1^2 + n_2\sigma_2^2 + n_3\sigma_3^2 + n_1d_1^2 + n_2d_2^2 + n_3d_3^2}{n_1 + n_2 + n_3}}$$

$$= \sqrt{\frac{50(8)^2 + 100(9)^2 + 120(10)^2 + 50(-12)^2 + 100(-3)^2 + 120(7.5)^2}{50 + 100 + 120}}$$

$$= \sqrt{\frac{3200 + 8100 + 12000 + 7200 + 900 + 6750}{270}}$$

$$= \sqrt{\frac{38150}{270}} = \sqrt{141.30} = 11.89.$$

Example 9. *The mean weight of 150 students is 60 kg. The mean weight of boys is 70 kg with a standard deviation of 10 kg. For the girls, the mean weight is 55 kg and the standard deviation is 15 kg. Find the number of boys and the combined standard deviation.*

Sol. Let $\bar{x}_1$ and $\bar{x}_2$ denotes the mean of boys and girls, σ_1 and σ_2 be their standard deviation respectively. Let $\bar{x}$ be the mean of all students.

Given $\bar{x}_1 = 70, \bar{x}_2 = 55$

$\sigma_1 = 10, \sigma_2 = 15$

Let n_1 = Number of boys, n_2 = Number of girls

such that $n_1 + n_2 = 150$ ...(1)

Using $\bar{x} = \dfrac{n_1\bar{x}_1 + n_2\bar{x}_2}{n_1 + n_2}$, we have $60 = \dfrac{70n_1 + 55n_2}{150}$

$\Rightarrow \quad 70n_1 + 55n_2 = 9000 \Rightarrow 14n_1 + 11n_2 = 1800$

$\Rightarrow \quad 14n_1 + 11(150 - n_1) = 1800 \Rightarrow 14n_1 + 1650 - 11n_1 = 1800$ | Using (1)

$\Rightarrow \quad 3n_1 = 1800 - 1650 = 150 \Rightarrow n_1 = 50$

$\therefore \quad n_2 = 150 - n_1 = 150 - 50 = 100$

Further, the combined standard deviation is given by

$$\sigma = \sqrt{\frac{n_1\sigma_1^2 + n_2\sigma_2^2 + n_1d_1^2 + n_2d_2^2}{n_1 + n_2}}$$

where σ_1^2 = variance of boys = 100, σ_2^2 = variance of girls = 225,

$d_1 = |\bar{x}_1 - \bar{x}| = |70 - 60| = 10, d_2 = |\bar{x}_2 - \bar{x}| = |55 - 60| = 5,$

σ = combined standard deviation

$$\sigma = \sqrt{\frac{50 \times 100 + 100 \times 225 + 50 \times 100 + 100 \times 25}{150}}$$

$$= \sqrt{\frac{5000 + 22500 + 5000 + 2500}{150}} = \sqrt{233.33} = 15.27 \text{ kg.}$$

Example 10. *The mean and standard deviation of a set of 100 observations were worked out as 40 and 5 respectively by a computer which by mistake took the value 50 in place of 40 for one observation. Find the correct mean and correct variance.*

Sol. Given, $\dfrac{\Sigma x}{100} = 40$

$\Rightarrow$ Incorrected $\Sigma x = 40 \times 100 = 4000$

Corrected value of Σx = Incorrected value of Σx – (Incorrected item) + (Corrected item)

$= 4000 - 50 + 40 = 3990$

$\therefore$ Corrected mean $= \dfrac{\text{Corrected } \Sigma x}{100} = \dfrac{3990}{100} = 39.90$

To find corrected value of variance

Given variance = 25 $\Rightarrow \dfrac{\Sigma x^2}{n} - (\bar{x})^2 = 25$

$\Rightarrow \quad \dfrac{\Sigma x^2}{100} - (40)^2 = 25 \Rightarrow \dfrac{\Sigma x^2}{100} = 25 + 1600 = 1625$

$\Rightarrow$ Incorrected $\Sigma x^2 = 1625 \times 100 = 162500$

$\therefore$ Corrected value of Σx^2

$= (\text{Incorrected value of } \Sigma x^2) - (\text{Incorrected item})^2 + (\text{Corrected item})^2$

$= 162500 - (50)^2 + (40)^2 = 162500 - 2500 + 1600$

$= 161600$

$$\therefore \quad \text{Corrected variance} = \frac{\text{Corrected } \Sigma x^2}{N} - (\text{Corrected } \bar{x})^2$$

$$= \frac{161600}{100} - (39.9)^2 = \frac{161600 - 159201}{100} = \frac{2399}{100} = 23.99.$$

Example 11. *The mean of 5 observations is 4.4 and the variance is 8.24. If three of the five observations are 1, 2 and 6. Find the other two.*

Sol. Let the required observations are x_1 and y_1.

Given mean of 5 observations = 4.4 $\Rightarrow \dfrac{1+2+6+x_1+y_1}{5} = 4.4$

$\Rightarrow \quad 9 + x_1 + y_1 = (4.4) \times 5 = 22$

$\Rightarrow \quad x_1 + y_1 = 22 - 9 = 13$ ...(1)

Also $\quad \sigma^2 = 8.24$

$\Rightarrow \quad \dfrac{\Sigma x^2}{n} - (\bar{x})^2 = 8.24 \quad \Rightarrow \quad \dfrac{\Sigma x^2}{5} - (4.4)^2 = 8.24$

$\Rightarrow \quad \dfrac{\Sigma x^2}{5} = 8.24 + (4.4)^2 \quad \Rightarrow \quad \Sigma x^2 = 41.2 + 96.8 = 138$

$\Rightarrow \quad 1^2 + 2^2 + 6^2 + x_1^2 + y_1^2 = 138$

$\Rightarrow \quad x_1^2 + y_1^2 = 138 - 41 = 97$ ...(2)

Consider $\quad (x_1 + y_1)^2 = x_1^2 + y_1^2 + 2x_1 y_1$

$\Rightarrow \quad 13^2 = 97 + 2x_1 y_1$ | Using (1) and (2)

$\Rightarrow \quad 2x_1 y_1 = 169 - 97 = 72$

$\Rightarrow \quad x_1 y_1 = 36$ ...(3)

Consider, $\quad (x_1 - y_1)^2 = x_1^2 + y_1^2 - 2x_1 y_1$

$= 97 - 2 \times 36 = 25$

$\Rightarrow \quad x_1 - y_1 = 5$ ...(4)

Adding (1) and (4), $\quad 2x_1 = 18 \Rightarrow x_1 = 9$

From (1), $\quad 9 + y_1 = 13 \Rightarrow y_1 = 4$

Hence the required observations are 9 and 4.

Example 12. *Mean and standard deviation of the following continuous series are 31 and 15.9 respectively. The distribution after taking step deviations is as follows :*

d	– 3	– 2	– 1	0	1	2	3
f	10	15	25	25	10	10	5

Determine the actual class intervals.

Sol. To find the actual classes, we first find the assumed mean and the class interval.

To find the class interval, consider the following table:

d	f	fd	fd^2
– 3	10	– 30	90
– 2	15	– 30	60
– 1	25	– 25	25
0	25	0	0
1	10	10	10
2	10	20	40
3	5	15	45
	$\Sigma f = 100 = N$	$\Sigma fd = -40$	$\Sigma fd^2 = 270$

Given standard deviation = 15.9 *i.e.*, $\sigma = 15.9$

$$\Rightarrow \quad \sqrt{\frac{\Sigma fd^2}{N} - \left(\frac{\Sigma fd}{N}\right)^2} \times h = 15.9$$

$$\Rightarrow \quad \sqrt{\frac{270}{100} - \left(\frac{-40}{100}\right)^2} \times h = 15.9$$

$$\Rightarrow \quad \sqrt{2.7 - 0.16} \times h = 15.9 \Rightarrow h = \frac{15.9}{1.59} = 10$$

To find the assumed mean. Given mean = 31

$$\Rightarrow \quad A + h\frac{\Sigma fd}{\Sigma f} = 31 \Rightarrow A + 10 \times \left(\frac{-40}{100}\right) = 31$$

$$\Rightarrow \quad A = 31 + 4 = 35$$

i.e., the class corresponds to this value would be 30–40. Thus the actual class group is as below :

Classes	*Frequency*
0–10	10
10–20	15
20–30	25
30–40	25
40–50	10
50–60	10
60–70	5

6.31. RELATION BETWEEN MEASURES OF DISPERSION

It has been observed that in frequency distribution, the following relation hold :

(*i*) **M.D.** $= \frac{4}{5}$ **S.D** (*ii*) **Q.D.** $= \frac{2}{3}$ **S.D.**

Example. *The mean and standard deviation of normal distribution are 60 and 5 respectively. Find the interquartile range and the mean deviation of the distribution.*

Sol. We know $\quad Q.D. = \frac{2}{3} S.D. \quad ...(1)$

Given $\quad \text{mean} = 60, \sigma = 5$

From (1), $\quad Q.D. = \frac{2}{3} \times 5 = \frac{10}{3} \Rightarrow \frac{Q_3 - Q_1}{2} = \frac{10}{3}$

$\Rightarrow \quad Q_3 - Q_1 = \frac{20}{3} = 6.67$

Hence interquartile range = 6.67.

6.32. MERITS OF S.D.

1. It is simple to understand.
2. It is well defined.
3. In the calculation of S.D., the signs of deviations of items, are also taken into account.
4. It is based on all the items.
5. It is capable of further algebraic treatment.
6. It has sampling stability.
7. It is very useful in the study of "Tests of Significance".

6.33. DEMERITS OF S.D.

1. It is not easy to calculate.
2. It is unduly affected by the extreme items, because the squares of deviations of extreme items would be either extremely low or extremely high.

6.34. DIFFERENCE BETWEEN MEAN DEVIATION AND STANDARD DEVIATION

M.D	*S.D*
In calculating mean deviation, algebraic signs are ignored.	In calculating standard deviation, signs are taken into account.
It can be computed from median as well as from mean.	It can be computed only from mean.

6.35. SIGNIFICANCE OF VARIANCE AND STANDARD DEVIATION

The variance and its square root *i.e.,* standard deviation are measures of variability in a population. The smaller the value of variance, the lesser is the variability or greater the uniformity in the population.

6.36. STANDARD DEVIATION IS BETTER THAN MEAN DEVIATION

(P.T.U. M.B.A. May, 2011)

In mean deviation, the algebraic signs are ignored while taking the deviations of the items. But, this is mathematically wrong and makes the method non-algebraic. In standard deviation, the signs of deviation are not ignored and the net sum of the deviations will be zero if the reference point is the mean or approximately zero if the reference point is median.

Also, mean deviation is not capable of further algebraic treatment, but standard deviation is capable of further algebraic treatment. Hence, standard deviation is a better measure as compared to mean deviation.

6.37. CASE STUDIES

Case Study I. Himgiri Hospital

The hospital recently has installed a new computer based, interactive, hospital communication system. The system fully integrates the communication activities of admitting, nursing, physician services, laboratory, radiology, pharmacy and assorted medication services, business office, medical records, central supply, dietary services, emergency and outpatient.

In special training sessions with physicians who were to use the system, the director of the hospital observed that one of the key variables affecting the physicians was the 'waiting time' they experienced between inputting data or information requests at a video matrix terminal and the response by the main-frame computer. One of the doctors who is a cardiologist was particularly vocal in his complaints about the system: 'Look, I can't wait all day for a machine. I need information that is accurate and in a form I can use. You can't expect me to also spend time learning how to use your machine–I have enough to do.'

To the physicians, sittings at a terminal and waiting for the computer to respond was simply 'intolerable'. The director of the hospital was sympathetic to the physicians' attitude and had negotiated a contract with the computer hardware vendor specifying that the average waiting time not to exceed 10 seconds.

After the system has been operating nearly 15 months, the director conducted a full-scale evaluation. In general, all aspects of the system looked either good or excellent with the exception that only about 60 percent of the physicians were actually using it, and over the past several months, there had been a number of complaints about excessive waiting times.

The director was considering the possibility of holding a new series of training sessions for the physicians, but he decided to first review the data collected on actual waiting times experienced by the physicians. These sets of data were available: those collected during the original training session in January, 2003 and those collected by staff analysts in March, 2004 and May, 2004. These waiting-time (in seconds) data are given below:

January 2003			*March 2004*				*May 2004*			
9	8	5	8	6	14	12	7	7	15	16
6	6	7	12	8	7	10	13	7	17	15
9	9	8	12	10			14	7		
7										

Questions for Discussion: *1. Calculate the mean waiting time for each of the three sets of data. Do the mean waiting times appear to be in conformance with the established standard?*

2. Calculate the median waiting times for each of the three sets of data. What general conclusion can you draw?

3. Determine the range and standard deviation for each of the three sets of data and consider the implications of the results.

Sol. We first arrange the given data in the following table.

For series I, take $d_i = x_i - 7.4$

For series II, take $d_i = x_i - 9.9$

For series III, take $d_i = x_i - 11.8$

Series 1	$d_i = x_i - 7.4$	d_i^2	*Series 2*	$d_i = x_i - 9.9$	d_i^2	*Series 3*	$d_i = x_i - 11.8$	d_i^2
9	1.6	2.56	8	–1.9	3.61	7	–4.8	23.04
6	–1.4	1.96	12	2.1	4.41	13	1.2	1.44
9	1.6	2.56	12	2.1	4.41	14	2.2	4.84
7	–0.4	0.16	6	–3.9	15.21	7	–4.8	23.04
8	0.6	0.36	8	–1.9	3.61	7	–4.8	23.04
6	–1.4	1.96	10	0.1	0.01	7	–4.8	23.04
9	1.6	2.56	14	4.1	16.81	15	3.2	10.24
5	–2.4	5.76	7	–2.9	8.41	17	5.2	27.04
7	–0.4	0.16	12	2.1	4.41	16	4.2	17.64
8	0.6	0.36	10	0.1	0.01	15	3.2	10.24
Total		18.4			60.9			163.6

1. **Calculation of Mean Waiting Time:** The mean waiting time of series I, II and III are calculated below.

Series I. Mean waiting time for January, 2003

$$= \frac{9+6+9+7+8+6+9+5+7+8}{10} = 7.4$$

Series II. Mean waiting time for March, 2003

$$= \frac{8+12+12+6+8+10+14+7+12+10}{10} = 9.9$$

Series III. Mean waiting time for May, 2004

$$= \frac{7+13+14+7+7+7+15+17+16+15}{10} = 11.8$$

Now, the mean waiting times as set by the computer hardware vendor should not exceed 10 seconds. Therefore, the mean waiting time for the series III (for March, 2004) does not appear in conformance with the established standards.

2. Calculation of Median Waiting Time

Series I. The number of observations is 10

$$\therefore \quad \text{Median waiting time} = \frac{\left(\frac{10}{2}\right)^{\text{th}} + \left(\frac{10}{2}+1\right)^{\text{th}}}{2} \text{ observation}$$

$$= \frac{5^{\text{th}} + 6^{\text{th}}}{2} \text{ observation} = \frac{7+8}{2} = \frac{15}{2} = 7.5$$

Series II. Median waiting time

$$= \frac{5^{th} + 6^{th}}{2} \text{ observation} = \frac{10 + 10}{2} = 10$$

Series III. Median waiting time

$$= \frac{5^{th} + 6^{th}}{2} \text{ observation} = \frac{13 + 14}{2} = \frac{27}{2} = 13.5$$

Conclusion. Since median is the middles most item, therefore,

For Series I. The waiting time of 5 physicians was less than or equal to 7.5 (As 6 items lie above the median value) and of 5 physicians was greater than 7.5 second.

For Series II. The waiting time of 6 physicians was less than or equal to 10 and of 4 physicians was greater than 10.

For Series III. The waiting time of 5 physicians was less than or equal to 13.5 and of 5 physicians was greater than 13.5.

Hence, a total of 16 out of 30 physicians (10 from series I and 6 from series II) had their waiting time less than the standard waiting time established by the director

3. Range. For series I, range $= 9 - 5 = 4$

For series II, range $= 14 - 6 = 8$

Also, For series III, range $= 17 - 7 = 10$

The series I has smallest range *i.e.,* 4 where as the series III has highest range *i.e.,* 10.

It means the waiting time of the physicians of series I are less dispersed and their mean waiting time is the most typical. (A series with smaller range has less dispersion and the average of that distribution is more typical).

Also, the waiting time of the physicians of series III are more dispersed and their mean waiting time is less typical.

We now find standard deviation for each series.

$$\text{S.D. of series I} = \sqrt{\frac{\Sigma d_i^2}{n}} = \sqrt{\frac{18.4}{10}} = \sqrt{1.84} = 1.357$$

$$\text{S.D. of series II} = \sqrt{\frac{\Sigma d_i^2}{n}} = \sqrt{\frac{60.9}{10}} = \sqrt{6.09} = 2.468$$

$$\text{S.D. of series III} = \sqrt{\frac{\Sigma d_i^2}{n}} = \sqrt{\frac{163.6}{10}} = \sqrt{16.36} = 4.045$$

To interpret the result, we find

$$\text{C.V. of series I} = \frac{\sigma}{\bar{x}} \times 100 = \frac{1.357}{7.4} \times 100 = 18.33$$

$$\text{C.V. of series II} = \frac{\sigma}{\bar{x}} \times 100 = \frac{2.468}{9.9} \times 100 = 24.92$$

$$\text{C.V. of series III} = \frac{\sigma}{\bar{x}} \times 100 = \frac{4.045}{11.8} \times 100 = 34.27$$

Conclusion. The coefficient of variation of series I is less than of series II and series III. The waiting time of the physicians of series I is more consistent or we can say the fluctuations in waiting time of series III is much higher than of series I and series II.

Case study II. ABC bank: The number of cheques cashed each day at the five branches of a bank during the past month has the following frequency distribution:

Number of cheques	*Frequency*
0– 199	10
200–399	13
400–599	17
600–799	42
800–999	18

The general manager, operations, for the bank, knows that a standard deviation in cheque cashing of more than 200 checks per day creates staffing problem at the branches because of the uneven workload.

Questions For Discussion

(i) Find the average no. of cheques cashed per day.

(ii) Should the manager worry about staffing next month?

Sol. Hint: (*i*) mean no. of cheques = 590 cheques/day

(*ii*) s.d. = 242.48 cheques/day > 200, hence the manager should worry.

Case Study III. Air Charter Company

An air-charter company has been requested to quote a realistic turn-round time for a contract to handle certain imports and exports of a fragile nature.

The contract manager has provided the management accountant with the following analysis of turn-round times for similar goods over a given twelve-monthly period.

Turn-round Time (in hours)	*Frequency*
Less than 2	25
2 and < 4	36
4 and < 6	66
6 and < 8	47
8 and < 10	26
10 and < 12	18
12 and < 14	2

Questions For Discussion: *As a managing directar of the company, you are required to (a) Calculate mean and standard deviation.*

(b) Advise the contract manager about the turn-round time to be quoted using.

(i) mean plus one standard deviation;

(ii) mean plus two standard deviations.

Sol. Hint: (*a*) mean = 5.68, s.d. = 2.88

(*b*) $\mu + \sigma = 5.68 + 2.88 = 8.56$ hrs

The chance of 8.56 hrs turn round time cover app. 84%

The chance of 11.44 hrs turn round time cover app. 97.7%

Case study IV. ABC Stores. ABC stores, a wholesaler, was contemplating becoming the supplier to three retailers, but inventory shortages have forced him to select only one. ABC's credit manager is evaluating the credit record of these three retailers. Over the past 5 years, these retailer's accounts receivable have been outstanding for the following average number of days. The credit manager feels that consistency, in addition to lowest average, is important. Based on relative dispersion, which retailer would make the best customer?

	Average number of days				
Lee:	62.60	61.80	63.40	63.00	61.70
Forest:	62.50	61.90	63.80	63.00	61.70
Devis:	62.00	61.90	63.00	63.90	61.50

Questions For Discussion: *As an inventory manager, you are required to find*

(i) mean and s.d. of each retailer

(ii) which retailer would you like to choose the best customer.

Sol. Hint: (*i*) Lee: mean = 62.42, s.d. = 0.7497

Forest: mean = 62.18, s.d. = 0.9257

Davis: mean = 62.46, s.d. = 0.9762

(*ii*) Lee (C.V. of Lee is highest)

TEST YOUR KNOWLEDGE 6.4

1. Find the mean and standard deviation for the following data using short-cut method.

x	60	61	62	63	64	65	66	67	68
f	2	1	12	29	25	12	10	4	5

2. The scores of 48 children in an intelligence test are shown in the frequency table below :

Score	71	76	79	83	86	89	92	97	101	103	107	110	114
Frequency	4	3	4	5	6	5	4	4	3	3	3	2	2

Calculate the variance σ^2 and find out the percentage of childern whose scores lie between $\bar{x} - \sigma$ and $\bar{x} + \sigma$.

3. The diameters of circles (in mm) drawn in a design are given below :

Diameter (in mm)	33–36	37–40	41–44	45–48	49–52
No. of Circles	15	17	21	22	25

Calculate the standard deviation and mean diameter of the circles.

4. If the values of the mean and S.D. of the following frequency distribution (using step deviation method) are 135.3 and 9.6 respectively. Find the actual class limits.

5. Find the mean, variance and standard deviation using short-cutmethod :

Class interval	10–20	20–30	30–40	40–50	50–60	60–70	70–80	80–90	90–100
Frequency	3	4	7	7	15	9	6	6	3

6. Calculate mean, standard deviation and its coefficient from the following data :

Wage up to (in ₹)	10	20	30	40	50	60	70	80
No. of persons	12	30	65	107	157	202	220	230

7. (*a*) Goals scored by two teams in a football season were as follows :

No. of goals scored in a match	*No. of matches*	
	Team A	*Team B*
0	15	20
1	10	10
2	07	05
3	05	04
4	03	02
5	02	01
Total	42	42

Calculate coefficient of variation and state which team is more consistent.

(*b*) Scores obtained by two batsmen in 10 matches are as follows:

A	30	44	66	62	60	34	80	46	20	38
B	34	46	70	38	55	48	60	34	45	30

Determine who is the most consistent batsman. (*P.T.U., M.B.A. May 2008*)

8. From the data given below, state which series is more variable :

Variable	10–20	20–30	30–40	40–50	50–60	60–70
Group A	10	18	32	22	40	18
Group B	18	22	40	18	32	10

9. The following table gives the distribution of wages in the two branches of an industrial concern. Find out which branch has greater variability in wages relating to the average wage :

Monthly wage (in ₹)	*No. of workers*	
	Branch A	*Branch B*
50–100	20	8
100–150	35	17
150–200	42	43
200–250	45	20
250–300	58	12
Total	200	100

10. From the data given below, state which group is more variable :

Class	10–20	20–30	30–40	40–50	50–60	60–70	70–80
Group A (freq.)	9	17	32	23	40	18	1
Group B (freq.)	18	22	40	18	32	8	2

11. For a group of 50 male workers, the mean and standard deviation of their weekly wages are ₹ 63 and ₹ 9 respectively. For a group of 40 female workers, these measures are respectively ₹ 54 and ₹ 6. Find the S.D. for the combined group of workers.

12. Calculate the S.D. of the combined group of 500 items from the following data :

	Group I	*Group II*	*Group III*
No. of items	100	150	250
A.M.	50	55	60
Variance	100	121	144

13. The first of two sub-groups has 100 items with mean 15 and standard deviation 3. If the whole group has 250 items with mean 15.6 and standard deviation 3.6, find the standard deviation of the second sub-group.

14. The arithmetic mean and standard deviation of a series of 20 items were calculated by a student as 20 and 5 respectively. But while calculating, an item 13 was misread as 30. Find the correct arithmetic mean and standard deviation.

15. The scores of two batsmen A and B in 10 innings during a certain session are as below :

A	32	28	47	63	71	39	10	60	96	14
B	19	31	48	53	67	90	10	62	40	80

Find which of the two batsmen A or B, is more consistent in scoring.

16. Given the daily wages paid to workers in two factories x and y, find out:

(*i*) which factory pays higher wages?

(*ii*) which factory has a more consistent wage structure?

Daily wages (₹)	*No. of workers*	
	Factory x	*Factory y*
120–130	15	25
130–140	30	40
140–150	44	60
150–160	60	35
160–170	30	12
170–180	14	15
180–190	7	5

(*P.T.U. M.B.A. May 2011*)

Answers

1. 64, 1.69 **2.** 140.70, 64.58% **3.** 5.55 mm, 43.5 mm

4.

Class limits	*Frequency*
109.5–115.5	2
115.5–121.5	5
121.5–127.5	8
127.5–133.5	18
133.5–139.5	22
139.5–145.5	13
145.5–151.5	8
151.5–157.5	4

5. 56, 422.33, 20.55 **6.** ₹ 40.52, ₹ 17.41, 0.43

7. (*a*) C.V. for $A = 102.13\%$; C.V. for $B = 124.54\%$; A is more consistent.

(*b*) C.V. for $A = 36.75$; C.V. for $B = 26.30$; The batsman B is more consistent.

8. C.V. for $A = 33.85\%$, C.V. for $B = 38.24\%$, Group B is more variable.

9. C.V. for $A = 33.90\%$, C.V. for $B = 29.81\%$; Variability is more in branch A.

10. C.V. for $A = 33.30\%$; C.V. for $B = 38.86\%$; Group B is more variable.

11. ₹ 59, ₹ 9. **12.** 11.98. **13.** 4 **14.** 19.15, 4.66.

15. C.V. for A = 55.42%, C.V. for B = 48.86% ; The batsman B is more consistent.

16. (*i*) Factory x pays higher wages since the mean wages for the factory x is larger than that of y

(*ii*) The wages of factory y are more consistent since the C.V. for x is less than that of y.

7 Moments

7.1. INTRODUCTION

The term "moment" in statistics gives the same meaning as in statics. In statics, the 'moment' refers to the tendency of a force to rotate a body about a point. In statistics, we define the 'moment' as below:

7.2. MOMENTS ABOUT AN ARBITRARY POINT

Let $x: \quad x_1 \quad x_2 \quad x_3 \quad ...... \quad x_n$

$f: \quad f_1 \quad f_2 \quad f_3 \quad ..... \quad f_n$, be a frequency distribution.

Then r^{th} moment μ_r' about the point $x = A$ is defined by

$$\mu_r' = \frac{1}{N}\sum_{i=1}^{n} f_i (x_i - A)^r, \text{ where } N = \sum_{i=1}^{n} f_i;\ r = 0, 1, 2, ...$$

Particular cases. Put $r = 0, 1, 2, 3, 4$, in above, we get

$$\mu_0' = \frac{1}{N}\sum_{i=1}^{n} f_i (x_i - A)^0 = \frac{1}{N}\sum_{i=1}^{n} f_i = \frac{N}{N} = 1$$

$$\Rightarrow \qquad \boxed{\mu_0' = 1}$$

Also $$\mu_1' = \frac{1}{N}\sum_{i=1}^{n} f_i (x_i - A)^1 = \frac{1}{N}\sum_{i=1}^{n} (f_i x_i - f_i A)$$

$$= \frac{1}{N}\sum_{i=1}^{n} f_i x_i - \frac{A}{N}\sum_{i=1}^{n} f_i = \overline{X} - \frac{A}{N} \times N = \overline{X} - A$$

$$\Rightarrow \qquad \boxed{\mu_1' = \overline{X} - A}$$

Similarly, $$\mu_2' = \frac{1}{N}\sum_{i=1}^{n} f_i (x_i - A)^2$$

$$\mu_3' = \frac{1}{N}\sum_{i=1}^{n} f_i (x_i - A)^3$$

$$\mu_4' = \frac{1}{N}\sum_{i=1}^{n} f_i (x_i - A)^4$$

7.3. MOMENTS ABOUT THE ORIGIN

Let $x: \; x_1 \quad x_2 \quad x_3 \quad ..... \quad x_n$

$f: \; f_1 \quad f_2 \quad f_3 \quad ...... \quad f_n,$ be a frequency distribution.

Then r^{th} moment about the origin, *i.e.*, about the point $x = 0$, is defined as

$$v_r = \frac{1}{N}\sum_{i=1}^{n} f_i x_i^r, \text{ where } N = \sum_{i=1}^{n} f_i, \; r = 0, 1, 2, ...$$

Particular cases. Put $r = 0, 1, 2, 3, 4$, in above, we get

$$v_0 = \frac{1}{N}\sum_{i=1}^{n} f_i x_i^0 = \frac{1}{N}\sum_{i=1}^{n} f_i = \frac{N}{N} = 1$$

$\Rightarrow \qquad v_0 = 1$

For $r = 1$, $\qquad v_1 = \frac{1}{N}\sum_{i=1}^{n} f_i x_i = \overline{X}$

Also $\qquad v_2 = \frac{1}{N}\sum_{i=1}^{n} f_i x_i^2$

$$v_3 = \frac{1}{N}\sum_{i=1}^{n} f_i x_i^3$$

$$v_4 = \frac{1}{N}\sum_{i=1}^{n} f_i x_i^4$$

or $\qquad v_1 = \mu_1' + A \qquad\qquad | \; \mu_1' = \overline{X} - A$

$$v_2 = \frac{1}{N}\sum_{i=1}^{n} f_i x_i^2 = \frac{1}{N}\sum_{i=1}^{n} f_i (x_i - \overline{X} + \overline{X})^2$$

$$= \frac{1}{N}\sum_{i=1}^{n} f_i (x_i - \overline{X})^2 + \frac{1}{N}\sum_{i=1}^{n} f_i \overline{X}^2 + \frac{2}{N}\sum_{i=1}^{n} f_i (x_i - \overline{X})\overline{X}$$

$$= \mu_2 + \overline{X}^2\left(\frac{1}{N}\sum_{i=1}^{n} f_i\right) + 0 = \mu_2 + \overline{X}^2$$

$\Rightarrow \qquad v_2 = \mu_2 + v_1^2 \qquad\qquad \left| \; \mu_1 = \frac{1}{N}\sum_{i=1}^{n} f_i (x_i - \overline{X}) = 0 \right.$

Similarly, $\qquad v_3 = \mu_3 + 3v_2 v_1 - 2v_1^3$

$$v_4 = \mu_4 + 4v_3 v_1 - 6v_2 v_1^2 + 3v_1^4 \text{ and so on}$$

7.4. CENTRAL MOMENTS (MOMENTS ABOUT MEAN)

Let $x: \; x_1 \quad x_2 \quad ...... \quad x_n$

$f: \; f_1 \quad f_2 \quad ...... \quad f_n,$ be a frequency distribution.

Then r^{th} moments μ_r about the mean $\overline{X}$, is defined by

$$\mu_r = \frac{1}{N}\sum_{i=1}^{n} f_i (x_i - \overline{X})^r, \text{ where } N = \sum_{i=1}^{n} f_i \, ; r = 0, 1, 2, ... \text{ and } \overline{X} = \frac{1}{N}\sum_{i=1}^{n} f_i \, x_i$$

Particular cases. Put $r = 0, 1, 2, 3, 4$, in above we get

$$\mu_0 = \frac{1}{N}\sum_{i=1}^{n} f_i (x_i - \overline{X})^0 = \frac{1}{N}\sum_{i=1}^{n} f_i = \frac{N}{N} = 1$$

$\Rightarrow$ $\mu_0 = 1$

For $r = 1$,

$$\mu_1 = \frac{1}{N}\sum_{i=1}^{n} f_i (x_i - \overline{X})^1 = \frac{1}{N}\sum_{i=1}^{n} f_i (x_i - \overline{X})$$

$$= \frac{1}{N}\sum_{i=1}^{n} f_i x_i - \frac{1}{N}\sum_{i=1}^{n} f_i \overline{X}$$

$$= \frac{1}{N}\sum_{i=1}^{n} f_i x_i - \overline{X}\left(\frac{1}{N}\cdot\sum_{i=1}^{n} f_i\right)$$

$$= \overline{X} - \overline{X} = 0 \qquad \Big| \sum_{i=1}^{n} f_i = N$$

$\Rightarrow$ $\mu_1 = 0$

Also, $$\mu_2 = \frac{1}{N}\sum_{i=1}^{n} f_i (x_i - \overline{X})^2 = \text{Variance (X)} = \sigma^2$$

Further, $$\mu_3 = \frac{1}{N}\sum_{i=1}^{n} f_i (x_i - \overline{X})^3$$

$$\mu_4 = \frac{1}{N}\sum_{i=1}^{n} f_i (x_i - \overline{X})^4 \text{ and so on}$$

Remarks. (*i*) The moments about the mean are known as central moments.

(*ii*) The results $\mu_0 = 1$, $\mu_1 = 0$ and $\mu_2 = \sigma^2$, are of fundamental importance and should be committed to memory.

(*iii*) In case of frequency distribution with class intervals, the values of X are the mid-points of the class-intervals.

7.5. RELATION BETWEEN MOMENTS ABOUT MEAN IN TERMS OF MOMENTS ABOUT ANY POINT AND VICE-VERSA

By definition, $\mu_r' = \frac{1}{N}\Sigma f(x - A)^r$, where A is any point

$$= \frac{1}{N}\Sigma fd^r, \text{ where } d = x - A \qquad \ldots(1)$$

Putting $r = 1$, $\mu_1' = \frac{1}{N}\Sigma fd$

$\therefore$ A.M. $M = A + \frac{1}{N}\Sigma fd = A + \mu_1'$

or $\mu_1' = M - A \qquad \ldots(2)$

Now $\mu_r = \frac{1}{N}\Sigma f(x - M)^r$

$$= \frac{1}{N}\Sigma f(x - A + A - M)^r = \frac{1}{N}\Sigma f(d - \mu_1')^r \qquad | \text{ Using (2)}$$

$$= \frac{1}{N} \Sigma f [d^r - {}^rC_1 d^{r-1}\mu_1' + {}^rC_2 d^{r-2}\mu_1'^2 - {}^rC_3 d^{r-3} \mu_1'^3 + \ldots\ldots + (-1)^r . \mu_1'^r]$$

$$= \frac{1}{N} \Sigma fd^r - {}^rC_1\mu_1' . \frac{1}{N} \Sigma fd^{r-1} + {}^rC_2\mu_1'^2 \frac{1}{N} \Sigma fd^{r-2}$$

$$- {}^rC_3\mu'^3 \frac{1}{N} \Sigma fd^{r-3} + \ldots\ldots + (-1)^r\mu_1'^r . \frac{1}{N} \Sigma f$$

$$= \mu_r' - {}^rC_1\mu_{r-1}' \mu_1' + {}^rC_2\mu_{r-2}' \mu_1'^2 - {}^rC_3\mu_{r-3}' \mu_1'^3 + \ldots\ldots + (-1)^r\mu_1'^r$$

| Using (1)

In particular, putting $r = 2, 3, 4$, we get

$$\mu_2 = \mu_2' - 2\mu_1'^2 + \mu_0' \mu_1'^2 = \mu_2' - \mu_1'^2 \qquad | \because \mu_0' = 1$$

$$\mu_3 = \mu_3' - 3\mu_2' \mu_1' + 3\mu_1'^3 - \mu_0' \mu_1'^3 = \mu_3' - 3\mu_2' \mu_1' + 2\mu_1'^3$$

$$\mu_4 = \mu_4' - 4\mu_3' \mu_1' + 6\mu_2' \mu_1'^2 - 4\mu_1' \mu_1'^3 + \mu_0' \mu_1'^4$$

$$= \mu_4' - 4\mu_3' \mu_1' + 6\mu_2' \mu_1'^2 - 3\mu_1'^4$$

Hence

$$\boldsymbol{\mu_1 = 0}$$

$$\boldsymbol{\mu_2 = \mu_2' - \mu_1'^2}$$

$$\boldsymbol{\mu_3 = \mu_3' - 3\mu_2' \mu_1' + 2\mu_1'^3} \qquad (\mu_1' = M - A)$$

$$\boldsymbol{\mu_4 = \mu_4' - 4\mu_3' \mu_1' + 6\mu_2' \mu_1'^2 - 3\mu_1'^4}$$

By using these formulae, we can find moments about mean, when moments about any point are given.

Conversely, $\mu_r = \frac{1}{N} \Sigma f(x - M)^r = \frac{1}{N} \Sigma fd^r$, where $d = x - M$ ...(3)

Now $\mu_r' = \frac{1}{N} \Sigma f(x - A)^r = \frac{1}{N} \Sigma f(x - M + M - A)^r = \frac{1}{N} \Sigma f(d + \mu_1')^r$ | Using (2)

$$= \frac{1}{N} \Sigma f(d^r + {}^rC_1 d^{r-1} \mu_1' + {}^rC_2 d^{r-2} \mu_1'^2 + {}^rC_3 d^{r-3} \mu_1'^3 + \ldots\ldots + \mu_1'^r)$$

$$= \frac{1}{N} \Sigma fd^r + {}^rC_1\mu_1' . \frac{1}{N} \Sigma fd^{r-1} + {}^rC_2 \mu_1'^2 \frac{1}{N} \Sigma fd^{r-2} + \ldots\ldots + \mu_1'^r . \frac{1}{N} \Sigma f$$

$$= \mu_r + {}^rC_1\mu_{r-1} \mu_1' + {}^rC_2\mu_{r-2} \mu_1'^2 + \ldots\ldots + \mu_1'^r$$

| Using (3)

In particular, putting $r = 2, 3, 4$ and noting that $\mu_1 = 0$, $\mu_0 = 1$, we get

$$\boldsymbol{\mu_2' = \mu_2 + 2\mu_1\mu_1' + \mu_0 \mu_1'^2 = \mu_2 + \mu_1'^2}$$

$$\boldsymbol{\mu_3' = \mu_3 + 3\mu_2\mu_1' + 3\mu_1\mu_1'^2 + \mu_0\mu_1'^3 = \mu_3 + 3\mu_2\mu_1' + \mu_1'^3}$$

$$\boldsymbol{\mu_4' = \mu_4 + 4\mu_3\mu_1' + 6\mu_2\mu_1'^2 + 4\mu_1\mu_1'^3 + \mu_0\mu_1'^4 = \mu_4 + 4\mu_3\mu_1' + 6\mu_2\mu_1'^2 + \mu_1'^4.}$$

By using these formulae, we can find moments about any point, when moments about mean are given.

7.6. EFFECT OF CHANGE OF ORIGIN AND SCALE ON MOMENTS

Let $u = \frac{x - A}{h}$, *i.e.*, $x = A + hu$

$\therefore$ $\bar{x} = A + h\bar{u}$, where bar denotes the mean of the respective variable.

$\therefore$ $x - \bar{x} = h(u - \bar{u})$

$$\mu_r' = \frac{1}{N} \Sigma f(x - A)^r = \frac{1}{N} \Sigma fh^r u^r = h^r . \frac{1}{N} \Sigma fu^r$$

Also $$\mu_r = \frac{1}{N}\Sigma f(x-\bar{x})^r = \frac{1}{N}\Sigma fh^r(u-\bar{u})^r = h^r \cdot \frac{1}{N}\Sigma f(u-\bar{u})^r$$

Hence, the rth moment of the variable x is h^r times the corresponding moment of the variable u.

7.7. SHEPPARD'S CORRECTIONS FOR MOMENTS

In the case of class intervals we assume that the frequencies are concentrated at mid-points of class intervals. Since this assumption is not true in general, some error is likely to creep into the calculation of moments. W.F. Sheppard gave the following formulae by which these errors may be corrected :

$$\mu_2 \text{ (corrected)} = \mu_2 - \frac{1}{12}h^2 ; \quad \mu_3 \text{ (corrected)} = \mu_3$$

$$\mu_4 \text{ (corrected)} = \mu_4 - \frac{1}{2}h^2\mu_2 + \frac{7}{240}h^4,$$ where h is the width of class intervals.

7.8. CHARLIER'S CHECK

To check the accuracy in the calculation of first four moments, we often use the following identities known as *Charlier checks* :

$$\Sigma f(x+1) = \Sigma fx + \Sigma f = \Sigma fx + N$$
$$\Sigma f(x+1)^2 = \Sigma fx^2 + 2\Sigma fx + N$$
$$\Sigma f(x+1)^3 = \Sigma fx^3 + 3\Sigma fx^2 + 3\Sigma fx + N$$
$$\Sigma f(x+1)^4 = \Sigma fx^4 + 4\Sigma fx^3 + 6\Sigma fx^2 + 4\Sigma fx + N.$$

7.9. PEARSON'S β AND γ CO-EFFICIENTS

Karl Pearson defined the following four co-efficients based upon the first four moments about mean.

$$\beta_1 = \frac{\mu_3^2}{\mu_2^3}, \gamma_1 = +\sqrt{\beta_1}; \qquad \beta_2 = \frac{\mu_4}{\mu_2^2}, \gamma_2 = \beta_2 - 3$$

These co-efficients are independent of units of measurement and therefore are pure numbers.

Based upon moments, co-efficient of skewness is $S_k = \dfrac{\sqrt{\beta_1}(\beta_2+3)}{2(5\beta_2 - 6\beta_1 - 9)}$

ILLUSTRATIVE EXAMPLES

Example 1. *The first three moments of a distribution about the value 2 of the variable are 1, 16 and –40. Show that mean = 3, variance = 15 and $\mu_3 = -86$.*

Sol. Let x_i/f_i ; $i = 1, 2, 3, \ldots, n$, be the given frequency distribution. Let μ_1', μ_2', μ_3' be the given moments about the point $x = 2$.

Then, as per given $\mu_1' = 1, \mu_2' = 16$

$\mu_3' = -40$

But $\mu_1' = \bar{X} - A$. Here, $A = 2$

$\therefore \quad 1 = \bar{X} - 2 \Rightarrow \bar{X} = 3$

Also, to find variance, we find μ_2

Now $\mu_2 = \mu_2' - \mu_1'^2 = 16 - 1 = 15$

$\Rightarrow$ variance = 15

Lastly $\mu_3 = \mu_3' - 3\mu_2' \mu_1' + 2\mu_1'^3 = -40 - 48 + 2 = -86.$

Example 2. *The first four moments of a distribution about $x = 2$ are 1, 2.5, 5.5 and 16. Calculate the first four moments about the mean and about zero.*

Sol. Let x_i/f_i ; $i = 1, 2, ..., n$ be the given frequency distribution. Let $\mu_1', \mu_2', \mu_3', \mu_4'$ be the first four moments about $x = 2$,

Then, as per given, $\mu_1' = 1, \mu_2' = 2.5$

$\mu_3' = 5.5, \mu_4' = 16, A = 2$

To find the first four moments about mean, *i.e.*, To find $\mu_1, \mu_2, \mu_3, \mu_4$.

By def. $\mu_1 = 0$

$$\mu_2 = \mu_2' - \mu_1'^2 = 2.5 - 1 = 1.5$$

$$\mu_3 = \mu_3' - 3\mu_2' + 2\mu_1'^3 = 5.5 - 3\ (2.5) + 2\ (1) = 5.5 - 7.5 + 2 = 0$$

$$\mu_4 = \mu_4' - 4\mu_3' \mu_1' + 6\mu_2' \mu_1' - 3\mu_1'^4$$

$$= 16 - 4 \times 5.5 \times 1 + 6 \times 2.5 \times 1 - 3 \times 1$$

$$= 16 - 22 + 15 - 3 = 6$$

Hence, $\mu_1 = 0, \mu_2 = 1.5, \mu_3 = 0, \mu_4 = 6$

Now to find the moments about $x = 0$. Let v_1, v_2, v_3, v_4 be the required moments about zero.

Then $v_1 = \mu_1' + A = 1 + 2 = 3$

$$v_2 = \mu_2 + v_1^2 = 1.5 + 9 = 10.5$$

$$v_3 = \mu_3 + 3v_2 v_1 - 2v_1^3 = 0 + 3 \times 10.5 \times 3 - 2 \times 3^3 = 40.5$$

$$v_4 = \mu_4 + 4v_3 v_1 - 6v_2 v_1^2 + 3v_1^4$$

$$= 6 + 4 \times 40.5 \times 3 - 6 \times 10.5 \times 9 + 3 \times 81 = 168.$$

Example 3. *The first four moments of a distribution about the value 4 of the variable are – 1.5, 17, – 30 and 108. Find the moments about mean, β_1 and β_2.*

Sol. Let $\mu_1', \mu_2', \mu_3', \mu_4'$ be the first four moments of the given distribution, then

$$A = 4, \mu_1' = -1.5, \mu_2' = 17, \mu_3' = -30, \mu_4' = 1.8$$

Let $\mu_1, \mu_2, \mu_3, \mu_4$ be the first four moments about the mean, then by def., $\mu_1 = 0$ (True for every distribution).

$$\mu_2 = \mu_2' - \mu_1'^2 = 17 - (-1.5)^2$$

$$= 17 - 2.25 = 14.75$$

$$\mu_3 = \mu_3' - 3\mu_2' \mu_1' + 2\mu_1'^3$$

$$= -30 - 3 \times 17 \times 1.5 + 2 \times (1.5)^3$$

$$= -30 - 76.5 - 6.75 = -113.25$$

Also $\mu_4 = \mu_4' - 4\mu_3' \mu_1' + 6\mu_2' \mu_1'^2 - 3\mu_1'^4$

$$= 108 - 4 \times (-30) \times (-1.5) + 6 \times 17 \times (-1.5)^2 - 3 \times (-1.5)^4$$

$$= 108 - 180 + 229.5 - 15.1875 = 142.3125$$

Lastly, $$\beta_1 = \frac{\mu_3^2}{\mu_2^3} = \frac{(-113.25)^2}{(14.75)^3} = \frac{12825.5625}{3209.04687} = 3.996$$

Also $$\beta_2 = \frac{\mu_4}{\mu_2^2} = \frac{(-113.25)^2}{(14.75)^3} = \frac{142.3125}{(14.75)^2} = 0.654$$

Example 4. *For a distribution the mean is 10, variance is 16, γ_1 is 1 and β_2 is 4. Find the first four moments about the mean.*

Sol. Let $\mu_1, \mu_2, \mu_3, \mu_4$ be the first four moments about the mean.

Here $\overline{X} = 10$, variance = 16 $\Rightarrow$ $\mu_2 = 16$

Also $\gamma_1 = 1 \Rightarrow \sqrt{\beta_1} = 1 \Rightarrow \beta_1 = 1 \Rightarrow \dfrac{\mu_3^2}{\mu_2^3} = 1$

$\Rightarrow$ $\mu_3^2 = \mu_2^3 = (16)^3 = (4^2)^3 = (4^3)^2$

$\Rightarrow$ $\mu_3 = 64$

Also $\beta_2 = 4 \Rightarrow \dfrac{\mu_4}{\mu_2^2} = 4 \Rightarrow \mu_4 = 4 \times \mu_2^2 = 4 \times 16^2 = 1024.$

Example 5. *Calculate the first four moments of the following distribution about the mean. Also find β_1 and β_2.*

X:	*0*	*1*	*2*	*3*	*4*	*5*	*6*	*7*	*8*
Y:	*1*	*8*	*28*	*56*	*70*	*56*	*28*	*8*	*1*

Sol. Let $\mu_1, \mu_2, \mu_3, \mu_4$ be the first four moments about the mean. Then by def.,

$$\left.\begin{aligned} \mu_1 &= 0 \\ \mu_2 &= \mu_2' - \mu_1' \\ \mu_3 &= \mu_3' - 3\mu_2'\,\mu_1' + 2\mu_1'^3 \\ \mu_4 &= \mu_4' - 4\mu_3'\,\mu_1' + 6\mu_2'\,\mu_1'^2 - 3\mu_1'^4 \end{aligned}\right\} \quad \ldots(1)$$

where $\mu_1', \mu_2', \mu_3', \mu_4'$ are first four moments about any point. We first find these moments. For this, consider the following table :

Take A = 4.

x_i	f_i	$x_i - A$	$f_i\,(x_i - A)$	$f_i\,(x_i - A)^2$	$f_i\,(x_i - A)^3$	$f_i\,(x_i - A)^4$
0	1	– 4	– 4	16	– 64	256
1	8	– 3	– 24	72	– 216	648
2	28	– 2	– 56	112	– 224	448
3	56	– 1	– 56	56	– 56	56
4	70	0	0	0	0	0
5	56	1	56	56	56	56
6	28	2	56	112	224	448
7	8	3	24	72	216	648
8	1	4	4	16	64	256
	$N = \Sigma f_i = 256$		$\Sigma f_i\,(x_i - A) = 0$	$\Sigma f_i (x_i - A)^2 = 512$	$\Sigma f_i\,(x_i - A)^3 = 0$	$\Sigma f_i\,(x_i - A)^4 = 2816$

Now, $$\mu_1' = \frac{1}{N}\sum_{i=1}^{n} f_i\,(x_i - A) = \frac{1}{N}\sum_{i=1}^{9} f_i\,(x_i - 4) = 0$$

$$\mu_2' = \frac{1}{N}\sum_{i=1}^{n} f_i\,(x_i - A)^2 = \frac{1}{N}\sum_{i=1}^{9} f_i\,(x_i - 4)^2 = \frac{512}{256} = 2$$

$$\mu_3' = \frac{1}{N}\sum_{i=1}^{n} f_i (x_i - A)^3 = \frac{1}{N}\sum_{i=1}^{9} f_i\ (x_i - 4)^3 = \frac{0}{256} = 0$$

$$\mu_4' = \frac{1}{N}\sum_{i=1}^{n} f_i (x_i - A)^4 = \frac{1}{N}\sum_{i=1}^{n} f_i (x_i - 4)^4 = \frac{2816}{256} = 11$$

Therefore, from (1), after using the above values,

$$\mu_1 = 0$$

$$\mu_2 = 2 - 0 = 2$$

$$\mu_3 = 0 - 3 \times 2 \times 0 + 2 \times 0 = 0$$

$$\mu_4 = 11 - 4 \times 0 + 6 \times 2 \times 0 - 3 \times 0 = 11$$

Hence $$\beta_1 = \frac{\mu_3^2}{\mu_2^3} = \frac{0}{8} = 0,\ \beta_2 = \frac{\mu_4}{\mu_2^2} = \frac{11}{4} = 2.75$$

Example 6. *Consider the following distribution :*

Variable :	*0–10*	*10–20*	*20–30*	*30–40*
Frequency :	*1*	*3*	*4*	*2*

Find (i) moments about assumed mean
(ii) moments about actual mean
(iii) moments about zero.

Sol. Let μ_1', μ_2', μ_3', μ_4' be the moments about any point, *i.e.*, assumed mean (Take A = 25). Consider the following table :

Variable	*Mid-points* x_i	*Frequency* f_i	$u_i = \frac{x_i - A}{h}$ *(A = 25, h = 10)*	$f_i u_i$	$f_i u_i^2$	$f_i u_i^3$	$f_i u_i^4$
0–10	5	1	– 2	– 2	4	– 8	16
10–20	15	3	–1	– 3	3	– 3	3
20–30	25	4	0	0	0	0	0
30–40	35	2	1	2	2	2	2
		$\Sigma f_i = 10$		$\Sigma f_i u_i = -3$	$\Sigma f_i u_i^2 = 9$	$\Sigma f_i u_i^3 = -9$	$\Sigma f_i u_i^4 = 21$

(*i*) Now $$\mu_1' = h\left(\frac{1}{N}\sum_{i=1}^{n} f_i u_i\right) = 10\left(\frac{1}{10}\times(0-3)\right) = -3$$

$$\mu_2' = h^2\left(\frac{1}{N}\sum_{i=1}^{n} f_i u_i^2\right) = 100\left(\frac{1}{10}\times 9\right) = 90$$

$$\mu_3' = h^3\left(\frac{1}{N}\sum_{i=1}^{n} f_i u_i^3\right) = 1000\left(\frac{1}{10}\times -9\right) = -900$$

$$\mu_4' = h^4\left(\frac{1}{N}\sum_{i=1}^{n} f_i u_i^4\right) = 1000 \times\left(\frac{1}{10}\times 21\right) = 2100$$

(*ii*) Let $\mu_1, \mu_2, \mu_3, \mu_4$ are the moments about the actual mean, then by definition,

$$\mu_1 = 0$$
$$\mu_2 = \mu_2' - \mu_1'^2 = 90 - (-3)^2 = 81$$
$$\mu_3 = \mu_3' - 3\mu_2' \mu_1' + 2\mu_1'^3 = -900 - 3 \times 90 \times (-3) + 2(-3)^3$$
$$= -900 + 810 - 54 = -144$$
$$\mu_4 = \mu_4' - 4\mu_3' \mu_1' + 6\mu_2' \mu_1'^2 - 3\mu_1'^4$$
$$= 2100 - 4 \times (-900) \times (-3) + 6 \times (90) \times (-3)^2 - 3 \times 81$$
$$= 2100 - 10800 + 4860 - 243 = -4083$$

(*iii*) Let v_1, v_2, v_3, v_4 be the moments about zero, then by definition,

$$v_1 = \mu_1' + A = -3 + 25 = 22$$
$$v_2 = \mu_2 + v_1^2 = 81 + (22)^2 = 565$$
$$v_3 = \mu_3 + 3v_2v_1 - 2v_1^3 = -144 + 3 \times 565 \times 22 - 2 \times (22)^3$$
$$= -144 + 37290 - 21296 = 15850$$
$$v_4 = \mu_4 + 4v_3v_1 - 6v_2v_1^2 + 3v_1^4$$
$$= -4083 + 4 \times 22 \times 15850 - 6 \times (22)^2 \times 565 + 3 \times (22)^4$$
$$= -4083 + 1394800 - 1640760 + 702768 = 452725.$$

Example 7. *Using moments, calculate a measure of relative skewness and a measure of relative kurtosis for the following distribution. Also comment on the result so obtained.*

Marks	*No. of students*
70 but below 90	*8*
90 but below 110	*11*
110 but below 130	*18*
130 but below 150	*9*
150 but below 170	*4*

Sol. The relative measure of skewness is given by $\beta_1 = \dfrac{\mu_3^2}{\mu_2^3}$ and the relative measure of kurtosis is given by $\beta_2 = \dfrac{\mu_4}{\mu_2^2}$

Calculation of μ_2, μ_3, and μ_4. Take assumed mean A = 120. Also $h = 20$.

Marks	*mid-point* x_i	*frequency* f_i	$u_i = \dfrac{x_i - A}{h}$	f_iu_i	$f_iu_i^2$	$f_iu_i^3$	$f_iu_i^4$
70–90	80	8	– 2	– 16	32	– 64	128
90–110	100	11	– 1	– 11	11	– 11	11
110–130	120	18	0	0	0	0	0
130–150	140	9	1	9	9	9	9
150–170	160	4	2	8	16	32	64
		$\Sigma f_i = 50 = N$		$\Sigma f_iu_i = -10$	$\Sigma f_iu_i^2 = 68$	$\Sigma f_iu_i^3 = -34$	$\Sigma f_iu_i^4 = 212$

$$\mu'_1 = h\left(\frac{1}{N}\sum_{i=1}^{n} f_i u_i\right) = 20\left(\frac{-10}{50}\right) = -4$$

$$\mu'_2 = h^2\left(\frac{1}{N}\sum_{i=1}^{n} f_i u_i^2\right) = 400\left(\frac{68}{50}\right) = 544$$

$$\mu'_3 = h^3\left(\frac{1}{N}\sum_{i=1}^{n} f_i u_i^3\right) = 800\left(\frac{-34}{50}\right) = -5440$$

$$\mu'_4 = h^4\left(\frac{1}{N}\sum_{i=1}^{n} f_i u_i^4\right) = 16000\left(\frac{212}{50}\right) = 678400$$

Further,
$$\mu_2 = \mu'_2 - \mu'^2_1 = 544 - 16 = 528$$
$$\mu_3 = \mu'_3 - 3\mu'_1\,\mu'_2 + 2\mu'^3_1$$
$$= -5440 - 3 \times (-4) \times 544 + 2 \times (-64)$$
$$= -5440 + 6528 - 128 = 960$$
$$\mu_4 = \mu'_4 - 4\mu'_1\,\mu'_3 + 6\mu'^2_1\,\mu'_2 - 3\mu'^4_1$$
$$= 678400 - 4 \times (-4) \times (-5440) + 6 \times 16 \times 544 - 3 \times 256$$
$$= 678400 - 87040 + 52224 - 768$$
$$= 730624 - 87808 = 642816$$

Hence
$$\beta_1 = \frac{\mu_3^2}{\mu_2^3} = \frac{960^2}{528^3} = \frac{921600}{147197952} = 0.006$$

Also
$$\beta_2 = \frac{\mu_4}{\mu_2^2} = \frac{642816}{528^2} = \frac{642816}{278784} = 2.305$$

Comment. Since $\beta_1 = 0.006 \cong 0$ $\therefore$ The distribution is symmetrical

Also $\beta_2 = 2.305 < 3$ $\therefore$ The distribution is platykurtic.

Example 8. *You are given the following values of moment :* $\mu_2 = 43.553$, $\mu_3 = -9.774$

$\mu_4 = 5508.567$

Find the correct value of each one of these, taking into account the class interval 3.

Sol. To find the correct value of μ_2, μ_3, μ_4, we use Sheppard's correction formulae.

Here
$$\mu_2\text{ (corrected)} = \mu_2\text{ (uncorrected)} - \frac{h^2}{12} = 43.553 - \frac{9}{12} = 42.603$$
$$\mu_3\text{ (corrected)} = \mu_3\text{ (uncorrected)} = -9.774$$
$$\mu_4\text{ (corrected)} = \mu_4\text{ (uncorrected)} - \frac{h^2}{2}\,\mu_2\text{ (uncorrected)} + \frac{7}{240}\,h^4$$
$$= 5508.567 - \frac{9}{2} \times 43.553 + \frac{7}{240} \times 3^4$$
$$= 5508.567 - 195.9885 + 2.3625 = 5314.941.$$

TEST YOUR KNOWLEDGE 7.1

1. What is the effect of change of origin and scale on moments about any point and central moments of a frequency distribution.
2. The first three moments about the point $x = 7$ are 3, 11, 47 respectively. Find mean, variance and β_1.
3. Calculate the first four moments about the mean for the following data:

Variate :	1	2	3	4	5	6	7	8	9
Frequency :	1	6	13	25	30	22	9	5	2

4. The first three moments of a distribution about the value 2 of the variable are 1, 16 and – 40. Show that the mean is 3, variance is 15 and $\mu_3 = -86$. Also show that the first three moments about $x = 0$ are 3, 24 and 76.
5. The first four moments of a distribution about the value 5 of the variable are 2, 20, 40 and 50. Find moments about the mean.
6. Show that for a discrete distribution :
   (*i*) $\beta_2 > 1$ (*ii*) $\beta_2 > \beta_1$.
7. Find the first four moments about the mean β_1 and β_2 from the following data :

Marks	0–10	10–20	20–30	30–40	40–50	50–60	60–70
No. of students	5	12	18	40	15	7	3

(P.T.U. M.B.A. Dec., 2010)

8. The first four central moments of a frequency distribution with class interval each having width $h = 10$, are 0, 11.372, – 8.69, 3522.44. Apply Sheppard's corrections to find the corrected value of the moments.
9. You are given the following information.
   $\mu_2 = 44.553$, $\mu_3 = -9.774$, $\mu_4 = 5508.567$.
   Find the corrected value of μ_2 and μ_4, it is given that the class interval is 3

Answers

1. The *r*th moment of the variable *x* is h^r times the corresponding moment of the variable *u*.
2. Mean = 10, variance = 2, $\beta_1 = 0.5$.
3. 0.249, 0.68, 18.26.
5. 0, 16, – 64, 162.
7. $\mu_1 = 0$, $\mu_2 = 177.39$, $\mu_3 = 47.982$, $\mu_4 = 95009.364$, $\beta_1 = 0.0004$, $\beta_2 = 3.02$.
8. $\mu_1 = 0$, $\mu_2 = 105.4$, $\mu_3 = -8.69$, $\mu_4 = 29830$.
9. μ_2 (corrected) = 42.603, μ_4 (corrected) = 5478.41.

8

Skewness and Kurtosis

8.1. SKEWNESS

(P.T.U.M.B.A., May 2006, Dec. 2008)

"Skewness means lack of symmetry or lopsideness in a frequency distribution". The object of measuring skewness is to estimate the extent to which a distribution is distorted from a perfectly symmetrical distribution. Skewness indicates whether the curve is turned more to one side than to other, *i.e.*, whether the curve has a longer tail on-one side.

Skewness can be positive as well as negative. **Skewness** is **positive** if the longer tail of the distribution lies towards the right and **negative** if it lies towards the left.

8.2. SYMMETRICAL DISTRIBUTION

A frequency distribution is called symmetric if the frequencies are symmetrically distributed on both sides of the centre point of the frequency curve. or A frequency distribution, in which the values of mean, median and mode are equal, is called symmetrical distribution.

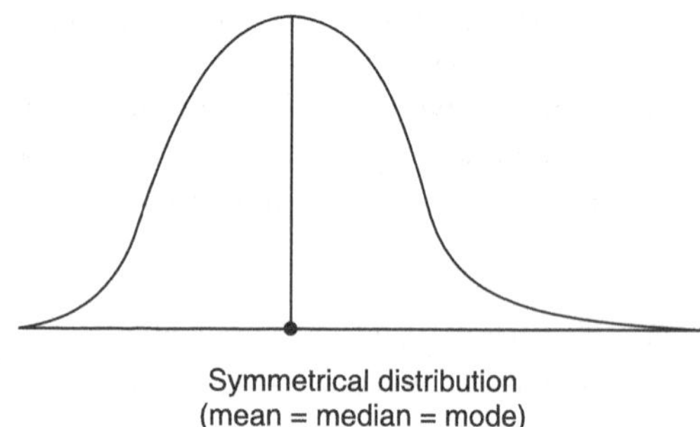

Symmetrical distribution
(mean = median = mode)

8.3. SKEWED DISTRIBUTION

A frequency distribution which is not symmetrical is called skewed distribution. It is of two types :

(*a*) **Positively skewed**

(*b*) **Negatively skewed**

Positively skewed distribution. A frequency distribution is said to be +ve skewed if the frequency curve, gives a longer tail to the right hand side.

or

In a +ve skewed distribution, the value of mean is maximum and that of mode is least, the median lies between mean and mode, *i.e.*,

Mean > Median > Mode.

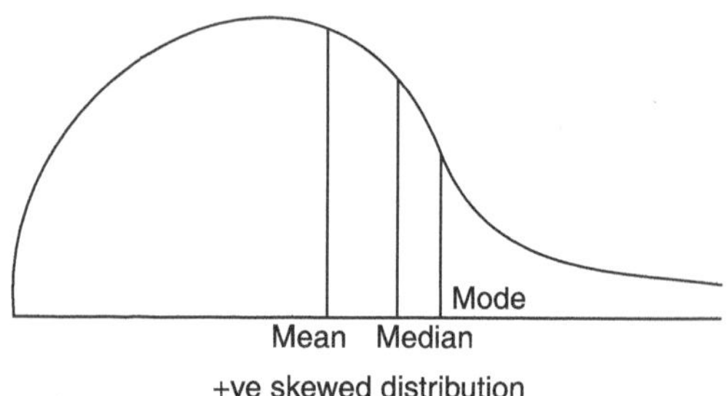

+ve skewed distribution

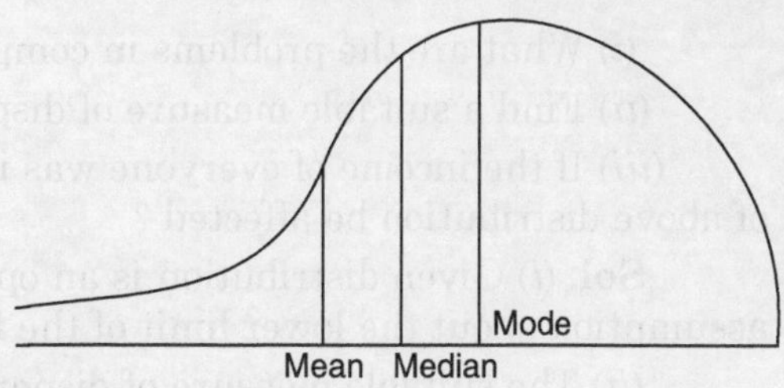

Negatively skewed distribution. A frequency distribution is said to be negatively skewed if the frequency curve gives a longer tail on the left hand side. In a –ve skewed distribution, the value of the mode is maximum and that of mean is least, the median lies between mode and mean, *i.e.*,

Mode > Median > Mean

8.4. MODERATELY SYMMETRICAL DISTRIBUTION

If in a frequency distribution, the interval between the mean and median is approximately one-third of the interval between the mean and mode, then the distribution is called moderately symmetrical distribution. Thus, for a moderate symmetrical distribution,

$$\text{Mean} - \text{Median} = \frac{1}{3}(\text{Mean} - \text{Mode})$$

or $$3(\text{Mean} - \text{Median}) = \text{Mean} - \text{Mode}$$

or $$\text{Mode} = 3\ \text{Median} - 2\ \text{Mean}.$$

8.5. TESTS OF SKEWNESS

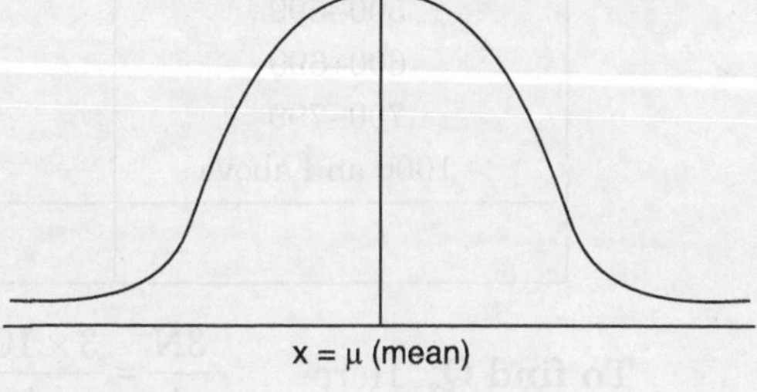

To check, whether a distribution is skewed or not, the following tests can be applied.

A skewed distribution satisfies

(1) The values of mean, median and mode do not coincide.

(2) Quartiles are not equidistant from the median.

(3) Frequencies are not symmetrically distributed on both sides of the centre point of the frequency curve.

(4) The graph of the given distribution is bell shaped. (see fig.)

ILLUSTRATIVE EXAMPLES

Example 1. *The following table gives the distribution of income of household.*

Income (₹)	*% of households*
Below 100	*7.2*
100–199	*11.7*
200–299	*12.1*
300–399	*14.8*
400–499	*15.9*
500–599	*14.9*
600–699	*10.4*
700–799	*9*
1000 and above	*4*

(*i*) What are the problems in computing standard deviation for *the given data* ?

(*ii*) Find a suitable measure of dispersion.

(*iii*) If the income of everyone was increased by a certain proportion, will the skewness of above distribution be affected ?

Sol. (*i*) Given distribution is an open-end distribution. It means, we need to make an assumption about the lower limit of the first class and the upper limit of the last class.

(*ii*) The suitable measure of dispersion is the quartile deviation *i.e.,*

$$Q.D = \frac{Q_3 - Q_1}{2}$$

Calculation of Q_3 and Q_1

(Income ₹)	*% of household* *f*	*Cumulative frequency* *c.f.*
Below 100	7.2	7.2
100–199	11.7	18.9
200–299	12.1	31
300–399	14.8	45.8
400–499	15.9	61.7
500–599	**14.9**	**76.6**
600–699	10.4	87
700–799	9	96
1000 and above	4	100
	$\Sigma f = 100$	

To find Q_3. Here $\frac{3N}{4} = \frac{3 \times 100}{4} = 75$

i.e., Q_3 lies in 500–599. But the actual limit should be 499.5–599.5

$$l = 499.5,\ C = 61.7,\ f = 14.9,\ h = 100$$

$$\therefore \quad Q_3 = l + \frac{\frac{3N}{4} - C}{f} \times h = 499.5 + \frac{75 - 61.7}{14.9} \times 100$$

$$= 499.5 + 89.26 = 588.76$$

To find Q_1 Here $\frac{N}{4} = \frac{100}{4} = 25$

i.e., Q_1 lies in 200–299. But the actual limit should be 199.5–299.5

$$l = 199.5,\ C = 18.9,\ f = 12.1,\ h = 100$$

$$\therefore \quad Q_1 = l + \frac{\frac{N}{4} - C}{f} \times h = 199.5 + \frac{25 - 18.9}{12.1} \times 100$$

$$= 199.5 + 50.41 = 249.91$$

Hence $Q.D = \frac{Q_3 - Q_1}{2} = \frac{588.76 - 249.91}{2} = 169.425$

(*iii*) If the income of every one is increased by a certain proportion, the skewness would not be affected, since it is independent of the charge of origin.

8.6. MEASURES OF SKEWNESS

There are various methods of measuring skewness of a distribution. These measures tell the direction and extent of asymmetry in a distribution. The following diagram classifies the different measures of skewness :

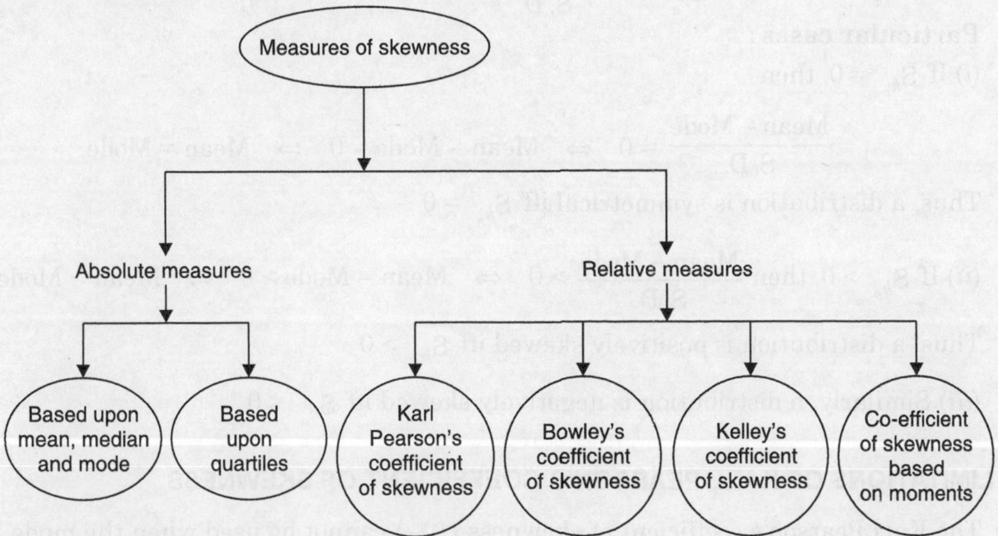

We now discuss in detail the various measures of skewness.

8.7. ABSOLUTE MEASURES OF SKEWNESS

The absolute measures of skewness (S_k)

Based upon mean, median and mode are

(*a*) S_k = Mean – Mode

(*b*) S_k = Mean – Median

8.8. BASED UPON QUARTILES ARE

(*a*) $S_k = Q_3 + Q_1 - 2Q_2$

(*b*) $S_k = Q_3 + Q_1 - 2$ Median

8.9. LIMITATIONS OF THE ABSOLUTE MEASURES OF SKEWNESS

The skewness computed by using any one of the above measures is expressed in the unit of value of the distribution, and hence we cannot compare the skewness of another distribution expressed in different units.

8.10. RELATIVE MEASURES OF SKEWNESS

To compare two or more distributions, the absolute measure of skewness cannot be used. To overcome this, we compute **relative measures of skewness,** which are known as "coefficients of skewness". The following are the coefficients of skewness :

(*a*) Karl Pearson's coefficient of skewness.

(*b*) Bowley's coefficient of skewness.

(*c*) Kelley's coefficient of skewness.

(*d*) Coefficient of skewness based on moments.

8.11. KARL PEARSON'S COEFFICIENT OF SKEWNESS (S_{k_p})

The Karl Pearson's coefficient of skewness S_{k_p} is given by

$$S_{k_p} = \frac{\text{Mean} - \text{Mode}}{\text{S.D}}, \text{ where } -1 \le S_{k_p} \le 1.$$

Particular cases :

(*i*) If $S_{k_p} = 0$, then

$$\frac{\text{Mean} - \text{Mode}}{\text{S.D.}} = 0 \Leftrightarrow \text{Mean} - \text{Mode} = 0 \Leftrightarrow \text{Mean} = \text{Mode}.$$

Thus, a distribution is symmetrical iff $S_{k_p} = 0$

(*ii*) If $S_{k_p} > 0$, then $\frac{\text{Mean} - \text{Mode}}{\text{S.D.}} > 0 \Leftrightarrow \text{Mean} - \text{Mode} > 0 \Leftrightarrow \text{Mean} > \text{Mode}.$

Thus, a distribution is positively skewed iff $S_{k_p} > 0$

(*iii*) Similarly, a distribution is negatively skewed iff $S_{k_p} < 0$.

8.12. LIMITATIONS OF KARL PEARSON'S COEFFICIENT OF SKEWNESS

The Karl Pearson's coefficient of skewness (S_{k_p}) cannot be used when the mode is ill-defined. But for a moderately skewed distribution, mean, median and mode are connected by the following relation :

Mean – Mode = 3 (Mean – Median)

Therefore, for a moderately skewed-distribution,

$$S_{k_p} = \frac{\text{Mean} - \text{Mode}}{\text{S.D.}} = \frac{3\,(\text{Mean} - \text{Median})}{\text{S.D.}},$$

where $-3 \le S_{k_p} \le 3$, for a moderately skewed distribution.

ILLUSTRATIVE EXAMPLES

Example 1. *Define skewness and hence compute coefficient of skewness from the values of the variables given below :*

25, 15, 23, 40, 27, 25, 23, 25, 20.

Sol. Skewness. Skewness means lack of symmetry or lopsideness in a frequency distribution.

The coefficent of skewness is given by $S_{k_p} = \frac{\text{Mean} - \text{Mode}}{\text{S.D.}}$.

$$\text{Mean} = \overline{x}$$

$$= \frac{25 + 15 + 23 + 40 + 27 + 25 + 23 + 25 + 20}{9} = \frac{223}{9} = 24.77$$

To find mode, arranging the given data in ascending order, we have

15, 20, 23, 23, 25, 25, 25, 27, 40.

Here maximum frequency is 25. Therefore, Mode = 25.

Also to find S.D. consider the table.

x_i	x_i^2
25	625
15	225
23	529
40	1600
27	729
25	625
23	529
25	625
20	400
223	5887

The standard deviation of the given values is given by

$$\sigma = \sqrt{\frac{1}{n}\sum_{i=1}^{n} x_i^2 - \left(\frac{1}{n}\sum_{i=1}^{n} x_i\right)^2} = \sqrt{\frac{5887}{9} - \left(\frac{223}{9}\right)^2}$$

$$= \sqrt{654.11 - 613.55} = \sqrt{40.56} = 6.36$$

Hence, the required coefficient of skewness (Karl Pearson's coefficient) is given by

$$S_{k_p} = \frac{\text{Mean} - \text{Mode}}{\text{S.D.}} = \frac{24.77 - 25}{6.36} = -\frac{0.23}{6.36} = -0.036.$$

Example 2. *For a moderate skewed distribution, the A.M. is 200, the coefficient of variation is 8 and Karl's Pearson coefficient of skewness is 0.3. Find the median and mode.*

Sol. Given mean $\bar{x} = 200$, C.V = 8, $S_{k_p} = 0.3$

Using C.V. $= \frac{\sigma}{\bar{x}} \times 100$, we have $8 = \frac{\sigma}{200} \times 100 = \frac{\sigma}{2} \Rightarrow \sigma = 16$

Also $S_{k_p} = \frac{\text{Mean} - \text{Mode}}{\sigma}$ gives $0.3 = \frac{200 - \text{Mode}}{16}$

$\Rightarrow$ 200 – Mode = 4.8 $\Rightarrow$ Mode = 200 – 4.8 = 195.2

Also Mode = 3 Median – 2 Mean, gives 195.2 = 3 Median – 2 × 200

$\Rightarrow$ 3 Median = 195.2 + 400 = 595.2 $\Rightarrow$ Median $= \frac{595.2}{3} = 198.4$

Example 3. *In a moderate skewed distribution, the mean is 20 and median is 18.5. If the coefficient of variation is 30%, find Karl Pearson's coefficient of skewness of the distribution.*

Sol. Given, Mean = 20, Median = 18.5,

Also C. V = 30%

$$\Rightarrow \quad \frac{\sigma}{\bar{x}} \times 100 = 30$$

$$\Rightarrow \quad \frac{\sigma}{20} \times 100 = 30$$

$\Rightarrow \qquad \sigma = 6. \Rightarrow$ S.D. = 6

Now, for a moderate skewed distribution

$$S_{k_p} = \frac{3(\text{Mean} - \text{Median})}{\text{S.D.}} = \frac{3\,(20 - 18.5)}{6} = 0.75.$$

Example 4. *For a group of 20 items, $\Sigma x_i = 200$, $\Sigma x_i^2 = 5000$ and median = 15. Find Karl Pearson's coefficient of skewness.*

Sol. Given $\qquad n = 20, \Sigma x_i = 200, \Sigma x_i^2 = 5000$

$$\therefore \qquad \text{Mean} = \frac{1}{n} \Sigma x_i = \frac{200}{20} = 10$$

$$\text{S.D.} = \sqrt{\frac{1}{n} \Sigma x_i^2 - \left(\frac{1}{n} \Sigma x_i\right)^2} = \sqrt{\frac{5000}{20} - 10^2}$$

$$= \sqrt{250 - 100} = \sqrt{150} = 12.24$$

Therefore, the required Karl's Pearson coefficient of skewness is given by

$$S_{k_p} = \frac{3\,(\text{Mean} - \text{Median})}{\text{S.D.}} = \frac{3(10 - 15)}{12.24} = \frac{-15}{12.24} = -1.22$$

$\Rightarrow \qquad S_{k_p} = \mathbf{-1.22.}$

Example 5. *Calculate Karl Pearson's coefficient of skewness from the data given below:*

x_i :	1	2	3	4	5	6	7
f_i :	10	18	30	25	12	3	2

Sol. The Karl Pearson's coefficient of skewness is given by

$$S_{k_p} = \frac{\text{Mean} - \text{Mode}}{\text{S.D.}} \qquad \ldots(1)$$

We first calculate Mean, Mode and S.D. of the given distribution.

Calculation of Mean. Take the assumed mean A = 4, and consider the following table :

x_i	f_i	$u_i = x_i - A$	$f_i u_i$	$f_i u_i^2$
1	10	– 3	– 30	90
2	18	– 2	– 36	72
3	30	– 1	– 30	30
4	25	0	0	0
5	12	1	12	12
6	3	2	6	12
7	2	3	6	18
	$\Sigma f_i = 100$		$\Sigma f_i u_i = -72$	$\Sigma f_i u_i^2 = 234$

The mean $\bar{x}$ is given by $\bar{x} = A + \frac{1}{N} \sum_{i=1}^{n} f_i u_i = 4 + \frac{1}{100}(-72) = \frac{328}{100} = 3.28$

Calculation of Mode. We know that Mode is that value of the variable which has the maximum frequency. Here the maximum frequency (which is 30) occurs corresponding to the value 3 of the variable x_i. $\therefore$ Mode = 3.

Calculation of standard deviation. We know that the S.D. is given by

$$\sigma = h\sqrt{\frac{1}{N}\sum_{i=1}^{n} f_i u_i^2 - \left(\frac{1}{N}\sum_{i=1}^{n} f_i u_i\right)^2}$$

$$= 1 \times \sqrt{\frac{1}{100} \times 234 - \left(\frac{1}{100} \times (-72)^2\right)} = \sqrt{\frac{234}{100} - \frac{5184}{10000}}$$

$$= \sqrt{\frac{23400 - 5184}{10000}} = \sqrt{\frac{18216}{10000}} = \sqrt{1.8216} = 1.3496.$$

$\therefore$ From (1), $\quad S_{k_p} = \dfrac{3.28 - 3}{1.3496} = 0.2074$

Example 6. *Compute Karl Pearson's coefficient of skewness from the following data :*

Marks	*0–10*	*10–20*	*20–30*	*30–40*	*40–50*
Frequency	*8*	*11*	*26*	*9*	*6*

Sol. The Karl Pearson's coefficient of skewness is given by

$$S_{k_p} = \frac{\text{Mean} - \text{Mode}}{\text{S.D.}} \qquad \ldots(1)$$

We calculate mean, mode and S.D. of the given distribution.

Consider the following table. Take assumed Mean A = 25 and $h = 10$.

Marks	*Mid-Values* (x_i)	f_i	$u_i = \dfrac{x_i - A}{h}$	$f_i u_i$	$f_i u_i^2$
0–10	5	8	– 2	– 16	32
10–20	15	11	– 1	– 11	11
20–30	25	26	0	0	0
30–40	35	9	1	9	9
40–50	45	6	2	2	24
		$\Sigma f_i = 60$		$\Sigma f_i u_i = -6$	$\Sigma f_i u_i^2 = 76$

Calculation of Mean. The Mean $\bar{x}$ is given by

$$\bar{x} = A + h\left(\frac{1}{N}\sum_{i=1}^{n} f_i u_i\right) = 25 + 10\left(-\frac{6}{60}\right) = 25 - 1 = 24$$

Calculation of Mode. Here, the maximum frequency is 26, corresponding to the modal class 20–30.

Therefore, $\quad l = 20, \qquad h = 10, f_m = 26, f_1 = 11$

Hence $\qquad \text{Mode} = l + \dfrac{f_m - f_1}{2f_m - f_1 - f_2} \times h$

$$= 20 + \frac{26 - 11}{52 - 11 - 9} \times 10 = 20 + \frac{15}{32} \times 10 = 24.69$$

Calculation of standard deviation. The standard deviation is given by

$$\sigma = h\left[\sqrt{\frac{1}{N}\Sigma f_i u_i^2 - \left(\frac{1}{N}\Sigma f_i u_i\right)^2}\right]$$

$$= 10\left[\sqrt{\frac{76}{60} - \left(\frac{-6}{60}\right)^2}\right] = 10 \times \sqrt{\frac{76}{60} - \frac{36}{3600}}$$

$$= 10 \times \sqrt{\frac{76 \times 60 - 36}{3600}} = 10 \times \sqrt{\frac{4524}{3600}}$$

$$= 10 \times \frac{67.26}{60} = \frac{67.26}{6} = 11.21$$

Hence from (1) the Karl Pearson's coefficient of correlation is given by

$$S_{k_p} = \frac{24 - 24.69}{11.21} = \frac{-0.69}{11.21} = -\ 0.062.$$

Example 7. *Calculate Karl Pearson's coefficient of skewness from the given data :*

Profit (in lacs)	*Below 20*	*40*	*60*	*80*	*100*
No. of firms	*8*	*20*	*50*	*64*	*70*

Sol. The given frequency distribution is a cumulative frequency distribution. Write this as a frequency distribution as follows :

Profits : (in lacs)	0–20	20–40	40–60	60–80	80–100
No. of firms	8	12	30	14	6

Proceeding as in above example, we get $\bar{x}$ = Mean = 49.42, Mode = 50.58

S.D. = 21.63

The Karl Pearson's coefficient of skewness is given by

$$S_{k_p} = \frac{\text{Mean} - \text{Mode}}{\text{S.D.}} = \frac{49.42 - 50.58}{21.63} = -\ 0.0536.$$

Example 8. *Following table gives the distributions of populations in towns A and B according to different age group.*

Age groups	*Population in (,000)*	
	Town A	*Town B*
0–10	*18*	*10*
10–20	*16*	*12*
20–30	*15*	*24*
30–40	*12*	*32*
40–50	*10*	*29*
50–60	*5*	*11*
60–70	*2*	*3*
> 70	*1*	*1*

(*i*) *Which town has more variation in age distribution ?*

(*ii*) *Which town is more skewed with regards to age distribution ?*

Sol. (*i*) To find which town is having more variation, we need to find the coefficient of variation for both the towns.

C.V. for town A. Take assumed mean A = 45, $h = 10$

Age groups	*frequency* f_i	*Mid-point* x_i	$d_i = x_i - A$	$u_i = \frac{x_i - A}{h}$	u_i^2	$f_i u_i$	$f_i u_i^2$
0–10	18	5	– 40	– 4	16	– 72	288
10–20	16	15	– 30	– 3	9	– 48	144
20–30	15	25	– 20	– 2	4	– 30	60
30–40	12	35	– 10	– 1	1	– 12	12
40–50	10	45	0	0	0	0	0
50–60	5	55	10	1	1	5	5
60–70	2	65	20	2	4	4	8
> 70	1	75	30	3	9	3	9
	$\Sigma f_i = 79$					$\Sigma f_i u_i = -150$	$\Sigma f_i u_i^2 = 526$

∴ Mean $\bar{x} = A + h \frac{\Sigma f_i u_i}{\Sigma f_i} = 45 + 10 \times \left(\frac{-150}{79}\right) = 45 - 18.98 = 26.01$

Also the standard deviation is given by

$$\sigma = \sqrt{\frac{\Sigma f_i u_i^2}{\Sigma f_i} - \left(\frac{\Sigma f_i u_i}{\Sigma f_i}\right)^2} \times h = \sqrt{\frac{526}{79} - \left(\frac{-150}{79}\right)^2} \times 10$$

$$= \sqrt{6.682 - 3.605} \times 10 = \sqrt{2.9770} \times 10 = 1.7253 \times 10 = 17.253$$

∴ C.V. for town A is given by $C.V = \frac{\sigma}{\bar{x}} \times 100 = \frac{17.253}{26.01} \times 100 = 66.336$

C.V for town B. Take assumed Mean A = 45

Age groups	*Frequency* f_i	*Mid point* x_i	$d_i = x_i - A$	$u_i = \frac{x_i - A}{h}$	u_i^2	$f_i u_i$	$f_i u_i^2$
0–10	10	5	– 40	– 4	16	– 40	160
10–20	12	15	– 30	– 3	9	– 36	108
20–30	24	25	– 20	– 2	4	– 48	96
30–40	32	35	– 10	– 1	1	– 32	32
40–50	29	45	0	0	0	0	0
50–60	11	55	10	1	1	11	11
60–70	3	65	20	2	4	6	12
> 70	1	75	30	3	9	3	9
	$\Sigma f_i = 122$					$\Sigma f_i u_i = -136$	$\Sigma f_i u_i^2 = 428$

∴ Mean $\bar{x} = A + h\,\frac{\Sigma f_i u_i}{\Sigma f_i} = 45 + 10 \times \left(\frac{-136}{122}\right)$

$= 45 - 11.147 = 33.852$

Also the standard deviation is given by

$$\sigma = \sqrt{\frac{\Sigma f_i u_i^{\,2}}{\Sigma f_i} - \left(\frac{\Sigma f_i u_i}{\Sigma f_i}\right)^2} \times h$$

$$= \sqrt{\frac{428}{122} - \left(\frac{-136}{122}\right)^2} \times 10 = \sqrt{3.508 - 1.242} \times 10$$

$$= \sqrt{2.266} \times 10 = 1.5053 \times 10 = 15.053$$

∴ $\text{C.V.} = \frac{\sigma}{\bar{x}} \times 100 = \frac{15.053}{34.836} \times 100 = 43.21$

Hence the coefficient of variation for town A is greater than the coefficient of variation for town B.

∴ The town A has more variation in age distribution.

(*ii*) To test which town is more skewed, we need to find the Karl Pearson's coefficient of skewness, given by

$$S_{k_p} = \frac{3(\bar{x} - \text{Median})}{\sigma}$$

Calculation of S_{k_p} for town A.

Age group	*Frequency* f_i	*Cumulative frequency* *c.f.*
0–10	18	18
10–20	16	34
20–30	15	49
30–40	12	61
40–50	10	71
50–60	5	76
60–70	2	78
> 70	1	79
	$N = \Sigma f_i = 79$	

Here $\frac{N}{2} = \frac{79}{2} = 39.5$

The cumulative frequency just greater than $\frac{N}{2} = 39.5$ is 49 and the corresponding median class is 20–30

$\therefore \qquad l = 20, h = 10, f = 15, C = 34$

$$\therefore \quad \text{Median} = l + \frac{\frac{N}{2} - C}{f} \times h = 20 + \frac{39.5 - 34}{15} \times 10$$

$$= 20 + 3.666 = 23.666$$

$\therefore$ The Karl Pearson's coefficient of skwness for town A is given by

$$S_{k_p} = \frac{3(\bar{x} - \text{Median})}{\sigma} = \frac{3(33.852 - 23.666)}{15.053} = 2.030$$

Calculation of S_{k_p} for town B.

Age group	*Frequency* f_i	*Cumulative frequency c.f.* c.f.
0–10	10	10
10–20	12	22
20–30	24	46
30–40	32	78
40–50	29	107
50–60	11	118
60–70	3	121
> 70	1	122
	$\Sigma f_i = 122$	

Here $\frac{N}{2} = \frac{122}{2} = 61$

The cumulative frequency just greater than $\frac{N}{2} = 61$ is 71 and the corresponding median class is 30–40

$\therefore \qquad l = 30, h = 10, f = 32, C = 46$

$$\therefore \quad \text{Median} = l + \frac{\frac{N}{2} - C}{f} \times h = 30 + \frac{61 - 46}{32} \times 10 = 40 + 4.68 = 44.68$$

The Karl Pearson's coefficient of skewness for town B is given by

$$S_{k_p} = \frac{3(\bar{x} - \text{Median})}{\sigma} = \frac{3(33.852 - 44.68)}{15.053} = -2.157$$

Here the Karl Pearson's coefficient of skewness for town A is greater than the Karl Pearson's coefficient of skewness for town B. Therefore the town A is more skewed with regards to age distribution.

TEST YOUR KNOWLEDGE 8.2

1. (*a*) Define skewness and mention absolute and relative measures of skewness.
   (*b*) Distinguish between dispersion and skewness (*P.T.U. M.B.A. Dec., 2010*)
2. Explain the main types of skewness. What is positive and negative skewness ?
3. What are the tests of skewness ?
4. Calculate the Karl pearson's coefficient of skewness from the data given below

x_i :	15	20	25	30	35	40
f_i :	12	28	25	24	20	21

5. Calculate the Karl Pearson's coefficient of skewness from the following data :

Marks :	0–10	10–20	20–30	30–40	40–50	50–60	60–70
No. of students :	10	12	24	32	28	11	3

6. For a moderately skewed distribution of retail prices for ladies footwear, it was found that the Mean price was ₹ 200 and Median price was ₹ 190. If the coefficient of variation was 20%, find the Karl Pearson's coefficient of skewness of the distribution.
7. A frequency distribution gives the following results :

$$\text{C.V.} = 5,\ S_{k_p} = 0.5,\ \text{S.D.} = 2.$$

   Find the Mean and Mode of the distribution.
8. Consider the following two series

   Series A : Mean = 22, Median = 24, S.D. = 10

   Series B : Mean = 22, Median = 25, S.D. = 12.

   Which of the series is symmetrical ?

   [**Hint.** Find S_{k_p} for series A and B. The series with smaller coefficient of skewness in magnitude will be more symmetrical.]

Answers

4. 0.9962 **5.** – 0.358 **6.** 0.25

7. Mean = 40, Mode = 39 **8.** Series A.

8.13. BOWLEY'S COEFFICIENT OF SKEWNESS

The Bowley's coefficient of skewness (S_{k_B}) is defined by

$$S_{k_p} = \frac{Q_3 + Q_1 - 2\text{ Median}}{Q_3 - Q_1} = \frac{(Q_3 - \text{Median}) + (Q_1 - \text{Median})}{Q_3 - Q_1}.$$

Particular cases

(*i*) If the distribution is symmetrical, then Median is equidistant from Q_1 and Q_3, *i.e.*,

Q_1 – Median = Median – Q_3

$\Leftrightarrow\ Q_1 + Q_3 - 2\text{ Median} = 0$

$\Leftrightarrow\ S_{k_b} = 0$

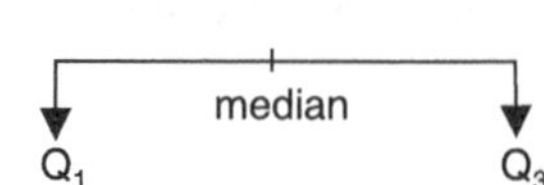

Hence the distribution is symme$\frac{3.12}{1.263}$trical iff $S_{k_b} = 0$

(*ii*) The distribution is positively skewed iff

Q_1 – Median > Median – Q_3

$\Leftrightarrow \quad Q_3 + Q_1 - 2\text{ Median} > 0$

$\Leftrightarrow \quad S_{k_B} > 0$

Similarly, the distribution is negatively skewed iff $S_{k_B} < 0$.

(*iii*) The Bowley's coefficient of skewness is also called "quartile measure of skewness" and its values lies between – 1 and 1, *i.e.*, $-1 \le S_{k_B} \le 1$.

Remark. In case of open-end distributions and where the extreme values are present, S_{k_B} is most effective tool to measure skewness.

ILLUSTRATIVE EXAMPLES

Example 1. *In a frequency distribution, the coefficient of skewness based on quartiles is 0.6. If the sum of the upper and lower quartiles is 100 and the median is 38. Find the value of the upper quartile.*

Sol. Given $S_{k_B} = 0.6$

Sum of upper and lower quartile = 100

$\Rightarrow \quad Q_3 + Q_1 = 100$ ...(1)

Also Median = 38

Using $S_{k_B} = \frac{Q_3 + Q_1 - 2\text{ Median}}{Q_3 - Q_1}$, we get

$$0.6 = \frac{100 - 76}{Q_3 - Q_1} = \frac{24}{Q_3 - Q_1}$$

$\Rightarrow \quad Q_3 - Q_1 = \frac{24}{0.6} = 40$ ...(2)

Adding (1) and (2), $2Q_3 = 140$

$\Rightarrow \quad Q_3 = 70$

$\therefore$ Upper quartile $Q_3 = 70$.

Example 2. *(a) In a distribution, the difference between two quartiles is 15, their sum is 35 and Median is 20. Find the coefficient of skewness.*

(b) In a frequency distribution, the median is 13, $Q_1 + Q_3 = 25$ and $Q_3 - Q_1 = 10$. Find Bowley's coefficient of skewness.

(c) In a frequency distribution, the median is 38, Bowley's coefficient is 0.6 and $Q_1 + Q_3 = 100$. Find Q_1 and Q_3.

Sol. (*a*) Given $Q_3 - Q_1 = 15$ ...(1)

$Q_3 + Q_1 = 35$ ...(2)

Median = 20

By def., $$S_{k_B} = \frac{Q_3 + Q_1 - 2\text{ Median}}{Q_3 - Q_1} = \frac{35 - 40}{15} = -\frac{1}{3} = -0.333.$$

(*b*) Given $Q_1 + Q_3 = 25$

$Q_3 - Q_1 = 10$

Median = 13

∴ Bowley's coefficient of skewness is given by

$$S_{k_B} = \frac{Q_3 + Q_1 - 2\,\text{Median}}{Q_3 - Q_1} = \frac{25 - 26}{10} = \frac{-1}{10} = -0.1$$

(*c*) Given Bowley's coefficient of skewness = 0.6 *i.e.*, $S_{k_B} = 0.6$

$$\Rightarrow \quad \frac{Q_3 + Q_1 - 2\,\text{Median}}{Q_3 - Q_1} = 0.6$$

$$\Rightarrow \quad \frac{100 - 76}{Q_3 - Q_1} = 0.6$$

$$\Rightarrow \quad Q_3 - Q_1 = \frac{24 \times 10}{6} = 40 \qquad ...(1)$$

Also $Q_3 + Q_1 = 100$ ...(2)

Adding (1) and (2) $2Q_3 = 140 \Rightarrow Q_3 = 70$

From (1), $Q_1 = Q_3 - 40 = 70 - 40 = 30.$

Example 3. *Compute the Bowley's coefficient of skewness for the marks obtained by 10 students in a class ; which are given below :*

43, 12, 31, 20, 17, 26, 35, 40, 5, 37.

Sol. The Bowley's coefficient of skewness is given by

$$S_{k_B} = \frac{Q_3 + Q_1 - 2\,(\text{Median})}{Q_3 - Q_1} \qquad ...(1)$$

We first compute Q_1, Q_3 and Median for the given data.

Computation of Q_1, Q_3

Given $n = 10$, and writing the data, in ascending order, we have

5, 12, 17, 20, 26, 31, 35, 37, 40, 43

$$\therefore \quad Q_1 = \text{Value of } \left(\frac{n+1}{4}\right)^{\text{th}} \text{ observation}$$

= Value of (2.75)th observation

= 2nd observation + (0.75) (3rd observation– 2nd observation)

= 12 + (0.75) (17 – 12) = 12 + 3.75 = 15.75

$$Q_3 = \text{Value of } \frac{3}{4}\,(n+1)^{\text{th}} \text{ observation}$$

= Value of 8.25^{th} observation

= 8th observation + (0.25) (9th observation – 8th observation)

= 37 + (0.25) (40 – 37) = 37 + .75 = 37.75

Also Median = Mean of 5th and 6th observation

$$= \frac{26 + 31}{2} = 28.5 \qquad (\because \; n = 10 \text{ is even})$$

∴ From (1), the required Bowley's coefficient of skewness is given by

$$S_{k_B} = \frac{37.75 + 15.75 - 2\,(28.5)}{37.75 - 15.75} = \frac{-3.5}{22} = -0.158.$$

Example 4. *Compute Bowley's coeficient of skewness from the data*

x_i :	5	15	25	35	45
f_i :	10	20	40	20	10

Sol. We know that Bowley's coefficient of skewness is given by

$$S_{k_B} = \frac{Q_3 + Q_1 - 2\,\text{Median}}{Q_3 - Q_1} \quad ...(1)$$

We first calculate Q_1, Q_3 and Median.

Consider the following table :

x_i	f_i	c.f.
5	10	10
15	20	30
25	40	70
35	20	90
45	10	100
	$\Sigma f_i = 100$	

Computation of Q_1 (lower quartile).

Here, $$N = \sum_{i=1}^{n} f_i = 100$$

∴ $$\frac{N}{4} = \frac{100}{4} = 25$$

The cumulative frequency just greater than 25 is 30 and the corresponding value of x is 15.

∴ $Q_1 = 15$

Computation of Median

Here, $$\frac{N}{2} = \frac{100}{2} = 50$$

The cumulative frequency just greater than 50 is 70 and the corresponding value of x is 25.

∴ Median = 25

Computation of Q_3 (upper quartile)

Here, $$\frac{3N}{4} = \frac{3 \times 100}{4} = 75$$

The comulative frequency just greater than 75 is 90 and the corresponding value of x is 35.

∴ $Q_3 = 35$

Hence, from (1), $$S_{k_B} = \frac{35 + 15 - 2\,(25)}{35 - 15} = \frac{50 - 50}{20} = 0$$

⇒ $S_{k_B} = 0$, *i.e.*, the distribution is **symmetric.**

Example 5. *Find Bowley's coefficient of skewness from the data given below :*

Marks in Pharm. Sc.	*30–40*	*40–50*	*50–60*	*60–70*	*70–80*	*80–90*	*90–100*
No. of students	*3*	*5*	*11*	*20*	*12*	*8*	*6*

Sol. The Bowley's coefficient of skewness is given by

$$S_{k_B} = \frac{Q_3 + Q_1 - 2\,\text{Median}}{Q_3 - Q_1} \qquad ...(1)$$

We first compute Q_1, Q_3 and median for the given data. Consider the following table :

Marks in Pharm. Sc.	*No. of students* f_i	*c.f.*
30–40	3	3
40–50	5	8
50–60	11	19
60–70	20	39
70–80	12	51
80–90	8	59
90–100	6	65
	$\Sigma f_i = 65$	

Computation of Q_1 (lower quartile).

Here, $\quad N = 65$

$$\therefore \quad \frac{N}{4} = \frac{65}{4} = 16.25$$

The cumulative frequency just greater than $\frac{N}{4} = 16.25$ is 19 and the corresponding quartile class is 50–60.

$$\therefore \quad l = 50, f = 11, C = 8, h = 10$$

$$\therefore \quad Q_1 = l + \frac{\frac{N}{4} - C}{f} \times h = 50 + \frac{16.25 - 8}{11} \times 10$$

$$= 50 + \frac{8.25}{11} \times 10 = 50 + \frac{82.5}{11} = \mathbf{57.5}$$

Computation of Median

Here, $\quad \frac{N}{2} = \frac{65}{2} = 32.5$

The cumulative frequency just greater than $\frac{N}{2} = 32.5$, is 39 and the corresponding median class is 60–70.

$$l = 60, h = 10, f = 20, C = 19$$

Hence, $\quad \text{Median} = l + \frac{\frac{N}{2} - C}{f} \times h = 60 + \frac{32.5 - 19}{20} \times 10$

$$= 60 + \frac{1.35}{2} \times 10 = 60 + \frac{13.5}{2} = 66.75$$

Computation of Q_3 (upper quartile)

Here, $\frac{3N}{4} = \frac{3 \times 65}{4} = 48.75$

The cumulative frequency just greater than 48.75 is 51, and the corresponding quartile class is 70–80

$\therefore$ $l = 70, h = 10, f = 12, C = 39$

Hence, $$Q_3 = l + \frac{\frac{3N}{4} - C}{f} \times h = 70 + \frac{48.75 - 39}{12} \times 10$$

$$= 70 + \frac{97.5}{12} = 78.125$$

Therefore, from (1), the required Bowley's coefficient of skewness is given by

$$S_{k_B} = \frac{78.125 + 57.5 - 2\,(66.75)}{78.125 - 57.5} = \frac{135.625 - 133.5}{78.125 - 57.5} = \frac{2.125}{20.625} = 0.1030$$

Example 6. *Calculate the quartile coefficient of skewness of the following distribution :*

Variate (x) :	*1–5*	*6–10*	*11–15*	*16–20*	*21–25*	*26–30*	*31–35*
Frequency (f) :	*3*	*4*	*68*	*30*	*10*	*6*	*2*

Sol.

Class	*f*	*c.f.*
1–5	3	3
6–10	4	7
11–15	68	75
16–20	30	105
21–25	10	115
26–30	6	121
31–35	2	123
		N = 123

Here, $\frac{N}{2} = 61.5.$

The cumulative frequency just greater than 61.5 is 75. Therefore Median class is 11–15, *i.e.*, 10.5–15.5

Hence, $$\text{Median } M_d = l + \frac{\frac{N}{2} - C}{f} \times h = 10.5 + \frac{5}{68}\,(61.5 - 7) = 10.5 + \frac{272.5}{68} = 14.5$$

Further, $\frac{N}{4} = 30.75$

∴ Class of lower quartile Q_1 is 11–15, *i.e.*, 10.5–15.5

Hence, $$Q_1 = l + \frac{\frac{N}{4} - C}{f} \times h = 10.5 + \frac{5}{68}(30.75 - 7)$$

$$= 10.5 + \frac{118.75}{68} = 12.25$$

Further, $$\frac{3N}{4} = 92.25$$

∴ Class of upper quartile Q_3 is 16–20. *i.e.*, 15.5–20.5

Hence, $$Q_3 = l + \frac{\frac{3N}{4} - C}{f} \times h = 15.5 + \frac{5}{30}(92.25 - 75)$$

$$= 15.5 + \frac{16.50}{6} = 18.25$$

Therefore Quartile coefficient of skewness S_{k_B} is given by

$$S_{k_B} = \frac{Q_3 + Q_1 - 2\,M_d}{Q_3 - Q_1} = \frac{30.50 - 29}{6} = \frac{1.50}{6} = 0.25.$$

Example 7. *Compute quartile coefficient of dispersion and skewness of the following data :*

Central size :	*1*	*2*	*3*	*4*	*5*	*6*	*7*	*8*	*9*	*10*
Frequency :	*2*	*9*	*11*	*14*	*20*	*24*	*20*	*16*	*5*	*2*

Sol. Arranging in groups, we have

Class	*f*	*c.f.*
0.5–1.5	2	2
1.5–2.5	9	11
2.5–3.5	11	22
3.5–4.5	14	36
4.5–5.5	20	56
5.5–6.5	24	80
6.5–7.5	20	100
7.5–8.5	16	116
8.5–9.5	5	121
9.5–10.5	2	123

Here, $$N = 123 \Rightarrow \frac{N}{2} = 61.5.$$

The cumulative frequency just greater than 61.5 is 80

∴ Median class is 5.5–6.5

Now, Median $$M_d = l + \frac{\frac{N}{2} - C}{f} \times h = 5.5 + \frac{1}{24}(61.5 - 56) = 5.5 + .23 = 5.73$$

Also, $$\frac{N}{4} = 30.75.$$

The cumulative frequency just greater than 30.75 is 36

$\therefore$ Class of lower quartile Q_1 is 3.5–4.5

Hence, $$Q_1 = l + \frac{\frac{N}{4} - C}{f} \times h = 3.5 + \frac{1}{14}(30.75 - 22) = 3.5 + 0.625 = 4.125$$

Also $$\frac{3N}{4} = 92.25$$

The cumulative frequency just greater than 92.25 is 100

$\therefore$ Class of upper quartile Q_3 is 6.5–7.5

Hence, $$Q_3 = l + \frac{\frac{3N}{4} - C}{f} \times h = 6.5 + \frac{1}{20}(92.25 - 80) = 6.5 + .61 = 7.11$$

Therefore, Quartile coefficient of dispersion

$$= \frac{Q_3 - Q_1}{Q_3 + Q_1} = \frac{7.11 - 4.125}{7.11 + 4.125} = \frac{2.985}{11.235} = 0.26$$

Also Quartile coefficient of skewness S_{k_B} is given by

$$S_{k_B} = \frac{Q_3 + Q_1 - 2M_d}{Q_3 - Q_1} = \frac{7.11 + 4.125 - 2(5.73)}{7.11 - 4.125} = -\frac{0.225}{2.985} = -0.075.$$

Example 8. *Find the Bowley's coefficient of skewness if difference of two quartiles is 8, mode is 11, sum of two quartile is 22 and mean is 8.*

Sol. We know Bowley's coefficient of skewness is given by

$$S_{k_B} = \frac{Q_3 + Q_1 - 2\,\text{Median}}{Q_3 - Q_1} \quad \ldots(1)$$

Also, $$\text{Mode} = 3\,\text{Median} - 2\,\text{Mean} \quad \ldots(2)$$

From (2), $$11 = 3\,\text{Median} - 2 \times 8$$

$$\Rightarrow \quad 3\,\text{Median} = 11 + 16 = 27$$

$$\Rightarrow \quad \text{Median} = 9$$

From (1), $$S_{k_B} = \frac{22 - 2 \times 9}{8} = \frac{4}{8} = \frac{1}{2} = 0.5.$$

TEST YOUR KNOWLEDGE 8.3

1. In a frequency distribution, the coefficient of skewness based upon the quartiles is 0.6. If the sum of the upper and lower quartile is 100 and median is 38, find the value of the upper and lower quartile.
2. For a distribution, the Bowley's coefficient of skewness is 0.36, $Q_1 = 8.6$ and Median = 12.3. Find the quartile coefficient of dispersion.
3. If the first quartile is 142 and semi-inter quartile range is 18. Find the Median, given that the distribution is symmetrical.
4. Compute Bowely's coefficient of skewness from the following data :
   25, 15, 23, 40, 27, 25, 23, 25, 20.

5. Find the measure of skewness based on quartiles and median from the following data.

x_i :	10–20	20–30	30–40	40–50	50–60	60–70	70–80
f_i :	358	2417	976	129	62	18	10

6. Find the Bowely's coefficient of skewness from the data :

Variate :	Below 200	200–400	400–600	600–800	800–1000	1000 and above
Frequency :	25	40	85	75	16	16

7. By using quartiles find the measure of skewness for the following data:

Annual sales ('000 ₹)	*No. of firms*
less than 20	30
less than 30	225
less than 40	465
less than 50	580
less than 60	634
less than 70	644
less than 80	650
less than 90	665
less than 100	680.

Answers

1. $Q_3 = 70, Q_1 = 30$ **2.** 0.24 **3.** 160

4. – 0.3 **5.** 0.131 **6.** 0.09 **7.** $S_{k_b} = 0.09$.

8.14. MEASURE OF SKEWNESS BASED UPON MOMENTS

Karl Pearson defined the following measures of skewness based upon moments, which are

$$\gamma_1 = \sqrt{\beta_1} = \frac{\mu_3}{\sqrt{\mu_2^{\,3}}} \; ; \; \gamma_2 = \beta_2 - 3 = \frac{\mu_4}{\mu_2^{\,2}} - 3$$

(*i*) If $\gamma_1 = 0$, then the distribution is symmetrical.
(*ii*) If $\gamma_1 > 0$, then the distribution is positively skewed.
(*iii*) If $\gamma_1 < 0$, then the distribution is negatively skewed.

ILLUSTRATIVE EXAMPLES

Example 1. *The first four moments about the mean are 0, 2, 0.7 and 18.75. Find the coefficient of skewness based upon these moments.*

Sol. Let $\mu_1, \mu_2, \mu_3, \mu_4$ be the moments about the mean. Then given,

$$\mu_1 = 0, \quad \mu_2 = 2, \mu_3 = 0.7, \quad \mu_4 = 18.75$$

The required coefficient of skewness based upon these moments is given by

$$\gamma_1 = \frac{\mu_3}{\sqrt{\mu_2^3}} = \frac{0.7}{\sqrt{8}} = \frac{0.7}{2.828} = \mathbf{0.24770.}$$

Remark. In the above example, $\gamma_1 = 0.24770 > 0$, it means the distribution is +ve skewed.

Example 2. *If the first three moments of a distribution about the value 2 are 1, 22 and 100. Find the moment measure of skewness.*

Sol. Let μ_1', μ_2', μ_3' are the moments about the value 2, then given

$$\mu_1' = 1, \mu_2' = 22, \mu_3' = 100.$$

Now,
$$\mu_2 = \mu_2' - \mu_1'^2 = 22 - 1 = 21$$
$$\mu_3 = \mu_3' - 3\mu_2'\mu_1' + 2\mu_1'^3 = 100 - 3 \times 22 \times 1 + 2 \times 1$$
$$= 100 - 66 + 2 = 36$$

The required moment measure of skewness is given by

$$\gamma_1 = \frac{\mu_3}{\sqrt{\mu_2^3}} = \frac{36}{\sqrt{9261}} = \frac{36}{96.23} = 0.374$$

$$\Rightarrow \quad \gamma_1 = 0.3740.$$

Remark. In the above example, $\lambda_1 = 0.3740 > 0$, it means the distribution is positively skewed.

Example 3. *The value of mean, variance and γ_1 for a distribution are 10, 16 and 1 respectively. Find the first three moments about the origin and discuss the nature of skewness.*

Sol. Let v_1, v_2, v_3 be the first three moments about the origin, then by def,

$$v_1 = \text{Mean} = 10$$
$$v_2 = \mu_2 + v_1^2 = \text{variance} + v_1^2 = 16 + 100 = 116$$

Also,
$$\gamma_1 = 1 \Rightarrow \sqrt{\beta_1} = 1 \Rightarrow \beta_1 = 1$$

$$\Rightarrow \quad \frac{\mu_3^2}{\mu_2^3} = 1 \Rightarrow \mu_3^2 = \mu_2^3 = 16^3 \qquad | \mu_2 = \text{variance}$$

$$\Rightarrow \quad \mu_3 = 16^{3/2} = 64$$

Hence,
$$v_3 = \mu_3 + 3v_2v_1 - 2v_1^3 = 64 + 3 \times 116 \times 10 - 2 \times 1000$$
$$= 64 + 3480 - 2000 = 1544$$

As $\gamma_1 = 1 > 0 \Rightarrow \gamma_1 > 0$, it means, the distribution is positively skewed.

Example 4. *In two distributions A and B, the second central moments are 9 and 16 respectively and the third central moments are – 8.1 and – 12.8 respectively. Which distribution is less skewed to the left ?*

Sol. The extent of skewness can be well determined by their coefficient of skewness.

For the distribution A, Given

$$\mu_2 = 9, \mu_3 = -8.1$$

$$\therefore \quad \gamma_1 = \sqrt{\beta_1} = \frac{\mu_3}{\sqrt{\mu_2^3}} = \frac{-8.1}{\sqrt{729}} = \frac{-8.1}{27} = -0.3$$

For the distribution B, Given $\mu_2 = 16, \mu_3 = -12.8$

$$\therefore \quad \gamma_1 = \sqrt{\beta_1} = \frac{\mu_3}{\sqrt{\mu_2^3}} = \frac{-12.8}{\sqrt{4096}} = \frac{-12.8}{64} = -0.2$$

Here, for the distribution A, $\gamma_1 = -0.3$ and for the distribution B, $\gamma_1 = -0.2$.

Clearly, the distribution B is less skewed to the left.

8.15. KELLEY'S CO-EFFICIENT OF SKEWNESS

Kelley's coefficient of skewness are based upon deciles and percentiles.

(*i*) **Based upon deciles.** The kelley's coefficient of skewness, based upon deciles is given by

$$S_{k_k} = \frac{D_1 + D_9 - 2\text{ Median}}{D_9 - D_1}$$

(*ii*) **Based upon percentiles.** The Kelley's coefficient of skewness, based upon percentiles is given by

$$S_{k_k} = \frac{P_{10} + P_{90} - 2\text{ Median}}{P_{90} - P_{10}}.$$

ILLUSTRATIVE EXAMPLES

Example 1. *The marks obtained by 15 students of M.B.A first year are*

10, 60, 36, 20, 5, 8, 19, 28, 16, 9, 46, 53, 14, 32, 40.

Find Kelley's coefficient of skewness based upon percentiles

Sol. Arranging the marks in ascending order, we get

5, 8, 9, 10, 14, 16, 19, 20, 28, 32, 36, 40, 46, 53, 60.

Also $n = 15$

$$\therefore \quad P_{10} = \text{Value of } \frac{10}{100}(n+1)^{\text{th}} \text{ observation}$$

$$= \text{Value of } 1.6^{\text{th}} \text{ observation}$$

$$= \text{Value of first observation} + (0.6)\,(2^{\text{nd}} \text{ observation} - \text{first observation})$$

$$= 5 + (0.6)\,(9 - 8) = 5 + 0.6 = 5.6$$

$$P_{50} = \text{Value of } \frac{50}{100}(n+1)^{\text{th}} \text{ observation}$$

$$= \text{Value of 8th observation} = 20$$

$$P_{90} = \text{Value of } \frac{90}{100}(n+1)^{\text{th}} \text{ observation}$$

$$= \text{Value of 14.4th observation}$$

$$= \text{14th observation} + (0.4)\,(15^{\text{th}} \text{ observation} - 14^{\text{th}} \text{ observation})$$

$$= 53 + (0.4)\,(60 - 53) = 53 + 2.8 = 55.8$$

The required Kelley's coefficient of skewness based upon percentiles is given by

$$S_{k_k} = \frac{P_{10} + P_{90} - 2\text{ Median}}{P_{90} - P_{10}} = \frac{5.6 + 55.8 - 2\,(20)}{55.8 - 5.6} \qquad |\; P_{50} = \text{Median}$$

$$= \frac{61.4 - 40}{50.2} = \frac{21.4}{50.2} = 0.42.$$

Example 2. *Find Kelley's coefficient of skewness based upon percentiles for the given data :*

Marks	*0–5*	*5–10*	*10–15*	*15–20*	*20–25*	*25–30*	*30–35*	*35–40*	*40–45*	*45–50*	*50–55*	*55–60*
Freq.	*4*	*9*	*32*	*108*	*127*	*176*	*158*	*185*	*130*	*48*	*20*	*3*

Sol. Consider the following table :

Marks	*Frequency*	*c.f.*
0–5	4	4
5–10	9	13
10–15	32	45
15–20	108	153
20–25	127	280
25–30	176	456
30–35	158	614
35–40	185	799
40–45	130	929
45–50	48	977
50–55	20	997
55–60	3	1000

To find P_{10}. Here N = 1000

$$\therefore \quad \frac{10N}{100} = \frac{10 \times 1000}{100} = 100$$

From the table, we observe that the comulative frequency just greater than $\frac{10N}{100} = 100$ is 153 and the corresponding percentiles class is 15–20.

$$\therefore \quad l = 15, f = 108, C = 45, h = 5$$

Now,
$$P_{10} = l + \frac{\frac{10N}{100} - C}{f} \times h = 15 + \frac{100 - 45}{108} \times 5 = 15 + \frac{275}{108}$$
$$= 15 + 2.54 = 17.54$$

To find P_{50}, *i.e.*, Median

Here, $\frac{N}{2} = \frac{1000}{2} = 500$

$\therefore$ The cumulative frequency just greater than $\frac{N}{2} = 500$ is 614 and the corresponding median class is 30–35. Therefore, $l = 30, f = 158, C = 456, h = 5$

Hence,
$$P_{50} = \text{Median} = l + \frac{\frac{N}{2} - C}{f} \times h$$
$$= 30 + \frac{500 - 456}{158} \times 5 = 30 + 1.39 = 31.39$$

To find P_{90}. Here, $\frac{90N}{100} = \frac{90}{100} \times 1000 = 900$

i.e., the cumulative frequency just greater than $\frac{90N}{100} = 900$ is 929 and hence, the 90th percentile class is 40–45.

$$\therefore \quad l = 40, f = 130, C = 799, h = 5$$

Hence, $$P_{90} = l + \frac{\frac{90N}{100} - C}{f} \times h = 40 + \frac{900 - 799}{130} \times 5$$

$$= 40 + 3.88 = 43.88$$

Hence, the required Kelley's coefficient of skewness based upon percentiles is given by

$$S_{k_k} = \frac{P_{90} + P_{10} - 2\,\text{Median}}{P_{90} - P_{10}} = \frac{43.88 + 17.54 - 2\,(31.39)}{43.88 - 17.54}$$

$$= \frac{-1.36}{26.34} = -\mathbf{0.0516.}$$

TEST YOUR KNOWLEDGE 8.4

1. What is the coefficient of skewness based upon moments, if the first three central moments of a distribution are 0, 12.25 and – 39.75 ?
2. Compute the moment coefficient of skewness of a distribution whose first four moments about the value 5 are 2, 20, 40 and 50.
3. For a frequency distribution, if $P_{10} = 5$, Median = 12 and $P_{90} = 22$.

   Find the Kelley's coefficient of skewness.
4. The heights (cms) of 11 students in a class of B. Pharm are

   149, 156, 141, 160, 152, 135, 146, 158, 154, 159, 143.

   Find the Kelley's coefficient of skewness based upon percentiles.
5. Find the Kelley's coefficient of skewness based upon moments from the given data :

x_i :	0	1	2	3	4	5	6	7	8
f_i :	1	8	28	56	70	56	28	8	1

6. Find Kelley's coefficient of skewness for the following frequency table :

Rains in mm :	85	90	95	100	105	110	115	120	125
No,. of days :	20	23	32	24	20	13	18	23	27

7. Find the Kelley's coefficient of skewness from the data given below :

Wages :	Below 50	60	70	80	90	100
No. of workers :	6	16	40	68	83	100

8. Find the Kelley's coefficient of skewness from the given data :

Marks is maths :	*more than* 0	10	20	30	40	50	60
No. of students :	100	96	89	70	55	37	10

Answers

1. – 0.927	**2.** – 1	**3.** 0.18
4. – 0.34	**5.** 0	**6.** – 0.14
7. 0.023	**8.** – 0.168	

KURTOSIS

8.16. DEFINE KURTOSIS

(P.T.U., M.B.A. May 2008)

Given two frequency distributions, which have the same variability as measured by the standard deviation, they may be relatively more or less flat topped than the "Normal curve". A frequency curve may be symmetrical but it may not be equally flat topped with the Normal curve. The relative flatness of the top is called **Kurtosis** or convexity of the frequency curve.

Kurtosis enables us to have an idea about the" flatness or peakedness" of the frequency curve.

8.17. NORMAL CURVES OR MESOKURTIC CURVES

The curves which are neither flat, nor sharply peaked, are known as Normal curves or mesokurtic curves (see curve A in figure given below).

8.18. PLATYKURTIC CURVES

The curves which are flatter than the Normal curves, are known as platykurtic curves (see curve B in figure given below).

8.19. LEPTOKURTIC CURVES

The curves which are more sharply peaked than the normal curve, are known as leptokurtic curves (see curve C in the figure given below).

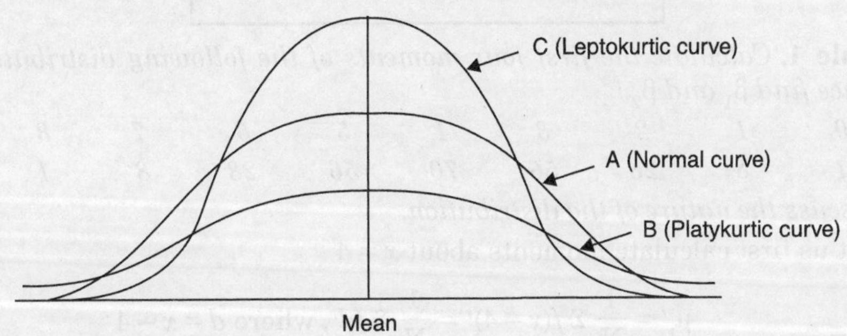

8.20. MEASURES OF KURTOSIS

(1) The kurtosis of a frequency curve is measured by the value of the Pearsonian coefficient β_2, given by

$$\beta_2 = \frac{\mu_4}{\mu_2^2}$$

(2) Another measure of kurtosis is γ_2, which is given by $\gamma_2 = \beta_2 - 3$

Remark.

(i) For Normal curve or mesokurtic curve, $\beta_2 = 3, \gamma_2 = 0$

(ii) For platykurtic curve, $\beta_2 < 3$ or $\gamma_2 < 0$

(iii) For leptokurtic curve, $\beta_2 > 3$ or $\gamma_2 > 0$

Theorem. *For a symmetrical distribution, all the moments of odd order about the mean vanish.*

Proof. Let $\bar{x}$ denote the mean of the variate x, then

$$\mu_{2r+1} = \frac{1}{N}\sum_{i=1}^{n} f_i(x_i - \bar{x})^{2r+1}, \ N = \Sigma f_i$$

In a symmetrical distribution, the values of the variate equidistant from the mean have equal frequencies.

$$\therefore \qquad f_1(x_1 - \bar{x})^{2r+1} + f_n(x_n - \bar{x})^{2r+1} = 0$$

[$\because$ $x_1 - \bar{x}$ and $x_n - \bar{x}$ are equal in magnitude but opposite in sign. Also $f_1 = f_n$]

Similarly, $f_2(x_2 - \bar{x})^{2r+1} + f_{n-1}(x_{n-1} - \bar{x})^{2r+1} = 0$ and so on.

$\therefore$ If n is even, all the terms in $\frac{1}{N}\sum_{i=1}^{n} f_i(x_i - \bar{x})^{2r+1}$ cancel in pairs. If n is odd, again the terms cancel in pairs and the middle term vanishes, since middle term = $\bar{x}$.

Hence, $\mu_{2r+1} = 0$

In particular $\mu_3 = 0$ and hence $\beta_1 = \dfrac{\mu_3^2}{\mu_2^3} = 0.$

Thus, β_1 gives a measure of departure from symmetry, *i.e.*, of skewness.

Remark. The above result does not hold for asymmetrical distribution.

ILLUSTRATIVE EXAMPLES

Example 1. *Calculate the first four moments of the following distribution about the mean and hence find β_1 and β_2 :*

x :	0	1	2	3	4	5	6	7	8
f :	1	8	28	56	70	56	28	8	1

Also discuss the nature of the distribution.

Sol. Let us first calculate moments about $x = 4$.

$$\mu_r' = \frac{1}{N}\Sigma f(x-4)^r = \frac{1}{N}\Sigma fd^r, \text{ where } d = x - 4$$

x	f	$d = x - 4$	fd	fd^2	fd^3	fd^4
0	1	– 4	– 4	16	– 64	256
1	8	– 3	– 24	72	–216	648
2	28	– 2	– 56	112	– 224	448
3	56	– 1	– 56	56	– 56	56
4	70	0	0	0	0	0
5	56	1	56	56	56	56
6	28	2	56	112	224	448
7	8	3	24	72	216	648
8	1	4	4	16	64	256
	N = 256		0	512	0	2816

$\mu_1' = \frac{1}{N}\Sigma fd = 0$; $\mu_2' = \frac{1}{N}\Sigma fd^2 = \frac{512}{256} = 2$

$\mu_3' = \frac{1}{N}\Sigma fd^3 = 0$; $\mu_4' = \frac{1}{N}\Sigma fd^4 = \frac{2816}{256} = 11$

Moments about mean are

$\mu_1 = 0$ (*always*) ; $\mu_2 = \mu_2' - \mu_1'^2 = 2$

$\mu_3 = \mu_3' - 3\mu_2'\mu_1' + 2\mu_1'^3 = 0$; $\mu_4 = \mu_4' - 4\mu_3'\mu_1' + 6\mu_2'\mu_1'^2 - 3\mu_1'^4 = 11$

$\beta_1 = \frac{\mu_3^2}{\mu_2^3} = 0$; $\beta_2 = \frac{\mu_4}{\mu_2^2} = \frac{11}{4} = 2.75.$

Here, $\beta_2 = 2.75$, it means, the distribution is symmetrical.

Also $\gamma_2 = \beta_2 - 3 = 2.75 - 3 = -0.25$.

It means, the distribution is platykurtic.

Example 2. *The second, third and the fourth central moments of a distribution are 2, 0.6 and 18.25 respectively. Test the skewness and kurtosis of the distribution.*

Sol. Given $\mu_2 = 2, \mu_3 = 0.6, \mu_4 = 18.25$

For skewness, $\gamma_1 = \sqrt{\beta_1} = \sqrt{\frac{\mu_3^2}{\mu_2^3}} = \frac{\mu_3}{\sqrt{\mu_2^3}} = \frac{0.6}{\sqrt{8}} = 0.21 > 0$

$\Rightarrow$ $\gamma_1 > 0$. Hence, the distribution is +ve skewed.

For kurtosis, $\beta_2 = \frac{\mu_4}{\mu_2^2} = \frac{18.25}{4} = 4.5673$

$\Rightarrow$ $\beta_2 > 3$. Hence, the distribution is leptokurtic.

Example 3. *The standard deviation of a symmetrical distribution is 3. Find the value of the fourth moment about the mean for which the distribution becomes mesokurtic, leptokurtic and platykurtic.*

Sol. Given S.D. = 3 $\Rightarrow$ variance = 9 $\Rightarrow$ $\mu_2 = 9$

(*i*) For the distribution to be mesokurtic, we know

$$\beta_2 = 3 \Rightarrow \frac{\mu_4}{\mu_2^2} = 3 \Rightarrow \mu_4 = 3 \times 9^2 = 243$$

Hence, the fourth moment about the mean of the distribution must be 243.

(*ii*) For the distribution to be leptokurtic, we know

$$\beta_2 > 3 \Rightarrow \mu_4 > 243$$ | As in part (*i*)

(*iii*) For the distribution to be platykurtic, we know

$$\beta_2 < 3 \Rightarrow \mu_4 < 243$$ | As in part (*i*)

Example 4. *Find the kurtosis of the following data :*

Marks :	*0–10*	*10–20*	*20–30*	*30–40*	*40–50*
Freq. :	*10*	*20*	*40*	*20*	*10*

Sol. Take assumed mean A = 25, h = 10. Consider the following table.

Marks	*Mid-value* x_i	f	$u_i = \frac{x_i - A}{h}$	$f_i u_i$	$f_i u_i^2$	$f_i u_i^3$	$f_i u_i^4$
0–10	5	10	– 2	–20	40	– 80	160
10–20	15	20	– 1	– 20	20	– 20	20
20–30	25	40	0	0	0	0	0
30–40	35	20	1	20	20	20	20
40–50	45	10	2	20	40	80	160
	Total	$\Sigma f = 100$		$\Sigma f_i u_i = 0$	$\Sigma f_i u_i^2 = 120$	$\Sigma f_i u_i^3 = 0$	$\Sigma f_i u_i^4 = 360$

We wish to find the value of β_2, where

$$\beta_2 = \frac{\mu_4}{\mu_2^2} \text{ ; where } \mu_4, \mu_2 \text{ are the moments about the mean.}$$

We first find $\mu_1', \mu_2', \mu_3', \mu_4'$.

Here,
$$\mu_1' = h\left(\frac{1}{N}\sum_{i=1}^{n} f_i u_i\right) = 10 \times \left(\frac{1}{100} \times 0\right) = 0$$

$$\mu_2' = h^2\left(\frac{1}{N}\sum_{i=1}^{n} f_i u_i^2\right) = 100\left(\frac{1}{100} \times 120\right) = 120$$

$$\mu_3' = h^3\left(\frac{1}{N}\sum_{i=1}^{n} f_i u_i^3\right) = 1000\left(\frac{1}{100} \times 0\right) = 0$$

$$\mu_4' = h^4\left(\frac{1}{N}\sum_{i=1}^{n} f_i u_i^4\right) = 10000\left(\frac{1}{100} \times 360\right) = 36000$$

$\therefore$
$$\mu_2 = \mu_2' - \mu_1'^2 = 120 - 0 = 120$$
$$\mu_4 = \mu_4' - 4\mu_3' + 6\mu_2' \mu_1'^2 - 3\mu_1'^4$$
$$= 36000 - 0 + 0 - 0 = 36000$$

Hence,
$$\beta_2 = \frac{\mu_4}{\mu_2^2} = \frac{36000}{120^2} = \frac{36000}{14400} = \frac{360}{144} = 2.5 < 3$$

$\Rightarrow$ The distribution is **platykurtic.**

Example 5. *Show that for discrete distribution, $\beta_2 > 1$.*

Sol. We know
$$\beta_2 = \frac{\mu_4}{\mu_2^2}$$

$\therefore$
$$\beta_2 > 1 \quad \text{if} \quad \frac{\mu_4}{\mu_2^2} > 1$$

or if
$$\mu_4 > \mu_2^2$$

or if $\frac{1}{N}\Sigma f(x-M)^4 > \left[\frac{1}{N}\Sigma f(x-M)^2\right]^2$

or if $\frac{1}{N}\Sigma fy^4 > \frac{1}{N^2}(\Sigma fy^2)^2$, where $y = x - M$

or if $N\Sigma fy^4 > (\Sigma fy^2)^2$

or if $(f_1 + f_2 + \ldots\ldots, + f_n)(f_1y_1^4 + f_2y_2^4 + \ldots\ldots + f_ny_n^4)$
$> (f_1y_1^2 + f_2y_2^2 + \ldots\ldots + f_ny_n^2)^2$

or if $f_1f_2(y_1^2 - y_2^2)^2 + f_1f_3(y_1^2 - y_3^2)^2 + \ldots\ldots > 0$

Since f_i ($i = 1, 2, \ldots\ldots, n$) is always +ve, therefore, the inequality is always true.

Hence, $\beta_2 > 1$.

Example 6. *Show that for a discrete distribution,* $\beta_2 > \beta_1$.

Sol. We know $\beta_2 = \frac{\mu_4}{\mu_2^2}$ $\beta_1 = \frac{\mu_3^2}{\mu_2^3}$

Now $\beta_2 > \beta_1$

if $\frac{\mu_4}{\mu_2^2} > \frac{\mu_3^2}{\mu_2^3}$

or if $\mu_2\mu_4 > \mu_3^2$

or if $\frac{1}{N}\Sigma f_i(x_i - \bar{x})^2, \frac{1}{N}\Sigma f_i(x_i - \bar{x})^4 > \left[\frac{1}{N}\Sigma f_i(x_i - \bar{x})^3\right]^2$

or if $\Sigma f_iy_i^2\,\Sigma f_iy_i^4 > (\Sigma f_iy_i^3)^2$ where $y_i = x_i - \bar{x}$

or if $(f_1y_1^2 + f_2y_2^2 + \ldots\ldots)(f_1y_1^4 + f_2y_2^4 + \ldots\ldots) > (f_1y_1^3 + f_2y_2^3 + \ldots\ldots)^2$

or if $f_1^2y_1^6 + f_2^2y_2^6 + f_1f_2y_1^2y_2^2(y_1^2 + y_2^2) + \ldots\ldots > f_1^2y_1^6 + f_2^2y_2^6 + 2f_1f_2y_1^3y_2^3 + \ldots\ldots$

or if $f_1f_2y_1^2y_2^2(y_1^2 + y_2^2) - 2f_1f_2y_1^3y_2^3 + \ldots\ldots > 0$

or if $f_1f_2y_1^2y_2^2(y_1^2 + y_2^2 - 2y_1y_2) + \ldots\ldots > 0$

or if $f_1f_2y_1^2y_2^2(y_1 - y_2)^2 + \ldots\ldots > 0$

Since f_i ($i = 1, 2, \ldots\ldots, n$) is always +ve, the inequality is always true.

Hence, $\beta_2 > \beta_1$.

TEST YOUR KNOWLEDGE 8.5

1. What do you understand by kurtosis ? How it is measured ?
2. The first four moments of a distribution about the value 5 of the variable are 2, 20, 40 and 50. Comment upon the nature of the distribution.
3. The first four central moments of a frequency distribution are 0, 60, – 50 and 80, 20 respectively. Discuss the Kurtosis of the distribution.
4. Compute the coefficients of skewness and Kurtosis based on moments for the following distribution.

x:	4.5	14.5	24.5	34.5	44.5	54.5	64.5	74.5	84.5	94.5
f:	1	5	12	22	17	9	4	3	1	1

5. Compute μ_2, μ_3 and μ_4 from the following data and determine whether the distribution is platykurtic, leptokurtic or mesokurtic

Wages :	0–10	10–20	20–30	30–40	40–50	50–60	60–70
No. of workers :	8	12	20	30	15	10	5

6. Compute β_1 and β_2 for the following distribution.

Marks :	25–30	30–35	35–40	40–45	45–50	50–55	55–60	60–65
f :	2	8	18	27	25	16	7	2

7. Prove that the frequency distribution curve of the following frequency distribution is leptokurtic.

Marks :	10–15	15–20	20–25	25–30	30–35	35–40	40–45	45–50	50–55
f :	1	4	8	19	35	20	7	5	1

8. Distinguish between skewness and kurtesis

Answers

2. $\beta_2 = 0.64$ **3.** $\beta_2 = 2.22$. Platykurtic **4.** $\beta_1 = 0.504$, $\beta_2 = 3.782$

5. $\mu_2 = 236.76$, $\mu_3 = 264.336$, $\mu_4 = 141290.11$, $\beta_2 = 2.52$, platykurtic.

6. $\beta_1 = 0.033$, $\beta_2 = -27$, platykurtic.

Unit-II
Sampling and Sampling Distribution

9
Concepts of Sampling

9.1. INTRODUCTION

We are well familiar with secondary data *i.e.,* the data which are obtained either from published or unpublished sources. But, sometimes, secondary data are not available for the problem under consideration. In such situation, a decision may be taken to collect primary data by using various methods like "Direct Personal Interviews", "Indirect Oral Interviews", "Information From Correspondents", "Mailed Questionnaire Method" etc. But there are some limitations in applying these methods. The required information may be obtained from the following discussed methods *viz.,* "Census Method" and "Sample Method"

9.2. CENSUS METHOD

This method is also known as "Complete Enumeration Survey Method". In this method, data are collected from each and every unit of the population. As an example, if we wish to calculate the average wages of all the workers working in a coal company, we would obtain the total wages of all the workers and then divide the total wages by the number of workers working in the coal company.

Merits of Census method: The following are the merits of census method:

(*a*) Data obtained from census method can be accepted as a basis for various surveys.

(*b*) It is an appropriate method of obtaining information on rare events.

Limitations of Census method:

(*a*) The time required for carrying out a complete survey is very large.

(*b*) In case of infinite population, this method can not be applied.

9.3. SAMPLE METHOD

In this method, instead of taking every unit of the population, we consider a sample of the population and obtain the required information based on this sample.

The conclusions for the entire population are then drawn from the information obtained from the sample. Briefly speaking, this method involves the following three steps.

I. Selection of the sample

II. Collection of information from the selected sample

III. Making an inference about the entire population

We first define two important terms—*population or universe* and *sampling.*

9.3.1. Population or Universe

An aggregate of objects (animate or inanimate) under study is called **population or universe.** It is thus a collection of individuals or of their attributes (qualities) or of results of operations which can be numerically specified.

A universe containing a finite number of individuals or members is called a **finite universe.** For example, the universe of the weights of students in a particular class.

A universe with infinite number of members is known as an **infinite universe.** For example, the universe of pressures at various points in the atmosphere.

In some cases, we may be even ignorant whether or not a particular universe is infinite *e.g.,* the universe of stars.

The universe of concrete objects is an **existent universe.** The collection of all possible ways in which a specified event can happen is called a **hypothetical universe.** The universe of heads and tails obtained by tossing a coin an infinite number of times (provided that it does not wear out) is a hypothetical one.

9.3.2. Sampling

The statistician is often confronted with the problem of discussing universe of which he cannot examine every member *i.e.,* of which complete enumeration is impracticable. For example, if we want to have an idea of the average per capita income of the people of India, enumeration of every earning individual in the country is a very difficult task. Naturally, the question arises: What can be said about a universe of which we can examine only a limited number of members? This question is the origin of the Theory of Sampling.

A finite subset of a universe is called a **sample.** A sample is thus a small portion of the universe. The number of individuals in a sample is called the **sample size.** The process of selecting a sample from a universe is called **sampling.**

The theory of sampling is a study of relationship existing between a population and samples drawn from the population. The fundamental object of sampling is to get as much information as possible of the whole universe by examining only a part of it. An attempt is thus made through sampling to give the maximum information about the parent universe with the minimum effort.

Sampling is quite often used in our day-to-day practical life. For example, in a shop we assess the quality of sugar, rice or any other commodity by taking only a handful of it from the bag and then decide whether to purchase it or not. A housewife, normally, tests the cooked products to find if they are properly cooked and contain the proper quantity of salt or sugar, by taking a spoonful of it.

9.4. SAMPLING METHODOLOGIES

Sampling methodologies are classified under two general categories:

1. Non-probability sampling (or non-random sampling) (P.T.U. M.B.A. Dec-2012)
2. Probability sampling (or random sampling) (P.T.U. M.B.A. Dec-2012)

In this, the researcher knows the exact possibility of selecting each member of the population while in the latter, the chance of being included in the sample is not known. A probability sample tends to be more difficult and costly to conduct. However, probability samples are the only type of samples where the results can be generalized from the sample to the population. In addition, probability samples allow the researcher to calculate the precision of the estimates obtained from the sample and to specify the sampling error.

Non-probability samples, incontrast, do not allow the study's findings to be generalized from the sample to the production. When discussing the results of a non-probability sample, the researchers must limit his/her findings to the persons or elements sampled.

This procedure also does not allow the researcher to calculate sampling statistics that provide information about the precision of the results. The advantages of non-probability sampling is the case in which it can be administered.

Non-probability samples tend to be less complicated and less time consuming than probability samples. If the researcher has no intention of generalizing beyond the sample, one of the non-probability sampling methodologies will provide the desired information.

I. Non-Probability Sampling: The three common types of non-probability sampling are:

(i) Convenience Sampling: As the name implies, convenience sampling involves choosing respondents at the convenience of the researcher. Examples of convenience sampling include sample in the street interviews—the sampling of people to which the researcher has easy access, each as a class of students and studies that use people who have volunteered to be questioned is a result of an advertisement or another type of promotion. A drawback to this methodology is the lack of sampling accuracy. Because the probability of inclusion in the sample is unknown to each respondent, none of the reliability or sampling precision statistics can be calculated. Convenience samples, however, are employed by researchers because the time and cost of collecting information can be reduced.

(ii) Quota Sampling: Quota sampling is often confused with stratified and cluster sampling—two probability sampling methodologies. All of these methodologies sample a population that has been divided into classes or categories.

The primary differences between the methodologies is that with stratified and cluster sampling, the classes are mutually exclusive and are isolated prior to sampling. Thus, the probability of being selected is known and members of the population selected to be sampled is not arbitrarily disqualified from being included in the results. In quota sampling, the data cannot be isolated prior to sampling and respondents are categorized into the classes as the survey proceeds. As each class fills or reaches its quota, additional respondents that would have fallen into these classes are rejected or excluded from the results.

An example of a quota sample would be a survey in which the researcher desires to obtain a certain number of respondents from various income categories. Generally, researchers donot know the income of the persons they are sampling until they ask about income. Therefore, the researcher is unable to subdivide the population from which the sample is drawn into mutually exclusive income categories prior to drawing the sample.

(iii) Judgemental Sampling: In judgemental or purposive sampling, the researcher employs his or her own expert judgement about whom to include in the sample frame. Prior knowledge and research skill are used in selecting the respondents or elements to be sampled.

An example of this type of sample would be a study of potential users of a new recreational facility that is limited to those persons who live within two miles of the new facility. Expert judgement based on past experience indicates that most of the use of this type of facility comes from persons living within two miles. However, by limiting the sample to only this groups, usage projections may not be reliable if the usage characteristics of the new facility vary from those previously experienced. As with all non-probability sampling methods, the degree and direction of error introduced by the researcher cannot be measured and the statistics that measure the precision of the estimates cannot be calculated.

Merits:

(*a*) This method is useful in those cases when the population is very small. Because, a simple random sample may miss the important elements whereas, this method would certainly consider those elements in the sample.

(*b*) This method gives a fast solution to those problems, in which the company executive cannot wait for sample designs due to shortage of time.

Limitations:

(*a*) It is not a scientific method.

(*b*) The judgement of a researcher may vary from a sample to sample.

II. Probability Sampling: Five methodologies are most commonly used for conducting probability sampling.

(i) Simple or unrestricted random sampling: Simple random sampling provides the base from which the other more complex sampling methodologies are derived.

To conduct a simple random sampling, the researcher must first prepare an exhaustive list (sampling frame) of all members of the population of interest. From this list, the sample is drawn so that each person or item has an equal chance of being drawn during each selection round. Samples may be drawn with or without replacement. In practice, however, most simple random sampling for survey research is done without replacement ; that is, a person or item selected for sampling is removed from the population for all subsequent selections. At any draw, the process for a simple random sample without replacement must provide an equal chance of inclusion to any member of the population not already drawn. To draw a simple random sample without introducing researcher bias, computerized sampling programs and random numbers tables are used to impartially select the members of the population to be sampled.

An example of a simple random sample would be a survey of County employees. An exhaustive list of all County employees as of a certain date could be obtained from the Department of Human Resources. If 100 names were selected from this list using a random number table or a computerized sampling program, then a simple random sample would be created. Such a random sampling procedure has the advantage of reducing bias and enables the researcher to estimate sampling errors and the precision of the estimates derived thought statistical calculations.

Merits:

(*a*) The personal bias does not affect the results since the selection of items in the sample totally depend on the chance.

(*b*) This method is much better than the judgement method as it represents the population in a better way.

Limitations:

(*a*) This method of sampling may give the most non-random looking results. For example, 13 cards from a well-shuffled pack of playing cards may be of one suit. But in practical, the occurrence of such event rarely happens.

(ii) Stratified random sampling: Stratified random sampling involves categorizing the members of the population into mutually exclusive and collectively exhaustive groups. An independent simple random sample is then drawn from each group. Stratified sampling techniques can provide more precise estimates if the population being surveyed is more heterogeneous than the categorized groups can enable the researcher to determine desired levels of sampling precision for each group, and can provide administrative efficiency.

An example of a stratified sample would be a sample conducted to determine the average income earned by families in the United States. To obtain more precise estimates of income, the researcher may want to stratify the sample by geographic region (northeast, mid-Atlantic etc.) and/or stratify the sample by urban, suburban, and rural groupings. If the differences in income among the regions or groupings are greater than the income differences within the regions or groupings, precision of the estimates is improved. In addition, if the research organization has branch offices located in these regions, the administration of the survey can be decentralized and perhaps conducted in a more cost-efficient manner.

Merits:

(*a*) This method of sampling has greater accuracy since each strata consists of uniform or homogeneous items.

(*b*) It is more representative since the population is first divided into various strata and then a sample is drawn from each stratum. Hence, there is a little chance of any important group of the population being completely ignored.

Limitations:

It is difficult to select items at random from each stratum.

(iii) Cluster Sampling: Cluster sampling is similar to stratified sampling because the population to be sampled is subdivided into mutually exclusive groups. However, in cluster sampling, the groups are defined so as to maintain the heterogeneity of the population. It is the researcher's goal to establish clusters that are representative of the population as a whole, although in practice this may be difficult to achieve. After the clusters are established, a simple random sample of the clusters is drawn and the members of the chosen clusters are sampled. If all of the elements (members) of the clusters selected are sampled, then the sampling procedure is defined as **one-stage cluster sampling.** If a random sample of the elements of each selected cluster is drawn, then the sampling procedure is defined as **two-stage cluster sampling.**

Cluster sampling is frequently employed when the researcher is unable to compile a comprehensive list of all the elements in the population of interest. A cluster sample might be used by a researcher attempting to measure the age distribution of persons residing in Mumbai. It would be much more difficult for the researcher to compile a list of every person residing in Mumbai than to compile a list of residential addresses. In this example, each address would represent a cluster of elements (persons) to be sampled. If the elements contained in the clusters are as heterogeneous as the population, then estimates derived from cluster sampling are as precise as those from simple random sampling. However, if the heterogeneity of the clusters is less than that of the population, the estimates will be less precise.

(iv) Systematic Sampling: Systematic sampling, a form of one-stage cluster sampling, is often used in place of simple random sampling. In systematic sampling, the researcher selects every n^{th} member after randomly selecting the first through n^{th} element as the starting point. For example, if the researcher decides to sample every 20th member of the population, a 5 per cent sample, the starting point for the sample is randomly selected from the first 20 members. A systematic sample is a type of cluster sample because each of the first 20 members of the sampling frame defines a cluster that contains 5 per cent of the population.

A researcher may choose to conduct a systematic sample instead of a simple random sample for several reasons. Systematic samples tend to be easier to draw and execute. The researcher does not have to jump backward and forward through the sampling frame to draw the members to be sampled. A systematic sample may spread the members selected for measurement more evenly across the entire population than simple random sampling.

Therefore, in some cases, systematic sampling may be more representative of the population mid more precise.

One of the most attractive aspects of systematic sampling is that this method can allow the researcher to draw a probability sample without complete prior knowledge of the sampling frame. For example, a survey of visitors to the County's publications desk could be conducted by sampling every 10th visitor after randomly selecting the first through 10th visitor as the starting point. By conducting the sample in this manner, it would not be necessary for the researcher to obtain a comprehensive list of visitors prior to drawing the sample.

As with other types of cluster sampling, systematic sampling is as precise as simple random sampling if the members contained in the clusters are as heterogeneous as the population. If this assumption is not valid, then systematic sampling will be less precise than simple random sampling. In conducting systematic sampling, it is also essential that the researcher does not introduce bias into the sample by selecting an inappropriate sampling interval. For instance, when conducting a sample of financial records, or other items that follow a calendar schedule, the researcher would not want to select "7" as the sampling interval because the sample would then be comprised of observations that were all on the same day of the week. Day-of-the-week influences may, cause contamination of the sample, giving the researcher biased results.

Merits:

(*a*) It is a simple and convenient method as the time required for sampling is relatively less.

(*b*) This method is also effective in those cases when the population is sufficiently large.

Limitations:

This method becomes less representative if some one deals with a population having hidden periodicities. For example, in the study of wages of the workers, the list may be such that every twelfth worker on the list may get a low salary than others.

(*v*) *Multi-Stage-Sampling:* Multi-stage sampling is like cluster sampling, but involves selecting a sample within each chosen cluster, rather than including all units in the cluster. Thus, multi-stage sampling involves selecting a sample in at least two stages. In the first-stage, large groups or clusters are selected. These clusters are designed to contain more population units than are required for the final sample.

In the second stage, population units are chosen from selected clusters to derive a final sample. If more than two stages are used, the process of choosing population units within clusters continues until the final sample is achieved.

An example of multi-stage sampling is where, firstly, electoral sub-divisions (clusters) are sampled from a city or state. Secondly, blocks of houses are selected from within the electoral sub-divisions and, thirdly, individual houses are selected from within the selected blocks of houses.

The advantages of multi-stage sampling are convenience, economy and efficiency. Multi-stage sampling does not require a complete list of members in the target population, which greatly reduces sample preparation cost. The list of members is required only for those clusters used in the final stage. The main disadvantage of multi-stage sampling is the same as for cluster sampling: lower accuracy due to higher sampling error.

Merits:

(*a*) This sampling method introduces flexibility in the sampling which is lacking in the other methods.

Limitations: This method in general is less accurate.

9.5. SAMPLE SIZE

We know that the number of individuals in a sample is called **sample size**. But a question arises. "What percentage of the size of population be included to consider a sample size?"

Some researchers suggested that the sample size should be 5% of the size of population while others suggested that it should be atleast 10%. But these views are of little use. Infact, there is no hard and fast rule to decide a sample size. A sample can be very small or very large. Briefly speaking, a sample size should be of 'Optimum Size' which can fulfill the requirements of flexibility, reliability and efficiency.

The following are the points which should be kept in mind while deciding the sample size:

(*i*) If the population is large, the sample size should also be large.

(*ii*) If the population contains homogeneous groups, we should choose a small sample. But, if the population consists of heterogeneous group, a large sample should be taken.

(*iii*) For greater degree of accuracy, the sample size should be large.

9.6. CALCULATION OF SAMPLE SIZE

The following formulae can be used to calculate the sample size.

(*i*) Let n be the sample size, σ be the standard deviation of the population, d be the difference between population mean and sample mean, Z_α denotes the critical value at α% level of significance. Then the sample size n can be calculated as:

$$n = \left(\frac{Z_\alpha \sigma}{d}\right)^2$$

(*ii*) When standard deviation of population is not known, but standard deviation of the sample is given, the following formula can be used to calculate the sample size, Let s denotes the standard deviation of the sample, then

$$n = \frac{s^2}{(\text{S.E.}(\bar{x}))^2}$$

(*iii*) We can also determine the sample size when standard error of proportion is known. The formula is

$$\text{S.E. (Proportion)} = \sqrt{\frac{pq}{n}}$$

where p = Probability of success in each trial

q = Probability of failure = $1 - p$

n = size of the sample.

ILLUSTRATIVE EXAMPLES

Example 1. *Calculate the size of sample drawn from a population whose standard deviation is 6, mean is 25 and sample mean is 23. (use 5% level of significance).*

Sol. Here $\sigma = 6$, d = difference between population mean and sample mean $= 25 - 23 = 23$

Z_α = The critical value of Z at 5% level of significance = 1.96

$$\therefore \qquad n = \left(\frac{Z_\alpha \sigma}{d}\right)^2 = \left(\frac{(1.96)\times 6}{2}\right)^2$$

$$= \left(\frac{11.76}{2}\right)^2 = (5.88)^2 = 34.57 \cong 35.$$

Example 2. *The standard error of mean of a random sample is found to be 1.311 while the standard deviation of the sample is 13.11. Calculate the sample size.*

Sol. Here,

$$\text{S.E.}(\bar{x}) = \text{standard error of mean} = 1.311$$

$$s = \text{standard deviation of sample} = 13.11$$

Using $n = \dfrac{s^2}{(\text{S.E.}(\bar{x}))^2}$, we get $n = \left(\dfrac{13.11}{1.311}\right)^2 = 100.$

Example 3. *A factory produces 5000 pairs of socks daily. From a sample of 500 socks, 3% were found to be of poor quality. Find the standard errors of proportion.*

Sol. Here the sample size $(n) = 500$

$$p = \text{The probability of success} = \frac{3}{100} = 0.03$$

$$q = 1 - 0.03 = 0.97$$

$\therefore$ The standard error of proportion is given as

$$\text{S.E.}(p) = \sqrt{\frac{pq}{n}} = \sqrt{\frac{(0.03)(0.97)}{500}} = 0.0076.$$

9.7. SAMPLING AND NON-SAMPLING ERRORS

According to **Patterson** "Sampling error is the difference between the result of studying a sample and inferring a result about the population and the result of the census of the whole population".

When we select a sample, the results obtained from the sample may not coincide with the true value in the population. The reason is that the selection of a sample is not completely random. Hence, sampling gives rise to certain errors, known as **sampling errors** or **sampling fluctuations.** Further, the sampling errors can be divided into two types:

(*i*) Biased and

(*ii*) Unbiased.

Biased Sampling Errors

These errors occur due to any bias while selecting a sample.

The bias may arise due to faulty process of a selection or faulty collection of data or faulty work during the collection.

The biased sampling error becomes a constant component of error and it does not decrease in a large population with the increase in sample size. Hence, the biased sampling error is also known as **non-compensating error**.

Unbiased Sampling Errors

These errors occur due to the difference between the number of individuals of the population included in the sample and those not included.

The unbiased sampling error decreases with the increase in sample size. Hence, this type of error is also known as *compensating error.*

9.8. RELATION BETWEEN SAMPLE SIZE AND SAMPLING ERRORS

The main objective of sampling is that it should be free of any bias. If any bias exists, we cannot draw a fully objective conclusion. The simplest method of avoiding any bias in selecting a sample is that the sample must be drawn at random. Once the absence of bias has been ensured, efforts should be made to reduce the random sampling errors. Reduction of errors is essential to attain the desired accuracy.

The accuracy of a sample can also be increased by increasing the sample size. The sampling errors usually decrease with the increase in sample size and this decrease is inversely proportional to the square root of the sample size as shown in the following diagram. (Fig. 9.1)

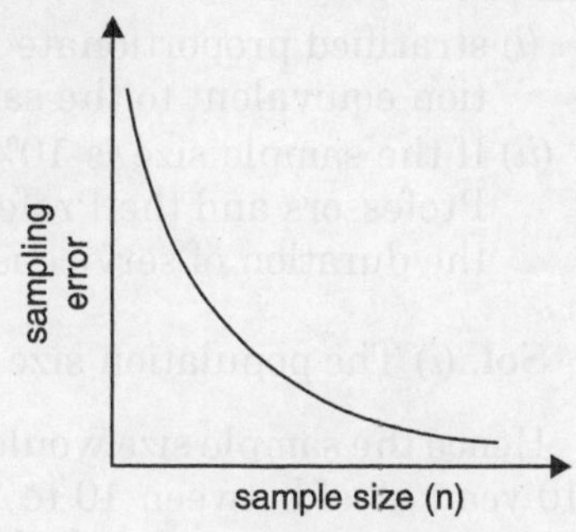

Fig. 9.1. Relation between sample size and sample errors.

From the diagram, we observe that if the sampling size is small, the degree of sampling error is high. But, when the sample size increases, the degree of sampling error also declines.

9.9. NON-SAMPLING ERRORS

According to *Petterson*, Non-sampling errors are those errors that occur in acquiring recording or tabulating a statistical data that cannot be ascribed to sampling error.

Non-sampling errors are likely to be more in case of complete enumeration survey than in case of a simple survey. The best method to reduce non-sampling errors is that we should use trained workers at the field and during tabulation. Non-sampling errors can occur at every stage of planning and execution of the census or survey. Other reasons of non-sampling errors are:

(*i*) defective methods of data collection
(*ii*) faulty methods of tabulation
(*iii*) incomplete coverage of population or sample.

9.10. RELATION BETWEEN SAMPLE SIZE AND NON-SAMPLING ERRORS

The non-sampling errors increase with the increase in sample size. The behaviour of non-sampling errors with the increase in sample size is just opposite of sampling errors.

9.11. CASE STUDY

You are given the following data of the number of Assistant professors, Associate professors and professors in Central Universities of India.

Duration of service	*Asst. Prof.*	*Asso. Prof.*	*Prof.*	*Total*
< 5 years	2000	250	50	2300
Between 5–10 years	3000	220	80	3300
Between 10–15 years	1500	170	30	1700
> 15 years	880	80	40	1000
Total	7380	720	200	8300

Questions for Discussion:

You, as an dean academics, are required to analyze the data and determine and discuss:

How many Assistant Professors, Associate Professors and Professors may be selected from each category if

(*i*) stratified proportionate sampling method is adopted by taking 10% of the population equivalent to the sample size.

(*ii*) If the sample size is 10% of the population but the Assistant Professors, Associate Professors and the Professors are to be in the ratio of 5 : 3 : 2 and the weightage of the duration of service is to be in the ratio of 4 : 3 : 2 : 1.

Sol. (*i*) The population size is 8300 and 10% of this size = $8300 \times \frac{10}{100} = 830.$

Hence the sample size would be 830. There will be 12 strata (3 of < 5 years, 3 of between 5 to 10 years, 3 of between 10 to 15 years and 3 of more than 15 years duration of service). Using the proportionate stratified sampling technique, the number of persons selected in each stratum is given below. (Taking 10% of each stratum).

Duration of service	*Asst. Prof.*	*Asso. Prof.*	*Prof.*	*Total*
< 5 years	$2000 \times \frac{10}{100} = 200$	25	5	230
Between 5–10 years	300	22	8	330
Between 10–15 years	150	17	3	170
> 15 years	88	8	4	100
Total	738	72	20	830

(*ii*) Here, again the sample size is 830. But the Assistant Professors, Associate Professors and Professors are to be selected in the ratio of 5 : 3 : 2 of the sample

$\therefore$ number of Assistant Professors $= 830 \times \frac{5}{10} = 415$

number of Associate Professors $= 830 \times \frac{3}{10} = 249$

number of Professors $= 830 \times \frac{2}{10} = 166$

Also, the weightage of the duration of service is in the ratio of 4 : 3 : 2 : 1. Therefore, the required number selected from each category is given below:

Duration of sevice	*Asst. Prof.*	*Asso. Prof.*	*Prof.*	*Total*
< 5 years	$415 \times \frac{4}{10} = 166$	$249 \times \frac{4}{10}$ $= 99.6 \cong 100$	$166 \times \frac{4}{10}$ $= 66.4 \cong 66$	332
Between 5–10 years	$415 \times \frac{3}{10}$ $= 124.5 \cong 124$	$249 \times \frac{3}{10}$ $= 74.7 \cong 74^*$	$166 \times \frac{3}{10}$ $= 49.80 \cong 50$	248
Between 10–15 years	$415 \times \frac{2}{10} = 83$	$249 \times \frac{2}{10}$ $= 49.8 \cong 50$	$166 \times \frac{2}{10} = 33.2$ $\cong 33$	166
> 15 years	$415 \times \frac{1}{10}$ $= 41.5 \cong 42$	$249 \times \frac{1}{10}$ $= 24.9 \cong 25$	$166 \times \frac{1}{10} = 16.6 \cong 17$	84
Total	415	249	166	830

Note: We take $74.7 \cong 74$ though it should be 75. The reason is that the total number of Associate Professors is 249, otherwise it would be 250.

TEST YOUR KNOWLEDGE 9.1

1. Distinguish between the "census" and "sampling" methods of data collection and compare their merits and demerits.
2. Explain the term 'population' and 'sample'.
3. What is random sampling? How can a random sample be selected?
4. Discuss the types of non-random sampling.
5. Write a note on biased and unbiased errors.
6. What are sampling errors? Is there any relation between sampling errors and sample size? Discuss in detail.
7. What is the best formula to determine the sample size?

10

Testing of Hypothesis

10.1. POPULATION OR UNIVERSE *(P.T.U., M.B.A. Dec., 2010)*

An aggregate of objects (animate or inanimate) under study is called **population or universe.** It is thus a collection of individuals or of their attributes (qualities) or of results of operations which can be numerically specified.

A universe containing a finite number of individuals or members is called a **finite inverse.** For example, the universe of the weights of students in a particular class or the universe of smokes in Rohtak district.

A universe with infinite number of members is known as an **infinite universe.** For example, the universe of pressures at various points in the atmosphere.

In some cases, we may be even ignorant whether or not a particular universe is infinite, *e.g.*, the universe of stars.

The universe of concrete objects is an **existent universe.** The collection of all possible ways in which a specified event can happen is called a **hypothetical universe.** The universe of heads and tails obtained by tossing a coin an infinite number of times (provided that it does not wear out) is a hypothetical one.

10.2. SAMPLING *(P.T.U., M.B.A. Dec., 2010)*

The statistician is often confronted with the problem of discussing universe of which he cannot examine every member, *i.e.*, of which complete enumeration is impracticable. For example, if we want to have an idea of the average per capita income of the people of India, enumeration of every earning individual in the country is a very difficult task. Naturally, the question arises : What can be said about a universe of which we can examine only a limited number of members ? This question is the origin of the Theory of Sampling.

A finite sub-set of a universe is called a **sample.** A sample is thus a small portion of the universe. The number of individuals in a sample is called the **sample size.** The process of selecting a sample from a universe is called **sampling.**

The theory of sampling is a study of relationship existing between a population and samples drawn from the population. The fundamental object of sampling is to get as much information as possible of the whole universe by examining only a part of it. An attempt is thus made through sampling to give the maximum information about the parent universe with the minimum effort.

Sampling is quite often used in our day-to-day practical life. For example, in a shop we asses the quality of sugar, rice or any other commodity by taking only a handful of it from the bag and then decide whether to purchase it or not. A housewife normally tests the cooked products to find if they are properly cooked and contain the proper quantity of salt or sugar, by taking a spoonful of it.

10.3. PARAMETERS OF STATISTICS

The statistical constants of the population such as mean, variance, etc., are known as parameters. The statistical concepts of the sample from the members of the sample to estimate the parameters of the population from which the sample has been drawn are known as *statistic*.

Population mean and variance are denoted by μ and σ^2, while those of the sample are given by $\bar{x}$, s^2.

10.4. STANDARD ERROR (S.E.)

(P.T.U., M.B.A. May 2003)

The standard deviation of the sampling distribution of a statistic is known as the standard error (S.E.).

It plays an important role in the theory of large samples and it forms a basis of the testing of hypothesis. If t is any statistic for large sample, then

$z = \dfrac{t - E(t)}{S.E(t)}$ is normally distributed with mean 0 and variance unity.

For large sample, the standard errors of some of the well known statistic are listed below :

n-sample size ; σ^2-population variance ; s^2-sample variance ; P-population proportion ; $Q = 1 - P$; n_1, n_2-are sizes of two independent random sample.

No.	*Statistic*	*Standard error*
1.	$\bar{x}$	$\sigma/\sqrt{n}$
2.	s	$\sqrt{\sigma^2/2n}$
3.	Difference of two sample means $\bar{x}_1 - \bar{x}_2$	$\sqrt{\dfrac{\sigma_1^2}{n_1} + \dfrac{\sigma_2^2}{n_2}}$
4.	Difference of two sample standard deviation $s_1 - s_2$	$\sqrt{\dfrac{\sigma_1^2}{2n_1} + \dfrac{\sigma_2^2}{2n_2}}$
5.	Difference of two sample proportions $p_1 - p_2$	$\sqrt{\dfrac{P_1Q_1}{n_1} + \dfrac{P_2Q_2}{n_2}}$
6.	Observed sample proportion p	$\sqrt{PQ/n}$

10.5. TEST OF SIGNIFICANCE

An important aspect of the sampling theory is to study the test of significance which will enable us to decide, on the basis of the results of the sample, whether

(i) the deviation between the observed sample statistic and the hypothetical parameter value or

(ii) the deviation between two sample statistics is significant or might be attributed due to chance or the fluctuations of the sampling.

Null Hypothesis *(P.T.U., M.B.A. Dec. 2008, May 2010,2006)*

For applying the tests of significance, we first set up a hypothesis which is a definite statement about the population parameter called **Null hypothes is** denoted by H_0.

Alternative Hypothesis *(P.T.U., M.B.A. May 2010, Dec. 2006)*

Any hypothesis which is complementary to the null hypothesis ($\mathbf{H_0}$) is called an **Alternative hypothesis** denoted by $\mathbf{H_1}$.

For example, if we want to test the null hypothesis that the population has a specified mean μ_0, then we have

$$\mathbf{H_0} : \mu = \mu_0$$

Alternative hypothesis will be

(*i*) $H_1 : \mu \neq \mu_0$ ($\mu > \mu_0$ *or* $\mu < \mu_0$) (two tailed alternative hypothesis).

(*ii*) $H_1 : \mu > \mu_0$ (right tailed alternative hypothesis (*or*) single tailed).

(*iii*) $H_1 : \mu < \mu_0$ (left tailed alternative hypothesis (*or*) single tailed).

Hence alternative hypothesis helps to know whether the test is two tailed test or one tailed test.

10.6. CRITICAL REGION

A region corresponding to a statistic t, in the sample space S which amounts to rejection of the null hypothesis H_0 is called as **critical region** or **region of rejection.** The region of the sample space S which amounts to the acceptance of H_0 is called *acceptance region*.

10.7. LEVEL OF SIGNIFICANCE *(P.T.U., M.B.A. May 2003, 2004, 2000, Dec. 2003)*

The probability of the value of the variate falling in the critical region is known as level of significance.

The probability α that a random value of the statistic t belongs to the critical region is known as the *level of significance* where

$$P(t \in \omega \mid H_0) = \alpha$$

i.e., the level of significance is the size of the type I error or the maximum producer's risk.

10.8. ERRORS IN SAMPLING *(P.T.U., M.B.A. May 2010, 2004, Dec. 2009)*

The main aim of the sampling theory is to draw a valid conclusion about the population parameters on the basis of the sample results. In doing this, we may commit the following two types of errors :

Type I Error. When H_0 is true, we may reject it, *i.e.*,

P(Reject H_0 when it is true) = P(Reject H_0/H_0) = α

α is called the size of the type I error also referred to as **producer's risk.**

Type II Error. When H_0 is wrong we may accept it. *i.e.*,

P(Accept H_0 when it is wrong) = P(Accept H_0/H_1) = β.

β is called the size of the type II error, also referred to as **consumer's risk.**

10.9. CRITICAL VALUES OR SIGNIFICANT VALUES

The values of the test statistic which separates the critical region and acceptance region is called the **critical values** or **significant value.**

This value is dependent on (*i*) the level of significance used and (*ii*) the alternative hypothesis, whether it is one tailed or two tailed.

10.10. TESTING OF HYPOTHESIS *(P.T.U., M.B.A. May 2004)*

For larger samples corresponding to the statistic t, the variable $z = \dfrac{t - E(t)}{S.E(t)}$ is Normally distributed with mean 0 and variance 1. The value of z given above under the null hypothesis is known as **test statistic.**

The critical value of z_α of the test statistic z at level of significance α for a two tailed test is given by

$$p(|\ z\ | > z_\alpha) = \alpha \qquad ...(1)$$

i.e., z_α is the value of z so that the total area of the critical region on both tails is α. Since the Normal curve is a symmetrical, from equation (1), we get

$$p(z > z_\alpha) + p(z < -z_\alpha) = \alpha \text{ ; } i.e., \ 2p(z > z_\alpha) = \alpha \ \Rightarrow \ p(z > z_\alpha) = \alpha/2$$

i.e., the area of each tail is $\alpha/2$.

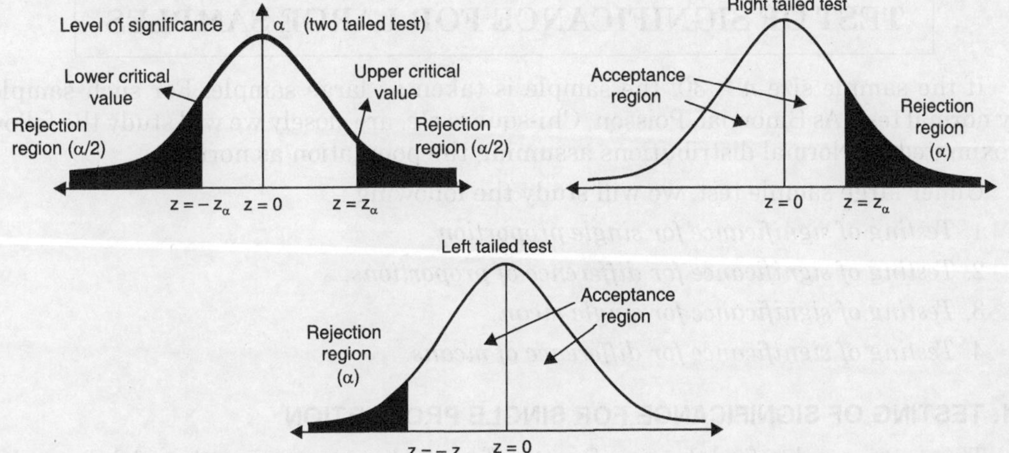

The critical value z_α is that value such that the area to the right of z_α is $\alpha/2$ and the area to the left of $-z_\alpha$ is $\alpha/2$.

In the case of one tailed test

$p(z > z_\alpha) = \alpha$ if it is right tailed ; $p(z < -z_\alpha) = \alpha$ if it is left tailed.

The critical value of z for a single tailed test (right or left) at level of significance α is same as the critical value of z for two-tailed test at level of significance 2α.

Using the equation, also using the normal tables, the critical value of z at different level of significance (α) for both single tailed and two tailed test are calculated and listed below. The equations are

$$p(|\ z\ | > z_\alpha) = \alpha \text{ ; } p(z > z_\alpha) = \alpha \text{ ; } p(z < -z_\alpha) = \alpha$$

	Critical value	*Level of significance*		
		1% (0.01)	*5% (0.05)*	*10% (1.1)*
Two tailed test	$\lvert z_\alpha \rvert$	2.58	1.96	1.645
Right tailed	z_α	2.33	1.645	1.28
Left tailed	z_α	– 2.33	1.645	– 1.28

Note. Steps in testing of hypothesis:

The following steps may be adopted in testing of statistical hypothesis :

(P.T.U. M.B.A. Dec. 2012)

Step 1. Null hypothesis. Set up H_0.

Step 2. Alternative hypothesis. Set up H_1 so that we could decide whether we should used one-tailed test or two tailed test.

Step 3. Level of significance. Select the appropriate level of significance in advance depending on the reliability of the estimates.

Step 4. Test statistic. Compute the test statistic $z = \dfrac{t - E(t)}{S.E(t)}$ under the null hypothesis.

Step 5. Conclusion. Compare the computed value of z with the critical value z_α at level of significance (α). If $|z| > z_\alpha$, we reject H_0 and conclude that there is significant difference. If $|z| < z_\alpha$, we accept H_0 and conclude that there is no significant difference.

TEST OF SIGNIFICANCE FOR LARGE SAMPLES

If the sample size $n > 30$, the sample is taken as large sample. For such sample we apply normal test. As Binomial, Poisson, Chi-square etc. are closely we will study the following approximated by Normal distributions assuming the population as normal.

Under large sample test, we will study the following :

1. *Testing of significance for single proportion.*
2. *Testing of significance for difference of proportions.*
3. *Testing of significance for single mean.*
4. *Testing of significance for difference of means.*

10.11. TESTING OF SIGNIFICANCE FOR SINGLE PROPORTION

This test is used to find the significant difference between proportion of the sample and the population.

Let X be the number of successes in n independent trials with constant probability P of success for each trial.

$$E(X) = nP \ ; \ V(X) = nPQ \ ; \ Q = 1 - P = \text{Probability of failure.}$$

Let $p = X/n$ called the observed proportion of success.

$$E(p) = E(X/n) = \frac{1}{n} E(X) = \frac{nP}{n} = P$$

$$V(p) = V(X/n) = \frac{1}{n^2} V(X) = \frac{nPQ}{n^2} = PQ/n$$

$$S.E(p) = \sqrt{\frac{PQ}{n}} \ ; \ z = \frac{p - E(p)}{S.E(p)} = \frac{p - P}{\sqrt{PQ/n}} \sim N(0, 1)$$

This z is called test statistic which is used to test the significant difference of sample and population proportion.

Note 1. The probable limit for the observed proportion of successes are $p \pm z_\alpha \sqrt{PQ/n}$, where z_α is the significant value at level of significance α.

2. If p is not known, the limits for the proportion in the population are $P \pm z_\alpha \sqrt{pq/n}$, $q = 1 - p$.

3. If α is not given, we can take safely 3σ limits.

ILLUSTRATIVE EXAMPLES

Example 1. *A coin was tossed 400 times and the head turned up 216 times. Test the hypothesis that the coin is unbiased.*

Sol. Null Hypothesis. H_0 : The coin is unbiased *i.e.,* P = 0.5.

Alternative Hypothesis. H_1 : The coin is not unbiased *i.e.,* P ≠ 0.5 (two tailed test)

Here $n = 400$, X = No. of success = 216

$$p = \text{proportion of success in the sample} = \frac{X}{n} = \frac{216}{400} = 0.54$$

Probability of success P = 0.5 (As the coin is unbiased) ; Q = 1 – P = 1 – 0.5 = 0.5

Under H_0, $$z = \frac{p - P}{\sqrt{PQ/n}}$$

$$z = \frac{0.54 - 0.5}{\sqrt{\dfrac{0.5 \times 0.5}{400}}} = 1.6 \quad \Rightarrow \quad |z| = 1.6$$

Conclusion. Since $|z| = 1.6 < 1.96$ *i.e.,* $|z| < z_\alpha$, z_α is the significant value of z at 5% level of significance *i.e.,* H_0 is accepted and hence the coin is unbiased.

Example 2. *A certain cubical die was thrown 9000 times and 5 or 6 was obtained 3240 times. On the assumption of certain throwing, do the data indicate an unbiased die ?*

Sol. Here $n = 9000$

P = probability of success (*i.e.,* getting 5 or 6 in die)

= 2/6 = 1/3, Q = 1 – 1/3 = 2/3

$$\text{Proportion of success } p = \frac{X}{n} = \frac{3240}{9000} = 0.36$$

Null Hypothesis H_0 : The die is unbiased, *i.e.,* P = 1/3

Alternative Hypothesis H_1 : P ≠ 1/3 (two tailed test)

Under H_0 $$z = \frac{p - P}{\sqrt{\dfrac{PQ}{n}}} = \frac{0.36 - 0.33}{\sqrt{\dfrac{1}{3} \times \dfrac{2}{3} \times \dfrac{1}{9000}}} = \frac{(0.03) \times \sqrt{81000}}{\sqrt{2}}$$

$$= \frac{(0.03) \times 284.60}{1.4142} = \frac{8.538}{1.4142} = 6.0374$$

$\Rightarrow$ $|z| = 6.0374$

Conclusion. Since $|z| = 6.0374 > 1.96$. Therefore H_0 is rejected *i.e.,* the die is not unbiased.

Example 3. *A manufacturer claims that only 4% of his products supplied by him are defective. A random sample of 600 products contained 36 defectives. Test the claim of the manufacturer.*

Sol. Let p = Observed proportion of success.

i.e., $$p = \text{Proportion of defective products in the sample} = \frac{36}{600} = 0.06$$

P = Probability of being defectives in the population = 0.04, Q = 1 – P = 0.96

Null Hypothesis H_0 : P = 0.04 is true *i.e.*, the claim of the manufacturer is accepted.

Alternative Hypothesis. H_1 : P ≠ 0.04 (two tailed test)

Under H_0,
$$z = \frac{p - P}{\sqrt{PQ/n}} = \frac{0.06 - 0.04}{\sqrt{\dfrac{0.04 \times 0.96}{600}}} = \frac{(0.02) \times \sqrt{6000000}}{\sqrt{384}} = \frac{48.98}{19.59} = 2.5.$$

Conclusion. Since | z | = 2.5 > 1.96, we reject the hypothesis H_0 at 5% level of significance *i.e.*, the manufacturer's claim is not acceptable.

Example 4. *A machine is producing bolts of which a certain fraction is defective. A random sample of 400 is taken from a large batch and is found to contain 30 defective bolts. Does this indicate that the proportion of defectives is larger than that claimed by the manufacturer where the manufacturer claims that only 5% of his product are defective. Find 95% confidence limits of the proportion of defective bolts in batch.*

Sol. Null hypothesis. H_0 : The manufacturer claim is accepted, *i.e.*,

$$P = \frac{5}{100} = 0.05,\ Q = 1 - P = 1 - 0.05 = 0.95$$

Alternative hypothesis. $\mathbf{H_1}$: P > 0.05 (Right tailed test).

Here
$$p = \text{Observed proportion of sample} = \frac{30}{400} = 0.075$$

Under H_0, the test statistic
$$z = \frac{p - P}{\sqrt{PQ/n}} = \frac{0.075 - 0.05}{\sqrt{\dfrac{0.05 \times 0.95}{400}}} = \frac{(0.025)\sqrt{4000000}}{\sqrt{475}}$$
$$= \frac{50}{21.79} = 2.2941.$$

⇒ $| z | = 2.2941$

Conclusion. The tabulated value of z at 5% level of significance for right tailed test is $z_\alpha = 1.645$. Since $| z | = 2.2941 > 1.645$ ∴ H_0 is rejected at 5% level of significance. *i.e.*, the proportion of defective is larger than the manufacturer claim.

To find 95% confidence limits of the proportion.

It is given by $p \pm z_\alpha \sqrt{PQ/n}$

$$= 0.075 \pm 1.645 \sqrt{\frac{0.05 \times 0.95}{400}} = 0.075 \pm 0.01792 = (0.09292, 0.05708)$$

Hence 95% confidence limits for the proportion of defective bolt are (0.05708, 0.09292).

Example 5. *A bag contains defective article, the exact number of which is not known. A sample of 100 from the bag gives 10 defective articles. Find the limits for the proportion of defective articles in the bag.*

Sol. Here p = Proportion of defective articles = $\frac{10}{100} = 0.1$; $q = 1 - p = 1 - 0.1 = 0.9$

Since the confidence limits is not given, we assume it is 95%.

∴ At 5% level of significance, = 1.96.

Also the probability of success P is not given. $\therefore$ we take $P = p = 0.1$.

To get the confidence limit, it is given by

$$P \pm z_\alpha \sqrt{pq/n} = 0.1 \pm 1.96 \sqrt{\frac{0.1 \times 0.9}{100}} = 0.1 \pm 0.0588 = 0.1588,\ 0.0412$$

Hence 95% confidence limits for defective article in the bag are (0.0412, 0.1588).

Example 6. *A manufacturer claims that only 10% of the articles produced are below the standard quality. Out of a random inspection of 300 articles, 37 are found to be of poor quality. Test the manufacturer's claim at 5% level of significance.* (P.T.U., M.B.A. Dec. 2001)

Sol. Let

Null Hypothesis:

H_0 = The claim of manufacturer is true

Alternative hypothesis:

H_1 = The claim of manufacturer is not true *i.e.*, $p \neq 0.1$ (two tailed test)

Now P = Proportion of defective articles in the population = 10% $= \frac{10}{100} = 0.1$

$Q = 1 - P = 1 - 0.1 = 0.9,\ n = 300$

p = Proportion of defective articles in the sample $= \frac{37}{300} = 0.1233$

Under H_0,
$$Z = \frac{p - P}{\sqrt{PQ/n}} = \frac{0.1233 - 0.1}{\sqrt{\frac{(0.1)(0.9)}{300}}} = \frac{0.0233}{0.0173} = 1.3468$$

$\Rightarrow$ $|z| = 1.3468 < 1.96$

Conclusion. H_0 is accepted *i.e.*, the manufacturer's claim is true.

TEST YOUR KNOWLEDGE 10.1

1. A sample of size of 600 persons selected at random from a large city shows that the percentage of males in the sample is 53. It is believed that the ratio of males to the total population in the city is 0.5. Test whether the belief is confirmed by the observation.
2. In a city a sample of 1000 people were taken and out of them 540 are vegetarian and the rest are non-vegetarian. Can we say that the both habits of eating (Vegetarian or non-vegetarian) are equally popular in the city at (*i*) 1% level of significance (*ii*) 5% level of significance.
3. 325 men out of 600 men chosen from a big city were found to be smokers. Does this information support the conclusion that the majority of men in the city are smokers?
4. A random sample of 500 bolts was taken from a large consignment and 50 were found to be defective. Find the percentage of defective bolts in the consignment.
5. In a hospital 475 female and 525 male babies were born in a week. Do these figure confirm the hypothesis that males and females are born in equal number.
6. 400 apples are taken at random from a large basket and 40 are found to be bad. Estimate the proportion of bad apples in the basket and assign limits within which the percentage most probably lies. *(P.T.U., M.B.A. May 2004)*
7. Distinguish between two tailed and one tailed test of hypothesis. *(P.T.U., M.B.A. May 2003)*

Answers

1. H_0 accepted at 5% level ($|z| = 1.5$) **2.** H_0 rejected at 5% level, accepted at 1% level ($|z| = 2.53$)
3. H_0 rejected at 5% level ($|z| = 2$) **4.** Between 8.5 and 17.5
5. H_0 accepted at 5% level ($|z| = 1.26$) **6.** (0.0706, 0.1294).

10.12. TEST OF DIFFERENCE BETWEEN PROPORTIONS

Consider two samples X_1 and X_2 of sizes n_1 and n_2 respectively taken from two different populations. To test the significance of the difference between the sample proportion p_1 and p_2, the test statistic under the null hypothesis H_0 : that there is no significant difference between the two sample proportion, is given by

$$z = \frac{p_1 - p_2}{\sqrt{PQ\left(\frac{1}{n_1} + \frac{1}{n_2}\right)}}, \qquad \text{where } P = \frac{n_1 p_1 + n_2 p_2}{n_1 + n_2} \text{ and } Q = 1 - P.$$

ILLUSTRATIVE EXAMPLES

Example 1. *Before an increase in excise duty on tea, 800 people out of a sample of 1000 persons were found to be tea drinkers. After an increase in the duty, 800 persons were known to be tea drinkers in a sample of 1200 people. Do you think that there has been a significant decrease in the consumption of tea after the increase in the excise duty ?*

Sol. Here $n_1 = 800, n_2 = 1200$

$$p_1 = \frac{X_1}{n_1} = \frac{800}{1000} = \frac{4}{5} \; ; \; p_2 = \frac{X_2}{n_2} = \frac{800}{1200} = \frac{2}{3}$$

$$P = \frac{p_1 n_1 + p_2 n_2}{n_1 + n_2} = \frac{X_1 + X_2}{n_1 + n_2} = \frac{800 + 800}{1000 + 1200} = \frac{8}{11} \; ; \; Q = \frac{3}{11}$$

Null hypothesis H_0 : $p_1 = p_2$, *i.e.*, there is no significant difference in the consumption of tea before and after increase of excise duty.

Alternative hypothesis H_1 : $p_1 > p_2$ (Right tailed test)

Under H_0, the test statistic
$$z = \frac{p_1 - p_2}{\sqrt{PQ\left(\frac{1}{n_1} + \frac{1}{n_2}\right)}} = \frac{0.8 - 0.6666}{\sqrt{\frac{8}{11} \times \frac{3}{11}\left(\frac{1}{1000} + \frac{1}{1200}\right)}}$$

$$= \frac{0.1334}{0.01906} = 6.99 .$$

$\Rightarrow$ $|z| = 6.99$

Conclusion. Since the calculated value of $|z| > 1.645$. Also $|z| > 2.33$. Hence H_0 is rejected at 5% and 1% level of significance, *i.e.*, there is a significant decrease in the consumption of tea due to increase in excise duty.

Example 2. *A machine produced 16 defective articles in a batch of 500. After overhauling it produced 3 defectives in a batch of 100. Has the machine improved ?*

Sol. $p_1 = \frac{16}{500} = 0.032 \; ; \; n_1 = 500$

$$p_2 = \frac{3}{100} = 0.03 \; ; \; n_2 = 100$$

Null hypothesis H_0 : The machine has not improved due to overhauling *i.e.*, $p_1 = p_2$.
Alternative Hypothesis H_1 : $p_1 > p_2$ (Right tailed test)

$$\therefore \qquad P = \frac{p_1 n_1 + p_2 n_2}{n_1 + n_2} = \frac{19}{600} \cong 0.032$$

Under H_0, the test statistic

$$z = \frac{p_1 - p_2}{\sqrt{PQ\left(\frac{1}{n_1} + \frac{1}{n_2}\right)}} = \frac{0.032 - 0.03}{\sqrt{(0.032)(0.968)\left(\frac{1}{500} + \frac{1}{100}\right)}}$$

$$= \frac{0.002}{\sqrt{(0.032)(0.968)(0.012)}} = \frac{0.002}{0.01927} = 0.104.$$

Conclusion. The calculated value of $|z| < 1.645$,

$\therefore$ H_0 is accepted at 5% level of significance, *i.e.*, the machine has not improved due to overhauling.

Example 3. *In two large populations there are 30% and 25% respectively of fair haired people. Is this difference likely to be hidden in samples of 1200 and 900 respectively from the two populations ?*

Sol. p_1 = proportion of fair haired people in the first population = 30% = 0.3 ; p_2 = 25% = 0.25 ; n_1 = 1200, n_2 = 900

Null hypothesis H_0 : Sample proportions are equal ($p_1 = p_2$) *i.e.*, the difference in population proportions is likely to be hidden in sampling.

Alternative hypothesis H_1 : $p_1 \neq p_2$ (two tailed test)

$$\therefore \qquad P = \frac{n_1 p_1 + n_2 p_2}{n_1 + n_2} = \frac{360 + 225}{2100} = 0.2785$$

$$Q = 1 - P = 1 - 0.2785 = 0.7215$$

Under H_0,

$$z = \frac{p_1 - p_2}{\sqrt{PQ\left(\frac{1}{n_1} + \frac{1}{n_2}\right)}} = \frac{0.3 - 0.25}{\sqrt{0.2785 \times 0.7215\left(\frac{1}{1200} + \frac{1}{900}\right)}}$$

$$= \frac{(0.05) \times 10}{\sqrt{(0.2785) \times (0.7215) \times 0.1944}} = \frac{0.5}{0.1976} = 2.530$$

Conclusion. Since $|z| > 1.96$ $\therefore$ H_0 is rejected at 5% level of significance. However $|z| < 2.58$ $\therefore$ H_0 is accepted at 1% level of significance. At 5% level, these samples will reveal the difference in the population proportions.

Example 4. *500 articles from a factory are examined and found to be 2% defective. 800 similar articles from a second factory are found to have only 1.5% defective. Can it reasonably be concluded that the product of the first factory are inferior to those of second ?*

Sol. $n_1 = 500$, $n_2 = 800$

p_1 = proportion of defective from first factory = 2% = 0.02

p_2 = proportion of defective from second factory = 1.5% = 0.015

Null Hypothesis H_0 : There is no significant difference between the two products, *i.e.*, the products do not differ in quality.

Alternative Hypothesis $H_1 : p_1 > p_2$ (right tailed test)

Under H_0, $$z = \frac{p_1 - p_2}{\sqrt{PQ\left(\frac{1}{n_1} + \frac{1}{n_2}\right)}}$$

Here, $$P = \frac{n_1p_1 + n_2p_2}{n_1 + n_2} = \frac{0.02(500) + (0.015)(800)}{500 + 800} = 0.01692 \; ; \; Q = 1 - P = 0.9830$$

$$\therefore \quad z = \frac{0.02 - 0.015}{\sqrt{0.01692 \times 0.983\left(\frac{1}{500} + \frac{1}{800}\right)}} = \frac{(0.005)(10)}{\sqrt{0.01692 \times 0.983 \times 0.325}}$$

$$= \frac{0.05}{0.0735} = 0.68$$

Conclusion. As $|z| < 1.645$ $\therefore$ H_0 is accepted at 5% level of significance *i.e.,* the products do not differ in quality.

Example 5. *A sample of 400 voters from city A and 300 voters from city B showed that 60% respectively in favour of a candidate. Test at 5% level of significance that the two cities do not show any difference in their preference for the candidate.* (P.T.U., M.B.A. May 2001)

Sol. 60% of 400 $= 400 \times \frac{60}{100} = 240$ and 60% of 300 $= 300 \times \frac{60}{100} = 180$

$$\therefore \quad p_1 = \frac{240}{400} = 0.6 \; ; \quad p_2 = \frac{180}{300} = 0.6$$

Null Hypothesis H_0 : Two cities do not show any difference in their preference *i.e.,* $p_1 = p_2$

Alternative Hypothesis $H_1 : p_1 > p_2$ (right tailed test)

Under H_0, $$z = \frac{p_1 - p_2}{\sqrt{PQ\left(\frac{1}{n_1} + \frac{1}{n_2}\right)}} = \frac{0.6 - 0.6}{\sqrt{PQ\left(\frac{1}{n_1} + \frac{1}{n_2}\right)}} = 0$$

Conclusion. The calculated value of $|z| < 1.96$. Therefore H_0 is accepted at 5% level of significance *i.e.,* there is no difference in the preference of the voters from the cities A and B.

TEST YOUR KNOWLEDGE 10.2

1. Random sample of 400 men and 600 women were asked whether they want to have a school near their residence. 200 men and 325 women were in favour of proposal. Test the hypothesis that the proportion of men and women in favour of the proposal are same at 5% level of significance.
2. In a town A, there were 956 births of which 52.5% was males while in towns A and B combined, this proportion in total of 1406 births was 0.496. Is there any significant difference in the proportion of male births in the two towns ?
3. In a referendum submitted to the students body at a university, 850 men and 560 women voted. 500 men and 320 women voted yes. Does this indicate a significant difference of opinion between men and women on this matter at 1% level ?
4. A manufacturing firm claims that its brand A product outsells its brand B product by 8%. If it is found that 42 out of a sample of 200 persons prefer brand A and 18 out of another sample of 100 person prefer brand B. Test whether the 8% difference is a valid claim.

Answers

1. H_0 is accepted *i.e.*, the proportion of men and women in favour of the proposal is same. ($|z| = 1.269$)
2. H_0 is rejected *i.e.*, There is a significant difference in the proportion of male births in the two towns. ($|z| = 2.829$)
3. H_0 is accepted *i.e.*, there is no significant difference of opinion between men and women on the matter at 1% level of significance. ($|z| = 0.46$)
4. H_0 is accepted *i.e.*, the manufacturer's claim is true. ($|z| = 0.625$)

10.13. TEST OF SIGNIFICANCE FOR SINGLE MEAN

To test whether the difference between sample mean and population mean is significant or not.

Let $X_1, X_2, ..., X_n$ be a random sample of size n from a large population $X_1, X_2, ..., X_N$ of size N with mean μ and variance σ^2. $\therefore$ the standard error of mean of a random sample of size n from a population with variance σ^2 is $\sigma/\sqrt{n}$.

To test whether the given sample of size n has been drawn from a population with mean μ *i.e.*, to test whether the difference between the sample mean and population mean is significant or not. Set up the null hypothesis that there is no difference between the sample mean and population mean.

The test statistic is $z = \dfrac{\bar{x} - \mu}{\sigma/\sqrt{n}}$, where σ is the standard deviation of the population.

If σ is not known, we use the test statistic $z = \dfrac{\bar{x} - \mu}{s/\sqrt{n}}$, where s is the standard deviation of the sample.

Note. If the level of significance is α and z_α is the critical value then, $-z_\alpha < |z| = \left|\dfrac{\bar{x} - \mu}{\sigma/\sqrt{n}}\right| < z_\alpha$

The limits of the population mean μ are given by $\bar{x} - z_\alpha \dfrac{\sigma}{\sqrt{n}} < \mu < \bar{x} + z_\alpha \sigma/\sqrt{n}$.

At 5% of level of significance, 95% confidence limits are $\bar{x} - 1.96 \dfrac{\sigma}{\sqrt{n}} < \mu < \bar{x} + 1.96 \dfrac{\sigma}{\sqrt{n}}$

At 1% level of significance, 99% confidence limits are $\bar{x} - 2.58 \dfrac{\sigma}{\sqrt{n}} < \mu < \bar{x} + 2.58 \dfrac{\sigma}{\sqrt{n}}$.

These limits are called **confidence limits** or **fiducial limits.**

ILLUSTRATIVE EXAMPLES

Example 1. *A normal population has a mean of 6.8 and standard deviation of 1.5. A sample of 400 members gave a mean of 6.75. Is the difference significant ?*

Sol. Null Hypothesis H_0 : There is no significant difference between $\bar{x}$ and μ. *i.e.*, $\bar{x} = \mu$

Alternative Hypothesis H_1 : There is significant difference between $\bar{x}$ and μ.

i.e., $\bar{x} \neq \mu$ (two tailed test).

Given $\mu = 6.8, \sigma = 1.5, \bar{x} = 6.75$ and $n = 400$

Under H_0 ; $z = \dfrac{\bar{x} - \mu}{\sigma/\sqrt{n}} = \dfrac{6.75 - 6.8}{1.5/\sqrt{400}} = -0.67 \Rightarrow |z| = 0.67$

Conclusion. As the calculated value of $|z| < z_\alpha = 1.96$ at 5% level of significance.

$\therefore$ H_0 is accepted, *i.e.*, there is no significant difference between $\bar{x}$ and μ.

Example 2. *A random sample of 900 members has a mean 3.4 cms. Can it be reasonably regarded as a sample from a large population of mean 3.2 cms and S.D. 2.3 cms ?*

Sol. Here $n = 900$, $\bar{x} = 3.4$, $\mu = 3.2$, $\sigma = 2.3$

Null Hypothesis H_0 : Assume that the sample is drawn from a large population with mean 3.2 *i.e.*, $\mu = 3.2$

Alternative Hypothesis H_1 : $\mu \neq 3.2$ (Two tailed test)

Under H_0 ; $$z = \frac{\bar{x} - \mu}{\sigma/\sqrt{n}} = \frac{3.4 - 3.2}{2.3/\sqrt{900}} = \frac{0.2}{2.3/30} = \frac{0.2}{2.3} \times 30 = 2.608.$$

Conclusion. $|z| = 2.608 > 1.96$

$\therefore$ H_0 is accepted at 5% level of significance *i.e.*, the sample is drawn from the population with mean 3.2 and s.d. = 2.3.

Example 3. *The mean weight obtained from a random sample of size 100 is 64 gms. The S.D. of the weight distribution of the population is 3 gms. Test the statement that the mean weight of the population is 67 gms at 5% level of significance. Also set up 99% confidence limits of the mean weight of the population.*

Sol. Here $n = 100$, $\mu = 67$, $\bar{x} = 64$, $\sigma = 3$

Null Hypothesis H_0 : There is no significant difference between sample and population mean. *i.e.*, $\mu = 67$.

Alternative Hypothesis H_1 : $\mu \neq 67$ (Two tailed test)

Under H_0, $$z = \frac{\bar{x} - \mu}{\sigma/\sqrt{n}} = \frac{64 - 67}{3/\sqrt{100}} = -10 \quad \therefore \quad |z| = 10.$$

Conclusion. Since the calculated value of $|z| > 1.96$

$\therefore$ H_0 is rejected at 5% level of significance *i.e.*, the sample is not drawn from the population with mean 67.

To find 99% confidence limits

It is given by $\bar{x} \pm 2.58\, \sigma/\sqrt{n} = 64 \pm 2.58 \times 3/\sqrt{100} = 64.774, 63.226$. Thus,

99% confidence limits of the mean weight are (63.226, 64.774)

Example 4. *The average marks in Mathematics of a sample of 100 students was 51 with a S.D. of 6 marks. Could this have been a random sample from a population with average marks 50 ?*

Sol. Here $n = 100$, $\bar{x} = 51$, $s = 6$, $\mu = 50$; σ is unknown.

Null Hypothesis H_0 : The sample is drawn from a population with mean 50 *i.e.*, $\mu = 50$

Alternative Hypothesis H_1 : $\mu \neq 50$ (Two tailed test)

Under H_0, $$z = \frac{\bar{x} - \mu}{s/\sqrt{n}} = \frac{51 - 50}{6/\sqrt{100}} = \frac{10}{6} = 1.6666$$

Conclusion. Since $|z| = 1.666 < 1.96$

$\therefore$ H_0, is accepted at 5% level of significance *i.e.*, the sample is drawn from the population with mean 50.

Example 5. *A manufacturer of iron rods estimates that standard deviation of rod lengths is 2.7 ft and average length is 30 ft. On the basis of a random sample of 300 rods, test the hypothesis that average length of rods manufactured by him is 32 ft at 5% level of significance.*

(P.T.U., M.B.A. May 2002)

Sol. Let H_0 = There is no significant difference between $\bar{x}$ and μ *i.e.*, $\bar{x} = \mu$

H_1 = There is a significant difference between $\bar{x}$ and μ *i.e.*, $\bar{x} \neq \mu$ (two tailed test)

Given $\mu = 30$, $\sigma = 2.7$, $n = 300$, $\bar{x} = 32$

Under H_0, $$z = \frac{\bar{x} - \mu}{\sigma/\sqrt{n}} = \frac{32 - 30}{2.7/\sqrt{300}} = \frac{2 \times 17.32}{2.7} = \frac{34.64}{2.7} = 12.82$$

Conclusion. The calculated value of $|z| > 1.96$ at 5% level of significance. H_0 is rejected *i.e.*, there is a significant difference between $\bar{x}$ and μ.

TEST YOUR KNOWLEDGE 10.3

1. A sample of 1000 students from a university was taken and their average weight was found to be 112 pounds with a S.D. of 20 pounds. Could the mean weight of students in the population be 120 pounds ?

2. A sample of 400 male students is found to have a mean height of 160 cms. Can it be reasonably regarded as a sample from a large population with mean height 162.5 cms and standard deviation 4.5 cms.

3. A random sample of 200 measurements from a large population gave a mean value of 50 and a S.D. of 9. Determine 95% confidence interval for the mean of population.

4. The guaranteed average life of certain type of bulbs is 1000 hours with a S.D. of 125 hours. It is decided to sample the output so as to ensure that 90% of the bulbs do not fall short of the guaranteed average by more than 2.5%. What must be the minimum size of the sample.

5. The heights of college students in a city are normally distributed with S.D. 6 cms. A sample of 1000 students has mean height 158 cms. Test the hypothesis that the mean height of college students in the city is 160 cms.

Answers

1. H_0 is rejected ($|z| = 12.64$)   **2.** H_0 accepted ($|z| = 11.11$)

3. (48.75, 51.2)   **4.** $n = 41$

5. H_0 rejected both at 1% to 5% level of significance. ($|z| = 10.54$)

10.14. TEST OF SIGNIFICANCE FOR DIFFERENCE OF MEANS OF TWO LARGE SAMPLES

Let $\bar{x}_1$ be the mean of a sample of size n_1 from a population with mean μ_1 and variance s_1^2. Let $\bar{x}_2$ be the mean of an independent sample of size n_2 from another population with mean μ_2 and variance s_2^2. The test statistic is given by $z = \dfrac{\bar{x}_1 - \bar{x}_2}{\sqrt{\dfrac{s_1^2}{n_1} + \dfrac{s_2^2}{n_2}}}$.

Under the null hypothesis that the samples are drawn from the same population where $\sigma_1 = \sigma_2 = \sigma$, the test statistic is given by $z = \dfrac{\bar{x}_1 - \bar{x}_2}{\sigma\sqrt{\dfrac{1}{n_1} + \dfrac{1}{n_2}}}$, where σ_1^2, σ_2^2 are population variances.

Note 1. If σ_1, σ_2 are known and $\sigma_1 \neq \sigma_2$ the test statistic in this case is $z = \dfrac{\bar{x}_1 - \bar{x}_2}{\sqrt{\dfrac{\sigma_1^2}{n_1} + \dfrac{\sigma_2^2}{n_2}}}$.

Note 2. If σ is not known and $\sigma_1 = \sigma_2$, use $\sigma^2 = \dfrac{n_1 s_1^2 + n_2 s_2^2}{n_1 + n_2}$.

ILLUSTRATIVE EXAMPLES

Example 1. *The average income of persons was ₹ 210 with a S.D. of ₹ 10 in sample of 100 people of a city. For another sample of 150 persons, the average income was ₹ 220 with S.D. of ₹ 12. The S.D. of incomes of the people of the city was ₹ 11. Test whether there is any significant difference between the average incomes of the localities.*

Sol. Here $n_1 = 100$, $n_2 = 150$, $\bar{x}_1 = 210$, $\bar{x}_2 = 220$, $s_1 = 10$, $s_2 = 12$.

Null hypothesis H_0 : The difference is not significant, *i.e.*, there is no difference between the incomes of the localities. *i.e.*, $H_0 : \bar{x}_1 = \bar{x}_2$

Alternative Hypothesis $H_1 : \bar{x}_1 \neq \bar{x}_2$ (Two tailed test)

Under H_0, $$z = \frac{\bar{x}_1 - \bar{x}_2}{\sqrt{\frac{s_1^2}{n_1} + \frac{s_2^2}{n_2}}} = \frac{210 - 220}{\sqrt{\frac{10^2}{100} + \frac{12^2}{150}}} = -7.1428 \quad \therefore \quad |z| = 7.1428.$$

Conclusion. As the calculated value of $|z| > 1.96$.

$\therefore$ H_0 is rejected at 5% level of significance *i.e.*, there is significant difference between the average incomes of the localities.

Example 2. *Intelligent tests were given to two groups of boys and girls.*

	Mean	*S.D.*	*Size*
Girls	*75*	*8*	*60*
Boys	*73*	*10*	*100*

Examine if the difference between mean scores is significant.

Sol. Null hypothesis H_0 : There is no significant difference between mean scores *i.e.*,

$$\bar{x}_1 = \bar{x}_2.$$

Alternative Hypothesis $H_1 : \bar{x}_1 \neq \bar{x}_2$ (Two tailed test)

Under H_0, $$z = \frac{\bar{x}_1 - \bar{x}_2}{\sqrt{\frac{s_1^2}{n_1} + \frac{s_2^2}{n_2}}} = \frac{75 - 73}{\sqrt{\frac{8^2}{60} + \frac{10^2}{100}}} = 1.3912.$$

Conclusion. As the calculated value of $|z| < 1.96$.

$\therefore$ H_0 is accepted at 5% level of significance *i.e.*, there is no significant difference between mean scores.

Example 3. *For sample I, $n_1 = 1000$, $\Sigma x = 49,000$, $\Sigma(x - \bar{x})^2 = 7,84,000$.*

For sample II, $n_2 = 1,500$, $\Sigma x = 70,500$, $\Sigma(x - \bar{x})^2 = 24,00,000$. Discuss the significance of the difference of the sample means.

Sol. Null hypothesis H_0 : There is no significant difference between the sample means.

$$i.e., \overline{x}_1 = \overline{x}_2$$

Alternative Hypothesis $H_1 : \overline{x}_1 \neq \overline{x}_2$ (Two tailed test)

To calculate sample variance,

$$s_1^2 = \frac{1}{n_1}\Sigma(x_1 - \overline{x}_1)^2 = \frac{784000}{1000} = 784$$

$$s_2^2 = \frac{1}{n_2}\Sigma(x_2 - \overline{x}_2)^2 = \frac{1}{1500}(2400000) = 1600$$

$$\overline{x}_1 = \frac{\Sigma x_1}{n_1} = \frac{49000}{1000} = 49 \; ; \; \overline{x}_2 = \frac{\Sigma x_2}{n_2} = \frac{70500}{1500} = 47$$

Under H_0 ; the test statistic is

$$z = \frac{\overline{x}_1 - \overline{x}_2}{\sqrt{\frac{s_1^2}{n_1} + \frac{s_2^2}{n_2}}} = \frac{49 - 47}{\sqrt{\frac{784}{1000} + \frac{1600}{1500}}} = 1.470.$$

Conclusion. $| z | = 1.47 < 1.96$.

$\therefore$ H_0 is accepted at 5% level of significance *i.e.*, there is no significant difference between the sample means.

Example 4. *From the data given below, compute the standard error of the difference of the two sample means and find out if the two means significantly differ at 5% level of significance.*

	No. of items	*Mean*	*S.D.*
Group I	*50*	*181.5*	*3.0*
Group II	*75*	*179*	*3.6*

Sol. Null hypothesis H_0 : There is no significant difference between the samples. *i.e.*,

$$\overline{x}_1 = \overline{x}_2$$

Alternative Hypothesis $H_1 : \overline{x}_1 \neq \overline{x}_2$ (Two tailed test)

Under H_0,

$$z = \frac{\overline{x}_1 - \overline{x}_2}{\sqrt{\frac{s_1^2}{n_1} + \frac{s_2^2}{n_2}}} = \frac{181.5 - 179.0}{\sqrt{\frac{9}{50} + \frac{(3.6)^2}{75}}} = 4.2089.$$

Conclusion. As $| z | = 4.2089 > 1.96$.

$\therefore$ H_0 is rejected at 5% level of significance *i.e.*, there is significant difference between the samples.

Example 5. *A random sample of 200 villages from Coimbatore district gives the mean population per village at 485 with a S.D. of 50. Another random sample of the same size from the same district gives the mean population per village at 510 with a S.D. of 40. Is the difference between the mean values given by the two samples statistically significant ? Justify your answer.*

Sol. Here $n_1 = 200$, $n_2 = 250$, $\bar{x}_1 = 485$, $\bar{x}_2 = 510$, $s_1 = 50$, $s_2 = 40$

Null hypothesis H_0. There is no significant difference between the mean values (*i.e.,*)

$$\bar{x}_1 = \bar{x}_2$$

Alternative Hypothesis H_1 : $\bar{x}_1 \neq \bar{x}_2$ (Two tailed test)

Under H_0, the test statistic is given by

$$z = \frac{\bar{x}_1 - \bar{x}_2}{\sqrt{\frac{s_1^2}{n_1} + \frac{s_2^2}{n_2}}} = \frac{485 - 510}{\sqrt{\frac{50^2}{200} + \frac{40^2}{200}}} = -5.53$$

$\therefore$ $|z| = 5.53.$

Conclusion. $|z| > 1.96.$

$\therefore$ H_0 is rejected at 5% level of significance *i.e.,* there is significant difference between the mean values of two samples.

Example 6. *The means of two large samples of 1,000 and 2,000 members are 67.5 inches and 68.0 inches respectively. Can the samples be regarded as drawn from the same population of standard deviation 2.5 inches ?* (P.T.U., M.B.A. Dec. 2003)

Sol. Given $n_1 = 1000$, $n_2 = 2000$, $\bar{x}_1 = 67.5$, $\bar{x}_2 = 68$, $\sigma = 2.5$

Assume

Null Hypothesis H_0 : The samples are drawn from the same population *i.e.,* $\bar{x}_1 = \bar{x}_2$

Alternative Hypothesis. H_1 : The samples are not drawn from the same population *i.e.,* $\bar{x}_1 \neq \bar{x}_2$ (Two tailed test)

Under H_0,

$$z = \frac{\bar{x}_1 - \bar{x}_2}{\sigma\sqrt{\frac{1}{n_1} + \frac{1}{n_2}}} = \frac{67.5 - 68}{(2.5)\sqrt{\left(\frac{1}{1000} + \frac{1}{2000}\right)}}$$

$$= \frac{-0.5}{(2.5)\sqrt{(.001 + 0.0005)}} = \frac{-0.5}{(2.5)(0.03872)} = \frac{-0.5}{0.09682} = -5.1642$$

$\Rightarrow$ $|z| = 5.1642$

Conclusion. Since $|z| > 1.96.$

$\therefore$ H_0 is rejected at 5% level of significance *i.e.* the samples are not drawn from the same population.

TEST YOUR KNOWLEDGE 10.4

1. Intelligence tests on two groups of boys and girls gave the following results. Examine if the difference is significant.

	Mean	*S.D.*	*Size*
Girls	*70*	*10*	*70*
Boys	*75*	*11*	*100*

2. Two random samples of sizes 1000 and 2000 farms gave an average yield of 2000 kg and 2050 kg respectively. The variance of wheat farms in the country may be taken as 100 kg. Examine whether the two samples differ significantly in yield ?

3. A sample of heights of 6400 soldiers has a mean of 67.85 inches and a S.D. of 2.56 inches. While another sample of heights of 1600 sailors has a mean of 68.55 inches with S.D. of 2.52 inches. Do the data indicate that the sailors are on the average taller than soldiers ?
4. In a survey of buying habits, 400 women shoppers are chosen at random in supermarket A. Their average weekly food expenditure is ₹ 250 with a S.D. of ₹ 40. For 500 women shoppers chosen at supermarket B, the average weekly food expenditure is ₹ 220 with a S.D. of ₹ 45 test at 1% level of significance whether the average food expenditures of the two groups are equal.
5. The number of accident per day were studied for 144 days in town A and for 100 days in town B and the following information was obtained.

	Mean number of accident	*S.D.*
Town A	4.5	1.2
Town B	5.4	1.5

Is the difference between the mean accidents of the two towns statistically significant ?
6. An examination was given to 50 students of a college A and to 60 students of college B. For A, the mean grade was 75 with S.D. of 9 and for B, the mean grade was 79 with S.D. of 7. Is there any significant difference between the performance of the students of college A and those of college B ?
7. A random sample of 200 measurements from a large population gave a mean value of 50 and S.D. of 9. Determine the 95% confidence interval for the mean of the population ?
8. The means of two large samples of 1000 and 2000 members are 168.75 cms and 170 cms respectively. Can the samples be regarded as drawn from the same population of standard deviation 6.25 cms ? *(P.T.U., M.B.A. Dec. 2003)*

Answers

1. H_0 is rejected at 5% and 1% level of significance. ($|z| = 3.08$)
2. Highly significant. ($|z| = 129.19$)
3. H_0 is rejected *i.e.*, the heights of the soldiers and sailers are highly significant ($|z| = 10$)
4. H_0 is rejected at 1% level of significance. ($|z| = 10.6$)
5. Highly significant. ($|z| = 4.687$)
6. Not significant. ($|z| = 2.56$)
7. (48.76, 51.24) **8.** Not significant *i.e.*, H_0 is rejected ($|z| = 5.20$)

10.15. TEST OF SIGNIFICANCE FOR THE DIFFERENCE OF STANDARD DEVIATIONS

If s_1 and s_2 are the standard deviations of two independent samples, then under the null hypothesis $H_0 : s_1 = s_2$, *i.e.*, the sample standard deviations do not differ significantly, the statistic is

$$z = \frac{s_1 - s_2}{\sqrt{\dfrac{\sigma_1^2}{2n_1} + \dfrac{\sigma_2^2}{2n_2}}}, \text{ where } \sigma_1 \text{ and } \sigma_2 \text{ are population standard deviations.}$$

Note: When population standard deviations are not known, then $z = \dfrac{s_1 - s_2}{\sqrt{\dfrac{s_1^2}{2n_1} + \dfrac{s_2^2}{2n_2}}}$.

ILLUSTRATIVE EXAMPLES

Example 1. *Random samples drawn from two countries gave the following data relating to the heights of adult males.*

	Country A	*Country B*
Mean height (in inches)	*67.42*	*67.25*
Standard deviation	*2.58*	*2.50*
Number in samples	*1000*	*1200*

(*a*) *Is the difference between the means significant ?*

(*b*) *Is the difference between the standard deviations significant ?*

Sol. Given : $n_1 = 1000$, $n_2 = 1200$, $\bar{x}_1 = 67.42$; $\bar{x}_2 = 67.25$, $s_1 = 2.58$, $s_2 = 2.50$

(*a*) **Null Hypothesis.** $H_0 : \mu_1 = \mu_2$, *i.e.*, sample means do not differ significantly.

Alternative hypothesis : $H_1 : \mu_1 \neq \mu_2$ (Two tailed test)

Under H_0 :
$$z = \frac{\bar{x}_1 - \bar{x}_2}{\sqrt{\frac{s_1^2}{n_1} + \frac{s_2^2}{n_2}}} = \frac{67.42 - 67.25}{\sqrt{\frac{(2.58)^2}{1000} + \frac{(2.50)^2}{1200}}} = 1.56$$

Conclusion. Since $|\ z\ | < 1.96$, we accept the null hypothesis at 5% level of significanc. *i.e.*, there is no significant difference between the sample means.

(*b*) **Null hypothesis.** $H_0 : \sigma_1 = \sigma_2$, *i.e.*, the sample S.D.'s do not differ significantly.

Alternative Hypothesis : $H_1 = \sigma_1 \neq \sigma_2$ (Two tailed test)

Under H_0, the test statistic is

$$z = \frac{s_1 - s_2}{\sqrt{\frac{\sigma_1^2}{2n_1} + \frac{\sigma_2^2}{2n_2}}} = \frac{s_1 - s_2}{\sqrt{\frac{s_1^2}{2n_1} + \frac{s_2^2}{2n_2}}} \qquad (\because \ \sigma_1 = s_1, \sigma_2 = s_2 \text{ for large samples})$$

$$= \frac{2.58 - 2.50}{\sqrt{\frac{(2.58)^2}{2 \times 1000} \times \frac{(2.50)^2}{2 \times 1200}}} = \frac{0.08}{\sqrt{\frac{6.6564}{2000} + \frac{6.25}{2400}}} = 1.0387$$

Conclusion. Since $|\ z\ | < 1.96$, we accept the null hypothesis at 5% level of significance. *i.e.*, there is no significant difference between the standard deviations.

Example 2. *Intelligence test of two groups of boys and girls gives the following results :*

Girls	*mean = 84*	*S.D. = 10*	*N = 121*
Boys	*mean = 81*	*S.D. = 12*	*N = 81*

(*a*) *Is the difference in mean scores significant ?*

(*b*) *Is the difference between the standard deviations significant ?*

Sol. Given : $n_1 = 121$, $n_2 = 81$, $\bar{x}_1 = 84$, $\bar{x}_2 = 81$, $s_1 = 10$, $s_2 = 12$

(*a*) **Null hypothesis.** $H_0 : \mu_1 = \mu_2$, *i.e.*, sample means do not differ significantly.

Alternative hypothesis : $H_1 = \mu_1 \neq \mu_2$ (Two tailed test)

Under H_0, the test statistic is $z = \dfrac{\bar{x}_1 - \bar{x}_2}{\sqrt{\dfrac{s_1^2}{n_1} + \dfrac{s_2^2}{n_2}}} = \dfrac{84 - 81}{\sqrt{\dfrac{(10)^2}{121} + \dfrac{(12)^2}{81}}} = 0.1859$

Conclusion. Since $|z| < 1.96$, we accept the null hypothesis at 5% level of significance. *i.e.*, there is no significant difference between the sample means.

(*b*) We set up the **Null hypothesis** $H_0 : \sigma_1 = \sigma_2$, *i.e.*, the sample S.D.'s do not differ significantly.

Alternative hypothesis : $H_1 = \sigma_1 \neq \sigma_2$ (Two tailed test)

Under H_0, the test statistic is $z = \dfrac{s_1 - s_2}{\sqrt{\dfrac{\sigma_1^2}{2n_1} + \dfrac{\sigma_2^2}{2n_2}}} = \dfrac{s_1 - s_2}{\sqrt{\dfrac{s_1^2}{2n_1} + \dfrac{s_2^2}{2n_2}}}$

($\because$ $\sigma_1 = s_1$, $\sigma_2 = \sigma_2$ for large samples)

$$= \frac{10 - 12}{\sqrt{\dfrac{100}{2 \times 121} + \dfrac{144}{2 \times 81}}} = -1.7526$$

$\therefore$ $|z| = 1.7526$

Conclusion. Since $|z| = 1.7526 < 1.96$, we accept the null hypothesis at 5% level of significance. *i.e.*, there is no significant difference between the standard deviations.

TEST YOUR KNOWLEDGE 10.5

1. The mean yield of two sets of plots and their variability are as given. Examine.
   (*i*) Whether the difference in the mean yield of the two sets of plots is significant ?
   (*ii*) Whether the difference in the variability in yields is significant ?

	Set of 40 plots	*Set of 60 plots*
Mean yield per plot	1258 lb	1243 lb
S.D. per plot	34	28

2. The yield of wheat in a random sample of 1000 farms in a certain area has a S.D. of 192 kg. Another random sample of 1000 farms gives a S.D. of 224 kg. Are the S.Ds significantly different ?

Answers

1. (*i*) $z = 2.318$. Difference significant at 5% level ; (*ii*) $z = 1.31$. Difference not significant at 5% level
2. $z = 4.850$. The S.D.s are significantly different.

10.16. TEST OF SIGNIFICANCE OF SMALL SAMPLES

When the size of the sample is less than 30, then the sample is called small sample. For such sample it will not be possible for us to assume that the random sampling distribution of a statistic is approximately normal and the values given by the sample data are sufficiently close to the population values and can be used in their place for the calculation of the standard error of the estimate.

t-TEST

10.17. STUDENT'S *t*-DISTRIBUTION (*P.T.U., M.B.A. May 2002, Dec. 2002, May 2000*)

This *t*-distribution is used when sample size is ≤ 30 and the population standard deviation is unknown. The *t*-statistic is defined as

$$t = \frac{\bar{x} - \mu}{s/\sqrt{n}} \sim t(n-1\ d.f.) \text{ where } s = \sqrt{\frac{\Sigma(X - \bar{X})^2}{n-1}}$$

By **degree of freedom** (d.f.). we mean the number '*n*' of independent observations minus the number '*m*' of parameters (required to compute the statistic). Thus,

$$\text{d.f. } \nu = n - m$$

Example. Suppose we are to choose any five numbers whose sum is 100. We can try any four numbers since the fifth number would be 100 minus sum of these four numbers (*i.e.*, if the four numbers are 10, 15, 20, 30, then the fifth number would be 100 – (10 + 15 + 20 + 30 = 25).

Though, we were to choose any five numbers but we have chosen any four numbers and hence our choice is reduced by one because of one condition placed in the data *i.e.*, "a total of 100", thus, in this case, d.f. = 5 – 1 = 4.

Remark. (*i*) When we fit a Binomial distribution, then d.f. = *n*, where *n* is the no. of observations.

(*ii*) When we fit a poisson distribution, then d.f. = *n* – 2 (we use two parameters viz total frequency and A.M.)

(*iii*) When we fit a normal curve, then d.f. = *n* – 3 (we use three parameters viz total frequency, A.M. and S.D.).

The *t*-table

The *t*-table given at the end is the probability integral of *t*-distribution. The *t*-distribution has different values for each degrees of freedom. When the degrees of freedom are infinitely large, the *t*-distribution is equivalent to Normal distribution and the probabilities shown in the Normal distribution tables are applicable.

10.18. APPLICATIONS OF T-DISTRIBUTION

Some of the applications of *t*-distribution are given below :

1. *To test if the sample mean* ($\bar{X}$) *differs significantly from the hypothetical value* μ *of the population mean.*
2. *To test the significance between two sample means.*
3. *To test the significance of observed partial and multiple correlation coefficients.*

10.19. PROPERTIES OF T-DISTRIBUTION

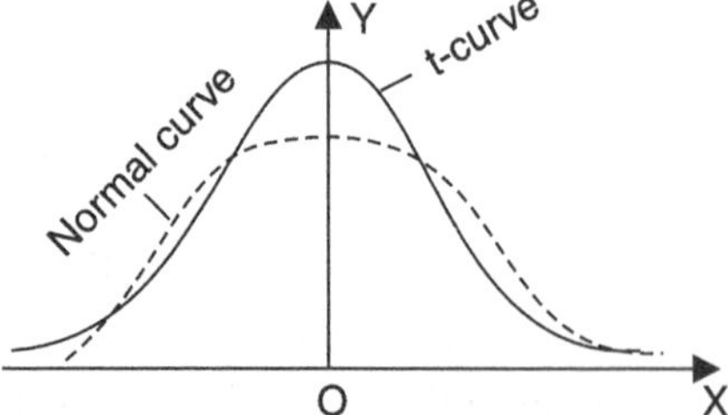

The following are the properties of *t*-distribution :

1. It is unimodal distribution.
2. The probability distribution curve is symmetrical about the line $t = 0$.
3. It is bell-shaped curve just like a Normal curve with its tail a little higher above the abscissa than the Normal curve (see fig.)
4. The limiting form of *t*-distribution, when its degree of freedom $\upsilon \to \infty$, is given by

$$y = y_0 e^{-\frac{1}{2}t^2}, \text{ which is a Normal curve.}$$

This means that *t* is normally distributed for large samples.

10.20. CRITICAL VALUE OF t

The critical value or significant value of t at level of significance α, degrees of freedom γ for two tailed test is given by

$$P[\mid t \mid > t_\gamma (\alpha)] = \alpha$$
$$P[\mid t \mid \le t_\gamma (\alpha)] = 1 - \alpha$$

The significant value of t at level of significance α for a single tailed test can be got from those of two tailed test by referring to the values at 2α.

10.21. TEST I : *t*-TEST OF SIGNIFICANCE OF THE MEAN OF A RANDOM SAMPLE

To test whether the mean of a sample drawn from a Normal population deviates significantly from a stated value when variance of the population is unknown.

H_0 : There is no significant difference between the sample mean $\bar{x}$ and the population mean μ *i.e.*, we use the statistic

$$t = \frac{\bar{x} - \mu}{s/\sqrt{n}}, \qquad \text{where } \bar{x} \text{ is mean of the sample.}$$

$$s^2 = \frac{1}{n-1} \sum_{i=1}^{n} (x_i - \bar{x})^2 \text{ with degrees of freedom } (n - 1).$$

At given level of significance α and degrees of freedom $(n - 1)$, we refer to t-table to find the critical value t_α (two tailed or one tailed).

If calculated value $\mid t \mid$ is such that $\mid t \mid < t_\alpha$, the null hypothesis is accepted and if $\mid t \mid > t_\alpha$, H_0 is rejected.

10.22. FIDUCIAL LIMITS OF POPULATION MEAN

If t_α is the tabulated value of t at α level of significance at $(n - 1)$ degrees of freedom. Then

$$\left| \frac{\bar{x} - \mu}{s/\sqrt{n}} \right| < t_\alpha \text{ for acceptance of } H_0.$$

$$\Rightarrow \quad \bar{x} - t_\alpha\, s/\sqrt{n} < \mu < \bar{x} + t_\alpha\, s/\sqrt{n} \text{ i.e.,}$$

95% confidence limits (level of significance 5%) are $\bar{x} \pm t_{0.05}\, s/\sqrt{n}$.

99% confidence limits (level of significance 1%) are $\bar{x} \pm t_{0.01}\, s/\sqrt{n}$.

Note. Instead of calculating s, we calculate S for the sample.

Since $s^2 = \frac{1}{n-1} \sum_{i=1}^{n} (x_i - \bar{x})^2 \;\therefore\; S^2 = \frac{1}{n} \sum_{i=1}^{n} (x_i - \bar{x})^2.$ $\left[(n - 1)s^2 = nS^2,\ s^2 = \frac{n}{n-1} S^2 \right]$

ILLUSTRATIVE EXAMPLES

Example 1. *A random sample of size 16 has 53 as mean. The sum of squares of the derivation from mean is 135. Can this sample be regarded as taken from the population having 56 as mean ? Obtain 95% and 99% confidence limits of the mean of the population.*

Sol. Null Hypothesis H_0 : There is no significant difference between the sample mean and hypothetical population mean. *i.e.*, $\mu = 56$

Alternative Hypothesis $H_1 : \mu \ne 56$ (Two tailed test)

Under H_0, $$t = \frac{\bar{x} - \mu}{s/\sqrt{n}} \sim t(n - 1 \text{ d.f.})$$

Given : $\bar{x} = 53, \mu = 56, n = 16, \Sigma(x - \bar{x})^2 = 135$

$$\therefore \quad s = \sqrt{\frac{\Sigma(x-\bar{x})^2}{n-1}} = \sqrt{\frac{135}{15}} = 3 \; ; \; t = \frac{53-56}{3/\sqrt{16}} = \frac{-3\times 4}{3} = -4 \;\Rightarrow\; |t| = 4.$$

Conclusion. The tabulated value of t at 5% level of significance is $t_{0.05} = 1.753$. for 15 d.f. (see t-table)

Since $|t| = 4 > t_{0.05} = 1.753$, *i.e.*, the calculated value of t is more than the tabulated value. The hypothesis H_0 is rejected. Hence the sample mean has not come from a population having 56 as mean.

95% confidence limits of the population mean is given by

$$\bar{x} \pm \frac{s}{\sqrt{n}} t_{0.05} \quad \text{or} \quad 53 \pm \frac{3}{\sqrt{16}} (1.725) = (51.706, 54.293)$$

99% confidence limits of the population mean is given by

$$\bar{x} \pm \frac{s}{\sqrt{n}} t_{0.01} \quad \text{or} \quad 53 \pm \frac{3}{\sqrt{16}} (2.602) = (51.048, 54.951).$$

Example 2. *The life time of electric bulbs for a random sample of 10 from a large consignment gave the following data :*

Item	*1*	*2*	*3*	*4*	*5*	*6*	*7*	*8*	*9*	*10*
Life in '000 hrs.	*4.2*	*4.6*	*3.9*	*4.1*	*5.2*	*3.8*	*3.9*	*4.3*	*4.4*	*5.6*

Can we accept the hypothesis that the average life time of bulb is 4000 hrs ?

Sol. Null Hypothesis H_0 : There is no significant difference in the sample mean and population mean. *i.e.*, $\mu = 4000$ hrs.

Alternative hypothes is $H_1 : \mu \neq 400$ hrs (two tailed test)

x	4.2	4.6	3.9	4.1	5.2	3.8	3.9	4.3	4.4	5.6
$x - \bar{x}$	− 0.2	0.2	− 0.5	− 0.3	0.8	− 0.6	− 0.5	− 0.1	0	1.2
$(x - \bar{x})^2$	0.04	0.04	0.25	0.09	0.64	0.36	0.25	0.01	0	1.44

Now $\quad \bar{x} = \frac{\Sigma x}{n} = \frac{44}{10} = 4.4 \,,\; \Sigma(x - \bar{x})^2 = 3.12$

$$\therefore \quad s = \sqrt{\frac{\Sigma(x-\bar{x})^2}{n-1}} = \sqrt{\frac{3.12}{9}} = 0.589 \; ;$$

$$\Rightarrow \quad t = \frac{4.4-4}{\frac{0.589}{\sqrt{10}}} = 2.123$$

Under H_0, $\quad t = \frac{\bar{x} - \mu}{s/\sqrt{n}} \sim t(10 - 1\ d.f.)$

Also, the tabulated value of t at 5% level of significance is $t_{0.05} = 2.26$ for 9 d.f. (see t-table)

Conclusion. Since the calculated value of t is less than tabulated value $t_{0.05}$.

$\therefore$ The hypothesis H_0 is accepted at 5% level of significance *i.e.*, the average life time of bulbs could be 4000 hrs.

Example 3. *A sample of 20 items has mean 42 units and S.D. 5 units. Test the hypothesis that it is a random sample from a normal population with mean 45 units.*

Sol. Null Hypothesis H_0 : There is no significant difference between the sample mean and the population mean. *i.e.*, $\mu = 45$ units

Alternative Hypothesis $H_1 : \mu \neq 45$ (Two tailed test)

Given : $n = 20, \bar{x} = 42, S = 5$

$$\therefore \quad s^2 = \frac{n}{n-1} S^2 = \left[\frac{20}{20-1}\right](5)^2 = 26.31 \quad \therefore \quad s = 5.129$$

Under H_0, $$t = \frac{\bar{x} - \mu}{s/\sqrt{n}} \sim t(n-1\,d.f.) = \frac{42-45}{5.129/\sqrt{20}} = -2.615$$

$\Rightarrow \quad |t| = 2.615$

The tabulated value of t at 5% level of significance for 19 d.f. is $t_{0.05} = 2.09$. (see t-table)

Conclusion. Since $|t| > t_{0.05}$, $\therefore$ the hypothesis H_0 is rejected ; *i.e.*, there is significant difference between the sample mean and population mean. *i.e.*, The sample could not have come from this population.

Example 4. *The 9 items of a sample have the following values 45, 47, 50, 52, 48, 47, 49, 53, 51. Does the mean of these values differ significantly from the assumed mean 47.5.*

(P.T.U. M.B.A., May 2008)

Sol. Null Hypothesis $H_0 : \mu = 47.5$ *i.e.*, there is no significant difference between the sample and population mean.

Alternative Hypothesis $H_1 : \mu \neq 47.5$ (two tailed test)

Given : $n = 9$, $\mu = 47.5$ consider The following table :

x	45	47	50	52	48	47	49	53	51
$x - \bar{x}$	– 4.1	– 2.1	0.9	2.9	– 1.1	– 2.1	– 0.1	3.9	1.9
$(x - \bar{x})^2$	16.81	4.41	0.81	8.41	1.21	4.41	0.01	15.21	3.61

$$\bar{x} = \frac{\Sigma x}{n} = \frac{442}{9} = 49.11 \,;$$

$$\Sigma(x - \bar{x})^2 = 54.89 \,; \; s^2 = \frac{\Sigma(x-\bar{x})^2}{(n-1)} = \frac{54.89}{8} = 6.86 \quad \therefore \quad s = 2.619$$

Under H_0, $$t = \frac{\bar{x} - \mu}{s/\sqrt{n}} \sim t(n-1\,d.f.) = \frac{49.1 - 47.5}{2.619/\sqrt{8}} = \frac{(1.6)\sqrt{8}}{2.619} = 1.7279$$

Also, the tabulated value of t at 5% level of significance is $t_{0.05} = 2.31$ for 8 d.f. (see t-table)

Conclusion. Since $|t| < t_{0.05}$, $\therefore$ The hypothesis H_0 is accepted, *i.e.*, there is no significant difference between their mean.

Example 5. *The following results are obtained from a sample of 10 boxes in biscuits.*

Mean weight content = 490 g, S.D. of the weight = 9 g

Could the sample come from a population having a mean of 500 g ?

Sol. Given : $n = 10, \bar{x} = 490 \,; S = 9$ g, $\mu = 500$

$$\therefore \quad s = \sqrt{\frac{n}{n-1}} S^2 = \sqrt{\frac{10}{9} \times 9^2} = 9.486$$

Null Hypothesis H_0 : The difference is not significant *i.e.*, $\mu = 500$

Alternative Hypothesis $H_1 : \mu \neq 500$ (Two tailed test)

Under H_0, $t = \frac{\bar{x} - \mu}{s/\sqrt{n}} = \frac{490 - 500}{9.486/\sqrt{10}} = -0.333 \Rightarrow |t| = 0.333$

Also, the tabulated value of t at 5% level of significance is $t_{0.05} = 2.26$ for 9 d.f. (see t-table)

Conclusion. Since $|t| = 0.333 > t_{0.05}$ $\therefore$ The hypothesis H_0 is rejected.

$\therefore$ The sample could not have come from the population having mean 500 gm.

TEST YOUR KNOWLEDGE 10.6

1. Ten individuals are chosen at random from a normal population of students and their marks found to be 63, 63, 66, 67, 68, 69, 70, 70, 71, 71. In the light of these data, discuss the suggestion that mean mark of the population of students is 66.
2. The following values give the lengths of 12 samples of egyptian cotton taken from a consignment : 48, 46, 49, 46, 52, 45, 43, 47, 47, 46, 45, 50. Test if the mean length of the consignment can be taken as 46.
3. A sample of 18 items has a mean 24 units and standard deviation 3 units. Test the hypothesis that it is a random sample from a Normal population with mean 27 units.
4. A random sample of 10 boys had the I.Q's 70, 120, 110, 101, 88, 83, 95, 98, 107 and 100. Do these data support the assumption of a population mean I.Q of 160 ?
5. A filling machine is expected to fill 5 kg of powder into bags. A sample of 10 bags gave the following weights : 4.7, 4.9, 5.0, 5.1, 5.4, 5.2, 4.6, 5.1, 4.6 and 4.7. Test whether the machine is working properly.

Answers

1. accepted ($|t| = 1.912$) 2. accepted ($|t| = 1.41$) 3. rejected ($|t| = 12.72$)
4. accepted ($|t| = 0.62$) 5. accepted. ($|t| = 0.8043$)

10.23. TEST II : t-TEST FOR DIFFERENCE OF MEANS OF TWO SMALL SAMPLES (FROM A NORMAL POPULATION)

This test is used to test whether the two samples $x_1, x_2, \ldots\ldots, x_{n_1}, y_1, y_2, \ldots\ldots, y_{n_2}$ of sizes n_1, n_2 have been drawn from two Normal populations with mean μ_1 and μ_2 respectively under the assumption that the population variance are equal. ($\sigma_1 = \sigma_2 = \sigma$).

H_0 : The samples have been drawn from the Normal population with means μ_1 and μ_2 *i.e.*, $\mu_1 \neq \mu_2$.

Let $\bar{x}, \bar{y}$ be their means of the two sample.

Under this H_0, the test statistic t is given by $t = \frac{(\bar{x} - \bar{y})}{s\sqrt{\frac{1}{n_1} + \frac{1}{n_2}}} \sim t(n_1 + n_2 - 2 \text{ d.f.})$

Note 1. If the two sample standard deviations s_1, s_2 are given, then we have $s^2 = \frac{n_1 s_1^2 + n_2 s_2^2}{n_1 + n_2 - 2}$.

Note 2. If $n_1 = n_2 = n$, $t = \frac{\bar{x} - \bar{y}}{\sqrt{\frac{s_1^2 + s_2^2}{n - 1}}}$ can be used as a test statistic.

10.24. TEST-III : PAIRED *t*-TEST FOR DIFFERENCE OF MEANS

This test is applied when the sample sizes of two samples are equal. In this case, the sample observations can be paired as (x_i, y_i), $i = 1, 2, \ldots n$. To test, whether the sample means differ significantly, the statistic is given by

$$t = \frac{\bar{d}}{s/\sqrt{n-1}} \sim t(n-1 \text{ d.f.}), \text{ where } \bar{d} = \text{Mean of paired differences}$$

$$s^2 = \frac{\Sigma d^2}{n} - (\bar{d})^2 \,;\; d = x_i - y_i,\ i = 1, 2 \ldots, n.$$

ILLUSTRATIVE EXAMPLES

Example 1. *Two samples of sodium vapour bulbs were tested for length of life and the following results were obtained* :

	Size	*Sample mean*	*Sample S.D.*
Type I	*8*	*1234 hrs*	*36 hrs*
Type II	*7*	*1036 hrs*	*40 hrs*

Is the difference in the means significant to generalise that type I is superior to type II regarding length of life ?

Sol. Null Hypothesis $H_0 : \mu_1 = \mu_2$, *i.e.,* two types of bulbs have same lifetime.

Alternative Hypothesis $H_1 : \mu_1 > \mu_2$, *i.e.,* type I is superior to type II (Right tailed test)

$$s^2 = \frac{n_1 s_1^2 + n_2 s_2^2}{n_1 + n_2 - 2} = \frac{8 \times (36)^2 + 7(40)^2}{8 + 7 - 2} = 1659.076$$

$$\Rightarrow \quad s = 40.7317$$

Under H_0,

$$t = \frac{\bar{x}_1 - \bar{x}_2}{s\sqrt{\dfrac{1}{n_1} + \dfrac{1}{n_2}}} \sim t(n_1 + n_2 - 2\, d.f.) = \frac{1234 - 1036}{40.7317\sqrt{\dfrac{1}{8} + \dfrac{1}{7}}} = \frac{198}{10.91}$$

$$= 9.393 \sim t(n_1 + n_2 - 2 \text{ d.f.})$$

Also, the tabulated value of t at 5% level of significance is $t_{0.05} = 1.77$ for 13 d.f. (one tailed test) (see t-table)

Conclusion. Since calculated $| t | > t_{0.05}$ $\therefore$ H_0 is rejected *i.e.,* H_1 is accepted.

$\therefore$ Type I is definitely superior to type II.

Example 2. *Samples of sizes 10 and 14 were taken from two normal populations with S.D. 3.5 and 5.2. The sample means were found to be 20.3 and 18.6. Test whether the means of the two populations are the same at 5% level.*

Sol. Null hypothesis $H_0 : \mu_1 = \mu_2$, *i.e.,* the means of the two populations are the same.

Alternative hypothesis $H_1 : \mu_1 \neq \mu_2$. (Two tailed test)

Given $\bar{x}_1 = 20.3$, $\bar{x}_2 = 18.6$; $n_1 = 10$, $n_2 = 14$, $s_1 = 3.5$, $s_2 = 5.2$

$$s^2 = \frac{n_1 s_1^2 + n_2 s_2^2}{n_1 + n_2 - 2} = \frac{10(3.5)^2 + 14(5.2)^2}{10 + 14 - 2} = 22.775 \quad \therefore \quad s = 4.772$$

$$t = \frac{\bar{x}_1 - \bar{x}_2}{s\sqrt{\frac{1}{n_1} + \frac{1}{n_2}}} \sim t(n_1 + n_2 - 2\, d.f.) = \frac{20.3 - 18.6}{\left(\sqrt{\frac{1}{10} + \frac{1}{14}}\right) 4.772} = 0.8604$$

The value of t at 5% level of significance for 22 d.f. is $t_{0.05} = 2.0739$. (see t-table)

Conclusion. Since $|t| = 0.8604 < t_{0.05}$ $\therefore$ The hypothesis H_0 is accepted, *i.e.*, there is no significant difference between their means.

Example 3. *The height of 6 randomly chosen sailors in inches are 63, 65, 68, 69, 71 and 72. Those of 9 randomly chosen soldiers are 61, 62, 65, 66, 69, 70, 71, 72 and 73. Test whether the sailors are on the average taller than soldiers.*

Sol. Let X_1 and X_2 be two samples denoting the heights of sailors and soldiers.

Given, $n_1 = 6$, $n_2 = 9$,

Null Hypothesis $H_0 : \mu_1 = \mu_2$. *i.e.*, the sailors are not on the average taller than sailors.

Alternative Hypothesis $H_1 : \mu_1 > \mu_2$ (One tailed test)

Calculation of two sample mean :

x_1	63	65	68	69	71	72
$x_1 - \bar{x}_1$	– 5	– 3	0	1	3	4
$(x_1 - \bar{x}_1)^2$	25	9	0	1	9	16

$$\bar{x}_1 = \frac{\Sigma x_1}{n_1} = 68\ ;\quad \Sigma(x_1 - \bar{x}_1)^2 = 60$$

x_2	61	62	65	66	69	70	71	72	73
$x_2 - \bar{x}_2$	– 6.66	– 5.66	– 2.66	1.66	1.34	2.34	3.34	4.34	5.34
$(x_2 - \bar{x}_2)^2$	44.36	32.035	7.0756	2.7556	1.7956	5.4756	11.1556	18.8356	28.5156

$$\bar{x}_2 = \frac{\Sigma x_2}{n_2} = 67.66\ ;\quad \Sigma(x_2 - \bar{x}_2)^2 = 152.0002$$

$$s^2 = \frac{1}{n_1 + n_2 - 2}\left[\Sigma(x_1 - \bar{x}_1)^2 + \Sigma(x_2 - \bar{x}_2)^2\right]$$

$$= \frac{1}{6 + 9 - 2}[60 + 152.0002] = 16.3077 \quad \therefore \quad s = 4.038$$

Under H_0,
$$t = \frac{\bar{x}_1 - \bar{x}_2}{s\sqrt{\frac{1}{n_1} + \frac{1}{n_2}}} = \frac{68 - 67.666}{4.0382\sqrt{\frac{1}{6} + \frac{1}{9}}} = 0.3031 \sim t(n_1 + n_2 - 2 \text{ d.f.})$$

The value of t at 5% level of significance ($\because$ the test is one tailed) for 13 d.f. is 2.16. (see t-table)

Conclusion. Since $|t| = 0.3031 < t_{0.05} = 2.16$ $\therefore$ The hypothesis H_0 is accepted. *i.e.*, there is no significant difference between their averages. *i.e.*, the sailors are not on the average taller than the soldiers.

Example 4. *Memory capacity of 9 students was tested before and after a course of meditation for a month. State whether the course was effective or not from the data below (in same units)*

Before	*10*	*15*	*9*	*3*	*7*	*12*	*16*	*17*	*4*
After	*12*	*17*	*8*	*5*	*6*	*11*	*18*	*20*	*3*

Sol. Since the data are correlated and concerned with the same set of students, we use paired t-test.

Null Hypothesis H_0 : Training was not effective *i.e.*, $\mu_1 = \mu_2$

Alternative Hypothesis $H_1 : \mu_1 \neq \mu_2$ (Two tailed test).

Before training (x)	*After training (y)*	$d = x - y$	d^2
10	12	– 2	4
15	17	– 2	4
9	8	1	1
3	5	– 2	4
7	6	1	1
12	11	1	1
16	18	– 2	4
17	20	– 3	9
4	3	1	1
		$\Sigma d = -7$	$\Sigma d^2 = 29$

Now $\qquad \overline{d} = \dfrac{\Sigma d}{n} = \dfrac{-7}{9} = -0.7778$; $s^2 = \dfrac{\Sigma d^2}{n} - (\overline{d})^2 = \dfrac{29}{9} - (-0.7778)^2 = 2.612$

Under H_0, $\qquad t = \dfrac{\overline{d}}{s/\sqrt{n-1}} \sim t(n-1)\,d.f. = \dfrac{-0.7778}{\sqrt{2.6172}/\sqrt{8}} = \dfrac{-0.7778 \times \sqrt{8}}{1.6177} = -1.359$

$\Rightarrow \qquad | t | = 1.359$

The tabulated value of $t_{0.05}$ at 8 d.f. is 2.31. (see t-table)

Conclusion. Since $| t | = 1.359 < t_{0.05}$, H_0 is accepted, *i.e.*, training was not effective in improving performance.

Example 5. *Ten workers were given a training programme with a view to shorten their assembly time for a certain mechanism. The results of the time and motion studies before and after the training programme are given below.*

Let x = Time taken for assembly before training, Y = Time taken for assembly after training.

	Workers									
Time	*1*	*2*	*3*	*4*	*5*	*6*	*7*	*8*	*9*	*10*
x	*15*	*18*	*20*	*17*	*16*	*14*	*21*	*19*	*13*	*22*
y	*14*	*16*	*21*	*10*	*15*	*18*	*19*	*16*	*14*	*30*

On the basis of this data, can it be concluded that the training programme has shortened the average assembly time ? (P.T.U., M.B.A. May 2006)

Sol. Null Hypothesis H_0 : The training programme has not shortened the average assembly time.

We apply paired t-Test. For this, consider the following table :

Training			
x	y	$d = x - y$	d^2
15	14	1	1
18	16	2	4
20	21	– 1	1
17	10	7	49
16	15	1	1
14	18	– 4	16
21	19	2	4
19	16	3	9
13	14	– 1	1
22	30	– 8	64
		$\Sigma d = 2$	$\Sigma d^2 = 150$

Here $$\bar{d} = \frac{\Sigma d}{n} = \frac{2}{10} = 0.2$$

$$s^2 = \frac{\Sigma d^2}{n} - (\bar{d})^2 = \frac{150}{10} - 4 = \frac{110}{10} = 11$$

$\Rightarrow$ $$s = \sqrt{11} = 3.3166$$

Under H_0, $$t = \frac{\bar{d}}{s/\sqrt{n-1}} \sim (n - 1 \text{ d.f.}) = \frac{0.2}{3.3166/\sqrt{9}}$$

$$= \frac{(0.2) \times 3}{3.3166} = \frac{0.6}{3.3166} = 0.1809$$

Also $t_{0.05}$ = The tabulated value of t at 5% level of significance for g.d.f. = 2.26 (see t-table)

Conclusion. Hence the calculated value of $t <$ the tabulated value of t at 5% level of significance for 9 d.f. $\therefore$ H_0 is accepted *i.e.,* the average assembly time was not shortened by the training programme.

Example 6. *The following figures refer to observations in live independent samples.*

Sample I	*25*	*30*	*28*	*34*	*24*	*20*	*13*	*32*	*22*	*38*
Sample II	*40*	*34*	*22*	*20*	*31*	*40*	*30*	*23*	*36*	*17*

Analyse whether the samples have been drawn from the population of equal means.

Sol. Null Hypothesis H_0 : The two samples have been drawn from the population of equal means. *i.e.,* there is no significant difference between their means *i.e.,* $\mu_1 = \mu_2$

Alternative Hypothesis $H_1 : \mu_1 \neq \mu_2$ (Two tailed test)

Given n_1 = Sample I size = 10 ; n_2 = Sample II size = 10

Calculation of sample means :

x_1	25	30	28	34	24	20	13	32	22	38
$x_1 - \bar{x}_1$	– 1.6	3.4	1.4	7.4	– 2.6	– 6.6	– 13.6	5.4	4.6	11.4
$(x_1 - \bar{x}_1)^2$	2.56	11.56	1.96	54.76	6.76	43.56	184.96	29.16	21.16	129.96
x_2	40	34	22	20	31	40	30	23	36	17
$x_2 - \bar{x}_2$	10.7	4.7	– 7.3	– 9.3	1.7	10.7	0.7	– 6.3	6.7	– 12.3
$(x_2 - \bar{x}_2)^2$	114.49	22.09	53.29	86.49	2.89	114.49	0.49	39.69	44.89	151.29

$$\bar{x}_1 = \sum_{i=1}^{10} \frac{x_1}{n_1} = \frac{266}{10} = 26.6 \; ; \qquad \bar{x}_2 = \sum_{i=1}^{10} \frac{x_2}{n_2} = \frac{293}{10} = 29.3$$

$$\Sigma(x_1 - \bar{x}_1)^2 = 486.4 \; ; \qquad \Sigma(x_2 - \bar{x}_2)^2 = 630.01$$

$$s^2 = \frac{1}{n_1 + n_2 - 2}[\Sigma(x_1 - \bar{x}_1)^2 + \Sigma(x_2 - \bar{x}_2)^2]$$

$$= \frac{1}{10 + 10 - 2} [486.4 + 630.01] = 62.022 \quad \therefore \quad s = 7.875$$

Under H_0, the test statistic is given by

$$t = \frac{\bar{x}_1 - \bar{x}_2}{s\sqrt{\frac{1}{n_1} + \frac{1}{n_2}}} \sim t(n_1 + n_2 - 2\, d.f.) = \frac{26.6 - 29.3}{7.875\sqrt{\frac{1}{10} + \frac{1}{10}}} = -\,0.7666$$

$$\Rightarrow \qquad | \, t \, | = 0.7666.$$

Conclusion. The tabulated value of t at 5% level of significance for 18 d.f. is 2.1 (see t-table). Since the calculated value $|\, t \,| = 0.7666 < t_{0.05}$, H_0 is accepted. *i.e.*, there is no significant difference between their means. *i.e.*, the two samples have been drawn from the populations of equal means.

Example 7. *A sample of 10 pigs fed on a diet A for a month showed an increase in their weights (in kgs) as 6, 3, 7, 10, 2, 4, 6, 4, 6, 2. For another random sample of 11 pigs fed on diet B for the same period, the increase in weights were 3, 4, 3, 8, 7, 6, 10, 5, 4, 14, 13. Test whether the two diets differ significantly as regards their effect on increasing the weights of pigs.*

Sol. Here $n_1 = 10$, $n_2 = 11$

Null Hypothesis $H_o : \bar{x} = \bar{y}$, *i.e.*, there is no significant difference as regards on increasing weights

Alternative Hypothesis $\quad H_1 : \bar{x} \neq \bar{y}$. (Two tailed test)

Using t-test, we know
$$t = \frac{\bar{x} - \bar{y}}{s\sqrt{\frac{1}{n_1} + \frac{1}{n_2}}} \sim t(n_1 + n_2 - 2 d.f.) \qquad \ldots(1)$$

Here
$$\bar{x} = \frac{6 + 3 + 7 + 10 + 2 + 4 + 6 + 4 + 6 + 2}{10} = \frac{50}{10} = 5$$

$$\bar{y} = \frac{3 + 4 + 3 + 8 + 7 + 6 + 10 + 5 + 4 + 14 + 13}{11} = \frac{77}{11} = 7$$

Consider the table

x	$(x-\bar{x})^2$	y	$(y-\bar{y})^2$
6	1	3	16
3	4	4	9
7	4	3	16
10	25	8	1
2	9	7	0
4	1	6	1
6	1	10	9
4	1	5	4
6	1	4	9
2	9	14	49
		13	36
	$\Sigma(x-\bar{x})^2 = 56$		$\Sigma(y-\bar{y})^2 = 150$

$\therefore$ $$s^2 = \frac{\Sigma(x-\bar{x})^2 + \Sigma(y-\bar{y})^2}{n_1+n_2-2} = \frac{56+150}{10+11-2} = \frac{206}{19} = 10.84$$

$\Rightarrow$ $$s = 3.292$$

$\therefore$ Under H_0, $$t = \frac{5-7}{3.292\sqrt{\frac{1}{10}+\frac{1}{11}}} = \frac{-2}{3.292\sqrt{0.1909}} = \frac{-2}{3.292\times 0.4369}$$

$$= \frac{-2}{1.4383} = -1.3905$$

$\Rightarrow$ $$|t| = 1.3905$$

Also for 19 d.f. $t_{0.05} = 2.09$ (see t-table)

Conclusion $\because$ Calculated value of $t >$ tabulated value of t.

$\therefore$ H_0 is accepted, *i.e.*, the diets do not differ significantly.

Example 8. *Two horses A and B were tested according to Time (in secs) to run a particular race with the following results :*

Horse A :	*28*	*30*	*32*	*33*	*33*	*29*	*34*
Horse B :	*29*	*30*	*30*	*24*	*27*	*29*	

Test whether you can discriminate between two horses.

Sol. Given $n_1 = 7$, $n_2 = 6$

Let $H_0 : \bar{x} = \bar{y}$, *i.e.*, there is no significant discrimination between two horses

$H_1 : \bar{x} \neq \bar{y}$ *i.e.*, there is a significant discrimination between two horses.

Using t-test, we know $$t = \frac{\bar{x}-\bar{y}}{s\sqrt{\frac{1}{n_1}+\frac{1}{n_2}}} \sim t(n_1+n_2-2 \text{ d.f.})$$

Here $$\bar{x} = \frac{28+30+32+33+33+29+34}{7} = \frac{219}{7} = 31.28$$

$$\bar{y} = \frac{29+30+30+24+27+29}{6} = \frac{169}{6} = 28.16$$

Consider the following table :

x	$(x-\bar{x})^2$	y	$(y-\bar{y})^2$
28	10.7584	29	0.705
30	0.0784	30	3.385
32	0.5184	30	3.385
33	2.958	24	17.30
33	2.958	27	1.345
29	5.1984	29	0.7056
34	7.3984	—	—
Total	$\Sigma(x-\bar{x})^2 = 29.868$		$\Sigma(y-\bar{y})^2 = 26.8256$

$$\therefore \quad s^2 = \frac{\Sigma(x-\bar{x})^2 + \Sigma(y-\bar{y})^2}{n_1+n_2-2}$$

$$= \frac{29.868 + 26.8256}{7+6-2} = \frac{56.6936}{11} = 5.15$$

$$\Rightarrow \quad s = \sqrt{5.15} = 2.270$$

Now using (1),
$$t = \frac{31.28 - 28.16}{2.270\sqrt{\frac{1}{7}+\frac{1}{6}}} = \frac{31.28-28.16}{2.270\sqrt{0.3095}} = \frac{3.12}{2.270\times(0.5563)}$$

$$= \frac{3.12}{1.263} = 2.47$$

$$\Rightarrow \quad |\, t \,| = 2.47$$

Also, for 11 d.f. $t_{0.05} = 2.20$ (see t-table)

i.e., the calculated value of t is greater than the tabulated value. Hence the hypothesis H_0 is rejected. Hence we can discriminate the two horses on the basis of given data.

Example 9. *Two types of drugs were used on 5 and 7 patients for reducing their weights. Drug A was impused and Drug B indigenous. The decrease in the weight after using drugs for six months are as follows.*

Drug A :	*10*	*12*	*13*	*11*	*14*		
Drug B :	*8*	*9*	*12*	*14*	*15*	*10*	*9*

Is there a significant difference in the efficiency of the two drugs ? If not, which drug you should buy ?

Sol. Here $n_1 = 5$, $n_2 = 7$

$$\bar{x} = \frac{10+12+13+11+14}{5} = \frac{60}{5} = 12$$

$$\bar{y} = \frac{8+9+12+14+15+10+9}{7} = \frac{77}{7} = 11$$

Let $H_0 : \bar{x} = \bar{y}$, *i.e.*, there is no significant difference in the efficiency of two drugs

$H_1 : \bar{x} \neq \bar{y}$, *i.e.*, there is a significant difference in the efficiency of two drugs

Consider the following table :

x	$(x - \bar{x})^2$	y	$(y - \bar{y})^2$
10	4	8	9
12	4	9	4
13	1	12	1
11	1	14	9
14	4	15	16
–	–	10	1
–	–	9	4
Total	$\Sigma(x - \bar{x})^2 = 10$		$\Sigma(y - \bar{y})^2 = 44$

$$\therefore \qquad s^2 = \frac{\Sigma(x-\bar{x})^2 + \Sigma(y-\bar{y})^2}{n_1 + n_2 - 2} = \frac{10+44}{5+7-2} = 5.4 \Rightarrow \quad s = 2.32$$

$\therefore$ Using t-test,

Under H_0,
$$t = \frac{\bar{x} - \bar{y}}{s\sqrt{\frac{1}{n_1} + \frac{1}{n_2}}} \sim t(n_1 + n_2 - 2 \text{ d.f.})$$

$$= \frac{12 - 11}{2.32\sqrt{\frac{1}{5} + \frac{1}{7}}} = \frac{1}{2.32(0.5855)} = \frac{1}{1.358} = 0.7363$$

Also, for 10 d.f., $t_{0.05} = 2.23$ (see t-table) *i.e.*, the calculated value of t is less than the tabulated value of t $\therefore$ H_o is accepted *i.e.*, there is no significant difference between the efficiency of two drugs, *i.e.*, we can buy any drug from drug A and drug B.

Example 10. *A group of seven-weak old chickens regred on a high protein diet weighing 12, 15, 11, 16, 14, 14 and 16 ounces. A second group of five chickens similarly treated except that they receive a low protein diet weighing 8, 10, 14, 10 and 13 ounces. Test whether the diet is significant evidence that additional protein has increased the weight of the chickens (given that for d.f. 13, $t_{0.05} = 2.23$.)*

Sol. Here $n_1 = 7$, $n_2 = 5$,

$$\bar{x} = \frac{12 + 15 + 11 + 16 + 14 + 14 + 16}{7} = \frac{98}{7} = 14$$

$$\bar{y} = \frac{8 + 10 + 14 + 10 + 13}{5} = \frac{55}{5} = 11$$

Let $\quad H_0 : \bar{x} = \bar{y}$, *i.e.*, there is no significant difference between the two diets

$H_1 : \bar{x} \neq \bar{y}$, *i.e.*, there is a significant difference between the two diets

Consider the following table :

x	$(x-\bar{x})^2$	y	$(y-\bar{y})^2$
12	4	8	9
15	1	10	1
11	9	14	9
16	4	10	1
14	0	13	4
14	0		
16	4		
Total	$\Sigma(x-\bar{x})^2 = 22$		$\Sigma(y-\bar{y})^2 = 24$

Using t-test, we have

$$t = \frac{\bar{x}-\bar{y}}{s\sqrt{\frac{1}{n_1}+\frac{1}{n_2}}} \sim t(n_1+n_2-2 \text{ d.f.}) \quad \ldots(1)$$

Here $$s^2 = \frac{\Sigma(x-\bar{x})^2+\Sigma(y-\bar{y})^2}{n_1+n_2-2} = \frac{22+24}{7+5-2} = \frac{46}{10} = 4.6$$

$\Rightarrow$ $$s = 2.1447$$

$\therefore$ from (1), $$t = \frac{22-24}{2.1447\sqrt{\frac{1}{7}+\frac{1}{5}}} = \frac{-2}{2.1447\sqrt{\frac{12}{35}}} = \frac{-2}{2.1447\sqrt{0.3428}}$$

$$= \frac{-2}{2.1447\,(0.5855)} = \frac{-2}{1.2557} = -1.5927$$

$\Rightarrow$ $$|t| = 1.5927$$

Also for 10 d.f., $t_{0.05} = 2.23$ (see t-table)

$\therefore$ The calculated value of t is less than the tabulated value of t at 5% level.

$\therefore$ H_0 is accepted, *i.e.*, there is no significant difference between the two diets.

Example 11. *A certain stimulus administered to each of 12 patients resulted in the following increases of blood pressure : 5, 2, 8, – 1, 3, 0, 6, – 2, 1, 5, 0, 4. Can it be concluded that the stimulus will in general be accompanied by an increase in blood pressure ?*

(P.T.U., M.B.A. Dec. 2000)

Sol. To test whether the mean increase in blood pressure of all patients to whom the stimulus is administered will be positive. We have to assume that this population is Normal with mean μ and S.D. σ which are unknown.

$$H_0 : \mu = 0; \qquad H_1 : \mu_1 > 0$$

The test statistic, under H_0

$$t = \frac{\bar{d}}{s/\sqrt{n-1}} \sim t(n-1 \text{ d.f.})$$

Here, $\bar{d} = \dfrac{5 + 2 + 8 + (-1) + 3 + 0 + 6 + (-2) + 1 + 5 + 0 + 4}{12} = 2.583$

$$s^2 = \frac{\Sigma d^2}{n} - \bar{d}^2$$

$$= \frac{1}{12}\,[5^2 + 2^2 + 8^2 + (-1)^2 + 3^2 + 0^2 + 6^2 + (-2)^2 + 1^2 + 5^2 + 0^2 + 4^2] - (2.583)^2$$

$$= 8.744 \quad \Rightarrow \quad s = 2.9571$$

$$t = \frac{\bar{d}}{s/\sqrt{n-1}} \sim t(n - 1\text{ d.f.}) = \frac{2.583}{2.9571/\sqrt{12-1}} = \frac{2.583\sqrt{11}}{2.9571} = 2.897$$

Conclusion. The tabulated value of $t_{0.05}$ at 5% level of significance for 11 d.f. is 2.2. (see t-table) $\therefore$ $|t| > t_{0.05}$, H_0 is rejected. *i.e.*, the stimulus does not increase the blood pressure. The stimulus in general will be accompanied by increase in blood pressure.

TEST YOUR KNOWLEDGE 10.7

1. The mean life of 10 electric motors was found to be 1450 hrs with S.D. of 423 hrs. A second sample of 17 motors chosen from a different batch showed a mean life of 1280 hrs with a S.D. of 398 hrs. Is there a significant difference between means of the two samples ?

2. The marks obtained by a group of 9 regular course students and another group of 11 part time course students in a test are given below :

Regular :	56	62	63	54	60	51	67	69	58		
Part-time :	62	70	71	62	60	56	75	64	72	68	66

Examine whether the marks obtained by regular students and part-time students differ significantly at 5% and 1% level of significance.

3. A group of 10 boys fed on diet A and another group of 8 boys fed on a different diet B recorded the following increase in weight (kgs).

Diet A :	5	6	8	1	12	4	3	9	6	10
Diet B :	2	3	6	8	10	1	2	8		

Does it show the superiority of diet A over the diet B ?

4. Two independent samples of sizes 7 and 9 have the following values :

Sample A :	10	12	10	13	14	11	10		
Sample B :	10	13	15	12	10	14	11	12	11

Test whether the difference between the mean is significant. (*P.T.U. B.Pharma May 2005*)

5. To compare the prices of a certain product in two cities, 10 shops when related at random in each town. The price was noted below :

City 1 :	61	63	56	63	56	63	59	56	44	61
City 2 :	55	54	47	59	51	61	57	54	64	58

Test whether the average prices can be said to be the same in two cities.

6. The average number of articles produced by two machines per day are 200 and 250 with standard deviation 20 and 25 respectively on the basis of records of 25 days production. Can you regard both the machines equally efficient at 5% level of significance ?

7. Two samples of 6 and 5 items respectively gave the following data :

	Sample I	*Sample II*
Mean	40	50
S.D.	8	10

Is the difference of mean significant ? (Test at 5% level of significance)

(*P.T.U., M.B.A. Dec. 2003*)

8. The change in sleeping hours of 7 patients after taking a medicine are as follows :

0.7, 0.1, – 0.3, 1.2, 1.0, 0.3 and – 0.4 hrs.

Do these data give evidence that the medicine produces additional hours of sleep ?

[**Hint.** $|t| = 1.439$]

9. Nine patients to whom a certain drug was administered, registered the following rise in blood pressure, 3, 7, 4, – 1, – 3, 6, – 4, 1, 5. Test the hypothesis that the drug does not raise the blood pressure.

[**Hint.** $|t| = 10.5$]

10. A sample of 11 rats from a central population had an average blood viscosity of 3.92 with a standard deviation of 0.61. Estimate the 95% confidence limits for the mean blood viscosity of the population.

Answers

1. There is no significant difference between means, ($|t| = 1.0369$)

2. There is a significant difference between the marks obtained by regular and part-time students ($|t| = 2.297$)

3. There is no significant difference between the two diets, ($|t| = 0.8717$)

4. There is no significant difference between the means, ($|t| = 0.6626$)

5. There is no significant difference between the two prices, ($|t| = 1.049$)

6. Both the machines are not equally significant, ($|t| = 4.686$)

7. Not significant

8. There is no significant difference in sleeping hours before and after taking the medicine

9. There is a significant difference between the blood pressure

10. 3.51 ± 4.33.

10.25. SNEDECOR'S VARIANCE RATIO TEST OR F-TEST (*P.T.U., M.B.A. Dec. 2010, 2005*)

In testing the significance of the difference of two means of two samples, we assumed that the two sample came from the same population or population with equal variance. The objective of the F-test is to discover whether two independent estimates of population variance differ significantly or whether the two samples may be regarded as drawn from the Normal populations having the same variance. Hence before applying the *t*-test for the significance of the difference of two means, we have to test for the equality of population variance by using F-test.

Let n_1 and n_2 be the sizes of two samples with variance s_1^2 and s_2^2. The estimate of the population variance based on these samples are $s_1^2 = \dfrac{n_1 S_1^2}{n_1 - 1}$ and $s_2^2 = \dfrac{n_2 S_2^2}{n_2 - 1}$. The degrees of freedom of these estimates are $\nu_1 = n_1 - 1$, $\nu_2 = n_2 - 1$.

To test whether these estimates s_1^2 and s_2^2 are significantly different or if the samples may be regarded as drawn from the same population or from two populations with same variance σ^2. We set up the null hypothesis $H_0 : \sigma_1^2 = \sigma_2^2 = \sigma^2$ *i.e.*, the independent estimates of the common population do not differ significantly.

To carry out the test of significance of the difference of the variances, we calculate the test statistic $F = \frac{s_1^2}{s_2^2}$, the numerator is greater than the denominator, *i.e.*, $s_1^2 > s_2^2$.

Conclusion. If the calculated value of F exceeds $F_{0.05}$ for $((n_1 - 1), (n_2 - 1))$ degrees of freedom, we conclude that the ratio is significant at 5% level. *i.e.*, we conclude that the sample could have come from two Normal population with same variance.

10.26. ASSUMPTIONS ON WHICH F-TEST IS BASED ARE

1. *The populations for each sample must be Normally distributed.*
2. *The samples must be random and independent.*
3. *The ratio of* σ_1^2 to σ_2^2 *should be equal to 1 or greater than 1. That is why we take the larger variance in the numerator of the ratio.*

10.27. METHOD TO APPLY F-TEST

We defined $F = \frac{s_1^2}{s_2^2}$, where

$$s_1^2 = \frac{\Sigma(x_i - \bar{x})^2}{n_1 - 1}; \; i = 1, 2, \ldots n$$

$$s_2^2 = \frac{\Sigma(y_j - \bar{y})^2}{n_2 - 1}, \; j = 1, 2, \ldots m$$

Here s_1^2, s_2^2 are called the unbiased estimates of the population variances.

If the calculated value of F exceeds the tabulated value (which depends on the degree of freedom $\nu_1 = (n_1 - 1)$ and $\nu_2 = (n_2 - 1)$, then the null hypothesis H_0 is rejected, If the calculated value of F is less than the tabulated value, then the null hypothesis H_0 is accepted.

ILLUSTRATIVE EXAMPLES

Example 1. *In two independent samples of sizes 8 and 10, the sum of squares of deviations of the sample values from the respective sample means were 84.4 and 102.6. Test whether the difference of variances of the populations is significant or not.*

Sol. Null hypothesis H_0 : $\sigma_1^2 = \sigma_2^2 = \sigma^2$, *i.e.*, there is no significant difference between population variance.

Under H_0 : $$F = \frac{s_1^2}{s_2^2} \sim F(\nu_1, \nu_2 \text{ d.f.}),$$

where $\nu_1 = n_1 - 1$, n_1 = Sample I size = 8 ; $\nu_2 = n_2 - 1$, n_2 = Sample II size = 10

$$\Sigma(x_1 - \bar{x}_1)^2 = 84.4 \,;\, \Sigma(x_2 - \bar{x}_2)^2 = 102.6$$

Here
$$s_1^2 = \frac{\Sigma(x_1 - \bar{x}_1)^2}{n_1 - 1} = \frac{84.4}{7} = 12.057\,;$$

$$s_2^2 = \frac{\Sigma(x_2 - \bar{x}_2)^2}{n_2 - 1} = \frac{102.6}{9} = 11.4$$

$$F = \frac{s_1^2}{s_2^2} = \frac{12.057}{11.4} = 1.0576. \quad \because \quad (s_1^2 > s_2^2)$$

Conclusion. The tabulated value of F at 5% level of significance for (7, 9) d.f. is 3.29

$\therefore$ $F_{0.05} = 3.29$ and $|\,F\,| = 1.0576 > 3.29 = F_{0.05}$ $\Rightarrow$ H_0 is accepted. *i.e.,* There is no significant difference between the variance of the populations.

Example 2. *Two random samples are drawn from 2 Normal populations are as follows :*

A	*17*	*27*	*18*	*25*	*27*	*29*	*13*	*17*
B	*16*	*16*	*20*	*27*	*26*	*25*	*21*	

Test whether the samples are drawn from the same Normal population.

Sol. To test if two independent samples have been drawn from the same population, we have to test (*i*) equality of the means by applying *t*-test and (*ii*) equality of population variance by applying F-test.

Since *t*-test assumes that the sample variances are equal, we shall first apply F-test.

Null hypothesis H_0 : $\sigma_1^2 = \sigma_2^2$, *i.e.*, the population variance do not differ significantly.

Alternative hypothesis. $H_1 : \sigma_1^2 \neq \sigma_2^2$.

Test statistic : $F = \frac{s_1^2}{s_2^2}$, (if $s_1^2 > s_2^2$)

Computations for s_1^2 and s_2^2

x_1	$x_1 - \bar{x}_1$	$(x_1 - \bar{x}_1)^2$	x_2	$x_2 - \bar{x}_2$	$(x_2 - \bar{x}_2)^2$
17	– 4.625	21.39	16	– 2.714	7.365
27	5.735	28.89	16	– 2.714	7.365
18	– 3.625	13.14	20	1.286	1.653
25	3.375	11.39	27	8.286	68.657
27	5.735	28.89	26	7.286	53.085
29	7.735	54.39	25	6.286	39.513
13	– 8.625	74.39	21	2.286	5.226
17	– 4.625	21.39			

$$\bar{x}_1 = 21.625 \,;\, n_1 = 8 \,;\, \Sigma(x_1 - \bar{x}_1)^2 = 253.87$$

$$\bar{x}_2 = 18.714 \,;\, n_2 = 7 \,;\, \Sigma(x_2 - \bar{x}_2)^2 = 182.859$$

$$s_1^2 = \frac{\Sigma(x_1 - \bar{x}_1)^2}{n_1 - 1} = \frac{253.87}{7} = 36.267\ ;$$

$$s_2^2 = \frac{\Sigma(x_2 - \bar{x}_2)^2}{n_2 - 1} = \frac{182.859}{6} = 30.47$$

$$F = \frac{s_1^2}{s_2^2} = \frac{36.267}{30.47} = 1.190.$$

Conclusion. The tabulated value of F for $\nu_1 = 7$ and $\nu_2 = 6$ degrees of freedom at 5% level is $F_{0.05} = 4.21$. (See F-table) The calculated value of F is less than the tabulated value of F. $\therefore$ H_0 is accepted. Hence we conclude that the variability in two populations is same.

***t*-test**

Null hypothesis. $H_0 : \mu_1 = \mu_2$, *i.e.*, the population means are equal.

Alternative hypothesis. $H_1 : \mu_1 \neq \mu_2$

$$s^2 = \frac{\Sigma(x_1 - \bar{x}_1)^2 + \Sigma(x_2 - \bar{x}_2)^2}{n_1 + n_2 - 2} = \frac{253.87 + 182.859}{8 + 7 - 2} = 33.594 \quad \therefore \quad s = 5.796$$

$$t = \frac{\bar{x}_1 - \bar{x}_2}{s\sqrt{\frac{1}{n_1} + \frac{1}{n_2}}} = \frac{21.625 - 18.714}{5.796\sqrt{\frac{1}{8} + \frac{1}{7}}} = 0.9704 \sim t(n_1 + n_2 - 2) \text{ d.f.}$$

Conclusion. The tabulated value of t at 5% level of significance for 13 d.f. is 2.16. (See t-table) the calculated value of t is less than the tabulated value.

H_0 is accepted, *i.e.*, there is no significant difference between the population mean ; *i.e.*, $\mu_1 = \mu_2$. $\therefore$ We conclude that the two samples have been drawn from the same normal population.

Example 3. *Two independent sample of sizes 7 and 6 have the following values :*

Sample A	*28*	*30*	*32*	*33*	*31*	*29*	*34*
Sample B	*29*	*30*	*30*	*24*	*27*	*28*	

Examine whether the samples have been drawn from Normal populations having the same variance.

Sol. Null Hypothesis H_0 : The variance are equal, *i.e.*, $\sigma_1^2 = \sigma_2^2$ *i.e.*, the samples have been drawn from Normal populations with same variance.

Alternative Hypothesis $H_1 : \sigma_1^2 \neq \sigma_2^2$

Computations for s_1^2 and s_2^2

x_1	$x_1 - \bar{x}_1$	$(x_1 - \bar{x}_1)^2$	x_2	$x_2 - \bar{x}_2$	$(x_2 - \bar{x}_2)^2$
28	– 3	9	29	1	1
30	– 1	1	30	2	4
32	1	1	30	2	4
33	2	4	24	– 4	16
31	0	0	27	– 1	1
29	– 2	4	28	0	0
34	3	9			
		28			26

$$\bar{x}_1 = 31, \quad n_1 = 7 ; \quad \Sigma(x_1 - \bar{x}_1)^2 = 28$$

$$\bar{x}_2 = 28, \quad n_2 = 6 ; \quad \Sigma(x_2 - \bar{x}_2)^2 = 26$$

$$s_1^2 = \frac{\Sigma(x_1 - \bar{x}_1)^2}{n_1 - 1} = \frac{28}{6} = 4.666 ; \quad s_2^2 = \frac{\Sigma(x_2 - \bar{x}_2)^2}{n_2 - 1} = \frac{26}{5} = 5.2$$

Under H_0, the test statistic $F = \frac{s_2^2}{s_1^2} = \frac{5.2}{4.666} = 1.1158.$ $(\because \; s_2^2 > s_1^2)$

Conclusion. (See F-table) The tabulated value of F at ($\nu_1 = 6 - 1, \nu_2 = 7 - 1$) d.f. for 5% level of significance is 4.39. Since the tabulated value of F is less than the calculated value, H_0 is accepted, *i.e.,* there is no significant difference between the variance, *i.e.,* the samples have been drawn from the Normal population with same variance.

Example 4. *The two random samples reveal the following data :*

Sample no.	*Size*	*Mean*	*Variance*
I	*16*	*440*	*40*
II	*25*	*460*	*42*

Test whether the samples come from the same normal population.

Sol. A Normal population has two parameters namely mean μ and variance σ^2. To test whether the two independent samples have been drawn from the same Normal population, we have to test

(*i*) the equality of means (*ii*) the equality of variance.

Since *t*-test assumes that the sample variance are equal, we first apply F-test.

Null hypothesis. $H_0 : \sigma_1^2 = \sigma_2^2$ *i.e.,* the population variance do not differ significantly.

Alternative hypothesis. $H_1 : \sigma_1^2 \neq \sigma_2^2$

Under H_0, the test statistic is given by $F = \frac{s_1^2}{s_2^2}, \; (s_1^2 > s_2^2)$

Given : $n_1 = 16, n_2 = 25 ; S_1^2 = 40, S_2^2 = 42$

$$\therefore \qquad F = \frac{s_1^2}{s_2^2} = \frac{\dfrac{n_1 S_1^2}{n_1 - 1}}{\dfrac{n_2 S_2^2}{n_2 - 1}} = \frac{16 \times 40}{15} \times \frac{24}{25 \times 42} = 0.9752.$$

$$\Rightarrow \qquad F = 0.9752$$

Conclusion. The calculated value of F is 0.9752. The tabulated value of F at (16 – 1, 25 – 1 d.f.) at 5% level of significance is 2.11 (see F-table). Since the calculated value is less than that of the tabulated value, H_0 is accepted ; *i.e.,* the population variances are equal.

***t*-test**

Null hypothesis. $H_0 : \mu_1 = \mu_2$, *i.e.,* the population means are equal.

Alternative hypothesis. $H_1 : \mu_1 \neq \mu_2$

Given : $n_1 = 16, n_2 = 25, \bar{x}_1 = 440, \bar{x}_2 = 460$

$$s^2 = \frac{n_1 s_1^{\ 2} + n_2 s_2^{\ 2}}{n_1 + n_2 - 2} = \frac{16 \times 40 + 25 \times 42}{16 + 25 - 2} = 43.333 \quad \therefore \quad s = 6.582$$

Under H_0, $$t = \frac{\bar{x}_1 - \bar{x}_2}{s\sqrt{\frac{1}{n_1} + \frac{1}{n_2}}} \sim (n_1 + n_2 - 2) \text{ d.f.} = \frac{440 - 460}{6.582\sqrt{\frac{1}{16} + \frac{1}{25}}} = -9.490$$

$\Rightarrow$ $\quad | t | = 9.490.$

Conclusion. The calculated value of $| t |$ is 9.490. The tabulated value of t at 39 d.f. for 5% level of significance is $F_{0.05} = 1.96$ (see t-table). Since the calculated value is greater than the tabulated value, H_0 is rejected. *i.e.*, there is significant difference between means, $\mu_1 \neq \mu_2$

Since there is significant difference between means and no significant difference between variance, we conclude that the samples do not come from the same Normal population.

Example 5. *Two independent samples of 8 and 7 items had the following values of the variables.*

Sample I	*9*	*11*	*13*	*11*	*15*	*9*	*12*	*14*
Sample II	*10*	*12*	*10*	*14*	*9*	*8*	*10*	

Do the estimates of population variance differ significantly?

(Given at 5% level, for 7 and 6 d.f. is $F_{0.05} = 4.20$) (P.T.U. M.B.A. May 2009)

Sol. Null Hypothesis: There is no significant difference between the population variances, *i.e.*, $(s_1^2 = s_2^2)$

Alternative Hypothesis: There is a significant difference between the population variances *i.e.*, $(s_1^2 \neq s_2^2)$

Consider the following table

x	$(x - \bar{x})$	$(x - \bar{x})^2$	y	$y - \bar{y}$	$(y - \bar{y})^2$
9	–2.75	7.5625	10	–0.42	0.1764
11	–.75	0.5625	12	1.58	2.4964
13	1.25	1.5625	10	–0.42	0.1764
11	–.75	0.5625	14	3.58	12.8164
15	3.25	10.5625	9	–1.42	2.0164
9	–2.75	7.5625	8	–2.42	5.8564
12	0.25	0.0625	10	–0.42	0.1764
14	2.25	5.0625	—	—	—
Total = 94		33.5	73		23.7148

$$\bar{x} = \frac{\Sigma x}{n_1} = \frac{94}{8} = 11.75; \bar{y} = \frac{\Sigma y}{n_2} = \frac{73}{7} = 10.42$$

$\therefore$ $$s_1^2 = \frac{1}{n_1 - 1}\Sigma(x - \bar{x})^2 = \frac{33.5}{7} = 4.78$$

$$s_2^2 = \frac{1}{n_2 - 1} - \Sigma(y - \bar{y})^2 = \frac{23.7148}{6} = 3.952$$

$$\therefore \qquad F = \frac{s_1^2}{s_2^2} = \frac{4.78}{3.952} = 1.2095$$

Conclusion: The calculated value of F is 1.2095. The given tabulated value of F for (7, 6) d.f. is $F_{0.05} = 4.20$. Since the calculated value is less than the tabulated value, H_0 is accepted. *i.e.*, the population variances do not differ significantly.

TEST YOUR KNOWLEDGE 10.8

1. From the following two sample values find out whether they have come from the same population :

Sample 1	17	27	18	25	27	29	27	23	17
Sample 2	16	16	20	16	20	17	15	21	

2. The daily wages in Rupees of skilled workers in two cities are as follows :

	Size of sample of workers	*S.D. of wages in the sample*
City A	16	25
City B	13	32

3. The standard deviation calculated from two random samples of sizes 9 and 13 are 2.1 and 1.8 respectively. Can the samples be regrated as drawn from normal populations with the same standard deviation ?
4. Two independent samples of size 8 and 9 have the following values of the variables :

Sample I	20	30	23	25	21	22	23	24	
Sample II	30	31	32	34	35	29	28	27	26

Do the estimates of the population variance differ significantly ?

Answers

1. rejected **2.** accepted **3.** accepted **4.** accepted.

10.28. CHI-SQUARE (χ^2) TEST *(P.T.U., M.B.A. May 2003, Dec. 2003, May 2002, Dec. 2001)*

When a coin is tossed 200 times, the theoretical considerations lead us to expect 100 heads and 100 tails. But in practice, these results are rarely achieved. The quantity χ^2 (a Greek letter, pronounced as chi-square) describes the magnitude of discrepancy between theory and observation. If $\chi = 0$, the observed and expected frequencies completely coincide. The greater the discrepancy between the observed and expected frequencies, the greater is the value of χ^2. Thus χ^2 **affords a measure of the correspondence between theory and observation.**

If O_i $(i = 1, 2, \ldots\ldots, n)$ is a set of observed (experimental) frequencies and E_i $(i = 1, 2, \ldots\ldots, n)$ is the corresponding set of expected (theoretical or hypothetical) frequencies, then, χ^2 is **defined as**

$$\chi^2 = \sum_{i=1}^{n} \left[\frac{(O_i - E_i)^2}{E_i} \right],$$

where $\Sigma O_i = \Sigma E_i = N$ (total frequency) and degrees of freedom (d.f.) = $(n - 1)$.

Note. (*i*) If $\chi^2 = 0$, the observed and theoretical frequencies agree exactly.

(*ii*) If $\chi^2 > 0$ they do not agree exactly.

10.29. APPLICATIONS OF χ^2 TEST

χ^2 test is one of the simplest and the most general test known. It is applicable to a very large number of problems in practice which can be summed up under the following heads :

(*i*) as a test of goodness of fit.

(*ii*) as a test of independence of attributes.

(*iii*) as a test of homogeneity of independent estimates of the population variance.

(*iv*) as a test of the hypothetical value of the population variance σ^2.

(*v*) as a list of the homogeneity of independent estimates of the population correlation coefficient.

10.30. CONDITIONS FOR APPLYING χ^2 TEST (*P.T.U., M.B.A. May 2008*)

Following are the conditions which should be satisfied before χ^2 test can be applied.

(*a*) N, the total number of frequencies should be large. It is difficult to say what constitutes largeness, but as an arbitrary figure, we may say that **N should be at least 50,** however, few the cells.

(*b*) No theoretical cell-frequency should be small. Here again, it is difficult to say what constitutes smallness, but 5 should be regarded as the very minimum and **10 is better.** If small theoretical frequencies occur (*i.e.*, < 10), the difficulty is overcome by grouping two or more classes together before calculating (O – E). **It is important to remember that the number of degrees of freedom is determined with the number of classes after regrouping.**

(*c*) The constraints on the cell frequencies, if any, should be linear.

10.31. THE χ^2 DISTRIBUTION

For large sample sizes, the sampling distribution of χ^2 can be closely approximated by a continuous curve known as the chi-square distribution. The probability function of χ^2 distribution is given by

$$f(\chi)^2 = c(\chi^2)^{(\nu/2-1)}\, e^{-x^2/2}$$

where $e = 2.71828$, ν = number of the degrees of freedom ; c = a constant depending only on ν.

Symbolically, the degrees of freedom are denoted by the symbol ν or by d.f. and are obtained by the rule $\nu = n - k$, where k refers to the number of independent constraints.

In general, when we fit a Binomial distribution, the number of degrees of freedom is one less than the number of classes. When we fit a Poisson distribution, the degrees of freedom are 2 less than the number of classes, because we use the total frequency and the arithmetic mean to get the parameter of the Poisson distribution. When we fit a Normal curve, the number of degrees of freedom are 3 less than the number of classes, but in this fitting, we use the total frequency, mean the standard deviation.

We may summarise the above explanation as follows :

If the data is given in series of "n" numbers. Then

In the case of Binomial distribution, d.f. $= n - 1$
In the case of Poisson distribution, d.f. $= n - 2$
In the case of Normal distribution, d.f. $= n - 3$.

10.32. χ^2 TEST AS A TEST OF GOODNESS OF FIT (*P.T.U., M.B.A. May 2001, Dec. 2001*)

χ^2 test enables us to ascertain how well the theoretical distributions such as Binomial, Poisson or Normal etc. fit empirical distributions, *i.e.*, distributions obtained from sample data. If the **calculated value of χ^2 is less than the table value** at a specified level (generally 5%) of significance, the **fit is considered to be good** *i.e.*, the divergence between actual and expected frequencies is attributed to fluctuations of simple sampling. If the calculated value of χ^2 is greater than the table value, the fit is considered to be poor.

ILLUSTRATIVE EXAMPLES

Example 1. *The following table gives the number of accidents that take place in an industry during various days of the week. Test if accidents are uniformly distributed over the week.*

Day	*Mon*	*Tue*	*Wed*	*Thu*	*Fri*	*Sat*
No. of accidents	*14*	*18*	*12*	*11*	*15*	*14*

Sol. Null hypothesis H_0. The accidents are uniformly distributed over the week.

Under this H_0, the expected frequencies of the accidents on each of these days

$$= \frac{14 + 18 + 12 + 11 + 15 + 14}{6} = \frac{84}{6} = 14$$

Observed frequency (O_i)	14	18	12	11	15	14
Expected frequency (E_i)	14	14	14	14	14	14
$(O_i - E_i)^2$	0	16	4	9	1	0
$\frac{(O_i - E_i)^2}{E_i}$	0	1.142	0.2857	0.6428	0.071	0

$$\therefore \qquad \chi^2 = \sum_{i=1}^{6} \left[\frac{(O_i - E_i)^2}{E_i} \right] = 0 + 1.142 + 0.2857 + 0.6428 + 0.071 + 0$$

$$\cong 2.14$$

Conclusion. The tabulated value of χ^2 at 5% level for (6 – 1 = 5 d.f.) is $\chi^2_{0.05} = 11.09$. (see χ^2-table)

Since the calculated value of χ^2 is less than the tabulated value, H_0 is accepted *i.e.*, the accidents are uniformly distributed over the week.

Example 2. *A die is thrown 270 times and the results of these throws are given below :*

No. appeared on the die	*1*	*2*	*3*	*4*	*5*	*6*
Frequency	*40*	*32*	*29*	*59*	*57*	*59*

Test whether the die is biased or not.

Sol. Null hypothesis H_0. Die is unbiased.
Under this H_0, the expected frequencies for each digit is

$$= \frac{40 + 32 + 29 + 59 + 57 + 59}{6} = \frac{276}{6} = 46.$$

To find the value of χ^2, consider the following table.

O_i	40	32	29	59	57	59
E_i	46	46	46	46	46	46
$(O_i - E_i)^2$	36	196	289	169	121	169
$\frac{(O_i - E_i)^2}{E_i}$	0.7826	4.2608	6.2826	3.6739	2.6304	3.6739

$$\chi^2 = \sum_{i=1}^{6} \left[\frac{(O_i - E_i)^2}{E_i}\right] = 0.7826 + 4.2608 + 6.2826 + 3.6739 + 2.6304 + 3.6739$$

$$= 28.3476 \cong 28.35$$

Conclusion. The tabulated value of χ^2 at 5% level of significance for (6 – 1 = 5) d.f. is $\chi^2_{0.05}$ = 11.09. (see χ^2-table) Since the calculated value of χ^2 = 28.35 > 11.07 (the tabulated value), H_0 is rejected. *i.e.,* Die is not unbiased or Die is biased.

Example 3. *The following table shows the distribution of digits in numbers chosen at random from a telephone directory :*

Digits	*0*	*1*	*2*	*3*	*4*	*5*	*6*	*7*	*8*	*9*
Frequency	*1026*	*1107*	*997*	*966*	*1075*	*933*	*1107*	*972*	*964*	*853*

Test whether the digits may be taken to occur equally frequently in the directory.

Sol. Null hypothesis H_0 : The digits taken in the directory occur equally frequency. *i.e.,* there is no significant difference between the observed and expected frequency.

Under H_0, the expected frequency is given by

$$= \frac{1026 + 1107 + 997 + 966 + 1075 + 933 + 1107 + 972 + 964 + 853}{10} = \frac{10{,}000}{10} = 1000$$

To find the value of χ^2

O_i	1026	1107	997	996	1075	933	1107	972	964	853
E_i	1000	1000	1000	1000	1000	1000	1000	1000	1000	1000
$(O_i - E_i)^2$	676	11449	9	16	5625	4489	11449	784	1296	21609
$\frac{(O_i - E_i)^2}{E_i}$	0.676	11.449	0.009	0.016	5.625	4.489	11.449	0.784	1.296	21.609

$$\chi^2 = \sum_{i=1}^{10} \left[\frac{(O_i - E_i)^2}{E_i}\right] = 0.676 + 11.449 + 0.009 + 0.016 + 5.625 + 4.489 + 11.449$$

$$+ 0.784 + 1.296 + 21.609 = 57.402$$

Conclusion. The tabulated value of χ^2 at 5% level of significance for 9 d.f. is $\chi^2_{0.05} = 16.919$ (see χ^2-table). Since the calculated value of χ^2 is greater than the tabulated value, H_0 is rejected. *i.e.*, there is significant difference between the observed and theoretical frequency. *i.e.*, the digits taken in the directory do not occur equally frequently.

Example 4. *200 digits are chosen at random from a set of table. The frequencies of the digits are as follows :*

Digit	*0*	*1*	*2*	*3*	*4*	*5*	*6*	*7*	*8*	*9*
Frequencies	*18*	*19*	*23*	*21*	*16*	*25*	*22*	*20*	*21*	*15*

Use chi-square test to asses the correctness of the hypothesis that the digits were distributed in equal numbers in the tables from where they are choosen. (P.T.U., M.B.A. May 2004)

Sol. Null hypothesis H_0 : The digits were distributed in equal numbers.

The expected frequencies of each digits $= \dfrac{200}{10} = 20$. To apply χ^2, consider the following table :

O_i	18	19	23	21	16	25	22	20	21	15
E_i	20	20	20	20	20	20	20	20	20	20
$(O_i - E_i)^2$	4	1	9	1	16	25	4	0	1	25
$\dfrac{(O_i - E_i)^2}{E_i}$	0.20	0.05	0.45	0.05	0.80	1.25	0.20	0	0.05	1.25

Under H_0, $\chi^2 = \displaystyle\sum_{i=1}^{10} \frac{(O_i - E_i)^2}{E_i}$

$$= 0.20 + 0.05 + 0.45 + 0.05 + 0.80 + 1.25 + 0.20 + 0.05 + 1.25 = 4.3$$

Also $\chi^2_{0.05}$ = The tabulated value of χ^2 at 5% level of significance for ($n - 1 = 9$ d.f.) = 16.22 (see χ^2-table)

Conclusion. The calculated value of χ^2 < the tabulated value of χ^2 at 5% level of significance for 9 d.f. $\therefore$ H_0 is accepted *i.e.*, the digits were distributed in equal numbers.

Example 5. *Records taken of the number of male and female births in 800 families having four children are as follows :*

No. of male births	*0*	*1*	*2*	*3*	*4*
No. of female births	*4*	*3*	*2*	*1*	*0*
No. of families	*32*	*178*	*290*	*236*	*94*

Test whether the data are consistent with the hypothesis that the Binomial law holds and the chance of male birth is equal to that of female birth, namely p = q = 1/2.

Sol. Null Hypothesis H_0 : The data are consistent with the hypothesis of equal probability for male and female births. *i.e.*, $p = q = 1/2$.

We use Binomial distribution to calculate theoretical frequency given by :

$$N(r) = N \times P(X = r)$$

where N is the total frequency, N(r) is the number of families with r male children and

$$P(X = r) = {}^nC_r p^r q^{n-r},$$

where p and q are probability of male and female birth, n is the number of children.

$$\therefore\ N(0) = \text{No. of families with 0 male children} = 800 \times {}^4C_0 \left(\frac{1}{2}\right)^4 = 800 \times 1 \times \frac{1}{2^4} = 50$$

$$N(1) = 800 \times {}^4C_1 \left(\frac{1}{2}\right)^1 \left(\frac{1}{2}\right)^3 = 200\ ;\ N(2) = 800 \times {}^4C_2 \left(\frac{1}{2}\right)^2 \left(\frac{1}{2}\right)^2 = 300$$

$$N(3) = 800 \times {}^4C_3 \left(\frac{1}{2}\right)^1 \left(\frac{1}{2}\right)^3 = 200\ ;\ N(4) = 800 \times {}^4C_4 \left(\frac{1}{2}\right)^0 \left(\frac{1}{2}\right)^4 = 50$$

Observed frequency O_i	32	178	290	236	94
Expected frequency E_i	50	200	300	200	50
$(O_i - E_i)^2$	324	484	100	1296	1936
$\dfrac{(O_i - E_i)^2}{E_i}$	6.48	2.42	0.333	6.48	38.72

$$\chi^2 = \sum_{i=1}^{5} \left[\frac{(O_i - E_i)^2}{E_i}\right] = 6.48 + 2.42 + 0.333 + 6.48 + 38.72 = 54.433$$

Conclusion. Table value of χ^2 at 5% level of significance for $5 - 1 = 4$ d.f. is $\chi^2_{0.05} = 9.49$ (see χ_2-table). Since the calculated value of χ^2 is greater than the tabulated value, H_0 is rejected. *i.e.*, the data are not consistent with the hypothesis that the Binomial law holds and that the chance of a male birth is not equal to that of a female birth.

Note. Since the fitting is Binomial, the degrees of freedom $\nu = n - 1$ *i.e.*, $\nu = 5 - 1 = 4$.

Example 6. *Verify whether Poisson distribution can be assumed from the data given below :*

No. of defects	*0*	*1*	*2*	*3*	*4*	*5*
Frequency	*6*	*13*	*13*	*8*	*4*	*3*

Sol. Null Hypothesis H_0 : Poisson fit is a good fit to the data.

$$\text{Mean of the given distribution} = \frac{\Sigma f_i x_i}{\Sigma f_i} = \frac{94}{47} = 2$$

To fit a Poisson distribution we, require m. Parameter $m = \bar{x} = 2$.
By Poisson distribution, the frequency of r success is

$$N(r) = N \times e^{-m} \cdot \frac{m^r}{r!},\ \text{N is the total frequency. } i.e.,$$

$$N(0) = 47 \times e^{-2} \cdot \frac{(2)^0}{0!} = 6.36\ ;\ N(1) = 47 \times e^{-2} \cdot \frac{(2)^1}{1!} = 12.72$$

$$N(2) = 47 \times e^{-2} \cdot \frac{(2)^2}{2!} = 12.72 \; ; \; N(3) = 47 \times e^{-2} \cdot \frac{(2)^3}{3!} = 8.48$$

$$N(4) = 47 \times e^{-2} \cdot \frac{(2)^4}{4!} = 4.24 \; ; \; N(5) = 47 \times e^{-2} \cdot \frac{(2)^5}{5!} = 1.696.$$

X	0	1	2	3	4	5
O_i	6	13	13	8	4	3
E_i	6.36	12.72	12.72	8.48	4.24	1.696
$\frac{(O_i - E_i)^2}{E_i}$	0.2037	0.00616	0.00616	0.02716	0.0135	1.0026

$$\chi^2 = \sum_{i=1}^{6} \left[\frac{(O_i - E_i)^2}{E_i}\right] = 0.2037 + 0.00616 + 0.00616 + 0.02716 + 0.0135 + 1.0026$$

$= 1.25928.$

Conclusion. The calculated value of χ^2 is 1.25928. Tabulated value of χ^2 at 5% level of significance for $\nu = 6 - 2 = 4$ d.f. is $\chi^2_{0.05} = 9.49$ (see χ^2-table). Since the calculated value of χ^2 is less than that of tabulated value. H_0 is accepted *i.e.*, Poisson distribution provides a good fit to the data.

Example 7. *The theory predicts the proportion of beans in the four groups G_1, G_2, G_3, G_4 should be in the ratio 9 : 3 : 3 : 1. In an experiment with 1600 beans, the numbers in the four groups were 882, 313, 287 and 118. Does the experimental result support the theory.*

Sol. Null Hypothesis H_0 : The experimental result support the theory. *i.e.*, there is no significant difference between the observed and theoretical frequency under H_0, the theoretical frequency can be calculated as follows :

$$E(G_1) = \frac{1600 \times 9}{16} = 900 \; ; \; E(G_2) = \frac{1600 \times 3}{16} = 300 \; ;$$

$$E(G_3) = \frac{1600 \times 3}{16} = 300 \; ; \; E(G_4) = \frac{1600 \times 1}{16} = 100$$

To calculate the value of χ^2.

Observed frequency O_i	882	313	287	118
Expected frequency E_i	900	300	300	100
$(O_i - E_i)$	324	169	169	324
$\frac{(O_i - E_i)^2}{E_i}$	0.36	0.5633	0.5633	3.24

$$\chi^2 = \sum_{i=1}^{4} \left[\frac{(O_i - E_i)^2}{E_i}\right] = 0.36 + 0.5633 + 0.5633 + 3.24 = 4.7266$$

Conclusion. The tabulated value of χ^2 at 5% level of significance for 3 d.f. is $\chi^2_{0.05} = 7.815$ (see χ^2-table). Since the calculated value of χ^2 is less than that of the tabulated value. Hence H_0 is accepted.

i.e., the experimental result supports the theory.

Example 8(a). *Calculate theoretical frequencies using Poisson's distribution:*

Deaths	*0*	*1*	*2*	*3*	*4*
Frequencies	*122*	*60*	*15*	*2*	*1*

(P.T.U. M.B.A. May 2009)

(b) In 1000 extensive sets of trials for an event of small probability, the frequency, of number of X successes proved to be. (P.T.U. M.B.A. Dec. 2007)

X	*0*	*1*	*2*	*3*	*4*	*5*	*6*	*7*
f	*305*	*365*	*210*	*80*	*28*	*9*	*2*	*1*

Assuming it to be a Poisson distribution, calculate the expected frequencies.

Sol. (*a*) Let X assumes the values 0, 1, 2, 3, 4. By Poisson distribution,

$$P(X = r) = N \times \frac{e^{-\lambda}\lambda^r}{r!}, r = 0, 1, 2, 3, 4$$

where $N = \Sigma f = 122 + 60 + 15 + 2 + 1 = 200,$

$$\lambda = \text{mean} = \frac{\Sigma fx}{\Sigma f} = \frac{0 + 1 \times 60 + 2 \times 15 + 3 \times 2 + 4 \times 1}{200}$$

$$= \frac{30 + 6 + 4}{200} = \frac{40}{200} = 0.2$$

The theoretical frequencies have been calculated in the following table.

r	$P(x = r)$	*Theoretical frequencies*
0	$200 \times e^{-0.2} = 163.800$	163
1	$200 \times e^{-0.2} \times 0.2 = 32.76$	33
2	$\frac{200 \times e^{-0.2} \times (0.2)^2}{2} = 3.276$	3
3	$\frac{200 \times e^{-0.2} \times (0.2)^3}{6} = 0.1092$	1
4	$\frac{200 \times e^{-0.2} \times (0.2)^4}{24} = 0.009$	0

Note: The second last frequency is taken as one since the total sum should be 200.

(*b*) By Poisson distribution, the frequency of r successes is given by

$$P(r) = N \times \frac{e^{-\lambda}\lambda^r}{r!} \text{ where } 0 \le r \le 7, \text{ where N is the total frequency.}$$

Consider the following table

x	0	1	2	3	4	5	6	7	Total
f	305	365	210	80	28	9	2	1	1000

Here $\lambda = \text{mean} = \dfrac{\Sigma f_i x_i}{\Sigma f_i} = \dfrac{0+365+420+240+112+45+12+7}{1000} = \dfrac{1201}{1000} = 1.201$

$$P(0) = 1000 \times \frac{e^{-1.201} \times (1.201)^0}{0!} = 1000 \times e^{-1.201} = 300.8931682 \cong 301$$

$$P(1) = 1000 \times \frac{e^{-1.201} \times (1.201)^1}{1!} = 361.3726951 \cong 361$$

$$P(2) = 1000 \times \frac{e^{-1.201} \times (1.201)^2}{2!} = 217.0043034 \cong 217$$

$$P(3) = 1000 \times \frac{e^{-1.201} \times (1.201)^3}{3!} = 86.87405612 \cong 87$$

$$P(4) = 1000 \times \frac{e^{-1.201} \times (1.201)^4}{4!} = 26.0083933535 \cong 26$$

$$P(5) = 1000 \times \frac{e^{-1.201} \times (1.201)^5}{5!} = 6.265361271 \cong 6$$

$$P(6) = 1000 \times \frac{e^{-1.201} \times (1.201)^6}{6!} = 1.25416481 \cong 1$$

$$P(7) = 1000 \times \frac{e^{-1.201} \times (1.201)^7}{7!} = 0.215170556 \cong 1$$

The last frequency is taken as 1 just to make the total sum 1000.

The expected frequencies E are shown in the following table.

X	0	1	2	3	4	5	6	7
E	301	361	217	87	26	6	1	1

Example 9. *Fit a Poisson distribution to the following :*

x :	*0*	*1*	*2*	*3*	*4*
f :	*46*	*38*	*22*	*9*	*1*

Sol. Null Hypothesis H_0 : Poisson fit is a good fit to the data.

Here mean of the given distribution $= \dfrac{\Sigma f_i x_i}{\Sigma f_i} = \dfrac{113}{116} = 0.97$

To fit a Poisson distribution, we require λ

Here $\lambda = \bar{x} = 0.97$

By Poisson distribution, the frequency of r success is

$$N(r) = N \times e^{-\lambda} \cdot \frac{\lambda^r}{r\,!}, \text{ N is the total frequency}$$

i.e., $N(0) = 116 \times e^{-0.97} = 116 \times 0.37 = 43.97$;

$$N(1) = 116 \times \frac{e^{-0.97}(0.97)}{\underline{|1}} = 41.76$$

$$N(2) = 116 \times e^{-0.97} \times \frac{(0.97)^2}{2} = 116 \times 0.17 = 19.72$$

$$N(3) = 116 \times e^{-0.97} \times \frac{(0.97)^3}{3!} = 6.688$$

$$N(4) = 116 \times e^{-0.97} \times \frac{(0.97)^4}{4!} = 1.62$$

X	0	1	2	3	4
O_i	46	38	22	9	1
E_i	43.97	41.76	19.72	6.68	1.62
$\frac{(O_i - E_i)^2}{E_i}$	0.093	0.338	0.263	0.805	0.23

$$\therefore \qquad \chi^2 = \sum_{i=1}^{5} \left[\frac{(O_i - E_i)^2}{E_i}\right] = 0.093 + 0.338 + 0.263 + 0.805 + 0.23 = 1.729$$

Conclusion. The calculated value of χ^2 is 1.729. Also the tabulated value of χ^2 at 5% level of significance for $\nu = 5 - 2 = 3$ *d.f.* is 7.815 (see χ^2-table). Since the calculated value of χ^2 at 5% level of significance is less than the tabulated value. Hence H_0 is accepted *i.e.*, Poisson distribution is a best fit to the given data.

Example 10. *Fit a Binomial distribution to the following frequency distribution.*

x	*0*	*1*	*2*	*3*	*4*	*5*	*6*
f	*13*	*25*	*52*	*58*	*32*	*16*	*4*

Sol. Null Hypothesis H_0 : Binomial distribution is a good fit to the given data.

We first find mean of the given distribution.

x_i	f_i	$f_i x_i$
0	13	0
1	25	25
2	52	104
3	58	174
4	32	128
5	16	80
6	4	24
	$N = \sum f_i = 200$	$\sum f_i x_i = 535$

Here mean $= \frac{\sum f_i x_i}{\sum f_i}$

$$\Rightarrow \qquad np = \frac{535}{200} = 2.675$$

$$\Rightarrow \qquad p = \frac{2.675}{7} = 0.38 \qquad | \; n = 7$$

$$\therefore \qquad q = 1 - p = 0.62$$

When $r = 0$, $P(X = 0) = 200 \times {}^7C_0\,(0.62)^7 = 7.043$
When $r = 1$, $P(X = 1) = 200 \times {}^7C_1\,(0.38)\,(0.62)^6$
$= 200 \times 7 \times 0.38 \times 0.0568 = 30.2176$
When $r = 2$, $P(X = 2) = 200 \times {}^7C_2\,(0.38)^2\,(0.62)^5$
$= 200 \times 21 \times 0.1444 \times 0.0916 = 55.55$
When $r = 3$, $P(X = 3) = 200 \times {}^7C_3\,(0.38)^3(0.62)^4$
$= 200 \times 35 \times 0.054 \times 0.1477 = 55.83$
When $r = 4$, $P(X = 4) = 200 \times {}^7C_4\,(0.38)^4(0.62)^3$
$= 200 \times 35 \times 0.020 \times 0.23 = 33.32$
When $r = 5$, $P(X = 5) = 200 \times {}^7C_5\,(0.38)^5\,(0.62)^2$
$= 200 \times 21 \times 0.0079 \times 0.3844 = 12.75$
When $r = 6$, $P(X = 6) = 200 \times {}^7C_6 \times (0.38)^6(0.62)^1$
$= 200 \times 7 \times 0.0030 \times 0.62 = 2.64$

E_i	O_i	$(O_i - E_i)^2$	$\frac{(O_i - E_i)^2}{E_i}$
7.043	13	35.48	178.73
30.21	25	27.144	24.38
55.55	52	12.60	2.85
55.83	58	4.70	0.39
33.32	32	1.74	0.09
12.75	16	10.56	8.74
2.64	4	1.84	1.28
	Total = 200		216.46

$$\chi^2 = \sum_{i=1}^{7} \frac{(O_i - E_i)^2}{E_i} = 216.46$$

Conclusion : The tabulated value of χ^2 at 5% level of significance for 7 – 1 = 6 d.f. is $\chi^2_{0.05} = 12.592$ (See-chi-square table). Since the calculated value of χ^2 is greater than the tabulated value of χ^2 at 5% level of significance.

Therefore H_0 is rejected *i.e.*, The Binomial law does not hold good according to the given data.

Example 11. *A survey of 320 families with 5 children each revealed the following distribution.*

No. of Boys	*No. of Girls*	*No. of Families*
5	*0*	*14*
4	*1*	*56*
3	*2*	*110*
2	*3*	*88*
1	*4*	*40*
0	*5*	*12*

Is this result consistent that the males and females births are equally probable ? (χ^2 at 5% level for 5 d.f. = 11.05). (P.T.U., M.B.A. Dec. 2004)

Sol. Null Hypothesis H_0 : The males and females births are equally probable.

As the males and females births are equally probable. $\therefore\ p = \frac{1}{2}, q = \frac{1}{2}$

The expected frequencies are the successive terms of the Binomial distribution

$$= N(q + p)^n = 320\left(\frac{1}{2} + \frac{1}{2}\right)^5$$

The successive terms are :

$$320 \times {}^5C_0 \times \left(\frac{1}{2}\right)^5, 320 \times {}^5C_1 \times \left(\frac{1}{2}\right)^5 ;$$

$$320 \times {}^5C_2 \times \left(\frac{1}{2}\right)^5, 320 \times {}^5C_3 \times \left(\frac{1}{2}\right)^5 ;$$

$$320 \times {}^5C_4 \times \left(\frac{1}{2}\right)^5, 320 \times {}^5C_5 \times \left(\frac{1}{2}\right)^5$$

or

10, 50, 100, 100, 50, 10.

To apply χ^2-test, consider the following table :

O_i	14	56	110	88	40	12
E_i	10	50	100	100	50	10
$(O_i - E_i)^2$	16	36	100	144	100	4
$\frac{(O_i - E_i)^2}{E_i}$	1.6	0.72	1	1.44	2	0.4

$$\chi^2 = \sum_{i=1}^{6}\left[\frac{(O_i - E_i)^2}{E_i}\right] = 1.6 + 0.72 + 1 + 1.44 + 2 + 0.4 = 7.16$$

Also $\chi^2_{0.05}$ = The tabulated value of χ^2 at 5% level of significance for $\upsilon = n - 1 = 6 - 1 = 5$ d.f. = 11.05 (see χ^2-table)

Conclusion. The calculated value of χ^2 is less than the tabulated value of χ^2 at 5% level of significance for 5 d.f. $\therefore$ H_0 is accepted *i.e.,* the males and females births are equally probable.

TEST YOUR KNOWLEDGE 10.9

1. The following table gives the frequency of occupance of the digits 0, 1, ..., 9 in the last place in four logarithm of numbers 10–99. Examine if there is any peculiarity.

Digits	:	0	1	2	3	4	5	6	7	8	9
Frequency	:	6	16	15	10	12	12	3	2	9	5

2. The sales in a supermarket during a week are given below. Test the hypothesis that the sales do not depend on the day of the week, using a significant level of 0.05.

Days	:	Mon	Tues	Wed	Thurs	Fri	Sat
Sales (in ₹ 1000)	:	65	54	60	56	71	84

3. Four coins were tossed at a time and this operation is repeated 160 times. It is found that 4 heads occur 6 times, 3 heads occur 43 times, 2 heads occur 69 times, one head occur 34 times. Discuss whether the coin may be regarded as unbiased ?

4. A survey of 800 families with 4 children each revealed the following distribution :

No. of boys	:	0	1	2	3	4
No. of girls	:	4	3	2	1	0
No. of families	:	32	178	290	236	64

Is this result consistent with the hypothesis that the male and female births are equally probable ?

5. Fit a Poisson distribution to the following data and best the goodness of fit :

x	:	0	1	2	3	4
f	:	109	65	22	3	1

6. Four coins were tossed 160 times and the following results were obtained.

No. of heads observed	:	0	1	2	3	4
Frequencies	:	17	52	54	31	6

Under the assumption that coins are balanced, find the expected frequencies of getting 0, 1, 2, 3 or 4 heads and test the goodness of fit.

7. A set of 5 coins is tossed 3200 times and the number of heads appearing each time is noted. The results are given below :

No. of heads	:	0	1	2	3	4	5
Frequencies	:	80	570	1100	900	50	50

Test the hypothesis that the coins are unbiased.

8. The number of scooter accidents per month in a certain town was as follows :

12	8	20	2	14	10	15	6	9	4

Use chi-square test to determine if these frequencies are in agreement with the belief that accident conditions were the same during 10-month period.

9. In the accounting department of bank, 100 accounts are selected at random and estimated for errors. The following results were obtained :

No. of errors	:	0	1	2	3	4	5	6
No. of accounts	:	35	40	19	2	0	2	2

Does this information verify that the errors are distributed according to the Poisson probability law ?

10. A sample analysis of examination results of 500 students, it was found that 220 students have failed, 170 have secured a third class, 90 have secured a second class and 20 got a first class. Do these figures support the general belief that above categories are in the ratio 4 : 3 : 2 : 1 respectively ?

Answers

1. There is no peculiarity in the occupance of the digits.

2. The sales donot depend on the day of the week.

3. Unbiased
4. The males and females births are not equally probable. ($\chi^2 = 19.633$)
5. Poisson law fits the data.
6. The coins are not balanced and the fit is not good ($\chi^2 = 12.725$)
7. The coins are biased ($\chi^2 = 58.80$)
8. The frequencies were not in agreement with the given belief $\chi^2 = 26.60$)
9. The errors are distributed according to the Normal distribution ($\chi^2 = 1.40$)
10. The observed results are not commensurate with the general examination result ($\chi^2 = 23.667$).

10.33. χ^2 TEST AS A TEST OF INDEPENDENCE

With the help of χ^2 test, we can find whether or not two attributes are associated. We take the null hypothesis that there is no association between the attributes under study, *i.e.*, **we assume that the two attributes are independent. If the calculated value of χ^2 is less than the table value** at a specified level (generally 5%) of significance, the hypothesis holds good, *i.e.*, **the attributes are independent** and do not bear any association. On the other hand, if the calculated value of χ^2 is greater than the table value at a specified level of significance, we say that the results of the experiment do not support the hypothesis. Thus a very useful application of χ^2 test is to investigate the relationship between trials or attributes which can be classified into two or more categories.

The sample data set out into two-way table, called **contingency table.**

Let us consider two attributes A and B divided into r classes $A_1, A_2, A_3, \ldots\ldots, A_r$ and B divided into s classes $B_1, B_2, B_3, \ldots\ldots, B_s$. If (A_i), (B_j) represents the number of persons possessing the attributes A_i, B_j respectively, ($i = 1, 2, \ldots\ldots, r, j = 1, 2, \ldots\ldots, s$) and $(A_i B_j)$ represent the number of persons possessing attributes A_i and B_j. Also we have $\sum_{i=1}^{r} A_i = \sum_{j=1}^{s} B_j = N$, where N is the total frequency. The contingency table for $r \times s$ is given below :

A \ B	A_1	A_2	A_3	...A_r	*Total*
B_1	(A_1B_1)	(A_2B_1)	(A_3B_1)	......(A_rB_1)	B_1
B_2	(A_1B_2)	(A_2B_2)	(A_3B_2)	......(A_rB_2)	B_2
B_3	(A_1B_3)	(A_2B_3)	(A_3B_3)	......(A_rB_3)	B_3
......	......	......	......	......	......
......	......	......	......	......	......
B_s	(A_1B_s)	(A_2B_s)	(A_3B_s)	......(A_rB_s)	(B_s)
Total	(A_1)	(A_2)	(A_3)	......(A_r)	N

H_0 : Both the attributes are independent. *i.e.*, A and B are independent under the null hypothesis, we calculate the expected frequency as follows :

$$P(A_i) = \text{Probability that a person possesses the attribute } A_i = \frac{(A_i)}{N} \quad i = 1, 2, \ldots\ldots, r$$

$$P(B_j) = \text{Probability that a person possesses the attribute } B_j = \frac{(B_j)}{N}$$

$P(A_iB_j)$ = Probability that a person possesses both attributes A_i and $B_j = \dfrac{(A_iB_j)}{N}$

If $(A_iB_j)_0$ is the expected number of persons possessing both the attributes A_i and B_j

$$(A_iB_j)_0 = NP(A_iB_j) = NP(A_i)(B_j)$$

$$= N\,\frac{(A_i)}{N}\,\frac{(B_j)}{N} = \frac{(A_i)(B_j)}{N} \qquad (\because \text{ A and B are independent})$$

Hence $$\chi^2 = \sum_{i=1}^{r}\sum_{j=1}^{s}\left[\frac{[(A_iB_j)_0 - (A_iB_j)]^2}{(A_iB_j)_0}\right]$$

which is distributed as a χ^2 variate with $(r-1)(s-1)$ degrees of freedom.

Note 1. For a 2 × 2 contingency table where the frequencies are $\dfrac{a/b}{c/d}$, χ^2 can be calculated from independent frequencies as $\chi^2 = \dfrac{(a+b+c+d)(ad-bc)^2}{(a+b)(c+d)(b+d)(a+c)}$.

Note 2. If the contingency table is not 2 × 2, then the formula for calculating χ^2 as given in note 1, can't be used. Hence, we have another formula for calculating the expected frequency $(A_iB_j)_0 = \dfrac{(A_i)(B_j)}{N}$

i.e., expected frequency in each cell is $= \dfrac{\text{Product of column total and row total}}{\text{whole total}}$.

Note 3. If $\dfrac{a\,|\,b}{c\,|\,d}$ is the 2 × 2 contingency table with two attributes, $Q = \dfrac{ad-bc}{ad+bc}$ is called the coefficient of association.

If the attributes are independent then $\dfrac{a}{b} = \dfrac{c}{d}$.

Note 4. Yate's Correction. In a 2 × 2 table, if the frequencies of a cell is small, we make Yate's correction to make χ^2 continuous.

Decrease by $\dfrac{1}{2}$ those cell frequencies which are greater than expected frequencies, and increase by $\dfrac{1}{2}$ those which are less than expectation. This will not affect the marginal columns. This correction is known as Yate's correction to continuity.

After Yate's correction, $$\chi^2 = \frac{N\left(bc - ad - \frac{1}{2}N\right)^2}{(a+c)(b+d)(c+d)(a+b)} \quad \text{when} \quad ad - bc < 0$$

$$\chi^2 = \frac{N\left(ad - bc - \frac{1}{2}N\right)^2}{(a+c)(b+d)(c+d)(a+b)} \quad \text{when} \quad ad - bc > 0.$$

ILLUSTRATIVE EXAMPLES

Example 1. *What are the expected frequencies of 2 × 2 contingency tables given below :*

(*i*)

a	*b*
c	*d*

(*ii*)

2	10
6	6

Sol. Observed frequencies — Expected frequencies

(*i*)

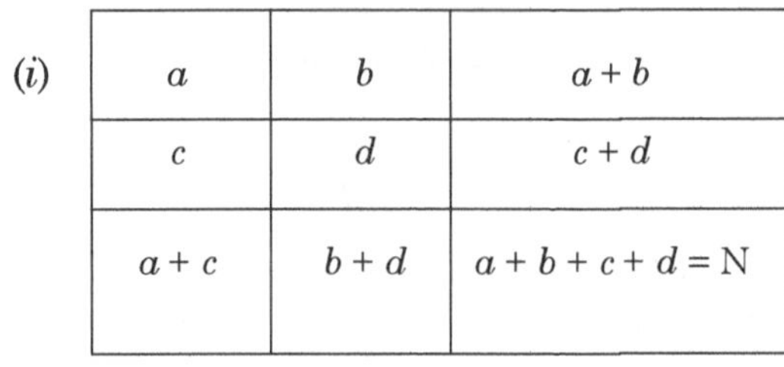

a	b	$a+b$
c	d	$c+d$
$a+c$	$b+d$	$a+b+c+d=\text{N}$

→

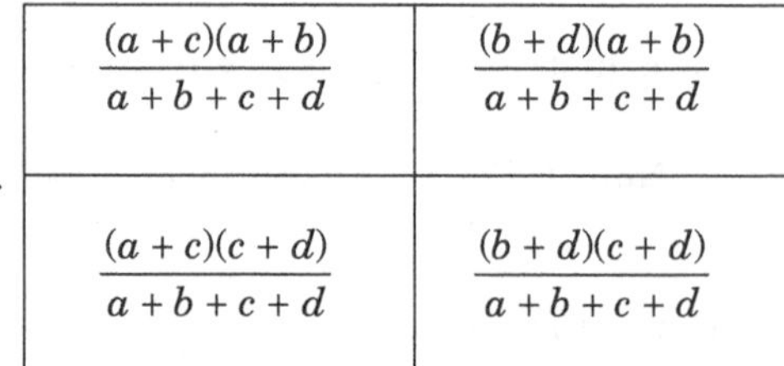

$\frac{(a+c)(a+b)}{a+b+c+d}$	$\frac{(b+d)(a+b)}{a+b+c+d}$
$\frac{(a+c)(c+d)}{a+b+c+d}$	$\frac{(b+d)(c+d)}{a+b+c+d}$

Observed frequencies — Expected frequencies

(*ii*)

2	10	12
6	6	12
8	16	24

→

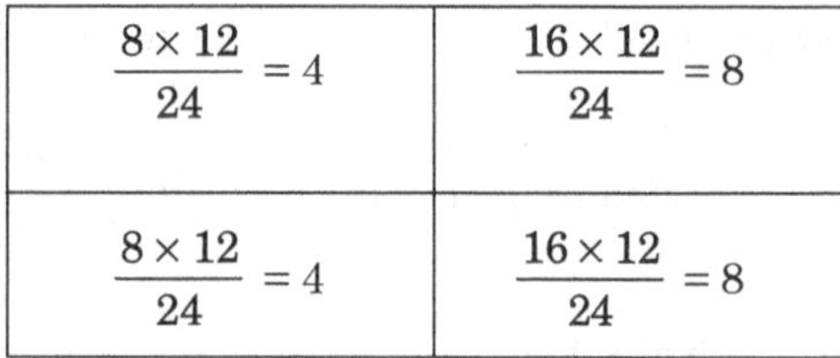

$\frac{8 \times 12}{24} = 4$	$\frac{16 \times 12}{24} = 8$
$\frac{8 \times 12}{24} = 4$	$\frac{16 \times 12}{24} = 8$

Example 2. *From the following table regarding the colour of eyes of fathers and sons test if the colour of son's eye is associated with that of the father.*

Eye colour of son

Eye colour of father		*Light*	*Not light*
	Light	*471*	*51*
	Not light	*148*	*230*

Sol. Null hypothesis H_0. The colour of son's eye is not associated with that of father. *i.e.,* they are independent.

Degree of freedom $v = (r-1)(s-1) = (2-1)(2-1) = 1$

Under H_0, we calculate the expected frequency in each cell as

$$= \frac{\text{Product of column total and row total}}{\text{Whole total}}$$

Expected frequencies are :

Eye colour of father \ Eye colour of son	*Light*	*Not light*	*Total*
Light	$\frac{619 \times 522}{900} = 359.02$	$\frac{289 \times 522}{900} = 167.62$	522
Not light	$\frac{619 \times 378}{900} = 259.98$	$\frac{289 \times 378}{900} = 121.38$	378
Total	619	289	900

$$\chi^2 = \sum_{i=1}^{4} \left[\frac{(O_i - E_i)^2}{E_i} \right]$$

$$= \frac{(471 - 359.02)^2}{359.02} + \frac{(51 - 167.62)^2}{167.62} + \frac{(148 - 259.98)^2}{259.98} + \frac{(230 - 121.38)^2}{121.38}$$

$= 261.498.$

Also $\chi^2_{0.05}$ = Tabulated value of χ^2 at 5% level for 1 d.f. is 3.841.

Conclusion. Since the calculated value of χ^2 > tabulated value of χ^2, H_0 is rejected. They are dependent *i.e.,* the colour of son's eye is associated with that of the father.

Example 3. *The following table gives the number of good and bad parts produced by each of the three shifts in a factors :*

	Good parts	*Bad parts*	*Total*
Day shift	*960*	*40*	*1000*
Evening shift	*940*	*50*	*990*
Night shift	*950*	*45*	*995*
Total	*2850*	*135*	*2985*

Test whether or not the production of bad parts is independent of the shift on which they were produced.

Sol. Null hypothesis H_0. The production of bad parts is independent of the shift on which they were produced.

Degree of freedom = $(r - 1)(s - 1) = (2 - 1)(3 - 1) = 2$

i.e., the two attributes, production and shifts are independent.

Under H_0,
$$\chi^2 = \sum_{i=1}^{2} \sum_{j=1}^{3} \left[\frac{[(A_iB_j)_0 - (A_iB_j)]^2}{(A_iB_j)_0} \right]$$

Calculation of Expected frequencies

Let A and B be the two attributes namely production and shifts. A is divided into two classes A_1, A_2 and B is divided into three classes B_1, B_2, B_3.

$$(A_1B_1)_0 = \frac{(A_1)(B_1)}{N} = \frac{(2850) \times (1000)}{2985} = 954.77$$

$$(A_1B_2)_0 = \frac{(A_1)(B_2)}{N} = \frac{(2850) \times (990)}{2985} = 945.226$$

$$(A_1B_3)_0 = \frac{(A_1)(B_3)}{N} = \frac{(2850) \times (995)}{2985} = 950$$

$$(A_2B_1)_0 = \frac{(A_2)(B_1)}{N} = \frac{(135) \times (1000)}{2985} = 45.27$$

$$(A_2B_2)_0 = \frac{(A_2)(B_2)}{N} = \frac{(135) \times (990)}{2985} = 44.773$$

$$(A_2B_3)_0 = \frac{(A_2)(B_3)}{N} = \frac{(135) \times (995)}{2985} = 45.$$

To calculate the value of χ^2

Class	O_i	E_i	$(O_i - E_i)^2$	$(O_i - E_i)^2/E_i$
(A_1B_1)	960	954.77	27.3529	0.02864
(A_1B_2)	940	945.226	27.3110	0.02889
(A_1B_3)	950	950	0	0
(A_2B_1)	40	45.27	27.7729	0.61349
(A_2B_2)	50	44.773	27.3215	0.61022
(A_2B_3)	45	45	0	0
Total				1.28126

$$\therefore \quad \chi^2 = \sum_{i=1}^{6} \left[\frac{(O_i - E_i)^2}{E_i} \right] = 1.28126$$

Also $\chi^2_{0.05}$ = The tabulated value of χ^2 at 5% level of significance for 2 d.f. = 5.991 (see χ^2-table)

Conclusion. The tabulated value of χ^2 at 5% level of significance for 2 degrees of freedom is 5.991. Since the calculated value of χ^2 is less than the tabulated value, we accept H_0. *i.e.,* the production of bad parts is independent of the shift on which they were produced.

Example 4. *A cigarette company interested in the effect of sex on the type of cigarettes smoked and has collected the following data from a random sample of 150 persons.*

Cigarette size	*Number of people smoked*		*Total*
	male	*female*	
Small	*25*	*30*	*55*
Medium	*40*	*15*	*55*
King size	*30*	*10*	*40*
Total	*95*	*55*	*150*

Test whether the type of cigarette smoked and sex are independent at level of significance $\alpha = 5\%$ *:* (P.T.U., M.B.A. Dec. 2006)]

Sol. Let H_0 : The type of cigarette smoked and sex are independent

$\therefore$ Degree of freedom = $(r - 1)(s - 1) = (2 - 1)(3 - 1) = 2$

The given data can be shown in the form of 3×2 contingency table.

Observed Frequencies

	Male	*Female*	*Total*
Small	25	30	55
Medium	40	15	55
King size	30	10	40
Total	95	55	150

Expected Frequencies

$\frac{95 \times 55}{150} = 34.83$	$\frac{55 \times 55}{150} = 20.16$
$\frac{95 \times 55}{150} = 34.83$	$\frac{55 \times 55}{150} = 20.16$
$\frac{95 \times 40}{150} = 38$	$\frac{55 \times 40}{150} = 14.66$

To calculate χ^2, we have the following table :

O_i	25	30	40	15	30	10
E_i	34.83	20.16	34.83	20.16	38	14.66
$\frac{(O_i - E_i)^2}{E_i}$	2.774	4.80	0.76	1.32	1.684	1.481

$$\therefore \quad \chi^2 = \sum_{i=1}^{6} \left[\frac{(O_i - E_i)^2}{E_i} \right] = 2.774 + 4.80 + 0.76 + 1.32 + 1.684 + 1.481$$

$$= 12.819$$

Also $\chi^2_{0.05}$ = The tabulated value of χ^2 at 5% level of significance for 2 d.f. = 5.991

Conclusion. The calculated value of χ^2 is greater than the tabulated value of χ^2 at 5% level of significance. Hence H_0 is rejected. *i.e.*, the type of cigarette smoked and sex depends on each other.

Example 5. *From the following data, find whether hair colour and sex are associated.*

Sex \ *Colour*	*Fair*	*Red*	*Medium*	*Dark*	*Black*	*Total*
Boys	*592*	*849*	*504*	*119*	*36*	*2100*
Girls	*544*	*677*	*451*	*97*	*14*	*1783*
Total	*1136*	*1526*	*955*	*216*	*50*	*3883*

Sol. Null hypothesis H_0. The two attributes (hair colour and sex) are not associated. *i.e.,* they are independent.

Let A and B be the attributes. A is divided into 5 classes ($r = 5$). B is divided into 2 classes ($s = 2$).

$\therefore$ Degrees of freedom $= (r-1)(s-1) = (5-1)(2-1) = 4$

Under H_0, we calculate $\chi^2 = \sum_{i=1}^{5}\sum_{j=1}^{2} \frac{[(A_iB_j)_0 - (A_iB_j)]^2}{(A_iB_j)_0}$

To calculate the expected frequency $(A_i B_j)_0$ as follows :

$$(A_1B_1)_0 = \frac{(A_1)(B_1)}{N} = \frac{1136 \times 2100}{3883} = 614.37$$

$$(A_1B_2)_0 = \frac{(A_1)(B_2)}{N} = \frac{1136 \times 1783}{3883} = 521.629$$

$$(A_2B_1)_0 = \frac{(A_2)(B_1)}{N} = \frac{1526 \times 2100}{3883} = 852.289$$

$$(A_2B_2)_0 = \frac{(A_2)(B_2)}{N} = \frac{1526 \times 1783}{3883} = 700.71$$

$$(A_3B_1)_0 = \frac{(A_3)(B_1)}{N} = \frac{955 \times 2100}{3883} = 516.482$$

$$(A_3B_2)_0 = \frac{(A_3)(B_2)}{N} = \frac{955 \times 1783}{3883} = 483.517$$

$$(A_4B_1)_0 = \frac{(A_4)(B_1)}{N} = \frac{216 \times 2100}{3883} = 116.816$$

$$(A_4B_2)_0 = \frac{(A_4)(B_2)}{N} = \frac{216 \times 1783}{3883} = 99.183$$

$$(A_5B_1)_0 = \frac{(A_5)(B_1)}{N} = \frac{50 \times 2100}{3883} = 27.04$$

$$(A_5B_2)_0 = \frac{(A_5)(B_2)}{N} = \frac{50 \times 1783}{3883} = 22.959$$

Calculation of χ^2

Class	O_i	E_i	$(O_i - E_i)^2$	$\frac{(O_i - E_i)^2}{E_i}$
(A_1B_1)	592	614.37	500.416	0.8145
(A_1B_2)	544	521.629	500.462	0.959
(A_2B_1)	849	852.289	10.8175	0.0127
(A_2B_2)	677	700.71	562.1641	0.8023

(A_3B_1)	504	516.482	155.800	0.3016
(A_3B_2)	451	438.517	155.825	0.3553
(A_4B_1)	119	116.816	4.7698	0.0408
(A_4B_2)	97	99.183	4.7654	0.0480
(A_5B_1)	36	27.04	80.2816	2.9689
(A_5B_2)	14	22.959	80.2636	3.495
				9.7981

$$\therefore \quad \chi^2 = \sum_{i=1}^{10} \frac{(O_i - E_i)^2}{E_i} = 9.7981.$$

Conclusion. Tabulated value of χ^2 at 5% level of significance for 4 d.f. is 9.488. (see χ^2-table) Since the calculated value of χ^2 < tabulated value H_0 is rejected. *i.e.,* the two attributes are not independent. *i.e.,* the hair colour and sex are associated.

Example 6. *Can vaccination be regarded as preventive measure of small-pox as evidenced by the following data of 1482 persons exposed to small-pox in a locality. 368 in all were attacked of these 1482 persons and 343 were vaccinated and of these only 35 were attacked.*

Sol. For the given data, we from the contingency table. Let the two attributes be vaccination and exposed to small-pox. Each attributes is divided into two classes.

Vaccination A / *Disease small pox B*	*Vaccinated*	*Not*	*Total*
Attacked	35	333	368
Not	308	806	1114
Total	343	1139	1482

Null hypothesis H_0. The two attributes are independent *i.e.,* vaccination can't be regarded as preventive measure of small pox.

Degrees of freedom $\nu = (r - 1)(s - 1) = (2 - 1)(2 - 1) = 1$

Under H_0,
$$\chi^2 = \sum_{i=1}^{2} \sum_{j=1}^{2} \frac{[(A_iB_j)_0 - (A_iB_j)]^2}{(A_iB_j)_0}$$

Calculation of expected frequency

$$(A_1B_1)_0 = \frac{(A_1)(B_1)}{N} = \frac{343 \times 368}{1482} = 85.1713$$

$$(A_1B_2)_0 = \frac{(A_1)(B_2)}{N} = \frac{343 \times 1114}{1482} = 257.828$$

$$(A_2B_1)_0 = \frac{(A_2)(B_1)}{N} = \frac{1139 \times 368}{1482} = 282.828.$$

$$(A_2B_2)_0 = \frac{(A_2)(B_2)}{N} = \frac{1139 \times 1114}{1482} = 856.171$$

Calculation of χ^2

Class	O_i	E_i	$(O_i - E_i)^2$	$\frac{(O_i - E_i)^2}{E_i}$
(A_1B_1)	35	85.1713	2517.159	29.554
(A_1B_2)	308	257.828	2517.229	8.1728
(A_2B_1)	333	282.828	2517.2295	7.5592
(A_2B_2)	806	856.171	2517.1292	2.9399
Total				48.2259

Calculated value of $\chi^2 = \sum_{i=1}^{4} \frac{(O_i - E_i)^2}{E_i} = 48.2259.$

Conclusion. Tabulated value of χ^2 at 5% level of significance for 1 d.f. is 3.841. (see χ^2-table). Since the calculated value of $\chi^2 >$ tabulated value H_0 is rejected. *i.e.*, the two attributes are not independent. *i.e.*, the vaccination can be regarded as preventive measure of small pox.

Example 7. *Three sales persons account for the following amount of sales (in thousand of rupees) over a period of 4 months. Test for the significant difference in their performance at $\alpha = 5\%$ level of significance :*

Sales person	*Monthly sales in' 000 ₹*				*Total*
X	*48*	*49*	*50*	*49*	*196*
Y	*47*	*49*	*48*	*48*	*192*
Z	*49*	*51*	*50*	*50*	*200*
Total	*144*	*149*	*148*	*147*	*588*

(P.T.U., M.B.A. May 2006)

Sol. Null Hypothesis H_0. There is no significant difference between the sales

Degree of freedom = $(r - 1)(s - 1) = (4 - 1)(3 - 1) = 6$

Under H_0,
$$\chi^2 = \sum_{i=1}^{6} \sum_{j=1}^{3} \left[\frac{[(A_iB_j)_0 - (A_iB_j)]^2}{(A_iB_j)_0} \right].$$

Calculation of Expected Frequencies

Let A and B be the two attributes namely sales and persons. A is divided into Four classes ($r = 4$) A_1, A_2, A_3 and A_4 and B is divided into three classes B_1, B_2, B_3 ($r = 3$).

$$\therefore \qquad (A_1B_1)_0 = \frac{(A_1B_1)}{N} = \frac{144 \times 196}{588} = 48$$

$$(A_1B_2)_0 = \frac{(A_1)(B_2)}{N} = \frac{144 \times 192}{588} = 47.02$$

$$(A_1B_3)_0 = \frac{(A_1)(B_3)}{N} = \frac{144 \times 200}{588} = 48.97$$

$$(A_2B_1)_0 = \frac{(A_2)(B_1)}{N} = \frac{149 \times 196}{588} = 49.66$$

$$(A_2B_2)_0 = \frac{(A_2)(B_2)}{N} = \frac{149 \times 192}{588} = 48.65$$

$$(A_3B_3)_0 = \frac{(A_2)(B_3)}{N} = \frac{149 \times 200}{588} = 50.68$$

$$(A_3B_1)_0 = \frac{(A_2)(B_1)}{N} = \frac{148 \times 196}{588} = 49.33$$

$$(A_3B_2)_0 = \frac{(A_3)(B_2)}{N} = \frac{148 \times 192}{588} = 48.32$$

$$(A_3B_3)_0 = \frac{(A_3)(B_3)}{N} = \frac{148 \times 200}{588} = 50.34$$

$$(A_4B_1)_0 = \frac{(A_4)(B_1)}{N} = \frac{147 \times 196}{588} = 49$$

$$(A_4B_2)_0 = \frac{(A_4)(B_2)}{N} = \frac{147 \times 192}{588} = 48$$

$$(A_4B_3) = \frac{(A_4)(B_3)}{N} = \frac{147 \times 200}{588} = 50$$

To calculate the value of χ^2, consider the following table :

Class	O_i	E_i	$(O_i - E_i)^2$	$\frac{(O_i - E_i)^2}{E_i}$
A_1B_1	48	48	0	0
A_1B_2	47	47.02	0.0002	0.00004
A_1B_3	49	48.97	0.0009	0.0001
A_2B_1	49	49.66	0.4356	0.087
A_2B_2	49	48.65	0.1225	0.025
A_2B_3	51	50.68	0.1024	0.020
A_3B_1	50	49.33	0.4489	0.09
A_3B_2	48	48.32	0.1024	0.021
A_3B_3	50	50.34	0.1156	0.022
A_4B_1	49	49	0	0
A_4B_2	48	48	0	0
A_4B_3	50	50	0	0
				Total = 0.26514

$$\chi^2 = \sum_{i=1}^{12} \frac{(O_i - E_i)^2}{E_i} = 0.2651$$

Also $\chi^2_{0.05}$ = the tabulated value of χ^2 at 5% level of significance for 6 d.f.
= 12.592 (see χ^2-table)

Conclusion. The calculated value of χ^2 is less than the tabulated value of χ^2 at 5% level of significance for 6 d.f. $\therefore$ H_0 is accepted *i.e.*, there is no significant difference between the sales.

Example 8. *In an experiment on immunization of cattle from tuberculosis, the following results were obtained.*

	Affected	*Not affected*
Inoculated	*12*	*26*
Not inoculated	*16*	*6*

Calculate χ^2 *and discuss the effect of vaccine in controlling the disease* ($\chi^2_{0.05}$ *for 1 d.f. = 3.84)*

Sol. Null Hypothesis H_0 : There is no effect of vaccine in controlling the disease.

Degree of freedom = $(r - 1)(s - 1) = (2 - 1)(2 - 1) = 1$

Since one of the frequency (observed) 6, is less than 10, apply Yate's correction, adding 0.5 in 6 and adjusting others, so that the total remains same.

Take the contingency table for observed frequencies as under :

Observed Frequencies

	Affected	*Not-affected*	*Total*
Inoculated	12.5	25.5	38
Not inoculated	15.5	6.5	22
Total	28	32	60

↓

Expected Frequencies

$\frac{28 \times 38}{60} = 17.73$	$\frac{32 \times 38}{60} = 20.26$
$\frac{28 \times 22}{60} = 10.26$	$\frac{32 \times 22}{60} = 11.73$

To calculate χ^2, we have the following table.

O_i	12.5	25.5	15.5	6.5
E_i	17.73	20.26	10.3	11.73
$\frac{(O_i - E_i)^2}{E_i}$	1.542	1.355	1.355	2.331

$$\therefore \qquad \chi^2 = \sum_{i=1}^{4} \frac{(O_i - E_i)^2}{E_i} = 1.542 + 1.355 + 1.355 + 2.33 = 6.583$$

Also, $\chi^2_{0.05}$ = The tabulated value of χ^2 at 5% level of significance for 1 d.f. = 3.84. *i.e.*, the calculated value of χ^2 is greater than the tabulated value of χ^2 at 5% level of significance. Therefore H_0 is rejected. Hence the vaccine is effected in controlling the disease.

Example 9. *From the following data, use χ^2-test and conclude whether inoculation is effective in preventing tuberculosis.*

	Attached	*Not-attached*	*Total*
Inoculated	*31*	*469*	*500*
Not-incoculated	*185*	*1315*	*1500*
Total	*216*	*1784*	*2000*

(P.T.U., M.B.A. May 2004)

Sol. Null Hypothesis H_0. The inoculation is not effective in preventing tuberculosis

Degree of freedom = $(r - 1)(s - 1) = (2 - 1)(2 - 1) = 1$

The given data can be shown in the form of 2 × 2 contingency table.

Observed Frequencies

	Attached	*Not-attached*	*Total*
Inoculated	31	469	500
Not-inoculated	185	1315	1500
Total	216	1784	2000

Expected Frequencies

$\frac{216 \times 500}{2000} = 54$	$\frac{1784 \times 500}{2000} = 446$
$\frac{216 \times 1500}{2000} = 162$	$\frac{1784 \times 1500}{2000} = 1338$

To calculate χ^2, we have the following table :

O_i	31	185	469	1315
E_i	54	162	446	1338
$(O_i - E_i)^2$	529	529	529	529
$\frac{(O_i - E_i)^2}{E_i}$	9.79	3.26	1.186	0.395

$$\therefore \quad \chi^2 = \sum_{i=1}^{4} \frac{(O_i - E_i)^2}{E_i} = 9.79 + 3.26 + 1.186 + 0.395 = 14.631$$

Also $\chi^2_{0.05}$ = The tabulated value of χ^2 at 5% level of significance for 1 d.f. = 3.841.

Conclusion. The calculated value of χ^2 is greater than the tabulated value of χ^2 at 5% level of significance for 1 d.f. $\therefore$ H_0 is rejected *i.e.,* the inoculation is effective in preventing tuberculosis.

Example 10. *A certain drug was administered to 500 people out of a total of 800. Out of these, 480 had an attack of typhoid and among them 200 were administered the drug. Test if the drug is effective in preventing the attack of typhoid ($\chi^2_{0.05}$ for 1 d.f. = 3.841)*

Sol. Null Hypothesis H_0 : There is no effect of drug in preventing the attack of typhoid. The given data can be shown in the form of 2 × 2 contingency table.

Observed Frequencies

	Affected	*Not affected*	*Total*
Administered	200	300	500
Not administered	280	20	300
Total	480	320	800

↓

Expected Frequencies

$\frac{480 \times 500}{800} = 300$	$\frac{480 \times 300}{800} = 180$
$\frac{320 \times 500}{800} = 200$	$\frac{320 \times 300}{800} = 120$

To calculate χ^2, we have the following table

O_i	200	300	280	20
E_i	300	180	200	120
$\frac{(O_i - E_i)^2}{E_i}$	33.33	80	32	83.33

$$\therefore \quad \chi^2 = \sum_{i=1}^{4} \frac{(O_i - E_i)^2}{E_i} = 33.33 + 80 + 32 + 83.33 = 228.66$$

Also, $\chi^2_{0.05}$ = The tabulated value of χ^2 at 5% level of significance at 1 d.f. = 3.841. The calculated value of χ^2 is greater than the tabulated value at 5% level of significance. Hence H_0 is rejected, *i.e.,* the drug is effective in controlling the attack of typhoid.

Example 11. *In a locality, 100 persons were randomly selected and asked about their educational achievements. The results are given below.*

		Education		
		Middle	*High School*	*College*
Sex	*Male*	*10*	*15*	*25*
	Female	*25*	*10*	*15*

Based on this information, can you say that the education depends on sex. ($\chi^2_{0.05}$ *for 2 d.f. = 5.991)*

Sol. Null Hypothesis H_0 : The two attributes 'education' and 'sex' are not associated.

Let A and B be the attributes. A is divided into 3 classes ($s = 3$) and B is divided into 2 classes ($s = 2$).

Degree of freedom $\quad v = (r \;\; 1)\,(s-1) = (3-1)\,(2-1) = 2$

Under H_0, we calculate

$$\chi^2 = \sum_{i=1}^{3}\sum_{i=1}^{2} \frac{[(A_iB_j)_0 - (A_iB_j)]^2}{(A_iB_j)_0}$$

Observed Frequencies

	Middle	High school	College	Total
Male	10	15	25	50
Female	25	10	15	50
Total	35	25	40	100

To calculate the expected frequencies $(A_iB_j)_0$, we have

$$(A_1B_1)_0 = \frac{(A_1)\,(B_1)}{N} = \frac{35 \times 50}{100} = 17.5$$

$$(A_1B_2)_0 = \frac{(A_1)\,(B_2)}{N} = \frac{35 \times 50}{100} = 17.5$$

$$(A_2B_1)_0 = \frac{(A_2)\,(B_1)}{N} = \frac{25 \times 50}{100} = 12.5$$

$$(A_2B_2)_0 = \frac{(A_2)\,(B_2)}{N} = \frac{25 \times 50}{100} = 12.5$$

$$(A_3B_1)_0 = \frac{(A_3)\,(B_1)}{N} = \frac{40 \times 50}{100} = 20$$

$$(A_3B_2)_0 = \frac{(A_3)\,(B_2)}{N} = \frac{40 \times 50}{100} = 20$$

Calculation of χ^2

Class	O_i	E_i	$(O_i - E_i)^2$	$\frac{(O_i - E_i)^2}{E_i}$
A_1B_1	10	17.5	56.25	3.26
A_1B_2	25	17.5	56.25	3.26
A_2B_1	15	12.5	6.25	0.5
A_2B_2	10	12.5	6.25	0.5
A_3B_1	25	20	25	1.25
A_3B_2	15	20	25	1.25

$$\therefore \qquad \chi^2 = \sum_{i=1}^{6}\left[\frac{(O_i - E_i)^2}{E_i}\right] = 3.26 + 3.26 + 0.5 + 0.5 + 1.25 + 1.25 = 10.02$$

Also $\chi^2_{0.05}$ = The tabulated value of χ^2 at 5% level of significance for 2 d.f. = 5.991

Thus the calculated value of χ^2 is greater than the tabulated value of χ^2 of 5% level of significance. Hence H_0 is rejected *i.e.*, the education depends on sex.

Example 12. *A sample of 200 people with a particular disease was selected. Out of these, 100 were given a drug and others were not given any drug. The results are as given :*

	With drug	*Without drug*	*Total*
Cured	*65*	*55*	*120*
Not cured	*35*	*45*	*80*
Total	*100*	*100*	*200*

Test whether the drug is effective or not at α = 5% level of significance.

(P.T.U., M.B.A. May 2006)

Sol. Null Hypothesis H_0 : The drug is not effective. Degree of freedom

$$= (r - 1)(s - 1) = (2 - 1)(2 - 1) = 1$$

The given data can be shown in the form of 2 × 2 contingency table :

Observed Frequencies

	With drug	*Without drug*	*Total*
Cured	65	55	120
Not cured	35	45	80
Total	100	100	200

Expected Frequencies

$\frac{100 \times 120}{200} = 60$	$\frac{100 \times 120}{200} = 60$
$\frac{100 \times 80}{200} = 40$	$\frac{100 \times 80}{200} = 40$

To calculate χ^2, we have the following table :

O_i	65	35	55	45
E_i	60	40	60	40
$(O_i - E_i)^2$	25	25	25	25
$\frac{(O_i - E_i)^2}{E_i}$	0.4166	0.625	0.4166	0.625

$$\therefore \quad \chi^2 = \sum_{i=1}^{4} \left[\frac{(O_i - E_i)^2}{E_i} \right]$$

$$= 0.4166 + 0.625 + 0.4166 + 0.625 = 2.0832$$

Also $\chi^2_{0.05}$ = the tabulated value of χ^2 at 5% level of significance at 1 d.f.

$$= 3.841 \text{ (see } \chi^2\text{-table)}$$

Conclusion. The calculated value of $\chi^2 <$ the tabulated value of χ^2 at 5% level of significance for 1 d.f. $\therefore$ H_0 is accepted *i.e.,* the drug is not effective.

TEST YOUR KNOWLEDGE 10.10

1. In a locality 100 persons were randomly selected and asked about their educational achievements. The results are given below :

		Education		
		Middle	*High school*	*College*
Sex	Male	10	15	25
	Female	25	10	15

Based on this information can you say the education depends on sex.

2. The following data is collected on two characters :

	Smokers	*Non smokers*
Literate	83	57
Illiterate	45	68

Based on this information can you say that there is no relation between habit of smoking and literacy.

3. 500 students at school were graded according to their intelligences and economic conditions of their homes. Examine whether there is any association between economic condition and intelligence, from the following data :

Economic conditions	*Intelligence*	
	Good	*Bad*
Rich	85	75
Poor	165	175

4. In an experiment on the immunisation of goats from anthrox, the following results were obtained. Derive your inferences on the efficiency of the vaccine.

	Died anthrox	*Survived*
Inoculated with vaccine	2	10
Not inoculated	6	6

5. From the adult male population of seven large cities, random samples of married and unmarried men as given below were taken. Can it be said that there is a significant variation among the people of different cities in the tendency to marry ?

City	A	B	C	D	E	F	G	Total
Married	170	285	165	106	153	125	146	1150
Unmarried	40	125	35	37	55	35	33	360
Total	210	410	200	143	208	160	179	1510

6. From the following data, find out whether there is any relationship between sex and preference of colour.

	Sex	
Colour	*Males*	*Females*
Red	10	40
White	70	30
Green	30	20

7. A survey among women was conducted to study the family life. The observation were as follows :

	Family Life	
	Happy	*Not happy*
Educated	70	30
Non Educated	60	40

Test whether there is any association between family life and education.

8. The following table shows the result of inoculation against Cholera in a certain test.

(P.T.U. M.B.A. Dec. 2007)

	Not attacked	*Attacked*	*Total*
Inoculated	267	37	304
Non inoculated	757	155	912
Total	1024	192	1216

Test whether inoculation against Cholera is effective or not.

9. A sample of 300 students of under-graduate and 300 students of post-graduate classes of a university were asked to give their opinion towards the autonomous colleges. 190 of the under-graduate and 210 of the post graduate students favoured the autonomous status. Present the above fact in the form of a frequency table and test that opinions of under-graduate and post-graduate students on autonomous status of colleges are independent.

Answers

1. Yes 2. No 3. No 4. No. effective
5. There is a difference in the tendency of people to marry in different cities. ($\chi^2 = 21.381$)
6. There is a relationship between sex and preference of colour. ($\chi^2 = 34.35$)
7. There is no association between family life and education. ($\chi^2 = 2.198$)
8. Effective.
9. The opinions of the under-graduate and post graduate students on autonomous status of colleges is independent. ($\chi^2 = 30$)

10.34. Z-TEST

This test is used to test the significance of the correlation co-efficient in small samples. If r is the correlation co-efficient of the sample and ρ, that of the population, calculate the value of

$$\frac{Z-\xi}{\frac{1}{\sqrt{n-3}}}, \quad \text{where } Z = \frac{1}{2}\tanh^{-1} r = \frac{1}{2}\log_e\left(\frac{1+r}{1-r}\right) \quad \text{or} \quad 1.1513 \log_{10}\left(\frac{1+r}{1-r}\right)$$

$$\xi = \frac{1}{2}\tanh^{-1}\rho = \frac{1}{2}\log_e\left(\frac{1+\rho}{1-\rho}\right) \quad \text{or} \quad 1.1513 \log_{10}\left(\frac{1+\rho}{1-\rho}\right)$$

$$\frac{1}{\sqrt{n-3}} = \text{S.E.}$$

If the absolute value of $\frac{Z-\xi}{\text{S.E.}}$ exceeds 1.96, the difference is significant at 5% level.

ILLUSTRATIVE EXAMPLES

Example 1. *Test the significance of the correlation $r = 0.5$ from a sample of size 18 against hypothetical correlation $\rho = 0.7$.*

Sol. Null Hypothesis H_0 : Correlation in the population is 0.7.

$$Z = 1.1513 \log_e\left(\frac{1+r}{1-r}\right) = 1.1513 \log_{10}\left(\frac{1+0.5}{1-0.5}\right)$$

$$= 1.1513 \log_{10} 3 = 1.1513 \times 0.4771 = 0.549$$

$$\xi = 1.1513 \log_{10}\left(\frac{1+\rho}{1-\rho}\right) = 1.1513 \log_{10}\left(\frac{1+0.7}{1-0.7}\right)$$

$$= 1.1513 \log_{10} 5.67 = 1.1513 \times 0.7536 = 0.868$$

$$Z - \xi = 0.549 - 0.868 = -0.319$$

$$\text{S.E.} = \frac{1}{\sqrt{n-3}} = \frac{1}{\sqrt{18-3}} = \frac{1}{\sqrt{15}} = 0.26$$

Absolute value of $\frac{Z-\xi}{\text{S.E.}} = \frac{0.319}{0.26} = 1.23$ which is less than 1.96 (5% level of significance)

$\therefore$ H_0 is accepted. Hence the sample may be regarded as coming from population with $\rho = 0.7$.

Example 2. *From a sample of 19 pairs of observations, the correlation is 0.5 and the corresponding population value is 0.3. Is the difference significant ?*

Sol. H_0 : There is no significant difference between the two correlation *i.e.*, $r = p$

Here $n = 19$, $r = 0.5$, $\rho = 0.3$

$$Z = 1.1513 \log_{10}\left(\frac{1+r}{1-r}\right) = 1.1513 \log_{10}\left(\frac{1+0.5}{1-0.5}\right)$$

$$= 1.1513 \log_{10} 3 = 1.1513 \times 0.4771 = 0.55$$

$$\xi = 1.1513 \log_{10}\left(\frac{1+\rho}{1-\rho}\right) = 1.1513 \log_{10}\left(\frac{1+0.3}{1-0.3}\right)$$

$$= 1.1513 \log_{10} 1.857 = 1.1513 \times 0.2695 = 0.31$$

$$Z - \xi = 0.55 - 0.31 = 0.24 ; \quad \text{S.E.} = \frac{1}{\sqrt{n-3}} = \frac{1}{\sqrt{19-3}} = \frac{1}{4} = 0.25$$

$$\therefore \qquad \frac{Z-\xi}{\text{S.E.}} = \frac{0.24}{0.25} = 0.96$$

which is less than 1.96 (5% level of significance) and is, therefore not significant. Hence the sample may be regarded as coming from population with $\rho = 0.3$.

10.35. TO TEST THE SIGNIFICANT DIFFERENCE BETWEEN TWO INDEPENDENT CORRELATION CO-EFFICIENTS.

To test the significance of two correlation co-efficient derived from two separate samples, the test statistic is $z = \dfrac{z_1 - z_2}{\sqrt{\dfrac{1}{n_1-3} + \dfrac{1}{n_2-3}}}$

where $z_1 = 1.1513 \log_{10}\left(\dfrac{1+r_1}{1-r_1}\right)$, $z_2 = 1.1513 \log_{10}\left(\dfrac{1+r_2}{1-r_2}\right)$

If $|z| > 1.96$, the difference will be significant at 5% level.

Example 3. *The following data gives sample sizes and correlation co-efficients. Test the significant of the difference between two values using z-test.*

Sample size	*r*
5	0.870
12	0.560

Sol. Let H_0 : The sample are drawn from same population.

Under H_0, $$z = \frac{z_1 - z_2}{\sqrt{\dfrac{1}{n_1-3} + \dfrac{1}{n_2-3}}}$$

where $$z_1 = 1.1513 \log_{10}\left(\frac{1+0.87}{1-0.87}\right)$$

$$= 1.1513 \log_{10}\left(\frac{1.87}{0.13}\right) = 1.1513 \log_{10} 14.385$$

$$= 1.1513 \times 1.1579 = 1.333$$

$$z_2 = 1.1513 \log_{10}\left(\frac{1+0.560}{1-0.560}\right) = 1.1513 \log_{10}\left(\frac{1.560}{0.44}\right)$$

$$= 1.1513 \log_{10} 3.545 = 1.1513 \times 0.5496 = 0.633$$

Also $n_1 = 5, n_2 = 12$

$$\therefore \quad z = \frac{1.333 - 0.633}{\sqrt{\frac{1}{2}+\frac{1}{9}}} = \frac{0.7}{0.782} = 0.895$$

$$\Rightarrow \quad |z| = 0.895 < 1.96$$

$\therefore$ **The difference is not significant *i.e*, the samples are not drawn from same population.**

TEST YOUR KNOWLEDGE 10.11

1. A correlation co-efficient of 0.72 is obtained from a sample of 29 pairs of observations. Can the sample be regarded as drawn from a bivariate normal population in which true correlation co-efficient is 0.8 ?

Answer

1. Yes.

11

F-Test and Analysis of Variance

ANOVA

11.1. ANALYSIS OF VARIANCE

We have studied *t*-test which is used to test the significance of the difference between two sample means. But, if the number of means is more than two, then *t*-test is not applicable. Hence, if we have a large number of means and we have to test the hypothesis that

(1) Means are homogeneous or not

(2) Means differ significantly or not

(3) Independency of errors

The techniques known as "Analysis of Variance" developed by 'Fisher' is useful.

11.2. TECHNIQUES OF ANOVA (ANALYSIS OF VARIANCE)

There are two types of techniques for the analysis of variance :

(1) One way classification

(2) Two way classification.

We now discuss the above classification in details.

11.3. ONE WAY CLASSIFICATION

Consider a set of N values of the variable x arranged into h rows and k columns so that $N = hk$. Assume the null hypothesis.

$H_0 : \mu_1 = \mu_2 = \mu_3 = \mu_4$ etc., *i.e.*, there is no significant difference between the sample means

$H_1 : \mu_1 \neq \mu_2 \neq \mu_3 \neq \mu_4$ etc., *i.e.*, there is a significant difference between the sample means.

For analysis of variance, we compute the following :

(*a*) **Calculation of Variance Between the Samples.** Let X_1, X_2, X_3, X_4, etc., are the samples, then

(*i*) Find the sum of squares between the samples, which can be calculated as under

Sum of squares between the samples

$$= \frac{(\Sigma X_1)^2}{N} + \frac{(\Sigma X_2)^2}{N} + \frac{(\Sigma X_3)^2}{N} + \frac{(\Sigma X_4)^2}{N} - \frac{T^2}{N}$$

where $\frac{T^2}{N}$ = Correction factor $= \frac{(\Sigma X_1 + \Sigma X_2 + \Sigma X_3 + \Sigma X_4)^2}{N}$

(*ii*) Find the degree of freedom between the samples which is given by

$$v_1 = h - 1$$

(*b*) **Calculation of Variance Within the Samples**

Let X_1, X_2, X_3, X_4, etc., are the samples. Then

(*i*) Find the total sum of squares which can be calculated as under.

Total sum of squares

$$= \Sigma X_1^2 + \Sigma X_2^2 + \Sigma X_3^2 + \Sigma X_4^2 - \frac{T^2}{N}$$

(*ii*) Find the sum of squares with in the samples which can be calculated as under.

Sum of squares with in the samples

= Total sum of squares – Sum of squares between the samples

(*iii*) Find the degree of freedom within the samples, which is given by

$$v_2 = N - h$$

(*c*) **Calculation of Mean Squares Between the Samples**

Find the mean squares between the samples and within the samples, which can be calculated as

$$\text{Mean squares} = \frac{\text{Sum of squares}}{\text{Degree of freedom}}$$

(*d*) **Value of F**

Calculate the value of F,

$$F = \frac{\text{Mean squares between the samples}}{\text{Mean squares within the sample}}, \text{ where}$$

(Numerator > denominator), Otherwise

$$F = \frac{\text{Mean squares within the samples}}{\text{Mean squares between the samples}}$$

Conclusion. If the calculated value of $|F|$ at 5% level of significance is less than the tabulated value of F for $(v_1 - 1, v_2 - 1)$ *d.f.* then the null hypothesis H_0 is accepted.

If the calculated value of $|F|$ at 5% level of significance is more than the tabulated value of F for $(v_1 - 1, v_2 - 1)$ *d.f.* then the null hypothesis is rejected, *i.e.*, H_1 is accepted.

Remark. The above results can be memorised with the help of the following 'ANOVA' table.

ANOVA Table

Source of variation	*Degree of freedom*	*Sum of squares*	*Mean squares*
	d.f.	*s.s.*	*s.s./d.f.*
Between samples	$v_1 = h - 1$	—	—
within samples	$v_2 = N - h$	—	—

ILLUSTRATIVE EXAMPLES

Example 1. *Four varieties of wheat are grown in 5 plots each and following yields, (in maunds, per acre) obtained.*

Plots/Varieties	*1*	*2*	*3*	*4*
I	*8*	*12*	*18*	*13*
II	*10*	*11*	*12*	*9*
III	*12*	*9*	*16*	*12*
IV	*8*	*14*	*6*	*16*
V	*7*	*4*	*8*	*15*

Test the significance of the difference between variety yields.

Sol. Consider the following table

Sample	*1*		*2*		*3*		*4*	
	X_1	X_1^2	X_2	X_2^2	X_3	X_3^2	X_4	X_4^2
I	8	64	12	144	18	324	13	169
II	10	100	11	121	12	144	9	81
III	12	144	9	81	16	256	12	144
IV	8	64	14	196	6	36	16	256
V	7	49	4	16	8	64	15	225
Total	$\Sigma X_1 = 45$	$\Sigma X_1^2 = 421$	$\Sigma X_2 = 50$	$\Sigma X_2^2 = 558$	$\Sigma X_3 = 60$	$\Sigma X_3^2 = 824$	$\Sigma X_4 = 65$	$\Sigma X_4^2 = 875$

Let H_0 : There is no significant difference between the varieties.

H_1 : There is a significant difference between the varieties.

Here, $h = 5, k = 4, N = hk = 20$

Under H_0,

$$\text{Correction factor} = \frac{T^2}{N} = \frac{(\Sigma X_1 + \Sigma X_2 + \Sigma X_3 + \Sigma X_4)^2}{N}$$

$$= \frac{(45 + 50 + 60 + 65)^2}{20} = \frac{(220)^2}{20} = \frac{48400}{20} = 2420$$

$\therefore$ Sum of squares between the samples

$$= \frac{(\Sigma X_1)^2}{N} + \frac{(\Sigma X_2)^2}{N} + \frac{(\Sigma X_3)^2}{N} + \frac{(\Sigma X_4)^2}{N} - \frac{T^2}{N}$$

$$= \frac{45^2}{20} + \frac{50^2}{20} + \frac{60^2}{20} + \frac{65^2}{20} - 2420$$

$$= \frac{2025 + 2500 + 3600 + 4225}{20} - 2420$$

$$= \frac{12350}{20} - 2420 = 617.5 - 2420 = -1802.5$$

Further,

$$\text{Total sum of squares} = \Sigma X_1^2 + \Sigma X_2^2 + \Sigma X_3^2 + \Sigma X_4^4 - \frac{T^2}{N}$$

$= 421 + 558 + 824 + 875 - 2420 = 2678 - 2420 = 258$

Hence sum of squares within the samples

$= \text{Total sum of squares} - \text{Sum of squares between the samples}$

$= 258 - (-1802.5) = 2060.5.$

Tabulating all the above values in ANOVA table, we get the following table.

ANOVA TABLE

Source of variation	*Degree of freedom d.f.*	*Sum of squares s.s*	*Mean squares s.s/d.f.*
Between samples	$v_1 = h - 1 = 4$	–1802.5	–450.625
Within samples	$v_2 = N - h = 15$	2060.5	137.36

One way classification

The value of $|F| = \left|\frac{-450.625}{137.36}\right| = 3.28$

Also $F_{0.05}$ = The tabulated value of F for $(v_1, v_2) = (4, 15)$ *d.f* at 5% level of significance

$= 3.06$ | The intersection of $v_1 = 4$ and $v_2 = 15$ (see F-table)

Hence, the calculated value of |F| is greater than the tabulated value of F at (4, 15) d.f. at 5% level of significance. Hence H_0 is rejected. *i.e.,* we conclude that the difference between the varities is significant.

Example 2. *Three different machines are used for a production. On the basis of output, test whether the machines are equally effective.*

Outputs

Machine I	*Machine II*	*MachineIII*
10	9	20
5	7	16
11	5	10
10	6	14

Sol. Consider the table :

Machines	*I*		*II*		*III*	
Output	X_1	X_1^2	X_2	X_2^2	X_3	X_3^2
	10	100	9	81	20	400
	5	25	7	49	16	256
	11	121	5	25	10	100
	10	100	6	36	14	196
Total	$\Sigma X_1 = 36$	$\Sigma X_1^2 = 346$	$\Sigma X_2 = 27$	$\Sigma X_2^2 = 191$	$\Sigma X_3 = 60$	$\Sigma X_3^2 = 952$

Let H_0 : There is no significant difference between the machines outputs

H_1 : There is a significant difference between the machines output

Here $h = 4$, $k = 3$, $N = hk = 12$

Under H_0, Correction factor

$$\frac{T^2}{N} = \frac{(\Sigma X_1 + \Sigma X_2 + \Sigma X_3)^2}{N} = \frac{(36+27+60)^2}{12}$$

$$= \frac{(123)^2}{12} \approx 1260.75 \cong 1260$$

Sum of squares between the samples

$$= \frac{(\Sigma X_1)^2}{N} + \frac{(\Sigma X_2)^2}{N} + \frac{(\Sigma X_3)^2}{N} - \frac{T^2}{N}$$

$$= \frac{1296}{12} + \frac{729}{12} + \frac{3600}{12} - 1260$$

$$= 108 + 60.75 + 300 - 1260 = -791.25$$

$$\text{Total sum of squares} = \Sigma X_1^2 + \Sigma X_2^2 + \Sigma X_3^2 - \frac{T^2}{N}$$

$$= 346 + 191 + 952 - 1260 = 229$$

Therefore, sum of squares within the samples

= Total sum of squares – Sum of squares within the samples

= 229 – (– 791.25) = 1020.25

Tabulating the above values in ANOVA Table, we get

ANOVA TABLE

Source of variation	*Degree of freedom (d.f)*	*Sum of squares (s.s)*	*Mean squares (s.s/d.f.)*
Between samples	$v_1 = h - 1 = 3$	– 791.25	– 263.75
within samples	$v_2 = N - h = 8$	1020.25	127.53

One way classification

The value of $$F = \frac{-263.75}{127.53} = -2.068$$

$\Rightarrow$ $|F| = 2.068$

Also $F_{0.05}$ = The tabulated value of F for $(v_1, v_2) = (3,8)$ *d.f* at 5 % level of significance

= 6.04 (intersection of 3 and 8 (see F-Table)

Hence the calculated value of $|F|$ is less than the tabulated value of F at (3,8) *d.f* at 5% level of significance.

$\therefore$ H_0 is accepted *i.e.* we conclude that machines are equally effective.

Example 3. *The following table represents the yield of wheat in bushels per acre for trial plots of land treated with four different levels of fertilizer. Each level was applied to 5 plots randomly choosen over a field :*

Treatment

Plot No.	*1*	*2*	*3*	*4*
1	*21*	*24*	*34*	*40*
2	*25*	*33*	*26*	*47*
3	*31*	*34*	*38*	*39*
4	*17*	*39*	*32*	*41*
5	*26*	*35*	*35*	*33*

Carry out an analysis of variance and state your conclusion

Sol. Consider the table :

Plots	*1*		*2*		*3*		*4*	
	X_1	X_1^2	X_2	X_2^2	X_3	X_3^2	X_4	X_4^2
1	21	441	24	576	34	1156	40	1600
2	25	625	33	1089	26	676	47	2209
3	31	961	34	1156	38	1444	39	1521
4	17	289	39	1521	32	1024	41	1681
5	26	676	35	1225	35	1225	33	1089
	$\Sigma X_1 = 120$	$\Sigma X_1^2 = 2992$	$\Sigma X_2 = 165$	$\Sigma X_2^2 = 5567$	$\Sigma X_3 = 165$	$\Sigma X_3^2 = 5525$	$\Sigma X_4 = 200$	$\Sigma X_4^2 = 8100$

Let H_0 : There is no significant difference between varieties.

H_1 : There is a significant difference between the varieties.

Here, $h = 5,\ k = 4,\ N = hk = 20$

Under H_0, correction factor $= \dfrac{T^2}{N}$

$$= \frac{(\Sigma X_1 + \Sigma X_2 + \Sigma X_3 + \Sigma X_4)^2}{N}$$

$$= \frac{(120 + 165 + 165 + 200)^2}{20} = 21125$$

Sum of squares between the samples

$$= \frac{(\Sigma X_1)^2}{N} + \frac{(\Sigma X_2)^2}{N} + \frac{(\Sigma X_3)^2}{N} + \frac{(\Sigma X_4)^2}{N} - \frac{T^2}{N}$$

$$= \frac{14400}{20} + \frac{27225}{20} + \frac{27225}{20} + \frac{40000}{20} - 21125$$

$$= 720 + 1361.25 + 1361.25 + 2000 - 21125$$

$$= 5442.5 - 21125 = -15682.5$$

Total sum of squares

$$= \Sigma X_1^2 + \Sigma X^2_2 + \Sigma X^2_3 + \Sigma X^2_4 - \frac{T^2}{N}$$

$$= 2992 + 5567 + 5525 + 8100 - 21125 = 1059$$

Hence sum of squares within the sample = Total sum of squares – Sum of squares between the sample

$$= 1059 - (-15682.5) = 16741.5$$

Tabulating the above data in the following Anova Table.

ANOVA TABLE

Source of variation	*Degree of freedom (d.f)*	*Sum of squares (s.s)*	*Mean squares (s.s/d.f.)*
Between samples	$v_1 = h - 1 = 4$	– 15682.5	– 3920.625
Within samples	$v_2 = N - h = 15$	16741.5	1116.1

One way classification

The Value of $F = \frac{-3920.625}{1116.1} = -3.5127$

$\Rightarrow$ $|F| = 3.5127$

Also $F_{0.05}$ = The tabulated value of F for (4, 15) *d.f.* at 5% level of significance

= 3.06 | The intersection of 4 and 15 (see F table)

Thus the calculated value of |F| is greater than the tabulated value of F at (4, 15) *d.f.* at 5% level of significance. Hence H_0 is rejected. *i.e.,* we conclude that the difference between the varities is significant.

Example 4. *Three fertilizers A, B and C are given to different number of plots of uniform area and their yield in kilograms are as given below. Test whether the average yields of different fertilizers is same at α = 5% level of significance.*

Fertilizers	*Yields*				
A	*7*	*11*	*9*	—	—
B	*4*	*6*	*8*	*5*	*2*
C	*10*	*8*	*6*	*8*	

(P.T.U., M.B.A. Dec. 2006)

Sol. Consider the following table

Fertilizers	*Yields*									
	I		*II*		*III*		*IV*		*V*	
	X_1	X_1^2	X_2	X_2^2	X_3	X_3^2	X_4	X_4^2	X_5	X_5^2
A	7	49	11	121	9	81	—	—	—	—
B	4	16	6	36	8	64	5	25	2	4
C	10	100	8	64	6	36	8	64		
Total	$\Sigma X_1 = 21$	$\Sigma X_1^2 = 165$	$\Sigma X_2 = 25$	$\Sigma X_2^2 = 221$	$\Sigma X_3 = 23$	$\Sigma X_3^2 = 181$	$\Sigma X_4 = 13$	$\Sigma X_4^2 = 89$	$\Sigma X_5 = 2$	$\Sigma X_5^2 = 4$

Let H_0 : The average yields of different fertilizers is same.

H_1 : The average yields of different fertilizers is not same.

Given h = Number of rows = 3 ; k = Number of columns = 5

$N = hk = 15$

Under H_0, Correction factor

$$= \frac{T^2}{N} = \frac{(\Sigma X_1 + \Sigma X_2 + \Sigma X_3 + \Sigma X_4 + \Sigma X_5)^2}{N}$$

$$= \frac{(21 + 25 + 23 + 13 + 2)^2}{15} = \frac{84^2}{15} = \frac{7056}{15} = 470.4$$

∴ Sum of squares between the samples

$$= \frac{(\Sigma X_1)^2}{N} + \frac{(\Sigma X_2)^2}{N} + \frac{(\Sigma X_3)^2}{N} + \frac{(\Sigma X_4)^2}{N} + \frac{(\Sigma X_5)^2}{N} - \frac{T^2}{N}$$

$$= \frac{21^2}{15} + \frac{25^2}{15} + \frac{23^2}{15} + \frac{13^2}{15} + \frac{2^2}{15} - 470.4$$

$$= 29.4 + 41.6 + 35.2 + 11.26 + 0.26 - 470.4$$

$$= 117.72 - 470.4 = -352.54$$

Further, total sum of squares

$$= \Sigma X_1^{\,2} + \Sigma X_2^{\,2} + \Sigma X_3^{\,2} + \Sigma X_4^{\,2} + \Sigma X_5^{\,2} - \frac{T^2}{N}$$

$$= 165 + 221 + 181 + 89 + 4 - 470.4 = 660 - 470.4 = 189.6$$

Hence sum of squares within the samples

= Total sum of squares – Sum of square between the samples

$= 189.6 - (-352.54)$

$= 542.14$

Tabulating all the above values in ANOVA table, we get the following table :

ANOVA TABLE

Source of variation	*Degree of freedom d.f.*	*Sum of squares s.s.*	*Mean squares s.s./d.f.*
Between samples	$v_1 = h - 1 = 2$	– 352.54	– 176.27
Within samples	$v_2 = N - h = 12$	542.14	45.17

One way classification

The value of $F = \dfrac{176.27}{45.17} = -3.902$

⇒ $|F| = 3.902$

Also $F_{0.05}$ = The tabulated value of F at 5% level of significance for (v_1, v_2)

= (2, 12) d.f. at 5% level of significance

= 19.4 (the intersection of $v_1 = 2$ and $v_2 = 12$ (see F-Table)

Since the calculated value of | F | is less than the tabulated value of F at 5% level of significance for (2, 15) d.f. Hence H_0 is accepted *i.e.,* the average yields of different fertilizers is same at $\alpha = 5\%$. level of significance.

11.4. TWO-WAY CLASSIFICATION

In two way classification of Analysis of Variance, we adopt the following procedure :

Consider a set of N values of the variables arranged into h rows and k columns so that $N = hk$.

Assume the null hypothesis

$H_0 : u_1 = u_2 = u_3 = u_4$ etc., *i.e.,* there is no significant difference between the sample means.

$H_1 : u_1 \neq u_2 \neq u_3 \neq u_4$ etc., *i.e.,* there is a significant difference between the sample means

For the analysis of variance, compute the following :

(*a*) **Calculation of Variance between Rows.** For this, find the sum of squares between rows, which is given by

Sum of squares between rows

$$= \frac{1}{k} \Sigma T_i^2 - \frac{T^2}{N}, \text{ where } \Sigma T_i = \text{rows total and } \frac{T^2}{N} = \text{correction factor}$$

Also degree of freedom $= k - 1$

(*b*) **Calculation of Variance between Columns.** For this, find the sum of squares between columns which is given by

Sum of squares between columns

$$= \frac{1}{h} \Sigma T_j^2 - \frac{T^2}{N}, \text{ where } \Sigma T_j = \text{column total}$$

Also degree of freedom $= k - 1$

(*c*) **Find the Error Sum of Squares,** which is given by

error sum of squares = total sum of squares – (Sum of squares between rows) – (Sum of squares between columns)

where total Sum of squares $= \Sigma X_1^2 + \Sigma X_2^2 + \Sigma X_3^2 + \Sigma X_4^2 - \dfrac{T^2}{N}$

Also degree of freedom $= (h - 1)(k - 1)$

(*d*) **Find the Value of F (F_1 or F_2)** which can be calculated as

$$F_1 = \frac{\text{Mean squares values between rows}}{\text{Error sum of squares}}$$

Otherwise $$F_2 = \frac{\text{Mean squares values between columns}}{\text{Error sum of squares}}$$

The above results can be summarized in the anova table given below :

ANOVA TABLE

Source of variation	*Degree of freedom (d.f.)*	*Sum of squares (s.s)*	*Mean square s.s/d.f.*	*F*
Between rows	$v_1 = h - 1$	—	—	F_1
Between columns	$v_2 = k - 1$	—	—	F_2
Error	$v = (h - 1)(k - 1)$	—	—	—

Two Way Classification

Conclusion. If calculated value of $|F_1|$ is less than the tabulated value of F_1 for (v_1, v) d.f., at 5% level of significance, then H_0 is accepted, otherwise rejected. If calculated value of $|F_2|$ is less than the tabulated value of F_2 for (v_2, v) d.f. at 5% level of significant, then H_0 is accepted, otherwise rejected.

Example 5. *Yields of 4 varieties of wheat in 3 blocks are given below :*

Varieties	*Blocks*		
I	*10*	*9*	*8*
II	*7*	*7*	*6*
III	*8*	*5*	*4*
IV	*5*	*4*	*4*

Is the difference between varieties significant ?

Is the difference between blocks significant ?

Sol. For varieties. Assume the null hypothesis as

H_0 : There is no significant difference between the varieties.

H_1 : There is a significant difference between the varities

For blocks. Assume the null hypothesis,

H_0 : There is no significant difference between the blocks.

H_1 : There is a significant difference between the blocks

Given h = Number of rows = 4

k = Number of columns = 3

$N = hk = 12$

Also for simplification, we subtract 5 from each element, the given data become

Varieties	*Blocks*			*Rows total*
	X_1	X_2	X_3	
I	5	4	3	12
II	2	2	1	5
III	3	0	–1	2
IV	0	– 1	– 1	– 2
Column total	10	5	2	Total = 17

(*a*) **Calculation of Variance between Rows**

Here, Correction factor $= \frac{T^2}{N} = \frac{17^2}{12} = \frac{289}{12} = 24.1$

$\therefore$ Sum of squares between rows

$$= \frac{1}{k} \Sigma T_i^2 - \frac{T^2}{N} = \frac{1}{3} [12^2 + 5^2 + 2^2 + (-2)^2] - 24.1$$

$$= \frac{177}{3} - 24.1 = 59 - 24.1 = 34.9$$

Also degree of freedom $v_1 = h - 1 = 4 - 1 = 3$

(*b*) **Calculation of variance between columns**

Here, Sum of squares between columns

$$= \frac{1}{h} \Sigma T_j^2 - \frac{T^2}{N} = \frac{1}{4} (10^2 + 5^2 + 2^2) - 24.1$$

$$= \frac{129}{4} - 24.1 = 32.5 - 24.1 = 8.15$$

Also degree of freedom $v_2 = k - 1 = 3 - 1 = 2$

(*c*) **Calculation of error sum of squares**

Here, Total sum of squares

$$= \Sigma X_1^2 + \Sigma X_2^2 + \Sigma X_3^2 - \frac{T^2}{N}$$

$= 38 + 21 + 12 - 24.1$

$= 71 - 24.1 = 46.9$

	X_1^2	X_2^2	X_3^2
	25	16	9
	4	4	1
	9	0	1
	0	1	1
Total	38	21	12

$\therefore$ Error sum of squares

= Total sum of squares – (Sum of squares between rows) – (Sum of squares between columns)

$= 46.9 - 34.9 - 8.15 = 3.85.$

Also degree of freedom $v = (h - 1)(k - 1) = 3 \times 2 = 6$

Tabulating all the above, we get the following 'ANOVA TABLE'.

ANOVA TABLE

Source of variation	*Degree of freedom (d.f.)*	*Sum of squares (s.s.)*	*Mean squares s.s./d.f.*
Varieties (between rows)	$v_1 = h - 1 = 3$	34.9	11.63
Blocks (between columns)	$v_2 = k - 1 = 2$	8.15	4.07
Error	$v = (h - 1)(k - 1) = 6$	3.85	0.64

Conclusion. From the table,

$$F_1 = \frac{\text{Mean squares between rows}}{\text{Error sum of squares}} = \frac{11.63}{0.64} = 18.17$$

$$F_2 = \frac{\text{Mean squares between columns}}{\text{Error sum of squares}} = \frac{4.07}{0.64} = 6.4$$

Also F_1 (tabulated) at 5% level of significance for (3, 6) d.f. = 4.76 (see F-table), *i.e.*, calculated value of $|F_1|$ is greater than the tabulated value of F_1 for (3, 6) d.f. at 5% level of significant.

Therefore H_0 is rejected, *i.e.*, the difference between varieties is highly significant.

Also $|F_2|$ (calculated) = 6.4 and F_2 (tabulated) at 5% level of significance for (2, 6) d.f. = 5.14(see F-table), *i.e.*, calculated value of F_2 is more than the tabulated value of F_2 for (2, 6) d.f. at 5% level of significant.

Therefore H_0 is rejected, *i.e.*, the difference between blocks is significant.

Example 6. *In a feeding experiment on swins, three rations R_1, R_2, R_3 were tried. The animals put into three classes of three each according to littre in lbs, in certain period.*

	Class I	*Class II*	*Class III*	*Total*
R_1	4	16	10	30
R_2	14	18	19	51
R_3	3	14	7	24
Total	21	48	36	105

Analyse the data and state your conclusion. Has division into classes proved effective ? (5% value of F for (2, 4) d.f. = 6.94).

Sol. For rations : ∴ Assume the null hypothesis as

$\mathbf{H_0}$ **:** There is no significant difference between rations

$\mathbf{H_1}$ **:** There is a significant difference rations

For classes : Assume null hypothesis as

$\mathbf{H_0}$ **:** The division into classes is not effective

$\mathbf{H_1}$ **:** The division into classes is effective.

For Analysis of Variance as Two Way Classification, we proceed as follows

Given h = Number of rows = 3

k = Number of columns = 3

$N = hk = 9$

(*a*) **Calculation of Variance between Rows**

$$\text{Correction factor} = \frac{T^2}{N} = \frac{105^2}{9} = 1225$$

∴ Sum of squares between rows

$$= \frac{1}{k}\Sigma T_i^2 - \frac{T^2}{N} = \frac{1}{3}(30^2 + 51^2 + 24^2) - 1225$$

$$= \frac{900 + 2601 + 576}{3} - 1225 = \frac{4077}{3} - 1225 = 1359 - 1225 = 134$$

Also degree of freedom $v_1 = h - 1 = 3 - 1 = 2$

(b) Calculation of Variance between Columns

Sum of squares between columns

$$= \frac{1}{h} \Sigma T_j^2 - \frac{T^2}{N} = \frac{1}{3}(21^2 + 48^2 + 36^2) - 1225$$

$$= \frac{441 + 2304 + 1296}{3} - 1225 = \frac{4041}{3} - 1225 = 1347 - 1225 = 122$$

Also degree of freedom $v_2 = k - 1 = 3 - 1 = 2$

(c) Calculation of Error Sum of Squares

	X_1^2	X_2^2	X_3^2
	16	256	100
	196	324	361
	9	196	49
Total	221	776	510

Here, Total sum of squares $= \Sigma X_1^2 + \Sigma X_2^2 + \Sigma X_3^2 - \frac{T^2}{N}$

$= 221 + 776 + 510 - 1225$

$= 282$

$\therefore$ Error sum of squares

= Total sum of squares – (Sum of squares between rows) – (Sum of squares between columns)

$= 282 - 134 - 122 = 26$

Also, degree of freedom

$v = (h - 1)(k - 1) = 4$

Tabulating all the above values, we get the following 'ANOVA TABLE'

ANOVA TABLE

Source of variation	*Degree of freedom (d.f.)*	*Sum of squares (s.s.)*	*Mean squares (s.s./d.f.)*
Between rations (rows)	$v_1 = h - 1 = 2$	134	67
Between classes (columns)	$v_2 = k - 1 = 2$	122	61
Error	$v = (h - 1)(k - 1) = 4$	26	6.5

Conclusion. From the table,

$$F_1 = \frac{\text{Mean squares between rations}}{\text{Error sum of squares}} = \frac{67}{6.5} = 10.30$$

$$F_2 = \frac{\text{Mean squares between classes}}{\text{Error sum of squares}} = \frac{61}{6.5} = 9.38$$

Here, F_1 (calculated) $= 10.30$

Also F_1 (tabulated) for $(v_1, v_2) = (2, 4)$ d.f. at 5% level of significance = 6.94 (see F-table) *i.e.*, the calculated value of $|F_1|$ is more than the tabulated value of F_1 at 5% level of significance for (2, 4) d.f.

H_0 is rejected and we conclude that the difference between the ratios is significant.

Also F_2 (calculated) = 9.38

F_2 (tabulated) at 5% level of significance for $(v_1, v_2) = 6.94$ (see F-table)

The calculated value of $|F_2|$ is greater than the tabulated value of F_2 at 5% level of significance. H_0 is rejected and hence we conclude that the divison into classes is effective

11.5. CASE STUDIES

Case study I : FMCG Company

A FMCG company wished to study the effects of four training programmes on the sales abilities of their sales personnel. Thirty-two people were randomly divided into four groups of equal size, and the groups were then subjected to the different sales training programmes. Because there were some dropouts during the training programmes due to illness, vacations, and so on, the number of trainees completing the programmes varied from group to group. At the end of the training programmes, each salesperson was randomly assigned a sales area from a group of sales areas that were judge to have equivalent sales potentials. The sales made by each of the four groups of salespeople during the first week after completing the training programme are listed in the table:

Training Programme

1	2	3	4
78	99	74	81
84	86	87	63
86	90	80	71
92	93	83	65
69	94	78	86
73	85	73	79
97	70	—	—
91	—	—	—
482	735	402	588

Questions for Discussion

1. Analyse the experiment using the appropriate method.
2. Identify the treatments or factors of interest to the researcher and investigate any significant effects.
3. What are the practical implications of this experiment?
4. Write a paragraph explaining the results of your analysis.

Sol. (1) **Analysing the given Experiment**

The given problem is about the effectiveness of four training programmes in terms of sales. The factor of interest means an independent variable that is controlled by the researcher. Here, the factor of interest is the training programme conducted by the FMCG company. The dependent (or response) variable of interest is the sales ability of the company's *sales personal.* The problem under study "whether the training programmes on the sales abilities of their *sales personals* have been effective or not" can be solved by applying techniques of ANOVA (analysis of variance)

(2) As stated above, the FMCG company plans to conduct a training programme in which "effectiveness" is the independent variable called factor of interest. The dependent variable is the "sales". Assume

Null Hypothesis H_0 : The training programmes have not been effective in promoting sales

Alternative Hypothesis : The training programme have been effective in promoting sales

We apply one way classification of ANOVA as there is only one factor of interest.

Here $h = 4$ (four training programmes)

$k = 4$(four groups of sales personal)

$N = hk = 16$

Consider the following table:

	Group 1		Group 2		Group 3		Group 4	
	X_1	X_1^2	X_2	X_2^2	X_3	X_3^2	X_4	X_4^2
	78	6084	99	9801	74	5476	81	6561
	84	7056	86	7396	87	7569	63	3969
	86	7396	90	8100	80	6400	71	5041
	92	8464	93	8649	83	6889	65	4225
	69	4761	94	8836	78	6084	86	7396
	73	5329	85	7225	73	5329	79	6241
	97	9409	70	4900	—	—	—	—
	91	8281	—	—	—	—	—	—
Total	482	56780	735	54907	402	37747	588	33433

Under H_0,

$$\text{Correction factor} = \frac{T^2}{N} = \frac{(\Sigma X_1 + \Sigma X_2 + \Sigma X_3 + \Sigma X_4)^2}{N}$$

$$= \frac{(482 + 735 + 402 + 588)^2}{16}$$

$$= \frac{4870849}{16} = 304428.06$$

Sum of squares between the samples

$$= \frac{(\Sigma X_1)^2}{N_2} + \frac{(\Sigma X_2)^2}{N_2} + \frac{(\Sigma X_3)^2}{N_3} + \frac{(\Sigma X_4)^2}{N} - \frac{T^2}{N}$$

$$= \frac{232324}{16} + \frac{540225}{16} + \frac{161604}{16} + \frac{345744}{16} - 304428.06$$

$= 14520.25 + 33764.06 + 10100.25 + 21609 - 304428.06$

$= - 224434.5$

Total sum of squares

$$= \Sigma X_1^2 + \Sigma X_2^2 + \Sigma X_3^2 + \Sigma X_4^2 - \frac{T^2}{N}$$

$= 56780 + 54907 + 37747 + 33433 - 304428.06$

$= - 121561.06$

$\therefore$ Sum of squares with in the samples

= Total sum of squares – Sum of squares between the samples

$$= -121561.06 - (-224434.5)$$
$$= 102873.44$$

Tabulating all the above values in the following ANOVA table.

ANOVA Table

Source of variation	Degree of freedom *d.f.*	Sum of squares *S.S.*	Mean squares *S.S./d.f.*
Between samples	$v_1 = h - 1 = 3$	– 224434.5	–74811.5
Within samples	$v_2 = N - h$ $= 16 - 4 = 12$	102873.44	8572.78

one way classification

The value of $$F = \frac{-74811.5}{8572.78} = -8.72$$

$\Rightarrow$ $|F| = 8.72$

Also $F_{0.05}$ = The tabulated value of F for $(v_1, v_2) = (3, 12)$ *d.f.* at 5% level of significance

$= 3.49$ (see F-table)

Since, the calculated value of $|F|$ is greater than the tabulated value of F at (3, 12) *d.f.* at 5% level of significance. H_0 is rejected which means the sales made after the training programmes differ significantly.

(3) and (4). The training programmes conducted by the FMCG company have been effective in increasing the sales of their sales personal:

Case study 2: *H.L.L. India Ltd. is manufacturing a new cosmetic powder for the Indian market. it is specially designed for the North Indian market where the moisture content (humidity) is usually quite high in summer months. The company has decided to conduct experiments so as to determine the moisture content in the powder, and therefore 6 consignments have been taken as samples. Four experiments are to be conducted after taking a sample from each of the 6 consignments. Four observers have been appointed for the task and their assessments were found to be as follows.*

	Consignments					
Observers	*1*	*2*	*3*	*4*	*5*	*6*
A	*9*	*10*	*9*	*10*	*11*	*11*
B	*12*	*11*	*9*	*11*	*10*	*10*
C	*11*	*10*	*10*	*12*	*11*	*10*
D	*12*	*13*	*11*	*14*	*12*	*10*

You as a manager are required to analyze the given data, and determine and subsequently discuss as to whether:

(i) The six consignments differ with respect to their moisture content.

(ii) The inspection results of the four observers are at variance with reference to each other. (P.T.U. M.B.A. December 2012)

Sol. For consignments. Assume the null hypothesis as H_0 : There is no significant difference between the consignments with respect to the moisture content.

For Observers. Assume the null hypothesis as H_0 : There is no significant difference between the observers.

Given h = Number of rows = 4 ; k = Number of columns = 6 ; N = hk = 24

Also for simplification, we subtract 10 from each element, the given data becomes

Observers	*Consignments*						*Rows Total*
	1	2	3	4	5	6	
1	– 1	0	– 1	0	1	1	0
2	2	1	– 1	1	0	0	3
3	1	0	0	2	1	0	4
4	2	3	1	4	2	0	12
Column Total	4	4	– 1	7	4	1	Total = 19

(*a*) **Calculation of variance between rows**

Here, correction factor $= \dfrac{T^2}{N} = \dfrac{19^2}{24} = \dfrac{361}{24} = 15.04$

∴ Sum of squares between rows

$$= \frac{1}{k} \Sigma T_i^2 - \frac{T^2}{N}$$

$$= \frac{1}{6} [0 + 9 + 16 + 144] - 15.04$$

$$= 28.16 - 15.04 = 13.12$$

Also degree of freedom $\upsilon_1 = h - 1 = 4 - 1 = 3$

(*b*) **Calculation of variance between columns**

Here, sum of squares between columns $= \dfrac{1}{h} \Sigma T_j^2 - \dfrac{T^2}{N}$

$$= \frac{1}{4} [16 + 16 + 1 + 49 + 16 + 1] - 15.04$$

$$= 24.75 - 15.04 = 9.71$$

Also degree of freedom $\upsilon_2 = k - 1 = 6 - 1 = 5$

(*c*) **Calculation of error sum of squares**

Here, total sum of squares

$$= \Sigma X_1^2 + \Sigma X_2^2 + \Sigma X_3^2 + \Sigma X_4^2 + \Sigma X_5^2 + \Sigma X_6^2 - \frac{T^2}{N}$$

$$= 10 + 10 + 3 + 21 + 6 + 1 - 15.04 = 51 - 15.04 = 35.96$$

X_1^2	X_2^2	X_3^2	X_4^2	X_5^2	X_6^2
1	0	1	0	1	−1
4	1	1	1	0	0
1	0	0	4	1	0
4	9	1	16	4	0
Total 10	10	3	21	6	1

∴ Error sum of squares

= Total sum of squares – (Sum of squares between rows) – (Sum of squares between columns)

= 35.96 – 13.12 – 9.71

= 35.96 – 22.83 = 13.13

Also degree of freedom $v_1 = (h-1)(k-1) = 3 \times 5 = 15$

Calculating all the above, we get the following 'ANOVA TABLE'.

ANOVA TABLE

Source of variation	*Degree of freedom (d.f.)*	*Sum of squares (s.s.)*	*Mean squares s.s./d.f.*
Observers (between rows)	$v_1 = h - 1 = 3$	13.12	4.37
Consignments (between columns)	$v_2 = k - 1 = 5$	9.71	1.942
Error	$v = (h-1)(k-1) = 15$	13.13	0.875

Two way classification

Conclusion : From the table

$$F_1 = \frac{\text{Mean squares between rows}}{\text{Error sum of squares}} = \frac{4.37}{0.875} = 4.99$$

$$F_2 = \frac{\text{Mean squares between columns}}{\text{Error sum of squares}}$$

$$= \frac{1.942}{0.875} = 2.219 \textit{ i.e.,}$$

F_1(Calculated) = 4.99

(*i*) Since F_1 (tabulated) at 5% level of significance for (3, 15) d.f. = 3.29 (see F-table) *i.e.,* the calculated value of $|F_1|$ is greater than the tabulated value of F_1 for (3, 15) d.f. at 5% level of significance.

∴ H_0 is rejected *i.e.,* the difference between consignments is highly significant.

(*ii*) Since $|F_2|$ (tabulated) at 5% level of significance for (5, 15) d.f. = 2.90 (see F-table) *i.e.,* the calculated value of F_2 is less than the tabulated value of F_2 for (5, 15) d.f. at 5% level of significance.

∴ H_0 is accepted *i.e.,* there is no significant difference between the observers.

TEST YOUR KNOWLEDGE

1. The following table gives yields on 15 sample plots under three varieties of seeds. Find out if the average yields of land under different variances show significance.

   A: 20, 21, 23, 16, 20.

   B: 18, 20, 17, 15, 25.

   C: 25, 28, 22, 28, 32. *(P.T.U., M.B.A. Dec. 2010)*

2. Set up the analysis of variance table for the two way classified data

Varieties	*Seeds (in metric tonnes)*		
A	*B*	*C*	
I	6	5	5
II	7	5	4
III	3	3	3
IV	8	7	4

   State whether variety differ significantly at 5% level ?

3. The following figures related to the number of units sold in five different areas by four salesman

Number of units

Area	*A*	*B*	*C*	*D*
1	80	100	95	70
2	82	110	90	75
3	88	105	100	82
4	85	115	105	88
5	75	90	80	65

   Is there a significant difference in the efficiency of these salesmen ?

   (Given : $F_{0.05}$ for $v_1 = 3$, $v_2 = 16$ is 3.24)

4. A test was given to 5 students choosen at random from the M.B.A. class of each of the three university in Punjab. Their scores were found as follows :

Universities	*Scores*				
A	90	70	60	50	80
B	70	40	50	40	50
C	60	50	60	70	60

   Perform analysis of variance and show if there is any significant difference between the scores of students in the three universities

   (Given F at 5%. = 3.44 for $v_1 = 2$, $v_2 = 12$ d.f.)

5. The following table gives the weights of 12 individuals drawn from four different sources situated in 3 different districts. Carry out an analysis of variance :

Sources	*Districts*		
	A	*B*	*C*
S_1	61	62	63
S_2	63	64	63
S_3	66	67	68
S_4	68	69	69

6. The following data represent the number of units of production per day turned out 2 by 5 different workers using 4 different type of machines :

	Machine type			
Workers	*A*	*B*	*C*	
1	44	38	47	36
2	46	40	52	43
3	34	36	44	32
4	43	38	46	33
5	38	42	49	39

Test (*i*) Whether the mean productivity is same different types of machines

(*ii*) Whether the five men differ with respect to mean productivity.

7. The following table gives the number of refrigerators sold by 4 salesmen in three months May, June, July

	Salesmen			
Months	*A*	*B*	*C*	*D*
May	50	40	48	39
June	46	48	50	45
July	39	44	40	39

(*a*) Is there any significant difference in the sales made by the four salesmen ?

(*b*) Is there a significant difference in the sales made during different months ?

8. What are the assumptions of ANOVA.

Answers

1. $F = 8.14 < 3.88 = F_{0.05}$. The average yields of land under different varities of seed show differences
2. The difference among varieties of seeds is significant
3. There is a significant difference in the efficiency of the four salesmen.

Hint. One way classification ANOVA TABLE (F = 10.61)

Source of variation	*Degree of freedom d.f.*	*Sum of squares s.s.*	*Mean squares s.s/d.f.*
Between samples	3	2340	780
With in samples	16	1176	735

4. There is no significant difference between the scores

Hint. One way classification ANOVA TABLE (F = 3.33)

Source of variation	*Degree of freedom d.f.*	*Sum of squares s.s.*	*Mean squares s.s/d.f.*
Between samples	2	1000	500
With in samples	12	1800	150

5. **ANOVA TABLE (shifting the origin to 64)**

Source of variation	*d. f.*	*Sum of squares*	*Mean squares*	*F*
Between rows	3	86.92	28.97	9.38
Between columns	2	3.5	1.75	10.30
Error	6	18.3	3.05	–
Total	11	92.25		

6. **ANOVA TABLE**

Source of variation	*d.f.*	*Sum of squares*	*Mean squares*	*F*
Between machine type	3	338.8	112.93	18.38
Between workers	4	161.5	40.37	6.57
Error	12	73.7	6.14	–

(*i*) Mean productivity is not same for four different types of machines

(*ii*) Workers differ with respect to mean productivity.

7. (*a*) The sales made by the four salesmen do not differ significantly

(*b*) The sales made during different months do not differ significantly.

[**Hint.** (For simplicity, subtract each element by 40)]

Two way classification ANOVA TABLE

Source of variation	*Degree of freedom d.f.*	*Sum of squares s.s.*	*Mean squares s.s/d.f.*
Between salesmen	3	42	14
Between months	2	91.5	45.75
Error	6	82.5	

Unit-III
Correlation Analysis

12 Correlation and Regression

12.1. UNIVARIATE DISTRIBUTIONS

Distributions involving one variable are called univariate distributions. For example, marks obtained in a particular subject, wages earned by a group of workers.

12.2. BIVARIATE DISTRIBUTIONS

Distributions involving two variables are called bivariate distributions. For example, heights and weights of a certain group of persons, ages of husband and wife at the time of marriage.

12.3. CORRELATION (*P.T.U., M.B.A. Dec., 2009*)

In a bivariate distribution, if the change in one variable affects a change in the other variable, the variables are said to be correlated.

12.4. POSITIVE OR NEGATIVE CORRELATION (*P.T.U., M.B.A. Dec. 2006*)

If the increase (or decrease) in one results in a corresponding increase (or decrease) in the other, correlation is said to be **direct** or **positive.** For example, the correlation between income and expenditure is **positive.**

If the two variables deviate in opposite directions, *i.e.*, if the increase (or decrease) in one results in a corresponding decrease (or increase) in the other, correlation is said to be **inverse** or **negative.** For example, the correlation between volume and pressure of a gas, correlation between price and demand, are **negative correlation.**

Correlation is said to be **perfect** if the deviation in one variable is followed by a corresponding and proportional deviation in the other.

12.5. LINEAR AND NON-LINEAR CORRELATION

The correlation between two variables is said to be **linear** if the ratio of change in one variable to the change in the other variable, is almost constant, otherwise, the correlation is called **non-linear.**

12.6. METHODS OF MEASURING CORRELATION

The various methods of measuring correlation between the two variables are

(1) Scatter or dot diagrams method

(2) Karl-Pearson's coefficient of correlation

(3) Spearman's rank coefficient of correlation.

We now discuss in details the above methods.

12.7. SCATTER OR DOT DIAGRAM METHOD

It is the simplest method of the diagrammatic representation of bivariate data. Let (x_i, y_i), $i = 1, 2, 3, \ldots\ldots, n$, be a bivariate distribution. Let the values of the variables x and y be plotted along the x-axis and y-axis on a suitable scale. Then corresponding to every ordered pair, there corresponds a point or dot in the xy plane. The diagram of dots so obtained is called a dot or **scatter diagrams.** The scatter diagrams of different type of correlation between the two variables x and y, is given below:

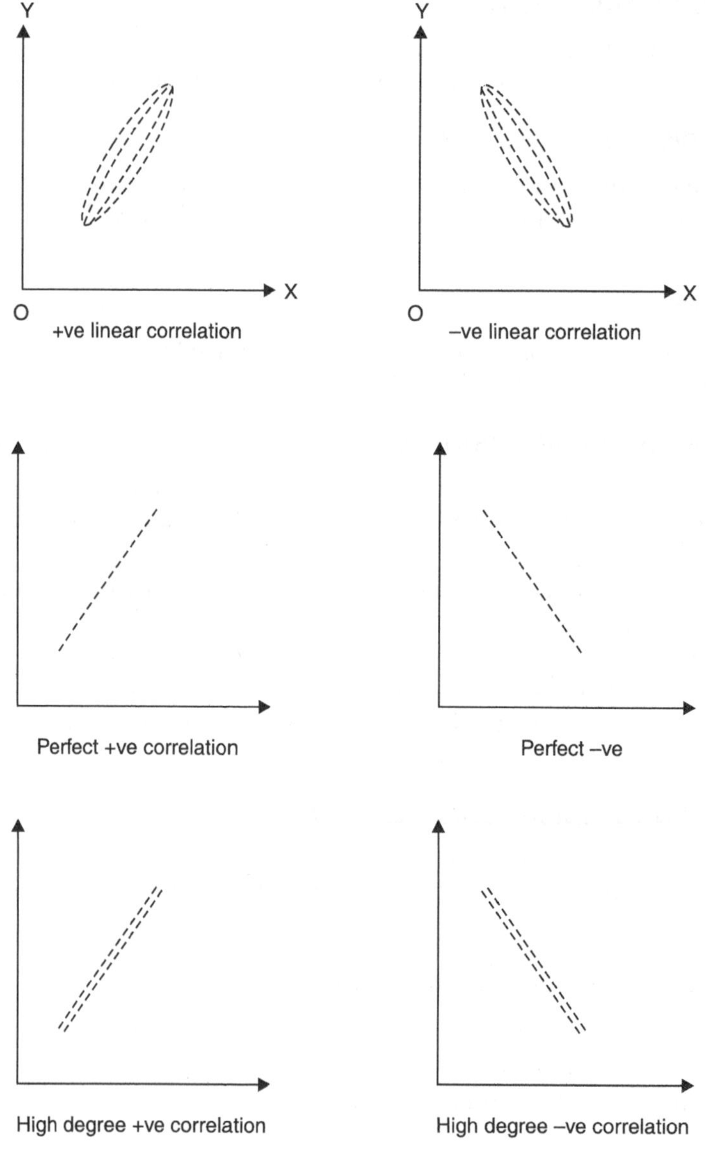

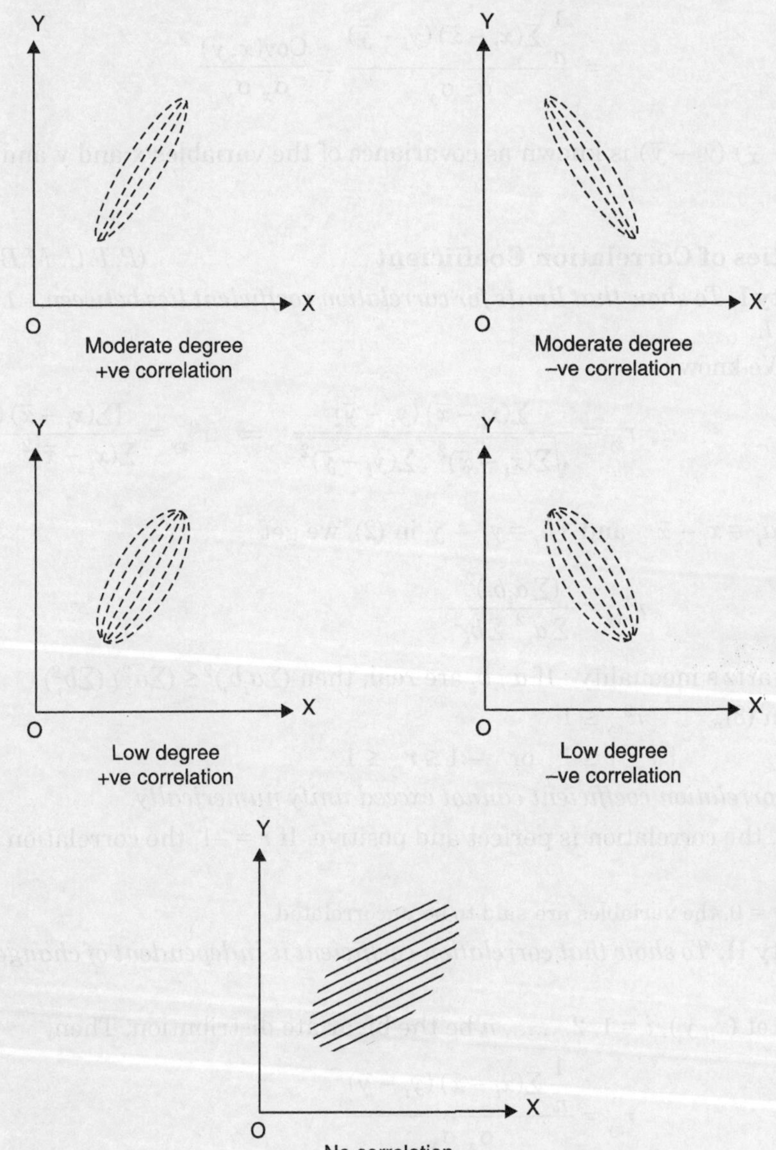

Note. This method is not suitable if the number of observations is large.

12.8. KARL PEARSON'S COEFFICIENT OF CORRELATION

Theorem I. *Define karl pearson's coefficient of correlation (or product moment correlation coefficient).* (P.T.U., M.B.A. Dec. 2010, 2005)

Proof. Correlation coefficient between two variables x and y, usually denoted by $r(x, y)$ or r_{xy} is a numerical measure of linear relationship between them and is defined as

$$r_{xy} = \frac{\Sigma(x_i - \overline{x})(y_i - \overline{y})}{\sqrt{\Sigma(x_i - \overline{x})^2 . \Sigma(y_i - \overline{y})^2}} = \frac{\frac{1}{n}\Sigma(x_i - \overline{x})(y_i - \overline{y})}{\sqrt{\frac{1}{n}\Sigma(x_i - \overline{x})^2 . \frac{1}{n}\Sigma(y_i - \overline{y})^2}}$$

$$= \frac{\frac{1}{n}\Sigma(x_i - \bar{x})(y_i - \bar{y})}{\sigma_x \sigma_y} = \frac{\text{Cov}(x, y)}{\sigma_x \sigma_y} \quad ...(1)$$

where $\frac{1}{n}\Sigma(x_i - \bar{x})(y_i - \bar{y})$ is known as covariance of the variables x and y and is denoted by Cov(x, y).

Properties of Correlation Coefficient *(P.T.U. M.B.A. Dec. 2012)*

Property I. *To show that limits for correlation coefficient lies between – 1 and 1 or show that* $-1 \le r_{xy} \le 1$.

Proof. We know

$$r_{xy} = \frac{\Sigma(x_i - \bar{x})(y_i - \bar{y})}{\sqrt{\Sigma(x_i - \bar{x})^2 \cdot \Sigma(y_i - \bar{y})^2}} \Rightarrow r^2_{xy} = \frac{[\Sigma(x_i - \bar{x})(y_i - \bar{y})]^2}{\Sigma(x_i - \bar{x})^2 \cdot \Sigma(y_i - \bar{y})^2} \quad ...(2)$$

Putting $a_i = x_i - \bar{x}$ and $b_i = y_i - \bar{y}$ in (2), we get

$$r^2_{xy} = \frac{(\Sigma a_i b_i)^2}{\Sigma a_i^2 \, \Sigma b_i^2} \quad ...(3)$$

By Schwartz's inequality : If a_i, b_i are real, then $(\Sigma a_i b_i)^2 \le (\Sigma a_i^2)(\Sigma b_i^2)$

$\therefore$ From (3), $r^2_{xy} \le 1$

or $|r_{xy}| \le 1$ or $-1 \le r_{xy} \le 1$

Hence, *correlation coefficient cannot exceed unity numerically.*

If $r = +1$, the correlation is perfect and positive. If $r = -1$, the correlation is perfect and negative.

Note. If $r = 0$, the variables are said to be uncorrelated.

Property II. *To show that correlation coefficient is independent of change of origin and scale.*

Proof. Let (x_i, y_i), $i = 1, 2, ..., n$ be the bivariate distribution. Then,

$$r_{xy} = \frac{\frac{1}{n}\Sigma(x_i - \bar{x})(y_i - \bar{y})}{\sigma_x \sigma_y} \quad ...(1)$$

Let us define two new variables u and v as $u = \frac{x - a}{h}$, $v = \frac{y - b}{k}$;

where a, b, h, k are constants, then

$$x = a + hu, \qquad y = b + kv$$

$$\therefore \quad \bar{x} = a + h\bar{u}, \qquad \bar{y} = b + k\bar{v}$$

$$\Rightarrow \quad x - \bar{x} = h(u - \bar{u}), \qquad y - \bar{y} = k(v - \bar{v})$$

$$\therefore \quad \sigma_x^2 = \frac{1}{n}\Sigma(x_i - \bar{x})^2 = \frac{h^2}{n}\Sigma(u_i - \bar{u})^2 = h^2\sigma_u^2$$

$$\therefore \quad \sigma_y^2 = \frac{1}{n}\Sigma(y_i - \bar{y})^2 = \frac{k^2}{n}\Sigma(v_i - \bar{v})^2 = k^2\sigma_v^2$$

$$\therefore \quad \text{from (1),} \qquad r_{xy} = \frac{\frac{1}{n}\Sigma(x_i - \bar{x})(y_i - \bar{y})}{\sigma_x \, \sigma_y} = \frac{\frac{1}{n}\Sigma\, hk\,(u_i - \bar{u})(v_i - \bar{v})}{h\sigma_u \,.\, k\sigma_v}$$

$$= \frac{\frac{1}{n}\Sigma(u_i - \bar{u})(v_i - \bar{v})}{\sigma_u \, \sigma_v} = r_{uv}, \text{ which is free from } a, b, h \text{ and } k.$$

Hence, we can say that the correlation coefficient is independent of the change of origin as well as scale.

12.9. COMPUTATION OF CORRELATION COEFFICIENT

We know that,
$$r_{xy} = \frac{\frac{1}{n}\Sigma(x_i - \bar{x})(y_i - \bar{y})}{\sigma_x \, \sigma_y} \qquad \ldots(1)$$

Now,
$$\frac{1}{n}\Sigma(x_i - \bar{x})(y_i - \bar{y}) = \frac{1}{n}\Sigma(x_i y_i - x_i \bar{y} - y_i \bar{x} + \bar{x}\,\bar{y})$$

$$= \frac{1}{n}\Sigma x_i y_i - \bar{y}\;\frac{1}{n}\Sigma x_i - \bar{x}\,.\,\frac{1}{n}\Sigma y_i + \frac{1}{n}(n\bar{x}\,\bar{y})$$

$$= \frac{1}{n}\Sigma x_i y_i - \bar{y}\,.\,\bar{x} - \bar{x}\,.\,\bar{y} + \bar{x}\,\bar{y} = \frac{1}{n}\Sigma x_i y_i - \bar{x}\,\bar{y}$$

$$\sigma_x^2 = \frac{1}{n}\Sigma(x_i - \bar{x})^2 = \frac{1}{n}\Sigma(x_i^2 - 2x_i\,\bar{x} + \bar{x}^2)$$

$$= \frac{1}{n}\Sigma x_i^2 - 2\bar{x}\,.\,\frac{1}{n}\Sigma x_i + \frac{1}{n}(n\bar{x}^2)$$

$$= \frac{1}{n}\Sigma x_i^2 - 2\bar{x}\,.\,\bar{x} + \bar{x}^2 = \frac{1}{n}\Sigma x_i^2 - \bar{x}^2$$

Similarly,
$$\sigma_y^2 = \frac{1}{n}\Sigma y_i^2 - \bar{y}^2$$

$$\therefore \qquad r_{xy} = \frac{\frac{1}{n}\Sigma x_i y_i - \bar{x}\,\bar{y}}{\sqrt{\left(\frac{1}{n}\Sigma x_i^2 - \bar{x}^2\right)\left(\frac{1}{n}\Sigma y_i^2 - \bar{y}^2\right)}} \qquad \ldots(2)$$

If
$$u = \frac{x - a}{h} \quad \text{and} \quad v = \frac{y - b}{k}$$

Then
$$r_{xy} = r_{uv} = \frac{\frac{1}{n}\Sigma u_i v_i - \bar{u}\,\bar{v}}{\sqrt{\left(\frac{1}{n}\Sigma u_i^2 - \bar{u}^2\right)\left(\frac{1}{n}\Sigma v_i^2 - \bar{v}^2\right)}} \qquad \ldots(3)$$

Note. The students are advised to calculate r_{xy} by arbitrary origin method given above rather than by the direct method.

12.10. CHARACTERISTICS OF KARL PEARSON'S COEFFICIENT OF CORRELATION (r_{XY})

The Karl Pearson's coefficient of correlation satisfies the following :

(*i*) The value of r_{xy} always lies between – 1 and 1, *i.e.*, $-1 \le r_{xy} \le 1$.

(*ii*) If $r_{xy} = -1$, then there is perfect negative correlation between x and y.

(*iii*) If $r_{xy} = +1$, then there is perfect +ve correlation between x and y.

(*iv*) If $r_{xy} = 0$, then there is no correlation between x and y.

(*v*) If $0 < r_{xy} < 1$, then there is positive correlation between x and y.

(*vi*) If $-1 < r_{xy} < 0$, then there is negative correlation between x and y.

12.11. DEGREE OF KARL PEARSON'S COEFFICIENT OF CORRELATION

For different values of r_{xy}, between – 1 and 1, we have different types of correlation as seen from the following table.

Value of r_{xy}	*Degree of correlation*
$+1$	Perfect +ve correlation
$.75 \le r_{xy} \le 1$	High degree +ve correlation
$.50 \le r_{xy} \le .75$	Moderate degree +ve correlation
$0 < r_{xy} < 0.50$	Low degree +ve correlation
$r_{xy} = 0$	No correlation
$-0.50 < r < 0$	Low degree –ve correlation
$-.75 < r \le -.50$	Moderate degree –ve correlation
$-1 < r \le -.75$	High degree –ve correlation
$r_{xy} = -1$	Perfect –ve correlation

12.12. PROBABLE ERROR

(P.T.U., M.B.A. May 2008, May 2009)

The probable error of the coefficient of correlation is defined as P.E. $= 0.6745 \dfrac{1-r^2}{\sqrt{n}}$,

where P.E. = Probable error ; r = Coefficient of correlation ; n = Number of pair of observations.

12.13. STANDARD ERROR

(P.T.U., M.B.A. May 2009 ; May 2010)

The standard error of the coefficient of correlation is defined as S.E. $= \dfrac{1-r^2}{\sqrt{n}}$,

where S.E. = Standard error ; r = Coefficient of correlation ; n = Number of pair of observations.

12.14. LIMITS OF CORRELATION

The limits of the correlation in the population is $r \pm$ P.E., where P.E. stands for probable error.

ILLUSTRATIVE EXAMPLES

Example 1. *Find the coefficient of correlation for the following data :*

$$n = 10, \Sigma x = 50, \Sigma y = -30, \Sigma x^2 = 290, \Sigma y^2 = 300, \Sigma xy = -115.$$

Sol. The coefficient of correlation r_{xy} is given by

$$r_{xy} = \frac{\frac{1}{n}\Sigma x_i y_i - \bar{x}\,\bar{y}}{\sqrt{\left(\frac{1}{n}\Sigma x_i^2 - \bar{x}^2\right)\left(\frac{1}{n}\Sigma y_i^2 - \bar{y}^2\right)}}$$

$$= \frac{\frac{1}{10}\times(-115) - 5\times(-3)}{\sqrt{\left(\frac{1}{10}\times 290 - 25\right)\left(\frac{1}{10}\times 300 - 9\right)}} \qquad \left| \begin{array}{l} \bar{x} = \frac{1}{n}\Sigma x_i = \frac{50}{10} = 5 \\ \bar{y} = \frac{1}{n}\Sigma y_i = \frac{-30}{10} = -3 \end{array} \right.$$

$$= \frac{-11.5 + 15}{\sqrt{4 \times 21}} = \frac{3.5}{\sqrt{84}} = \frac{3.5}{9.165} = 0.38.$$

Remark. There is moderate degree +ve correlation

Example 2. *If X and Y are the deviations from the actual mean and $\Sigma X^2 = 10, \Sigma XY = 12, \Sigma Y^2 = 24$. Find the coefficient of correlation between the variables.*

Sol. Given, X and Y are deviations from the actual mean, say, $\bar{x}$ and $\bar{y}$, then

$$\Sigma(x - \bar{x})^2 = 10 \qquad \left| \; X = x - \bar{x}, Y = y - \bar{y} \right.$$

$$\Sigma(x - \bar{x})(y - \bar{y}) = 12$$

$$\Sigma(y - \bar{y})^2 = 24$$

The required coefficient of correlation is given by

$$r_{xy} = \frac{\frac{1}{n}\Sigma(x_i - \bar{x})(y_i - \bar{y})}{\sqrt{\frac{1}{n}\Sigma(x_i - \bar{x})^2 \cdot \frac{1}{n}\Sigma(y_i - \bar{y})^2}} = \frac{\frac{1}{n}.(12)}{\sqrt{\frac{1}{n}.(10)\times\frac{1}{n}.24}}$$

$$= \frac{12}{\sqrt{240}} = \frac{12}{15.49} = 0.7746$$

Remark. In the given data, there is high degree +ve correlation.

Example 3. *The coefficient of correlation between two variables X and Y is 0.64, their covariance is 6.72. If the standard deviation of Y is 3.5, find the variance of X.*

Sol. Given $\quad r_{xy} = 0.64, \text{Cov}(x, y) = 6.72, \sigma_y = 3.5$

By def, $\quad r_{xy} = \dfrac{\text{Cov}(x, y)}{\sigma_x\,\sigma_y}$

$$0.64 = \frac{6.72}{\sigma_x(3.5)} \Rightarrow \quad \sigma_x = \frac{6.72}{(0.64)(3.5)} = \frac{6.72}{2.24} = 3.$$

Example 4. (*a*) *Give the range of possible values of correlation coefficient and explain the meaning of r = 0, 1 and –1. Calculate Karl Pearson's coefficient of correlation between x and y :*

x :	65	66	67	68	69	70	71
y :	67	68	66	69	72	72	69

(*b*) *Calculate Karl Pearson's coefficient of correlation between marks in two subjects from the following data :*

Roll No.	*1*	*2*	*2*	*4*	*5*
Marks in Accountancy	*48*	*35*	*17*	*23*	*47*
Marks in statistics	*45*	*20*	*40*	*25*	*45*

(P.T.U., M.B.A. Dec. 2005)

Sol. (*a*) The value of r_{xy} lies between – 1 and 1, *i.e.*, $-1 \le r_{xy} \le 1$.

When $r_{xy} = 0$, there is no correlation.

$r_{xy} = 1$, there is perfect +ve correlation between the variables x and y.

$r_{xy} = -1$, there is perfect –ve correlation between the variables x and y.

Take A = 68, B = 69 as assumed means.

Consider the table

x	y	$u = x - A$	$v = y - B$	u^2	v^2	uv
65	67	– 3	– 2	9	4	6
66	68	– 2	– 1	4	1	2
67	66	– 1	– 3	1	9	3
68	69	0	0	0	0	0
69	72	1	3	1	9	3
70	72	2	3	4	9	6
71	69	3	0	9	0	3
	Total	$\Sigma u = 0$	$\Sigma v = 0$	$\Sigma u^2 = 28$	$\Sigma v^2 = 32$	$\Sigma uv = 23$

Here, $$\bar{u} = \frac{\Sigma u_i}{n} = 0, \; \bar{v} = \frac{\Sigma v_i}{n} = 0$$

Now, $$r_{uv} = \frac{\frac{1}{n}\Sigma u_i v_i - \bar{u}\bar{v}}{\sqrt{\left(\frac{1}{n}\Sigma u_i^2 - \bar{u}^2\right)\left(\frac{1}{n}\Sigma v_i^2 - \bar{v}^2\right)}}$$

$$= \frac{\frac{1}{7} \times 23 - 0}{\sqrt{\left(\frac{1}{7} \times 28 - 0\right)\left(\frac{1}{7} \times 32 - 0\right)}} = \frac{23}{\sqrt{28 \times 32}}$$

$$= \frac{23}{\sqrt{644}} = \frac{23}{25.37} = 0.9065$$

Hence, $r_{xy} = r_{uv} = 0.9065$ | r_{xy} is independent of change of origin and scale.

(*b*) Denote the marks in accountancy by *x* and marks in statistics by *y*. Take A = 34, B = 35. Consider the following Table:

Roll No.	*x*	*y*	$u = x - A$	$v = y - B$	u^2	v^2	uv
1	48	45	14	10	196	100	140
2	35	20	1	– 15	1	225	– 15
3	17	40	– 17	5	289	25	– 85
4	23	25	– 11	– 10	121	100	110
5	47	45	13	10	169	100	130
			$\Sigma u = 0$	$\Sigma v = 0$	$\Sigma u^2 = 776$	$\Sigma v^2 = 550$	$\Sigma uv = 280$

Here, $\bar{u} = \frac{1}{n}\Sigma u = 0,\ \bar{v} = \frac{1}{n}\Sigma v = 0$

$$\therefore \quad r_{uv} = \frac{\frac{1}{n}\Sigma uv - \bar{u}\,\bar{v}}{\sqrt{\left(\frac{1}{n}\Sigma u^2 - (\bar{u})^2\right)\left(\frac{1}{n}\Sigma v^2 - (\bar{v})^2\right)}}$$

$$= \frac{\frac{1}{5}\times 280 - 0}{\sqrt{\left(\frac{1}{5}\times 776 - 0\right)\left(\frac{1}{5}\times 550 - 0\right)}}$$

$$= \frac{280}{\sqrt{776 \times 550}} = \frac{280}{\sqrt{426800}} = \frac{280}{653.299}$$

$$= 0.4285 = 0.429.$$

Example 5. *Find the coefficient of correlation for the following table :*

(P.T.U., M.B.A. May 2009)

x	*10*	*14*	*18*	*22*	*26*	*30*
y	*18*	*12*	*24*	*6*	*30*	*36*

Sol. Let $u = \frac{x - 22}{4},\ v = \frac{y - 24}{6}$.

Consider the following table.

x	*y*	*u*	*v*	u^2	v^2	uv
10	18	– 3	– 1	9	1	3
14	12	– 2	– 2	4	4	4
18	24	– 1	0	1	0	0
22	6	0	– 3	0	9	0
26	30	1	1	1	1	1
30	36	2	2	4	4	4
Total		$\Sigma u = -3$	$\Sigma v = -3$	$\Sigma u^2 = 19$	$\Sigma v^2 = 19$	$\Sigma uv = 12$

Here, $\bar{u} = \frac{1}{n} \Sigma u_i = \frac{1}{6} (-3) = -\frac{1}{2}$; $\bar{v} = \frac{1}{n} \Sigma v_i = \frac{1}{6} (-3) = -\frac{1}{2}$

$$\therefore \quad r_{uv} = \frac{\frac{1}{n} \Sigma u_i v_i - \bar{u}\bar{v}}{\sqrt{\left(\frac{1}{n} \Sigma u_i^2 - \bar{u}^2\right)\left(\frac{1}{n} \Sigma v_i^2 - \bar{v}^2\right)}}$$

$$= \frac{\frac{1}{6}(12) - \frac{1}{4}}{\sqrt{\left[\frac{1}{6}(19) - \frac{1}{4}\right]\left[\frac{1}{6}(19) - \frac{1}{4}\right]}} = \frac{\frac{7}{4}}{\frac{35}{12}} = \frac{3}{5} = 0.6.$$

Hence, $r_{xy} = r_{uv} = 0.6.$ $\quad | \, r_{xy}$ is independent of change of origin and scale

Example 6. *A computer while calculating correlation coefficient between two variables X and Y from 25 pairs of observations obtained the following results :*

$n = 25, \quad \Sigma X = 125, \quad \Sigma X^2 = 650,$

$\Sigma Y = 100, \quad \Sigma Y^2 = 460, \quad \Sigma XY = 508.$

It was, however, later discovered at the time of checking that he had copied down two pairs as

X	*Y*
6	*14*
8	*6*

while the correct values were

X	*Y*
8	*12*
6	*8*

Obtain the correct value of correlation coefficient.

Sol. Corrected $\Sigma X = 125 - 6 - 8 + 8 + 6 = 125$

Corrected $\Sigma Y = 100 - 14 - 6 + 12 + 8 = 100$

Corrected $\Sigma X^2 = 650 - 6^2 - 8^2 + 8^2 + 6^2 = 650$

Corrected $\Sigma Y^2 = 460 - 14^2 - 6^2 + 12^2 + 8^2 = 436$

Corrected $\Sigma XY = 508 - 6 \times 14 - 8 \times 6 + 8 \times 12 + 6 \times 8 = 520$

(Subtract the incorrect values and add the corresponding correct values)

$\therefore$ Corrected $\bar{X} = \frac{1}{n} \Sigma X = \frac{1}{25} \times 125 = 5$; $\bar{Y} = \frac{1}{n} \Sigma Y = \frac{1}{25} \times 100 = 4$

$$\text{Hence, Corrected } r_{XY} = \frac{\frac{1}{n} \Sigma XY - \bar{X}\bar{Y}}{\sqrt{\left(\frac{1}{n} \Sigma X^2 - \bar{X}^2\right)\left(\frac{1}{n} \Sigma Y^2 - \bar{Y}^2\right)}}$$

$$= \frac{\frac{1}{25} \times 520 - 5 \times 4}{\sqrt{\left(\frac{1}{25} \times 650 - 25\right)\left(\frac{1}{25} \times 436 - 16\right)}}$$

$$= \frac{\frac{4}{5}}{\sqrt{(1)\left(\frac{36}{25}\right)}} = \frac{4}{5} \times \frac{5}{6} = \frac{2}{3} = 0.67.$$

Example 7. *Calculate correlation coefficient from the following results :*
$n = 10, \Sigma x = 140, \Sigma y = 150, \Sigma(x - 10)^2 = 180, \Sigma(y - 15)^2 = 215, \Sigma(x - 10)(y - 15) = 60$.

Sol. We know that the correlation coefficient between two series x and y is given by

$$r = \frac{\frac{1}{n}\Sigma xy - \bar{x}\,\bar{y}}{\sqrt{\left(\frac{1}{n}\Sigma x^2 - (\bar{x})^2\right)\left(\frac{1}{n}\Sigma y^2 - (\bar{y})^2\right)}} \quad ...(1)$$

Given $\Sigma(x - 10)^2 = 180$

$\Rightarrow \Sigma(x^2 + 100 - 20x) = 180$

$\Rightarrow \Sigma x^2 + 100 \times 10 - 20\,\Sigma x = 180$

$\Rightarrow \Sigma x^2 = 180 - 1000 + 20 \times 140 = 1980 \quad ...(2)$

Also $\Sigma(y - 15)^2 = 215$

$\Rightarrow \Sigma(y^2 + 225 - 30y) = 215$

$\Rightarrow \Sigma y^2 + 225 \times 10 - 30\,\Sigma y = 215$

$\Rightarrow \Sigma y^2 = 215 - 2250 + 30 \times 150 = 2465 \quad ...(3)$

Further, $\Sigma(x - 10)(y - 15) = 60$

$\Rightarrow \Sigma(xy - 15x - 10y + 150) = 60$

$\Rightarrow \Sigma xy - 15\,\Sigma x - 10\,\Sigma y + 150 \times 10 = 60$

$\Rightarrow \Sigma xy - 15 \times 140 - 10 \times 150 + 1500 = 60$

$\Rightarrow \Sigma xy = 60 + 2100 + 1500 - 1500 = 2160 \quad ...(4)$

Also $\bar{x} = \frac{\Sigma x}{n} = \frac{140}{10} = 14, \ \bar{y} = \frac{\Sigma y}{10} = \frac{150}{10} = 15 \quad ...(5)$

Using (2), (3), (4), (5) in (1), we have

$$r = \frac{\frac{1}{10} \times 2160 - (14)(15)}{\sqrt{\left(\frac{1}{10} \times 1980 - (14)^2\right)\left(\frac{1}{10} \times 2465 - (15)^2\right)}}$$

$$= \frac{216 - 210}{\sqrt{(198 - 196)(246.5 - 225)}} = \frac{6}{\sqrt{(2)(21.5)}} = \frac{6}{6.557} = 0.915.$$

Example 8. *If $r = 0.6$ and $n = 64$. Find the probable error of the coefficient of correlation and determine the limits for the population r.*

Sol. We know $\quad \text{P.E.} = 0.6745 \left(\frac{1 - r^2}{\sqrt{n}}\right) \quad ...(1)$

Given $\quad r = 0.6, n = 64$

$\therefore$ (1) gives $\quad \text{P.E.} = 0.6745 \left(\frac{1 - (0.6)^2}{\sqrt{64}}\right) = \frac{(0.6745) \times (0.64)}{8} = 0.054$

Also the limits of population correlation $= r \pm$ P.E. $= 0.6 \pm 0.054 = (0.546, 0.654)$.

Example 9. *A student calculates the value of r (correlation coefficient) as + 0.72 for a question comprising 5 pair of observations and concludes that there is high degree of correlation between the variables. Do you justify his conclusion ?*

Sol. The value of r is considered to be significant if it is more than 6 times the probable error. The probable error (P.E.) is given by

$$\text{P.E.} = (0.6745)\ \frac{1-r^2}{\sqrt{n}} \qquad \ldots(1)$$

Given $r = 0.72$, $n = 5$

$$\therefore \quad \text{(1) gives} \qquad \text{P.E.} = (0.6745)\left(\frac{1-(0.72)^2}{\sqrt{5}}\right)$$

$$= (0.6745)\left(\frac{0.4816}{2.236}\right) = 0.145$$

$$\therefore \qquad \frac{r}{\text{P.E.}} = \frac{0.72}{0.145} = 4.97 \not> 6$$

i.e., the value of r calculated by the student is not significant.

12.15. RANK CORRELATION

Sometimes we have to deal with problems in which data cannot be quantitatively measured but qualitative assessment is possible.

Let a group of n individuals be arranged in order of merit or proficiency in possession of two characteristics A and B. The ranks in the two characteristics are, in general, different. For example, if A stands for intelligence and B for beauty, it is not necessary that the most intelligent individual may be the most beautiful and *vice versa.* Thus an individual who is ranked at the top for the characteristic A *may be* ranked at the bottom for the characteristic B. Let (x_i, y_i), $i = 1, 2, \ldots, n$ be the ranks of the n individuals in the group for the characteristics A and B respectively. Pearsonian coefficient of correlation between the ranks x_i' s and y_i' s is called the *rank correlation coefficient* between the characteristics A and B for that group of individuals.

Thus rank correlation coefficient

$$r = \frac{\Sigma(x_i - \bar{x})(y_i - \bar{y})}{\sqrt{\Sigma(x_i - \bar{x})^2\ \Sigma(y_i - \bar{y})^2}} = \frac{\frac{1}{n}\Sigma(x_i - \bar{x})(y_i - \bar{y})}{\sigma_x\, \sigma_y} \qquad \ldots(1)$$

Now x_i' s and y_i' s are merely the permutations of n numbers from 1 to n. *Assuming that no two individuals are bracketed for tied in either classification, i.e.,* $(x_i, y_i) \neq (x_j, y_j)$ *for* $i \neq j$, *both x and y take all integral values from 1 to n.*

$$\therefore \qquad \bar{x} = \bar{y} = \frac{1}{n}(1 + 2 + 3 + \ldots + n) = \frac{1}{n}\cdot\frac{n(n+1)}{2} = \frac{n+1}{2}$$

$$\Sigma x_i = 1 + 2 + 3 + \ldots + n = \frac{n(n+1)}{2} = \Sigma y_i$$

$$\Sigma x_i^2 = 1^2 + 2^2 + \ldots + n^2 = \frac{n(n+1)(2n+1)}{6} = \Sigma y_i^2$$

If d_i denotes the difference in ranks of the ith individual, then

$$d_i = x_i - y_i = (x_i - \bar{x}) - (y_i - \bar{y}) \qquad |\because\ \bar{x} = \bar{y}|$$

$$\frac{1}{n}\Sigma d_i^2 = \frac{1}{n}\Sigma[(x_i - \overline{x}) - (y_i - \overline{y})]^2$$

$$= \frac{1}{n}\Sigma(x_i - \overline{x})^2 + \frac{1}{n}\Sigma(y_i - \overline{y})^2 - 2 \cdot \frac{1}{n}\Sigma(x_i - \overline{x})(y_i - \overline{y})$$

$$= \sigma_x^2 + \sigma_y^2 - 2r\sigma_x\sigma_y \quad ...(2) \quad |\text{Using (1)}$$

But $$\sigma_x^2 = \frac{1}{n}\Sigma x_i^2 - \overline{x}^2 = \frac{1}{n}\Sigma y_i^2 - \overline{y}^2 = \sigma_y^2$$

$\therefore$ From (2) $$\frac{1}{n}\Sigma d_i^2 = 2\sigma_x^2 - 2r\sigma_x^2 = 2(1-r)\sigma_x^2$$

$$= 2(1-r)\left[\frac{1}{n}\Sigma x_i^2 - \overline{x}^2\right]$$

$$= 2(1-r)\left[\frac{1}{n}\cdot\frac{n(n+1)(2n+1)}{6} - \frac{(n+1)^2}{4}\right]$$

$$= (1-r)(n+1)\left[\frac{4n+2-3n-3}{6}\right] = \frac{(1-r)(n^2-1)}{6}$$

or $$1 - r = \frac{6\Sigma d_i^2}{n(n^2-1)}$$

Hence, $$r = 1 - \frac{6\Sigma d_i^2}{n(n^2-1)}.$$

Note. This is called *Spearman's Formula* for Rank Correlation.

$\Sigma d_i = \Sigma(x_i - y_i) = \Sigma x_i - \Sigma y_i = 0$ always. This serves as a check on calculations.

ILLUSTRATIVE EXAMPLES

Example 1. *If $d_i = 0$ for all i, show that $r = 1$ and conversely if $r = 1$, then $d_i = 0$ for all i.*

Sol. $d_i = 0$ for all $i \Rightarrow \Sigma d_i^2 = 0$

$$\therefore \quad r = 1 - \frac{6\Sigma d_i^2}{n(n^2-1)} = 1$$

Conversely, if $r = 1$, then $\Sigma d_i^2 = 0$

$\Rightarrow d_1^2 + d_2^2 + ... + d_n^2 = 0$

$\Rightarrow \quad d_1 = d_2 = ... = d_n = 0$

$\Rightarrow \quad d_i = 0$ for all i.

Example 2. *Show that the rank correlation coefficient varies between –1 and +1.*

Sol. Spearman's Rank Correlation Co-efficient is given by

$$r = 1 - \frac{6\Sigma d_i^2}{n(n^2-1)} \quad ...(1)$$

(*i*) r is maximum, when Σd_i^2 is minimum

i.e., when $\Sigma d_i^2 = 0$

i.e., when $d_i = x_i - y_i = 0$ for each i

i.e., when $x_i = y_i$ for each i.

This happens when ever y individual gets the same rank in the two characteristics.

$\therefore$ Maximum value of $r = 1 - 0 = 1$.

(*ii*) r is minimum, when Σd_i^2 is maximum.

Σd^2 is maximum when $| d_i | = | x_i - y_i |$ is maximum.

This happens when an individual getting the highest rank in one characteristic gets the lowest rank in the second characteristic ; *i.e.*, when the ranks (x_i, y_i) are $(1, n)$, $(2, n-1)$, $(3, n-2)$, ..., $(n, 1)$.

$\therefore$ Σd^2 is maximum when $x_i + y_i = n + 1$ for each i.

Proceeding as in example 2, $r = -1$.

Hence $-1 \le r \le +1$

i.e., r varies between -1 and $+1$.

Example 3. *The ranking of ten students in two subjects A and B are as follows :*

A :	*3*	*5*	*8*	*4*	*7*	*10*	*2*	*1*	*6*	*9*
B :	*6*	*4*	*9*	*8*	*1*	*2*	*3*	*10*	*5*	*7*

What is the coefficient of rank correlation ? (P.T.U., M.B.A. May 2009)

Sol.

Ranks in A (x)	3	5	8	4	7	10	2	1	6	9	Total
Ranks in B (y)	6	4	9	8	1	2	3	10	5	7	
$d = x - y$	-3	1	-1	-4	6	8	-1	-9	1	2	0
d^2	9	1	1	16	36	64	1	81	1	4	214

$$\therefore \qquad r = 1 - \frac{6\Sigma d^2}{n(n^2-1)}, \qquad | \text{ Here, } n = 10$$

$$= 1 - \frac{6 \times 214}{10 \times 99} = -\frac{147}{495} = -0.3.$$

Example 4. *Calculate the coefficient of correlation using Rank method,*

x	*78*	*89*	*97*	*69*	*59*	*79*	*68*	*57*
y	*125*	*137*	*156*	*112*	*107*	*136*	*123*	*108*

(P.T.U., M.B.A. Dec. 2008)

Sol. Write down the ranks in each series. The item with the largest size is ranked 1, next largest 2 and so on.

x:	78	89	97	69	59	79	68	57
y:	125	137	156	112	107	136	123	108
Ranks in X(x)	4	2	1	5	7	3	6	8
Ranks in Y(y)	4	2	1	6	8	3	5	7
$d = x - y$	0	0	0	-1	-1	0	1	1
d^2	0	0	0	1	1	0	1	1

By **Rank method,** the coefficient of correlation is given as

$$r = 1 - \frac{6\sum d^2}{n(n^2-1)} = 1 - \frac{6 \times 4}{8(64-1)} = 1 - \frac{3}{63} = 1 - 0.047 = 0.953.$$

Example 5. *The ranks of same 16 students in Mathematics and Physics are as follows : Two numbers within bracket denote the ranks of the students in Mathematics and Physics :*

(1, 1), (2, 10), (3, 3), (4, 4), (5, 5), (6, 7), (7, 2), (8, 6), (9, 8), (10, 11), (11, 15), (12, 9), (13, 14), (14, 12), (15, 16), (16, 13).

Calculate the rank correlation coefficient for proficiencies of this group in Mathematics and Physics.

Sol. Consider the following table :

Ranks in Math. (*x*)	1	2	3	4	5	6	7	8	9	10	11	12	13	14	15	16	Total
Ranks in Physics (*y*)	1	10	3	4	5	7	2	6	8	11	15	9	14	12	16	13	
$d = x - y$	0	–8	0	0	0	–1	5	2	1	–1	–4	3	–1	2	–1	3	0
d^2	0	64	0	0	0	1	25	4	1	1	16	9	1	4	1	9	136

$$\therefore \quad r = 1 - \frac{6\Sigma d^2}{n(n^2-1)} \qquad | \text{ Here, } n = 16$$

$$= 1 - \frac{6 \times 136}{16 \times 255} = 1 - \frac{816}{4080} = 1 - \frac{1}{5} = \frac{4}{5} = 0.8.$$

Example 6. *The coefficient of rank correlation between marks in Statistics and marks in Mathematics by a certain group of students is 0.8. If the sum of the squares of the difference in ranks is given to be 33, find the number of students in the group.*

Sol. Here $\quad r = 0.8, \quad \Sigma d^2 = 33, \quad n = ?$

Using $r = 1 - \dfrac{6\Sigma d^2}{n(n^2-1)}$, we have

$$0.8 = 1 - \frac{6 \times 33}{n(n^2-1)}$$

$$\Rightarrow \quad \frac{198}{n(n^2-1)} = 1 - 0.8 = 0.2 = \frac{1}{5} \quad \Rightarrow \quad n(n^2-1) = 990$$

$$\Rightarrow \quad n^3 - n - 990 = 0. \quad \Rightarrow \quad n(n^2-1) = 990 = 10(10^2-1) \quad \Rightarrow \quad n = 10$$

Example 7. *The coefficient of rank correlation of the marks obtained by 10 students in Mathematics and Statistics was found to be 0.5. It was later discovered that the difference in ranks in two subjects obtained by one of the students was wrongly taken as 3 instead of 7. Find the correct coefficient of rank correlation.*

Sol. Here, $n = 10$, Incorrected $r = 0.5$

Using $r = 1 - \dfrac{6\Sigma d_i^2}{n(n^2-1)}$, we have $0.5 = 1 - \dfrac{6\Sigma d_i^2}{10 \times 99}$

$$\Rightarrow \qquad 6\Sigma d_i^2 = 990 \times 0.5 = 495$$

$$\therefore \text{ Incorrected } \qquad \Sigma d_i^2 = \frac{495}{6} = 82.5$$

$$\text{Corrected } \qquad \Sigma d_i^2 = 82.5 - 3^2 + 7^2 = 122.5$$

$$\therefore \text{ Corrected value of } \quad r = 1 - \frac{6 \times \text{corrected } \Sigma d_i^2}{n(n^2 - 1)} = 1 - \frac{6 \times 122.5}{10 \times 99} = 0.2576.$$

Example 8. *The coefficient of rank correlation of the marks obtained by 10 students in statistics and accountancy was found to be 0.2. It was later discovered that the difference in ranks in the two subjects obtained by one of the students was wrongly taken as 9 instead of 7. Find the correct coefficient of rank correlation.*

Sol. We know
$$r = 1 - \frac{6\Sigma d^2}{n(n^2 - 1)} \qquad \text{...(1)}$$

Given $r = 0.2$, $n = 10$

$$\therefore \quad \text{(1) gives} \quad 0.2 = 1 - \frac{6\Sigma d^2}{10 \times 99}$$

$$\Rightarrow \quad \frac{6\Sigma d^2}{990} = 1 - 0.2 = 0.8 \quad \Rightarrow \quad \Sigma d^2 = \frac{0.8 \times 990}{6} = 132$$

i.e., Incorrected value of $\Sigma d^2 = 132$

$\therefore$ Corrected value of $\Sigma d^2 = 132 -$ (Incorrected item)^2 + (Corrected item)^2

$$= 132 - 9^2 + 7^2 = 100$$

Hence the corrected value of r is given by

$$r = 1 - \frac{6\,(\text{Corrected value of } \Sigma d^2)}{n(n^2 - 1)}$$

$$= 1 - \frac{6 \times 100}{9 \times 10} = 1 - 0.606 = 0.394.$$

Example 9. *Ten competitors in a beauty contest are ranked by three Judges in the following order :*

1st Judge	*1*	*6*	*5*	*10*	*3*	*2*	*4*	*9*	*7*	*8*
2nd Judge	*3*	*5*	*8*	*4*	*7*	*10*	*2*	*1*	*6*	*9*
3rd Judge	*6*	*4*	*9*	*8*	*1*	*2*	*3*	*10*	*5*	*7*

Use the rank correlation coefficient to discuss which pair of Judges have the nearest approach to common test in beauty.

Sol. In order to know which pair of Judges have the nearest approach to common test in beauty, we compare the Rank correlation coefficient between the Judgements of (*i*) 1st and 2nd Judge (*ii*) 1st and 3rd Judge (*iii*) 2nd and 3rd Judge.

Ranking by 1st Judge R_1	*Ranking by 2nd Judge* R_2	*Ranking by 3rd Judge* R_3	$(R_1 - R_2)^2$ d^2	$(R_2 - R_3)^2$ d^2	$(R_3 - R_1)^2$ d^2
1	3	6	4	9	25
6	5	4	1	1	4
5	8	9	9	1	16
10	4	8	36	16	4
3	7	1	16	36	4
2	10	2	64	64	0
4	2	3	4	1	1
9	1	10	64	81	1
7	6	5	1	1	4
8	9	7	1	4	1
			$\Sigma d^2 = 200$	$\Sigma d^2 = 214$	$\Sigma d^2 = 60$

Rank correlation coefficient between the Judgements of 1st and 2nd Judge is given by

$$R_1 = 1 - \frac{6\Sigma d^2}{n(n^2-1)} = 1 - \frac{6 \times 200}{10 \times 99} = 1 - \frac{1200}{990}$$

$$= 1 - 1.212 = -0.212$$

Rank correlation coefficient between the Judgements of 2nd and 3rd Judge is given by

$$R_2 = 1 - \frac{6\Sigma d^2}{n(n^2-1)} = 1 - \frac{6 \times 214}{10 \times 90} = 1 - \frac{1284}{990}$$

$$= 1 - 1.297 = -0.297$$

Rank correlation coefficient between the Judgements of 1st and 3rd Judge is given by

$$R_3 = 1 - \frac{6\Sigma d^2}{n(n^2-1)} = 1 \frac{6 \times 60}{10 \times 99} = 1 - \frac{360}{990} = 0.636$$

Here we observe that the rank correlation coefficient is maximum in the Judgements of the 1st and 3rd Judges.

Conclusion: The pair of 1st and 3rd Judges have the nearest approach to common test in beauty.

12.16. REPEATED RANKS

If any two or more individuals have the same rank or the same value in the series of marks, then the above formula fails and requires an adjustment. In such cases, each individual is given an average rank. This common average rank is the average of the ranks which these individuals would have assumed if they were slightly different from each other. Thus, if two individuals are ranked equal at the sixth place, they would have assumed the 6th and 7th ranks if they were ranked slightly different. Their common rank $= \frac{6+7}{2} = 6.5$. If three individuals are ranked equal at fourth place, they would have assumed the 4th, 5th and 6th ranks if they were ranked slightly different. Their common rank = $\frac{4+5+6}{3} = 5$.

Adjustment. Add $\frac{1}{12}$ $m(m^2 - 1)$ to Σd^2, where m stands for the number of times an item is repeated.

This adjustment factor is to be added for each repeated item.

Thus,
$$r = 1 - \frac{6\left\{\Sigma d^2 + \frac{1}{12} m(m^2 - 1) + \frac{1}{12} m(m^2 - 1) + ...\right\}}{n(n^2 - 1)}.$$

Example 10. *Obtain the rank correlation coefficient for the following data :*

X	*68*	*64*	*75*	*50*	*64*	*80*	*75*	*40*	*55*	*64*
Y	*62*	*58*	*68*	*45*	*81*	*60*	*68*	*48*	*50*	*70*

Sol. Here, marks are given, so write down the ranks.

X	68	64	75	50	64	80	75	40	55	64	Totals
Y	62	58	68	45	81	60	68	48	50	70	
Ranks in X (x)	4	6	2.5	9	6	1	2.5	10	8	6	
Ranks in Y (y)	5	7	3.5	10	1	6	3.5	9	8	2	
$d = x - y$	– 1	– 1	– 1	– 1	5	– 5	– 1	1	0	4	0
d^2	1	1	1	1	25	25	1	1	0	16	72

In the X-series, the value 75 occurs twice. Had these values been slightly different, they would have been given the ranks 2 and 3. Therefore, the common rank given to them is $\frac{2+3}{2} = 2.5$. The value 64 occurs thrice. Had these values been slightly different, they would have been given the ranks 5, 6 and 7. Therefore, the common rank given to them is $\frac{5+6+7}{3} = 6$. Similarly, in the Y-series, the value 68 occurs twice. Had these values been slightly different, they would have been given the ranks 3 and 4. Therefore, the common rank given to them is $\frac{3+4}{2} = 3.5$.

Thus, m has the values 2, 3, 2.

$$\therefore \qquad r = 1 - \frac{6\left\{\Sigma d^2 + \frac{1}{12} m(m^2 - 1) + \frac{1}{12} m\,(m^2 - 1) + ...\right\}}{n(n^2 - 1)}$$

$$= 1 - \frac{6\left[72 + \frac{1}{12} . 2(2^2 - 1) + \frac{1}{12} . 3(3^2 - 1) + \frac{1}{12} . 2(2^2 - 1)\right]}{10(10^2 - 1)}$$

$$= 1 - \frac{6\left[72 + \frac{1}{2} + 2 + \frac{1}{2}\right]}{990} = 1 - \frac{6 \times 75}{990} = \frac{6}{11} = 0.545.$$

TEST YOUR KNOWLEDGE 12.1

1. (*a*) Calculate the correlation coefficient for the following heights in inches of fathers (X) and their sons (Y).

X :	65	66	67	67	68	69	70	72
Y :	67	68	65	68	72	72	69	71

(*b*) Find the correlation coefficient between x and y from the given data :

x :	78	89	97	69	59	79	68	57
y :	125	137	156	112	107	138	123	108

(*P.T.U., M.B.A. Dec. 2006, Dec. 2008*)

(*c*) Find the correlation coefficient from the following data :

x :	92	89	87	86	83	77	71	63	53	50
y :	86	88	91	77	68	85	52	82	37	57

(*d*) Find the regression coefficients of y on x and x on y from the following data :

$\Sigma x = 50$, $\bar{x} = 5$, $\Sigma y = 60$, $\bar{y} = 6$

$\Sigma xy = 350$, $6x^2 = 4$, $6y^2 = 9$, $n = 10$

2. (*a*) Calculate Rank correlation coefficient of correlation from the following data and interpret its value.

Roll No. of students	1	2	3	4	5	6	7
Marks in mathematics	41	23	24	56	45	34	46
Marks in physics	23	45	65	23	12	36	78

(*b*) The following data shows the ages (X) and Blood pressure (Y) of 8 persons.

X	52	63	45	36	72	65	47	25
Y	62	53	51	25	79	43	60	33

Find Karl Pearson's coefficient of correlation between age and blood pressure.

(*c*) Calculate Karl Pearson's coefficient of correlation from the following data and interpret its value.

Roll No. of students	1	2	3	4	5
Marks in mathematics	48	35	17	23	47
Marks in physics	45	20	40	25	45

(*d*) You are given the following information regarding a frequency distribution of 10 observations. $\bar{x} = 5.5$, $\bar{y} = 4.0$, $\Sigma x^2 = 385$, $\Sigma y^2 = 192$, $\Sigma(x + y)^2 = 947$. Find r_{xy}.

3. Calculate the coefficient of correlation for the following ages of husbands and wives :

Husband's age x	23	27	28	28	29	30	31	33	35	36
Wife's age y	18	20	22	27	21	29	27	29	28	29

4. Establish the formula $(\sigma_x - \sigma_y)^2 = \sigma_x^2 + \sigma_y^2 - 2r\sigma_x\sigma_y$, where r is the correlation coefficient between x and y.

5. (*a*) Calculate the coefficient of correlation for the following table :

y \ x	*16–18*	*18–20*	*20–22*	*22–24*
10–20	2	1	1	
20–30	3	2	3	2
30–40	3	4	5	6
40–50	2	2	3	4
50–60	—	1	2	2
60–70	—	1	2	1

(*b*) Find the correlation between x (marks is Mathematics) and y (marks in Engineering Drawing) given in the following data :

y \ x	*10–40*	*40–70*	*70–100*	*Total*
0–30	5	20	—	25
30–60	—	28	2	30
60–90	—	32	13	45
Total	5	80	15	100

6. Ten students got the following percentage of marks in Chemistry and Physics :

Students	1	2	3	4	5	6	7	8	9	10
Marks in Chemistry	78	36	98	25	75	82	90	62	65	39
Marks in Physics	84	51	91	60	68	62	86	58	63	47

Calculate the rank correlation coefficient.

7. Two Judges in a beauty contest rank the ten competitors in the following order :

1st Judge	6	4	3	1	2	7	9	8	10	5
2nd Judge	4	1	6	7	5	8	10	9	3	2

Do the Judges agree in their standard ?

8. The following is record of ranking to 8 participants in a music contest by three Judges A, B, C.

A	3	5	8	4	7	2	1	6
B	6	4	8	1	2	3	5	7
C	1	6	5	3	2	4	7	8

Use Spearman's Rank correlation to see which pair of Judges is more consistent.

9. Ten competitors in a musical test were ranked by the three judges x, y and z in the following order :

Ranks by x	1	6	5	10	3	2	4	9	7	8
Ranks by y	3	5	8	4	7	10	2	1	6	9
Ranks by z	6	4	9	8	1	2	3	10	5	7

Using rank correlation method, discuss which pair of judges has the nearest approach to common likings in music.

10. A sample of 12 fathers and their eldest sons gave the following data about their heights in inches :

Father	65	63	67	64	68	62	70	66	68	67	69	70
Son	68	66	68	65	69	66	68	65	71	67	68	70

Calculate the coefficient of rank correlation.

11. Obtain the rank correlation coefficient between the variables x and y from the following pair of observed values :

x	50	55	65	50	55	60	50	65	70	75
y	110	110	115	125	140	115	130	120	115	160

Answers

1. (*a*) 0.603 (*b*) 0.96 (*c*) 0.7291
(*d*) $b_{xy} = 0.5555$, $b_{yx} = 1.25$

2. (*a*) $r = -0.55$. *i.e.*, the correlation is – ve moderate (*b*) 0.70
(*c*) $r = 0.429$ *i.e.*, the correlation is + ve and low degree. (*d*) $r_{xy} = -0.681$

3. 0.82 **5.** (*a*) 0.28 (*b*) 0.4517

6. 0.84 **7.** $r = 0$ *i.e.*, the Judges do not agree as there is no correlation.

8. 2nd and 3rd Judges **9.** x and z **10.** 0.722

11. 0.155.

12.17. REGRESSION

(*P.T.U., M.B.A. Dec. 2009*)

Regression is the estimation or prediction of unknown values of one variable from known values of another variable.

After establishing the fact of correlation between two variables, it is natural curiosity to know the extent to which one variable varies in response to a given variation in the other variable, *i.e.*, one is interested to know the nature of relationship between the two variables. Thus **Regression measures the nature and extent of correlation.**

12.18. LINEAR REGRESSION

If two variates x and y are correlated, *i.e.*, there exists an association or relationship between them, then the *scatter diagram* will be more or less concentrated round a curve. This curve is called the *curve of regression* and the relationship is said to be expressed by means of *curvilinear regression.* In the particular case, when the curve is a straight line, it is called a *line of regression* and the regression is said to be *linear.*

A line of regression is the straight line which gives the best fit in the least square sense to the given frequency.

If the line of regression is so chosen that the sum of squares of deviations parallel to the axis of y is minimised [See. Fig. (a)], it is called *the line of regression of y on x* and it gives the *best estimate of y for any given value of x.*

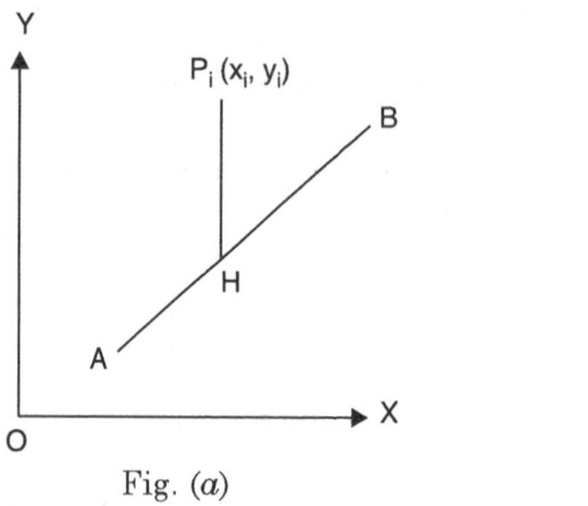

Fig. (a)

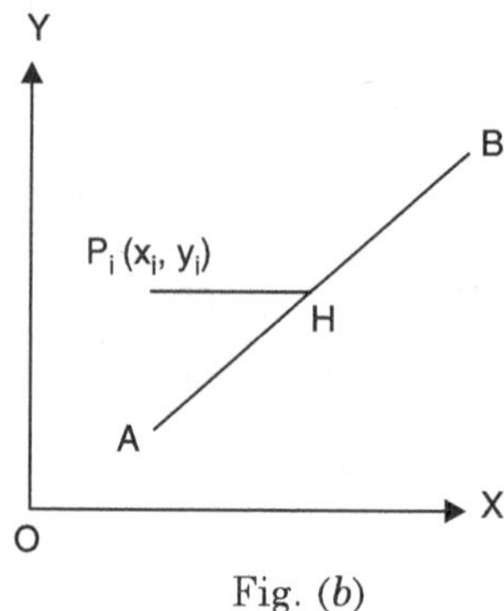

Fig. (b)

If the line of regression is so chosen that the sum of squares of deviations parallel to the axis of x is minimised [See Fig. (b)], it is called *the line of regression of x on y* and it gives the *best estimate of x for any given value of y.*

12.19. EQUATIONS TO THE LINES OF REGRESSION

Let $$y = a + bx \qquad \text{...(1)}$$
be the equation of the line of regression of y on x so that corresponding to $x = x_i$, the expected value of y is Y_i $(= a + bx_i)$ and S, the sum of the squares of deviations of observed value y_i from expected value Y_i is given by

$$S = \sum_{i=1}^{n} (y_i - Y_i)^2 = \sum_{i=1}^{n} (y_i - a - bx_i)^2$$

According to the principle of least squares, we have to choose a and b so that S is minimum. The normal equations are

$$\frac{\partial S}{\partial a} = 0, \qquad \frac{\partial S}{\partial b} = 0$$

or $$-2\Sigma(y_i - a - bx_i) = 0 \quad \text{and} \quad -2\Sigma x_i (y_i - a - bx_i) = 0$$

or $$\Sigma y_i = na + b\Sigma x_i \qquad [\because \ \Sigma a = na] \quad \text{...(2)}$$

and $$\Sigma x_i y_i = a\Sigma x_i + b\Sigma x_i^2 \qquad \text{...(3)}$$

Dividing (2) by n, we have

$$\frac{1}{n} \Sigma y_i = a + b \cdot \frac{1}{n} \Sigma x_i$$

or $$\bar{y} = a + b\bar{x} \qquad \text{...(4)}$$

Subtracting (4) form (1) [to eliminate a, we get

$$y - \bar{y} = b(x - \bar{x}) \qquad \text{...(5)}$$

To find b $$r = \frac{\frac{1}{n}\Sigma x_i y_i - \bar{x}\,\bar{y}}{\sigma_x \sigma_y}$$

$$\Rightarrow \quad \frac{1}{n} \Sigma x_i y_i = r\,\sigma_x\,\sigma_y + \bar{x}\,\bar{y} \qquad \text{...(6)}$$

Dividing (3) by n, we have

$$\frac{1}{n}\Sigma x_i y_i = a \cdot \frac{1}{n}\Sigma x_i + b \cdot \frac{1}{n}\Sigma x_i^2$$

Using (6), $r\sigma_x \sigma_y + \bar{x}\,\bar{y} = a\bar{x} + b \cdot \frac{1}{n}\Sigma x_i^2$ ...(7)

Multiplying (4) by $\bar{x}$, we get

$$\bar{x}\,\bar{y} = a\,\bar{x} + b\,\bar{x}\,\bar{y} \quad ...(8)$$

Subtracting (8) from (7), we get

$$r\sigma_x\sigma_y = b\left(\frac{1}{n}\Sigma x_i^2 - \bar{x}\,\bar{y}\right)$$

or $\quad r\sigma_x\sigma_y = b\sigma_x^2 \qquad \therefore \quad b = \dfrac{r\sigma_y}{\sigma_x}$

$\therefore$ From (5), the line of regression of y on x is

$$y - \bar{y} = \frac{r\sigma_y}{\sigma_x}(x - \bar{x})$$

Similarly, the equation to the line of regression of x on y is

$$x - \bar{x} = \frac{r\sigma_y}{\sigma_x}(y - \bar{y}).$$ *(P.T.U., M.B.A. Dec., 2008)*

Note. From the equations of the two lines of regression, it is clear that both the lines pass through the point $(\bar{x}, \bar{y})$.

Thus, to find the mean of x and y series, solve the equations of the two lines of regression.

Note. $$\frac{r\sigma_x}{\sigma_y} = r \cdot \frac{\sigma_x}{\sigma_y} = \frac{\frac{1}{n}\Sigma xy - \bar{x}\,\bar{y}}{\sigma_x\,\sigma_y} \cdot \frac{\sigma_x}{\sigma_y}$$

$$= \frac{\frac{1}{n}\Sigma xy - \bar{x}\,\bar{y}}{\sigma_y^2} = \frac{\frac{1}{n}\Sigma xy - \bar{x}\,\bar{y}}{\frac{1}{n}\Sigma y^2 - \bar{y}^2}$$

Similarly, $$\frac{r\sigma_y}{\sigma_x} = \frac{\frac{1}{n}\Sigma xy - \bar{x}\,\bar{y}}{\frac{1}{n}\Sigma x^2 - \bar{x}^2}.$$

12.20. REGRESSION COEFFICIENTS

The equation to the line of regression of y on x is $y - \bar{y} = \dfrac{r\sigma_y}{\sigma_x}(x - \bar{x})$

and the equation to the line of regression of x on y is $x - \bar{x} = \dfrac{r\sigma_x}{\sigma_y}(y - \bar{y})$ where $\dfrac{r\sigma_y}{\sigma_x}$ is called the regression co-efficient of y on x and is denoted by b_{yx} and $\dfrac{r\sigma_x}{\sigma_y}$ is called the regression co-efficient of x on y and is denoted by b_{xy}.

Note. If $r = 0$, the two lines of regression become $y = \bar{y}$ an $x = \bar{x}$ which are two straight lines parallel to X and Y-axes respectively and passing through their means $\bar{y}$ and $\bar{x}$. They are mutually perpendicular.

If $r = \pm 1$, the two lines of regression will coincide.

12.21. PROPERTIES OF REGRESSION CO-EFFICIENTS

Property I. *Correlation coefficient is the geometric mean between the regression coefficients or* $r^2 = b_{xy} \cdot b_{yx}$ (P.T.U., M.B.A. Dec. 2007)

Proof. The regression coefficients are $\dfrac{r\sigma_y}{\sigma_x}$ and $\dfrac{r\sigma_x}{\sigma_y}$.

G.M., between them $= \sqrt{\dfrac{r\sigma_y}{\sigma_x} \times \dfrac{r\sigma_x}{\sigma_y}} = \sqrt{r^2} = r =$ Correlation coefficient.

Property II. *If one of the regression coefficients is greater than unity numerically, the other must be less than unity numerically.*

Proof. The two regression coefficients are

$$b_{yx} = \frac{r\sigma_y}{\sigma_x} \quad \text{and} \quad b_{xy} = \frac{r\sigma_x}{\sigma_y}.$$

Let $b_{yx} > 1$, then $\dfrac{1}{b_{yx}} < 1$ ...(1)

Since $b_{yx} \cdot b_{xy} = r^2 \le 1$ $(\because \; -1 \le r \le 1)$

$\therefore$ $b_{xy} \le \dfrac{1}{b_{yx}} < 1$ | Using (1)

Similarly, if $b_{xy} > 1$, then $b_{yx} < 1$.

Property III. *Arithmetic mean of regression coefficients is greater than the correlation coefficient.*

Proof. We have to prove that

$$\frac{b_{yx} + b_{xy}}{2} > r \quad \text{or} \quad \frac{\dfrac{r\sigma_y}{\sigma_x} + \dfrac{r\sigma_x}{\sigma_y}}{2} > r$$

or $\sigma_y^2 + \sigma_x^2 > 2\sigma_x\sigma_y$ or $\sigma_y^2 + \sigma_x^2 - 2\sigma_x\sigma_y > 0$

or $(\sigma_y - \sigma_x)^2 > 0$ which is true.

Hence, the result.

Second Method. We know that A.M. > G.M.

$\therefore$ $\dfrac{b_{yx} + b_{xy}}{2} > \sqrt{b_{yx} \cdot b_{xy}}$ or $\dfrac{b_{yx} + b_{xy}}{2} > r$ $[\because \; r = \sqrt{b_{yx} \cdot b_{xy}}\,]$

$\therefore$ A.M. of regression coefficients is greater than correlation coefficient.

Property IV. *Regression coefficients are independent of the origin but not of the scale.*

Proof. Let $u = \dfrac{x - a}{h}$, $v = \dfrac{y - b}{k}$, where a, b, h and k are constants.

Now, $b_{yx} = \dfrac{r\sigma_y}{\sigma_x} = r \cdot \dfrac{k\sigma_v}{h\sigma_u} = \dfrac{k}{h}\left(\dfrac{r\sigma_v}{\sigma_u}\right) = \dfrac{k}{h}\, b_{vu}$

Similarly, $b_{xy} = \frac{h}{k}\, b_{uv}.$

Thus, b_{yx} and b_{xy} are both independent of a and b but not of h and k.

Property V. *The correlation coefficient and the two regression coefficients have same sign.*

Proof. Regression coefficient of y on $x = b_{yx} = r\frac{\sigma_y}{\sigma_x}$

Regression coefficient of x on $y = b_{xy} = r\frac{\sigma_x}{\sigma_y}$

Since σ_x and σ_y are both positive, b_{yx}, b_{xy} and r have same sign.

12.22. ANGLE BETWEEN TWO LINES OF REGRESSION

Statement. *If θ is the acute angle between the two regression lines in the case of two variables x and y, show that*

$$\tan\theta = \frac{1-r^2}{|r|}\cdot\frac{\sigma_x\sigma_y}{\sigma_x^{\,2}+\sigma_y^{\,2}},$$ *where r, σ_x, σ_y have their usual meanings.*

Explain the significance of the formula when r = 0 and r = ± 1.

(P.T.U., M.B.A. May 2008, Dec. 2008)

Proof. Equations to the lines of regression of y on x and x on y are

$$y-\bar{y} = \frac{r\sigma_y}{\sigma_x}(x-\bar{x}) \quad\text{and}\quad x-\bar{x} = \frac{r\sigma_x}{\sigma_y}(y-\bar{y})$$

Their slopes are $m_1 = \frac{r\sigma_y}{\sigma_x}$ and $m_2 = \frac{\sigma_y}{r\sigma_x}$.

$$\therefore \quad \tan\theta = \left|\frac{m_2-m_1}{1+m_2\,m_1}\right| = \left|\frac{\dfrac{\sigma_y}{r\sigma_x}-\dfrac{r\sigma_y}{\sigma_x}}{1+\dfrac{\sigma_y^2}{\sigma_x^2}}\right|$$

$$= \left|\frac{1-r^2}{r}\cdot\frac{\sigma_y}{\sigma_x}\cdot\frac{\sigma_x^2}{\sigma_y^2+\sigma_y^2}\right| = \frac{1-r^2}{|r|}\cdot\frac{\sigma_x\,\sigma_y}{\sigma_x^2+\sigma_y^2}$$

Since $r^2 < 1$, and σ_x, σ_y are positive.

Hence, $$\tan\theta = \frac{1-r^2}{|r|}\cdot\frac{\sigma_x\sigma_y}{\sigma_x^2+\sigma_y^2}$$

Significance of the formula

When r = 0, $\theta = \frac{\pi}{2}$

∴ The two lines of regression are perpendicular to each other.

Hence, the estimated value of y is the same for all values of x and *vice versa.*

When r = ± 1, $\tan\theta = 0$ so that, $\theta = 0$ or π.

Hence, the lines of regression coincide and there is perfect correlation between the two variates x and y.

ILLUSTRATIVE EXAMPLES

Example 1. *From two series x and y, Cov (x, y) = 25. r = 0.6, $\sigma_x^2 = 36$. Calculate standard deviation of y.*

Sol. We know $r_{xy} = \frac{\text{Cov}(x, y)}{\sigma_x \cdot \sigma_y} \Rightarrow 0.6 = \frac{25}{6 . \sigma_y}$

$$\Rightarrow \quad \sigma_y = \frac{25}{(0.6)(6)} = 6.944.$$

Example 2. (*a*) *Find the value of the correlation coefficient if $b_{yx} = -6$ and $b_{xy} = -1.35$.*

(*b*) *If $\sigma_x^2 = 9$, $\sigma_y^2 = 1600$, $r_{xy} = 0.5$, find b_{xy}.*

(*c*) *If $\sigma_x^2 = 9$, $\sigma_y^2 = 4$, $b_{xy} = 1.5$, find r.*

Sol. (*a*) We know that the correlation coefficient is the geometric mean of the regression coefficients, *i.e.*, $r_{xy} = \sqrt{b_{xy}\, b_{yx}} = \sqrt{(-6) \times (-1.35)} = \sqrt{8.1} = 2.846.$

(*b*) We know, $b_{xy} = \frac{r\,\sigma_x}{\sigma_y} \Rightarrow b_{xy} = \frac{(0.5)\,3}{40} = \frac{0.15}{40} = 0.00375.$ $\quad | \; r = r_{xy}$

(*c*) We know, $b_{xy} = \frac{r\sigma_x}{\sigma_y} \Rightarrow 1.5 = \frac{r\,(3)}{2}$

$\Rightarrow \quad r = \frac{(1.5)(2)}{3} = 1$, *i.e.*, there is perfect +ve correlation.

Example 3. *If r = 0, show that the two lines of regression are parallel to the axes.*

Sol. Equations to the two lines of regression are

$$y - \bar{y} = \frac{r\sigma_y}{\sigma_x}(x - \bar{x}) \quad \text{and} \quad x - \bar{x} = \frac{r\sigma_x}{\sigma_y} = (y - \bar{y})$$

When $r = 0$, they reduce to $y = \bar{y}$ and $x = \bar{x}$ which are equations of lines parallel to x-axis and y-axis respectively.

Example 4. *If the two regression coefficients are 0.8 and 1.2, what would be the value of coefficient of correlation ?*

Sol. Since the coefficient of correlation is the G.M. between the regression coefficients

$\therefore \quad r^2 = 0.8 \times 0.2 = 0.16, \quad r = \pm 0.4$

Since r has same sign as the two regression coefficients.

$\therefore$ r must be +ve. Hence, $r = 0.4$.

Example 5. *Is the following statement correct ? Give reasons. The regression coefficient of x on y is 3.2 and that of y on x is 0.8.*

Sol. $b_{xy} = 3.2,\ b_{yx} = 0.8$

Now $r^2 = b_{xy} \times b_{yx} = 3.2 \times 0.8 = 2.56 > 1$

Since $r^2 \le 1$ always, the given statement is false.

Example 6. (*a*) *Is the following statement true ? Give reasons.*

$$40x - 18y = 5 \quad \text{and} \quad 8x - 10y + 6 = 0$$

are respectively the regression equations of y on x and x on y.

(*b*) *Two random variables have the regression equations :*

$3x + 2y - 26 = 0,\ 6x + y - 31 = 0$ (P.T.U., M.B.A. May 2009)

Find the mean values and the coefficient of correlation between x and y. If the variance of x is 25, find the standard deviation of y from the data given above.

Sol. (*a*) Regression equation of y on x is

$$40x - 18y = 5 \quad \text{or} \quad 18y = 40x - 5$$

or $$y = \frac{20}{9}x - \frac{5}{18}$$

$\Rightarrow$ Regression coefficient of y on $x = b_{xy} = \dfrac{20}{9}$

Regression equation of x and y is $8x - 10y + 6 = 0$

or $$8x = 10y - 6$$

or $$x = \frac{5}{4}y - \frac{3}{4}$$

$\Rightarrow$ Regression coefficient of x on $y = b_{xy} = \dfrac{5}{4}$

Now $$r^2 = b_{yx} \cdot b_{xy} = \left(\frac{20}{9}\right)\left(\frac{5}{4}\right) = \frac{25}{9} > 1$$

But r^2 is always ≤ 1.

$\therefore$ The statement is false.

(*b*) Given $3x + 2y - 26 = 0$ ...(1)

$6x + y - 31 = 0$ ...(2)

The mean values of x and y are the values of x and y given by (1) and (2). Multiplying (2) by 2 and subtracting from (1), we get

$$-9x + 36 = 0$$

$\Rightarrow$ $x = 4$ *i.e.*, $\overline{x} = 4$

From (1), $12 + 2y - 26 = 0$

$\Rightarrow$ $y = 7$ *i.e.*, $\overline{y} = 7$.

Calculation of correlation coefficient.

From (1), $2y = -3y + 26$

$$\Rightarrow \quad y = -\frac{3}{2}x + 13 = -\frac{3}{2}\left(x - \frac{26}{3}\right)$$

i.e., $$r\frac{\sigma_y}{\sigma_x} = -1.5 \qquad \text{...(3)}$$

Also from (2), $6x = -y + 31$, $x = -\dfrac{y}{6} + 31 = -\dfrac{1}{6}(y - 186)$

i.e., $$r\frac{\sigma_x}{\sigma_y} = -\frac{1}{6} \qquad \text{...(4)}$$

From (3), (4), $r^2 = (-1.5)\left(-\dfrac{1}{6}\right) \Rightarrow r^2 = 0.25 \Rightarrow r = \pm 0.5$

Take $r = -0.5$ | The sign of r and regression coefficients are same.

Again, from (3), $r\dfrac{\sigma_y}{\sigma_x} = -1.5$

$$\Rightarrow \quad (-0.5)\frac{\sigma_y}{5} = -1.5 \Rightarrow \sigma_y = \frac{(1.5)(5)}{0.5} = 15.$$

Example 7. (*a*) *Consider the two regression lines $3x + 2y = 26$, $6x + y = 31$. Find the mean values of the series x and y.*

(*b*) *From the following data, compute the value of y when $x = 2.5$*

$$\bar{x} = 5,\ \bar{y} = 6,\ \Sigma xy = 350,\ \Sigma x^2 = 290,\ \Sigma y^2 = 450,\ n = 10.$$

Sol. (*a*) We know that, the mean value of the given series, say, $(\bar{x}, \bar{y})$ satisfies the regression lines, *i.e.*, $3\bar{x} + 2\bar{y} = 26$ ...(1)

$$6\bar{x} + \bar{y} = 31 \quad ...(2)$$

Operating (1) – 2 × (2), we get $-9\bar{x} = -36 \Rightarrow \bar{x} = 4$

Form (2) $\bar{y} = 31 - 24 = 7$, *i.e.*, $\bar{x} = 4$, $\bar{y} = 7$.

(*b*) Let r_{xy} be the correlation coefficient between the two variables *x* and *y*, then

$$r_{xy} = \frac{\frac{1}{n}\Sigma x_i y_i - \bar{x}\,\bar{y}}{\sqrt{\left(\frac{1}{n}\Sigma x_i^2 - \bar{x}^2\right)\left(\frac{1}{n}\Sigma y_i^2 - \bar{y}^2\right)}} \quad ...(1)$$

Here, $\bar{x} = 5 \Rightarrow \frac{\Sigma x}{n} = 5 \Rightarrow \Sigma x = 50.$

Also, $\bar{y} = 6$

$\Rightarrow \frac{\Sigma y}{n} = 6 \Rightarrow \Sigma y = 60$ | $n = 10$

∴ Using all these values in (1), we have

$$r_{xy} = \frac{\frac{1}{10}(350) - (5)(6)}{\sqrt{\left(\frac{1}{10}(290) - 25\right)\left(\frac{1}{10}(450) - 36\right)}} = \frac{5}{\sqrt{(4)(9)}} = \frac{5}{6}$$

Also, $\sigma_x^2 = \frac{1}{n}\Sigma x_i^2 - \bar{x}^2 = \frac{1}{10}(290) - 25 = 4 \Rightarrow \sigma_x = 2$

$$\sigma_y^2 = \frac{1}{n}\Sigma y_i^2 - \bar{y}^2 = \frac{1}{10}(450) - 36 = 45 - 36 = 9 \Rightarrow \sigma_y = 3$$

∴ $b_{xy} = \frac{r_{xy}\,\sigma_x}{\sigma_y} = \frac{5}{6} \cdot \frac{2}{3} = \frac{5}{9}$

$$b_{yx} = \frac{r_{xy}\,\sigma_y}{\sigma_x} = \frac{5}{6} \cdot \frac{3}{2} = \frac{5}{4}$$

Now the lines of regression of *y* on *x* is

$$y - \bar{y} = b_{yx}(x - \bar{x})$$

or $y - 6 = \frac{5}{4}(x - 5) \Rightarrow 4y - 24 = 5x - 25$

$\Rightarrow 5x - 4y - 1 = 0$ ...(2)

When $x = 2.5$, from (2), $5 - 4y - 1 = 0 \Rightarrow 4 = 4y \Rightarrow y = 1.$

Example 8. *Calculate the coefficient of correlation and obtain the least square regression lines for the following data :*

x	1	2	3	4	5	6	7	8	9
y	9	8	10	12	11	13	14	16	15

Also obtain an estimate of y which should correspond on the average to x = 6.2.

Sol. Take Assumed mean A = 5, B = 12

x	y	$u = x - 5$	$v = y - 12$	u^2	v^2	uv
1	9	– 4	– 3	16	9	12
2	8	– 3	– 4	9	16	12
3	10	– 2	– 2	4	4	4
4	12	– 1	0	1	0	0
5	11	0	1	0	1	0
6	13	1	1	1	1	1
7	14	2	2	4	4	4
8	16	3	4	9	16	12
9	15	4	3	16	9	12
Total		$\Sigma u = 0$	$\Sigma v = 0$	$\Sigma u^2 = 60$	$\Sigma v^2 = 60$	$\Sigma uv = 57$

$$r_{xy} = r_{uv} = \frac{\frac{1}{n}\Sigma uv - \bar{u}\,\bar{v}}{\sqrt{\left(\frac{1}{n}\Sigma u^2 - \bar{u}^2\right)\left(\frac{1}{n}\Sigma v^2 - \bar{v}^2\right)}} \qquad \left|\ \bar{u} = \frac{\Sigma u}{n} = 0,\quad \bar{v} = \frac{\Sigma v}{n} = 0\right.$$

$$= \frac{\frac{1}{9}(57) - 0}{\sqrt{\left[\frac{1}{9}(60) - 0\right]\left[\frac{1}{9}(60) - 0\right]}} = \frac{\frac{1}{9}(57)}{\frac{1}{9}(60)} = \frac{19}{20} = 0.95$$

$$\therefore \qquad r\frac{\sigma_y}{\sigma_x} = \frac{r\sigma_v}{\sigma_u} = \frac{\frac{1}{n}\Sigma uv - \bar{u}\,\bar{v}}{\frac{1}{n}\Sigma u^2 - \bar{u}^2} = \frac{\frac{1}{9}(57) - 0}{\frac{1}{9}(60) - 0} = \frac{19}{20} = 0.95 \quad |\ r = r_{xy}$$

Also, $\bar{x} = A + \frac{1}{n}\Sigma u = 5 + \frac{1}{9}\Sigma u = 5$, $\quad \bar{y} = B + \frac{1}{n}\Sigma v = 12 + \frac{1}{9}\Sigma v = 12$

Equation to the line of regression of y on x is

$$y - \bar{y} = \frac{r\sigma_y}{\sigma_x}(x - \bar{x})$$

or $\qquad y - 12 = 0.95\,(x - 5)$

or $\qquad y = 0.95x + 7.25$

When $x = 6.2$, estimated value of $y = 0.95 \times 6.2 + 7.25 = 5.89 + 7.25 = 13.14$

$$\text{Now} \qquad r\frac{\sigma_x}{\sigma_y} = r\frac{\sigma_u}{\sigma_v} = \frac{\frac{1}{n}\Sigma uv - \bar{u}\,\bar{v}}{\frac{1}{n}\Sigma v^2 - \bar{v}^2} = \frac{\frac{1}{9}(57) - 0}{\frac{1}{9}(60) - 0} = \frac{19}{20} = 0.95$$

Equation to the line of regression of x on y is

$$x - \bar{x} = \frac{r\sigma_x}{\sigma_y}(y - \bar{y})$$

or $$x - 5 = 0.95\,(y - 12) \quad \text{or} \quad x = 0.95y - 6.4.$$

Example 9. *A panel of Judges A and B graded seven debators and independently awarded the following marks :*

Debators	*1*	*2*	*3*	*4*	*5*	*6*	*7*
Marks by A	*40*	*34*	*28*	*30*	*44*	*38*	*31*
Marks by B	*32*	*39*	*26*	*30*	*38*	*34*	*28*

An 8th debator was awarded 36 marks by Judge A while Judge B was not present. If Judge B were also present, how many marks would you expect him to award to the 8th debator assuming that the same degree of relationship exists in their judgement ?

Sol. Denote the marks of A by x and marks of B by y. The marks expected to be awarded by Judge B can be determined by fitting regression line of y on x.

Calculation of regression line of y on x. Take Assumed means A = 35, B = 30

x	$u = x - 35$	u^2	y	$v = y - B$	u^2	uv
40	5	25	32	2	4	10
34	1	1	39	9	81	9
28	– 7	49	26	– 4	16	28
30	– 5	25	30	0	0	0
44	9	81	38	8	64	72
38	3	9	34	4	16	12
31	– 4	16	28	– 2	4	8
$\Sigma x = 245$	$\Sigma u = 0$	$\Sigma u^2 = 206$	$\Sigma y = 227$	$\Sigma v = 17$	$\Sigma v^2 = 185$	$\Sigma uv = 139$

The regression equation of y on x is given by

$$y - \bar{y} = r\frac{\sigma_y}{\sigma_x}(x - \bar{x}) \qquad \text{...(1)}$$

Here, $$\bar{y} = \frac{\Sigma y}{n} = \frac{227}{7} = 32.43\ ;\ \bar{x} = \frac{\Sigma x}{n} = \frac{245}{7} = 35$$

$$\bar{u} = \frac{\Sigma u}{n} = 0, \bar{v} = \frac{\Sigma v}{n} = \frac{17}{7} = 2.42$$

$\therefore$ $$r\frac{\sigma_y}{\sigma_x} = \frac{\frac{1}{n}\Sigma uv - \bar{u}\,\bar{v}}{\frac{1}{n}\Sigma u^2 - (\bar{u})^2}, = \frac{\frac{1}{7}\times 139 - 0}{\frac{1}{7}\times 206 - 0} = \frac{139}{206} = 0.6747$$

$\therefore$ From (1), $y - 32.43 = 0.6747(x - 35) = 0.6747x - 23.61$

$\Rightarrow$ $$y = 8.38 + 0.6747x \qquad \text{...(2)}$$

Now, if $x = 36$, (2) gives $y = 8.38 + 0.6747\ (36)$

$= 32.6692 \cong 33$

Thus if Judge B were also present, he would have awarded 33 marks to the 8th debator.

Example 10. *From the data given below. Find*

(i) The coefficient of correlation between marks in economics and statistics

(ii) The two regression equations

(iii) The most likely marks in statistics when the marks in economics are 30.

Marks in Eco.	*25*	*28*	*35*	*32*	*31*	*36*	*29*	*38*	*34*	*32*
Marks in Sta.	*43*	*46*	*49*	*41*	*36*	*32*	*31*	*30*	*33*	*39*

Sol. (*i*) Denote the marks in economics by x and of statistics by y.

Take Assumed mean A = 31, B = 36.

Consider the following table :

x	y	$u = x - 31$	$v = y - 36$	u^2	v^2	uv
25	43	− 6	7	36	49	− 42
28	46	− 3	10	9	100	− 30
35	49	4	13	16	169	52
32	41	1	5	1	25	5
31 = A	36 = B	0	0	0	0	0
36	32	5	− 4	25	16	− 20
29	31	− 2	− 5	4	25	10
38	30	7	− 6	49	36	− 42
34	33	3	−3	9	9	− 9
32	39	1	3	1	9	3
Total		$\Sigma u = 10$	$\Sigma v = 20$	$\Sigma u^2 = 150$	$\Sigma v^2 = 438$	$\Sigma uv = -73$

Here $\quad \bar{u} = \dfrac{\Sigma u}{n} = \dfrac{10}{10} = 1\ ;\ \bar{v} = \dfrac{\Sigma v}{n} = \dfrac{20}{10} = 2$

$$\therefore \qquad r_{xy} = r_{uv} = \frac{\frac{1}{n}\Sigma\, uv - \bar{u}\,\bar{v}}{\sqrt{\left(\frac{1}{n}\Sigma u^2 - \bar{u}^2\right)\left(\frac{1}{n}\Sigma v^2 - \bar{v}^2\right)}}$$

$$= \frac{\frac{1}{10} \times (-73) - 2}{\sqrt{\left(\frac{1}{10} \times 150 - 1\right)\left(\frac{1}{10} \times 438 - 4\right)}}$$

$$= \frac{-9.3}{\sqrt{(14)\,(39.8)}} = \frac{-9.3}{23.60}$$

$$= -0.3940$$

(*ii*) **Calculation of regression equations. We know**

$$r\frac{\sigma_y}{\sigma_x} = r\frac{\sigma_v}{\sigma_u} = \frac{\frac{1}{n}\Sigma uv - \bar{u}\,\bar{v}}{\frac{1}{n}\Sigma u^2 - \bar{u}^2} = \frac{\frac{1}{10}(-73) - 2}{\frac{1}{10}\times(150) - 1} = \frac{-9.3}{14} = -0.6642$$

Also
$$\bar{x} = A + \frac{1}{n}\Sigma u = 31 + \frac{1}{10}\times 10 = 32$$
$$\bar{y} = B + \frac{1}{n}\Sigma v = 36 + \frac{1}{10}\times 20 = 38$$

∴ The equation to the line of regression of y on x is

$$y - \bar{y} = r\frac{\sigma_y}{\sigma_x}(x - \bar{x})$$

$$\Rightarrow \quad y - 38 = (-0.6642)(x - 32) = -0.6642x + 21.25$$

$$\Rightarrow \quad 0.6642x + y - 59.25 = 0 \quad \ldots(1)$$

Further,
$$r\frac{\sigma_x}{\sigma_y} = r\frac{\sigma_u}{\sigma_v} = \frac{\frac{1}{u}\Sigma uv - \bar{u}\,\bar{v}}{\frac{1}{n}\Sigma v^2 - \bar{v}^2} = \frac{\frac{1}{10}(-73) - 2}{\frac{1}{10}(438) - 4} = \frac{-9.3}{39.8} = -0.2336$$

∴ The equation to the line of regression of x on y is

$$x - \bar{x} = r\frac{\sigma_x}{\sigma_y}(y - \bar{y})$$

$$\Rightarrow \quad x - 32 = (-0.2336)(y - 38) = -0.2336y + 8.8768$$

$$\Rightarrow \quad x + 0.2336y - 40.8768 = 0 \quad \ldots(2)$$

The equations (1) and (2) are the required equations of regressions.

(*iii*) When the marks in economics are 30 *i.e.*, $x = 30$ then from (1),

$$(0.6642)\times 30 + y - 59.25 = 0$$

$$\Rightarrow \quad y = 59.25 - 19.92 \cong 39.33.$$

Example 11. *Heights of fathers and sons is given. Form the two lines of regressing using this data:* (P.T.U., M.B.A. May 2009)

Height of fathers (inches)	*65*	*66*	*67*	*67*	*68*	*69*	*71*	*73*
Height of sons (inches)	*67*	*68*	*64*	*68*	*72*	*70*	*69*	*70*

Sol. Let x and y denote the heights of fathers and sons respectively. Take assumed means A = 67, B = 68.

x	y	$u = x - A$	$v = y - B$	u^2	v^2	uv
65	67	–2	–1	4	1	2
66	68	–1	0	1	0	0
67	64	0	– 4	0	16	0
67	68	0	0	0	0	0
68	72	1	4	1	16	4
69	70	2	2	4	4	4
71	69	4	1	16	1	4
73	70	6	2	36	4	12
Total		$\Sigma u = 10$	$\Sigma v = 4$	$\Sigma u^2 = 62$	$\Sigma v^2 = 42$	$\Sigma uv = 26$

Here $\bar{u} = \frac{\Sigma u}{n} = \frac{10}{8} = 1.25 \,; \bar{v} = \frac{\Sigma v}{n} = \frac{4}{8} = 0.50$

$$r\frac{\sigma_y}{\sigma_x} = r\frac{\sigma_v}{\sigma_u} = \frac{\frac{1}{n}\Sigma uv - \bar{u}\,\bar{v}}{\frac{1}{n}\Sigma u^2 - \bar{u}^2} = \frac{\frac{1}{8}\times 26 - (1.25)(0.50)}{\frac{1}{8}\times 62 - (1.25)^2}$$

$$= \frac{3.25 - 0.0625}{7.75 - 1.5625} = \frac{3.1875}{6.1875} = 0.5151$$

Also $$r\frac{\sigma_x}{\sigma_y} = r\frac{\sigma_u}{\sigma_v} = \frac{\frac{1}{n}\Sigma uv - \bar{u}\,\bar{v}}{\frac{1}{n}\Sigma v^2 - \bar{v}^2} = \frac{\frac{1}{8}\times 26 - (1.25)(0.50)}{\frac{1}{8}\times 42 - (0.50)^2}$$

$$= \frac{3.1875}{5.25 - 0.25} = \frac{3.1875}{5} = 0.6375$$

The equation of line of regression of y on x is

$$y - \bar{y} = r\frac{\sigma_y}{\sigma_x}(x - \bar{x}) \quad \text{...(1)}$$

where $\bar{x} = A + \frac{1}{n}\Sigma u = 67 + \frac{10}{8} = 68.25$

and $\bar{y} = B + \frac{1}{n}\Sigma v = 68 + \frac{4}{8} = 68.50$

(1) gives $y - 68.50 = (0.5151)(x - 68.25)$

or $y - 0.5151x - 68.50 + 35.155 = 0$

or $y - 0.5151x - 33.375 = 0$ ...(2)

The equation of line of regression of x on y is

$$x - \bar{x} = r\frac{\sigma_x}{\sigma_y}(y - \bar{y})$$

or $x - 68.25 = 0.6375(y - 68.50)$

or $x - 68.25 - 0.6375 + 43.66 = 0$

or $x - 0.6375y - 24.59 = 0$ ...(3)

Equations (2) and (3) are the required lines of regressions.

Example 12. *(a) Following table gives average daily per capita expenditure on food items (Y) and average per capita total daily expenditure (X) for different income classes.*

Y	11.7	7.8	6.3	13.7	15.2	18.1	24.2	30.8	52.9	50.2	54.0
X	195	230	274	312	344	491	645	863	1175	1180	1500

Find linear regression of Y on X and interpret the results.

(b) Also find correlation coefficient between X and Y and interpret.

(P.T.U. M.B.A. December 2009)

Sol. (*a*) Take assumed means A = 491, B = 18.1. Consider the following table:

X	$U = X - A$	u^2	y	$v = y - B$	v^2	uv
195	–296	87616	11.7	–6.4	40.96	1894.4
230	–261	68121	7.8	–10.3	106.09	2688.3
274	–217	47089	6.3	–11.8	139.24	2560.6
312	–179	32041	13.7	–4.4	19.36	787.6
344	–147	21609	15.2	–2.9	8.41	426.3
491	0	0	18.1	0	0	0
645	154	23716	24.2	6.1	37.21	939.4
863	372	138384	30.8	12.7	161.29	4724.4
1175	684	467856	52.9	34.8	1211.04	23803.2
1180	689	474721	50.2	32.1	1030.41	22116.9
1500	1009	1018081	54.0	35.9	1288.81	36223.9
$\Sigma X = 7209$	$\Sigma u = 1808$	$\Sigma u^2 = 2379234$	$\Sigma y = 284.9$	$\Sigma v = 85.8$	$\Sigma v^2 = 4042.82$	$\Sigma uv = 96164.2$

The regression equation of y on x is given by $y - \bar{y} = r\dfrac{\sigma_y}{\sigma_x}(x - \bar{x})$ ...(1)

where $\bar{y} = \dfrac{284.9}{11} = 25.9, \bar{x} = \dfrac{7209}{11} = 655.36$

and
$$r\frac{\sigma_y}{\sigma_x} = \frac{\frac{1}{n}\Sigma uv - \bar{u}\,\bar{v}}{\frac{1}{n}\Sigma u^2 - (\bar{u})^2} = \frac{\frac{96164.2}{11} - (164.36)(7.8)}{\frac{2379234}{11} - (164.36)^2} = \frac{8742.2 - 1282.008}{216294 - 27014.20}$$

$$= \frac{7460.172}{189279.8} = 0.3941, \quad \bar{u} = \frac{\Sigma u}{n} = \frac{1808}{11} = 164.36, \bar{v} = \frac{\Sigma v}{n} = \frac{85.8}{11} = 7.8$$

∴ (1) gives $y - 25.9 = 0.3941\ (x - 655.36)$

or $(0.3941)x - 258.27 - y + 25.9 = 0$ or $(0.3941)\ x - y - 232.37 = 0$

(*b*) Further, the correlation coefficient between X and Y is given by

$$r_{xy} = r_{uv} = \frac{\frac{1}{n}\Sigma uv - \bar{u}\,\bar{v}}{\sqrt{\frac{1}{n}\Sigma u^2 - (\bar{u})^2}\sqrt{\frac{1}{n}\Sigma v^2 - \bar{v}^2}} = \frac{7460.192}{\sqrt{189279.8}\sqrt{306.68}} \quad |\text{proceeding as above}$$

$$= \frac{7460.192}{(435.00)(17.51)} = \frac{7460.192}{7617.1} = 0.9792$$

Example 13. *Why regression is known as a cause-and-effect analysis?*

(P.T.U. M.B.A. May 2011)

Sol. In regression analysis, one variable is taken as dependent variable and other variable as independent variable. Due to this, we can study the casuse and effect relationship. Hence, regression analysis is, some times, known as cause-and-effect analysis.

Example 14. *Distinguish between correlation and regression*

(P.T.U. M.B.A. Dec. 2010)

Sol.

	Correlation	*Regression*
1.	It is used to measure the degree of covariability between two variables.	It is used to study the nature of relationship between the two variables.
2.	It is a tool of ascertaining the degree of relationship between the two variables and due to this, we cannot say that one variable is cause and other is effect.	In regression, one variable is dependent and the other is independent. Due to this, we can study the cause and effect relationship.
3.	In correlation, r_{xy} is a measure of direction and degree of linear relationship between the two variables x and y. Also r_{xy} and r_{yx} are symmetric. Due to this, any one variable may be treated as independent variable and the other as dependent variable.	In regression, the coefficients b_{xy} and b_{yx} are not symmetric. Due to this, it makes a difference as to which variable is dependent and which is independent.
4.	We can have non-sense correlation between the two variables which is purely due to chance and has no practical relevance. Example, increase in income and increase in weight of a group of people.	There is nothing like non-sense regression.
5.	Correlation coefficient is independent of change of scale and origin.	Regression coefficients are independent of change of origin but not of scale.

TEST YOUR KNOWLEDGE 12.2

1. If $r = 0$, show that the two lines of regression are paralled to the axes.

2. If the two regression coefficients are 0.8 and 0.2, what would be the value of coefficient of correlation.

3. (*a*) Find the correlation coefficient and the equations of regression lines for the following values of x and y :

x :	1	2	3	4	5
y :	2	5	3	8	7

(*b*) Find the correlation coefficient between x and y for the given values. Find also the two regression lines.

x :	1	2	3	4	5	6	7	8	9	10
y :	10	12	16	28	25	36	41	49	40	50

(*c*) Discuss uses of regression analysis.

4. The two regression equations of the variables x and y are $x = 19.13 - 0.87$ and $y = 11.64 - 0.50x$. Find (*i*) mean of x's, (*ii*) mean of y's and (*iii*) the correlation coefficient between x and y.

5. Two random variables have the regression lines with equations $3x + 2y = 26$ and $6x + y = 31$. Find the mean values and the correlation coefficient between x and y.

6. In a partially destroyed laboratory data, only the equations giving the two lines of regression of y on x and x on y are available and are respectively $7x - 16y + 9 = 0$, $5y - 4x - 3 = 0$.

Calculate the coefficient of correlation, $\overline{x}$ and $\overline{y}$.

7. Find the most likely production corresponding to a rainfall 40″ from the following data :

	Rainfall	*Production*
Average	30″	500 kg
Standard Deviation	5″	100 kg

Co-efficient of correlation = 0.8.

8. You are given the following information about advertising and sales :

	Adv. Exp (X) ₹ crores	*Sales (Y) ₹ crores*
Mean	20	100
S.D.	5	12

Correlation coefficient = 0.8

(*i*) Calculate the two regression lines

(*ii*) Find the likely sales when advertisement expenditure is ₹. 25 crores

(*iii*) What should be advertisement expenditure if the company wants to attain sales target of ₹ 130 crores ?

9. By using the following data, find out the two lines of regression and from them compute the Karl Pearson's coefficient of correlation.

$$\Sigma x = 250,\ \Sigma xy = 7900,\ \Sigma x^2 = 6500,\ \Sigma y^2 = 10000,\ n = 10.$$

10. For a given set of bivariate data, the following results were obtained.

$\overline{x} = 53.2$, $\overline{y} = 27.9$, Regression coefficient of y on $x = -1.5$,

Regression coefficient of x on $y = -0.2$. Find the most probable error of y when $x = 60$.

11. Given two regression lines: $x = \dfrac{y}{2}$ and $y = 6x - 4$ and standard deviation of x is 3. Find the coefficient of correlation, standard deviation of y. What percentage of variation is not explained by the variables? (*P.T.U. M.B.A. May 2011*)

Answers

2. 0.4

3. (*a*) $r = 0.8$; $y = 1.3x + 1.1$; $x = 0.5y + 0.5$

(*b*) $r = 0.96$; $y = 1.3x + 1.1$; $x = 0.2y - 0.64$

4. (*i*) 15.79 (*ii*) 3.74 (*iii*) – 0.66

5. $\overline{x} = 9.06$, $\overline{y} = 5.52$, $r = 0.46$ **6.** $r = 0.7395$, $\overline{x} = -0.1034$, $\overline{y} = 0.5172$

7. The most likely production corresponding to a rainfall of 30″ is 660 kg.

8. (*i*) $x = -13.3 + 0.333y$; $y = 61.6 + 1.92x$

(*ii*) Advertisement expenditure = ₹. 109.6 crores

(*iii*) ₹. 29.99 crores.

9. $x = 13 + (0.4)y$; $y = 1.6x + 10$; $r = 0.8$

10. 17.7

11. $\sigma y = 11\sqrt{3}$ and $r = 0.03$ means 0.03% o the total variation can be explained by the variables *i.e.*, 99.97% of the total variation cannot be explained.

12.23. CASE STUDIES

Made in China : The phrase 'Made in China' has become an issue of concern in the last few years, as Indian Companies try to protect their products from overseas competition. In these years a major trade imbalance in India has been caused by a flood of imported goods that enter the country and are sold at lower price than comparable Indian made goods. One prime concern is the electronic goods in which total imported items have steadily increased during the year 1990s to 2004s. The Indian companies have been worried on complaints about product quality, worker layoffs, and high prices and has spent millions in advertising to produce electronic goods that will satisfy consumer demands. Have these companies been successful in stopping the flood of these imported goods purchased by Indian consumers? The given data represent the volume of imported goods sold in India for the years 1999-2004. To simplify the analysis, we have coded the year using the coded variable x = Year 1989.

Year	*x = Year 1989*	*Volume of Import (in ₹ billion)*
1989	0	1.1
1990	1	1.3
1991	2	1.6
1992	3	1.6
1993	4	1.8
1994	5	1.4
1995	6	1.6
1996	7	1.5
1997	8	2.1
1998	9	2.0
1999	10	2.3
2000	11	2.4
2001	12	2.3
2002	13	2.2
2003	14	2.4
2004	15	2.4

Questions for Discussion

1. *Find the least-squares line for predicting the volume of import as a function of year for the years 1989-2000.*
2. *Is there a significant linear relationship between the volume of import and the year?*
3. *Predict the volume of import of goods using 95% prediction intervals for each of the years 2001, 2002, 2003 and 2004.*
4. *Do the predictions obtained in step 3 provided accurate estimates of the actual values observed in these years? Explain.*
5. *Add the data for 1989-2004 to your database, and recalclate the regression line. What effect have the new data points had on the slope? What is the effect of SSE?*
6. *Given the form of the scattered diagram for the years 1989-2004, does it appear that a straight line provides an accurate model for the data? What other types of model might be more appropriate?*

Sol. Let y denotes the volume of imported goods sold in India and x denotes the year. Consider the following Table.

Year	x	y	y^2	x^2	xy
1989	0	1.1	1.21	0	0
1990	1	1.3	1.69	1	1.3
1991	2	1.6	2.56	4	3.2
1992	3	1.6	2.56	9	4.8
1993	4	1.8	3.24	16	7.2
1994	5	1.4	1.96	25	7
1995	6	1.6	2.56	36	9.6
1996	7	1.5	2.25	49	10.5
1997	8	2.1	4.41	64	16.8
1998	9	2	4	81	18
1999	10	2.3	5.29	100	23
2000	11	2.4	5.76	121	26.4
Total	66	20.7	37.49	506	127.8

From the above table,

$$\bar{x} = \frac{66}{12} = 5.5, \ \bar{y} = \frac{20.7}{12} = 1.725$$

$$\sigma_x = \sqrt{\frac{1}{n}\Sigma x_i^2 - \bar{x}^2} = \sqrt{\frac{506}{12} - (5.5)^2}$$

$$= \sqrt{42.167 - 30.25} = 3.452$$

$$\sigma_y = \sqrt{\frac{1}{n}\Sigma y_i^2 - \bar{y}^2} = \sqrt{\frac{37.49}{12} - (1.725)^2}$$

$$= \sqrt{3.124 - 2.975} = \sqrt{0.149} = 0.386$$

The Karl Pearson's coefficient of correlation is given as

$$r = \frac{\frac{1}{n}\Sigma x_i y_i - \bar{x}\,\bar{y}}{\sqrt{\left(\frac{1}{n}\Sigma x_i^2 - \bar{x}^2\right)\left(\frac{1}{n}\Sigma y_i^2 - \bar{y}^2\right)}}$$

$$= \frac{\frac{1}{12} \times 127.8 - (5.5)(1.725)}{(3.452)(0.386)}$$

$$= \frac{10.65 - 9.4875}{1.332} = \frac{1.1625}{1.332} = 0.873$$

(1) The least squares line to predict the volume of imported goods (y) as a function of year (x) is given as

$$y - \bar{y} = \frac{r\sigma_y}{\sigma_x}(x - \bar{x})$$

$$\Rightarrow \quad y - 1.725 = \frac{(0.873)(0.386)}{3.452}(x - 5.5)$$

$$= \frac{0.337}{3.452}(x - 5.5) = 0.097(x - 5.5) = 0.097x - 0.5335$$

$$\Rightarrow \quad y = 0.097x + 1.1915 \qquad \text{...(1)}$$

is the required line

(2) Since $r = 0.873$, there is a high degree +ve correlation between the volume of import and the year.

(3) **Prediction of volume of import of goods**

(*i*) For the year 2001, put $x = 12$ in (1), we get

$$y = 0.097(12) + 1.1915$$
$$= 2.3555 \cong 2.35$$

(*ii*) For the year 2002, put $x = 13$ in (1), we get

$$y = 0.097\ (13) + 1.1915$$
$$= 1.261 + 1.1915$$
$$= 2.4525 \cong 2.5$$

(*iii*) For the year 2003, put $x = 14$ in (1), we get

$$y = 0.097(14) + 1.1915$$
$$= 1.358 + 1.1915$$
$$= 2.5495 \cong 2.5$$

(*iv*) For the year 2004, put $x = 15$ in (1), we get

$$y = (0.097)\ (15) + 1.1915$$
$$= 1.455 + 1.1915$$
$$= 2.6465 \cong 2.6$$

(4) The estimated and accurate volume of imported goods for the years 2001, 2002, 2003 and 2004 is given below

Years	*Estimated* y_E	*Accurate* y_A	*Difference* $y_E - y_A$
2001	2.3	2.3	0.0
2002	2.5	2.2	0.3
2003	2.5	2.4	0.1
2004	2.6	2.4	0.2

Since, there is a little difference between the estimated and accurate volume of imported goods for the years 2001, 2002, 2003 and 2004, we can say that the estimated volume of imported goods for the years 2001, 2002, 2003 and 2004 is quite accurate.

(5) After adding the data for 1989–2004, the required regression line of y on x is given as

$$y - \overline{y} = r\frac{\sigma_y}{\sigma_x}(x - \overline{x}) \qquad \text{...(2)}$$

Consider the following table

Year	x	y	y^2	x^2	xy
1989	0	1.1	1.21	0	0
1990	1	1.3	1.69	1	1.3
1991	2	1.6	2.56	4	3.2
1992	3	1.6	2.56	9	4.8
1993	4	1.8	3.24	16	7.2
1994	5	1.4	1.96	25	7
1995	6	1.6	2.56	36	9.6
1996	7	1.5	2.25	49	10.5
1997	8	2.1	4.41	64	16.8
1998	9	2	4	81	18
1999	10	2.3	5.29	100	23
2000	11	2.4	5.76	121	26.4
2001	12	2.3	5.29	144	27.6
2002	13	2.2	4.84	169	28.6
2003	14	2.4	5.76	196	33.6
2004	15	2.4	5.76	225	36
Total	120	30	59.14	1240	253.6

From the table,

$$\bar{x} = \frac{\Sigma x}{n} = \frac{120}{16} = 7.5;\ \bar{y} = \frac{\Sigma y}{n} = \frac{30}{16} = 1.875$$

$$\sigma_x = \sqrt{\frac{1}{n}\Sigma x_i^2 - \bar{x}^2} = \sqrt{\frac{1240}{16} - 56.25} = \sqrt{77.5 - 56.25} = \sqrt{21.25} = 4.61$$

$$\sigma_y = \sqrt{\frac{1}{n}\Sigma y_i^2 - \bar{y}^2} = \sqrt{\frac{1}{16} \times (59.14) - (1.875)^2}$$

$$= \sqrt{3.69625 - 3.515625} = \sqrt{0.180625} = 0.425$$

Also,
$$r = \frac{\frac{1}{n}\Sigma x_i y_i - \bar{x}\,\bar{y}}{\sqrt{\left(\frac{1}{n}\Sigma x_i^2 - \bar{x}^2\right)\left(\frac{1}{n}\Sigma y_i^2 - \bar{y}^2\right)}}$$

$$= \frac{\frac{253.6}{16} - (7.5)(1.875)}{(4.61)(0.425)} = \frac{15.85 - 14.0625}{1.95925} = \frac{1.7875}{1.95925} = 0.9123$$

The required equation of regression line of y on x is given as (using (2))

$$y - 1.875 = \frac{(0.9123)(0.425)}{4.61}(x - 7.5) = 0.084\ (x - 7.5)$$

$$\Rightarrow \quad y = 0.084x - 0.63 + 1.875 = 0.084x + 1.245 \quad \ldots(3)$$

$$= a + bx, \text{ where } a = 1.245,\ b = 0.084$$

As the value of $r = 0.9123$, which is +ve and near to unity, the volume of imported goods will go on increasing with increase in the number of years.

Calculation of SSE: The standard error of estimate (SSE) of volume of imported goods (y) for different years (x) is given as

$$\text{SSE} = \sqrt{\frac{\Sigma y_i^2 - a\Sigma y_i - b\,\Sigma x_i y_i}{n-2}} \qquad | \text{ Using (3)}$$

$$= \sqrt{\frac{59.14 - 1.245(30) - 0.084(253.6)}{14}}$$

$$= \sqrt{\frac{59.14 - 37.35 - 21.3024}{14}}$$

$$= \sqrt{\frac{0.4876}{14}} = 0.1866$$

Effect of SSE: The large value of SSE indicates a large amount of scatter or dispersion of dot points around the line. Smaller the value of SSE, the closer the dot points (y-values) fall around the regression line and better the line fits the data and describes the better average relationship between the two variables.

(6) The scatter diagram is shown below. From this diagram, we observe that there is a positive linear relationship between the volume of imported goods (y) and the years (x). It means the volume of imported goods will increase with the increasing years.

The linear relationship can also be checked by finding the probable error (PE_r) where

$$\text{PE}_r = (0.675)\left(\frac{1-r^2}{\sqrt{n}}\right)$$

If $r < \text{PE}_r$, then there would be no linear relationship between the two variables y and x.

If $r > \text{PE}_r$, then there is a linear relationship between the two variables

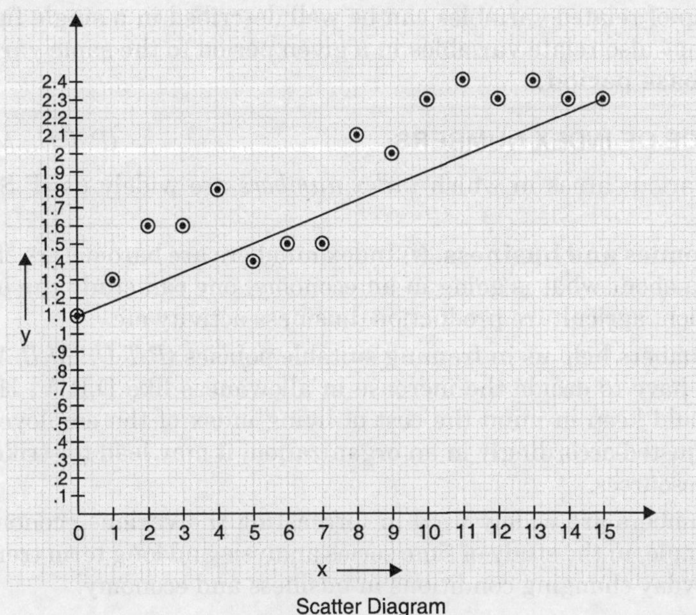

Scatter Diagram

13

Index Numbers

13.1. INDEX NUMBERS (*P.T.U., M.B.A. Dec. 2005, 2009, Dec. 2012*)

Index numbers are devices to measure the differences in the magnitude of a group of related variables. In 1764, they were first developed for measuring the effect of change in prices. Today, *index numbers* are one of the most widely used statistical instrument to measure various activities like growth or decay of prices, rise or fall in industrial production, agriculture production, business activity etc.

In fact, *index numbers* may be well described as " Barometers of Economics Activity".

According to *Spiegel*,

"An Index number is a statistical measure designed to show changes in a variable with respect to time, geographical location or other characteristics such as income, prices, etc."

13.2. INDEX NUMBERS AS A SPECIALIZED AVERAGE

When two or more series are expressed in different units, or there are different types of items in a given series *index numbers* are best measure to obtain an average of all the items expressed in different units in a given series. Thus index numbers are *specialized averages.*

13.3. INDEX NUMBERS AS A MEASURE

Index numbers measure the net change in a group of related variables. The increase or decrease in a group of related variables can be well described in a single figure by means of index numbers. They also relate variables in a given period to the same variables in another period, called the **base period.**

13.4. SIGNIFICANCE OF INDEX NUMBERS (*P.T.U., M.B.A. May 2010*)

There are various areas in which *index numbers* are widely used. Some of them are listed below :

(*a*) **In economics and business.** (*i*) Index numbers are barometers of economic activities. To get an idea about what is going in an economy, one can study the index numbers in industrial production, agriculture production, business activity etc.

(*ii*) Index numbers help us in framing suitable policies (*P.T.U., M.B.A. Dec. 2012*). For example when we have to decide the increase in allowances like D.R.A., H.R.A. etc., of the employees, we should keep in mind the cost of living index of the employees. If wages and salaries are not adjusted accordingly in an organization, it may lead to strikes, which in turn cause wastage of resources.

(*iii*) Index numbers are widely used in forecasting the various economic and business activities. For example, in the study of time series analysis and long term trend, one may keep pace with the everyday changing conditions in business and economy.

(*b*) **In deflating.** Index numbers are used in deflating. *i.e.,* they are used to adjust the original data for price changes, to adjust the wages for the cost of living changes etc.

13.5. CONSTRUCTION OF INDEX NUMBERS (*P.T.U., M.B.A. May 2009*)

There are several methods for the construction of index numbers. The following diagram illustrates the various methods.

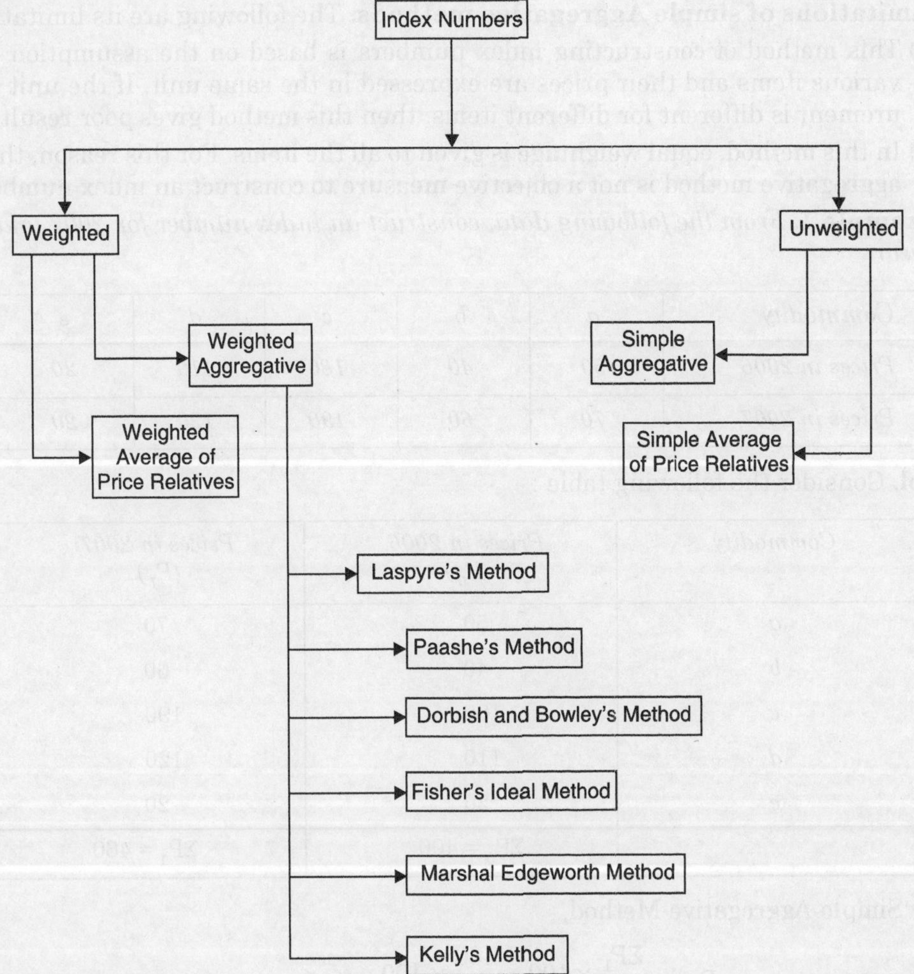

We now explain the various methods in details. There are mainly two classes of index numbers, namely

(*i*) Unweighted index numbers

(*ii*) Weighted index numbers.

13.6. UNWEIGHTED INDEX NUMBERS

These are the index numbers to which weights are not assigned. To construct unweighted index numbers, there are basically two methods which are discussed as :

I. This is the most simplest method of constructing index numbers.

Let P_{01} = The index for time '1' on time '0'.

P_1 = The current year price of a commodity or an item.

P_0 = The base year price of a commodity or an item. Then

$$P_{01} = \frac{\Sigma P_1}{\Sigma P_0} \times 100$$

Limitations of simple Aggregative methods. The following are its limitations.

(*i*) This method of constructing index numbers is based on the assumption that the various items and their prices are expressed in the same unit. If the unit of measurement is different for different items, then this method gives poor results.

(*ii*) In this method, equal weightage is given to all the items. For this reason, the simple aggregative method is not a objective measure to construct an index number.

Example 1. *From the following data, construct an index number for 2007 taking 2006 as base year*

Commodity	*a*	*b*	*c*	*d*	*e*
Prices in 2006	*50*	*40*	*180*	*110*	*20*
Prices in 2007	*70*	*60*	*190*	*120*	*20*

Sol. Consider the following table :

Commodity	*Prices in 2006* (P_0)	*Prices in 2007* (P_1)
a	50	70
b	40	60
c	180	190
d	110	120
e	20	20
	$\Sigma P_0 = 400$	$\Sigma P_1 = 460$

By Simple Aggregative Method,

$$P_{01} = \frac{\Sigma P_1}{\Sigma P_0} \times 100 = \frac{460}{400} \times 100 = 115.$$

It means that there is a net increase in the prices of various commodities in the year 2007 as compared to 2006 and the increase is 15%.

Example 2. *For the given data, find the index number by taking*

(*i*) *1999 as the base year* (*ii*) *2006 as base year*

(*iii*) *1999 to 2004 as the base period.*

Years	*1999*	*2000*	*2001*	*2002*	*2003*	*2004*	*2005*	*2006*	*2007*
Price (₹)	*4*	*5*	*6*	*7*	*9*	*10*	*9*	*12*	*11*

Sol. Consider the following table :

Year	*Price of commodity*	*(i)* *Index numbers (1999 = 100)*	*(ii)* *Index numbers (2006 = 100)*	*(iii)* *Index numbers* (2002 = 100)*
1999	(4)	100	$\frac{4}{12} \times 100 = 33.33$	$\frac{4}{5} \times 100 = 80$
2000	5	$\frac{5}{4} \times 100 = 125$	$\frac{5}{12} \times 100 = 41.66$	$\frac{5}{5} \times 100 = 100$
2001	6	$\frac{6}{4} \times 100 = 150$	$\frac{6}{12} \times 100 = 50$	$\frac{6}{5} \times 100 = 120$
2002	(7)	$\frac{7}{4} \times 100 = 175$	$\frac{7}{12} \times 100 = 58.33$	$\frac{7}{5} \times 100 = 140$
2003	9	$\frac{9}{4} \times 100 = 225$	$\frac{9}{12} \times 100 = 75$	$\frac{9}{5} \times 100 = 180$
2004	10	$\frac{10}{4} \times 100 = 250$	$\frac{10}{12} \times 100 = 83.33$	$\frac{10}{5} \times 100 = 200$
2005	9	$\frac{9}{4} \times 100 = 225$	$\frac{9}{12} \times 100 = 75$	$\frac{9}{5} \times 100 = 180$
2006	(12)	$\frac{12}{4} \times 100 = 300$	$\frac{12}{12} \times 100 = 100$	$\frac{12}{5} \times 100 = 240$
2007	11	$\frac{11}{4} \times 100 = 275$	$\frac{11}{12} \times 100 = 91.66$	$\frac{11}{5} \times 100 = 220$

(*iii*) ***When 1999 to 2004 is taken as base year.** We take average price of 1999, 2000, 2001, 2002, 2003 and 2004.

$$\text{Here average price} = \frac{4+5+6\ +7+9+10}{6} = \frac{41}{6} = 6.8 \cong 7$$

It means 2002 will be taken as base year. The index numbers are given in the last column of the above table

II. Simple Average of Price Relative Method

We first define Price Relative.

A **price relative** is the ratio of the price of a single commodity in a given period to its price in another period (base period).

Let P_1 = The commodity price in a given period

P_0 = The commodity price in a base period. Then

$$\text{Price Relative} = \frac{P_1}{P_0}$$

To construct an index number by **'Simple Average of Price Relative Method'**. We first find price relatives of the various items or commodities and then averages of these relatives is obtained by using any one of the measures of central tendency. (*i.e.,* A.M. Median, Mode, G.M., H.M.).

Case I. When A.M. is used for averaging the relatives, the formula for constructing the index number is

$$P_{01} = \frac{\sum \left(\frac{P_1}{P_0} \times 100\right)}{N}, \text{ N = Number of items (commodities)}$$

Case II. When G.M. is used for averaging the price relatives, the formula for constructing the index number is

$$\log P_{01} = \frac{\sum \log\left(\frac{P_1}{P_0} \times 100\right)}{N}, \text{ N = Number of items (commodities)}$$

Although any measure of central tendency can be used to obtain the averages of prices relatives, generally A.M. and G.M. are used.

Merits of Simple Average of Price Relative Method

This method is superior as compared to 'Simple Aggregative Method' because of the following :

(*i*) In this method, equal weightage is given to all the commodities.

(*ii*) The index number constructed by this method is not influenced by the extreme items.

Limitations: The following are the demerits of 'Simple Average of Price Relative Method'.

(*i*) Only A.M. and G.M. are used in averaging the price relatives of the commodities. Other measures of central tendency are ignored.

(*ii*) The price relatives are assumed to have equal importance.

13.7. WEIGHTED INDEX NUMBERS

These are index numbers to which weights are assigned to each items or commodities. They are of two types, namley (*a*) Weighted Aggregative (*b*) Weighted Average of Price Relatives.

(*a*) Weighted Aggregative Index Numbers

There are so many methods to construct *weighted aggregative index numbers* in which weights are assigned to various items or commodities.

I. Laspeyre's Method. The *Laspeyre's price index* is a weighted price index in which the weights are determined by the quantities in the *base period.*

Let P_1 = The current year price of a commodity or an item

P_0 = The base year price of a commodity or an item

Q_1 = The current year weight

Q_0 = The base year weight. Then

$$P_{01} = \frac{\Sigma P_1 Q_0}{\Sigma P_0 Q_0} \times 100$$

The Laspeyre's method of constructing an index number has an upward bias.

It means, when prices increase, the consumption of the higher priced items are reduced. Therefore, by using base year weights *too much weight* may be given to those items whose prices have been increased most.

Limitations of Laspeyre's Method

(*i*) It does not take into consideration the consumption pattern.

(*ii*) The Laspeyres index has an upward bias.

Uses

This method is useful in calculating the change in aggregate value of the base period list of items when valued at given period prices.

II. Paasche's method. It is a weighted aggregative price index in which the weights are determined by the quantities in the *given year*.

Let P_1 = The current year price of a commodity or an item.

P_0 = The base year price of a commodity or an item.

Q_1 = The current year weight

Q_0 = The base year weight. Then,

$$P_{01} = \frac{\Sigma P_1 Q_1}{\Sigma P_0 Q_1} \times 100$$

The Paasche's method of constructing an index number has a downward bias.

It means, when prices decrease, the consumers purchase those items which decline the most. Therefore, by using base year weights, **too little weight** is given to those items whose prices have been decreased most.

Limitations of Paasche's Method (*i*) The Paasche index numbers can be constructed only when up-to-date for the weights are available.

(*ii*) It cannot be used frequently where the number of commodities or items is large.

Uses

(*i*) It has an downward bias.

(*ii*) This method is useful in calculating the value of the given period list of items when valued at base periods prices.

Comparison of Laspeyre's and Paasche's Methods

Laspeyre's Method	*Paasche's Method*
(*i*) The base year weights (Q_0) do not change from one period to the next.	(*i*) The base year weights are changed from the year under consideration to the next year.
(*ii*) It has an upward bias.	(*ii*) It has an downward bias.
(*iii*) It measures the change in the aggregate value of the base period list of items when valued at given period prices.	(*iii*) It measures the change in the aggregate value of the given period list of items when valued at base period prices.

III. Dorbish and Bowley's method. The formula for constructing the index number given by **Dorbish** and **Bowley** is

$$P_{01} = \frac{L+P}{2}, \text{ where } L = \text{Laspeyre's index},$$

$$P = \text{Paasche's index}$$

i.e., Dorbish and Bowley's index is the arithmetic mean of Laspeyres's and Paasche's index.

Also
$$P_{01} = \frac{\dfrac{\Sigma P_1 Q_0}{\Sigma P_0 Q_0} + \dfrac{\Sigma P_1 Q_1}{\Sigma P_0 Q_1}}{2} \times 100$$

IV. Fisher's Ideal Method *(P.T.U., M.B.A. May 2002, Dec. 2002, May 2004)*

The Fisher Ideal Index, due to Prof. Irving Fisher is given by

$$P_{01} = \sqrt{LP},$$

where L = Laspeyre's index P = Paasche's index

i.e., Fisher ideal index is the geometric mean of Laspeyre's and Paasche's index.

Also
$$P_{01} = \sqrt{\frac{\Sigma P_1 Q_0}{\Sigma P_0 Q_0} \times \frac{\Sigma P_1 Q_1}{\Sigma P_0 Q_1}} \times 100$$

Merits of Fisher's Ideal Index *(P.T.U., M.B.A. Dec. 2002)*

The Fisher's index is considered an **'Ideal index'** because of the following reasons.

(*i*) It is based on G.M. which is the best average to construct index numbers.

(*ii*) It is free from bias *i.e.,* it has neither upward bias like Laspeyre's index, nor downward bias like Passche's index.

(*iii*) It accounts both current year as well as base years prices and quantities.

(*iv*) It satisfies both the time reversal test as well as the factor reversal test.

Limitation : It is not used practically because it is laborious.

V. Marshall Edgeworth Method. This method of constructing index numbers uses both the current year as well as base year prices and quantities.

Let P_1 = The current year price of a commodity or an item

P_0 = The base year price of a commodity or an item

Q_1 = The current year weight

Q_0 = The base year weight. Then

$$P_{01} = \frac{\Sigma P_1 Q_0 + \Sigma P_1 Q_1}{\Sigma P_0 Q_0 + \Sigma P_0 Q_1} \times 100$$

VI. Kelley's Method. This method is also known as **fixed weight aggregative** method of constructing index numbers.

Let P_1 = The current year price of a commodity or an item

P_0 = The base year price of a commodity or an item

Q = The average of base year as well as current year quantity. Then

$$P_{01} = \frac{\Sigma P_1 Q}{\Sigma P_0 Q} \times 100.$$

Uses. Kelley's method has an important advantage.

It does not demand yearly changes in the weights. Also the base year can be changed without making changes in the weights.

(*b*) **Weighted Averages of Price Relatives**

As in case of unweighted price relative method, it is also possible to compute weighted average of price relatives. The averages of these relatives can be obtained by using the A.M. or G.M.

Case I. When A.M. used for averaging the relatives.

Let P = The price relative $= \frac{P_1}{P_0} \times 100$

V = Value weights

$$= \begin{cases} P_0 Q_0 \text{ or } P_1 Q_1, & \text{if theoretical values are used as weights} \\ P_1 Q_1, & \text{if current year values are used as weights} \end{cases}$$ Then

$$P_{01} = \frac{\Sigma PV}{\Sigma V}$$

Case II. When G.M. is used for averaging the relatives, then

$$P_{01} = \text{antilog}\left(\frac{\Sigma V \log_{10} P}{\Sigma V}\right), \text{where } P = \frac{P_1}{P_0} \times 100$$

13.8. MERITS OF WEIGHTED AVERAGE OF PRICE RELATIVES METHOD

The following are the merits of weighted average of price relatives over weighted aggregate index numbers.

(*i*) The index numbers having the same base, constructed by the averages of price relatives can be combined to find a new index number.

(*ii*) When an index number is computed by selecting one item from each of the many sub-groups of items, the values of each subgroup may be used as weights. The most appropriate method of computing such index numbers is the weighted average of price relatives.

(*iii*) By using this method, we can splice the relatives of new items to the relatives of old items after the new items are introduced to replace the one formerly used.

ILLUSTRATIVE EXAMPLES

Example 1. *Calculate the price index numbers of 1994 using Laspeyre's methods with base 1984 from the following data :*

Commodity	*1984*		*1994*	
	Quantity	*Price*	*Quantity*	*Price*
A	*40*	*4*	*50*	*5*
B	*30*	*3*	*35*	*3*
C	*20*	*1*	*15*	*2*

(P.T.U., M.B.A. May 2002)

Sol. Let P_1 = The current year price

P_0 = The base year price

Q_1 = The current year quantity

Q_0 = The base year quantity.

Here base year is 1984. Consider the following table :

Commodity	P_0	Q_0	P_1	Q_1	P_1Q_1	P_0Q_1
A	4	40	5	50	250	200
B	3	30	3	35	105	105
C	1	20	2	15	30	15
					$\Sigma P_1Q_1 = 385$	$\Sigma P_0Q_1 = 320$

The required index number is given by

$$P_{01} = \frac{\Sigma P_1 Q_1}{\Sigma P_0 Q_1} \times 100 = \frac{385}{320} \times 100 = 120.31$$

Example 2. *Construct Fisher's Ideal index numbers for the following data :*

Commodity	*1986*		*1987*	
	Quantity	*Price*	*Quantity*	*Price*
A	*20*	*12*	*30*	*14*
B	*13*	*14*	*15*	*20*
C	*12*	*10*	*20*	*15*
D	*8*	*6*	*10*	*4*
E	*5*	*8*	*5*	*6*

(P.T.U., M.B.A. May 2003)

Sol. Let P_1 = The current year price

P_0 = The base year price

Q_1 = The current year quantity

Q_0 = The base year quantity. Consider the following table.

Take the base year as 1986.

Commodity	P_0	Q_0	P_1	Q_1	P_1Q_0	P_0Q_1	P_0Q_0	P_1Q_1
A	12	20	14	30	280	360	240	420
B	14	13	20	15	260	210	182	300
C	10	12	15	20	180	200	120	300
D	6	8	4	10	32	60	48	40
E	8	5	6	5	30	40	40	30
					$\Sigma P_1Q_0 = 782$	$\Sigma P_0Q_1 = 870$	$\Sigma P_0Q_0 = 630$	$\Sigma P_1Q_1 = 1090$

The Fisher's Ideal index number is given by

$$P_{01} = \sqrt{\frac{\Sigma P_1 Q_0}{\Sigma P_0 Q_0} \times \frac{\Sigma P_1 Q_1}{\Sigma P_0 Q_1}} \times 100 = \sqrt{\frac{782}{630} \times \frac{1090}{870}} \times 100$$

$$= \sqrt{1.241 \times 1.252} \times 100 = \sqrt{1.553} \times 100$$

$$= 1.246 \times 100 = 124.64.$$

Example 3. *Calculate*

(i) Laspeyre's *(ii) Paasche's*

(iii) Bowley's and *(iv) Fisher's Index numbers for following data.*

Items	*2005*		*2006*	
	Quantity	*Value*	*Quantity*	*Value*
A	*10*	*12*	*12*	*13*
B	*50*	*14*	*40*	*15*
C	*15*	*16*	*25*	*19*
D	*12*	*18*	*15*	*16*

(P.T.U., M.B.A. Dec. 2007)

Sol. Let P_0 = The base year price

Q_0 = The base year quantity

P_1 = The current year price

Q_1 = The current year quantity

Commodity	Q_0	P_0	P_0Q_0	Q_1	P_1	P_1Q_1	Q_1P_0	Q_0P_1
A	10	12	120	12	13	156	144	130
B	50	14	700	40	15	600	560	750
C	15	16	240	25	19	475	400	285
D	12	18	216	15	16	240	270	192
Total			1276			1471	1374	1357

(i) Laspeyre's quantity index is given by

$$Q_{01} = \frac{\Sigma Q_1P_0}{\Sigma Q_0P_0} \times 100 = \frac{1374}{1276} \times 100 = 107.68$$

(ii) Paasche's quantity index is given by

$$Q_{01} = \frac{\Sigma Q_1P_1}{\Sigma Q_0P_1} \times 100 = \frac{1471}{1357} \times 100 = 108.4$$

(iii) Bowley's quantity index is given by

$$Q_{01} = \frac{\frac{\Sigma Q_1P_0}{\Sigma Q_0P_0} + \frac{\Sigma Q_1P_1}{\Sigma Q_0P_1}}{2} \times 100$$

$$= \frac{\frac{1374}{1276} + \frac{1471}{1357}}{2} \times 100 = \frac{1.0768 + 1.084}{2} \times 100 = 108.04$$

(iv) Fisher's quantity index is given by $Q_{01} = \sqrt{LP}$

Where L = Laspeyre's quantity index

P = Paasche's quantity index

$$Q_{01} = \sqrt{107.68 \times 108.4} = \sqrt{11672.512} = 108.03$$

Example 4. *Construct Index numbers of price from the following data, by using*
(a) Laspeyre's Method
(b) Paasche's Method
(c) Bowley's Method
(d) Fisher's Ideal Method
(e) Marshall Edgeworth Method.

Commodity	*Year 2005*		*Year 2006*	
	Price	*Quantity*	*Price*	*Quantity*
I	*4*	*8*	*6*	*8*
II	*6*	*12*	*4*	*5*
III	*8*	*14*	*5*	*10*
IV	*5*	*16*	*8*	*12*

Sol. Let P_0 = The base year price
Q_0 = The base year quantity
P_1 = The current year price
Q_1 = The current year quantity.

Consider the following table. Take base year as 2005.

Commodity	*Year 2005*		*Year 2006*					
	P_0	Q_0	P_1	Q_1	P_1Q_1	P_0Q_0	P_1Q_0	P_0Q_1
I	4	8	6	8	48	32	48	32
II	6	12	4	5	20	72	48	30
III	8	14	5	10	50	112	70	80
IV	5	16	8	12	96	80	128	60
			Total		$\Sigma P_1Q_1 = 214$	$\Sigma P_0Q_0 = 296$	$\Sigma P_1Q_0 = 294$	$\Sigma P_0Q_1 = 202$

(*a*) **By Laspeyre's Method:**

$$P_{01} = \frac{\Sigma P_1Q_0}{\Sigma P_0Q_0} \times 100 = \frac{294}{296} \times 100 = 99.32$$

(*b*) **Paasche's Method:**

$$P_{01} = \frac{\Sigma P_1Q_1}{\Sigma P_0Q_1} \times 100 = \frac{214}{202} \times 100 = 105.94$$

(*c*) **Bowley's Method**

$$P_{01} = \frac{\frac{\Sigma P_1Q_0}{\Sigma P_0Q_0} + \frac{\Sigma P_1Q_1}{\Sigma P_0Q_1}}{2} \times 100 = \frac{\frac{294}{296} + \frac{214}{202}}{2} \times 100$$

$$= \frac{0.99 + 1.05}{2} \times 100 = 102$$

(*d*) **Fisher's Ideal Method**

$$P_{01} = \sqrt{\frac{\Sigma P_1Q_0}{\Sigma P_0Q_0} \times \frac{\Sigma P_1Q_1}{\Sigma P_0Q_1}} \times 100 = \sqrt{\frac{294}{296} \times \frac{214}{202}} \times 100$$

$$= \sqrt{0.99 \times 1.05} \times 100 = 1.03 \times 100 = 103$$

(*e*) **Marshall Edgeworth Method :**

$$P_{01} = \frac{\Sigma P_1Q_0 + \Sigma P_1Q_1}{\Sigma P_0Q_0 + \Sigma P_0Q_1} \times 100 = \frac{294 + 214}{296 + 202} \times 100$$

$$= \frac{508}{498} \times 100 = 102.$$

Example 5. *Construct a Index number for the price of the group of four commodities by using the suitable formula.*

Commodity	*Base Year*		*Current Year*	
	Price	*Expenditure*	*Price*	*Expenditure*
a	*3*	*40*	*6*	*85*
b	*5*	*16*	*7*	*50*
c	*2*	*10*	*3*	*24*
d	*6*	*24*	*12*	*60*

Sol. From the given data, the base year and current year prices and expenditure are available to us.

∴ Fisher's Ideal formula is most suitable. Consider the following table :

Commodity	P_0	Q_0	P_1	Q_1	P_1Q_1	P_1Q_0	P_0Q_1	P_0Q_0
a	3	40	6	85	510	240	255	120
b	5	16	7	50	350	112	250	80
c	2	10	3	24	72	30	48	20
d	6	24	12	60	720	288	360	144
					$\Sigma P_1Q_1 = 1652$	$\Sigma P_1Q_0 = 670$	$\Sigma P_0Q_1 = 913$	$\Sigma P_0Q_0 = 364$

We apply Fisher's Ideal index method. The required index number is

$$\therefore \quad P_{01} = \sqrt{\frac{\Sigma P_1Q_0}{\Sigma P_0Q_0} \times \frac{\Sigma P_1Q_1}{\Sigma P_0Q_1}} \times 100 = \sqrt{\frac{670}{364} \times \frac{1652}{913}} \times 100$$

$$= \sqrt{1.84 \times 1.80} \times 100 = 1.81 \times 100 = 181.$$

Example 6. *By using the average of the quantities of two years as weights, find the price index for the given data.*

Commodity	*Quantity*		*Price*	
	2005	*2006*	*2005*	*2006*
A	*10*	*16*	*20*	*25*
B	*9*	*7*	*25*	*28*
C	*20*	*24*	*40*	*40*

Sol. We apply Kelly's method because in the given data, average quantity of two years 2005 and 2006 are used.

Consider the following table. Take the base year as 2005.

Commodity	Q_0	Q_1	$Q = \frac{Q_0 + Q_1}{2}$	P_0	P_1	P_1Q	P_0Q
A	10	16	13	20	25	325	260
B	9	7	8	25	28	224	200
C	20	24	22	40	40	880	880
						$\Sigma P_1Q = 1429$	$\Sigma P_0Q = 1340$

Let Q = The average of base year as well as current year quantity.
P_0 = The base year price.
P_1 = The current year price.

By Kelly's method,

$$P_{01} = \frac{\Sigma P_1 Q}{\Sigma P_0 Q} \times 100 = \frac{1429}{1340} \times 100 = 106.64$$

Example 7. *From the following data, calculate index number in 1984 and 1985, using price in 1983 as basis :*

Commodities	*Units*	*Prices in ₹*		
		1983	*1984*	*1985*
A	*Quintals*	*200*	*180*	*220*
B	*kg.*	*20*	*22*	*18*
C	*km.*	*10*	*12*	*8*
D	*Litres*	*8*	*10*	*4*
E	*Dozen*	*2*	*6*	*2*

(P.T.U., M.B.A. May 2003)

Sol. Let P_1 = The current year price.
Q_1 = The current year quantity.
P_0 = The base year price.
Q_0 = The base year quantity.

To find Index number in 1984. The base year is 1983. Since the quantities are not given in the data, we calculate the required index numbers by using 'Simple Aggregate of Actual Prices. Consider the following table :

Commodity	P_0	P_1
A	200	180
B	20	22
C	10	12
D	8	10
E	2	6
	$\Sigma P_0 = 240$	$\Sigma P_1 = 230$

$$\therefore \quad P_{01} = \frac{\Sigma P_1}{\Sigma P_0} \times 100$$

$$= \frac{230}{240} \times 100 = 95.83.$$

To find Index number in 1985. Consider the following table. Here the base year is 1983.

Commodity	P_0	P_1
A	200	220
B	20	18
C	10	8
D	8	4
E	2	2
	$\Sigma P_0 = 240$	$\Sigma P_1 = 252$

$$\therefore \quad P_{01} = \frac{\Sigma P_1}{\Sigma P_0} \times 100$$

$$= \frac{252}{240} \times 100 = 105.83$$

Example 8. *Consider the following data :*

Commodity	*Year 2002*		*Year 2003*	
	P_0	Q_0	P_1	Q_1
A	*1*	*10*	*2*	*5*
B	*1*	*5*	*k*	*2*

where P and Q stands for price and quantity and subscripts stand for time period. Find the value of k if the ratio between Laspeyre's (L) and Paasche's (P) index numbers is 28:27.

Sol. We first find Laspeyre's and Paasche's index numbers. Take the base year as 2002. Consider the following data.

Commodity	P_0	Q_0	P_1	Q_1	P_1Q_0	P_0Q_1	P_0Q_0	P_1Q_1
A	1	10	2	5	20	5	10	10
B	1	5	k	2	$5k$	2	5	$2k$
					$\Sigma P_1Q_0 = 20 + 5k$	$\Sigma P_0Q_1 = 7$	$\Sigma P_0Q_0 = 15$	$\Sigma P_1Q_1 = 10 + 2k$

$$\therefore \quad L = P_{01} = \frac{\Sigma P_1Q_0}{\Sigma P_0Q_0} \times 100 = \frac{20+5k}{15} \times 100 \quad \text{...(1)}$$

$$P = P_{01} = \frac{\Sigma P_1Q_1}{\Sigma P_0Q_1} = \frac{10+2k}{7} \times 100 \quad \text{...(2)}$$

Given $\frac{L}{P} = \frac{28}{27}$

$$\therefore \quad \frac{20+5k}{15} \times \frac{7}{10+2k} = \frac{28}{27} \qquad | \text{ Using (1) and (2)}$$

$$\Rightarrow \quad \frac{140+35k}{150+30k} = \frac{28}{27}$$

$$\Rightarrow \quad 3780 + 945k = 4200 + 840k \quad \Rightarrow \quad 945k - 840k = 4200 - 3780$$

$$\Rightarrow \quad 105k = 420 \quad \Rightarrow \quad k = \frac{420}{105} = 4.$$

Example 9. *It is stated that Marshall-Edgeworth index number is a good approximation to the Ideal index number. Verify this statement for the following data :*

Commodity	2005		2006	
	Price	Quantity	Price	Quantity
A	2	74	3	82
B	5	125	4	140
C	7	60	6	53

Sol. We find Marshall Edgeworth and Fisher's ideal index number for the given data. Consider the following table :

Commodity	P_0	Q_0	P_1	Q_1	P_0Q_1	P_1Q_0	P_0Q_0	P_1Q_1
A	2	74	3	82	164	222	148	246
B	5	125	4	140	700	500	625	560
C	7	60	6	53	371	360	420	318
					ΣP_0Q_1 = 1235	ΣP_1Q_0 = 1082	ΣP_0Q_0 = 1193	ΣP_1Q_1 = 1124

Marshall Edgeworth index number is given by

$$P_{01} = \frac{\Sigma P_1Q_0 + \Sigma P_1Q_1}{\Sigma P_0Q_0 + \Sigma P_0Q_1} \times 100 = \frac{1082 + 1124}{1193 + 1235} \times 100$$

$$= \frac{2206}{2428} \times 100 = 90.8 \qquad ...(1)$$

Fisher's ideal index number is given by

$$P_{01} = \sqrt{\frac{\Sigma P_1Q_0}{\Sigma P_0Q_0} \times \frac{\Sigma P_1Q_1}{\Sigma P_0Q_1}} \times 100 = \sqrt{\frac{1082}{1193} \times \frac{1124}{1235}} \times 100$$

$$= \sqrt{0.90 \times 0.91} \times 100 = 0.904 \times 100 = 90.4 \qquad ...(2)$$

Hence from (1) and (2), we observe that both Index numbers have almost same value. Hence the given statement is true.

Example 10. *Find the weighted Price index for the following data :*

Materials Required	Units	Quantity Required	Price in ₹	
			Year 2005	Year 2006
Bricks	Per' 000	20,000	12	24
Steel Sheets	cu. wt.	50 cu. wt	34	42
Timber	cu. ft.	2000 cu. ft.	9.5	14.2
Cement	per' 00 lb.	500 lb	5	8

Sol. Given weights are fixed weights. So we apply Kelley's Method to compute the required index number. Consider the following Table. Take the base year as 2005.

Materials req.	*Quantity req. (Q)*	P_0	P_1	P_0Q	P_1Q
Bricks	20	12	24	240	480
Steel sheets	50	34	42	1700	2100
Timber	2000	9.5	14.2	19000	28400
Cement	5	5	8	25	40
				$\Sigma P_0Q = 20965$	$\Sigma P_1Q = 31020$

$$\therefore \quad \text{By Kelly's Method, } P_{01} = \frac{\Sigma P_1Q}{\Sigma P_0Q} \times 100$$

$$= \frac{31020}{20965} \times 100 = 147.96.$$

Example 11. *Compute Index number of the following data, by using Weighted Average of Price Relative method. When*

(a) The averages are obtained from A.M. *(b) The averages are obtained from G.M.*

Commodity	*Price in ₹*		*Quantity Required*
	Year 2004	*Year 2005*	*in 2004*
A	*3*	*4*	*20*
B	*1.5*	*1.7*	*40*
C	*2*	*1.8*	*12*

Sol. (*a*) When the average is taken from A.M.

Consider the following Table. Take the base year as 2004.

Commodity	P_0	P_1	Q_0	$V = P_0Q_0$	$P = \frac{P_1}{P_0} \times 100$	PV
A	3	4	20	60	133.33	7999.8
B	1.5	1.7	40	60	113.33	6799.8
C	2	1.8	12	24	90	2160
				$\Sigma V = 144$		$\Sigma PV = 16959.6$

$\therefore$ Required Index number is

$$P_{01} = \frac{\Sigma PV}{\Sigma V} = \frac{16959.6}{144} = 117.77 \quad \Big| \text{ Here } V = P_0Q_0,\ P = \frac{P_1}{P_0} \times 100$$

(*b*) **When the average is taken from G.M.**

Consider the following table.

V	P	$\log_{10} P$	$V \log_{10} P$
60	133.33	2.124	127.44
60	113.33	2.054	123.24
24	90	1.9542	46.9
$\Sigma V = 144$			$\Sigma V \log_{10} P = 297.58$

The required index number is given by

$$P_{01} = \text{antilog}_{10}\left(\frac{\Sigma V \log_{10} P}{\Sigma V}\right) = \text{antilog}_{10}\left(\frac{297.58}{144}\right)$$

$$= \text{antilog}_{10}\,(2.066) = 116.41.$$

13.9. PROBLEMS FOR CONSTRUCTING INDEX NUMBERS (*P.T.U., M.B.A. May 2003*)

There are several methods to construct various index number like weighted index numbers, unweighted index numbers. But in constructing these index numbers, there are various problems which are discussed below.

(*a*) **In the selection of a base Period** (*P.T.U., M.B.A. Dec. 2012*)**.** The **base period** or **reference period** of an index number is the period against which comparisons are made. It may be a day or a month or a year. Generally, it is always taken as 100. The problems in the selection of a base period for the construction of index numbers are

(*i*) Whether the base period is normal or not.

(*ii*) Whether the base period is fixed or not.

(*i*) While selecting a base period, the base should be taken as normal. It means that it should be free from abnormalities like floods, natural disasters, earthquakes etc. In some cases, a year which is normal in one respect may be abnormal in another aspect. In such cases, an average of a number of years may be taken as base.

(*ii*) While selecting a base period, the main problem is to decide whether the base is fixed or not *i.e.,* whether we have a fixed base index or chain base index. In the fixed base method, the base period to which all other prices are related is constant for all times. In the chain base method, the prices of a year are linked with those of the proceeding years and not with the fixed year. Generally, the chain base method gives a better result as compared to fixed base method.

(*b*) **In the selection of number of items.** In the construction of an index number, the main problem is the selection of number of items. We cannot include every item while constructing index numbers. The number of items should be selected by the purpose for which the index number is being constructed. For example, in the construction of price index, if the number of commodities is large, the cost and time taken would also be large. Therefore, the number of items should be selected in such a manner that they may be identified after a time lapse.

(*c*) **In the selection of an average.** While calculating price relatives of various items or commodities, the averaging of relatives is much important. But the averages of these relatives may be obtained by using any one of the measure of central tendency (A.M. Median, Mode, G.M., H.M.). But mean, Median and Mode are never used for the construction of various index numbers as they do not give accurate results. Generally, we use A.M and G.M for averaging the relatives. But G.M is the best average in the construction of various index numbers because of the following reasons.

(*i*) It is less affected by the fluctuations of various items.

(*ii*) Index numbers calculated by using G.M. as an average satisfies Time Reversal Test and Factor Reversal Test and hence base shifting is also possible.

In some cases, A.M is also used for the construction of index numbers as it is much more easy to compute than the G.M.

(*d*) **In the selection of an appropriate weight.** In the construction of index numbers, the problem of selecting suitable weight is quite important.

There are two types of index numbers namely (*i*) Unweighted index number (*ii*) Weighted index numbers.

In the former case, no weights are assigned to the various items whereas in the latter case, weights are assigned to the various items. The term 'weight' refers to the relative importance of the different items in the construction of index numbers *i.e.,* all items are not equally important in constructing index numbers. The varying importance of the different items can be taken into account by allocating weights to them. There are two methods to assign weights namely

(*i*) Implicit Method

(*ii*) Explicit Method.

In implicit method, a commodity or its variety is included in the index a number of times. For example, if wheat is to be given in an index twice as much as milk, then two varities of wheat against one of milk may be included in the data.

In case of explicit method, two types of weights can be included namely

(*i*) Quantity weights (*b*) Value weights.

A **quantity weights** (Q) means the amount of item produced, distributed or consumed in some time period.

A **value weight** is the product of price (P) and quantity weight (Q). But the problem in the selection of weights is whether to choose quantity weights or value weights. If the Aggregative Method is used while constructing index numbers, then quantity weight is much better. In averaging price relative methods, value weights are much better.

(*e*) **In the selection of an appropriate formula.** There are several methods for the construction of index numbers. But the problem is how to select the most appropriate formula. The selection of these formulae depend upon the data available. The best formula is that which satisfies Time Reversal Test and Factor Reversal Test. Based upon these, **Fisher's ideal number** is the most appropriate index number. But there are some limitations of **Fisher's Ideal** index number as it is not used practically as it is laborious.

(*f*) **In the selection of price quotations.** It is a common fact that prices of many items vary from place to place and even from shop to shop in the same market. Therefore, it is not an easy job to obtain price quotations of a commodity from the market.

There are two methods of quoting prices namely

(*i*) Money Prices

(*ii*) Quantity Prices.

In Money Prices method, prices are quoted per unit of commodity or item. In Qnantity prices, prices are quoted per unit of money. Generally, money price method is used in quoting prices as it is free from any confusion.

TEST YOUR KNOWLEDGE 13.1

1. What are Index numbers and why they are called 'Business Barometers' ?
(P.T.U., M.B.A. Dec. 2002, 03 ; May 2004)
2. Discuss various methods of constructing index numbers and discuss their merits and demerits.
(P.T.U., M.B.A. Dec. 2002)
3. Why is Fisher's Index number is called Ideal Index number ?
(P.T.U., M.B.A. May 2002, 03 ; Dec. 2002)
4. Discuss briefly the problems faced in the construction of index numbers of prices.
(P.T.U., M.B.A. May 2001)
5. Explain the following statement 'Laspeyre's formula has an upward bias and Paasche's a downward bias". Do you agree with the statement ? Give reasons.
6. Consider the following data.

Items	*Base year*		*Current year*	
	Price (₹)	*Quantity*	*Price (₹)*	*Quantity*
A	5	25	6	30
B	3	8	4	10
C	2	10	3	8
D	10	4	3	5

Calculate
(*i*) Laspeyre's Index number (*ii*) Paasche's Index number
(*iii*) Fisher's Index number (*iv*) Marshall-Edgeworth's Index number.

7. From the following data, construct Fisher's ideal index number.

Commodity	*1996*		*2006*	
	Price	*Value (₹)*	*Price*	*Value (₹)*
A	5	50	6	72
B	7	84	10	80
C	10	80	12	96
D	4	20	5	30
E	8	56	8	64

8. From the data given below, calculate price index number using appropriate method for the year 2002 with base 2000.

Commodity	*2000*		*2002*	
	Quantity	*Price*	*Quantity*	*Price*
A	15	40	20	35
B	10	30	15	25
C	7	15	7	20
D	8	10	6	20
E	2	25	1	40

9. Compute (*i*) Laspeyre's (*ii*) Paasche's and (*iii*) Fisher's Ideal index numbers for the following data :

Items	*Base year*		*Current year*	
	Price	*Qty.*	*Price*	*Qty.*
A	12	10	15	12
B	15	7	20	5
C	24	5	20	9
D	5	10	5	14

10. Compute the price index P_{01} using Marshall-Edgeworth formula :

Items	P_0	Q_0	P_1	Q_1
A	20	10	30	12
B	4	9	4	16
C	14	17	25	23

11. Calculate weighted index number for 1999 by (*i*) Weighted Aggregate Method (*ii*) Weighted Average of Price Relative Method, for the following data:

Item	*Quantity*	*Price in ₹*	
		1998	*1999*
Bricks	10 units	100	161
Timber	7 units	200	210
Boards	15 units	50	60
Sand	9 units	20	30
Cement	10 units	10	14

12. For the data, construct a price index number of the group of four commodities by using Fisher's Ideal formula :

Commodity	*Base year*		*Current year*	
	Price	*Expenditure*	*Price*	*Expenditure*
A	2	40	5	75
B	4	16	8	40
C	1	10	2	60
D	5	25	10	60

13. Find out quarterly seasonal indices using moving average method for the following data of no. of defects per quarter for 2005 to 2008. (*P.T.U. M.B.A. Dec. 2009*)

	Quarter			
Year	Q_1	Q_2	Q_3	Q_4
2005	25	20	22	18
2006	27	23	20	19
2007	18	19	18	17
2008	17	16	15	15

Answers

6. (*i*) 107.17 (*ii*) 105.28 (*iii*) 106.22 (*iv*) 106.15

7. 121.86 **8.** 101.45 **9.** (*i*) 118.82 (*ii*) 112.77

(*iii*) 115.76 **10.** 160 **11.** (*i*) 127.69 (*ii*) 137.7

12. 219.1 **13.** 112.63, 100.98, 97.09, 87.33.

Hints

7. Since price and value are given in the data. ∴ To find quantities of various items, divide values by prices, we get the quantities.

12. To get quantities, divide expenditure by price of the four commodities.

13. For the computation of seasonal indices, consider the following table.

Year	Q_1	Q_2	Q_3	Q_4
2005	25	20	22	18
2006	27	23	20	19
2007	18	19	18	17
2008	17	16	15	15
Total	87	78	75	69
Average	$\frac{87}{4} = 21.75$	$\frac{78}{4} = 19.5$	$\frac{75}{4} = 18.75$	$\frac{69}{4} = 17.25$

Grand average $= \frac{21.75 + 19.5 + 18.75 + 17.25}{4} = \frac{77.25}{4} = 19.31$

Seasonal index for 1st quarter $Q_1 = \frac{\text{Average of First quarter}}{\text{Grand Average}} \times 100 = \frac{21.75}{19.31} \times 100 = 112.63$

Seasonal index for 2nd quarter $Q_2 = \frac{19.5}{19.31} \times 100 = 100.98$

Seasonal index for 3rd quarter $Q_3 = \frac{18.75}{19.31} \times 100 = 97.09$

Seasonal index for 4th quarter $Q_4 = \frac{17.25}{19.31} \times 100 = 87.33.$

13.10. QUANTITY INDEX NUMBERS

In our previous section, we studied and discussed **price index numbers** (denoted by P_{01}) which measure and compare the prices of various commodities. Similary, quantity index numbers measure the physical volume of production, construction etc. **Price index numbers** are also called **volume index numbers.**

Quantity index numbers can be obtained easily by changing P to Q and Q to P in the various formulae discussed in the previous section. Thus,

(*i*) When Laspeyre's method is used, the quantity index number is given by

$$Q_{01} = \frac{\Sigma Q_1 P_0}{\Sigma Q_0 P_0} \times 100$$

(*ii*) When Paasche's method is used, the quantity index number is given by

$$Q_{01} = \frac{\Sigma Q_1 P_1}{\Sigma Q_0 P_1} \times 100$$

(*iii*) When Dorbish and Bowley's method is used, the quantity price index is the arithmetic mean of Laspeyre's and Paasche's Index *i.e.*,

$$Q_{01} = \frac{\dfrac{\Sigma Q_1 P_0}{\Sigma Q_0 P_0} + \dfrac{\Sigma Q_1 P_1}{\Sigma Q_0 P_1}}{2} \times 100$$

(*iv*) When Fisher's ideal method is used, the quantity index number is given by

$$Q_{01} = \sqrt{LP}$$

where L = Laspeyre's Index, P = Paasche's Index.

(*v*) When Marshall-Edgeworth method is used, the quantity index number is given by

$$Q_{01} = \frac{\Sigma Q_1 P_0 + \Sigma Q_1 P_1}{\Sigma Q_0 P_0 + \Sigma Q_0 P_1} \times 100$$

13.11. VALUE INDEX NUMBERS

The value V of a single item or commodity is defined as

$$V = \frac{\Sigma P_1 Q_1}{\Sigma P_0 Q_0} \times 100$$

where P_1 = The current year price

Q_1 = The current year quantity

P_0 = The base year price

Q_0 = The base year quantity.

i.e., the value index number is the sum of the values of a given year divided by the sum of the values of the base year.

A **value index number** measures the change in actual values between the base and given period.

13.12. TESTS OF ADEQUACY OF INDEX NUMBER FORMULAE

(*P.T.U., M.B.A. Dec. 2005*)

There are various methods to construct index numbers. But the main problem is that of selecting the most appropriate one in a given situation. The below are some tests which help us for choosing a most suitable index.

I. Unit Test: According to this test, the formula for the construction of an index number should be independent of units in which prices and quantities are used. The only test which does not satisfy this test is the Unweighted Aggregative Method. All others test satisfies the unit test.

II. Time Reversal Test *(P.T.U., M.B.A. Dec. 2009)*

According to Prof. Irving Fisher,

"Time Reversal Test is that the formula for calculating the index number should be such that it will give the same ratio between one point comparison and the other, no matter which of the two is taken as base".

In other words, when the data for any two years are treated by the same method but with their bases reversed, the two index numbers obtained should be reciprocals of each other so that their product is unity.

Mathematically, $P_{01} \times P_{10} = 1$

where P_{01} = The index number for time '1' on time '0' as base

P_{10} = The index number for time '0' on time '1' as base.

Theorem I. *Show that Laspeyre's method does not satisfy time reversal test.*

Proof. Let P_1 = The current year price

Q_1 = The base year quantity

P_0 = The base year price

Q_0 = The base year quantity.

(*i*) By using Laspeyre's method, the price index number is given by

$$P_{01} = \frac{\Sigma P_1 Q_0}{\Sigma P_0 Q_0}$$

Also $$P_{10} = \frac{\Sigma Q_1 P_0}{\Sigma Q_1 P_1}$$ | Changing time *i.e.*, '0' to 1 and '1' to '0'

∴ $$P_{01} \times P_{10} = \frac{\Sigma P_1 Q_0}{\Sigma P_0 Q_0} \times \frac{\Sigma Q_1 P_0}{\Sigma Q_1 P_1} \neq 1.$$

i.e., Time reversal test is not satisfied.

Theorem II. *Show that Paasche's method does not satisfy time reversal test.*

Proof. By using Paasche's method, the price index number is given by

$$P_{01} = \frac{\Sigma P_1 Q_1}{\Sigma P_0 Q_1}$$

Also $$P_{10} = \frac{\Sigma Q_0 P_0}{\Sigma Q_0 P_1}$$

∴ $$P_{01} \times P_{10} = \frac{\Sigma P_1 Q_1}{\Sigma P_0 Q_1} \times \frac{\Sigma Q_0 P_0}{\Sigma Q_0 P_1} \neq 1.$$

i.e., Time reversal test is not satisfied.

Theorem III. *Show that Fisher's Ideal method satisfies time reversal test.*

(P.T.U., M.B.A., Dec., 2009)

Proof. Let P_1 = The current year price

Q_1 = The current year quantity

P_0 = The base year price

Q_0 = The base year quantity

By using Fisher's Ideal method

$$P_{01} = \sqrt{\frac{\Sigma P_1Q_0}{\Sigma P_0Q_0} \times \frac{\Sigma P_1Q_1}{\Sigma P_0Q_1}} \qquad | \text{ Changing P to Q and Q to P}$$

$$P_{10} = \sqrt{\frac{\Sigma Q_1P_0}{\Sigma Q_1P_1} \times \frac{\Sigma Q_0P_0}{\Sigma Q_0P_1}}$$

$$\therefore \quad P_{01} \times P_{10} = \sqrt{\frac{\Sigma P_1Q_0}{\Sigma P_0Q_0} \times \frac{\Sigma P_1Q_1}{\Sigma P_0Q_1}} \times \sqrt{\frac{\Sigma Q_0P_1}{\Sigma Q_1P_1} \times \frac{\Sigma Q_0P_0}{\Sigma Q_0P_1}}$$

$$= \sqrt{\frac{\Sigma P_1Q_0}{\Sigma P_0Q_0} \times \frac{\Sigma P_1Q_1}{\Sigma P_0Q_1} \times \frac{\Sigma Q_1P_1}{\Sigma Q_1P_1} \times \frac{\Sigma Q_0P_0}{\Sigma Q_0P_1}} = \sqrt{1} = 1.$$

Hence Fisher's Ideal method satisfies time reversal test.

III. Factor Reversal Test *(P.T.U., M.B.A. Dec. 2009)*

Let P_1 = The current year price

Q_1 = The current year quantity

P_0 = The base year price

Q_0 = The base year quantity.

Then, the total value of a given commodity in a given year is the product of the quantity and the price in that year (*i.e.* total value = P × Q)

According to **Fisher, "Factor Reversal Test"** is that the change in price multiplied by the change in quantity should be equal to the total change in value.

Let P_{01} = The change in price in the current year

Q_{01} = The change in quantity in the current year.

Then, according to 'Factor Reversal Test'

$$P_{01} \times Q_{01} = \frac{\Sigma P_1Q_1}{\Sigma P_0Q_0} \text{ must be true.}$$

Theorem IV. *Show that Fisher's ideal index is satisfied by the Factor Reversal Test*

(P.T.U., M.B.A., Dec. 2009)

Proof. By Fisher's Ideal Method,

$$P_{01} = \sqrt{\frac{\Sigma P_1Q_0}{\Sigma P_0Q_0} \times \frac{\Sigma P_1Q_1}{\Sigma P_0Q_1}}$$

$$Q_{01} = \sqrt{\frac{\Sigma Q_1P_0}{\Sigma Q_0P_0} \times \frac{\Sigma Q_1P_1}{\Sigma Q_0P_1}} \qquad | \text{ Changing P to Q and Q to P}$$

$$\therefore \qquad P_{01} \times Q_{01} = \sqrt{\frac{\Sigma P_1Q_0}{\Sigma P_0Q_0} \times \frac{\Sigma P_1Q_1}{\Sigma P_0Q_1}} \times \sqrt{\frac{\Sigma Q_1P_0}{\Sigma Q_0P_0} \times \frac{\Sigma Q_1P_1}{\Sigma Q_0P_1}}$$

$$= \sqrt{\frac{\Sigma P_1Q_0}{\Sigma P_0Q_0} \times \frac{\Sigma P_1Q_1}{\Sigma P_0Q_1} \times \frac{\Sigma Q_1P_0}{\Sigma Q_0P_0} \times \frac{\Sigma Q_1P_1}{\Sigma Q_0P_1}}$$

$$= \sqrt{\frac{(\Sigma P_1Q_1)^2}{(\Sigma P_0Q_0)^2}} = \frac{\Sigma P_1Q_1}{\Sigma P_0Q_0}.$$

Hence the result *i.e., Fisher's Ideal Index* is satisfied by *Factor Reversal Test.*

Uses of Factor Reversal Test. If any Index number formula satisfies *Factor Reversal Test,* then that formula can be used to construct index numbers of quantities as well as of prices. Only Fisher's Ideal Index satisfies Factor Reversal Test. Therefore Fisher's Ideal Index serves equally well for constructing index numbers of quantities and prices.

IV. Circular Test

This test is an extension of the 'Time Reversal Test'. Let P_{01}, P_{12}, P_{20} be three index numbers. Then we say that the circular test is satisfied if $P_{01} \times P_{12} \times P_{20} = 1$.

In other words, **'Circular Test'** is that if an index number is constructed for the year '*a*' on the base year '*b*', and for the year '*b*' on the base year '*c*', then the result should be same if we calculated the same index number for the year '*a*' on the base year '*c*' without going through '*b*' as an intermediary.

Theorem V. *Show that Laspeyre's Index number does not satisfy 'circular test'.*

Proof. By Laspeyre's Index formula,

$$P_{01} = \frac{\Sigma P_1Q_0}{\Sigma P_0Q_0}$$

$$P_{12} = \frac{\Sigma P_2Q_1}{\Sigma P_1Q_1}$$

$$P_{20} = \frac{\Sigma P_0Q_2}{\Sigma P_2Q_2}$$

$$\therefore \qquad P_{01} \times P_{12} \times P_{20} = \frac{\Sigma P_1Q_0}{\Sigma P_0Q_0} \times \frac{\Sigma P_2Q_1}{\Sigma P_1Q_1} \times \frac{\Sigma P_0Q_2}{\Sigma P_2Q_2} \neq 1$$

i.e., The Circular Test is not satisfied by Laspeyre's Index.

Theorem VI. *Show that Paasche's Index and Fisher's Ideal Index do not satisfy the circular test.*

Proof. (*i*) By Paasche's Index formula,

$$P_{01} = \frac{\Sigma P_1Q_1}{\Sigma P_0Q_1}$$

$$P_{12} = \frac{\Sigma P_2Q_2}{\Sigma P_1Q_2}$$

$$P_{20} = \frac{\Sigma P_0Q_0}{\Sigma P_2Q_0}$$

$$\therefore \quad P_{01} \times P_{12} \times P_{20} = \frac{\Sigma P_1 Q_1}{\Sigma P_0 Q_1} \times \frac{\Sigma P_2 Q_2}{\Sigma P_1 Q_2} \times \frac{\Sigma P_0 Q_0}{\Sigma P_2 Q_0} \neq 1$$

Hence the Circular Test is not satisfied by the Paasche's Index.

(*ii*) By Fisher's Ideal Index formula,

$$P_{01} = \sqrt{\frac{\Sigma P_1 Q_0}{\Sigma P_0 Q_0} \times \frac{\Sigma P_1 Q_1}{\Sigma P_0 Q_1}}$$

$$P_{12} = \sqrt{\frac{\Sigma P_2 Q_1}{\Sigma P_1 Q_1} \times \frac{\Sigma P_2 Q_2}{\Sigma P_1 Q_2}}$$

$$P_{20} = \sqrt{\frac{\Sigma P_0 Q_2}{\Sigma P_2 Q_2} \times \frac{\Sigma P_0 Q_0}{\Sigma P_2 Q_0}}$$

$$\therefore \quad P_{01} \times P_{12} \times P_{20} = \sqrt{\frac{\Sigma P_1 Q_0}{\Sigma P_0 Q_0} \times \frac{\Sigma P_1 Q_1}{\Sigma P_0 Q_1}} \times \sqrt{\frac{\Sigma P_2 Q_1}{\Sigma P_1 Q_1} \times \frac{\Sigma P_2 Q_2}{\Sigma P_1 Q_2}} \times \sqrt{\frac{\Sigma P_0 Q_2}{\Sigma P_2 Q_2} \times \frac{\Sigma P_0 Q_0}{\Sigma P_2 Q_0}} \neq 1$$

Hence the Circular Test is not satisfied by Fisher's Ideal Index.

Theorem VII. *Show that 'Simple Aggregative Method' and 'Fixed weight Aggregative Method' satisfies the circular test.*

Proof. (*i*) by 'Simple Aggregative Method',

$$P_{01} = \frac{\Sigma P_1}{\Sigma P_0}$$

$$P_{12} = \frac{\Sigma P_2}{\Sigma P_1}$$

$$P_{20} = \frac{\Sigma P_0}{\Sigma P_2}$$

$$\therefore \quad P_{01} \times P_{12} \times P_{20} = \frac{\Sigma P_1}{\Sigma P_0} \times \frac{\Sigma P_2}{\Sigma P_1} \times \frac{\Sigma P_0}{\Sigma P_2} = 1$$

Hence *Simple Aggregative Method* is satisfied by *Circular Test.*

(*ii*) By 'Fixed Weight Aggregative Method',

$$P_{01} = \frac{\Sigma P_1 Q}{\Sigma P_0 Q}$$

$$P_{12} = \frac{\Sigma P_2 Q}{\Sigma P_1 Q}$$

$$P_{20} = \frac{\Sigma P_0 Q}{\Sigma P_2 Q}$$

$$\therefore \quad P_{01} \times P_{12} \times P_{20} = \frac{\Sigma P_1 Q}{\Sigma P_0 Q} \times \frac{\Sigma P_2 Q}{\Sigma P_1 Q} \times \frac{\Sigma P_0 Q}{\Sigma P_2 Q} = 1$$

Hence *Fixed Weight Aggregative Method* is satisfied by *circular test.*

Uses of Circular Test. If an index is satisfied by the Circular Test, then the index number under consideration can be adjusted from year to year without refering each time to the original base.

Limitations of Circular Test. The Circular Test is not meet by any of the weighted aggregative methods with changing weights. Similarly Laspeyre's, Paasche, Durbish and Bowley's, Fisher's Ideal, Marshall-Edge worth, Kelley's index numbers do not meet the Circular Test because the weights in all these methods depend on the period between which comparisons are being made. If these periods change, the weights change.

13.13. CHAIN INDEX NUMBERS

(P.T.U., M.B.A. Dec. 2010)

The **chain index number** is one in which the figures for each year (or sub-period) are first expressed as percentages of the proceeding year. These percentages are then chained together by successive multiplication to form a chain index.

In other words, in chain index numbers, the base period does not remain same where as in fixed base method, the base period remains same.

13.14. CONSTRUCTION OF CHAIN INDEX NUMBERS

We first define **'Link Relatives'**. The link relative of a commodity is defined to be the ratio of the current year price and the previous year price multiplied by 100. *i.e.,*

$$\text{Link Relative} = \frac{\text{The current year price}}{\text{The previous year price}} \times 100.$$

To construct chain index numbers, the following steps are to be followed.

Step I. Obtain the Link Relatives.

Step II. Find the average Link Relative. Then chain index of any year is the average link of that year multiplied by chain index of previous year divided by 100. *i.e.*

Chain index for current year

$$= \frac{\text{Average Link Relative of current year} \times \text{Chain index of previous year}}{100}$$

13.15. DIFFERENCE BETWEEN CHAIN RELATIVES AND FIXED-BASE RELATIVES

Chain relatives are computed from Link Relatives whereas fixed base relatives are computed directly from the original data.

Remark. Chain relatives should be used when the original data is not available and link relatives are given.

13.16. TO CONVERT CHAIN INDEX TO FIXED-BASE INDEX

To covert chain-base index number to a fixed-base index number, the following steps are to be followed.

Step I. For the first year, the fixed base index = Chain base Index.

i.e., If the index numbers are to be constructed by taking first year as base, then the index number for the first year is taken as 100.

Step II. To find the index number for other years, use the following formula.

Fixed-Base Index for the current year

$$= \frac{\text{Chain - Base Index for the current year} \times \text{Fixed - Base Index for the previous year}}{100}$$

or $$\text{Current's year F.B.I.} = \frac{\text{Current's year C.B.I.} \times \text{Previous's year F.B.I.}}{100}$$

where F.B.I. = Fixed-Base Index, C.B.I. = Chain-Base Index.

13.17. ADVANTAGES OF CHAIN-BASE METHOD (*P.T.U., M.B.A. Dec. 2001 ; May 2004*)

The following are the main advantages of Chain-Base Method.

(*i*) This method is highly practicable in economics and business where we are to compare the data with the previous period and not with any distant past.

(*ii*) By using Chain-Base Method, we can add new commodities and delete old commodities without changing the entire data.

(*iii*) In the construction of consumer price index and the whole sale price index, chain-base index number is most suitable.

(*iv*) By using Chain-Base Index number, weights can be adjusted as frequently as possible.

(*v*) Index numbers obtained by Chain-Base Method are free from seasonal variations than those obtained by other methods.

13.18. LIMITATIONS OF CHAIN-BASE METHOD

The main disadvantage of the Chain-Base index number is that while the percentage of previous year figures give accurate comparisons of year-to-year changes, the long-range comparisons of chained percentage are not too much accurate.

ILLUSTRATIVE EXAMPLES

Example 1. *Find the quantity index for the following data. Interpret the result.*

Commodity	*Quantity*		*Price in*
	2004	*2005*	*2004*
A	*30*	*25*	*30*
B	*20*	*30*	*40*
C	*10*	*15*	*20*

Sol. Take the base year as 2004

Let P_0 = The base year price

Q_0 = The base year quantity

Q_1 = The current year quantity. Consider the following table :

Commodity	P_0	Q_0	Q_1	Q_0P_0	Q_1P_0
A	30	30	25	900	750
B	40	20	30	800	1200
C	20	10	15	200	300
				ΣQ_0P_0 = 1900	ΣQ_1P_0 = 2250

The required quantity index is given by

$$Q_{01} = \frac{\Sigma Q_1P_0}{\Sigma Q_0P_0} \times 100 = \frac{2250}{1900} \times 100 = 118.42.$$

Interpretation. The quantity index for the current year 2004 is 118.42. It means that the quantity index in 2004 has increased by 18.42% as compared to the quantity index in 2003.

Example 2. *Compute the quantity index by using Fisher's Ideal Index formula for the following data.*

Commodity		*Base year*	*Current year*	
	Price	*Total value*	*Price*	*Total value*
A	*10*	*100*	*8*	*96*
B	*16*	*96*	*12*	*96*
C	*12*	*48*	*10*	*40*

Sol. Let P_0 = The base year price

P_1 = The current year price

Q_0 = The base year quantity

Q_1 = The current year quantity.

The quantity for each commodity can be obtained by dividing the total value by the price. *i.e.* the quantity for the commodity A for the base year are $\frac{100}{10} = 10$ $\frac{96}{16} = 6$, $\frac{48}{12} = 4$ etc.

Consider the following table.

Commodity	P_0	Q_0	P_1	Q_1	Q_0P_0	Q_1P_0	Q_1P_1	Q_0P_1
A	10	10	8	12	100	120	96	80
B	16	6	12	8	96	128	96	72
C	12	4	10	4	48	48	40	40
					$\Sigma Q_0P_0 = 244$	$\Sigma Q_1P_0 = 296$	$\Sigma Q_1P_1 = 232$	$\Sigma Q_0P_1 = 192$

The required quantity index is given by

$$Q_{01} = \sqrt{\frac{\Sigma Q_1P_0}{\Sigma Q_0P_0} \times \frac{\Sigma Q_1P_1}{\Sigma Q_0P_1}} \times 100 = \sqrt{\frac{296}{244} \times \frac{232}{192}} \times 100$$

$$= \sqrt{1.2131 \times 1.2083} \times 100 = 1.21 \times 100 = 121.$$

Example 3. *Find Laspeyre's Price index and Paasche's quantity index number for the following data :*

Commodity	*Price*		*Quantity*	
	Base year	*Current year*	*Base year*	*Current year*
A	*2*	*5*	*20*	*15*
B	*4*	*8*	*4*	*5*
C	*1*	*3*	*12*	*12*
D	*5*	*10*	*6*	*8*

Sol. Let P_0 = The base year price

Q_0 = The base year quantity

P_1 = The current year price

Q_1 = The current year quantity.

Consider the table.

Commodity	P_0	Q_0	P_1	Q_1	P_0Q_0	P_1Q_0	P_0Q_1	P_1Q_1
A	2	20	5	15	40	100	30	75
B	4	4	8	5	16	32	20	40
C	1	12	3	12	12	36	12	36
D	5	6	10	8	30	60	40	80
					$\Sigma P_0Q_0 = 98$	$\Sigma P_1Q_0 = 228$	$\Sigma P_0Q_1 = 102$	$\Sigma P_1Q_1 = 231$

(*a*) Laspeyre's price index is given by

$$P_{01} = \frac{\Sigma P_1Q_0}{\Sigma P_0Q_0} \times 100 = \frac{228}{98} \times 100 = 232.65$$

(*b*) Paasche's quantity index is given by

$$Q_{01} = \frac{\Sigma Q_1P_1}{\Sigma Q_0P_1} \times 100 = \frac{231}{228} \times 100 = 101.31.$$

Example 4. *Construct a Fisher's Ideal index from the following data. Show that it satisfies :*

(*i*) *Time Reversal Test*

(*ii*) *Factor Reversal Test.*

Commodity	*2005*		*2006*	
	P_0	Q_0	P_1	Q_1
A	*10*	*40*	*12*	*45*
B	*11*	*50*	*11*	*52*
C	*14*	*30*	*17*	*30*
D	*8*	*28*	*10*	*29*
E	*12*	*15*	*13*	*20*

Sol. Let P_0 = The base year price

Q_0 = The base year quantity

P_1 = The current year price

Q_1 = The current year quantity.

Consider the Table

Commodity	P_0	Q_0	P_1	Q_1	P_0Q_0	P_0Q_1	P_1Q_0	P_1Q_1
A	10	40	12	45	400	450	480	540
B	11	50	11	52	550	572	550	572
C	14	30	17	30	420	420	510	510
D	8	28	10	29	224	232	280	290
E	12	15	13	20	180	240	195	260
					$\Sigma P_0Q_0 = 1774$	$\Sigma P_0Q_1 = 1914$	$\Sigma P_1Q_0 = 2015$	$\Sigma P_1Q_1 = 2172$

The Fisher's Ideal index is given by

$$P_{01} = \sqrt{\frac{\Sigma P_1Q_0}{\Sigma P_0Q_0} \times \frac{\Sigma P_1Q_1}{\Sigma P_0Q_1}} \times 100 = \sqrt{\frac{2015}{1774} \times \frac{2172}{1914}} \times 100$$

$$= \sqrt{1.135 \times 1.134} \times 100 = \sqrt{1.287} \times 100 = 1.1344 \times 100 = 113.44$$

Further, the Time Reversed Test is satisfied if $P_{01} \times P_{10} = 1$

Here $$P_{01} = \sqrt{\frac{\Sigma P_1Q_0}{\Sigma P_0Q_0} \times \frac{\Sigma P_1Q_1}{\Sigma P_0Q_1}} = \sqrt{\frac{2015}{1774} \times \frac{2172}{1914}} \quad ...(1)$$

$$P_{10} = \sqrt{\frac{\Sigma P_0Q_1}{\Sigma P_1Q_1} \times \frac{\Sigma P_0Q_0}{\Sigma P_1Q_0}} = \sqrt{\frac{1914}{2172} \times \frac{1774}{2015}} \quad ...(2)$$

From (1) and (2),

$$\therefore \quad P_{01} \times P_{10} = \sqrt{\frac{2015}{1774} \times \frac{2172}{1914} \times \frac{1914}{2172} \times \frac{1774}{2015}}$$

$= \sqrt{1} = 1$, which is true.

Also, the Factor Reversal Test is satisfied if $P_{01} \times Q_{01} = \frac{\Sigma P_1Q_1}{\Sigma P_0Q_0}$

Here $$Q_{01} = \sqrt{\frac{\Sigma Q_1P_0}{\Sigma Q_0P_0} \times \frac{\Sigma Q_1P_1}{\Sigma Q_0P_1}} = \sqrt{\frac{1914}{1774} \times \frac{2172}{2015}} \quad ...(3)$$

From (1) and (3),

$$\therefore \quad P_{01} \times Q_{01} = \sqrt{\frac{2015}{1774} \times \frac{2172}{1914} \times \frac{1914}{1774} \times \frac{2172}{2015}}$$

$$= \sqrt{\frac{2172 \times 2172}{1774 \times 1774}} = \frac{2172}{1774} = \frac{\Sigma P_1Q_1}{\Sigma P_0Q_0}$$

Hence the Factor Reversal Test is satisfied.

Example 5. *From the data given of the whole sale prices of Rice for six years, construct index numbers by chain-base method.*

Year	*Price of Rice*
1998	*50*
1999	*60*
2000	*62*
2001	*65*
2002	*70*
2003	*78*

Sol. To find the Chain index numbers, consider the following table :

Year	*Price*	*Link Relatives* $= \frac{\text{Current Year Price}}{\text{Previous Year Price}} \times 100$	*Chain Index Numbers*
1998	50	100	100
1999	60	$\frac{60}{50} \times 100 = 120$	$\frac{120 \times 100}{100} = 120$
2000	62	$\frac{62}{60} \times 100 = 103.33$	$\frac{103.33 \times 120}{100} = 124$
2001	65	$\frac{65}{62} \times 100 = 104.84$	$\frac{104.84 \times 124}{100} = 130$
2002	70	$\frac{70}{65} \times 100 = 107.69$	$\frac{107.69 \times 130}{100} = 140$
2003	78	$\frac{78}{70} \times 100 = 111.43$	$\frac{111.43 \times 140}{100} = 156$

Example 6. *From the chain-base index numbers, find the fixed-based index numbers for the following data :*

Year	*2001*	*2002*	*2003*	*2004*	*2005*
Chain Index Numbers	*110*	*120*	*90*	*80*	*140*

Sol. We know that Fixed base index for the current year

$$= \frac{\text{Chain-base index for the current year} \times \text{Fixed base index for the previous year}}{100}$$

∴ The fixed-base index number are given below :

Year	*Chain base Index numbers*	*Fixed base Index numbers*
2001	110	110
2002	120	$\frac{120 \times 110}{100} = 132$
2003	90	$\frac{90 \times 132}{100} = 118.8$
2004	80	$\frac{80 \times 118.8}{100} = 95.04$
2005	140	$\frac{140 \times 95.04}{100} = 133.05$

Example 7. *Compute the Chain index numbers with 2002 as base from the following data given the average whole sale prices of the commodities A, B and C as below :*

Commodity	*Average whole sale price*				
	2002	*2003*	*2004*	*2005*	*2006*
A	*20*	*16*	*28*	*35*	*21*
B	*25*	*30*	*24*	*36*	*45*
C	*20*	*25*	*30*	*24*	*30*

Sol. We know that Chain Index number for the current year

$$= \frac{\text{Average link relative of current year} \times \text{Chain Index number of previous year}}{100}$$

Also Link Relative for the current year $= \frac{\text{The current year price}}{\text{The previous year price}} \times 100$

Consider the following tables I and II.

Table I

		Link relatives			
Commodity	*Base year 2002*	*Year 2003*	*Year 2004*	*Year 2005*	*Year 2006*
A	100	$\frac{16}{20} \times 100 = 80$	$\frac{28}{16} \times 100 = 175$	$\frac{35}{28} \times 100 = 125$	$\frac{21}{35} \times 100 = 60$
B	100	$\frac{30}{25} \times 100 = 120$	$\frac{24}{30} \times 100 = 80$	$\frac{36}{24} \times 100 = 150$	$\frac{45}{36} \times 100 = 125$
C	100	$\frac{25}{20} \times 100 = 125$	$\frac{30}{25} \times 100 = 120$	$\frac{24}{30} \times 100 = 80$	$\frac{30}{24} \times 100 = 125$
Total of Link relatives	300	325	375	355	310
Average	$\frac{300}{3} = 100$	$\frac{325}{3} = 108.33$	$\frac{375}{3} = 125$	$\frac{355}{3} = 118.33$	$\frac{310}{3} = 103.33$

Table II

Construction of Chain Index numbers

Year	Average of link relatives	Chain Index number
2002	100	100
2003	108.33	$\frac{108.33 \times 100}{100} = 108.33$
2004	125	$\frac{125 \times 108.33}{100} = 135.41$
2005	118.33	$\frac{118.33 \times 135.41}{100} = 160.23$
2006	103.33	$\frac{103.33 \times 160.23}{100} = 165.57$

TEST YOUR KNOWLEDGE 13.2

1. Discuss various tests of adequacy of index numbers (*P.T.U., M.B.A. Dec. 2005*)
2. What is Time Reversal Test ? Show that Fisher's Ideal number satisfies time Reversal test. (*P.T.U., M.B.A Dec. 2003*)
3. What is Factor Reversal Test ? Is Fisher's Ideal index number satisfies it ? (*P.T.U., M.B.A Dec. 2003*)
4. What are chain-base indices ? Discuss its advantages over fixed-base index numbers. (*P.T.U., M.B.A Dec. 2001 ; May 2004*)
5. Define Factor Reversal Test used for index numbers. Examine whether this test is satisfied by Edgeworth's index numbers.
6. Define Index numbers. Distinguish between 'Fixed-base' and 'Chain-base index numbers with their merits and demerits.
7. Construct Fisher's Ideal index number for the following data and show how it satisfies Time and Factor Reserve Test

Commodity	2004		2005	
	Quantity	Price	Quantity	Price
M	20	12	30	14
N	13	14	15	20
O	12	10	20	15
P	8	6	10	4
Q	5	8	5	6

(*P.T.U., M.B.A May 2010*)

8. Calculate the Fisher's Ideal index from the following data and prove that it satisfies both the time reversal and factor reversal tests:

Commodity	*2002*		*2003*	
	Price	*Expenditure*	*Price*	*Expenditure*
A	8	80	10	120
B	10	120	12	96
C	5	40	5	50
D	4	56	3	60
E	20	100	25	150

(*P.T.U., M.B.A Dec. 2010*)

9. From the following data, construct quantity index numbers by
(*i*) Fisher's Method (*ii*) Marshall-Edgeworth method.

Commodity	*Base year*		*Current year*	
	Price	*Quantity*	*Price*	*Quantity*
A	25	40	2000	50
B	22	18	1200	30
C	54	16	1320	44
D	20	40	1350	45
E	18	30	630	15

10. From the Chain-base index numbers given below, prepare Fixed-base index numbers.

Year	2000	2001	2002	2003	2004	2005
Chain-base Index numbers	92	102	104	98	193	101

Answers

8. 112.8 **9.** (*i*) 136.85 (*ii*) 134.94
10. 92, 93, 84, 95, 65, 98, 52, 99.5.

13.19. CONCEPT OF BASE SHIFTING

The changing of reference base of an index number from one period to another period without recomputing the entire series and returning to the original raw data is called Base Shifting.

13.20. ADVANTAGES OF BASE SHIFTING

The following are the main advantages of 'Base Shifting'.

(*i*) When the previous base becomes useless for the purpose of comparison, the base shifting helps in stating the series in terms of a more recent period.

(*ii*) To compare several index numbers which have been computed on different base periods, it is necessary that all index numbers must have the same base period. For this reason, base shifting is important.

13.21. METHOD OF SHIFTING THE BASE PERIOD

Divide all index numbers (for the various years corresponding to the old base period) by the index number corresponding to the new base period and then express the results as percentages.

This method is applicable only if the index numbers satisfy the Circular Test.

Illustration : Consider the following index numbers of prices with 1996 as base year.

Year	1996	1997	1998	1999	2000	2001	2002	2003
Index	100	110	120	200	400	410	400	380

We shift the base from 1996 to 2000.

The index numbers for the various years (when the base year = 2000) are shown in the following table.

Year	*Index Numbers (1996 = 100)*	*Index Numbers (2000 = 100)*
1996	100	$\frac{100}{400} \times 100 = 25$
1997	110	$\frac{110}{400} \times 100 = 27.5$
1998	120	$\frac{120}{400} \times 100 = 30$
1999	200	$\frac{200}{400} \times 100 = 50$
2000	**400**	$\frac{400}{400} \times 100 = 100$
2001	410	$\frac{410}{400} \times 100 = 102.5$
2002	400	$\frac{400}{400} \times 100 = 100$
2003	380	$\frac{380}{400} \times 100 = 95$

13.22. CONCEPT OF SPLICING

Consider a series of index numbers with weights and we desire to construct another series of index numbers with new weights. The process of converting these two index numbers into a continuous series is called **splicing.**

Mathematically, Spliced Index number

$$= \frac{\text{Index number of current year} \times \text{Old Index number of New Base Year}}{100}$$

Illustration. The following table contains the series of index numbers with reference base of 2001 and another series of index numbers with reference base of 2003.

Year	*Old price index (Base Year = 2001)*	*Revised price index (Base Year = 2001)*
2000	96	—
2001	100	—
2002	110	—
2003	120	100
2004	—	104
2005	—	106
2006	—	112

We splice the two series *i.e.,* we obtain a continuous series with base year 2001. The spliced index numbers for the various years (with reference to base year 2003, are shown in the following table :

Year	*Old price index (2001 = 100)*	*Revised price index (2003 = 100)*	*Spliced index numbers (2003 = 100)*
2000	96	—	$\frac{96}{120} \times 100 = 80$
2001	100	—	$\frac{100}{120} \times 100 = 83.33$
2002	110	—	$\frac{110}{120} \times 100 = 91.66$
2003	**120**	100	$\frac{120}{120} \times 100 = 100$
2004	—	104	$\frac{104}{100} \times 100 = 104$
2005	—	106	$\frac{106}{100} \times 100 = 106$
2006	—	112	$\frac{112}{100} \times 100 = 112$

13.23. USES OF SPLICING

Splicing has the following uses :

1. It helps us for comparision between old and new index numbers.
2. It gives most accurate result when G.M. is used as an average in the construction of index numbers.
3. It is the only practical method for comparison of index numbers over different time periods.

13.24. PURCHASING POWER OF MONEY

The purchasing power of money is the reciprocal of the price index *i.e.,*

$$\text{Purchasing Power of Money} = \frac{1}{\text{Price Index}}$$

It means, if prices increase, the value of rupee will decrease.

13.25. REAL WAGE

The real wage is defined by the following formula *i.e.,*

$$\text{Real Wage} = \frac{\text{Money Wage}}{\text{Price Index}} \times 100.$$

13.26. DEFLATING

The process of calculating real wages by using the purchasing power of money or the price index is called deflating.

13.27. CONSUMER PRICE INDEX NUMBERS

The consumer price index numbers, also known as **cost of living index numbers** or **price of living index numbers** are those index numbers which help us in determining the effect of rise and fall in prices on different classes of consumers living in different areas.

13.28. NEED OF CONSUMER PRICE INDEX NUMBERS

The general index numbers are not able to give an exact idea of the effect of the change in the general price level on the cost of living of different classes of people. Different classes of people consume different type of commodities and even the same type of commodities are not consumed in the same proportion by different classes of people. The consumer price index numbers become necessary to measure these types of changes in price level on the cost of living of different classes of people.

13.29. LIMITATIONS

The **consumer price index numbers** or the **cost of living index numbers** do not measure the actural cost of living. These numbers also fail to measure the fluctuations in the cost of living due to causes other than the change in the price level.

13.30. USES OF THE CONSUMER PRICE INDEX NUMBERS

(i) These index numbers are very useful in wage negotiations and wage contracts. Dearness allowance component of wages are governed in many countries by consumer price index numbers.

(ii) These index numbers help us in framing various policies like wage policy, price policy, rent control, taxation policies, etc.

(iii) The consumer price index numbers are used to measure the changing purchasing power of the rupee, real income, etc.

13.31. METHOD OF CONSTRUCTING THE CONSUMER PRICE INDEX NUMBER

There are mainly two methods for constructing the consumer price index numbers, given by

(i) Aggregate Expenditure Method or Aggregative Method.

(ii) Family Budget Method or Method of Weighted Relatives.

I. Aggregate Expenditure Method. According to this method,

$$\text{Consumer price index number} = \frac{\Sigma P_1 Q_0}{\Sigma P_0 Q_0} \times 100$$

where P_1 = The current year price of a commodity.
P_0 = The base year price
Q_0 = The base year quantity.

The Aggregative Expenditure method is infact the Laspeyre's method and is the most power method for constructing consumer price index numbers.

II. Family Budget Method. According to this method,

$$\text{Consumer price index number} = \frac{\Sigma PV}{\Sigma V}$$

where $P = \frac{P_1}{P_0} \times 100, \quad V = P_0 Q_0$

P_1 = The current year price
P_0 = The base year price
Q_0 = The base year quantity.

This method is infact the weighted average of price relatives method as discussed earlier.

ILLUSTRATIVE EXAMPLES

Example 1. *Shift the base year from 1997 to 1999 in the following series of index numbers.*

Year	*1997*	*1998*	*1999*	*2000*	*2001*	*2002*	*2003*
Index	*100*	*115*	*125*	*130*	*140*	*185*	*200*

(P.T.U., M.B.A. Dec. 2004)

Sol. The index numbers for the various years with base 1999 are given in the following table :

Year	*Index number (1997 = 100)*	*Index numbers (1997 = 100)*
1997	100	$\frac{100}{125} \times 100 = 80$
1998	115	$\frac{115}{125} \times 100 = 92$
1999	**125**	$\frac{125}{125} \times 100 = 100$
2000	130	$\frac{130}{125} \times 100 = 104$
2001	140	$\frac{140}{125} \times 100 = 112$
2002	185	$\frac{185}{125} \times 100 = 148$
2003	200	$\frac{200}{125} \times 100 = 160$

Example 2. *A price index number series was started in 1993 as base. By 1997, it rose by 25%. The link relative for 1998 was 95. In this year, a new series was started. This new series rose by 15% by next year. But during next four years, the rise was not rapid. During 2001 the price level was only 8% higher than 2000 and in 2003, they were 5% higher than 2001. Splice the two series and calculate the index numbers for the various years by shifting the base to 2000.*

Sol. In the first series, the index number for the year 1993 = 100. It rose by 25% by 1997.

∴ Index number for the year 1997 = 125

For the year 1995, the link relative = 95

∴ The index number for the year 1998 $= 125 \times \frac{95}{100} = 118.75$

In the second series, the base year is 1998.

∴ The index number in this year = 100.

Now the index number for the year 2000 = 15% of the year 1998 = 115.

Also 8% of 115 = 9.2 ∴ Index number for the year 2001 = 115 + 9.2 = 124.20

Further 5% of 124.20 = 6.21.

∴ Index number for the year 2003 = 124.20 + 6.21 = 130.41

Tabulating the above data, we get the following table :

Year	*Index Number (1993 = 100)*	*Index Number (1998 = 100)*	*Spliced Index Numbers*
1993	100	—	$\frac{100}{118.75} \times 100 = 84.21$
1997	125	—	$\frac{125}{118.75} \times 100 = 105.26$
1998	**118.75**	**100**	$\frac{100}{100} \times 100 = 100$
2000	—	115	$\frac{115}{100} \times 100 = 115$
2001	—	124.20	$\frac{124.20}{100} \times 100 = 124.20$
2003	—	130.41	$\frac{130.41}{100} \times 100 = 130.41$

We now shift the base year from 1993 to 2000.

The Index numbers for the various years are shown in the following table :

Year	*Index Numbers (1993 = 100)*	*Index Numbers (2000 = 100)*
1993	84.21	$\frac{84.21}{115} \times 100 = 73.23$
1997	105.26	$\frac{105.26}{115} \times 100 = 91.53$
1998	100	$\frac{100}{115} \times 100 = 86.96$
2000	**115**	$\frac{115}{115} \times 100 = 100$
2001	124.20	$\frac{124.20}{115} \times 100 = 108$
2003	130.41	$\frac{130.41}{115} \times 100 = 113.40$

Example 3. *From the following data, calculate cost of living index number :*

Commodity	*Price (Base year)*	*Price (Current year)*	*Weighted Quantity*
A	*50*	*80*	*200 Qtls.*
B	*40*	*60*	*40 kg.*
C	*10*	*20*	*4 kg*
D	*5*	*10*	*120 m*
E	*2*	*5*	*6 m*
F	*8*	*14*	*10 Dozen*

(P.T.U., M.B.A. May 2001)

Sol. Let P_0 = The base year price

Q_0 = The base year quantity

P_1 = The current year price.

Consider the following table :

Commodity	*Weighted Quantity* Q_0	P_0	P_1	P_0Q_0	P_1Q_0
A	200	50	80	10000	16000
B	40	40	60	1600	2400
C	4	10	20	40	80
D	120	5	10	600	1200
E	6	2	5	12	30
F	10	8	14	80	140
				$\Sigma P_0Q_0 = 12332$	$\Sigma P_1Q_0 = 19850$

Using Aggregate Expenditure Method,

$$\text{Consumer price index number} = \frac{\Sigma P_1Q_0}{\Sigma P_0Q_0} \times 100 = \frac{19850}{12332} \times 100 = 160.96$$

Alternative : We can also compute the Consumer Price index by Family Budget Method. Consider the following table :

Commodity	*Weighted Quantity* Q_0	P_0	P_1	$P = \frac{P_1}{P_0} \times 100$	$V = P_0Q_0$	PV
A	200	50	80	160	10000	1600000
B	40	40	60	150	1600	240000
C	4	10	20	200	40	8000
D	120	5	10	200	600	120000
E	6	2	5	250	12	3000
F	10	8	14	175	80	14000
					ΣV = 12332	ΣPV = 1985000

$$\therefore \text{ Consumer Index Number} = \frac{\Sigma PV}{\Sigma V} = \frac{1985000}{12332} = 160.96.$$

Remark. The value of consumer price index number computed by the Aggregate Expenditure Method and Family Budget Method is same.

Example 4. *Construct a cost of living index for the year 2001, 2002 and 2003 from the following index numbers, the weights being food 55, rent 20, clothing 15, fuel and lighting 15 and miscellaneous 5.*

Year	*Food*	*Rent*	*Clothing*	*Fuel and Lighting*	*Misc.*
2000	*100*	*100*	*100*	*100*	*100*
2001	*105*	*104*	*98*	*100*	*110*
2002	*110*	*112*	*102*	*101*	*115*
2003	*112*	*115*	*105*	*103*	*120*

Sol. By Weighted Average of Relatives method,

$$\text{Price Index} = \frac{\Sigma PW}{\Sigma W},$$

where W = Value weights, PW = Weighted relatives

Calculation of Cost of Living index numbers

Commodity	Weights	2001		2002		2003	
	W	*Index Number*	*Weighted Relatives PW*	*Index Number*	*Weighted Relatives PW*	*Index Number*	*Weighted Relatives PW*
Food	55	105	55 × 105 = 5775	110	55 × 110 = 6050	112	55 × 112 = 6160
Rent	20	104	2080	112	2240	115	2300
Clothing	15	98	1470	102	1530	105	1575
Fuel and Lighting	15	100	1500	101	1515	103	1545
Misc.	5	110	550	115	575	120	600
	ΣW = 110		ΣPW = 11375		ΣPW = 11910		ΣPW =12180

By Family Budget Method,

$$\text{Cost of living index number for the year 2001} = \frac{\Sigma PW}{\Sigma W} = \frac{11375}{110} = 103.40$$

$$\text{Cost of living index number for the year 2002} = \frac{\Sigma PW}{\Sigma W} = \frac{11910}{110} = 108.27$$

$$\text{Cost of living index number for the year 2003} = \frac{\Sigma PW}{\Sigma W} = \frac{12180}{110} = 110.73.$$

Example 5. *The budgets of a middle class family of a particular city gave the following information :*

Items	*Food*	*Rent*	*Clothing*	*Fuel*	*Misc.*
Expenses	*35%*	*15%*	*20%*	*10%*	*20%*
Prices in 2004	*150*	*50*	*100*	*25*	*70*
Prices in 2005	*174*	*70*	*120*	*30*	*95*

What is the change in the cost of living figure of 2005 as compared to 2004.

Sol. Calculation of cost of living Index. Take the base year as 2004.

Items	*Price in 2004* P_0	*Price in 2005* P_1	$P = \frac{P_1}{P_0} \times 100$	*W*	*PW*
Food	150	174	116	35	4060
Rent	50	70	140	15	2100
Clothing	100	120	120	20	2400
Fuel	25	30	120	10	1200
Misc.	70	95	135	20	2700
				ΣW = 100	ΣPW = 12460

By Family Budget Method,

$$\text{Consumer Price Index} = \frac{\Sigma PW}{\Sigma W} = \frac{12460}{100} = 124.6$$

Hence as compared to 2005, the cost of living index number has risen by 24.6%.

Example 6. *Compute the cost of living index number using the weighted geometric mean. The data is given as under :*

Items	*Index Numbers*	*Weights*
Food	*350*	*10*
Fuel	*150*	*2*
Clothing	*200*	*2*
Rent	*150*	*3*
Misc.	*225*	*4*

Sol. Calculation of cost of living Index Number

Items	*I = Index Number*	*W = Weights*	$\log_{10} I$	$W \log_{10} I$
Food	350	10	2.5441	25.441
Fuel	150	2	2.1761	4.3522
Clothing	200	2	2.3010	4.602
Rent	150	3	2.1761	6.5283
Misc.	225	4	2.3522	9.4088
		$\Sigma W = 21$		$\Sigma W \log_{10} I = 50.3323$

∴ Cost of living Index number

$$= \text{Antilog}_{10}\left(\frac{\Sigma W \log_{10} I}{\Sigma W}\right) = \text{Antilog}\left(\frac{50.3323}{21}\right)$$

$$= \text{Antilog}_{10}\ (2.3967) = 249.28.$$

Example 7. *Given the following data :*

Year	*Weekly Wages*	*Consumer Price Index*
2000	*109.50*	*112.8*
2001	*112.20*	*118.2*
2002	*116.40*	*127.4*
2003	*125.08*	*138.2*
2004	*135.40*	*143.5*
2005	*138.10*	*149.8*

(a) Find the real weekly wage for each year

(b) In which year did the employees have the greatest buying power ?

(c) Find the increase in Percentage of the weekly wages for the year 2005 to provide the same buying power that the employees enjoyed in 2000.

Sol. (*a*) We know that real weekly wage is given by

$$\text{Real weekly wage} = \frac{\text{Money wage}}{\text{Price Index}} \times 100$$

Calculation of Real weekly wages.

Year	*Weekly Wages*	*Consumer Price Index*	*Real weekly Wages*
2000	109.50	112.8	$\frac{109.50}{112.8} \times 100 = 97.07$
2001	112.20	118.2	$\frac{112.20}{118.2} \times 100 = 94.92$
2002	116.40	127.4	$\frac{116.40}{127.4} \times 100 = 91.37$
2003	125.08	138.2	$\frac{125.08}{138.2} \times 100 = 90.51$
2004	135.40	143.2	$\frac{135.40}{143.2} \times 100 = 94.36$
2005	138.10	149.8	$\frac{138.10}{149.8} \times 100 = 92.19$

(*b*) From the table, we observe that real weekly wage is maximum for the year 2000. Therefore the employees were having the greatest buying power in the year 2000.

(*c*) Required percentage = 97.07 – 92.19 = 4.88.

TEST YOUR KNOWLEDGE 13.3

1. Discuss the concept of 'Base Shifting' and 'Deflating' with illustration, used in index numbers. (*P.T.U., M.B.A. May 2004*)

2. The following are the index numbers of prices. Shift the base from 1992 to 2001 and recast the index number

Year	*Index Number*
1992	100
1993	110
1994	110
1995	200
1996	320
1997	400
1998	410
1999	400
2000	380
2001	370

3. Given below are two sets of index numbers. One with 1995 as base and the other with 1998 as base.

Year	*Index No. (old)*	*Index Number New*
1995	100	—
1996	103	—
1997	108	—
1998	**110**	100
1999	—	104
2000	—	112
2001	—	110
2002	—	115

4. Compute the cost of living index number of the following data :

Commodity	*Weights*	*Price*	
		Base year	*Current year*
Food	42	12	28
Fuel	8	7	12
Clothing	13	25	70
Rent	15	10	26
Education	6	16	40
Misc.	16	9	36

5. Calculate the cost of living index number by using (*a*) the Weighted A.M. (*b*) the Weighted G.M. for the following data :

Items	*Index Number*	*Weights*
Food	352	48
Fuel	200	10
Clothing	230	18
Rent	160	12
Misc.	190	15

6. The following table gives the cost of living index numbers for different groups in their respective weights for the year 2002 (Base year 1992)

Items	*Cost of living index*	*Weight*
Food	525	40
Clothing	325	16
Fuel	240	15
Rent	180	20
Misc.	200	9

(*a*) Find the overall cost of living index number.

(*b*) If a person gets the salary of ₹ 550 in 1992. Determine how much he should have to receive the salary in 2002 to maintain same standard of living in 1992.

7. Given below are two sets of index numbers. For the purpose of continuity of record, you are required to construct a combined series with the year 1993 as the base :

Year	*Set I* *Price Relatives*	*Set II* *Link Relatives*
1990	100	—
1991	120	—
1992	125	—
1993	150	—
1994	—	110
1995	—	120
1996	—	95
1997	—	105

8. From the following data, compute the consumer price index number using
   (*i*) Aggregate Expenditure Method
   (*ii*) Family budget Method.

Items	*Units consumed in base year*	*Price*	
		Base year	*Current year*
Rice	20	1	1.2
Wheat	50	3	3.5
Pulses	50	4	5
Ghee	20	20	30
Sugar	40	2.5	5
Oil	50	10	15
Fuel	60	2	2.5
Vegetable	40	15	18

Hence show that the value of consumer price index number in (*i*) and (*ii*) is same.

Answers

2. 25, 27.5, 30, 50, 100, 102.5, 100, 95, 92.5, 85

4. 266.11

5. (*a*) 276 (*b*) 261.1

6. (*a*) ₹ 352 (*b*) ₹ 1936

8. 66.6, 80, 83.3, 100, 110, 120, 95, 105.

Unit-IV
Time Series Analysis

14 Time Series Analysis

14.1. INTRODUCTION

The term **'Time Series'** consists of quantitative data which are arranged in the order of their occurrence. For example when we collect the data regarding population per capita income, sales and prices of a commodity, etc. for a particular time period and arrange the data so obtained in a series, called **time series.** Thus, according to **'Spiegel'.**

'A time series is a set of observations taken at specified times, usually at equal intervals.'

In the analysis of time series, time is the most important variable which may be either year, month, week, day, hour or even minutes or seconds.

14.2. SIGNIFICANCE OF TIME SERIES ANALYSIS (*P.T.U., M.B.A. Dec. 2012*)

The analysis of time series is of great importance because of the following reasons.

(*a*) **To understand past behaviour.** With the help of time series analysis, we can observe data over a period of time and easily understand the changes which have taken place in the past. This helps us in predicting the future behaviour.

(*b*) **To predict future behaviour.** With the help of time series analysis, we can plan for the future business activities. There are so many statistical techniques by means of which we can analyse the time series so obtained regarding the prediction of various future variations in business and economics.

(*c*) **To evaluate current accomplishments.** By using time series analysis, we can investigate the cause for the growth and decay of the achievements in business activities.

14.3. COMPONENTS OF TIME SERIES (*P.T.U., M.B.A. Dec. 2007, Dec. 2012, May 2013*)

We first explain the term **'Trend'.** The term **'Trend',** is the basic tendency of production, sales and income etc. to grow or decline over a period of time. Trend does not include short-range oscillations, it includes steady movements over a long period of time. In business activities, we come across many economic time series. Some series increase slowly and some increase fast. Some others series decrease at varying rates, some remain constant for a long period of time. That is to say, we have two types of trends which are :

(*i*) Linear or Straight Line Trend

(*ii*) Non-Linear Trend.

We now discuss the various components of time series. There are mainly four types of components or patterns, or movements of a time series, given as (*a*) Secular Trend

(*b*) Seasonal Variations

(*c*) Cyclical Variations

(*d*) Irregular Variations (*P.T.U. M.B.A. Dec., 2008*)

(*a*) **Secular Trend.** The trends that occur as a result of general tendency of the data to increase or decrease, over a long period of time, are known as *secular trends*. When we say that secular trend refers to the general tendency of the data to increase or decrease over a long period of time, it means, we are to find what constitutes a long period of time. It does not mean several years.

A particular period can be regarded as long or not in the study of secular trend, depends upon the nature of the data. For example if we study the yearly salaries of employees for 2005 and 2006, we find that in 2006, the salaries are more as compared to that in 2005. This increment cannot be taken as secular trend since the time period from 2005 to 2006 is too short and in this small period, we cannot conclude that the salaries have shown an increasing tendency. Consider another example. In a culture, the number N of bacteria grows to a rate proportional to N. Suppose it becomes doubles in 10 seconds. We are interested to count the number of bacteria after 8 minutes. This increase in number shows a secular trend. It is clear from this example that in first case, two years could not be regarded as a long period whereas in second example, even 8 minutes constitute a long period. Hence it is the nature of the data which decides whether a particular period would be called long or not.

Also, for secular trend, it is not necessary that the data shows upward tendency or downward tendency. For example, if we study the trend of sales of cars over a period of 20 years, and find that except for a year or two, the sales are increasing continuously, we will call it '*a secular increase in sales*'.

(*b*) **Seasonal Variations** (*P.T.U. M.B.A. Dec., 2009*)

The trends that take place during a period of 12 months as a result of change in climate, weather conditions etc. are called *seasonal variations* or season variations are those periodic movements in business activity which occur regularly every year and have their origin in the nature of the year itself. There are some factors causing *seasonal variation* which are as under :

(*i*) **Weather and climate changes.** It is the most important factor causing seasonal variations. The change in the climate and weather conditions such as rainfall, humidity, etc. effects the different products differently. For example, there is a greater demand of soft drinks and cotton clothes in summer whereas, there is a greater demand of hot drinks and wollen clothes in winter.

(*ii*) **Traditions and habits of a culture.** For *seasonal variations* in time series, customs, traditions and habits are important factor. For example, on certain occasions like Deepawali, there is a big demand for sweets and also there is a great demand for cash before the festivals. Similarly, most of the students buy their books in the first few months after the opening of schools and colleges. Hence the sales of books, sweets etc. show seasonal variations.

(*c*) **Cyclic Variations.** Cyclic variations refer to the oscillatory variations in a time series which have a duration any where between 2 to 10 years. These variations arise due to **trade cycles** or **business cycles.** A *business cycle* has four phases namely (*i*) **Prosperity,** (*ii*) **Recession,** (*iii*) **Depression** (*iv*) **Recovery.** These phases are illustrated in the Fig. 14.1.

From the given graph, it is clear that the business activities (like production, sales, prices etc.) tend to be at their peak during prosperity. These business activities start recessing or falling and come to the lowest limit of decline. This level is called **depression level.** Thus, each phase changes gradually into the phase which follows it in the order given.

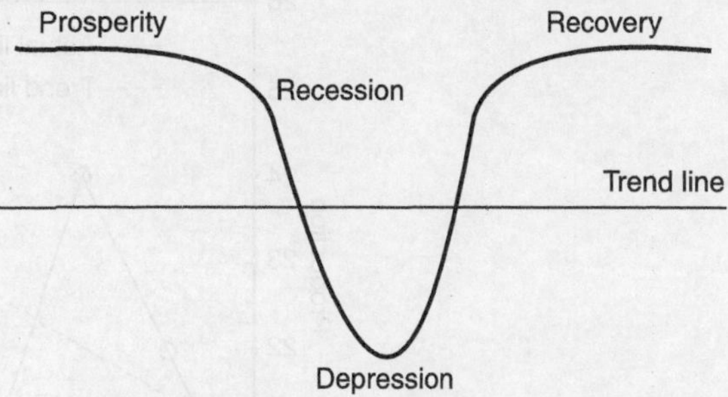

Fig. 14.1 Phases of business cycle

The study of *cyclic variations* is highly useful in framing best policies for stabilizing the level of business activity. For example, their study help us for checking periods of booms and depressions as these periods may bring a complete disaster to the economy.

The cyclic variations are the most typical type of economic fluctuations as they do not show regular periodicity.

(*d*) **Irregular Variations.** The variations in business activity which do not repeat in a definite pattern are called *irregular variations*. They are also called *erratic variations* or *accidental variations* or *random variations*.

Irregular variations take place due to special causes like floods, earth quakes, strikes, wars, etc. The declination in industrial output due to the strike in a factory is an example of irregular variations.

14.4. METHODS OF MEASURING TREND

Given any time series, we can determine its direction which it takes—is it growing or declining?

There are various methods that can be used for determining trend which are listed below:

1. Freehand or Graphic Method
2. Semi-Average Method
3. Moving Average Method
4. Method of Least Square.

We now discuss in details the above mentioned methods.

I. Freehand or Graphic Method. This is the simplest method of studying trends. The various steps involved are given below.

Step I. Plot the given time series on a graph paper and examine the direction of the trend based on the plotted information.

Step II. Draw a straight line (dotted) which will best fit to the data.

The curve so obtained is called **freehand curve** and this method is also called **trend fitting by inspection.**

ILLUSTRATIVE EXAMPLES

Example 1. *Fit a trend line to the following data by Freehand or graphic method.*

Year	*2000*	*2001*	*2002*	*2003*	*2004*	*2005*	*2006*	*2007*
Production (million tonnes)	*20*	*22*	*24*	*21*	*23*	*25*	*23*	*26*

Sol. Plot the given time series on a graph paper. The required trend line is shown by the dotted line in the Fig. 14.2 given below

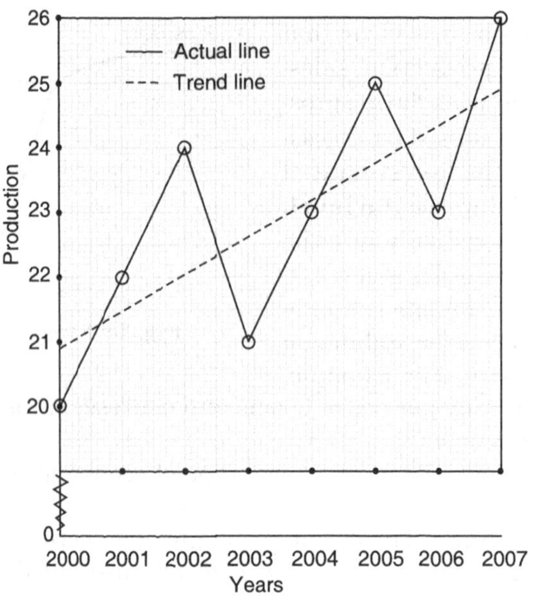

Fig. 14.2. Trend Line

Example 2. *Fit a trend line by 'Freehand Curve Method' to the data given below :*

Year	*1991*	*1992*	*1993*	*1994*	*1995*	*1996*	*1997*	*1998*	*1999*	*2000*
Sales ('000 ₹)	*150*	*155*	*165*	*152*	*174*	*150*	*174*	*175*	*160*	*180*

Sol. Plot the given time series on a graph paper, the required trend line is shown by the dotted line in the given Fig. 14.3.

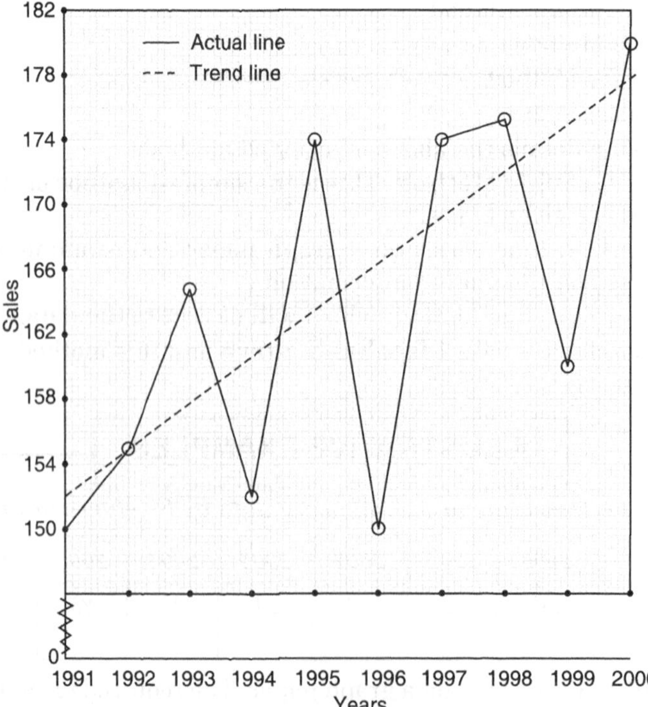

Fig. 14.3. Trend Line

14.5. MERITS AND DEMERITS OF FREEHAND CURVE METHOD

Merits. (*i*) It is the simplest method to measure trend.

(*ii*) It is flexible to use whether the trend is a straight line or a curve.

(*iii*) It requires no mathematical computations

(*iv*) It can be used to predict the future behaviour of business activity.

Demerits. (*i*) This method is subjective in nature as the trend line depends on the personal judgement. It means different persons may draw different trend lines or curves from the same set of given information.

(*ii*) It is time consuming

(*iii*) It lacks accuracy.

II. Semi-Average Method. In this method, the given data is divided into two parts. The various steps involved are

Step I. After dividing the data into two parts, find A.M. of each part.

Step II. Plot the two values of A.M. obtained in step. I on the graph paper corresponding to the time periods. Join these two points by a straight line, the straight line so obtained is the required trend line.

'Semi-Average Method' can be applied in two situations given below :

(*a*) When the number of years given is even

(*b*) When the number of years given is odd.

Example 3. *Fit a trend line to the following data by using semi-average method :*

Years	*1999*	*2000*	*2001*	*2002*	*2003*	*2004*	*2005*
Sales ('000 ₹)	*102*	*105*	*114*	*110*	*108*	*116*	*112*

Sol. The number of years given is odd (= 7). So we leave the middle year and we find the A.M. of first three years sales and the last three years sales.

$$\text{A.M. of first three years sales} = \frac{102+105+114}{3} = \frac{321}{3} = 107$$

$$\text{A.M. of last three years sales} = \frac{108+116+112}{3} = \frac{336}{3} = 112.$$

Year	*Sales*	*A.M.*	*Middle year*
1999	102		
2000	105	107	2000
2001	114		
2002	110		
2003	108		
2004	116	112	2004
2005	112		

Thus, we get two points 107 and 112. Plot these points corresponding to their respective middle years *i.e.,* corresponding to 2000 and 2004. Join these two points. The required trend is shown by the dotted line in the given Fig. 14.4.

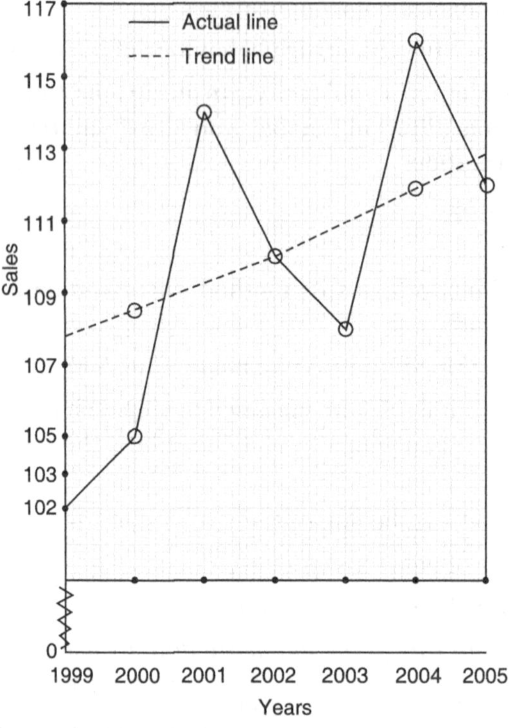

Fig. 14.4. Trend Line

Example 4. *Using semi-Average Method, fit a trend line for the data given below :*

Years	*1999*	*2000*	*2001*	*2002*	*2003*	*2004*	*2005*
Sales ('000 ₹)	*20*	*22*	*27*	*26*	*30*	*29*	*40*

Sol. The number of years given is odd (= 7). So we leave the middle year 2002 and calculate the A.M. of the two parts given as.

Year	*Profit ('000 ₹)*	*Semi-Average*	*Middle Year*
1999	20		
2000	22	$\frac{20+22+27}{3} = \frac{69}{3} = 23$	2000
2001	27		
2002	26		
2003	30		
2004	29	$\frac{30+29+40}{3} = \frac{99}{3} = 33$	2004
2005	40		

Thus we get two points 23 and 33. Plot these points corresponding to their respective middle years *i.e.,* corresponding to 2000 and 2004. Join these points, the required trend is shown by the dotted line in the Fig. 14.5.

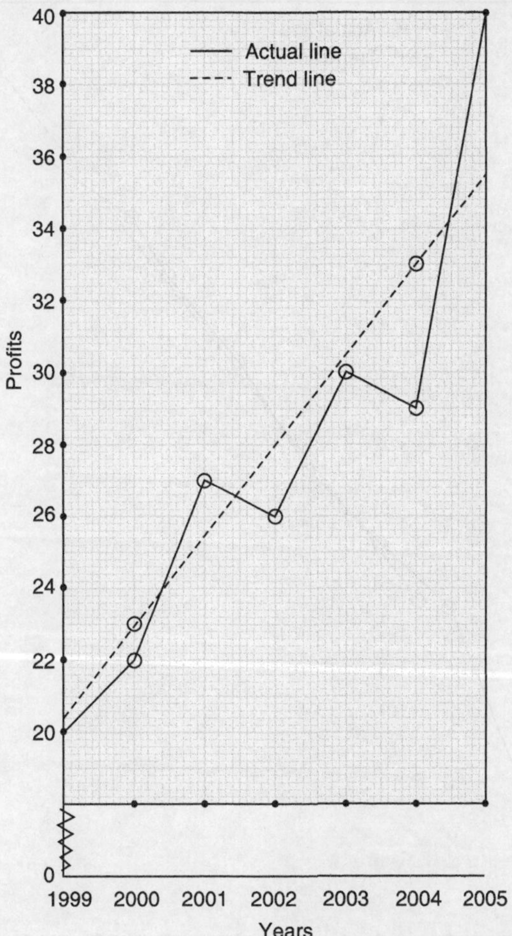

Fig. 14.5. Trend Line

Example 5. *The sales of a company in lakhs varied from 1998 to 2005 in the following manner.*

Years	*1998*	*1999*	*2000*	*2001*	*2002*	*2003*	*2004*	*2005*
Sales (₹ Lakhs)	*412*	*438*	*444*	*454*	*470*	*482*	*490*	*500*

Fit a trend line by the method of semi-average. Estimate the sales for the year 2006, if the actual sales for that year is ₹ 520 lakhs. Justify the difference between the two figures.

Sol. The number of years given is even (= 8). We find the A.M.s of the two parts as below :

$$\text{A.M. of the sales of first four years} = \frac{412 + 438 + 444 + 454}{4} = \frac{1748}{4} = 437$$

$$\text{A.M. of the sales of last four years} = \frac{470 + 482 + 490 + 500}{4} = \frac{1942}{4} = 485.5$$

Thus we get two points 437 and 485.5. Plot these two points corresponding to their respective middle years *i.e.,* middle of 1999 and 2000 and that of 2003 and 2004. Join these points, the required trend is shown by the dotted line in the Fig. 14.6.

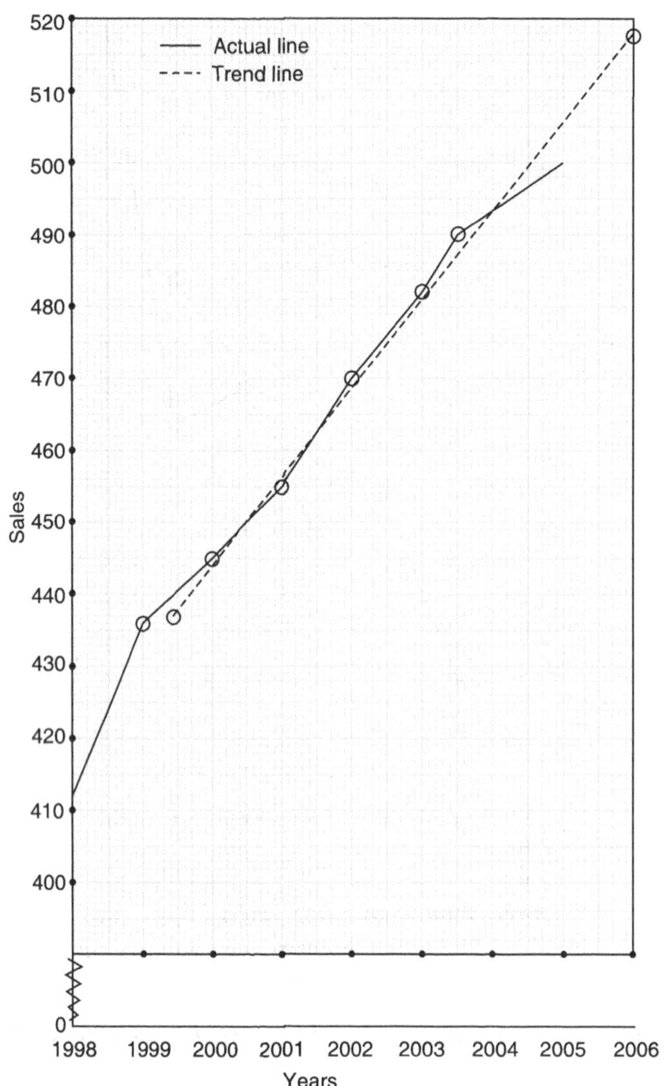

Fig. 14.6. Trend Line

The estimated sales for the year 2006 is ₹ 518 lakhs. But the actual sales for this year is ₹ 520 lakhs. The difference is due to the fact that time series analysis helps us to get the best possible estimates on certain assumptions which may or may not be true depending upon how far these assumptions have been realised in practice.

Example 6. *The sale of a commodity in tonnes varied from January 2005 to December 2005 in the manner given below:*

Jan.	*Feb.*	*March*	*April*	*May*	*June*	*July*	*Aug.*	*Sep.*	*Oct.*	*Non.*	*Dec.*
280	*300*	*280*	*280*	*270*	*240*	*230*	*230*	*220*	*200*	*210*	*200*

Fit a trend line by using semi-average method.

Sol. The number of months given is even (= 12). We calculate the A.M. of the two parts as below :

$$\text{A.M. of the sales of first six months} = \frac{280 + 300 + 280 + 280 + 270 + 240}{6} = \frac{1650}{6} = 275$$

$$\text{A.M. of the sales of last six months} = \frac{230 + 230 + 220 + 200 + 210 + 200}{6} = \frac{1290}{6} = 215$$

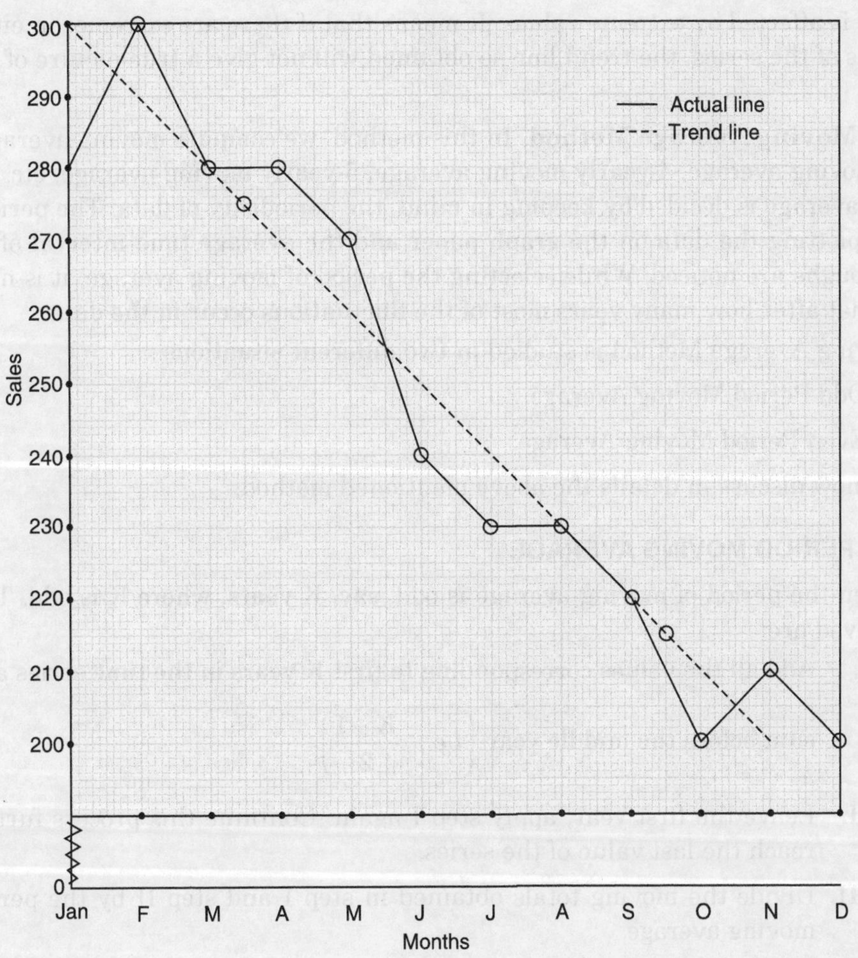

Fig. 14.7. Trend Line

Thus we get two points 275 and 215. Plot these two points corresponding to their respective middle months *i.e.,* at the middle of *March-April* and that of *September–October,* 2005. Join these two points, the required trend is shown by the dotted line in the Fig. 14.7 given above.

14.6. MERITS AND DEMERITS OF 'SEMI-AVERAGE METHOD'

Merits :

1. It is the simplest method as compared to other methods like Moving Average Method and Method of Least Squares.

2. It is objective in nature as everyone will get the same trend for a given data.

3. It is time saving.

Demerits :

1. It is based on straight line relationship between the plotted points. But this relationship may or may not exist.

2. It is affected by extreme values. It means that if there are extremes in either half or both halves of the series, the trend line so obtained will not give a true picture of the growth factor.

III. Moving Average Method. In this method, we compute moving averages such as 3-yearly moving average, 4-yearly moving average, 5-yearly moving average, etc. The period of moving average is decided by keeping in mind the periodicity of data. The period is determined by plotting the data on the graph paper and the average time interval of successive peaks or toughs are noticed. While selecting the period of moving average, it is necessary to consider that after how many years most of the fluctuations occur in the data.

Moving Average Method is studied in two different situations.

(*a*) Odd Period Moving Average

(*b*) Even Period Moving Average.

We now discuss in details the above mentioned method.

14.7. ODD PERIOD MOVING AVERAGE

When the period of moving average is odd, say, K years, where K is odd. The various steps involved are:

Step I. Add all the values corresponding to first K years in the time series and put the sum before the middle year $\left(i.e., \frac{K+1}{2}\right)$.

Step II. Leave the first year, apply step I again. Continue this process further till we reach the last value of the series.

Step III. Divide the moving totals obtained in step I and step II by the periods of the moving average.

Step IV. The trend values (or moving averages) of different years.

Example 7. *Obtain trend values using 3-yearly moving average for the following data :*

Year	*2000*	*2001*	*2002*	*2003*	*2004*	*2005*	*2006*
Production	*412*	*438*	*446*	*454*	*470*	*483*	*490*

Also plot the original and trend values on the same graph paper.

Sol. Here, the period of moving average is odd (= 3). The trend values are obtained in the following table. The trend line is shown by the dotted line in the given Fig. 14.8.

$$\left(k = 3 \;\Rightarrow\; \frac{k+1}{2} = 2\right)$$

Years	*Production*	*3-yearly moving totals*	*3-years moving averages (or Trend values)*
2000	412	—	—
2001	438	$\rightarrow 412 + 438 + 446 = 1296$	$\frac{1296}{3} = 432$
2002	446	$\rightarrow 438 + 446 + 454 = 1338$	$\frac{1338}{3} = 446$
2003	454	$\rightarrow 446 + 454 + 470 = 1370$	$\frac{1370}{3} = 456.66 \cong 457$
2004	470	$\rightarrow 454 + 470 + 483 = 1407$	$\frac{1407}{3} = 469$
2005	483	$\rightarrow 470 + 483 + 490 = 1443$	$\frac{1443}{3} = 481$
2006	490		

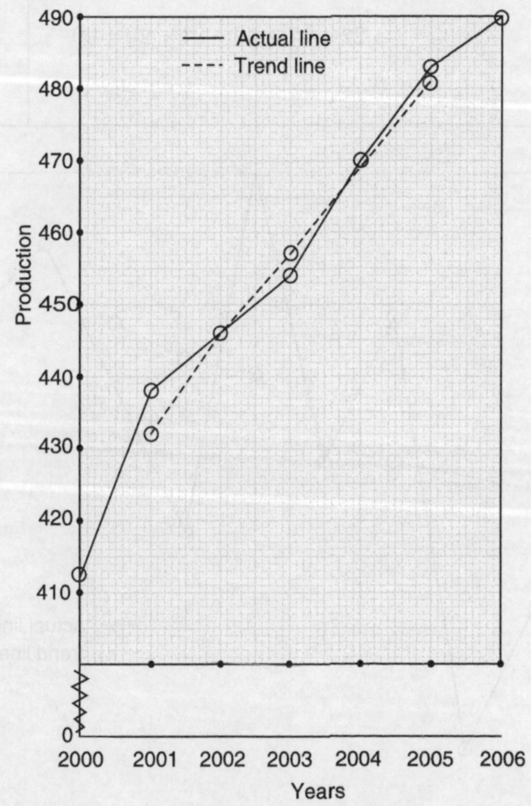

Fig. 14.8. Trend Values

Example 8. *From the data given below, obtain 5-yearly moving average.*

Year	*1998*	*1999*	*2000*	*2001*	*2002*	*2003*	*2004*	*2005*	*2006*
Sales ('000 ₹)	*16*	*14*	*20*	*18*	*22*	*17*	*19*	*21*	*20*

Also plot the original and trend values on the same graph paper.

Sol. Here, the period of moving average is odd (= 5). The trend values are obtained in the following table. Also the original line and trend line (dotted line) are shown in the given Fig. 14.9 ($k = 5 \Rightarrow \frac{k+1}{2} = 3$).

Years	*Sales ('000 ₹)*	*5-yearly moving totals*	*5-yearly moving averages (or Trend values)*
1998	16	—	—
1999	14	—	—
2000	20	→ 16 + 14 + 20 + 18 + 22 = 90	$\frac{90}{5} = 18$
2001	18	→ 14 + 20 + 18 + 22 + 17 = 91	$\frac{91}{5} = 18.2$
2002	22	→ 20 + 18 + 22 + 17 + 19 = 96	$\frac{96}{5} = 19.2$
2003	17	→ 18 + 22 + 17 + 19 + 21 = 97	$\frac{97}{5} = 19.4$
2004	19	→ 22 + 17 + 19 + 21 + 20 = 99	$\frac{99}{5} = 19.8$
2005	21	—	—
2006	20	—	—

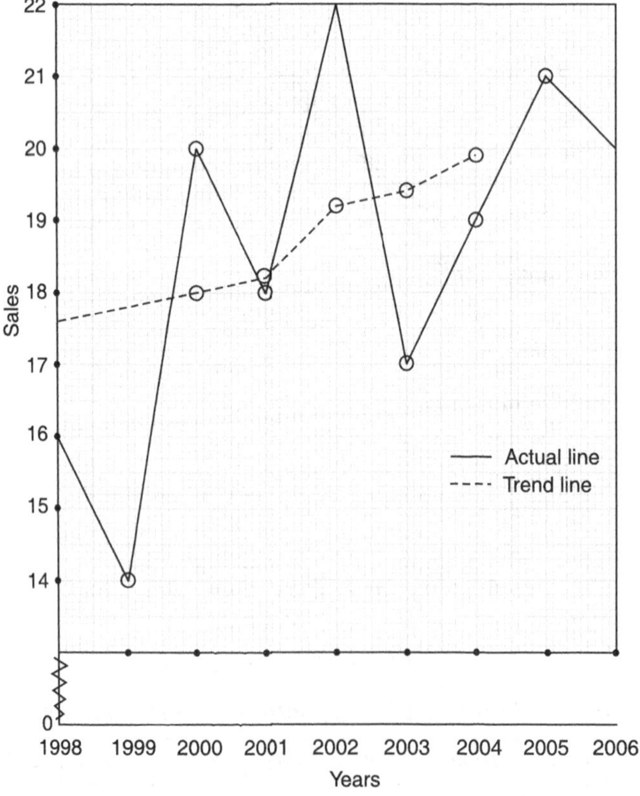

Fig. 14.9. Trend Values

Example 9. *Calculate 7-yearly moving averages for the following data of the numbers of commercial and industrial failures in a country during 1990 to 2006.*

Year	*No. of failures*	*Year*	*No. of failures*
1990	*23*	*1998*	*9*
1991	*26*	*1999*	*13*
1992	*28*	*2000*	*11*
1993	*32*	*2001*	*14*
1994	*20*	*2002*	*12*
1995	*12*	*2003*	*9*
1996	*12*	*2004*	*3*
1997	*10*	*2005*	*1*

Also plot the actual and trend values on the same graph paper.

Sol. Here, the period of moving average is odd (= 7). The trend values are obtained in the following Table. The actual line and the trend line (dotted line) are shown in the given Fig. 14.10

$$\left(k = 7 \quad \Rightarrow \quad \frac{k+1}{2} = 4 \right)$$

Year	*No. of failures*	*7-yearly moving total*	*7-yearly moving averages or Trend values*
1990	23		
1991	26		
1992	28		
1993	32	$\rightarrow 23 + 26 + 28 + 32 + 20 + 12 + 12 = 153$	$\frac{153}{7} = 21.9$
1994	20	$\rightarrow 26 + 28 + 32 + 20 + 12 + 12 + 10 = 140$	$\frac{140}{7} = 20$
1995	12	$\rightarrow 28 + 32 + 20 + 12 + 12 + 10 + 9 = 123$	$\frac{123}{7} = 17.6$
1996	12	$\rightarrow 32 + 20 + 12 + 12 + 10 + 9 + 13 = 108$	$\frac{108}{7} = 15.4$
1997	10	$\rightarrow 20 + 12 + 12 + 10 + 9 + 13 + 11 = 87$	$\frac{87}{7} = 12.4$
1998	9	$\rightarrow 12 + 12 + 10 + 9 + 13 + 11 + 14 = 81$	$\frac{81}{7} = 11.6$
1999	13	$\rightarrow 12 + 10 + 9 + 13 + 11 + 14 + 12 = 81$	$\frac{81}{7} = 11.6$
2000	11	$\rightarrow 10 + 9 + 13 + 11 + 14 + 12 + 9 = 78$	$\frac{78}{7} = 11.1$
2001	14	$\rightarrow 9 + 13 + 11 + 14 + 12 + 9 + 3 = 71$	$\frac{71}{7} = 10.9$
2002	12	$\rightarrow 13 + 11 + 14 + 12 + 9 + 13 + 1 = 63$	$\frac{63}{7} = 9$
2003	9		
2004	3		
2005	1		

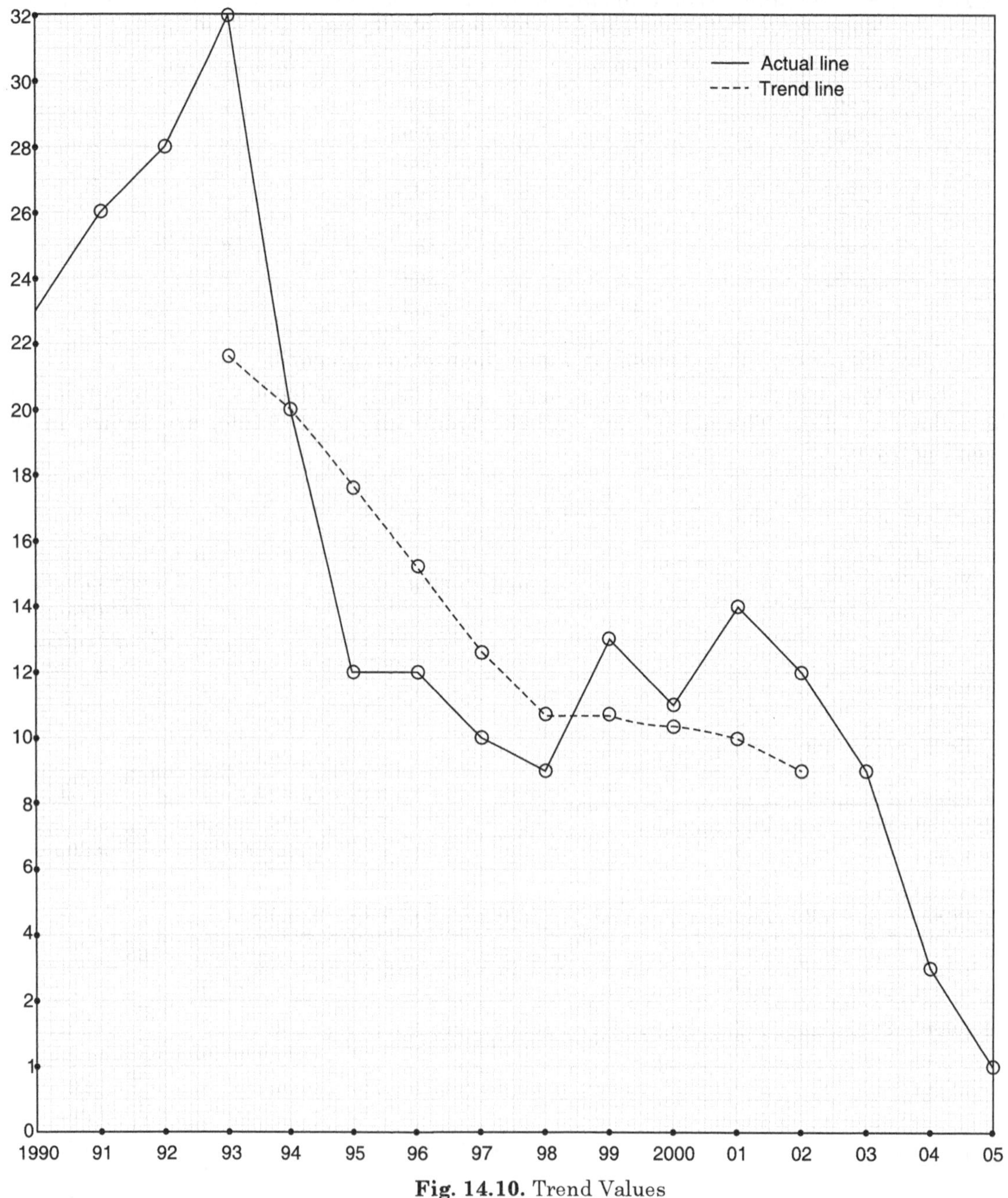

Fig. 14.10. Trend Values

14.8. EVEN PERIOD MOVING AVERAGE

If the moving average is an even period say, four-yearly or six-yearly, the moving averages are placed at the centre of the time span. This can be done by the following two methods :

(*a*) Moving average by centering the totals

(*b*) Moving average by centering the averages.

We now discuss in details the above mentioned methods.

14.9. MOVING AVERAGE BY CENTERING THE TOTALS

Consider the case of four-yearly moving average. The various steps involved are :

Step I. Add all the values corresponding to the first four years and put the sum in between second and third year. After this, the next total (from 2nd to 5th year total) is to be placed in between 3rd and 4th year. Continue this process upto the last value of the series.

Step II. Add the first and second 4-yearly totals and put them in front of 3rd year. Similarly, add second and third 4-yearly total and put them in front of 4th year. Continue this process upto the last value of the series.

Step III. Divide the values obtained in step II by 8, we get the 4-yearly moving averages or trend values.

Example 10. *Obtain trend values using 4-yearly moving average from the data given below* :

Year	*1995*	*1996*	*1997*	*1998*	*1999*	*2000*	*2001*	*2002*	*2003*	*2004*
Sales (in millions)	*7*	*8*	*9*	*11*	*10*	*12*	*8*	*6*	*5*	*10*

Sol. Here, the period of moving average is even (= 4). We find the trend values by *centering the totals*.

Year	*Sales (in millions)*	*4-yearly moving totals*	*2 period moving totals of 4-yearly moving totals*	*Trend values or 4-yearly moving average centered*
1995	7			
1996	8			
		→ 7 + 8 + 9 + 11 = 35		
1997	9		→ 35 + 38 = 73	$\frac{73}{8} = 9.12$
		→ 8 + 9 + 11 + 10 = 38		
1998	11		→ 38 + 42 = 80	$\frac{80}{8} = 10$
		→ 9 + 11 + 10 + 12 = 42		
1999	10		→ 42 + 41 = 83	$\frac{83}{8} = 10.37$
		→ 11 + 10 + 12 + 8 = 41		
2000	12		→ 41 + 36 = 77	$\frac{77}{8} = 9.62$
		→ 10 + 12 + 8 + 6 = 36		
2001	8		→ 36 + 31 = 67	$\frac{67}{8} = 8.37$
		→ 12 + 8 + 6 + 5 = 31		
2002	6		→ 31 + 29 = 60	$\frac{60}{8} = 7.5$
		→ 8 + 6 + 5 + 10 = 29		
2003	5	—	—	
2004	10	—	—	

14.10. MOVING AVERAGE BY CENTERING THE AVERAGE

Consider the case of 4-yearly moving averages. The various steps involved are :

Step I. Add all the values corresponding to the first 4 years and put the sum in between 2nd and 3rd year. After this, the next total (from 2nd to 5th year total) is put in between 3rd and 4th year. Continue this process upto the last value of the series.

Step II. Divide the 4-yearly totals obtained in step I by 4, we get the 4-yearly uncentered moving averages.

Step III. Add Ist and 2nd 4-yearly moving averages obtained in step II and divide it by 2. Put this sum in front of 3rd year, we get the 4-yearly centred moving averages.

Similarly, add 2nd and 3rd year moving average and divide it by 2 and put this average in front of 4th year. Continue this process upto the last value of the series. These values so obtained are known as *4-yearly centred moving averages or trend values.*

Example 11. *Obtain trend values using 4-yearly moving average from the data given below :*

Year	*1995*	*1996*	*1997*	*1998*	*1999*	*2000*	*2001*	*2002*	*2003*	*2004*
Sales (in crores)	*7*	*8*	*9*	*11*	*10*	*12*	*8*	*6*	*5*	*10*

Sol. Here, the period of moving average is even (= 4). We find the trend values by *centering the average.*

Year	*Sales (in crores)*	*4-yearly moving totals*	*4-yearly moving average (not centered)*	*2 period moving total of Column IV*	*4-yearly moving averages centered or trend values*
1995	7	—	—	—	—
1996	8	—	—	—	—
		→ 7 + 8 + 9 + 11 = 35	$\frac{35}{4} = 8.75$		
1997	9			→ 8.75 + 9.50 = 18.25	$\frac{18.25}{2} = 9.125$
		→ 8 + 9 + 11 + 10 = 38	$\frac{38}{4} = 9.50$		
1998	11			→ 9.50 + 10.50 = 20	$\frac{20}{2} = 10$
		→ 9 + 11 + 10 + 12 = 42	$\frac{42}{4} = 10.50$		
1999	10			→ 10.50 + 10.25 = 20.75	$\frac{20.75}{2} = 10.375$
		→ 11 + 10 + 12 + 8 = 41	$\frac{41}{4} = 10.25$		
2000	12			→ 10.25 + 9 = 19.25	$\frac{19.25}{2} = 9.625$
		→ 10 + 12 + 8 + 6 = 36	$\frac{36}{4} = 9$		

2001	8			→ 9 + 7.75 = 16.75	$\frac{16.75}{2} = 8.375$
		→ 12 + 8 + 6 + 5 = 31	$\frac{31}{4} = 7.75$		
2002	6			→ 7.75 + 7.25 = 15	$\frac{15}{2} = 7.5$
		→ 8 + 6 + 5 + 10 = 29	$\frac{29}{4} = 7.25$		
2003	5	—	—	—	—
2004	10	—	—	—	—

Example 12. *Assuming 4 yearly cycle, calculate the trend values by the method of moving averages and plot the actual data and the trend values:*

Year	*1987*	*1988*	*1989*	*1990*	*1991*	*1992*	*1993*	*1994*	*1995*
Sales (1000 ₹)	*285*	*320*	*310*	*362*	*355*	*336*	*350*	*342*	*359*

(P.T.U. M.B.A. May 2009)

Sol.

Year	*Sales (1000 ₹)*	*4-yearly moving totals*	*2-period moving totals of 4-yearly moving totals*	*Trend values*
1987	285			—
1988	320			—
		→ 285 + 320 + 310 + 362 = 1277		
1989	310		→ 2624	$\frac{2624}{8} = 328$
		→ 320 + 310 + 362 + 355 = 1347		
1990	362		→ 2710	$\frac{2710}{8} = 338.75$
		→ 310 + 362 + 355 + 336 = 1363		
1991	355		→ 2766	$\frac{2766}{8} = 345.75$
		→ 362 + 355 + 336 + 350 = 1403		
1992	336		→ 2786	$\frac{2786}{8} = 348.25$
		→ 355 + 336 + 350 + 342 = 1383		
1993	350		→ 2770	$\frac{2770}{8} = 346.25$
		→ 336 + 350 + 342 + 359 = 1387		
1994	342			—
1995	359			—

The Plot of Actual Values and the Trend Values are shown in the following Fig. 14.11.

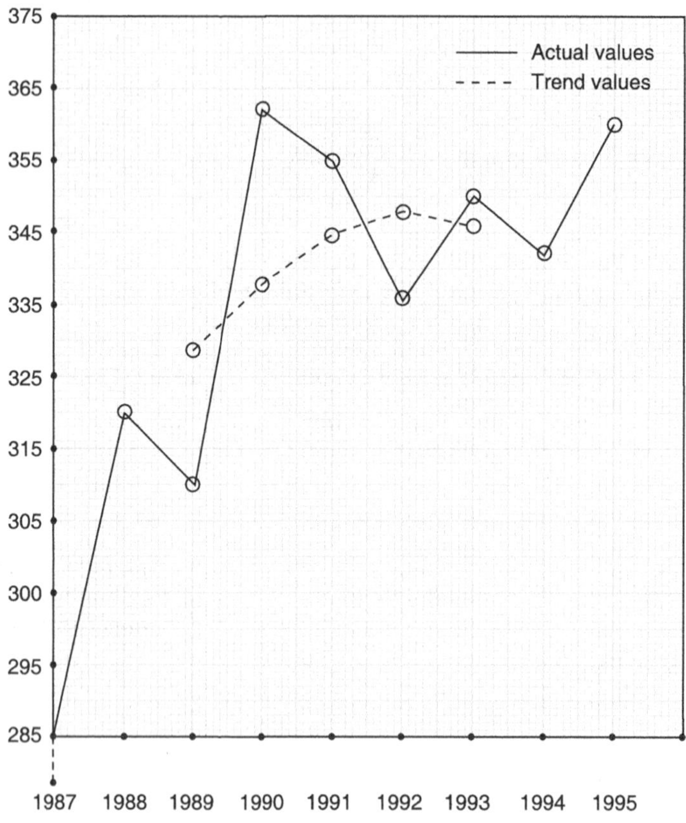

Fig. 14.11. Trend Values

14.11. PERIOD OF MOVING AVERAGE

In time series analysis, we may come across some situations when the period of moving average is not known. The period of the moving average for determining the trend values may be either 3-yearly, or 4-yearly of 5-yearly etc. or some other period. The basic principle in determining the period of moving average is that it should be equal to the period of cyclic variations so that all type of cyclical fluctuations are either eliminated or reduced to minimum.

In some other cases, the period of moving average in a series is not uniform. The cycle may complete in five years or in seven years or in eight or nine years. Under such circumstances, the average duration of the cycle is calculated and this calculated average is taken as the period of moving average.

In most of the cases, the duration of the cycle is found out by plotting original data on a graph paper and reading the time distances between various peaks or troughs. The average of these time distances would give the average duration of the cycle and this is taken as the period of moving average.

The following examples illustrates the above procedure.

Example 13. *Obtain the period of moving average for the following data and hence obtain trend values by using moving average method :*

Year	*Sales (in lakhs)*	*Year*	*Sales in (lakhs)*
1990	*390*	*1998*	*435*
1991	*381*	*1999*	*474*
1992	*372*	*2000*	*459*
1993	*405*	*2001*	*438*
1994	*420*	*2002*	*435*
1995	*396*	*2003*	*492*
1996	*387*	*2004*	*510*
1997	*381*	—	—

Sol. From the given data, we observe that there are peak values *viz.* 390, 420, 474 and 510 for the year 1990, 1994, 1999 and 2004 respectively. Hence the data exhibits a regular cyclic movement with period 5 (length of cycle (1990 – 1994 or 1994 – 1999 or 1999 – 2004 etc.)

Thus, the period of moving average is odd (= 5). The trend values are obtained in the following table:

Year	*Sales (in lakhs)*	*5-yearly moving totals*	*5-yearly moving Averages or trend values*
1990	390	—	—
1991	381	—	—
1992	372	→ 390 + 381 + 372 + 405 + 420 = 1968	$\frac{1968}{5} = 393.6$
1993	405	→ 381 + 372 + 405 + 420 + 396 = 1974	$\frac{1974}{5} = 394.8$
1994	420	→ 372 + 405 + 420 + 396 + 387 = 1980	$\frac{1980}{5} = 396$
1995	396	→ 405 + 420 + 396 + 387 + 381 = 1989	$\frac{1989}{5} = 397.8$
1996	387	→ 420 + 396 + 387 + 381 + 435 = 2019	$\frac{2019}{5} = 403.8$
1997	381	→ 396 + 387 + 381 + 435 + 474 = 2073	$\frac{2073}{5} = 414.6$
1998	435	→ 387 + 381 + 435 + 474 + 459 = 2136	$\frac{2136}{5} = 427.2$
1999	474	→ 381 + 435 + 474 + 459 + 438 = 2187	$\frac{2187}{5} = 437.4$
2000	459	→ 435 + 474 + 459 + 438 + 435 = 2241	$\frac{2241}{5} = 448.2$
2001	438	→ 474 + 459 + 438 + 435 + 492 = 2298	$\frac{2298}{5} = 459.6$
2002	435	→ 459 + 438 + 435 + 492 + 510 = 2334	$\frac{2334}{5} = 466.8$
2003	492	—	—
2004	510	—	—

Example 14. *Determine the period of moving average for the data given below:*

Year	*Sales (in lakhs)*	*Year*	*Sales in (lakhs)*
1987	*40*	*1997*	*42*
1988	*42*	*1998*	*45*
1989	*40*	*1999*	*46*
1990	*44*	*2000*	*52*
1991	*49*	*2001*	*58*
1992	*46*	*2002*	*56*
1993	*42*	*2003*	*51*
1994	*44*	*2004*	*57*
1995	*44*	*2005*	*54*
1996	*50*	*2006*	*65*

Also find the trend values by using moving average method.

Sol. The given data does not reveal a regular cycle of any fixed period. To determine the most appropriate period of moving average, we first plot the original data as shown in the given figure. Examining the graph carefully, we observe that the data has peaks at the following points.

Year	1988	1991	1996	1998	2001	2004	2006
Peak Point	42	49	50	45	58	57	63
Period	3	5	2	3	3	2	

The cycle from 1988 to 1991 is of period 3.
The cycle from 1991 to 1996 is of period 5.
The cycle from 1996 to 1998 is of period 2.
The cycle from 1998 to 2001 is of period 3.
The cycle from 2001 to 2004 is of period 3.
The cycle from 2004 to 2006 is of period 2.

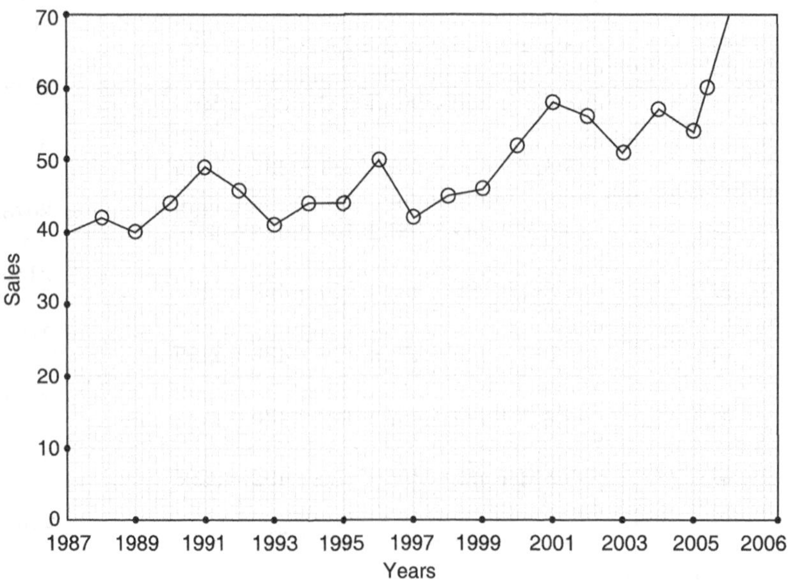

Fig. 14.12. Trend Values

The most appropriate period of moving average is given by the arithmetic mean of periods of different cycles. Thus, the required period of moving average

$$= \frac{3+5+2+3+3+2}{6} = \frac{18}{6} = 3$$

Hence we find 3-yearly moving average. The period of moving average is odd. The trend values are obtained in the following table. $\left(k = 3 \Rightarrow \frac{k+1}{2} = 2\right)$

Year	*Sales in Lakhs*	*3-yearly moving totals*	*3-yearly moving averages (or trend values)*
1987	40	—	—
1988	42	$\rightarrow 40 + 42 + 40 = 122$	$\frac{122}{3} = 40.66$
1989	40	$\rightarrow 42 + 40 + 44 = 126$	$\frac{126}{3} = 42.00$
1990	44	$\rightarrow 40 + 44 + 49 = 133$	$\frac{133}{3} = 44.33$
1991	49	$\rightarrow 44 + 49 + 46 = 139$	$\frac{139}{3} = 46.33$
1992	46	$\rightarrow 49 + 46 + 42 = 137$	$\frac{137}{3} = 45.66$
1993	42	$\rightarrow 46 + 42 + 44 = 132$	$\frac{132}{3} = 44.00$
1994	44	$\rightarrow 42 + 44 + 44 = 130$	$\frac{130}{3} = 43.33$
1995	44	$\rightarrow 44 + 44 + 50 = 138$	$\frac{138}{3} = 46.00$
1996	50	$\rightarrow 44 + 50 + 42 = 136$	$\frac{136}{3} = 45.33$
1997	42	$\rightarrow 50 + 42 + 45 = 137$	$\frac{137}{3} = 45.66$
1998	45	$\rightarrow 42 + 45 + 46 = 133$	$\frac{133}{3} = 44.33$
1999	46	$\rightarrow 45 + 46 + 52 = 143$	$\frac{143}{3} = 47.66$
2000	52	$\rightarrow 46 + 52 + 58 = 156$	$\frac{156}{3} = 52.00$
2001	58	$\rightarrow 52 + 58 + 56 = 166$	$\frac{166}{3} = 55.33$
2002	56	$\rightarrow 58 + 56 + 51 = 165$	$\frac{165}{3} = 55.00$
2003	51	$\rightarrow 56 + 51 + 57 = 164$	$\frac{164}{3} = 54.60$
2004	57	$\rightarrow 51 + 57 + 54 = 162$	$\frac{162}{3} = 54.00$
2005	54	$\rightarrow 57 + 54 + 63 = 174$	$\frac{174}{3} = 58.00$
2006	63	—	—

14.12. MEASUREMENT OF SHORT TERM FLUCTUATIONS

The term *'Short-term fluctuations'* may be defined as the difference of trend values and the original data. The following examples illustrate the concept of short-term fluctuations more briefly.

Example 15. *From the given data, compute "Trend' and 'short-term variations' by moving average method assuming 'a four-yearly cycle'.*

Years	*Sale*
1970	*75*
1971	*60*
1972	*55*
1973	*60*
1974	*65*
1975	*70*
1976	*70*
1977	*75*
1978	*85*
1979	*100*
1980	*70*

(P.T.U., M.B.A. Dec. 2002)

Sol. The period of moving average is even (= 4). We find the trend values by *centering* the totals and short-term fluctuations in the following table.

Years	*Sales* *Y*	*4-yearly moving totals*	*2 period moving totals of 4-yearly moving totals*	*4-yearly moving average centered (or trend values)* *T*	*Short-term fluctuations* *Y—T*
1970	75	—	—	—	—
1971	60	—	—	—	—
		→ 75 + 60 + 55 + 60 = 250			
1972	55		→ 250 + 240 = 490	$\frac{490}{8} = 61.25$	– 6.25
		→ 60 + 55 + 60 + 65 = 240			
1973	60		→ 240 + 250 = 490	$\frac{490}{8} = 61.25$	– 1.25
		→ 55 + 60 + 65 + 70 = 250			
1974	65		→ 250 + 255 = 455	$\frac{455}{8} = 56.87$	8.13
		→ 60 + 65 + 70 + 70 = 255			
1975	70		→ 255 + 280 = 535	66.87	3.13
		→ 65 + 70 + 70 + 75 = 280			
1976	70		→ 280 + 300 = 580	72.5	– 2.5
		→ 70 + 70 + 75 + 85 = 300			

1977	75		→ 300 + 330 = 630	78.75	− 3.75
		→ 70 + 75 + 85 + 100 = 330			
1978	85		—	—	—
		→ 75 + 85 + 100 + 70 = 330			
1979	100		—	—	—
1980	70	—			—

Example 16. *Using three year moving average determine 'trend' and short-term fluctuations for the following data :*

Years	*Production*
1968	*21*
1969	*22*
1970	*23*
1971	*24*
1972	*24*
1973	*22*
1974	*25*
1975	*26*
1976	*27*
1977	*26*

(P.T.U., M.B.A. June 2003)

Sol. Here, the period of moving average is odd (= 3). The trend values and short-term fluctuations are obtained in the following table:

Years	*Production* Y	*3-yearly moving totals*	*3-yearly moving average (or trend values)* (T)	*Short-term fluctuations* $Y—T$
1968	21	—	—	—
1969	22	21 + 22 + 23 = 66	$\frac{66}{3} = 22$	0
1970	23	22 + 23 + 24 = 69	$\frac{69}{3} = 23$	0
1971	24	23 + 24 + 24 = 71	$\frac{71}{3} = 23.66$	0.34
1972	24	24 + 24 + 22 = 70	$\frac{70}{3} = 23.33$	0.67
1973	22	24 + 22 + 25 = 71	$\frac{71}{3} = 23.66$	− 1.66
1974	25	22 + 25 + 26 = 73	$\frac{73}{3} = 24.33$	0.67
1975	26	26 + 26 + 27 = 79	$\frac{79}{3} = 26.33$	− 0.33
1976	27	26 + 27 + 26 = 79	$\frac{79}{3} = 26.33$	0.67
1977	26	—	—	—

14.13. MERITS AND DEMERITS OF MOVING AVERAGE METHOD

Merits :

The method of *moving average* has the following advantages.

1. It is a simple method if compared to the method of least squares.
2. It is a flexible method. It means, if some more figures are added to the data, the previous calculations will not change. But we will get some more trend values.
3. It is most suitable method in eliminating cyclic fluctuations. If the period of moving average happens to coincide with the period of cyclic fluctuations in the given data, cyclic fluctuations are automatically eliminated.

Demerits :

There are some limitations of this method which are given below.

1. Trend values cannot be obtained for all the years. For example, in a 3-yearly moving average, trend values cannot be obtained for the first year and the last year.
2. There is no hard and fast rule in selecting the period of moving average. One has to select the period of moving average based on his own judgement.
3. It cannot be used in forecasting as this method is not represented by a mathematical function.
4. It gives no appropriate computations when the trend is a straight line. The moving average lies either above or below the true sweep of the data.

TEST YOUR KNOWLEDGE 14.1

1. What is meant by time series ? Discuss its importance in business.
2. Explain the meaning and importance of time series.
3. Discuss the various components of time series. *(P.T.U., M.B.A. May 2004)*
4. Distinguish between secular trend and periodic movement of time series. *(P.T.U., M.B.A. May 2002)*
5. Fit a trend line for the following data, using 'Freehand curve method'.

Year	1996	1997	1998	1999	2000	2001	2002	2003	2004
Sales (in lakhs)	22	28	24	30	18	26	20	32	16

6. Fit a trend line by the method of semi-average to the following data:

Year	1998	1999	2000	2001	2002	2003
Production ('000 units)	22	26	24	30	28	32

7. Fit a trend line by the method of semi-average to the following data:

Year	1999	2000	2001	2002	2003	2004	2005
Sales (in lakhs)	30	26	24	38	40	30	46

8. Plot the following data on a graph paper and fit a trend line by the method of semi-averages:

Year	2000	2001	2002	2003	2004	2005	2006
Production (in million tonnes)	100	120	95	105	108	102	112

9. Calculate the trend values by the method of 4-yearly moving averages for the following data.

Year	1997	1998	1999	2000	2001	2002	2003	2004
Production	464	515	518	467	502	540	557	571

10. Calculate *3-yearly moving averages* of the production figures given below and draw the trend.

Year	*Production*	*Year*	*Production*
1991	15	1999	63
1992	21	2000	70
1993	30	2001	74
1994	36	2002	82
1995	42	2003	90
1996	46	2004	95
1997	50	2005	102
1998	56		

11. Construct *5-yearly moving averages* of the number of students studying in a college shown below.

Year	*No. of students*	*Year*	*No. of students*
1996	332	2001	405
1997	317	2002	410
1998	357	2003	427
1999	392	2004	405
2000	402	2005	438

12. Assume a *four yearly cycle*, calculate the trend by the method of moving averages from the following data relating to the production of tea in India

Year	*Production (m. lbs)*	*Year*	*Production (m. lbs)*
1994	464	1999	540
1995	515	2000	557
1996	518	2001	571
1997	467	2002	586
1998	502	2003	612

13. From the following data, calculate *3-yearly, 5-yearly and 7-yearly* moving averages and plot the data on a graph paper.

Year	1991	1992	1993	1994	1995	1996	1997
Cyclic fluctuations	+ 2	+ 1	0	− 2	− 1	+ 2	+ 1

Year	1998	1999	2000	2001	2002	2003	2004	2005
Cyclic fluctuations	0	– 2	– 1	+ 2	+ 1	0	– 2	– 1

14. Using three-yearly moving averages, determine the 'trend' and short-term fluctuations. Plot the original data and trend values on the same graph paper.

Year	*Production (in '000 tonnes)*	*year*	*Production ('000 tonnes)*
1997	21	2002	22
1998	22	2003	25
1999	23	2004	27
2000	25	2005	27
2001	24	2006	26

15. Determine the period of moving average for the data given below

Year	1980	1981	1982	1983	1984	1985	1986	1987
Sales (in lakhs)	130	127	124	135	140	132	129	127

Year	1988	1989	1990	1991	1992	1993	1994
Sales (in lakhs)	145	158	153	146	145	164	170

16. Calculate the trend values of the following data by using *4-yearly* moving average

Year	*Value*	*Year*	*Value*
1992	41	2000	67
1993	61	2001	73
1994	55	2002	78
1995	48	2003	76
1996	53	2004	84
1997	67	—	—
1998	62	—	—
1999	60	—	—

17. Using *3-yearly* moving average, determine the 'Trend' and 'Short-term fluctuations' for the following data:

Year	*Production in('000 tonnes)*	*year*	*Production in ('000 tonnes)*
1993	21	1998	22
1994	22	1999	25
1995	23	2000	26
1996	25	2001	27
1997	24	2002	26

18. From the given data, find 'trend' and 'short-term fluctuations' by moving average method of periodicity 4 years

Year	1995	1996	1997	1998	1999	2000	2001	2002	2003	2004
Production (in Qtls.)	462	510	525	470	515	550	575	560	580	645

19. Estimate the trend values using the data given by taking a *four-yearly moving average*:

(P.T.U., M.B.A. Dec., 2010)

Year	*Value*	*Year*	*Value*
1990	12	1997	100
1991	25	1998	82
1992	39	1999	65
1993	54	2000	49
1994	70	2001	34
1995	87	2002	20
1996	105	2003	7

Answers

5.

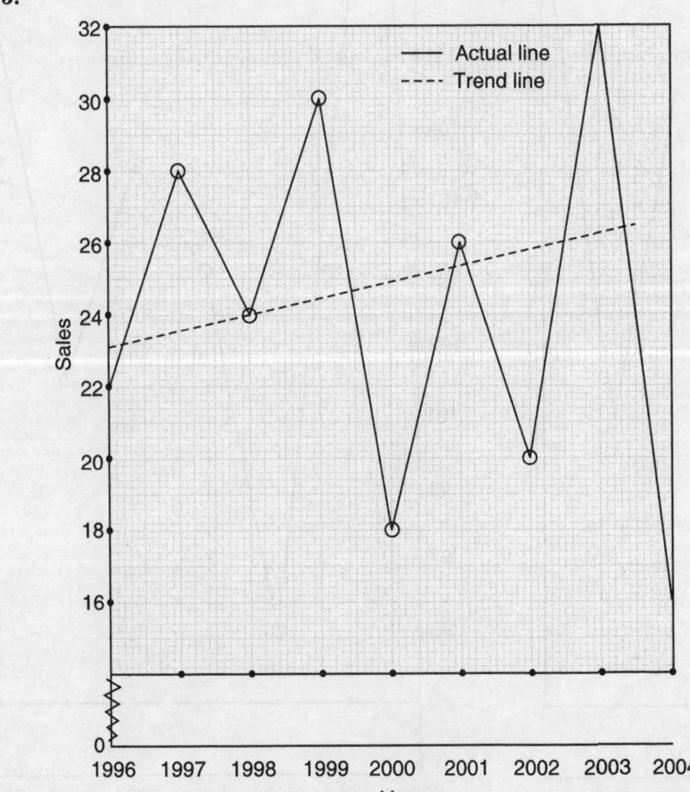

6.

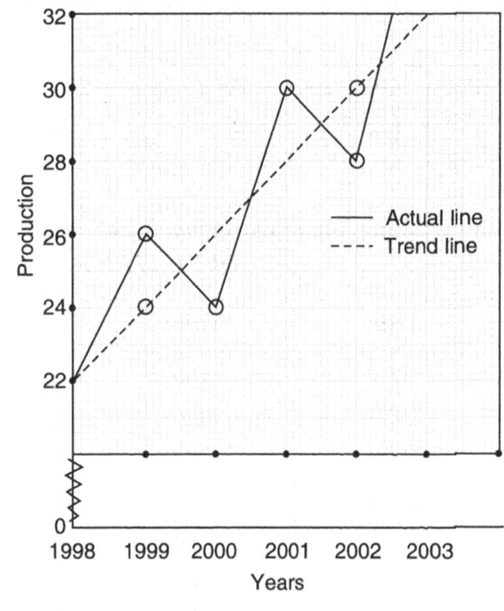
32
30
28
26
24
22
0
Production
Actual line
Trend line
1998
1999
2000
2001
2002
2003
Years

7.

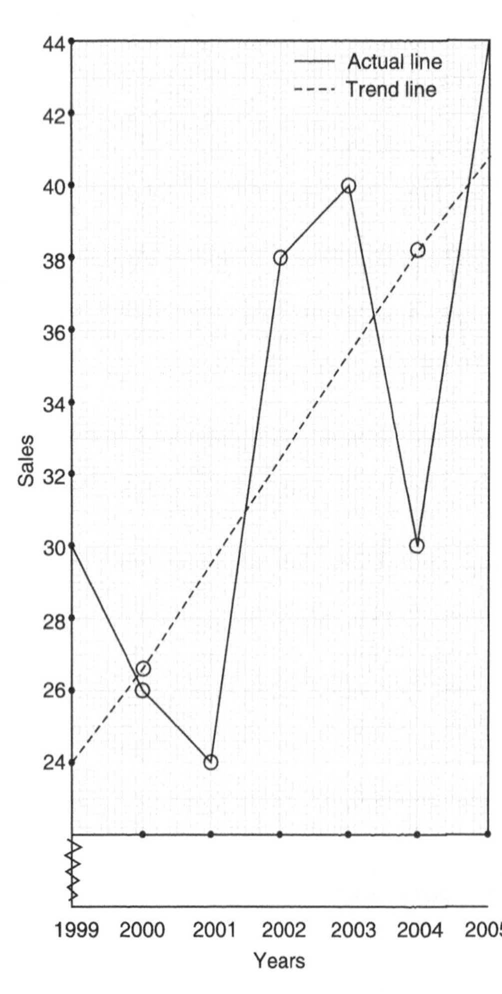
44
42
40
38
36
34
32
30
28
26
24
Sales
Actual line
Trend line
1999
2000
2001
2002
2003
2004
2005
Years

8.

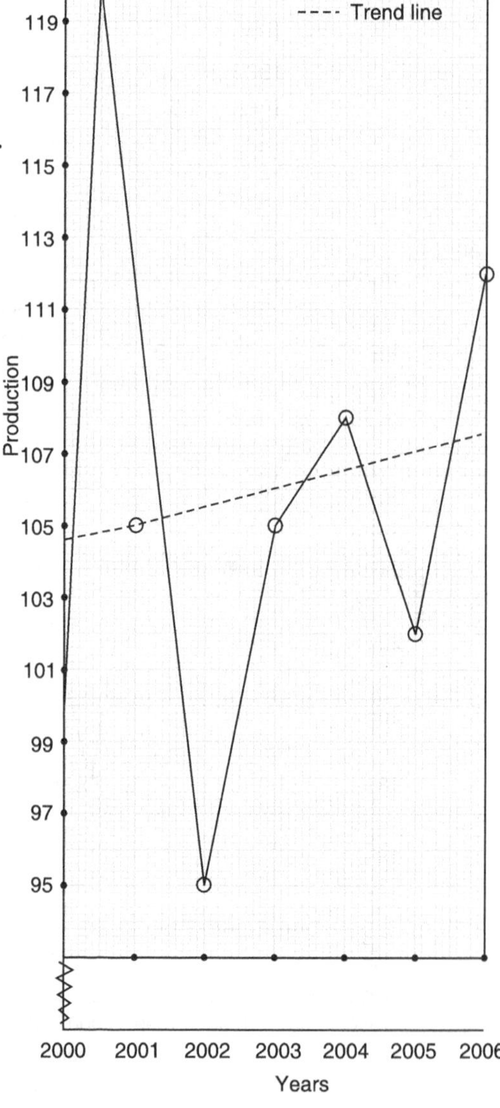
121
119
117
115
113
111
109
107
105
103
101
99
97
95
Production
Actual line
Trend line
2000
2001
2002
2003
2004
2005
2006
Years

9. Trend values: 495.75, 503.63, 511.63, 529.5, 553, 572.5

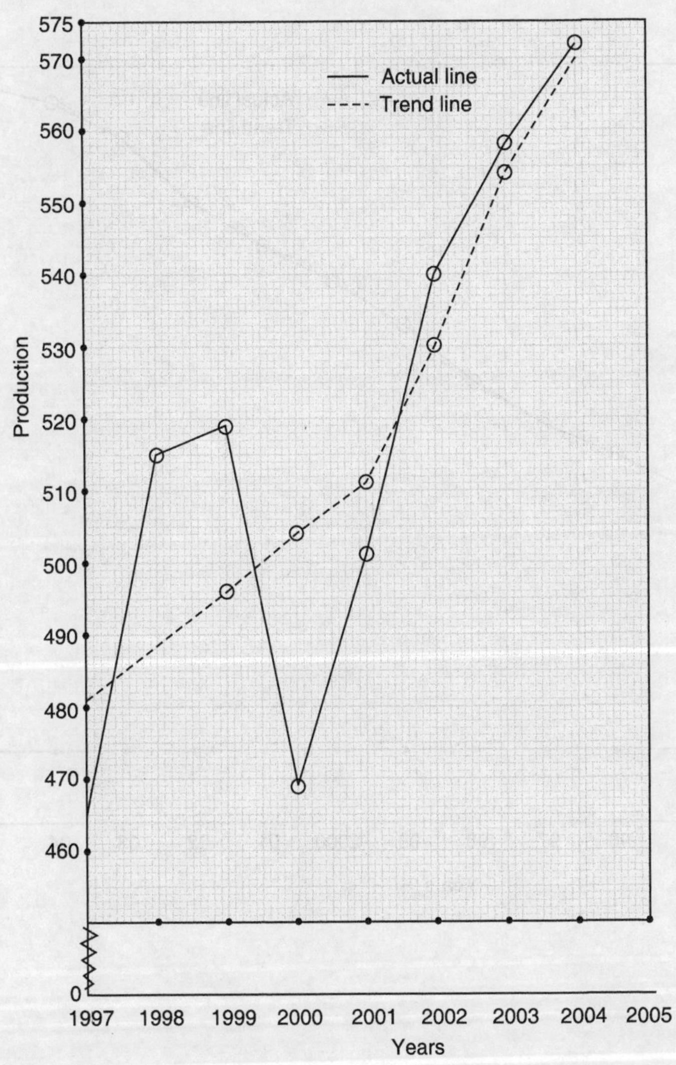

10. *3-yearly* moving averages or trend values: 22, 29, 36, 41.33, 46, 50.67, 56.33, 63, 69, 75.33, 82, 89, 95.67

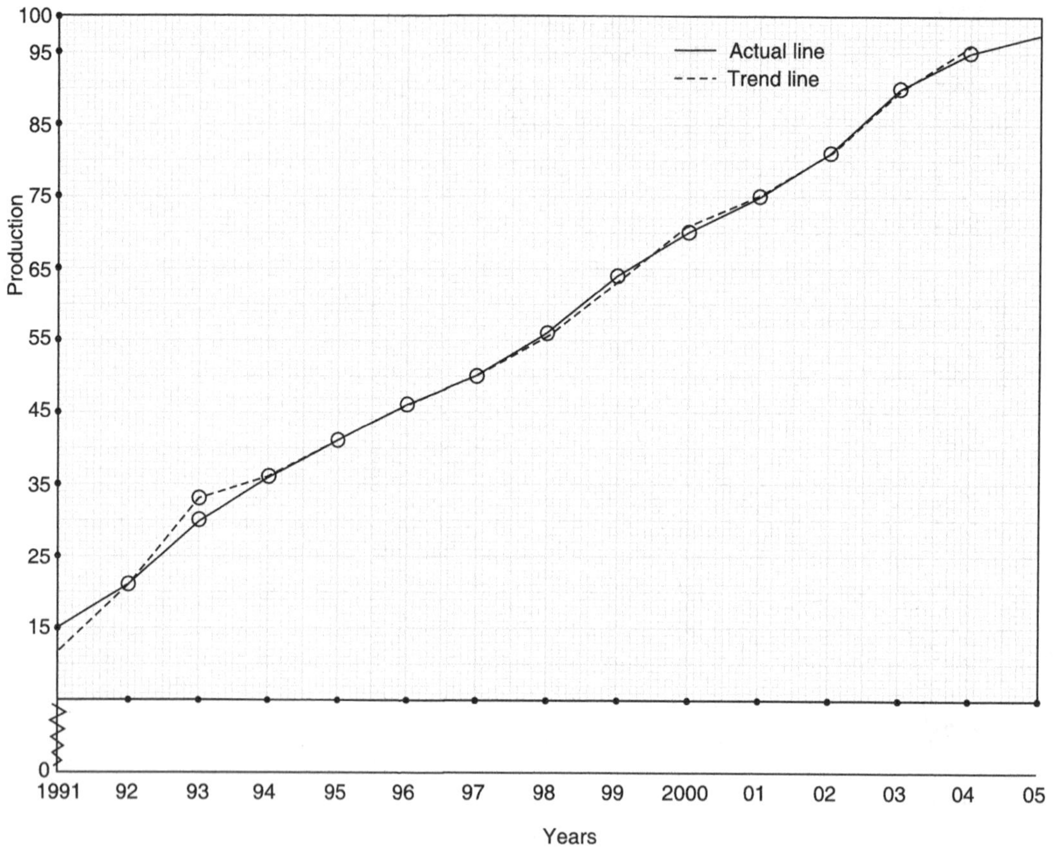

11. *5-yearly* moving averages or trend values :

360, 374.6, 393.2, 407.2, 409.8, 417

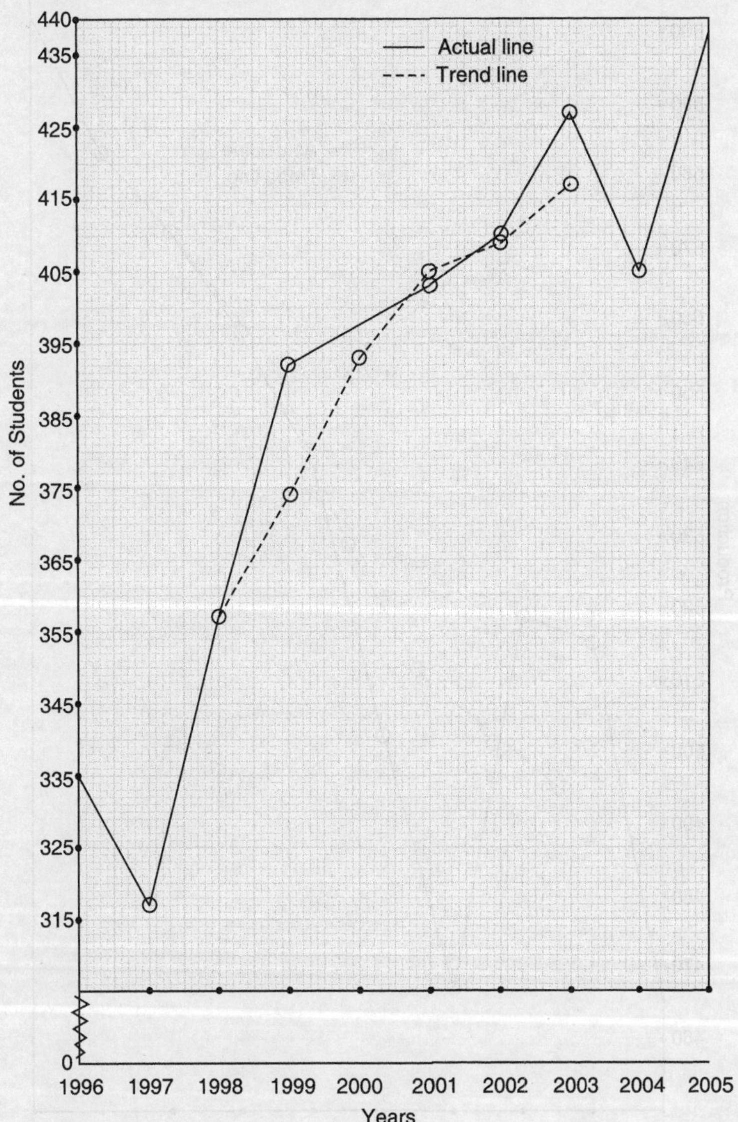

12. *4-yearly* moving averages or trend values: 495.75, 503.62, 511.62, 529.5, 553, 572.5

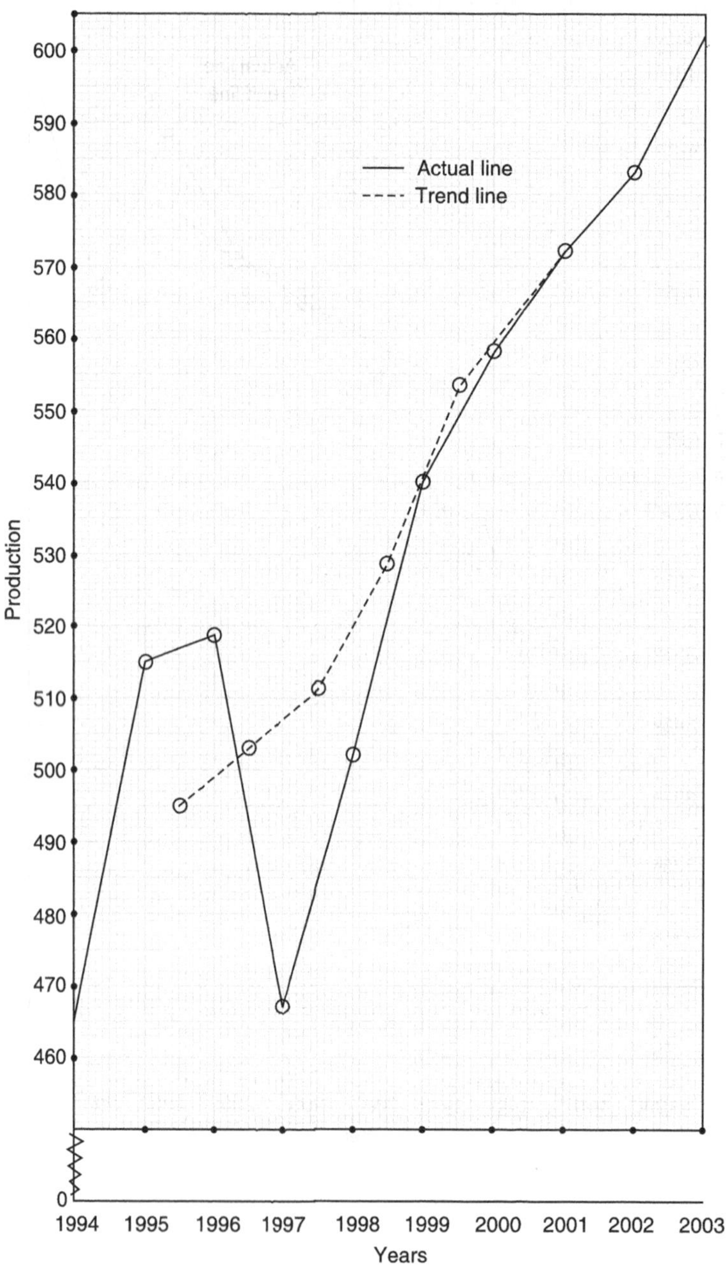

13. *3-yearly* moving averages : 1, – 3.3, – 1, .67, 1, – .33, – 1, – .33, .67, 1, – .33, – 1

5-yearly moving averages: 0, 0, 0, 0, 0, 0, 0, 0, 0, 0, 0

7-yearly moving averages: .43, .14, – .28, – .43, – .14, – .43, .14, – .28, – .43

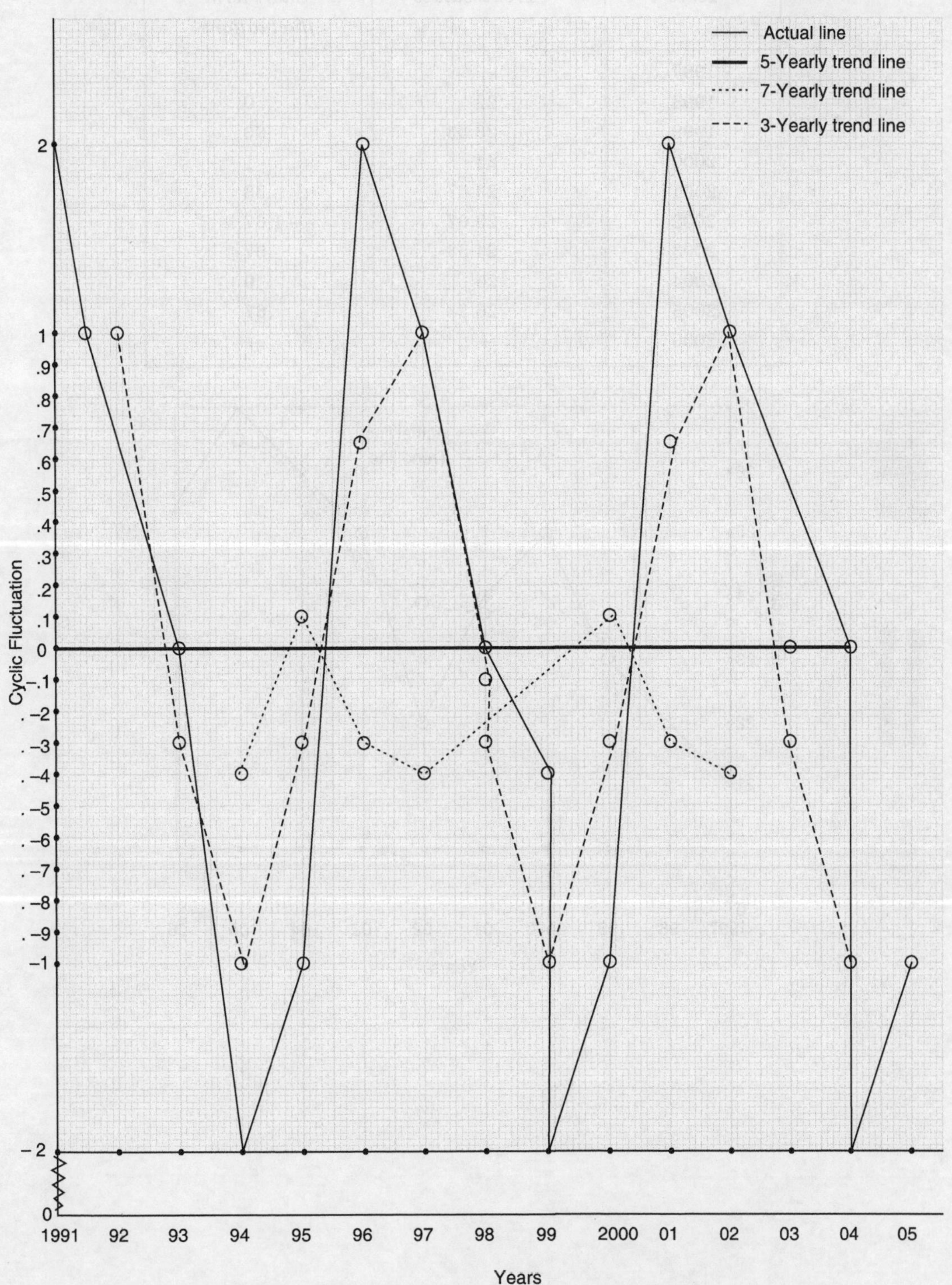
Actual line
5-Yearly trend line
7-Yearly trend line
3-Yearly trend line
Cyclic Fluctuation
2
1
.9
.8
.7
.6
.5
.4
.3
.2
.1
0
-.1
. -2
. -3
. -4
. -5
. -6
. -7
. -8
. -9
-1
- 2
0
1991
92
93
94
95
96
97
98
99
2000
01
02
03
04
05
Years

14.

Years	*Trend values*	*Short-term fluctuations*
1997	—	—
1998	22	0
1999	23.33	.33
2000	24	1
2001	23.67	.33
2002	23.67	– 1.67
2003	24.33	.67
2004	26	0
2005	26.33	.67
2006	—	—

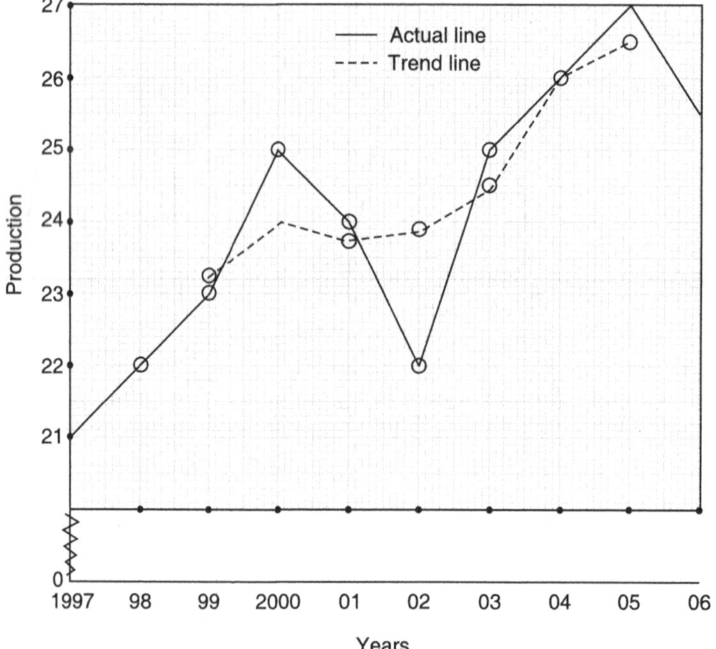

15. Period of moving average = 15

5-yearly moving averages: 131.2, 131.6, 132, 132.6, 134.6, 138.2, 142.4, 145.8, 149.4, 153.2, 155.6

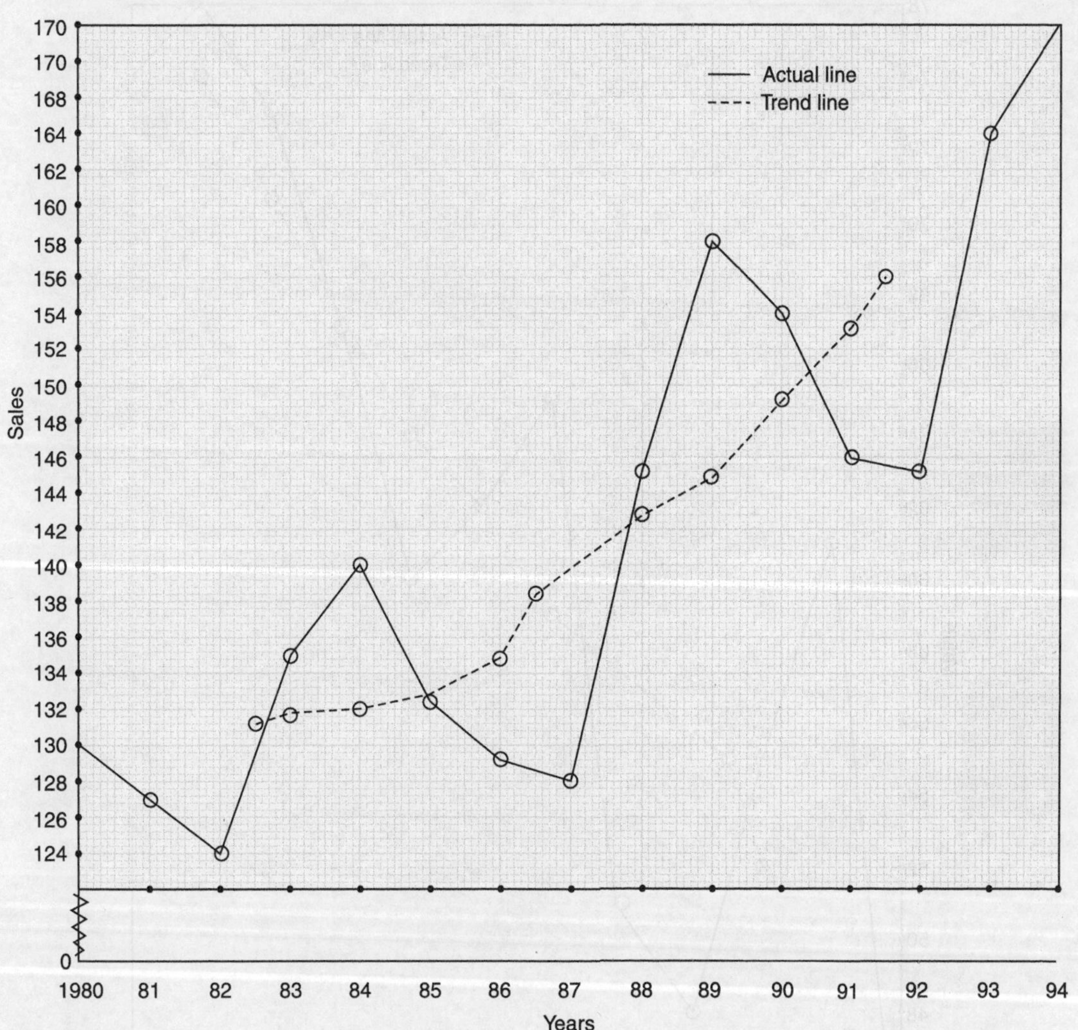

16. *4-yearly* moving averages : 52.75, 55, 56.62, 59, 62.25, 64.25, 67.5

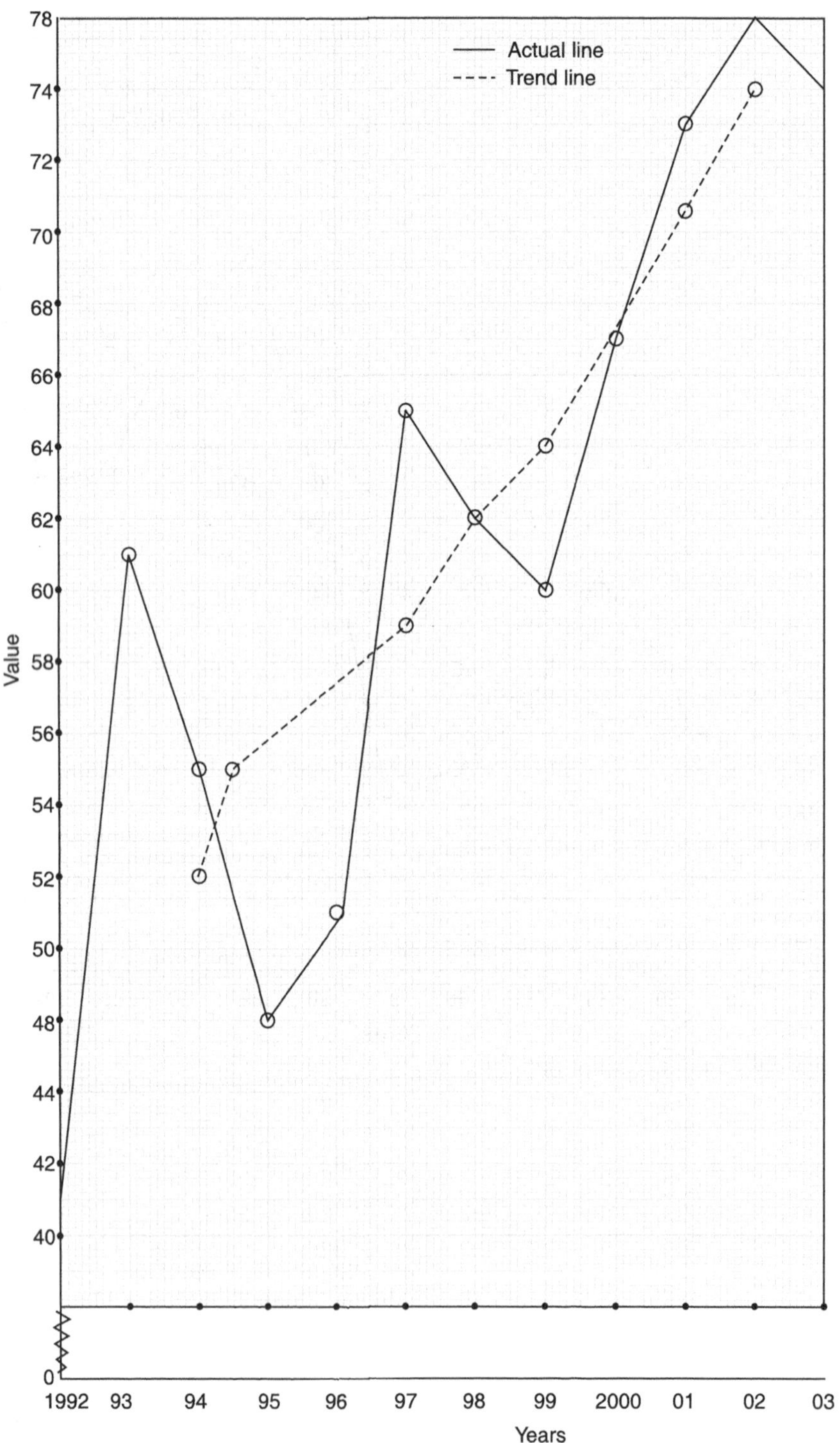

17.

Years	*Trend Values*	*Short term fluctuation*
1993	—	—
1994	22	0
1995	23.33	– .33
1996	24	1
1997	23.67	.33
1998	23.67	– 1.67
1999	24.33	– .67
2000	26	0
2001	26.33	.67
2002	—	—

18.

Years	*Trend values*	*Short-term fluctuations*
1995		
1996	—	—
1997	498.37	26.625
1998	510	– 40
1999	521.25	– 6.25
2000	538.75	11.25
2001	558.12	16.875
2002	575	– 15
2003	592.5	– 12.5
2004	—	—
2005	—	—

19.

Years	*Values*	*4-yearly moving average centred*
1990	12	—
1991	25	—
1992	39	→ 39.75
1993	54	→ 54.75
1994	70	→ 70.75
1995	87	→ 84.75
1996	105	→ 92
1997	100	→ 90.75
1998	82	→ 81
1999	65	→ 65.75
2000	49	→ 49.75
2001	34	→ 34.75
2002	20	—
2003	7	—

14.14. METHOD OF LEAST SQUARES

One of the best method of trend fitting in a time series analysis is the method of least squares. This method is widely used in practice. To fit a trend line, consider the following conditions.

(*i*) Sum of the deviations of the actual value and computed trend value is zero *i.e.*, $\Sigma(Y - Y_c) = 0$, where

$$Y = \text{the actual values}$$

$$Y_c = \text{the trend values}$$

(*ii*) Sum of the squares of the deviations of the actual values Y and computed trend values Y_c is least from this line, *i.e.*, $\Sigma(Y - Y_c)^2 = 0$.

The line obtained satisfying the conditions (*i*) and (*ii*) is known as '**line of best fit.**' '**Method of least squares**' can also be used to fit **parabolic trend** or exponential trend.

I. Fitting of a straight line trend :

Step I. Consider a straight line trend given by

$$Y = a + bX, \text{ where } Y = \text{trend values and } X = \text{unit of time.}$$

To find the *line of best fit,* we need to determine the constants a and b satisfying the normal equations given below

(*i*) $\Sigma Y = na + b\Sigma X$, where n = number of years

(*ii*) $\Sigma XY = a\Sigma X + b\Sigma X^2$

Step II. Find the trend values corresponding to different years and plot these values on a graph paper, we get the required straight line trend.

Year of origin. To fit a straight line trend by the method of least squares, we are also supposed to assign any year as the **year of origin.** There are two methods to predict which year should be taken as year of origin.

(*a*) **Direct method.** Any year can be taken as the year of origin. But generally, first year or before that is taken as year of origin. Let X denotes the time deviations. Then X will take the values 0 for the year of origin, 1 for the next year, 2 for the second next and so on, provided there is no gap in the given data.

(*b*) **Short cut method.** In this method, the middle year is taken as the year of origin. It should be noted that in case of odd number of years, when the deviations are taken from the middle year, ΣX would always be zero provided there is no gap in the given data. However, in case of even years also, ΣX will be zero if the year of origin is placed midway between the two middle years.

ILLUSTRATIVE EXAMPLES

Example 1. *Below are given the figures of production (in thousand quintals) of a rice factory*

Years	*2000*	*2001*	*2002*	*2003*	*2004*	*2005*	*2006*
Production (in '000 qtls)	*80*	*90*	*92*	*83*	*94*	*99*	*92*

(a) Fit a straight line trend to the data

(b) Show the trend line on a graph paper.

Sol. (*a*) Let the required straight line of best fit is

$$Y = a + b X \qquad ...(1)$$

Here $n = 7$ (odd) ∴ We take 2003 as the year of origin. Consider the following table. (Apply Direct method)

Years	*Production ('000 qtls) Y*	*Deviation (year of origin = 2003) X*	*XY*	X^2
2000	80	– 3	– 240	9
2001	90	– 2	– 180	4
2002	92	– 1	– 92	1
2003	83	0	0	0
2004	94	1	94	1
2005	99	2	198	4
2006	92	3	276	9
	$\Sigma Y = 630$	$\Sigma X = 0$	$\Sigma XY = 56$	$\Sigma X^2 = 28$

The normal equations are

$$\Sigma Y = 7a + b\Sigma X$$

and $\Sigma XY = a\Sigma X + b\Sigma X^2$ or $630 = 7a \Rightarrow a = 90$

and $56 = 28b \Rightarrow b = 2$

∴ From (1), the required equation of the straight line trend is $Y = 90 + 2X$.

(*b*) **To obtain Trend Values.** We know that if $Y = a + bX$ represents a straight line trend, then Y represents the trend values corresponding to X unit of time.

∴ The trend values are obtained in the following table.

Years Y	*X*	*Trend Values (Y_c) Y = 90 + 2X*
2000	– 3	84
2001	– 2	86
2002	– 1	88
2003	0	90
2004	1	92
2005	2	94
2006	3	96

The trend line is shown by the dotted line in the given figure

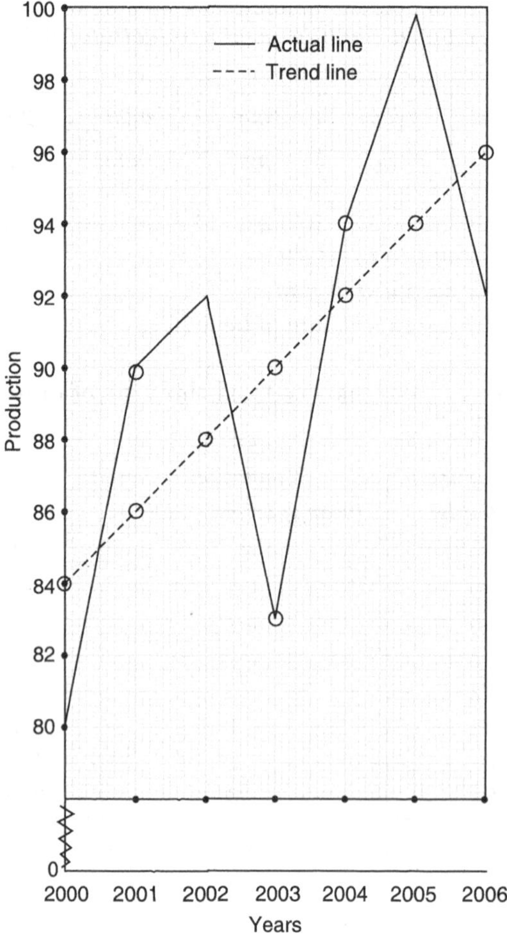

Fig. 14.13. Trend Values

Example 2. *From the data given below,*

Year	*1999*	*2000*	*2001*	*2002*	*2003*	*2004*	*2005*	*2006*
Sales	*80*	*90*	*92*	*83*	*94*	*99*	*92*	*104*

(a) Fit a straight line trend to the data

(b) Show the trend line on a graph paper.

Sol. (*a*) Let the required straight line trend of best fit is

$$Y = a + bX \qquad \ldots(1)$$

Here $n = 8$ (even), there are two middle years namely 2002 and 2003.

$$\text{A.M. of 2002 and 2003} = \frac{2002 + 2003}{2} = 2002.5$$

Hence we take year of origin as 2002.5. Consider the following table.

Years	*Sales* Y	*Deviations from 2002.5* x	*Deviations multiplied by 2* X = 2x	*XY*	X^2
1999	80	– 3.5	– 7	– 560	49
2000	90	– 2.5	– 5	– 450	25
2001	92	– 1.5	– 3	– 276	9
2002	83	– .5	– 1	– 83	1
2003	94	.5	1	94	1
2004	99	1.5	3	297	9
2005	92	2.5	5	460	25
2006	104	3.5	7	728	49
	ΣY = 734		ΣX = 0	ΣXY = 210	$\Sigma X^2 = 168$

The normal equations are

$$\Sigma Y = na + b\Sigma X \quad \text{and} \quad \Sigma XY = a\Sigma X + b\Sigma X^2$$

or
$$734 = 8a \Rightarrow a = \frac{734}{8} = 91.75$$

and
$$210 = 168b \Rightarrow b = \frac{210}{168} = 1.25$$

∴ From (1), the required equation of straight line trend is

$$Y = 91.75 + (1.25)X \quad \text{or} \quad Y = 91.75 + 2.5x \qquad | \; X = 2x$$

(*b*) **To obtain trend values.** We know that if Y = a + bX represents a straight line trend, then Y represents the trend values corresponding to X unit of time. The trend values are obtained in the following table:

Years	*Y*	*X = 2x*	*Trend values* (Y_c) *Y = 91.75 + (1.25)X*
1999	80	– 7	83
2000	90	– 5	85.5
2001	92	– 3	88
2002	83	– 1	90.5
2003	94	1	93
2004	99	3	95.5
2005	92	5	98
2006	104	7	100.5

The trend line is shown by the dotted line in the given figure.

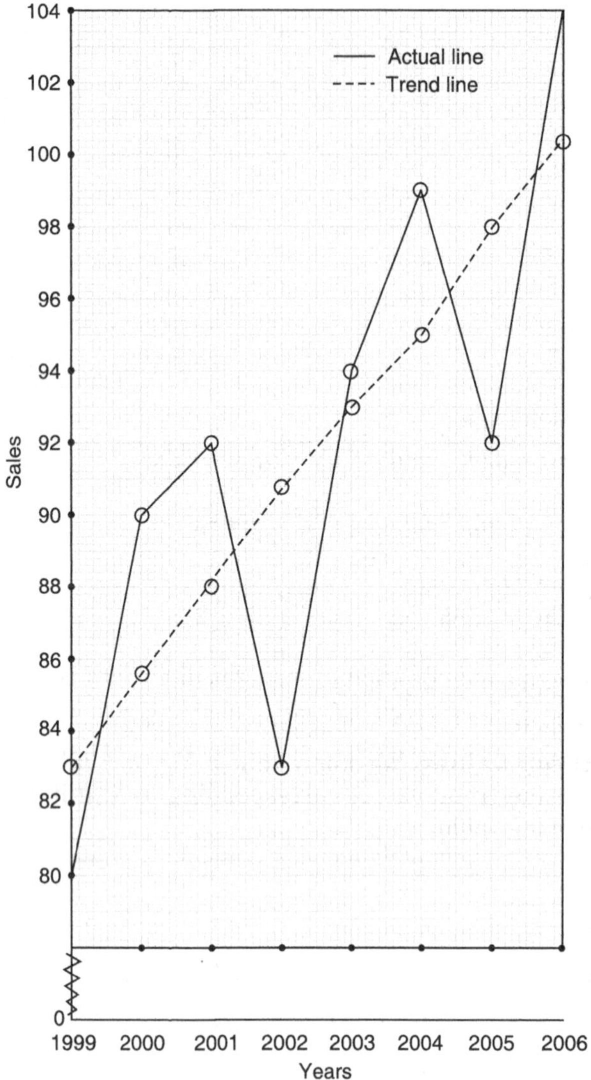

Fig. 14.14. Trend Line

Note. The same result will be obtained if we do not multiply the deviations by 2. But in that case our computations would be more difficult as could be seen in the table:

Years		*Deviations from 2002.5*		
	Y	*X*	*XY*	*X*^{2}
1999	80	– 3.5	– 280	12.25
2000	90	– 2.5	– 225	6.25
2001	92	– 1.5	– 138	2.25
2002	83	– .5	– 41.5	0.25
2003	94	.5	47	0.25
2004	99	1.5	148.5	2.25
2005	92	2.5	230	6.25
2006	104	3.5	364	12.25
		$\Sigma X = 0$	$\Sigma XY = 105$	$\Sigma X^2 = 42$

$\therefore$ The normal equations are

$$\Sigma Y = na + b\Sigma X \quad \text{and} \quad \Sigma XY = a\Sigma X + b\Sigma X^2$$

or $$734 = 8a \Rightarrow a = \frac{734}{8} = 91.75 \quad \text{and} \quad 105 = 42b \Rightarrow b = \frac{105}{42} = 2.5$$

$\therefore$ $Y = 91.75 + 2.5\ X$, which is same.

Example 3. *Fit a straight line trend by the method of least squares to the following data.*

Year	*1999*	*2000*	*2001*	*2002*	*2003*	*2004*	*2005*	*2006*
Sales (in lakhs)	*38*	*40*	*65*	*72*	*69*	*60*	*87*	*95*

Assume that the same rate of change will continue, predict the sale for the year 2008. Also plot the trend value on the graph and show the trend line.

Sol. Let the required straight line trend is

$$Y = a + bX \quad \text{...(1)}$$

Here $n = 8$(even), $\therefore$ there are two middle years namely 2002 and 2003.

A.M. of 2002 and 2003 $= \frac{2002 + 2003}{2} = 2002.5$

Hence we take year of origin as 2002.5. Consider the following table.

Year	*Sales (in lakhs)* *Y*	*Deviations from 2002.5* *x*	*Deviations multiplied by 2* *X = 2x*	*XY*	*X*^{2}
1999	38	– 3.5	– 7	– 266	49
2000	40	– 2.5	– 5	– 200	25
2001	65	– 1.5	– 3	– 195	9
2002	72	– 0.5	– 1	– 72	1
2003	69	0.5	1	69	1
2004	60	1.5	3	180	9
2005	87	2.5	5	435	25
2006	95	3.5	7	665	49
	$\Sigma Y = 526$		$\Sigma X = 0$	$\Sigma XY = 616$	$\Sigma X^2 = 168$

The normal equations are

$$\Sigma Y = na + b\Sigma X$$

and $$\Sigma XY = a\Sigma X + b\Sigma X^2$$

or $$526 = 8a \quad \Rightarrow \quad a = \frac{526}{8} = 65.75$$

and $$616 = 168b \quad \Rightarrow \quad b = \frac{616}{168} = 3.66$$

∴ from (1), the required equation of the straight line trend is

$$Y = 65.75 + (3.66)X \qquad \ldots(2)$$

To obtain trend values. We know that if $Y = a + bX$ represents a straight line trend. Then Y represents the trend values corresponding to X unit of time. The trend values are obtained in the following table.

Years	*Y*	*X*	*Trend values* (Y_C) $Y = 65.75 + (3.66)X$
1999	38	– 7	40.13
2000	40	– 5	47.45
2001	65	– 3	54.77
2002	72	– 1	62.09
2003	69	1	69.41
2004	60	3	76.73
2005	87	5	84.05
2006	95	7	91.37

To predict the sale for the year 2008.

For 2008, $X = 11$

∴ from (2) $Y_1 = 65.75 + (3.66)(11) = 106.01$

Hence the estimated sale for the year 2008 are ₹ 106.01 lakhs.

Finally, the trend line is shown in the given figure.

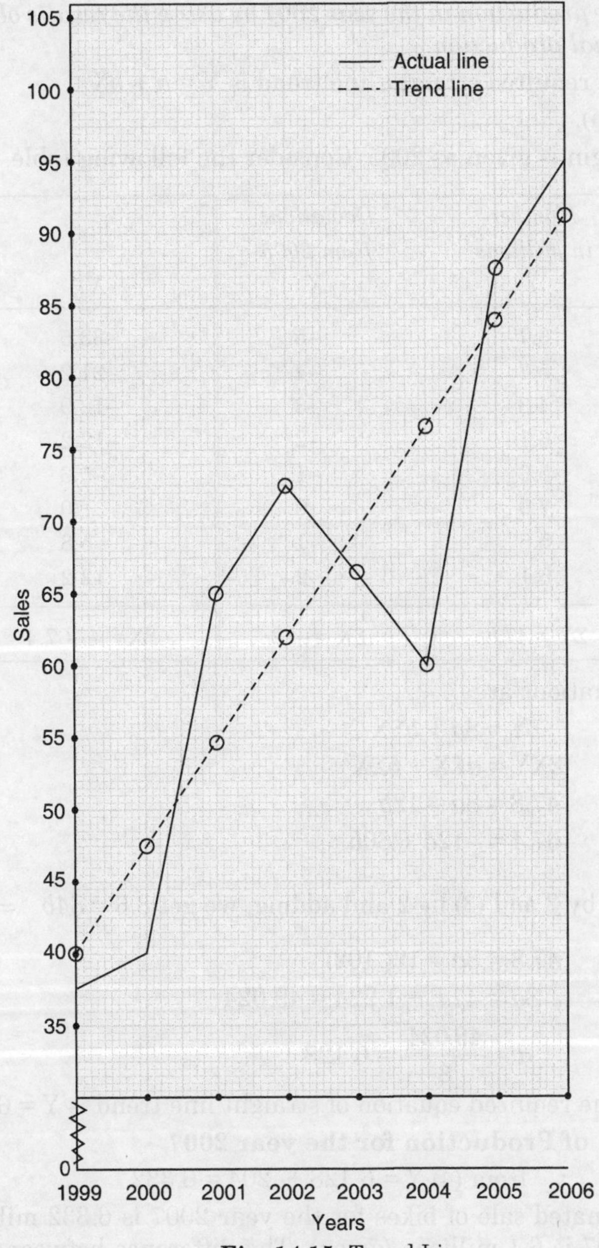

Fig. 14.15. Trend Line

Note. The same result will be obtained if we do not multiply the deviations by 2.

Example 4. *Consider the following data relating to the number of bikes (in millions) sold from 2000 to 2007.*

Years	*2000*	*2001*	*2002*	*2003*	*2004*	*2005*	*2006*	*2007*
No.	*6.7*	*5.3*	*4.3*	*6.1*	*5.6*	*7.9*	*5.8*	*6.1*

(a) Fit a straight line trend to the data through 2005 only.

(b) Estimate the production in the year 2007 by using the results obtained in part (a) and compare with the actual production.

Sol. (*a*) Let the required straight line trend is $Y = a + bX$ ...(1)

Here $n = 8$(even).

The year of origin is given as 2005. Consider the following table.

Years	*Number in millions* Y	*Deviations from 2005* X	XY	X^2
2000	6.7	–5	–33.5	25
2001	5.3	–4	–21.2	16
2002	4.3	–3	–12.9	9
2003	6.1	–2	–12.2	4
2004	5.6	–1	–5.6	1
2005	7.9	0	0	0
2006	5.8	1	5.8	1
2007	6.1	2	12.2	4
	$\Sigma Y = 47.8$	$\Sigma X = -12$	$\Sigma XY = -67.4$	$\Sigma X^2 = 60$

The normal equations are

$$\Sigma Y = 8a + b\Sigma X$$

and $$\Sigma XY = a\Sigma X + b\Sigma X^2$$

or $$47.8 = 8a - 12b \quad ...(2)$$

and $$-67.4 = -12a + 60b \quad ...(3)$$

Multiplying (2) by 3 and (3) by 2 and adding, we get $8.6 = 84b \Rightarrow b = \frac{8.6}{84} = .102$

From (2), $$47.8 = 8a - 12(.102)$$

$$\Rightarrow \quad 8a = 47.8 + 1.224 = 49.024$$

$$\Rightarrow \quad a = \frac{49.024}{8} = 6.128$$

$\therefore$ From (1), the required equation of straight line trend is $Y = 6.128 + (.102)\ X$ ...(4)

(*b*) Estimation of Production for the year 2007

For 2007, $X = 2$ $\therefore$ from (4) $Y = 6.128 + .204 = 6.332$

Hence the estimated sale of bikes for the year 2007 is 6.332 millions. But the actual sales for the year 2007 is 6.1 millions (given). The difference between the actual sales and estimated sales is due to the fact that estimated sales are based on certain assumptions. There is hardly a chance when actual and estimated figures may completely coincide.

Case of Gap Years in the Given Series

Example 5. *Below are given figures of production (in thousand litres) of a milk plant.*

Year	*1999*	*2001*	*2002*	*2003*	*2004*	*2005*	*2006*
Production (in '000 litres)	*77*	*88*	*94*	*85*	*91*	*98*	*90*

(a) *Fit a straight line by the method of least square and tabulate the trend values.*

(b) *Eliminate the trend, what components of the series are thus left over ?*

(c) *What is monthly increase in the production of milk ?*

(d) *Show the trend line on the graph paper.*

Sol. (a) Let the required equation of the straight line trend is $Y = a + bX$ ...(1)

Here $n = 7$(odd).

$\therefore$ The year of origin is 2003. Consider the following table.

Years	*Production (in '1000 litres) Y*	*Deviations from 2003 X*	*XY*	*X^2*
1999	77	– 4	– 308	16
2001	88	– 2	– 176	4
2002	94	– 1	– 94	1
2003	85	0	0	0
2004	91	1	91	1
2005	98	2	196	4
2006	90	3	270	9
	$\Sigma Y = 623$	$\Sigma X = -1$	$\Sigma XY = -21$	$\Sigma X^2 = 35$

The normal equations are

$$\Sigma Y = 7a + b\Sigma X$$

and $$\Sigma XY = a\Sigma X + b\Sigma X^2$$

or $$623 = 7a - b \quad \text{...(2)}$$

and $$-21 = -a + 35b \quad \text{...(3)}$$

Multiplying (3) by 7 and adding to (2), we get

$$476 = 244b \Rightarrow b = \frac{476}{244} = 1.95$$

From (2), $623 + 1.95 = 7a$

$$\Rightarrow \quad 7a = 624.95 \Rightarrow a = \frac{624.95}{7} = 89.27$$

$\therefore$ From (1), the required straight line trend is $Y = 89.27 + 1.95\,X$

(b) **To obtain trend values.** We know that if $Y = a + bX$ represents a straight line trend then Y represents the trend values corresponding to X unit of time. The trend values are obtained in the following table.

Years	*Y*	*X*	*Trend values Y_c*	*$Y = Y - Y_c$*
1999	77	– 4	81.47	– 4.47
2001	88	– 2	85.37	2.63
2002	94	– 1	87.32	6.68
2003	85	0	89	– 4

2004	91	1	91.22	– .22
2005	98	2	93.17	4.83
2006	90	3	95.12	– 5.12

From the last column of the above table, we observe that the variations like – 4.47, 2.63, 6.68 etc. are irregular. Hence after eliminating the trend, we are left with cyclical and irregular variations.

(*c*) The monthly increase in the production of milk is $\frac{b}{12} = \frac{1.95}{12} = 0.1625$ thousand litres

(*d*) The required trend line is shown by the dotted line in the figure.

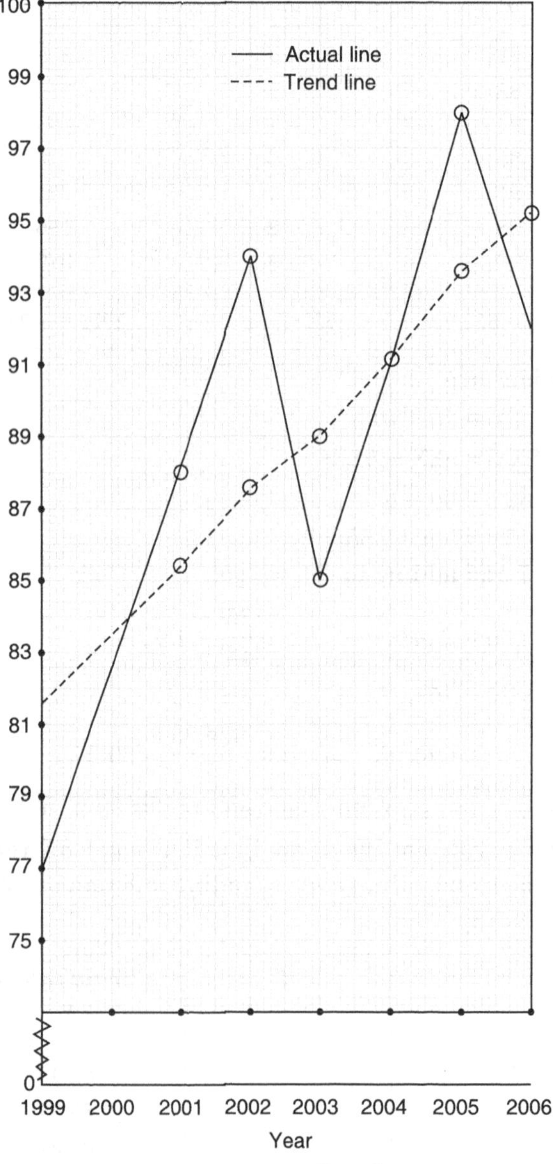

Fig. 14.16. Trend Line

Merits and Demerits of Method of Least Squares.

Merits. The following are the merits.

1. It is purely mathematical method to measure trend.
2. The straight line so obtained is the line of best fit.
3. Trend values can be obtained for all the given time periods in the series. But this is not possible in other methods like method of moving average, semi-average method etc.

Demerits. There are some limitations which are given below.

1. It requires great care in selecting the type of trend curve to be fitted.
2. It is a time-consuming method as compared to other methods.
3. It ignores impact of cyclical, seasonal and irregular variations. Also forecasting is based only on long-term variations.
4. It cannot be used to fit various curves like logistic curve, growth curve, Gompertz curve etc.

II. Fitting of parabolic trend. By a parabolic trend, we mean an equation of the form

$$Y = a + bX + cX^2$$

where a = Y-intercept

b = slope of the curve at the origin

c = rate of change in the slope.

By the method of least squares, the values of the constants a, b, c can be obtained by the normal equations given below. (Take n = number of years in the series).

$$\Sigma Y = na + b\Sigma X + c\Sigma X^2$$
$$\Sigma XY = a\Sigma X + b\Sigma X^2 + c\Sigma X^3$$
$$\Sigma X^2Y = a\Sigma X^2 + b\Sigma X^3 + c\Sigma X^4$$

A second degree trend is considered to be an appropriate mode for the secular trend component of time series when the data do not appear to fall in a straight line.

Example 6. *Fit a second degree parabolic trend to the following data*

Year	*2001*	*2002*	*2003*	*2004*	*2005*
Sales (in crores)	*5*	*7*	*4*	*9*	*12*

Also compute the trend values and predict the sales for the year 2006. Show the trend line on the graph paper.

Sol. Let the required parabolic trend is

$$Y = a + bX + cX^2 \quad \text{...(1)}$$

Here $n = 5$ (odd) $\therefore$ the year of origin is 2003. Consider the following table.

Years	*Sales (in crores) Y*	*Deviations from 2003 X*	X^2	X^3	X^4	*XY*	X^2Y
2001	5	– 2	4	8	16	– 10	20
2002	7	– 1	1	– 1	1	– 7	7
2003	4	0	0	0	0	0	0
2004	9	1	1	1	1	9	9
2005	12	2	4	8	16	24	48
	$\Sigma Y = 37$	$\Sigma X = 0$	$\Sigma X^2 = 10$	$\Sigma X^3 = 0$	$\Sigma X^4 = 34$	$\Sigma XY = 16$	$\Sigma X^2Y = 84$

The normal equations are

$$\Sigma Y = 5a + b\Sigma X + c\Sigma X^2$$

$$\Sigma XY = a\Sigma X + b\Sigma X^2 + c\Sigma X^3$$

and $$\Sigma X^2Y = a\Sigma X^2 + b\Sigma X^3 + c\Sigma X^4$$

or $$37 = 5a + 10c \quad \text{...(2)}$$

$$16 = 10b \quad \text{...(3)}$$

$$84 = 10a + 34c \quad \text{...(4)}$$

From (3), $$b = \frac{16}{10} = 1.6$$

Multiplying (2) by 2 and subtracting to (4), we get

$$74 - 84 = 20c - 14c = 6c \quad \Rightarrow \quad c = \frac{-10}{6} = -1.66$$

From (2), $37 - 10\,(-1.66) = 5a$

$$\Rightarrow \quad 5a = 37 + 16.6 = 53.6$$

$$\Rightarrow \quad a = \frac{53.6}{5} = 10.72$$

$\therefore$ from (1), the required parabolic trend is given by

$$Y = 10.72 + 1.6\,X - 1.66\,X^2 \quad \text{...(5)}$$

To obtain trend values. The trend values for the corresponding years are obtained in the following table.

Years	*Y*	*X*	*Trend values* (Y_c) $Y = 10.72 + 1.6X - 1.66X^2$
2001	5	– 2	0.88
2002	7	– 1	7.46
2003	4	0	10.72
2004	9	1	10.66
2005	12	2	7.28

To predict the sale for 2006. For the year 2006, X = 3

$\therefore$ from (5) $$Y = 10.72 + (1.6)3 - (1.66)(9)$$

$$= 10.72 + 4.8 - 14.94 = 0.58$$

The trend line is shown by the dotted line in the given figure.

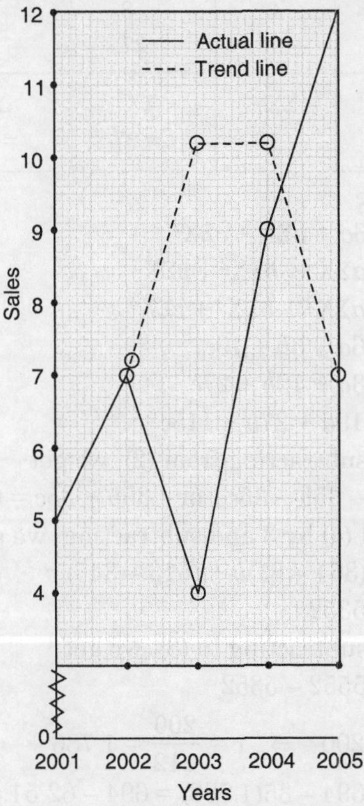

Fig. 14.17. Trend Line

Example 7. *The prices of a commodity during 2000–2005 are given below.*

Year	*2000*	*2001*	*2002*	*2003*	*2004*	*2005*
Prices (in ₹)	*100*	*107*	*128*	*140*	*181*	*192*

(a) Fit a parabola $Y = a + bX + cX^2$ *to these data.*

(b) Estimate the price of the commodity for the year 2006.

(c) Also plot the actual and trend values on the graph paper.

Sol. (*a*) Given equation of the parabola is

$$Y = a + bX + cX^2 \qquad \text{...(1)}$$

Here $n = 6$(even).

∴ We can take year of origin either 2002 or 2003. Consider the following table.

Years	*Prices (in ₹) Y*	*Deviations from 2002 X*	X^2	X^3	X^4	*XY*	X^2Y
2000	100	– 2	4	– 8	16	– 200	400
2001	107	– 1	1	– 1	1	– 107	107
2002	128	0	0	0	0	0	0

2003	140	1	1	1	1	140	140
2004	181	2	4	8	16	362	724
2005	192	3	9	27	81	576	1728
	$\Sigma Y = 848$	$\Sigma X = 3$	$\Sigma X^2 = 19$	$\Sigma X^3 = 27$	$\Sigma X^4 = 115$	$\Sigma XY = 771$	$\Sigma X^2 Y = 3099$

The normal equations are

$$\Sigma Y = 6a + b\Sigma X + c\Sigma X^2$$

$$\Sigma XY = a\Sigma X + b\Sigma X^2 + c\Sigma X^3$$

$$\Sigma X^2 Y = a\Sigma X^2 + b\Sigma X^3 + c\Sigma X^4$$

or

$$848 = 6a + 3b + 19c \quad \text{...(2)}$$

$$771 = 3a + 19b + 27c \quad \text{...(3)}$$

$$3099 = 19a + 27b + 115c \quad \text{...(4)}$$

Multiplying (3) by 2 and subtracting from (2), we get

$$-694 = -35b - 35c \quad \text{or} \quad 35b + 35c = 694 \quad \text{...(5)}$$

Multiplying (3) by 19 and (4) by 3 and subtracting, we get

$$14649 - 9297 = (361 - 81)b + (513 - 345)c$$

$$280b + 168c = 5352 \quad \text{...(6)}$$

Multiplying (5) by 8 and subtracting to (6), we get

$$280c - 168c = 5552 - 5352$$

$$\Rightarrow \quad 112c = 200 \Rightarrow c = \frac{200}{112} = 1.786$$

From (5), $35b = 694 - 35(1.786) = 694 - 62.51 = 631.49$

$$\Rightarrow \quad b = \frac{631.49}{35} = 18.042$$

From (2), $848 = 6a + 54.126 + 33.934$

$$\Rightarrow \quad 6a = 848 - 88.06 = 759.94$$

$$\Rightarrow \quad a = \frac{759.94}{6} = 126.656$$

$\therefore$ From (1), the required parabola is $Y = 126.656 + 18.042X + 1.786X^2$ ...(7)

(*b*) For the year 2006, X = 4

$\therefore$ The estimate price of the commodity for the year 2006 is given by (using (7))

$$Y = 126.656 + (18.042)(4) + (1.786)(16)$$

$$= 126.656 + 72.168 + 28.576 = ₹\ 227.4$$

(*c*) The trend values are obtained in the following table

Years	*Y*	*X*	*Trend values* (Y_c) $Y = 126.656 + 18.042X + 1.786X^2$
2000	100	−2	97.717
2001	107	−1	110.401
2002	128	0	126.656
2003	140	1	146.485
2004	181	2	169.885
2005	192	3	196.857

The trend line is shown in the given figure.

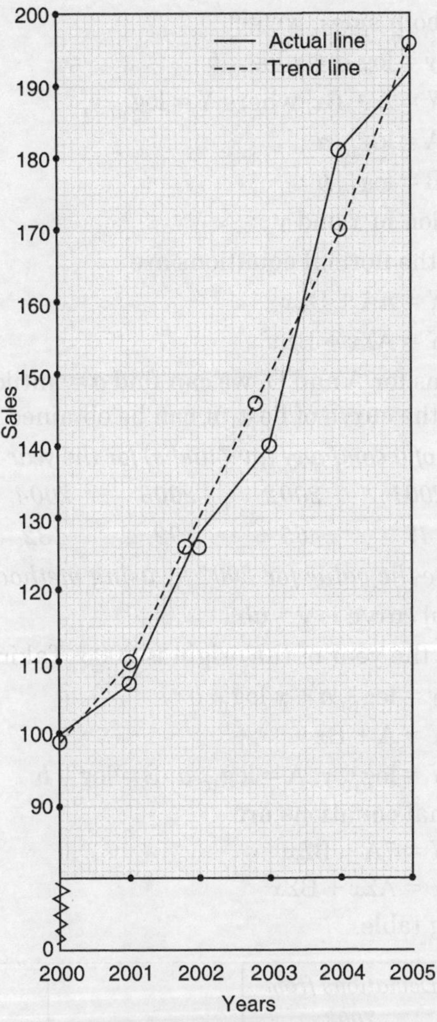

Fig. 14.18. Trend Line

Some other curves. While analysing an economic data in time series analysis, we may come across some situations when the growth is very slow. Also the demand increases every year by a large amount and at the same time, the amount of growth becomes less. The curve grows more and more slowly and tends to approach the upper limit. Such curves are known as **growth curves.** The growth curves do not reach a maximum and trend to second degree parabola. There are different number of growth curves to measure secular trend but the most commonly used curves to describe growth, are **Gompertz curves** and the **logistic curves.** Both these curve give a S-shaped representation when plotted on a graph paper.

The curve of the form $y = ka^{b^x}$, where k, a, b are constants, is known as **Gompertz** curve.

The curve of the form $\frac{1}{y} = k + ab^x$, where k, a, b are constants, is known as **logistic curves.**

The curve of the form $y = k + ab^x$, where k, a, b are constants, is known as **modified exponential curve.**

The curve of the form $y = ab^x$, where a, b are constants, is known as **exponential curve.**

III. Fitting of exponential curve. The curve to be fitted is $y = ab^x$ ...(1)

Taking logarithm on both sides, we get

$$\log_{10} y = \log a + x \log_{10} b$$

or $$Y = A + Bx, \text{ where } Y = \log_{10} y,$$

$$A = \log_{10} a$$

$$B = \log_{10} b$$

This is a linear equation in x and y.

To compute A and B, the normal equations are

$$\Sigma Y = nA + B\Sigma x$$

$$\Sigma xY = A\Sigma x + B\Sigma x^2$$

Solving these equations for A and B, we can find $a = \text{antilog}_{10}$ A, $b = \text{antilog}_{10}$ B. Using the values of a and b in (1), the curve of best fit can be obtained.

Example 8. *The sales of a company (in ₹ lakhs) for the year 2000 to 2006 are given below :*

Years	*2000*	*2001*	*2002*	*2003*	*2004*	*2005*	*2006*
Sales	*32*	*47*	*65*	*92*	*132*	*190*	*275*

for the curve $y = ab^x$, estimate the value for 2007 by using method of least squares.

Sol. Given exponential curve is $y = ab^x$ ...(1)

Here $n = 7$ (odd) ∴ the year of the origin is 2003. Taking logarithm of (1), we get

$$\log_{10} y = \log_{10} a + x \log_{10} b$$

or $$Y = A + Bx \quad ...(2)$$

where $$Y = \log_{10} y,\ A = \log_{10} a,\ B = \log_{10} b$$

To find A, B, the normal equations are

$$\Sigma Y = 7A + B\Sigma x \quad ...(3)$$

$$\Sigma xY = A\Sigma x + B\Sigma x^2 \quad ...(4)$$

Consider the following table.

Years	*Sales* y	*Deviations from 2003* x	$Y = \log_{10} y$	x^2	xY
2000	32	– 3	1.5051	9	– 4.5153
2001	47	– 2	1.6721	4	– 3.3442
2002	65	– 1	1.8129	1	– 1.8129
2003	92	0	1.9638	0	0
2004	132	1	2.1206	1	2.1206
2005	190	2	2.2788	4	4.5576
2006	275	3	2.4393	9	7.3149
	Σy = 833	Σx = 0	ΣY = 13.7926	Σx^2 = 28	ΣxY = 4.3237

From (3), $\quad 13.7926 = 7A \quad \Rightarrow \quad A = \dfrac{13.7926}{7} = 1.9704$

From (4), $\quad 4.3237 = 28\,B \quad \Rightarrow \quad B = \dfrac{4.3237}{28} = 0.154$

$\therefore$ from (2) $\quad Y = 1.9704 + (0.154)\, x$ ...(5)

For the year 2007, $x = 4$ $\therefore$ from (5), the estimated value is given by

$Y = 1.9704 + (0.154)(4) = 2.5864$

$\Rightarrow \quad \log_{10} y = 2.5864$

$\Rightarrow \quad y = \text{antilog}_{10}\,(2.5864) = 385.833 \cong$ ₹ 385.9 lakhs.

Example 9. *Consider the given figures of production (lakh litres) of a milk plant.*

Year	*2001*	*2002*	*2003*	*2004*	*2005*	*2006*
Production	*77*	*88*	*95*	*114*	*119*	*127*

Fit a trend $y = ab^x$ to this data and tabulate the trend values. Also plot the trend line on a graph paper.

Sol. Given curve is $\quad y = ab^x$ ...(1)

$\Rightarrow \quad \log_{10} y = \log_{10} a + x \log_{10} b$

$\Rightarrow \quad Y = A + Bx$ ...(2)

where $\quad Y = \log_{10} y \quad A = \log_{10} a \quad B = \log_{10} b$

Here $n = 6$ (even). $\therefore$ The year of the origin is the A.M. of 2003 and 2004.

$$\text{A.M. of 2003 and 2004} = \frac{2003 + 2004}{2} = 2003.5$$

To find A and B, the normal equations are

$$\Sigma Y = 6A + B\Sigma x \quad \text{...(3)}$$

$$\Sigma xY = A\Sigma x + B\Sigma x^2 \quad \text{...(4)}$$

Consider the following table.

Years	*Production* y	*Deviations from 2003.5*	*Deviations from (2003.5) × 2* x	x^2	$Y = \log_{10} y$	xY
2001	77	– 2.5	– 5	25	1.8865	– 9.4325
2002	88	– 1.5	– 3	9	1.9445	– 5.8335
2003	95	– 0.5	– 1	1	1.9777	– 1.9777
2004	114	0.5	1	1	2.0569	2.0569
2005	119	1.5	3	9	2.0755	6.2265
2006	127	2.5	5	25	2.1038	10.519
	Σy = 620		Σx = 0	Σx^2 = 70	ΣY = 12.0449	ΣxY = 1.5587

From (3), $\quad 12.0449 = 6A \Rightarrow A = \dfrac{12.0449}{6} = 2.0075$

From (4), $\quad 1.5587 = 70\,B \Rightarrow B = \dfrac{1.5587}{70} = 0.0223$

Hence $\quad A = \log_{10} a = 2.0075$

$\Rightarrow \quad a = \text{antilog}_{10}\ 2.0075 = 101.74$

$B = \log_{10} b = 0.0223$

$\Rightarrow \quad b = \text{antilog}_{10}\ 0.0223 = 1.053$

$\therefore$ From (1), the required curve of best fit is $y = (101.74)\,(1.053)^x.z$

The trend values are given in the following table

Years	x	*Trend values* (Y_c) $y = (101.74)\ (1.053)^x$
2001	– 5	78.7
2002	– 3	87.22
2003	– 1	96.65
2004	1	107.1
2005	3	118.7
2006	5	131.5

The trend line is shown by the dotted line in the following figure.

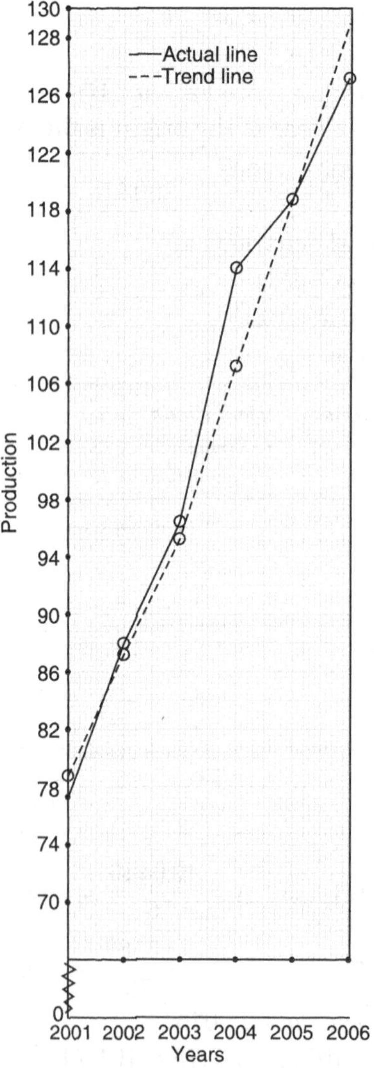

Fig. 14.19. Trend Line

Note. The same result will be obtained if we do not multiply the deviations by 2. But in that case, our computations would be more difficult.

TEST YOUR KNOWLEDGE 14.2

1. Consider the figures of production of steel given below

Years	2000	2001	2002	2003	2004	2005	2006
Production (metric tonnes)	60	72	75	65	80	85	95

Fit a straight line trend and estimate the production for the year 2007.

2. The following table relates to the tourists arrivals (in millions) during 2003 to 2006 in India.

Years	2000	2001	2002	2003	2004	2005	2006
Number of tourists (in millions)	18	20	23	25	24	28	30

Fit a straight line trend by the method of least squares and estimate the number of arrivals in the year 2010.

3. Consider the following data

Years	2000	2001	2002	2003	2004	2005	2006
Sales (in lakhs)	12	10	14	11	13	15	16

(*a*) Fit a straight line trend by the method of least squares.

(*b*) Obtain the trend values and show the trend line on the graph paper.

4. Fit a straight line trend by the method of least squares for the following data

Years	2000	2001	2002	2003	2004	2005	2006
Sales (in tonnes)	77	88	94	85	91	98	90

Obtain the trend values and plot the same on the graph paper.

5. Apply the method of least squares to obtain the trend values from the following data

Years	2001	2002	2003	2004	2005
Sales (in lakhs)	100	120	110	140	80

Estimate the sales for the year 2007.

6. The owner of Sun Solar Heater is examining the number of solar homes started in northern Indian villages in each of the first 8 months :

Months	Jan.	Feb.	March	April	May	June	July	August
No. of homes	351	366	362	400	419	420	450	518

Develop the linear equation and find that what will be the number of homes with solar heater in November.

7. Below are given the number of units produces (in lakhs) during as below

Years	1999	2000	2001	2002	2003	2004	2005	2006
Produced (in lakhs)	56	55	51	47	42	38	35	32

(*a*) Fit a straight line and obtain the trend values.

(*b*) Eliminate the trend. What components of the time series are thus left over ?

(*c*) What is the monthly increase in the number of units produced ?

8. Fit an equation of the form

$Y = a + bX + cX^2$, by using method of least squares. The data is

X :	1	2	3	4	5
Y :	25	28	33	39	46

9. The following table gives the number of eggs produced by hens for 5 years ending 2006.

Years	2002	2003	2004	2005	2006
No. of eggs (in thousands)	1.6	4.5	13.8	40.2	125

Fit an equation of the form $Y = ab^x$.

10. The sales of a company for the last eight years are given below.

Years	2000	2001	2002	2003	2004	2005	2006	2007
Sales ('000 ₹)	52	45	98	92	110	185	175	220

Estimate the sales for the year 2008 by using an equation of the form $Y = ab^X$, where X = year, Y = sales.

11. Fit a parabolic trend to the following time-series data.

Years	2000	2001	2002	2003	2004	2005	2006
Production ('000 units)	42	49	62	75	92	122	158

Estimate the production in 2011.

12. Fit a straight line trend by the method of least squares.

Years	1999	2001	2002	2003	2004	2005	2007
Sales (in lakhs)	57	68	74	65	71	78	70

Answers

1. Y = 76 + 4.857 X, Estimate production = 95.428 in tonnes

2. Y = 24 + 1.893 X, Estimate number of arrivals = 37.251 million

3. (*a*) Y = 13 + 0.75 X

(*b*) Trend values: 10.75, 11.5, 12.25, 13, 13.75, 14.5, 15.25

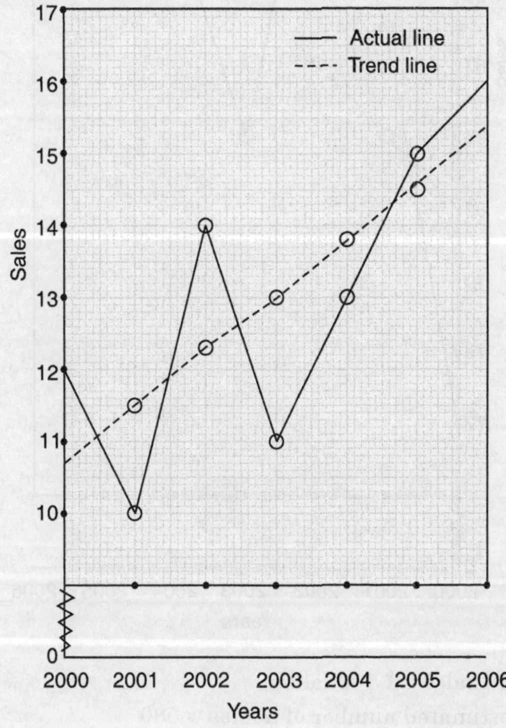

4. Y = 89 + 2X, trend values: 83, 85, 87, 89, 91, 93, 95.

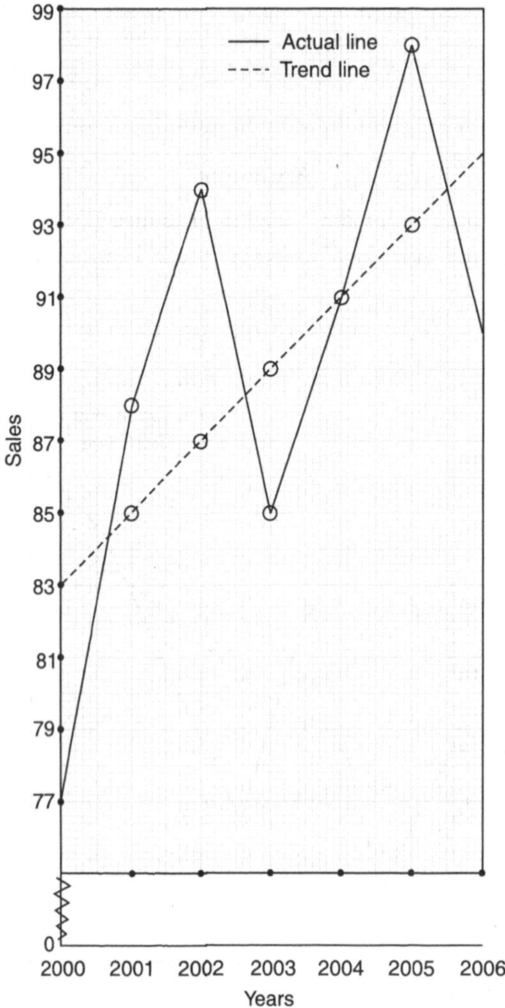

5. Y = 110 – 2X, estimated sales = ₹ 100 lakhs

6. Y = 406.84 + 21.23X, estimated number of homes = 580

7. (*a*) Y = 44.4 – 1.8X

(*b*)

Years	*Y*	*Deviations* *X*	*Trend values* (Y_c) $Y = 44.4 - 1.8X$	*Elimination of Trend* $Y - Y_c$
1999	56	– 4	51.6	4.4
2000	55	– 3	49.8	5.2
2001	51	– 2	48	3
2002	47	– 1	46.2	0.8

2003	42	1	42.6	−0.6
2004	38	2	40.8	−2.8
2005	35	3	39	−4
2006	32	4	37.2	−5.2

From the last column, we observe that the variations are irregular. Hence after eliminating the trend, we are left with cyclic and irregular variations.

(c) Monthly increase = – 0.15 lakhs.

8. $Y = 22.78 + 1.46X + 0.64X^2$

9. $Y = (13.79)(2.978)^X$

10. $Y = (106.414)(1.119)^X$, estimate sales = ₹ 293.76 crores

11. $Y = 74.39 + 18.71X + 2.83X^2$, estimate production = 405.19 thousand units.

12. $Y = 69 + 1.64X$. Trend values: 62.64, 65.72, 67.36, 69, 70.74, 72.28, 75.56.

14.15. SHIFTING THE ORIGIN

For simplicity of computation, we generally fit the trends to annual data with the middle of the series as origin. However, to study cyclic or seasonal variations, it is necessary to change the origin of the trend equation to some other point in the series. Annual trend may be changed to monthly trend or quarterly trend.

Case I. Shifting the origin for a straight line.

The equation of straight line is $Y = a + bX$

Here a is called Y-intercept.

After shifting the origin, the new straight line trend is $Y_t = a + b(X + k)$, provided k is positive and k = number of times unit shifted forward or $Y_t = a + b(X - k)$, provided k is negative and k = number of times unit shifted backward.

Case II. Shifting of origin for parabolic curves. The equation of the parabolic trend is

$$Y = a + bX = cX^2$$

After shifting the origin, the new parabolic trend is $Y_t = a + b(X + k) + c(X + k)^2$ where k = number of time units shifted.

Also take k positive if the number of times unit shifted forward and negative if shifted backward.

Case III. Shifting of origin for exponential curve. The equation of the exponential trend is

$$Y = ab^X$$

After shifting the origin, the new exponential trend is $Y = ab^{(X+k)}$, if k = number of times unit shifted forward.

or $$Y = ab^{(X-k)}, \text{ if } k \text{ is shifted backward.}$$

14.16. CONVERSION OF ANNUAL TREND EQUATION TO MONTHLY TREND EQUATION

Given annual trend equation, we can convert it into monthly trend equation.

Case I. When the trend equation is a straight line given by $Y = a + bX$ ...(1)

Assume (1) is given in annual totals. To convert (1) into monthly trend equation, divide $\boldsymbol{a}$ by 12 and $\boldsymbol{b}$ by 144. (Since the data are sums of 12 months and hence $\boldsymbol{a}$ and $\boldsymbol{b}$ must be divided by 12 and b is again divided by 12 so that the time units (X's) will be in months as well)

Thus the monthly trend equation is

$$Y = \frac{a}{12} + \frac{b}{144} X$$

Similarly, the annual trend equation (1) can be converted to quarterly trend equation by dividing ***a*** by 4 and ***b*** by 48. Thus the quarterly trend equation is

$$Y = \frac{a}{4} + \frac{b}{48} X$$

Case II. When the trend equation is a parabola given by

$$Y = a + bX + cX^2 \qquad \text{...(1)}$$

Assume (1) is given in annual totals. To convert (1) into monthly trend equation, divide ***a*** by 12, ***b*** by 12 × 12 = 144 and ***c*** by 12 × 12 × 12 = 1728.

Thus the monthly trend equation is

$$Y = \frac{a}{12} + \frac{b}{144} X + \frac{c}{1728} X^2$$

Similarly, the annual trend equation (1) can be converted to quarterly trend equation by dividing ***a*** by 4, ***b*** by 48 and ***c*** by 576. Thus the quarterly trend equation is

$$Y = \frac{a}{4} + \frac{b}{48} X + \frac{c}{576} X^2.$$

ILLUSTRATIVE EXAMPLES

Example 1. *Consider the trend equation Y = 110 + 2X, where year of origin is 1999 and time unit = 1 year Shift the origin to 2003.*

Sol. Given year of origin is 1999 and we are required to shift it to 2003, *i.e.,* 4 years forward.

Here $k = 4$ ∴ The required equation is

$$Y_t = 110 + 2\,(X + k) = 110 + 2(X + 4) = 118 + 2X.$$

Example 2. *Consider the trend equation Y = 210 – 1.5 X, where year of origin is 2003 and time unit = 1 year shift the origin to 1999.*

Sol. Given year of origin is 2003 and we are required to shift the origin from 2003 to 1999 as means going back by 4 years.

∴ $k = -4$. Hence the required equation is

$$\begin{aligned} Y_t &= 210 - 1.5\,(X - k) \\ &= 210 - 1.5\,(X - 4) \\ &= 216 - 1.5X. \end{aligned}$$

Example 3. *You are given the following equation $Y = 126.55 + 18.04X + 1.786X^2$, take the year of origin as 2002–2003. Shift the origin to 2003.*

Sol. Year of origin 2002–2003 means half of the annual increment *i.e.,* 0.5.

After shifting the origin to 2003, the new equation is

$$\begin{aligned} Y_t &= 126.55 + 18.04\,(X + 0.5) + 1.786\,(X + 0.5)^2 \\ &= 126.55 + 18.04X + 9.02 + 1.786(X^2 + 0.25 + X) \\ &= 136.0165 + 19.826X + 1.786X^2. \end{aligned}$$

Example 4. *Consider the trend equation: Y = 240 + 3.8X, where origin = 2000*

X units = one year

Y units = annual production of cement

Shift the origin to 2002–2003.

Sol. 2002–2003 means January 1, 2003, which means half of the annual increment.

∴ After shifting the origin from 2000 to 2002 – 2003, K = (2002 – 2000) + 0.5 = 2.5

∴ The required equation is

$$Y_t = 240 + 3.8\,(X + 2.5) = 240 + 3.8X + 9.5 = 249.5 + 3.8X.$$

Example 5. *Consider the trend equation: Y = 20 + 0.8X,*

where origin = 2002, X units = one year, Y units = production in million tonnes. Shift the origin to January 1, 2003.

Sol. To shift the origin from 2002 to January 1, 2003 means shift the origin from 2002 to 2002 – 2003 which means half of the annual increment *i.e.*, K = 0.5.

∴ The required equation is

$$Y_t = 20 + 0.8\,(X + 0.5) = 20 + 0.8X + 0.4 = 20.4 + 0.8X$$

Example 6. *Consider the trend equation: Y = 25 (2.8)^X, where origin = 2003, X unit = 1 year. Shift the origin forward by 2 years.*

Sol. For shifting the origin forward by 2 years, change X to X + 2 ∴ The new equation is

$$Y_t = 25\,(2.8)^{X+2} = 25\,(2.8)^X\,(2.8)^2 = 196\,(2.8)^X.$$

Example 7. *Consider the trend equation: Y = 280 + 10X + 0.6X^2,*

where origin = 1976, X unit = 1 year, Y = annual production of steel. Shift the origin to 1978–79.

Sol. 1978–1979 means January, 1 1979, which means half of the annual increment therefore, after shifting the origin from 1976 to 1978-1979,

$$K = (1978 - 1976) + 0.5 = 2.5$$

Hence the required equation is

$$\begin{aligned} Y_t &= 280 + 10\,(X + 2.5) + 0.6\,(X + 2.5)^2 \\ &= 280 + 10X + 25 + 0.6(X^2 + 6.25 + 5X) \\ &= 280 + 10X + 25 + 0.6X^2 + 3.75 + 3X \\ &= 308.75 + 13X + 0.6X^2. \end{aligned}$$

Example 8. *Consider the trend equation Y = 26 + 2.8X, where origin = 2003, X unit = 6 months, Y unit = Annual production in m. tonnes. Convert this to a monthly trend equation.*

Sol. Here, Y represents annual production and the time unit is $\frac{1}{2}$ year. To convert the given trend equation to a monthly trend equation, divide *a* by 12 and *b* by 12 × 6 = 72, we get

$$Y = \frac{26}{12} + \frac{2.8}{72} X = 2.167 + 0.039X$$

where origin: July 1, 2003, X unit = 1 month, Y unit = monthly production in m. tonnes.

Example 9. *Consider the trend equation: Y = 86 + 3.6X, where origin: Jan. 2003, X unit = 1 month, Y unit = monthly production in thousands. Convert it to annual trend equation.*

Sol. Given is monthly trend equation

$$Y = 86 + 3.6X \qquad ...(1)$$

To convert (1) to annual trend equation, we first shift the origin from middle January 2003 to July 1, 2003. $\therefore$ K = 5.5

$\therefore$ (1) reduces to

$$Y_t = 86 + 3.6 (X + 5.5)$$

$$= 86 + 3.6X + 19.8 = 105.8 + 3.6X \qquad ...(2)$$

To get annual trend equation, multiply a by 12, and b by 144, (2) gives

$$Y_t = (105.8) \times 12 + 3.6 \times 144X = 1269.6 + 518.4X$$

where origin : 2003, X unit = 1 year, Y unit = annual production.

Example 10. *Consider the annual production (in thousand tonnes) of a sugar factory.*

Year	*2000*	*2001*	*2002*	*2003*	*2004*	*2005*	*2006*
Production	*70*	*75*	*90*	*91*	*95*	*98*	*100*

(a) Fit a straight line by the method of least squares. Also obtain the trend values and show it on the graph paper.

(b) Convert your annual trend equation to a monthly trend equation.

Sol. (*a*) Let the required straight line to be fitted is Y = a + bX ...(1)

Here n = 7 (odd) $\therefore$ Year of origin is 2003. Consider the following table.

Years	*Production in thousands Y*	*Deviations from 2003 X*	*XY*	*X²*
2000	70	– 3	– 210	9
2001	75	– 2	– 150	4
2002	90	– 1	– 90	1
2003	91	0	0	0
2004	95	1	95	1
2005	98	2	196	4
2006	100	3	300	9
	$\Sigma Y = 619$	$\Sigma X = 0$	$\Sigma XY = 141$	$\Sigma X^2 = 28$

The normal equations are

$$\Sigma Y = 7a + b\Sigma X,$$
$$\Sigma XY = a\Sigma X + b\Sigma X^2$$

or $\quad 619 = 7a \quad \Rightarrow \quad a = \dfrac{619}{7} = 88.43$

and $\quad 141 = 28b \quad \Rightarrow \quad b = \dfrac{141}{28} = 5.04$

$\therefore$ From (1), the required straight line is

$$Y = 88.43 + 5.04X$$

The trend values are obtained in the following table.

Year	*X*	*Trend values* (Y_c) $Y = 88.43 + 5.04X$
2000	– 3	73.31
2001	– 2	78.35
2002	– 1	83.39
2003	0	88.43
2004	1	93.47
2005	2	98.51
2006	3	103.55

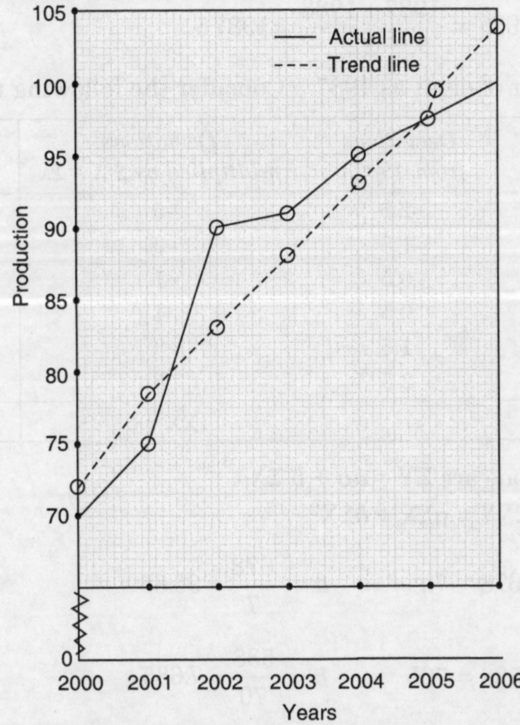

Fig. 14.20. Trend Values

(*b*) From part (*a*) Y = 88.43 + 5.04X converting it to a monthly trend equation $\left(\text{changing } a \text{ to } \frac{a}{12} \text{ and } b \text{ to } \frac{b}{144}\right)$, we get

$$Y = \frac{88.43}{12} + \frac{5.04}{144} X = 7.369 + 0.035X.$$

Example 11. *Convert the following annual trend equation to a monthly trend equation:*

$$Y = 10.6 + 0.8X + 0.64X^2.$$

Sol. To convert annual trend equation of second degree parabola ($Y = a + bX + cX^2$) divide *a* by 12, *b* by 144 (= 12 × 12) and *c* by 1728 (= 144 × 12), we get

$$Y = \frac{10.6}{12} + \frac{0.8}{144} X + \frac{0.64}{1728} X^2 = 0.883 + 0.0056X + 0.00037X^2.$$

Example 12. *Fit a straight line trend by least squares method to the following data and calculate short time fluctuations:* (P.T.U. M.B.A. May 2008)

Year	*1985*	*1986*	*1987*	*1988*	*1989*	*1990*
Production ('000 tons)	*75*	*83*	*109*	*129*	*134*	*148*

Sol. Let the required straight line is

$$y = a + bX \qquad \ldots(1)$$

Here $n = 6$ (even) ∴ There are two middle years namely 1987 and 1988

$$\text{A.M. of 1987 and 1988} = \frac{1987 + 1988}{2} = 1987.5$$

Hence we take year of oigin as 1987.5 Consider the following table.

Year	*Production ('000 tons)*	*Deviations from 1987.5*	*Deviations multiplied by 2 X = 2x*	*XY*	*X²*
1985	75	–2.5	–5	–375	25
1986	83	–1.5	–3	–249	9
1987	109	–0.5	–1	–109	1
1988	129	0.5	1	129	1
1989	134	1.5	3	402	9
1990	148	2.5	5	740	25
	ΣY = 678		ΣX = 0	ΣXY = 538	ΣX² = 70

The normal equations are $\Sigma Y = na + b\,\Sigma X$

and $$\Sigma XY = a\Sigma X + b\Sigma X^2$$

or $$678 = 7a \quad \Rightarrow \quad a = \frac{678}{7} = 96.85$$

and $$538 = 70b \quad \Rightarrow \quad b = \frac{538}{70} = 7.685$$

∴ From (1) The required equation of the straight line trend is

$$y = 96.85 + 7.685X.$$

To obtain short time fluctuations. We obtain the trend values and short term fluctuations which are given in the following table.

Year	*Y*	*X*	*Trend values* $Y_C = 96.85 + 7.685X$	*Short time fluctuations* $Y - Y_C$
1985	75	–5	58.425	16.575
1986	83	–3	73.795	9.205
1987	109	–1	89.165	19.835
1988	129	1	104.535	24.465
1989	134	3	119.905	14.095
1990	148	5	135.225	12.775

TEST YOUR KNOWLEDGE 14.3

1. Consider the straight line trend Y = 84.26 + 5.8X, where origin: 2002, X unit = 1 year, Y unit = annual production of steel.
Change the origin (*i*) to 1999 (*ii*) to Jan. 1, 2003.

2. Given the following equation
Y = 45 + 2.6X, where origin : 1975, X unit = 1 year, Y unit = Annual production of steel.
Shift the origin to 1978.

3. Given the equation: Y = 25 + 2.2X, where origin: 1983, X unit = 1 year
Shift the origin forward by 3 years.

4. You are given that: $Y = 480 + 10X + 0.8X^2$, where origin : 1998, X unit = 1 year
Y unit = annual production of sugar in tonnes. Shift the origin to 2003.

5. Given the following equation: Y = 148 + 24.4X, where origin : 2002, X unit = 1 year
Y unit = annual sales of steel.
Obtain the monthly trend equation.

6. The trend of annual sales of a company is given by the following Y = 15 + 0.5X, where origin : 1987, X unit = 1 year
Y unit = annual production, convert it to quarterly trend equation.

7. The trend of the annual sales of XYZ Co. Ltd. is described by the following equation.
Y = 30 + 3.6X [origin : 2001, X unit = 1 year, Y unit = annual sales] Convert it to monthly basis.

Answers

1. (*i*) $Y_t = 66.86 + 5.8X$ [origin : 1999, X unit = 1 year]
(*ii*) $Y_t = 87.16 + 5.8X$ [origin : Jan. 1, 2003, X unit = 1 year]

2. $Y_t = 52.8 + 2.6X$ [origin : 1978, X unit = 1 year, Y unit = Annual production of steel]

3. $Y_t = 31.6 + 2.2X$ [origin : 1986, X unit = 1 year]

4. $Y_t = 550 + 18X + 0.8X^2$ [origin 2003]

5. $Y_t = 12.333 + 0.1694X$ [origin : July 1, 2002, X unit = 1 month, Y unit = monthly sales of steel]

6. $Y_t = 3.75 + 0.03125X$

7. $Y_t = 2.5 + 0.025X$ [X unit = 1 month, Y unit = monthly sales].

14.17. MEASUREMENT OF SEASONAL VARIATIONS

Most of the phenomena in economics and business show seasonal patterns. But if the data is expressed annually then there is no seasonal variation. Only monthly or quarterly expressed data exhibit strong seasonal movements. To measure seasonal variations, it is necessary to first free the data from the effects of trend, cycles and irregular variation. A measure of seasonal variations which is free from the effects of trend, cycles and irregular variations etc. is known as **seasonal index**, the unit of seasonal index is per cent.

There are different methods for measuring seasonal variations. Some of them are:

1. Method of simple averages (weekly or monthly or quarterly)
2. Method of moving average
3. Ratio-to-trend method
4. Ratio-to-moving average
5. Link relative method.

We now discuss in details these methods.

I. Method of Simple Averages. (Weekly or monthly or quarterly)

This is the simplest method of obtaining a seasonal index. The various steps involved are

Step I. Arrange the given data by years and month-wise or quarter-wise (if quarterly data is given)

Step II. Obtain the totals of each month of quarter for different years. Obtain the average of each month or quarter.

Step III. Obtain an average of monthly averages by dividing the total of monthly averages by 12. In case of quarters, obtain an average of quarterly averages by dividing the total of quarterly averages by 4.

Step IV. Compute the percentages of various monthly average (take the general average as base) by using the following formula

$$(a) \text{ Seasonal Index for any month} = \frac{\text{Monthly average of that month}}{\text{Average of monthly average}} \times 100$$

$$(b) \text{ Seasonal Index for any quarter} = \frac{\text{Average of that quarter}}{\text{General Average}} \times 100.$$

ILLUSTRATIVE EXAMPLES

Example 1. *Assume that the trend is absent, determine, if any, seasonality in the data given below.*

Years	*Quarters*			
	I	*II*	*III*	*IV*
2002	*37*	*41*	*33*	*35*
2003	*37*	*39*	*36*	*36*
2004	*40*	*43*	*33*	*31*

Find the seasonal indices for each quarters by using method of simple averages.

Sol. To find seasonal indices. Consider the following table.

Years	*Quarters*			
	I	*II*	*III*	*IV*
2002	37	41	33	35
2003	37	39	36	36
2004	40	43	33	31
Total	114	123	102	102
Quarterly Average	$\frac{114}{3} = 38$	$\frac{123}{3} = 41$	$\frac{102}{3} = 34$	$\frac{102}{3} = 34$

Hence average of quarterly averages $= \frac{38+41+34+34}{4} = 36.75$

$\therefore$ Seasonal Index for quarter I $= \frac{38}{36.75} \times 100 = 103.4$

Seasonal Index for quarter II $= \frac{41}{36.75} \times 100 = 111.56$

Seasonal Index for quarter III $= \frac{34}{36.75} \times 100 = 92.52$

Seasonal Index for quarter IV $= \frac{34}{36.75} \times 100 = 92.52.$

Example 2. *Compute the seasonal averages, seasonal variations and seasonal indices for the following time series by using method of simple averages*

Years	*Months*											
	Jan.	*Feb.*	*Mar.*	*Apr.*	*May*	*June*	*July*	*Aug.*	*Sept.*	*Oct.*	*Nov.*	*Dec.*
2003	*15*	*16*	*18*	*18*	*23*	*23*	*20*	*28*	*29*	*33*	*33*	*38*
2004	*23*	*22*	*28*	*27*	*31*	*28*	*22*	*28*	*32*	*37*	*34*	*44*
2005	*25*	*25*	*35*	*36*	*36*	*30*	*30*	*34*	*38*	*47*	*41*	*53*

Sol. To find seasonal averages, seasonal variations, seasonal indices, consider the following table.

Months	*Years*			*3-yearly totals*	*Monthly average*	=	*Seasonal Index* $= \frac{\textit{Monthly average}}{\textit{Average of monthly average}} \times 100$
	2003	*2004*	*2005*				
Jan.	15	23	25	$15+23+25=63$	$\frac{63}{3} = 21$		$\frac{21}{30} \times 100 = 70$
Feb.	16	22	25	63	21		$\frac{21}{30} \times 100 = 70$

March	18	28	35	81	27	$\frac{27}{30} \times 100 = 90$
April	18	27	36	81	27	90
May	23	31	36	90	30	100
June	23	28	30	81	27	90
July	20	22	30	72	24	80
Aug.	28	28	34	90	30	100
Sept.	29	32	38	99	33	110
Oct.	33	37	47	117	39	130
Nov.	33	34	41	108	36	120
Dec.	38	44	53	135	45	150
Total					360	

Here, Average of monthly average = $\frac{360}{12} = 30.$

Merits and demerits of method of simple averages

Merits

It is the simplest method as compared to all other methods of measuring seasonality .

Demerits

It is not a very good method as it assumes that there is no trend component in the series.

II. Method of moving averages. It is a superior method as compared to method of simple averages. The various steps involved are

Step I. Compute moving average from the given data. If data are given on monthly basis, compute *12-monthly* moving averages and in case of quarterly basis. Compute *4-quarterly* moving averages.

Step II. Obtain trend values from the moving averages obtained in step I. We *denote* the trend values by 'T'.

Step III. Obtain short-term fluctuations by using trend values obtained in step-II.

Step IV. To find seasonal variations, use the formula :

Seasonal variations = Quarterly average – General average

where General average = Average of monthly or quarterly averages

Example 3. *Compute seasonal variations for the following data by using method of moving average.*

Years	*Quarters*			
	I	*II*	*III*	*IV*
2001	*30*	*81*	*62*	*119*
2002	*33*	*104*	*86*	*171*
2003	*42*	*153*	*99*	*221*
2004	*56*	*172*	*129*	*235*
2005	*67*	*201*	*136*	*302*

Sol. To find seasonal variations, consider the following table

Years	*Quarters*	*Y*	*4-quarterly moving totals*	*2-period moving totals of 4-quarterly moving totals*	*Trend values or quarterly moving average (T)*	*Short term fluctuations Y–T*
2001	I	30	—	—	—	—
	II	81	—	—	—	—
			→ 30 + 81 + 62 + 119 = 292			
	III	62		→ 299 + 295 = 587	$\frac{587}{8}$ = 73.37	– 11.37
			→ 81 + 62 + 119 + 33 = 295			
	IV	119		→ 295 + 318 = 613	$\frac{613}{8}$ = 76.62	42.38
			→ 62 + 119 + 33 + 104 = 318			
2002	I	33		→ 318 + 342 = 660	$\frac{660}{8}$ = 82.5	– 49.5
			→ 119 + 33 + 104 + 86 = 342			
	II	104		→ 342 + 394 = 736	$\frac{736}{8}$ = 92	12
			→ 33 + 104 + 86 + 171 = 394			
	III	86		→ 394 + 403 = 797	$\frac{797}{8}$ = 99.62	– 13.62
			→ 104 + 86 + 171 + 42 = 403			
	IV	171		→ 403 + 452 = 855	$\frac{855}{8}$ = 106.87	64.13
			→ 86 + 171 + 42 + 153 = 452			
2003	I	42		→ 452 + 465 = 917	$\frac{917}{8}$ = 114.62	– 72.62
			→ 171 + 42 + 153 + 99 = 465			
	II	153		→ 465 + 515 = 980	$\frac{980}{8}$ = 122.5	30.5
			→ 42 + 153 + 99 + 221 = 515			
	III	99		→ 515 + 529 = 1044	$\frac{1044}{8}$ = 130.5	– 31.5
			→ 153 + 99 + 221 + 56 = 529			
	IV	221		→ 529 + 548 = 1077	$\frac{1077}{8}$ = 134.62	86.38
			→ 99 + 221 + 56 + 172 = 548			
2004	I	56		→ 548 + 578 = 1126	$\frac{1126}{8}$ = 140.75	– 84.75
			→ 221 + 56 + 172 + 129 = 578			
	II	172		→ 578 + 592 = 1170	$\frac{1170}{8}$ = 146.25	25.75
			→ 56 + 172 + 129 + 235 = 592			

	III	129		→ 592 + 603 = 1195	$\frac{1195}{8}$ = 149.37	– 20.37
			→ 172 + 129 + 235 + 67 = 603			
	IV	235		→ 603 + 632 = 1235	$\frac{1235}{8}$ = 154.37	80.63
			→ 129 + 235 + 67 + 201 = 632			
2005	I	67		→ 632 + 639 = 1271	$\frac{1271}{8}$ = 158.87	– 91.87
			→ 235 + 67 + 201 + 136 = 639			
	II	201		→ 639 + 706 = 1345	$\frac{1345}{8}$ = 168.12	32.88
			→ 67 + 201 + 136 + 302 = 706			
	III	136	—	—		
	IV	302	—	—		

We now calculate seasonal variations by using short-term fluctuations obtained in last column of the above table.

Short-Term Fluctuations

Years	*Quarters*			
	I	*II*	*III*	*IV*
2001	—	—	– 11.37	42.38
2002	– 49.5	12	– 13.62	64.13
2003	– 72.62	30.5	– 31.5	86.38
2004	— 84.75	25.75	– 20.37	80.63
2005	– 91.87	32.88	—	—
Total	– 298.74	101.13	– 76.86	273.52
Quarterly Average	$\frac{-298.74}{4}$ = – 74.68	$\frac{101.13}{4}$ = 25.28	$\frac{-76.86}{4}$ = – 19.215	$\frac{273.52}{4}$ = 68.38

Hence, average of quarterly averages

$$= \frac{-74.68 + 25.28 - 19.215 + 68.38}{4} = \frac{-0.235}{4} = -0.05875$$

∴ Seasonal variations for quarter I

$$= -74.68 - (-0.05875) = -74.62$$

Seasonal variation for quarter II

$$= 25.28 - (-0.05875) = 25.33$$

Seasonal variation for quarter III

$$= -19.215 - (-0.05875) = -19.156$$

Seasonal variation for quarter IV

$$= 68.38 - (-0.05875) = 68.43.$$

III. Ratio-to-Trend Method. It is a method of calculate seasonal index. This method is also known as *percentage-to-trend* method. The various steps involved are

Step I. Find trend values (T) month wise or quarterly by the method of least squares.

Step II. Denote the original value by Y. Then find *ratio-to-trend* value for each period where

$$\text{Ratio-to-trend} = \frac{Y}{T} \times 100$$

Step III. Obtain the A.M. of each quarterly or monthly period ratio-to-trend.

Step IV. The seasonal index is given by seasonal index

$$= \frac{\text{Quarterly (or monthly) average}}{\text{General average}} \times 100.$$

Example 4. *By using Ratio-to-trend method, compute seasonal indices for each quarter of the following data.*

Years	*Quarters*			
	I	*II*	*III*	*IV*
2001	*30*	*40*	*36*	*34*
2002	*34*	*52*	*50*	*44*
2003	*40*	*58*	*54*	*48*
2004	*54*	*76*	*68*	*62*
2005	*80*	*92*	*86*	*82*

Sol. We first find the trend values by using method of least squares. Consider the following table. Here, $n = 5$(odd) $\therefore$ year of origin is 2003

Years	*Yearly totals*	*Yearly average* Y	*Deviations from 2003* X	*XY*	X^2
2001	30 + 40 + 36 + 34 = 140	$\frac{140}{4} = 35$	– 2	– 70	4
2002	34 + 52 + 50 + 44 = 180	$\frac{180}{4} = 45$	– 1	– 45	1
2003	40 + 58 + 54 + 48 = 200	$\frac{200}{4} = 50$	0	0	0
2004	54 + 76 + 68 + 62 = 260	$\frac{260}{4} = 65$	1	65	1
2005	80 + 92 + 86 + 82 = 340	$\frac{340}{4} = 85$	2	170	4
		$\Sigma Y = 280$	$\Sigma X = 0$	$\Sigma XY = 120$	$\Sigma X^2 = 10$

We first find the trend values yearly and will it convert it to quarterly. The equation of the straight line is

$$Y = a + bX \qquad \ldots(1)$$

To find *a*, *b*. The normal equations are

$$\Sigma Y = 5a + b\Sigma X$$

and $$\Sigma XY = a\Sigma X + b\Sigma X^2$$

or $$280 = 5a \Rightarrow a = \frac{280}{5} = 56$$

and $$120 = 10b \Rightarrow b = 12$$

$\therefore$ From (1), $$Y = 56 + 12X \qquad \ldots(2)$$

To find the trend values. Consider the following table.

Year	*X*	*Trend values* (Y_c) $Y = 56 + 12X$
2001	– 2	32
2002	– 1	44
2003	0	56
2004	1	68
2005	2	80

Conversion to quarterly trend values. From (2), b = yearly increment = 12

$\Rightarrow$ quarterly increment $= \frac{12}{4} = 3$

Consider the year 2001. Trend values for the middle quarter *i.e.,* half of the II quarter and half of the III quarter is 32. Also quarterly increment is 3. Therefore, the trend value of quarter II is $32 - \frac{3}{2} = 30.5$ and for quarter III is $32 + \frac{3}{2} = 33.5$. Similarly trend value for the quarter I is $30.5 - 3 = 27.5$ and for the quarter IV is $33.5 + 3 = 36.5$. Thus quarterly trend values for each year is given in the following table.

Trend values

Years	*Quarters*			
	I	*II*	*III*	*IV*
2001	27.5	30.5	33.5	36.5
2002	39.5	42.5	45.5	48.5
2003	51.5	54.5	57.5	60.5
2004	63.5	66.5	69.5	72.5
2005	75.5	78.5	81.5	84.5

Quarterly values as % of trend values. Consider the following table.

Years	*Quarters*			
	I	*II*	*III*	*IV*
2001	$\frac{30}{27.5} \times 100 = 109.09$	$\frac{40}{30.5} \times 100 = 131.14$	107.46	93.15
2002	$\frac{34}{39.5} \times 100 = 86.07$	$\frac{52}{42.5} \times 100 = 122.35$	109.89	90.72
2003	$\frac{40}{51.5} \times 100 = 77.66$	$\frac{58}{54.5} \times 100 = 106.42$	93.91	79.34
2004	$\frac{54}{63.5} \times 100 = 85.03$	$\frac{76}{66.5} \times 100 = 114.28$	97.84	85.52
2005	$\frac{80}{75.5} \times 100 = 105.96$	$\frac{92}{78.5} \times 100 = 117.19$	105.52	97.04
Total	463.84	591.41	514.62	445.77
Quarterly Average	$\frac{463.84}{5} = 92.77$	$\frac{591.41}{5} = 118.28$	$\frac{514.62}{5} = 102.92$	$\frac{445.77}{5} = 89.15$

$$\text{Now the general average} = \frac{92.77 + 118.28 + 102.92 + 89.15}{4}$$

$$= \frac{403.12}{4} = 100.78$$

$$\therefore \quad \text{Seasonal Index for quarter I} = \frac{92.77}{100.78} \times 100 = 92.05$$

$$\text{Seasonal Index for quarter II} = \frac{118.28}{100.78} \times 100 = 117.36$$

$$\text{Seasonal Index for quarter III} = \frac{102.92}{100.78} \times 100 = 102.12$$

$$\text{Seasonal Index for quarter IV} = \frac{89.15}{100.78} \times 100 = 88.46.$$

IV. Ratio-to-moving average method. It is the most commonly used method to measure seasonal variations. It is also known as **percentages of moving average** method. The various steps involved are

Step I. Obtain the trend values by applying **moving average method.** If the data are quarterly, find *4-quarterly* moving averages. In case of monthly data, find *12-monthly* moving averages.

Step II. Find ratio-to-moving averages by using the following formula

$$\text{Ratio-to-moving average} = \frac{Y}{T} \times 100,$$

where Y = original value,

T = moving average.

Step III. Obtain quarterly averages after arranging the ratio-to-moving averages corresponding to different periods.

Step IV. Obtain general average.

Step V. Obtain seasonal indices by using the following formula.

$$\text{Seasonal Index} = \frac{\text{Quarterly average}}{\text{General average}} \times 100$$

Example 5. *Compute seasonal indices by Ratio-to-moving average method from the following data.*

Years	*Quarters*			
	I	*II*	*III*	*IV*
2004	*68*	*62*	*61*	*63*
2005	*65*	*58*	*66*	*61*
2006	*68*	*63*	*63*	*67*

(P.T.U., M.B.A.Dec. 2004)

Sol. We first find the trend values by using *moving average method*. Consider the following table.

Years	*Q*	*Given value* Y	*4-quarterly moving totals*	*2-quarterly moving totals*	*Trend values or 4-quarterly moving average* T	*Ratio-to-moving average* $= \frac{Y}{T} \times 100$
2004	I	68	—	—	—	—
	II	62	—	—	—	—
			68 + 62 + 61 + 63 = 254			
	III	61		505	$\frac{505}{8} = 63.125$	$\frac{61}{63.125} \times 100 = 96.63$
			62 + 61 + 63 + 65 = 251			
	IV	63		498	$\frac{498}{8} = 62.25$	$\frac{63}{62.25} \times 100 = 101.21$
			61 + 63 + 65 + 58 = 247			
2005	I	65		499	$\frac{499}{8} = 62.375$	$\frac{65}{62.375} \times 100 = 104.2$
			63 + 65 + 58 + 66 = 252			
	II	58		502	$\frac{502}{8} = 62.75$	$\frac{58}{62.75} \times 100 = 92.43$
			65 + 58 + 66 + 61 = 250			
	III	66		503	$\frac{503}{8} = 62.875$	$\frac{66}{62.875} \times 100 = 104.97$
			58 + 66 + 61 + 68 = 253			
	IV	61		511	$\frac{511}{8} = 63.875$	$\frac{61}{63.875} \times 100 = 95.49$
			66 + 61 + 68 + 63 = 258			

2006	I	68		513	$\frac{513}{8} = 64.125$	$\frac{68}{64.125} \times 100 = 106.04$
			61 + 68 + 63 + 63 = 255			
	II	63		516	$\frac{516}{8} = 64.5$	$\frac{63}{64.5} \times 100 = 97.67$
			68 + 63 + 63 + 67 = 261			
	III	63	—			
	IV	67	—	—	—	—

We now obtain quarterly average for each quarter. Consider the following table :

Years	*Quarters*			
	I	*II*	*III*	*IV*
2004	—	—	96.63	101.2
2005	104.2	92.43	104.97	95.49
2006	106.04	97.67	—	—
Totals	210.24	190.1	201.16	196.69
Quarterly Average	$\frac{210.24}{2}$ = 105.12	$\frac{190.1}{2}$ = 95.05	$\frac{201.16}{2}$ = 100.58	$\frac{196.69}{2}$ = 98.345

$$\therefore \text{ General average } = \frac{\text{Quarterly average}}{4} = \frac{105.12 + 95.05 + 100.58 + 98.345}{4}$$

$$= \frac{399.095}{4} = 99.77$$

$$\therefore \text{ Seasonal Index for quarter I } = \frac{105.12}{99.77} \times 100 = 105.36$$

$$\text{Seasonal Index for quarter II } = \frac{95.05}{99.77} \times 100 = 95.26$$

$$\text{Seasonal Index for quarter III } = \frac{100.58}{99.77} \times 100 = 100.81$$

$$\text{Seasonal Index for quarter IV } = \frac{98.345}{99.77} \times 100 = 98.57$$

14.18. MERITS AND DEMERITS OF RATIO-TO-TREND METHOD

Merits :

1. It is a simple method and easy to compute and understand.

2. For measuring seasonal variations, it is more logical as compared to method of monthly average. For, it has a ratio-to-trend value for each month for which data are available. Hence there is no loss of data as occurs in the case of moving averages.

Demerits :

In case of cyclic fluctuations. The trend (a straight line or a curve) does not follow the actual data as closely as a 12-month moving average does. Hence the seasonal index so obtained is more biased as compared to ratio-to-moving average method.

V. Link Relative method. It is the most difficult method as compared to all other methods of measuring seasonal variations. The various steps involved are

Step I. Obtain link relatives of the seasonal figure monthly or quarterly by using the following formula

$$\text{Link relative} = \frac{\text{Current season's figure}}{\text{Previous season's figure}} \times 100$$

where the word 'season' means time period. In case of monthly data, season refers to a 'month' and in case of quarterly data to a 'quarter'.

Step II. Compute average of the link relatives for each month or quarter.

Step III. Convert the averages obtained in step II into chain relatives by using the following formula.

$$\text{Chain relatives} = \frac{[\text{Average of link relative of the current season's figure}] \times [\text{Chain relative of the previous seasons's figure}]}{100}$$

Assume chain relative of the first quarter = 100

Step IV. Calculate chain relative for the first term on the basis of chain relative of the last season's figure by using the following formula

Chain relatives of the first term

$$= \frac{[\text{Chain relative of the last seasons's figure}] \times [\text{Average of link relative of the first season's figure}]}{100}$$

Step V. Correct chain relative. Chain relative of the first period should be 100, But due to influence of the trend, it can be more or less than 100. Obtain the difference by deducing 100 from the revised chain relative of the first term. Divide this difference by the number of periods and multiply the quotient by 1, 2, 3 and so on. Subtract these values from the chain relative of second term, chain relative of third term 1 chain relative of fourth term and so on.

The above process is called *correcting of chain relative.*

Step VI. Compute A.M. of the corrected chain relatives.

Step VII. Obtain seasonal index by using the following formula.

$$\text{Seasonal Index} = \frac{\text{Correct chain relatives}}{\text{General average}} \times 100$$

Example 6. *Obtain seasonal indices by using link relative method for the following data.*

Link relative

Years	*Quarters*			
	I	*II*	*III*	*IV*
2001	—	*120*	*133*	*83*
2002	*80*	*117*	*113*	*89*
2003	*88*	*129*	*111*	*93*
2004	*80*	*125*	*115*	*96*
2005	*83*	*117*	*120*	*79*

Sol. Since link relatives is given to us, we find average of the link relatives for each quarter.

Now we find chain relatives by using the formula:

$$\text{Chain relatives} = \frac{[\text{Average of link relative of the current season's figure}] \times [\text{Chain relative of the previous season's figure}]}{100}$$

[Assume chain relative of the first quarter = 100] the chain relatives so obtained are shown in the following table.

Table I

Years	*Quarters*			
	I	*II*	*III*	*IV*
2001 2002 2003 2004 2005	— 80 88 80 83	120 117 129 125 117	133 113 111 115 120	83 89 93 96 79
Total of link of relatives	331	608	592	440
Average of link relatives	$\frac{331}{4} = 82.75$	$\frac{608}{5} = 121.6$	$\frac{592}{5} = 118.4$	$\frac{440}{5} = 88$
Chain relatives	100	$\frac{121.6 \times 100}{100} = 121.6$	$\frac{118.4 \times 121.6}{100} = 143.97$	$\frac{88 \times 143.97}{100} = 126.69$
Corrected chain relatives	100	$121.6 - 1 \times 1.21^* = 120.39$	$143.97 - 2 \times 1.21 = 141.55$	$126.69 - 3 \times 1.21 = 123.06$

* See "difference per quarter" as calculated below.

We next compute corrected (or adjusted) chain relatives (see the table). For this, chain relative of the first quarter (on the basis of last quarter)

$$= \frac{[\text{Chain relative of the last season's figure}] \times [\text{Average of the link relative of the first season's figure}]}{100}$$

$$= \frac{126.69 \times 82.75}{100} = 104.84$$

Difference between chain relative of the first quarter based on the last quarter and chain relative of the first quarter based on the first quarter

$$= 104.84 - 100 = 4.84$$

$\Rightarrow$ Difference per quarter $= \frac{4.84}{4} = 1.21.$

$\therefore$ Corrected (or adjusted) chain relatives for each quarter are obtained by subtracting 1×1.21, 2×1.21, 3×1.21, from the chain relatives of the II, III and IV quarters respectively. (See the table I).

Finally, general average (Average of corrected chain relatives)

$$= \frac{100 + 120.39 + 141.55 + 123.06}{4} = 121.25$$

$\therefore$ Seasonal Index for quarter I $= \frac{\text{Corrected chain relative of quarter I}}{\text{General average}} \times 100$

$$= \frac{100}{121.25} \times 100 = 82.47$$

Seasonal Index for quarter II $= \frac{120.39}{121.25} \times 100 = 99.29$

Seasonal Index for quarter III $= \frac{141.55}{121.25} \times 100 = 116.74$

Seasonal Index for quarter IV $= \frac{123.06}{121.25} \times 100 = 101.5.$

Example 7. *Apply the method of link relatives to the following data and calculate seasonal indices.*

Years	*Quarters*			
	I	*II*	*III*	*IV*
2003	—	6.5	7.8	8.7
2004	5.4	7.9	8.4	7.3
2005	6.8	6.5	9.3	6.4
2006	7.2	5.8	7.5	8.5
2007	6.6	7.3	8	7.1

Sol. We first find the link relatives of each quarter by using the follwoing formula.

$$\text{Link relative} = \frac{\text{Current season's figure}}{\text{Previous year's figure}} \times 100$$

The link relatives of each figure is shown in the following Table I.

Link relatives

Table I

Years	*Quarters*			
	I	*II*	*III*	*IV*
2003	—	$\frac{6.5}{6} \times 100 = 108.33$	$\frac{7.8}{6.5} \times 100 = 120$	$\frac{8.7}{7.8} \times 100 = 111.53$
2004	$\frac{5.4}{8.7} \times 100 = 62.06$	$\frac{7.9}{5.4} \times 100 = 146.29$	$\frac{8.4}{7.9} \times 100 = 106.32$	$\frac{7.3}{8.4} \times 100 = 86.9$
2005	$\frac{6.8}{7.3} \times 100 = 93.15$	$\frac{6.5}{6.8} \times 100 = 95.58$	$\frac{9.3}{6.5} \times 100 = 143.07$	$\frac{6.4}{9.3} \times 100 = 68.81$
2006	$\frac{7.2}{6.4} \times 100 = 112.15$	$\frac{5.8}{7.2} \times 100 = 80.55$	$\frac{7.5}{5.8} \times 100 = 129.31$	$\frac{8.5}{7.5} \times 100 = 113.33$
2007	$\frac{6.6}{8.5} \times 100 = 77.64$	$\frac{7.3}{6.6} \times 100 = 110.6$	$\frac{8}{7.3} \times 100 = 109.58$	$\frac{7.1}{8} \times 100 = 88.75$
Average of link relatives	$\frac{345.35}{4} = 86.33$	$\frac{541.35}{5} = 108.27$	$\frac{608.28}{5} = 121.65$	$\frac{469.32}{5} = 93.86$
Chain relatives	100	$\frac{100 \times 108.27}{100} = 108.27$	$\frac{108.27 \times 121.65}{100} = 131.71$	$\frac{131.71 \times 93.86}{100} = 123.62$
Corrected chain relatives	100	$108.27 - 1.68^* = 106.59$	$131.71 - 2 \times 1.68 = 128.35$	$123.62 - 3 \times 1.68 = 118.58$

* Difference per quarter is 1.68 as calculated below.

Calculation of Corrected chain relatives

Chain relative of quarter I on the basis of first quarter = 100

$$\text{Chain relative of quarter I on the basis of last quarter} = \frac{86.33 \times 123.62}{100} = 106.72$$

Difference between these chain relatives = 106.72 – 100 = 6.72

$$\Rightarrow \quad \text{Difference per quarter} = \frac{6.72}{4} = 1.68$$

$\therefore$ Corrected (or adjusted) chain relatives are obtained by subtracting 1 × 1.68, 2 × 1.68, 3 × 1.68 from the chain relatives of quarters II, III and IV respectively. (See the table I).

Hence average of corrected chain relatives (or General Average)

$$= \frac{100 + 106.59 + 128.35 + 118.58}{4} = \frac{453.52}{4} = 113.38$$

$$\therefore \quad \text{Seasonal Index for quarter I} = \frac{\text{Corrected chain relatives of quarter}}{\text{General average}} \times 100$$

$$= \frac{100 \times 100}{113.38} = 88.19$$

$$\text{Seasonal Index for quarter II} = \frac{106.59}{113.38} \times 100 = 94.01$$

$$\text{Seasonal Index for quarter III} = \frac{128.35}{113.38} \times 100 = 113.2$$

$$\text{Seasonal Index for quarter IV} = \frac{118.58}{113.38} \times 100 = 104.58.$$

TEST YOUR KNOWLEDGE 14.4

1. Calculate the seasonal index for the following data by using simple average method assuming trend is absent:

Years	*Ist Quarter*	*2nd Quarter*	*3rd Quarter*	*4th Quarter*
1987	3.7	4.1	3.3	3.5
1988	3.7	3.9	3.6	3.6
1989	4.0	4.1	3.3	3.1
1990	3.3	4.4	4.0	4.0

2. Calculate the seasonal index for the following data by using simple average method for the following data:

Years	*Summer*	*Monsoon*	*Autumn*	*Winter*
1981	112	110	120	115
1982	80	145	105	90
1983	95	100	140	80
1984	110	90	130	100

3. Find the seasonal fluctuations by the method of moving averages from the following data:

Years	*Ist Quarter*	*2nd Quarter*	*3rd Quarter*	*4th quarter*
1983	74	76	74	80
1984	82	68	50	62
1985	70	74	70	82

4. Find the seasonal fluctuations by using the following data:

Years	*1st Quarter*	*2nd Quarter*	*3rd Quarter*	*4th Quarter*
1983	16.00	13.50	14.70	17.00
1984	15.90	12.20	15.60	18.00
1985	16.30	11.90	16.90	19.20
1986	17.10	13.20	15.00	18.70

5. Using 'Ratio to Trend' method, determine the quarterly seasonal indices for the following data:

Years	*1st Quarter*	*2nd Quarter*	*3rd Quarter*	*4th Quarter*
1984	60	80	72	68
1985	68	104	100	88
1986	80	116	108	96
1987	108	152	136	124
1988	160	184	172	164

6. Calculate the seasonal index for the data given below by Ratio to Moving Average Method.

Years	*1st Quarter*	*2nd Quarter*	*3rd Quarter*	*4th Quarter*
1980	68	62	61	63
1981	65	58	56	61
1982	68	63	63	67
1983	70	59	56	62
1984	60	55	51	58

7. Eliminate 'trend' by moving average method from the quarterly data :

Years	*1st Quarter*	*2nd Quarter*	*3rd Quarter*	*4th Quarter*
1995	40	35	38	40
1996	42	37	39	38
1997	41	35	38	42

8. Apply method of link relatives to the following data and calculate seasonal indices :

Quarters	*Quarterly Figures*				
	1992	*1993*	*1994*	*1995*	*1996*
I	6.0	5.4	6.8	7.2	6.6
II	6.5	7.9	6.6	5.8	7.4
III	7.8	8.4	9.3	7.5	8.0
IV	8.7	7.3	6.4	8.5	7.1

9. Apply the method of link relatives to the following data and obtain seasonal indices.

Link Relatives

Years	*Ist Quarter*	*2nd Quarter*	*3rd Quarter*	*4th Quarter*
1987	—	120	133	83
1988	80	117	113	89
1989	88	129	111	92
1990	80	125	115	96
1991	83	117	120	79

Answers

1. 98.7, 110.7, 95.3, 95.3 **2.** 92.2, 103.39, 114.5, 89.4

3. 6.25, 1.375, – 8.50, 0.875 **4.** 754, – 3.33, .087, 2.4

5. 92.03, 117.33, 102.10, 88.44 **6.** 107.0, 96.4, 94.5, 102.1

7. 98.7, 102.56, 106.66, 94.2675, 100.32, 98.7, 107.54, 90.9

8. 88.09, 94.44, 113.05, 104.43 **9.** 82.5, 99.4, 116.8, 101.4.

15

Theory of Probability

15.1. INTRODUCTION

The words **'Probability'** and **'Chance'** are quite familiar to everyone. Many a times, we come across statements like "Probably it may rain today", Chances of his visit to the university are very few", "It is possible that he may pass the examination with good marks". In the above statements, the words *probably, chance, possible* etc., convey the sense of uncertainty about the occurrence of some event. Ordinarily, it may appear that there cannot be any exact measurement for these uncertainties, but in Mathematics, we do have methods for calculating the degree of certainty of events in numerical values, provided certain conditions are satisfied.

RANDOM EXPERIMENT AND THE SAMPLE SPACE

15.2. RANDOM EXPERIMENT

When we perform experiments in science and engineering, repeatedly under very nearly identical conditions, we get almost the same result. Such experiments are called **deterministic experiments.**

There also exist experiments in which the results may not be essentially the same even if the experiment is performed under very nearly identical conditions. Such experiments are called **random experiments.** If we toss a coin, we may get 'head' or 'tail'. This is a random experiment. Throwing of a die is also a random experiment as any of the six faces of the die may come up. In this experiment, there are six possibilities (1 or 2 or 3 or 4 or 5 or 6).

A random experiment is also known as a **probabilistic experiment** or as a **non-deterministic experiment.**

Remark 1. A *die* is a small cube used in gambling. On its six faces, dots are marked as shown below :

 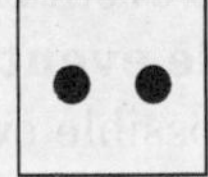 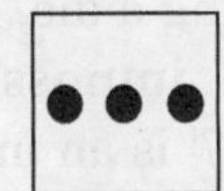 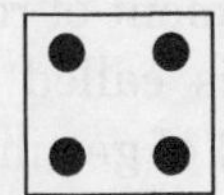 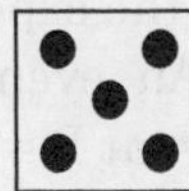 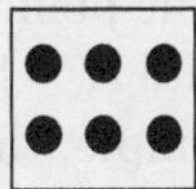

Numbers on a die

Plural of the word die is *dice*. The outcome of throwing a die is the number of dots on its upper most face.

Remark 2. A *pack of cards* consists of four suits called *Spades, Hearts, Diamonds* and *Clubs.* Each suit consists of 13 cards, of which nine cards are numbered from 2 to 10, an ace, a king, a queen and a jack (or knave). Spades and clubs are *black faced cards,* while hearts and diamonds are *red faced cards.* The kings, queens and jacks are called **face cards.**

15.3. SAMPLE SPACE

The **sample space** of a random experiment is defined as the set of all possible outcomes of the experiment. The possible outcomes are called **sample points.** The sample space is generally denoted by the letter S. We list the sample space of some random experiments.

Random Experiment	Sample Space
1. Tossing of an unbiased coin	S = {H, T}
2. Tossing of unbiased coin twice	S = {HH, HT, TH, TT}

In S, the sample point HT represent 'head' on first toss and tail on second toss.

3. Tossing of two unbiased coins	S = {HH, HT, TH, TT}

In S, the sample point HT represent 'head' on first coin and 'tail' on second coin.

4. Tossing of three unbiased coins	S = {HHH, HHT, HTH, THH, HTT, THT, TTH, TTT}*
5. A family of two children	S = {BB, BG, GB, GG}.

In S, the sample point BG represent elder child, 'Boy' and younger child 'Girl'.

6. Throwing of a fair die	S = {1, 2, 3, 4, 5, 6}.
7. Throwing of two fair dice	S = {(1,1) (1, 2), (1, 3), (1,4), (1, 5), (1, 6), (2, 1), (2, 2), (2, 3), (2, 4), (2, 5), (2, 6), (3, 1), (3, 2), (3, 3), (3, 4), (3, 5), (3, 6), (4, 1), (4, 2), (4, 3), (4, 4), (4, 5), (4, 6), (5, 1), (5, 2), (5, 3), (5, 4), (5, 5), (5, 6), (6, 1), (6, 2), (6, 3), (6, 4) (6, 5), (6, 6)}.

In S, the sample point (1, 2) represent the situation that 1 appeared on the first die and 2 on the second die. This sample space has $6 \times 6 = 36$ sample points.

Note. The sample space of a random experiment is either finite or infinite. In our present course, we shall restrict ourselves only to finite sample spaces.

EVENTS AS SUBSETS OF SAMPLE SPACE

15.4. EVENT

An **event** of a random experiment is defind as a subset of the sample space of the random experiment. If the outcome of an experiment is an element of an event A, we say that the event A has occurred. An event is called an **elementary** (*or* **simple**) **event,** if it contains only one sample point. In the experiment of rolling a die, the event A of getting '3' is a simple event. We write A′ = {3}. An event is called an **impossible event,** if it can never occur. In the above example, the event B = {7} of getting '7' is an impossible event. On the other hand, an event which is sure to occur is called a **sure event.** In the above example of rolling a die, the event C of getting a number less than 7 is a sure event. A sure event is also called a **certain event.**

---

*If n coins are tossed, then the number of elements in its sample space is equal to 2^n.

** If n dice are thrown, then number of elements in its sample space is 6^n.

PROBABILITY OF AN EVENT

15.5. EQUALLY LIKELY OUTCOMES

The outcomes of a random experiment are called **equally likely,** if all of these have equal preferences. In the experiment of tossing a unbiased coin, the outcomes, 'Head' and 'Tail' are equally likely.

15.6. EXHAUSTIVE OUTCOMES

The outcomes of a random experiment are called **exhaustive,** if these cover all the possible outcomes of the experiment. In the experiment of rolling a die, the outcomes 1, 2, 3, 4, 5, 6 are exhaustive.

15.7. PROBABILITY OF AN EVENT *(P.T.U., M.B.A. Dec. 2010)*

Suppose in a random experiment, there are n exhaustive, equally likely outcome. Let A be an event and there are m outcomes (cases) favourable to the happening of it. The **probability** P(A) of the happening of the event A is defined as :

$$P(A) = \frac{\text{Total number of cases favourable to the happening of A}}{\text{Total number of exhaustive equally likely cases}} = \frac{m}{n}.$$

It may be observed from this definition, that $0 \le m \le n$.

$$\therefore \quad 0 \le \frac{m}{n} \le 1 \quad \text{or} \quad \mathbf{0 \le P(A) \le 1.}$$

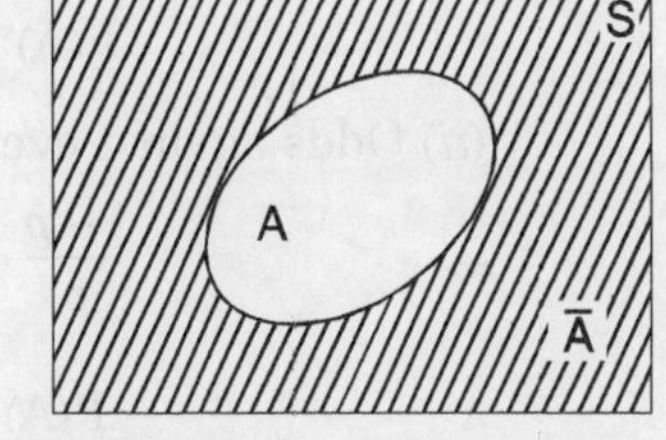

The number of cases favourable of the non-happening of the event A is $n - m$.

$$\therefore \quad P(\text{not } A) = \frac{n-m}{n} = \frac{n}{n} - \frac{m}{n} = 1 - \frac{m}{n} = 1 - P(A).$$

$$\therefore \quad P(A) + P(\text{not } A) = 1 \ \textit{i.e.,} \ P(A) + P(\bar{A}) = 1$$

If A is a sure event, then $P(A) = \frac{n}{n} = 1$ and if A happens to be an impossible event, then $P(A) = \frac{0}{n} = 0$.

From now onward, we shall always assume that the outcomes of any given random experiment are equally likely unless the contrary is stated explicitely.

ILLUSTRATIVE EXAMPLES

Example 1. *Three coins are tossed simultaneously. Write the sample space and the probabilities of getting (i) no head and (ii) two heads.*

Sol. Here S = {HHH, HHT, HTH, THH, HTT, THT, TTH, TTT}

(*i*) P(no head) $= P(\{TTT\}) = \frac{n(|TTT|)}{n(S)} = \frac{1}{8}$.

(*ii*) P(two heads) $= P(\{HHT, HTH, THH\}) = \frac{3}{8}$.

Remark. For the sake of simplicity, P({TTT}) is written as P(TTT).

15.8. 'ODDS IN FAVOUR' AND 'ODDS AGAINST' AN EVENT

Let A be an event of a random experiment. The ratio $P(A) : P(\overline{A})$ is called the **odds in favour** of happening of the event A. The ratio $P(\overline{A}) : P(A)$ is called the **odds against** the happening of the event A.

Let odds in favour of an event A be $m : n$.

Let $P(A) = p$. $\therefore$ $p : 1 - p = m : n$

$$\Rightarrow \frac{p}{1-p} = \frac{m}{n} \Rightarrow np = m - mp \Rightarrow p = \frac{m}{m+n} \text{ i.e., } P(A) = \frac{m}{m+n}.$$

$\therefore$ **If odds in favour of A are m : n, then** $\mathbf{P(A) = \frac{m}{m+n}}$.

Similarly, if odds against A are $m : n$ then odds in favour of A are $n : m$ and $P(A) = \frac{n}{n+m}$.

Remark. Odds in favour of event A are same as odds against the complement A′ of A and *vice-versa.*

Example 2. *Find the probability of the event A if (i) odds in favour of event A are 5 : 7 (ii) odds against A are 3 : 4.*

Sol. (*i*) Odds in favour of event A are 5 : 7. Let $P(A) = p$. $\therefore$ $p : 1 - p = 5 : 7$

$$\Rightarrow \frac{p}{1-p} = \frac{5}{7} \Rightarrow 7p = 5 - 5p \Rightarrow 12p = 5 \Rightarrow p = \frac{5}{12}$$

$$\therefore \quad P(A) = \frac{5}{12}.$$

(*ii*) Odds against event A are 3 : 4. Let $P(A) = p$. $\therefore$ $1 - p : p = 3 : 4$

$$\Rightarrow \frac{1-p}{p} = \frac{3}{4} \Rightarrow 4 - 4p = 3p \Rightarrow 7p = 4 \Rightarrow p = \frac{4}{7}$$

$$\therefore \quad P(A) = \frac{4}{7}.$$

15.9. WORKING RULES FOR SOLVING PROBLEMS

I. Find the number of elements in the sample space S of the given random experiment. Write the sample space, if it is feasible to do so.

II. Out of the elements of the sample space, identify the elements which are favourable to the event, A (say), whose probability is required. Write the event A, if it is feasible to do so.

III. Divide $n(A)$ by $n(S)$. This is equal to the required probability, P(A).

Example 3. *A bag contains 5 white, 7 black and 8 red balls. A ball is drawn at random. Find the probability of getting :*

(*i*) *red ball* (*ii*) *non-white ball* (*iii*) *white ball or black ball.*

Sol. No. of white balls = 5

No. of black balls = 7

No. of red balls = 8

5 White 7 Black 8 Red

$\therefore$ Total number of balls = 5 + 7 + 8 = 20.

(*i*) Let R = event of getting red ball

$$\therefore \quad P(\text{red ball}) = P(R) = \frac{n(R)}{n(S)} = \frac{8}{20} = \frac{2}{5}.$$

(*ii*) Let W = event of getting white ball

$\therefore$ P(non-white ball) = $P(\overline{W}) = \dfrac{\text{no. of non-white balls}}{\text{total no. of balls}} = \dfrac{7+8}{20} = \dfrac{15}{20} = \dfrac{3}{4}$.

(*iii*) Let A = event of getting a white ball or a black ball

$\therefore$ P(white ball or black ball) = $P(A) = \dfrac{n(A)}{n(S)} = \dfrac{5+7}{20} = \dfrac{12}{20} = \dfrac{3}{5}$.

Example 4. *A card is drawn from a pack of 52 playing cards, each card being equally likely to be drawn. Let A be the event, "card drawn is red". B the event "card drawn is a king or a queen" and C the event " card drawn is a king". Find the value of $P(A \cap B \cap C)$.*

Sol. A = event of getting a red card
B = event of getting a king or a queen
C = event of getting a king.

$\therefore$ $B \cap C$ = event of getting a king.

$\therefore$ $A \cap (B \cap C)$ = event of getting a red king *i.e.*, king of hearts or king of diamonds.

$\therefore$ $P(A \cap B \cap C) = \dfrac{2}{52} = \dfrac{1}{26}$.

Example 5. *Two unbiased coins are tossed simultaneously. Find the probability of getting :*

(*i*) *one head* (*ii*) *one tail* (*iii*) *at most one head*
(*iv*) *at least one tail* (*v*) *more than 2 heads* (*vi*) *less than 3 tails.*

Sol. Here S = (HH, HT, TH*, TT).

(*i*) Let A = event of getting one head. $\therefore$ A = {HT, TH}

$\therefore$ P(one head) = $P(A) = \dfrac{n(A)}{n(S)} = \dfrac{2}{4} = \dfrac{1}{2}$.

(*ii*) Let A = event of getting one tail. $\therefore$ A = {HT, TH}

$\therefore$ P(one tail) = $P(A) = \dfrac{n(A)}{n(S)} = \dfrac{2}{4} = \dfrac{1}{2}$.

(*iii*) Let A = event of getting at most one head. $\therefore$ A = {HT, TH, TT}

$\therefore$ P(at most one head) = $P(A) = \dfrac{n(A)}{n(S)} = \dfrac{3}{4}$.

(*iv*) Let A = event of getting at least one tail. $\therefore$ A = {HT, TH, TT}

$\therefore$ P(at least one tail) = $P(A) = \dfrac{n(A)}{n(S)} = \dfrac{3}{4}$.

(*v*) Let A be the event of getting more than 2 heads. $\therefore$ $A = \phi$.

$\therefore$ P(more than 2 heads) = $P(A) = \dfrac{n(A)}{n(S)} = \dfrac{0}{4} = 0$.

(*vi*) Let A be the event of getting less than 3 tails. $\therefore$ A = {HH, HT, TH, TT}

$\therefore$ P(less than 3 tails) = $P(A) = \dfrac{n(A)}{n(S)} = \dfrac{4}{4} = 1$.

***Why this step.** HT and TH are distinct sample points because HT represent head on the first coin and tail on the second coin whereas TH represent tail on the first coin and head on the second coin.

Example 6. *An unbiased die is thrown. Find the probability of getting :*

(*i*) *number greater than 4* (*ii*) *an even number*

(*iii*) *a number less than 8* (*iv*) *a multiple of 4.*

Sol. Here S = {1, 2, 3, 4, 5, 6}.

(*i*) Let A = event of getting number greater than 4. ∴ A = {5, 6}.

$$\therefore \quad P(\text{no.} > 4) = P(A) = \frac{n(A)}{n(S)} = \frac{2}{6} = \frac{1}{3}.$$

(*ii*) Let A = event of getting an even number. ∴ A = {2, 4, 6}

$$\therefore \quad P(\text{even number}) = P(A) = \frac{n(A)}{n(S)} = \frac{3}{6} = \frac{1}{2}.$$

(*iii*) Let A = event of getting number less than 8. ∴ A = {1, 2, 3, 4, 5, 6}

$$\therefore \quad P(\text{no.} < 8) = P(A) = \frac{n(A)}{n(S)} = \frac{6}{6} = 1.$$

(*iv*) Let A = event of getting a multiple of 4. ∴ A = {4}

$$\therefore \quad P(\text{multiple of } 4) = P(A) = \frac{n(A)}{n(S)} = \frac{1}{6}.$$

Example 7. *Two unbiased dice are thrown simultaneously. Find the probability of :*

(*i*) *getting sum 10*

(*ii*) *not getting same number on the dice*

(*iii*) *getting a multiple of 3 as the sum*

(*iv*) *an even number on the first die and an odd number on the second die.*

Sol. Here S = {(1, 1), (1, 2), (1, 3), ... , (6, 5), (6, 6)}.

∴ No. of possible outcomes = 6 × 6 = 36.

(*i*) Let A = event of getting sum '10'. ∴ A = {(4, 6), (5, 5), (6, 4)}

$$\therefore \quad P(A) = \frac{n(A)}{n(S)} = \frac{3}{36} = \frac{1}{12}.$$

(*ii*) Let A = event of getting the same number on both dice.

∴ A = {(1, 1), (2, 2), (3, 3), (4, 4), (5, 5), (6, 6)}

$$\therefore \quad P(A) = \frac{6}{36} = \frac{1}{6}$$

Required probability = P(different numbers on the dice) = $P(\overline{A}) = 1 - P(A) = 1 - \frac{1}{6} = \frac{5}{6}$.

(*iii*) Let A be the event of getting a multiple of 3 as the sum.

∴ Favourable multiples of 3 are 3, 6, 9, 12.

∴ A = {(1, 2), (2, 1), (1, 5), (2, 4), (3, 3), (4, 2), (5, 1), (3, 6), (4, 5), (5, 4), (6, 3), (6, 6)}

$$\therefore \quad P(A) = \frac{n(A)}{n(S)} = \frac{12}{36} = \frac{1}{3}.$$

(*iv*) Let A = event of getting an even number on the first die and an odd number on the second die.

∴ A = {(2, 1), (2, 3), (2, 5), (4, 1), (4, 3), (4, 5), (6, 1), (6, 3), (6, 5)}

$$\therefore \quad P(A) = \frac{n(A)}{n(S)} = \frac{9}{36} = \frac{1}{4}.$$

Example 8. *Find the probability that a leap year, selected at random, will contain 53 sundays.* (P.T.U., M.B.A. May 2008)

Sol. There are 366 days in a leap year. Now $366 = 7 \times 52 + 2$.

∴ This leap year will contain at least 52 sundays. The possible combinations for the remaining two days are :

(*i*) sunday and monday
(*ii*) monday and tuesday
(*iii*) tuesday and wednesday
(*iv*) wednesday and thursday
(*v*) thursday and friday
(*vi*) friday and saturday
(*vii*) saturday and sunday.

Let A be the event of getting 53 sundays in the leap year. Therefore, only those combinations will be favourable to the event A which contain 'sunday'.

∴ The combinations (*i*) and (*vii*) are favourable to the happening of A.

$$\therefore \qquad P(A) = \frac{2}{7}.$$

TEST YOUR KNOWLEDGE 15.1

1. What is the probability of getting an even number in the throw of an unbiased die ?
2. There are 2 children in a family. Find the probability that :
   (*i*) both children are boys
   (*ii*) only one of the children is a girl
3. (*i*) From a bag containing 5 red and 4 black balls, a ball is drawn at random. What is the probability that it is a red ball ?
   (*ii*) A bag contains 4 red, 3 white, 5 yellow and 7 green balls. A ball is drawn at random. Find the probability that the ball drawn is not red.
4. Find the probability of getting a 'king' or a 'queen' in a draw of one card, from a well-shuffled pack of playing cards.
5. Find the probability that an ordinary year has 53 fridays.
6. Three unbiased coins are tossed simultaneously. Find the probability of getting :
   (*i*) exactly two heads
   (*ii*) all heads
   (*iii*) all tails
   (*iv*) at least one head and one tail.
7. An unbiased die is thrown. Find the probability of getting :
   (*i*) number greater than 2
   (*ii*) number between 2 and 5
   (*iii*) a prime number
   (*iv*) number greater than 7.
8. In a single throw of two unbiased dice, find the probability of getting :
   (*i*) sum 7
   (*ii*) sum 7 or 9
   (*iii*) sum 9 or 11 (*P.T.U., M.B.A. Dec. 2000*)
   (*iv*) sum at least 10.
   (*v*) sum as a prime number
   (*vi*) sum as an odd number greater than 5.
9. In a single throw of three dice, find the probability of getting :
   (*i*) same number on all dice
   (*ii*) sum 5
   (*iii*) sum greater than 16
   (*iv*) sum less than 6.

10. From a bag containing 20 tickets, numbered from 1 to 20, two tickets are drawn at random. Find the probability that :

(*i*) both the tickets have prime numbers on them ;

(*ii*) on one there is a prime number and on the other there is a multiple of 4.

11. Two cards are drawn from a well shuffled pack of 52 cards. Find the probability of getting :

(*i*) one king and one jack

(*ii*) one card of spades and one queen of red colour

(*iii*) A red queen and a king of black colour.

12. (*i*) Four cards are drawn from a pack of playing cards. Find the probability that none is a king.

(*ii*) Four cards are drawn from a pack of playing cards. Find the probability of getting all the four cards of the same suit.

14. An urn contains 7 white, 5 black and 3 red balls. Two balls are drawn at random. Find the probability that :

(*i*) both balls are red (*ii*) one ball is red, the other is black

(*iii*) one ball is white.

14. 3 cards are drawn at random from a pack of well shuffled 52 cards. Find the probability that :

(*i*) all the three cards are of the same suit ;

(*ii*) one is a king, the other is a queen and the third is jack.

15. Three bulbs are chosen at random from 15 bulbs of which 5 are defective. Find the probability that (*i*) none is defective (*ii*) exactly one is defective (*iii*) at least one is defective.

16. A bag contains 8 red, 3 white and 9 blue balls. If three balls are drawn at random, determine the probability that

(*i*) all the three balls are blue balls.

(*ii*) all the balls are of different colours.

17. A bag contains tickets numbered from 1 to 22. Two tickets are drawn. Find the probability that both the numbers are prime.

18. What is the probability that in a group of :

(*i*) 2 people, both will have the same birthday ?

(*ii*) 3 people, at least 2 will have the same birthday ?

Assume that there are 365 days in a year and no one has his/her birthday on 29th February.

Answers

1. 1/2

2. (*i*) 1/4 (*ii*) 1/2 **3.** (*i*) 5/9 (*ii*) 15/19 **4.** 2/13

5. $\frac{1}{7}$ **6.** (*i*) $\frac{3}{8}$ (*ii*) $\frac{1}{8}$ (*iii*) $\frac{1}{8}$ (*iv*) $\frac{3}{4}$

7. (*i*) $\frac{2}{3}$ (*ii*) $\frac{1}{3}$ (*iii*) $\frac{1}{2}$ (*iv*) 0

8. (*i*) $\frac{1}{6}$ (*ii*) $\frac{5}{18}$ (*iii*) $\frac{1}{6}$ (*iv*) $\frac{1}{6}$ (*v*) $\frac{5}{12}$

(*vi*) $\frac{1}{3}$ **9.** (*i*) $\frac{1}{36}$ (*ii*) $\frac{1}{36}$ (*iii*) $\frac{1}{54}$ (*iv*) $\frac{5}{108}$

10. (*i*) $\frac{14}{95}$ (*ii*) $\frac{4}{19}$ **11.** (*i*) $\frac{8}{663}$ (*ii*) $\frac{1}{51}$ (*iii*) $\frac{2}{663}$

12. (*i*) $\frac{38916}{54145}$ (*ii*) $\frac{44}{4165}$ **13.** (*i*) $\frac{1}{35}$ (*ii*) $\frac{1}{7}$ (*iii*) $\frac{8}{15}$

14. (*i*) $\frac{22}{425}$ (*ii*) $\frac{48}{16575}$ **15.** (*i*) $\frac{24}{91}$ (*ii*) $\frac{45}{91}$ (*iii*) $\frac{67}{91}$

16. (*i*) $\frac{7}{95}$ (*ii*) $\frac{18}{95}$ **17.** $\frac{4}{33}$ **18.** (*i*) $\frac{1}{365}$

(*ii*) $1-\frac{364 \times 363}{(365)^2}$

Hints

10. (*i*) Reqd. prob. $= \frac{{}^8C_2}{{}^{20}C_2} = \frac{28}{190}$ (*ii*) Reqd. prob. $= \frac{8 \times 5}{{}^{20}C_2}$

11. (*ii*) Reqd. prob. $= \frac{{}^{13}C_1 \times {}^2C_1}{{}^{52}C_2} = \frac{13 \times 2}{26 \times 51}$. **12.** (*i*) Reqd. prob. $= \frac{{}^3C_2}{{}^{15}C_2} = \frac{3}{105}$

(*ii*) Reqd. prob. $\frac{{}^3C_1 \times {}^5C_1}{{}^{15}C_2} = \frac{3 \times 5}{105}$ (*iii*) Reqd. prob. $= \frac{{}^7C_1 \times {}^{5+3}C_1}{{}^{15}C_2} = \frac{7 \times 8}{105}$.

15. (*iii*) Reqd. prob. = 1 –P(none is defective) $= 1 - \frac{{}^{10}C_3}{{}^{15}C_3}$.

16. (*i*) Reqd. prob. $= \frac{{}^9C_3}{{}^{20}C_3}$ (*ii*) Reqd. prob. $= \frac{{}^8C_1 \times {}^3C_1 \times {}^9C_1}{{}^{20}C_3}$.

18. (*i*) Reqd. prob. $= \frac{365}{365 \times 365}$

(*ii*) Reqd. prob. = 1 – P(all have different birthdays) $= 1 - \frac{365 \times 364 \times 363}{365 \times 365 \times 365}$.

ADDITION THEOREMS

15.10. MUTUALLY EXCLUSIVE EVENTS (*P.T.U., M.B.A. Dec. 2000*)

Two events associated with a random experiment are said to be **mutually exclusive,** if both cannot occur together in the same trial. In the experiment of throwing a die, the events A = {1, 4} and B = {2, 5, 6} are mutually exclusive events. In the same experiment, the events A = {1, 4} and C = {2, 4, 5, 6} are not mutually exclusive because, if 4 appear on the die, then it is favourable to both events A and C. The definition of mutually exclusive events can also be extended to more than two events. We say that more than two events are mutually exclusive, if the happening of one of these, rules out the happening of all other events. The events A = {1, 2}, B = {3} and C = {6}, are mutually exclusive in connection with the experiment of throwing a single die.

n events $A_1, A_2, ..., A_n$ associated with a random experiment are said to **mutually exclusive events** if $A_i \cap A_j = \phi$ for all *i*, *j* and $i \neq j$.

For example, let a pair of dice be thrown and let A, B, C be the events that the sum is 7, sum is 8, sum is greater than 10 respectively,

$\therefore$ A = {(1, 6), (2, 5), (3, 4), (4, 3), (5, 2), (6, 1)}

B = {(2, 6), (3, 5), (4, 4), (5, 3), (6, 2)}

and C = {(5, 6), (6, 5), (6, 6)}

The events A, B and C are mutually exclusive.

Example. *Two dice are rolled. A is the event that the sum of the numbers shown on the two dice is 5. B is the event that at least one of the dice show up a 3. Are the two events A and B (i) mutually exclusive, (ii) exhaustive ? Give arguments in support of your answer.*

Sol. Here S = {(1, 1), (1, 2), (1, 3) ,......., (6, 5), (6, 6)}

We have A = {(1, 4), (2, 3), (3, 2), (4, 1)}

and B = {(3, 1), (3, 2), (3, 3), (3, 4), (3, 5), (3, 6), (1, 3), (2, 3), (4, 3), (5, 3), (6, 3)}

(*i*) The events A and B are not mutually exclusive because (2, 3), (3, 2) lies in both A and B.

(*ii*) The events A and B are not exhaustive because there are same elements in S (like (1, 1), (1, 2), (1, 5)) which are neither in A nor in B.

15.11. ADDITION THEOREM (FOR MUTUALLY EXCLUSIVE EVENTS)

(P.T.U., M.B.A. Dec. 2012)

Statement. *If A and B are two mutually exclusive events associated with a random experiment, then*

$$P(A \cup B) = P(A) + P(B).$$

Proof. Let n be the total number of exhaustive, equally likely cases of the experiment.

Let m_1 and m_2 be the number of cases favourable to the happening of the events A and B respectively.

$$\therefore \quad P(A) = \frac{m_1}{n} \quad \text{and} \quad P(B) = \frac{m_2}{n}.$$

S

A B

Since the events are given to be mutually exclusive, therefore, there cannot be any sample point common to both events A and B.

$\therefore$ The event $A \cup B$ can happen in exactly $m_1 + m_2$ ways.

$$\therefore \quad P(A \cup B) = \frac{m_1 + m_2}{n} = \frac{m_1}{n} + \frac{m_2}{n} = \mathbf{P(A) + P(B).}$$

Hence, $\mathbf{P(A \cup B) = P(A) + P(B).}$

Remark. This theorem can also be extended to more than two events.

Theorem I. *If A, B, C are three mutually exclusive events associated with a random experiment, then* $P(A \cup B \cup C) = P(A) + P(B) + P(C)$.

Proof. A, B, C are mutually exclusive elements.

$$\therefore \quad A \cap B = \phi, \; B \cap C = \phi, \; A \cap C = \phi.$$

We have $A \cap (B \cup C) = (A \cap B) \cup (A \cap C) = \phi \cup \phi = \phi$

$\therefore$ The events A and $B \cup C$ are mutually exclusive.

$\therefore$ By *addition theorem*, we have

$$P(A \cup (B \cup C)) = P(A) + P(B \cup C)$$
$$= P(A) + (P(B) + P(C))$$

(By applying ***addition theorem***, for the ***m.e.*** events B and C)

$$\therefore \quad \mathbf{P(A \cup B \cup C) = P(A) + P(B) + P(C).}$$

Theorem II. *If A and B be two events associated with a random experiment, then show that :*

(*i*) $P(\overline{A} \cap B) = P(B) - P(A \cap B)$

(*ii*) $P(A \cap \overline{B}) = P(A) - P(A \cap B)$.

Proof. (*i*) $(\overline{A} \cap B) \cup (A \cap B) = (\overline{A} \cup A) \cap B = S \cap B = B$ ...(1)

Also $(\overline{A} \cap B) \cap (A \cap B) = (\overline{A} \cap A) \cap (B \cap B) = \phi \cap B = \phi$

$\therefore$ The events $\overline{A} \cap B$ and $A \cap B$ are *m.e.*

By *addition theorem*, we have

$$P((\overline{A} \cap B) \cup (A \cap B)) = P(\overline{A} \cap B) + P(A \cap B)$$

$$\Rightarrow \quad P(B) = P(\overline{A} \cap B) + (P \cap B) \qquad \text{(Using (1))}$$

$$\Rightarrow \quad \mathbf{P(\overline{A} \cap B) = P(B) - P(A \cap B).}$$

(*ii*) $(A \cap \overline{B}) \cup (A \cap B) = A \cap (\overline{B} \cup B)$
$= A \cap S = A$ ...(1)

Also $(A \cap \overline{B}) \cap (A \cap B) = (A \cap A) \cap (\overline{B} \cap B)$
$= A \cap \phi = \phi$.

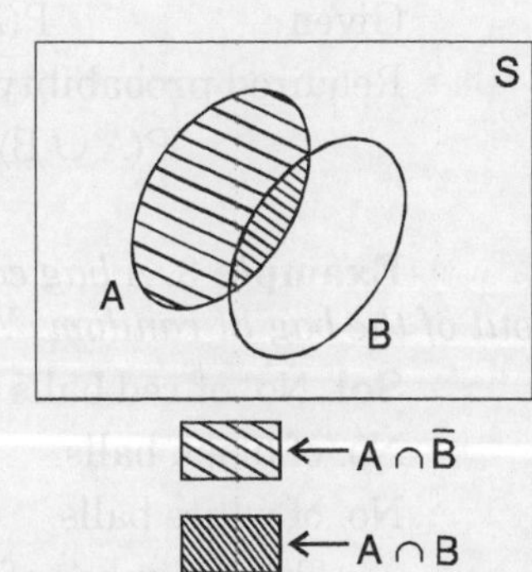

$\therefore$ The events $A \cap \overline{B}$ and $A \cap B$ are *m.e.*

$\therefore$ By *addition theorem*, we have

$$P((A \cap \overline{B}) \cup (A \cap B)) = P(A \cap \overline{B}) + P(A \cap B)$$

$$\Rightarrow \quad P(A) = P(A \cap \overline{B}) + P(A \cap B) \qquad \text{(Using (1))}$$

$$\Rightarrow \quad \mathbf{P(A \cap \overline{B}) = P(A) - P(A \cap B).}$$

15.12. WORKING RULES FOR SOLVING PROBLEMS

I. Find the number of elements in the sample space S of the given random experiment. Write the sample space, if it is feasible to do so.

II. Designate the events as A and B the probability of whose union, $A \cup B$ is to be found out. Out of the elements of the sample space, identify the elements which are favourable to the events A and B both.

III. Make sure that the events A and B are mutually exclusive *i.e.*, the set $A \cap B$ in the empty set.

IV. Use $P(A \cup B) = P(A) + P(B)$. This gives the required probability.

ILLUSTRATIVE EXAMPLES

Example 1. *If A and B are mutually exclusive events associated with a random experiment such that P(A) = 0.4 and P(B) = 0.5, then find :*

(*i*) $P(\overline{A})$ (*ii*) $P(\overline{B})$ (*iii*) $P(A \cup B)$

(*iv*) $P(A \cap \overline{B})$ (*v*) $P(\overline{A} \cap B)$ (*vi*) $P(\overline{A} \cap \overline{B})$.

Sol. We have P(A) = 0.4 and P(B) = 0.5.

(*i*) $P(\overline{A}) = 1 - P(A) = 1 - 0.4 = 0.6.$

(*ii*) $P(\overline{B}) = 1 - P(B) = 1 - 0.5 = 0.5.$

(*iii*) $P(A \cup B) = P(A) + P(B) = 0.4 + 0.5 = 0.9.$ ($\because$ A and B are *m.e.* events)

(*iv*) $P(A \cap \overline{B}) = P(A)^* = 0.4.$ ($\because A \cap B = \phi \Rightarrow A \subseteq \overline{B} \Rightarrow A \cap \overline{B} = A$)

(*v*) $P(\overline{A} \cap B) = P(B) = 0.5.$ ($\because A \cap B = \phi \Rightarrow B \subseteq \overline{A} \Rightarrow \overline{A} \cap B = B$)

(*vi*) $P(\overline{A} \cap \overline{B}) = P(\overline{A \cup B}) = 1 - P(A \cup B) = 1 - (P(A) + P(B)) = 1 - (0.4 + 0.5) = 0.1.$

Example 2. *The probability that a bread prepared in a hotel is well baked is 0.81 and that it will have sufficient proteins is 0.54. Again the probability that it has both is 0.18. Find the probability that a well-baked bread will contain sufficient proteins.*

(P.T.U., M.B.A. Dec. 2001)

Sol. Let A = The event that a bread is baked

B = The event that a bread has sufficient proteins.

Given P(A) = 0.81, P(B) = 0.54, $P(A \cap B) = 0.18$.

Required probability that a well baked bread will contain sufficient proteins

$$P(A \cup B) = P(A) + P(B) - P(A \cap B)$$
$$= 0.81 + 0.54 - 0.18 = 1.53.$$

Example 3. *A bag contains 5 red balls, 3 black balls and 4 white balls. A ball is drawn out of the bag at random. What is the probability that the ball drawn is either red or white ?*

Sol. No. of red balls = 5

No. of black balls = 3

No. of white balls = 4

5 Red 3 Black 4 White

∴ Total number of balls = 5 + 3 + 4 = 12

Let R and W be the events of drawing red ball and white ball respectively.

$$\therefore \quad P(R) = \frac{5}{12} \quad \text{and} \quad P(W) = \frac{4}{12} = \frac{1}{3}.$$

The events R and W are mutually exclusive.

∴ By *addition theorem, for mutually exclusive events*

$$P(\text{red ball or white ball}) = P(R \cup W) = P(R) + P(W) = \frac{5}{12} + \frac{1}{3} = \frac{9}{12} = \frac{3}{4}.$$

---

*We can also find the value of $P(A \cap \overline{B})$ as follows :

$P(A \cap \overline{B}) = P(A) - P(A \cap B) = P(A) - 0 = P(A)$, because A and B are *m.e.* events.

Example 4. *In a single throw of 2 dice, determine the probability of getting total 7 or 9.*

Sol. Here S = {(1, 1), (1, 2), ... (6, 5), (6, 6)}.

Let A and B be the events of getting total 7 and 9 respectively.

$\therefore$ A = {(1, 6), (2, 5), (3, 4), (4, 3), (5, 2), (6, 1)} and B = {(3, 6), (4, 5), (5, 4), (6, 3)}

The events A and B are mutually exclusive and $P(A) = \frac{6}{36} = \frac{1}{6}$ and $P(B) = \frac{4}{36} = \frac{1}{9}$.

$\therefore$ By *addition theorem, for mutually exclusive events*

$$P(\text{total is 7 or 9}) = P(A \cup B) = P(A) + P(B) = \frac{1}{6} + \frac{1}{9} = \frac{3+2}{18} = \frac{5}{18}$$

Example 5. *There are 2 red and 3 black balls in a bag, 3 balls are taken out at random from the bag. Find the probability of getting 2 red and 1 black balls or 1 red and 2 black balls.*

Sol. There are 2 red and 3 black balls in the bag.

2 Red
3 Black

Let A = event of drawing 2 red and 1 black balls

and B = event of drawing 1 red and 2 black balls.

$$\therefore \quad P(A) = \frac{^2C_2 \times {^3C_1}}{^5C_3} = \frac{1 \times 3}{10} = \frac{3}{10} \text{ and } P(B) = \frac{^2C_1 \times {^3C_2}}{^5C_3} = \frac{2 \times 3}{10} = \frac{3}{5}$$

The events A and B are mutually exclusive.

$\therefore$ Required probability $= P(A \cup B) = P(A) + P(B)$ (Addition theorem)

$$= \frac{3}{10} + \frac{3}{5} = \frac{9}{10}.$$

Example 6. *In a group there are 3 women and 3 men. 4 persons are selected at random from the group. Find the probability that 3 women and 1 man or 1 woman and 3 men are selected.*

Sol. There are 3 women and 3 men in the group.

3 Women
3 Men

Let A = event of selecting 3 women and 1 man

and B = event of selecting 1 woman and 3 men.

$$\therefore \quad P(A) = \frac{^3C_3 \times {^3C_1}}{^6C_4} = \frac{1 \times 3}{15} = \frac{1}{5} \text{ and } P(B) = \frac{^3C_1 \times {^3C_3}}{^6C_4} = \frac{3 \times 1}{15} = \frac{1}{5}$$

The events A and B are mutually exclusive.

$\therefore$ Required probability $= P(A \cup B) = P(A) + P(B)$ (Addition theorem)

$$= \frac{1}{5} + \frac{1}{5} = \frac{2}{5}.$$

Example 7. *In a single throw of two dice, find the probability that neither a doublet nor a total of 9 will appear.*

Sol. Here S = {(1, 1), (1, 2), ... , (6, 5), (6, 6)}.

$\therefore$ Number of possible outcomes = 6 × 6 = 36.

Let E = event that doublet is occurred and F = event that sum is 9.

$\therefore$ E = {(1, 1), (2, 2), (3, 3), (4, 4), (5, 5), (6, 6)} and F = {(3, 6), (4, 5), (5, 4), (6, 3)}.

$$\therefore \quad P(E) = \frac{6}{36} = \frac{1}{6} \text{ and } P(F) = \frac{4}{36} = \frac{1}{9}.$$

P (neither a doublet nor a total of 9)

$$= P(E^c \cap F^c) = P((E \cup F)^c) = 1 - P(E \cup F) \quad ...(1)$$

Since the events E and F are *mutually exclusive*

∴ By *addition theorem, for mutually exclusive events,*

$$P(E \cup F) = P(E) + P(F) = \frac{1}{6} + \frac{1}{9} = \frac{5}{18}$$

∴ (1) implies $P(E^c \cap F^c) = 1 - \frac{5}{18} = \frac{13}{18}$.

Example 8. *There are three events A, B, C one of which must happen and only one can happen at a time. The odds are 8 to 3 against A, 5 to 2 against B, find the odds against C.*

Sol. The given events A, B and C are mutually exclusive and exhaustive.

∴ $P(A \cup B \cup C) = P(A) + P(B) + P(C)$ and $P(A \cup B \cup C) = 1$

∴ $P(A) + P(B) + P(C) = 1$ ...(1)

Odds against A are 8 : 3. ∴ $P(A) = \frac{3}{8+3} = \frac{3}{11}$

Odds against B are 5 : 2 ∴ $P(B) = \frac{2}{5+2} = \frac{2}{7}$

∴ (1) $\Rightarrow \frac{3}{11} + \frac{2}{7} + P(C) = 1 \Rightarrow P(C) = 1 - \frac{3}{11} - \frac{2}{7} = \frac{77-21-22}{77} = \frac{34}{77}$

∴ Odds against C $= P(\bar{C}) : P(C) = 1 - \frac{34}{77} : \frac{34}{77} = \frac{43}{77} : \frac{34}{77} = 43 : 34.$

TEST YOUR KNOWLEDGE 15.2

1. A and B are mutually exclusive events of an experiment. If P('not A') = 0.65, $P(A \cup B) = 0.65$, and $P(B) = p$, find the value of p.
2. A box contains 4 red balls, 4 green balls and 7 white balls. What is the probability that a ball drawn is either red or white ?
3. In a class of 25 students with roll numbers 1 to 25, a student is picked up at random to answer a question. Find the probability that the roll number of the selected student is either a multiple of 5 or of 7.
4. In a single throw of three dice, find the probability of getting a total of 17 or 18.
5. (*i*) A bag contains 5 red, 6 white and 7 black balls. Two balls are drawn at random. What is the probability that both balls are red or both are black.

   (*ii*) A bag contains 3 red, 4 black and 2 green balls. Two balls are drawn at random from the bag. Find the probability that both balls are of different colours.
6. There are 3 red and 3 black balls in a bag. 3 balls are taken out at random from the bag. Find the probability of getting 2 red and 1 black balls or 1 red and 2 black balls.
7. In a group there are 3 men and 2 women. 3 persons are selected at random from this group. Find the probability that 1 man and 2 women or 2 men and 1 woman are selected.
8. A, B, C are three mutually exclusive and exhaustive events associated with a random experiment.

   Find P(A), given that $P(B) = \frac{3}{2} P(A)$ and $P(C) = \frac{1}{2} P(B)$.
9. In a class there are 10 boys and 8 girls. A committee of 3 students is constituted. What is the probability that the committee has at most one girl ?

Answers

1. 0.3	**2.** 11/15	**3.** 8/25	**4.** 1/54
5. (*i*) 31/153	(*ii*) 13/18	**6.** 9/10	**7.** 9/10
8. 4/13	**9.** 10/17		

Hints

1. Use P(A ∪ B) = (1 – P(not (A)) + P(B).

5. (*i*) Reqd. prob. $= \frac{{}^5C_2}{{}^{18}C_2} + \frac{{}^7C_2}{{}^{18}C_2}$ (*ii*) Reqd. prob. $= 1 - \left(\frac{{}^3C_2}{{}^9C_2} + \frac{{}^4C_2}{{}^9C_2} + \frac{{}^2C_2}{{}^9C_2}\right)$.

6. Reqd. prob. $= \frac{{}^3C_2 \times {}^3C_1}{{}^6C_3} + \frac{{}^3C_1 \times {}^3C_2}{{}^6C_3}$.

9. Reqd. prob. $= 1 - \frac{{}^{10}C_3 \times {}^8C_0}{{}^{18}C_3}$.

15.13. ADDITION THEOREM (GENERAL) (*P.T.U., M.B.A. Dec. 2009*)

Statement. *If A and B are two events not necessarily mutually exclusive, associated with a random experiment, then*

$$P(A \cup B) = P(A) + P(B) - P(A \cap B).$$

Proof. Let n be the total number of exhaustive, equally likely cases of the experiment. Let m_1 and m_2 be the number of cases favourable to the happening of the events A and B respectively.

$$\therefore \quad P(A) = \frac{m_1}{n} \quad \text{and} \quad P(B) = \frac{m_2}{n}.$$

Since the events are given to be not necessarily mutually exclusive, there may be some sample points common to both events A and B.

Let m_3 be the number of these common sample points. m_3 will be zero in case A and B are mutually exclusive.

S, A ∩ B, A, B

$$\therefore \quad P(A \cap B) = \frac{m_3}{n}.$$

The m_3 sample points, which are common to both events A and B, are included in the events A and B separately.

∴ Number of sample points in the event A ∪ B = $m_1 + m_2 - m_3$.

m_3 is subtracted from $m_1 + m_2$ to avoid counting of common sample points twice.

$$\therefore \quad P(A \cup B) = \frac{m_1 + m_2 - m_3}{n} = \frac{m_1}{n} + \frac{m_2}{n} - \frac{m_3}{n} = P(A) + P(B) - P(A \cap B).$$

Hence, **P(A ∪ B) = P(A) + P(B) – P(A ∩ B).**

Corollary. If events A and B happen to be mutually exclusive events, then P(A ∩ B) = 0 and in this case *addition theorem* implies

$$P(A \cup B) = P(A) + P(B) - P(A \cap B) = P(A) + P(B) - 0 = P(A) + P(B)$$

This is the same as the *addition theorem* for mutually exclusive events.

Remark. This theorem can also be extended to more than two events.

Theorem I. *If A, B, C are three events associated with a random experiment, then*

$$P(A \cup B \cup C) = P(A) + P(B) + P(C) - P(A \cap B) - P(B \cap C) - P(A \cap C) + P(A \cap B \cap C).$$

Proof. Considering '$B \cup C$' as one event and applying addition theorem to the events 'A' and '$B \cup C$', we have

$$P(A \cup B \cup C) = P(A \cup (B \cup C))$$

$$= P(A) + P(B \cup C) - P(A \cap (B \cup C))$$

$$= P(A) + (P(B) + P(C) - P(B \cap C)) - P((A \cap B) \cup (A \cap C))$$

(By using *addition theorem* for the events B and C)

$$= P(A) + P(B) + P(C) - P(B \cap C) - (P(A \cap B) + P(A \cap C) - P((A \cap B) \cap (A \cap C)))$$

(By applying *addition theorem* for the events $A \cap B$ and $A \cap C$)

$$= P(A) + P(B) + P(C) - P(B \cap C) - P(A \cap B) - P(A \cap C) + P(A \cap B \cap C)$$

$$(\because \quad (A \cap B) \cap (A \cap C) = (A \cap A) \cap B \cap C = A \cap B \cap C)$$

$\therefore$ $\mathbf{P(A \cup B \cup C) = P(A) + P(B) + P(C) - P(A \cap B) - P(B \cap C) - P(A \cap C) + P(A \cap B \cap C).}$

15.14. WORKING RULES FOR SOLVING PROBLEMS

I. Find the number of elements in the sample space S of the given random experiment. Write the sample space, if it is feasible to do so.

II. Designate the events as A and B the probability of whose union, $A \cup B$ is to be found out. Out of the elements of the sample space, identify the elements which are favourable to the events A and B both.

III. Write the event $A \cap B$ and find its probability.

IV. Use $P(A \cup B) = P(A) + P(B) - (A \cap B)$. This gives the required probability.

ILLUSTRATIVE EXAMPLES

Example 1. *Let A and B be events associated with a random experiment. State which of the following statements are true :*

(*i*) $P(A) = \frac{1}{3}$, $P(B) = \frac{2}{3}$, *A and B are mutually exclusive and exhaustive events.*

(*ii*) $P(A) = 0.4$, $P(B) = 0.25$, $P(A \text{ or } B) = 0.65$. *A and B are mutually exclusive events.*

(*iii*) $P(A) = 0.3$, $P(B) = 0.45$, $P(A \text{ and } B) = 0.2$ *A and B are not mutually exclusive events.*

(*iv*) $P(A) = 0.35$, $P(B) = 0.65$. *A and B are complementary events.*

Sol. (*i*) We have $P(A) = \frac{1}{3}$, $P(B) = \frac{2}{3}$. The events A and B are not necessarily mutually exclusive.

In case A and B are *m.e.* then $P(A \text{ or } B) = P(A) + P(B) = \frac{1}{3} + \frac{2}{3} = 1$ *i.e.*, A and B are exhaustive events.

$\therefore$ The statement is **not true.**

(*ii*) We have P(A) = 0.4, P(B) = 0.25, P(A or B) = 0.65.

By **addition theorem**

$$P(A \text{ or } B) = P(A) + P(B) - P(A \cap B)$$

$$\Rightarrow \quad 0.65 = 0.4 + 0.25 - P(A \cap B) \quad \Rightarrow \quad P(A \cap B) = 0$$

∴ A and B cannot happen simultaneously.

∴ A and B are mutually exclusive events.

∴ The statement is **true.**

(*iii*) We have P(A) = 0.3, P(B) = 0.45, P(A ∩ B) = 0.2.

Since P(A ∩ B) ≠ 0, the events A and B can happen simultaneously.

∴ A and B are not mutually exclusive events.

∴ The statement is **true.**

(*iv*) We have P(A) = 0.35, P(B) = 0.65. A and B would be complementary events only when A ∩ B = φ and A ∪ B = S.

The given data imply neither A ∩ B = φ nor A ∪ B = S.

∴ The statement is **not true.**

Example 2. *Find the probability of 4 turning up for at least once in two tosses of a fair die.*

Sol. Here S = {(1, 1), (1, 2), ..., (6, 5), (6, 6)}.

Let A = event of getting 4 on the first die

and B = event of getting 4 on the second die.

∴ A = {(4, 1), (4, 2), (4, 3), (4, 4), (4, 5), (4, 6)}

and B = {(1, 4), (2, 4), (3, 4), (4, 4), (5, 4), (6, 4)}.

$$\therefore \quad P(A) = \frac{n(A)}{n(S)} = \frac{6}{36} = \frac{1}{6} \quad \text{and} \quad P(B) = \frac{n(B)}{n(S)} = \frac{6}{36} = \frac{1}{6}.$$

The events A and B are not mutually exclusive because the sample (4, 4) is common to both.

$$\therefore \quad A \cap B = \{(4, 4)\} \quad \therefore \quad P(A \cap B) = \frac{1}{36}$$

By *addition theorem,* the required probability of getting four at least once is

$$P(A \cup B) = P(A) + P(B) - P(A \cap B) = \frac{1}{6} + \frac{1}{6} - \frac{1}{36} = \frac{11}{36}.$$

Example 3. *Two dice are thrown once. Find the probability of getting an even number on the first die or a total of 8.*

Sol. Here S = {(1, 1), (1, 2),......, (6, 5), (6, 6)}

Let A = event of getting an even number on the first die

and B = event of getting a total 8.

∴ A = {(2, 1), (2, 2), (2, 3), (2, 4), (2, 5), (2, 6), (4, 1), (4, 2), (4, 3), (4, 4), (4, 5), (4, 6), (6, 1), (6, 2), (6, 3), (6, 4), (6, 5), (6, 6)}

and B = {(2, 6), (3, 5), (4, 4), (5, 3), (6, 2)}

$$\therefore \quad P(A) = \frac{18}{36} = \frac{1}{2} \quad \text{and} \quad P(B) = \frac{5}{36}$$

The events A and B are not mutually exclusive because the sample points (2, 6), (4, 4), (6, 2) are common to both.

$$\therefore \quad A \cap B = \{(2, 6), (4, 4), (6, 2)\} \quad \therefore \quad P(A \cap B) = \frac{3}{36} = \frac{1}{12}$$

By *addition theorem,* the required probability of getting an even number on the first die or a total 8 is

$$P(A \cup B) = P(A) + P(B) - P(A \cap B) = \frac{1}{2} + \frac{5}{36} - \frac{1}{12} = \frac{5}{9}.$$

Example 4. *The probability of two events A and B are 0.25 and 0.50 respectively. The probability of their simultaneous occurrence is 0.14. Find the probability that neither A nor B occurs.*

Sol. We have $P(A) = 0.25$, $P(B) = 0.50$ and $P(A \cap B) = 0.14$.

By *addition theorem,*

$$P(A \cup B) = P(A) + P(B) - P(A \cap B) = 0.25 + 0.50 - 0.14 = 0.61$$

Now, $P(\text{neither A nor B}) = P(\overline{A} \cap \overline{B}) = P(\overline{A \cup B}) = 1 - P(A \cup B) = 1 - 0.61 = 0.39.$

Example 5. *A and B are two non-mutually exclusive events. If $P(A) = \frac{1}{4}$, $P(B) = \frac{2}{5}$ and $P(A \cup B) = \frac{1}{2}$, find the values of $P(A \cap B)$ and $P(A \cap B^c)$.*

Sol. We have $P(A) = \frac{1}{4}$, $P(B) = \frac{2}{5}$, $P(A \cup B) = \frac{1}{2}$

By *addition theorem,* $P(A \cup B) = P(A) + P(B) - P(A \cap B)$.

$$\therefore \quad \frac{1}{2} = \frac{1}{4} + \frac{2}{5} - P(A \cap B)$$

$$\therefore \quad P(A \cap B) = \frac{1}{4} + \frac{2}{5} - \frac{1}{2} = \frac{5 + 8 - 10}{20} = \frac{3}{20}.$$

We have, $(A \cap B^c) \cap (A \cap B) = A \cap (B^c \cap B) = A \cap \phi = \phi$

$\therefore$ The events $A \cap B^c$ and $A \cap B$ are mutually exclusive and

$(A \cap B^c) \cup (A \cap B) = A \cap (B^c \cup B) = A \cap S = A$ (S is the sample space)

$\therefore$ By *addition theorem,* $P(A) = P(A \cap B^c) + P(A \cap B)$.

$$\therefore \quad \frac{1}{4} = P(A \cap B^c) + \frac{3}{20} \quad \text{or} \quad P(A \cap B^c) = \frac{1}{4} - \frac{3}{20} = \frac{1}{10}.$$

Example 6. *A, B, C are events such that $P(A) = 0.3$, $P(B) = 0.4$, $P(C) = 0.8$, $P(A \cap B) = 0.08$, $P(A \cap C) = 0.28$, $P(A \cap B \cap C) = 0.02$. If $P(A \cup B \cup C) \geq 0.75$, then find the minimum value of the probability of the event $B \cap C$.*

Sol. We have $0.75 \leq P(A \cup B \cup C) \leq 1$.

Using *addition theorem,* we have

$$0.75 \leq P(A) + P(B) + P(C) - P(A \cap B) - P(B \cap C) - P(A \cap C) + P(A \cap B \cap C) \leq 1$$

$$\Rightarrow \quad 0.75 \leq 0.3 + 0.4 + 0.8 - 0.08 - P(B \cap C) - 0.28 + 0.02 \leq 1$$

$$\Rightarrow \quad 0.75 \leq 1.16 - P(B \cap C) \leq 1$$

$$\Rightarrow \quad 0.75 - 1.16 \leq - P(B \cap C) \leq 1 - 1.16$$

$$\Rightarrow \quad -0.41 \leq - P(B \cap C) \leq -0.16$$

$$\Rightarrow \quad 0.41 \geq P(B \cap C) \geq 0.16$$

i.e., $0.16 \leq P(B \cap C) \leq 0.41.$

$\therefore$ Minimum value of $P(B \cap C) = 0.16$.

TEST YOUR KNOWLEDGE 15.3

1. One card is drawn from a pack of 52 cards, each of the 52 cards being equally likely to be drawn. Find the probability of :
   (*i*) the card drawn is red (*ii*) the card drawn is a king
   (*iii*) the card drawn is red and a king (*iv*) the card drawn is either red or a king.
2. In a single throw of two dice, what is the probability of getting at least one ace ?
3. 100 students appeared for two examinations. 60 passed the first, 50 passed the second and 30 passed both. Find the probability that a student selected at random has failed in both examinations.
4. (*i*) If A and B are two events defined on a sample space such that $P(A \cup B) = \frac{5}{6}$, $P(A \cap B) = \frac{1}{3}$, $P(B^c) = \frac{1}{3}$, find P(A).
   (*ii*) If A and B are two events such that $P(A) = \frac{1}{4}$, $P(B) = \frac{1}{2}$ and $P(A \text{ and } B) = \frac{1}{8}$, find (*a*) P(A or B), (*b*) P(not A and not B).
5. From 30 tickets marked with first 30 numerals, one is drawn at random. Find the probability that it is a :
   (*i*) multiple of 5 or 7
   (*ii*) multiple of 3 or 7
6. A bag contains 100 identical tokens on which 1 to 100 are marked. A token is drawn randomly. What is the probability that the number on the token is either a multiple of 3 or of 5 ?
7. For any two events A and B, prove that $P(A \cap B) \le P(A) \le P(A \cup B) \le P(A) + P(B)$.
8. (*i*) Two dice are tossed together. Find the probability of getting a doublet or a total of 6.
   (*ii*) A pair of dice is rolled. Find the probability of getting a doublet or sum of numbers to be at least 10.
9. An integer is chosen at random from the numbers ranging from 1 to 50. What is the probability that the integer chosen is a multiple of either 2 or 3 or 10 ?

Answers

1. (*i*) $\frac{1}{2}$ (*ii*) $\frac{1}{13}$ (*iii*) $\frac{1}{26}$ (*iv*) $\frac{7}{13}$ **2.** $\frac{11}{36}$

3. $\frac{1}{5}$ **4.** (*i*) $\frac{1}{2}$ (*ii*) (*a*) $\frac{5}{8}$ (*b*) $\frac{3}{8}$

5. (*i*) $\frac{1}{3}$ (*ii*) $\frac{13}{30}$ **6.** 0.47 **8.** (*i*) $\frac{5}{18}$ (*ii*) $\frac{5}{18}$

9. $\frac{33}{50}$.

Hints

1. (*iv*) Reqd. prob. $= \frac{26}{52} + \frac{4}{52} - \frac{2}{52}$

2. Reqd. prob. $= \frac{6}{36} + \frac{6}{36} - \frac{1}{36}$ **3.** Reqd. prob. $= 1 - \left(\frac{60}{100} + \frac{50}{100} - \frac{30}{100}\right)$

4. (*i*) Use : $\frac{5}{6} = P(A) + \left(1 - \frac{1}{3}\right) - \frac{1}{3}$

7. $A \cap B \subseteq A \subseteq A \cup B \Rightarrow P(A \cap B) \le P(A) \le P(A \cup B)$

Also $P(A \cup B) = P(A) + P(B) - P(AB)$ implies $P(A \cup B) \le P(A) + P(B)$.

8. (*i*) Reqd. prob. = $\frac{6}{36} + \frac{5}{36} - \frac{1}{36}$ (*ii*) Reqd. prob. = $\frac{6}{36} + \frac{6}{36} - \frac{2}{36}$.

9. Let A, B, C be the events that the sum chosen is a multiple of 2, 3, 10 respectively.

$P(A) = \frac{25}{50}$, $P(B) = \frac{16}{50}$, $P(C) = \frac{5}{50}$, $P(A \cap B) = \frac{8}{50}$, $P(B \cap C) = \frac{1}{50}$, $P(A \cap C)$

$= \frac{5}{50}$, $P(A \cap B \cap C) = \frac{1}{50}$.

INDEPENDENT EVENTS

15.15. INTRODUCTION

In the present chapter, we shall study the method of evaluating probabilities of events relating to independent events and independent experiments. We shall also study random variables and their probability distributions.

15.16. CONDITIONAL PROBABILITY *(P.T.U., M.B.A. May 2010)*

Let us consider the random experiment of throwing a die. Let A be the event of getting an odd number on the die.

$\therefore$ $S = \{1, 2, 3, 4, 5, 6\}$ and $A = \{1, 3, 5\}$.

$\therefore$ $P(A) = \frac{3}{6} = \frac{1}{2}$.

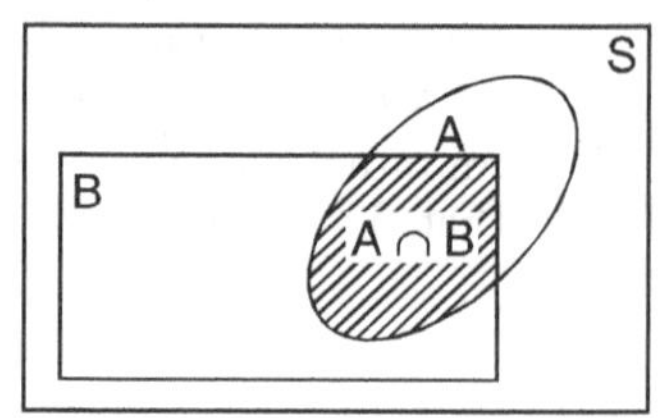

Let B = {2, 3, 4, 5, 6}. If, after the die is thrown, we are given the information that the event B has occurred, then the probability of event A will no more be $\frac{1}{2}$, because in this case, the favourable cases are three and the total number of possible outcomes will be five and not six. The probability of event A, with the condition that event B has happened will be 3/5. This conditional probability is denoted as P(A/B). Let us define the concept of conditional probability in a formal manner.

Let A and B be any two events associated with a random experiment. The probability of occurrence of event A when the event B has already occurred is called the **conditional probability** of A when B is given and is denoted as P(A/B). The conditional probability P(A/B) is meaningful only when $P(B) \ne 0$, *i.e.*, when B is not an impossible event.

By definition,

P(A/B) = Probability of occurrence of event A when the event B as already occurred.

$$= \frac{\text{No. of cases favourable to B which are also favourable to A}}{\text{No. of cases favourable to B}}$$

$$\therefore \quad \mathbf{P(A/B) = \frac{\textbf{No. of cases favourable to } A \cap B}{\textbf{No. of cases favourable to B}}}$$

$$\text{Also,} \quad P(A/B) = \frac{\dfrac{\text{No. of cases favourable to } A \cap B}{\text{No. of cases in the sample space}}}{\dfrac{\text{No. of cases favourable to B}}{\text{No. of cases in the sample space}}}$$

$$\therefore \quad \mathbf{P(A/B) = \frac{P(A \cap B)}{P(B)}, \text{ provided } P(B) \neq 0.}$$

Similarly, we have

$$\mathbf{P(B/A) = \frac{P(A \cap B)}{P(A)}, \text{ provided } P(A) \neq 0.}$$

15.17. INDEPENDENT EVENTS

(P.T.U., M.B.A. Dec. 2001, 2003)

Let A and B be two events associated with a random experiment. We have

$$P(B/A) = \frac{P(A \cap B)}{P(A)}, \text{ provided } P(A) \neq 0.$$

$$\therefore \quad P(A \cap B) = P(A)\, P(B/A).$$

In general P(B/A) may or may not be equal to P(B). When P(B/A) and P(B) are equal, then the events A and B are of special importance.

Two events associated with a random experiment are said to be **independent events** if the occurrence or non-occurrence of one event does not affect the probability of the occurrence of the other event. For example, the events A and B are independent events when P(A/B) = P(A) and P(B/A) = P(B).

Theorem II. *Let A and B be events associated with a random experiment. The events A and B are independent if and only if* $P(A \cap B) = P(A)\, P(B)$.

Proof. Let A and B be independent events.

$$\therefore \quad P(A \cap B) = \left(\frac{P(A \cap B)}{P(B)}\right) P(B) = P(A/B)\, P(B) \qquad \left(\because \; P(A/B) = \frac{P(A \cap B)}{P(B)}\right)$$

$$= P(A)\, P(B) \qquad (\because \; P(A/B) = P(A))$$

$$\therefore \quad P(A \cap B) = P(A)\, P(B).$$

Conversely, let $P(A \cap B) = P(A)\, P(B)$.

$$\therefore \quad P(A/B) = \frac{P(A \cap B)}{P(B)} = \frac{P(A)\, P(B)}{P(B)} = P(A)$$

and
$$P(B/A) = \frac{P(B \cap A)}{P(A)} = \frac{P(A \cap B)}{P(A)} = \frac{P(A)\, P(B)}{P(A)} = P(B).$$

$$\therefore \quad P(A/B) = P(A) \text{ and } P(B/A) = P(B).$$

∴ A and B are independent events.

Remark 1. $P(A \cap B) = P(A)\, P(B)$ is the necessary and sufficient condition for the events A and B to be independent.

Remark 2. Let A and B be events associated with a random experiment.

(*i*) Let A and B be mutually exclusive ∴ $P(A \cap B) = 0$

∴ $P(A \cap B) \neq P(A)\, P(B)$ *i.e.,* A and B are not independent events.

∴ **Mutually exclusive events cannot be independent.**

(*ii*) Let A and B be independent.

∴ $P(A \cap B) = P(A)\, P(B)$ *i.e.,* $P(A \cap B) \neq 0$.

∴ A and B are not mutually exclusive events.

∴ **Independent events cannot be mutually exclusive.**

Important observation. If A and B be any two events associated with a random experiment, then their physical description is not sufficient to decide if A and B are independent events or not. A and B are declared to be independent events only when we have $P(A \cap B) = P(A)\,P(B)$.

15.18. DEPENDENT EVENTS

Let A and B be two events associated with a random experiment. If A and B are not independent events, then these are called **dependent events.**

$\therefore$ In case of dependent events, we have $\mathbf{P(A \cap B) = P(A)\,P(B/A)}$.

15.19. MULTIPLICATION RULE OF PROBABILITY *(P.T.U., M.B.A. Dec. 2009, 2010, 2012)*

If A and B be any two events associated with a random experiment, then we have

$$\mathbf{P(A \cap B) = P(A)\,P(B/A).}$$

This is called the **multiplication rule of probability.**

In particular, if the events A and B are independent, then the *multiplication rule of probability* becomes

$$\mathbf{P(A \cap B) = P(A)\,P(B).}$$

Theorem I. *If A, B, C are three events associated with a random experiment, then*

$$P(A \cap B \cap C) = P(A)\,P(B/A)\,P(C/A \cap B).$$

Proof. We have

$$P(C/A \cap B) = \frac{P(C \cap (A \cap B))}{P(A \cap B)} = \frac{P(A \cap B \cap C)}{P(A \cap B)}$$

$$\therefore \quad P(A \cap B \cap C) = P(A \cap B)\,P(C/A \cap B) \qquad ...(1)$$

Also, $$P(B/A) = \frac{P(B \cap A)}{P(A)} = \frac{P(A \cap B)}{P(A)}$$

$$\therefore \quad P(A \cap B) = P(A)\,P(B/A) \qquad ...(2)$$

(1) and (2) implies $\mathbf{P(A \cap B \cap C) = P(A)\,P(B/A)\,P(C/A \cap B)}$.

Definition. Three events A, B, C associated with a random experiment are called **independent** if A, B, C are pairwise independent and $P(A \cap B \cap C) = P(A)\,P(B)\,P(C)$.

Theorem II. *Let A and B be events associated with a random experiment. If A and B are independent, then show that the events (i)* $\overline{A}, B$ *(ii)* $A, \overline{B}$ *(iii)* $\overline{A}, \overline{B}$ *are also independent.*

Proof. The events A and B are independent.

$$\therefore \quad P(A \cap B) = P(A)\,P(B) \qquad ...(1)$$

(*i*) $$(A \cap B) \cap (\overline{A} \cap B) = (A \cap \overline{A}) \cap (B \cap B) = \phi \cap B = \phi$$

and $$(A \cap B) \cup (\overline{A} \cap B) = (A \cup \overline{A}) \cap B = S \cap B = B.$$

$\therefore$ The events $A \cap B$ and $\overline{A} \cap B$ are mutually exclusive and their union is B.

$\therefore$ By *addition theorem,* we have $P(B) = P(A \cap B) + P(\overline{A} \cap B)$.

$$\Rightarrow \quad P(\overline{A} \cap B) = P(B) - P(A \cap B) = P(B) - P(A)\,P(B) \qquad \text{(Using (1))}$$

$$= (1 - P(A))\,P(B) = P(\overline{A})\,P(B)$$

$\therefore$ $\mathbf{P(\overline{A} \cap B) = P(\overline{A})\,P(B)}$ *i.e.,* $\overline{A}$ and B are independent.

(*ii*) $(A \cap B) \cap (A \cap \overline{B}) = (A \cap A) \cap (B \cap \overline{B}) = A \cap \phi = \phi$

and $(A \cap B) \cup (A \cap \overline{B}) = A \cap (B \cup \overline{B}) = A \cap S = A.$

$\therefore$ The events $A \cap B$ and $A \cap \overline{B}$ are mutually exclusive and their union is A.

$\therefore$ By *addition theorem,* we have

$$P(A) = P(A \cap B) + P(A \cap \overline{B}).$$

$$\Rightarrow \quad P(A \cap \overline{B}) = P(A) - P(A \cap B) = P(A) - P(A)\,P(B) \quad \text{(Using (1))}$$

$$= P(A)(1 - P(B)) = P(A)P(\overline{B})$$

$\therefore$ $\mathbf{P(A \cap \overline{B}) = P(A)\ P(\overline{B})}$ *i.e.,* A and $\overline{B}$ are independent.

(*iii*) $(\overline{A} \cap B) \cap (\overline{A} \cap \overline{B}) = (\overline{A} \cap \overline{A}) \cap (B \cap \overline{B}) = \overline{A} \cap \phi = \phi$

and $(\overline{A} \cap B) \cup (\overline{A} \cap \overline{B}) = \overline{A} \cap (B \cup \overline{B}) = \overline{A} \cap S = \overline{A}.$

$\therefore$ The events $\overline{A} \cap B$ and $\overline{A} \cap \overline{B}$ are mutually exclusive and their union is $\overline{A}$.

$\therefore$ By *addition theorem,* we have

$$P(\overline{A}) = P(\overline{A} \cap B) + P(\overline{A} \cap \overline{B}) \quad \text{...(1)}$$

$$\Rightarrow \quad P(\overline{A} \cap \overline{B}) = P(\overline{A}) - P(\overline{A} \cap B) = P(\overline{A}) - P(\overline{A})\,P(B) \quad \text{(Using part (i))}$$

$$= P(\overline{A})\,(1 - P(B)) = P(\overline{A})\,P(\overline{B}).$$

$\therefore$ $\mathbf{P(\overline{A} \cap \overline{B}) = P(\overline{A})\ P(\overline{B})}$ *i.e.,* $\overline{A}$ and $\overline{B}$ are independent.

15.20. WORKING RULES FOR SOLVING PROBLEMS

I. Find the number of elements in the sample paper S of the given random experiment. Write the sample space, if it is feasible to do so.

II. Designate the events, as A and B whose 'independence' is to be checked. Out of the elements of the sample space, identify the elements which are favourable to the events A and B. Also find, the event $A \cap B$.

III. Find P(A), P(B) and $P(A \cap B)$.

IV. Find P(A) P(B). If P(A) P(B) is equal to $P(A \cap B)$, then declare that the given events A and B are independent events.

Example 1. *If A and B are independent events such that $P(A \cup B) = 0.6$ and $P(A) = 0.2$, find P(B).*

Sol. We have $P(A \cup B) = 0.6$ and $P(A) = 0.2$.

By *addition theorem,* we have

$$P(A \cup B) = P(A) + P(B) - P(A \cap B)$$

$$\Rightarrow \quad P(A \cup B) = P(A) + P(B) - P(A)\,P(B) \quad (\because \text{ A and B are independent})$$

$$\Rightarrow \quad 0.6 = 0.2 + P(B) - (0.2)\,P(B)$$

$$\Rightarrow \quad 0.4 = P(B)\,(1 - 0.2)$$

$$\Rightarrow \quad (0.8)\,P(B) = 0.4 \Rightarrow P(B) = \frac{0.4}{0.8} = \frac{1}{2} = 0.5.$$

Example 2. *A pair of dice is thrown. A is the event: "the sum is 8" and B is the event: "at least one odd number is obtained". Show that the events A and B are dependent.*

Sol. Let S be the sample space.

$\therefore \quad S = \{(1, 1), (1, 2), \ldots\ldots, (6, 5), (6, 6)\}.$

$A = \{(2, 6), (3, 5), (4, 4), (5, 3), (6, 2)\}$

$B = \{(1, 1), (1, 2), (1, 3), (1, 4), (1, 5), (1, 6), (3, 1), (3, 2), (3, 3), (3, 4), (3, 5), (3, 6), (5, 1), (5, 2), (5, 3), (5, 4), (5, 5), (5, 6), (2, 1), (2, 3), (2, 5), (4, 1), (4, 3), (4, 5), (6, 1), (6, 3), (6, 5)\}.$

$$\therefore \quad P(A) = \frac{5}{36} \text{ and } P(B) = \frac{27}{36} = \frac{3}{4}$$

Also, $A \cap B = \{(3, 5), (5, 3)\}$. $\quad \therefore \quad P(A \cap B) = \frac{2}{36} = \frac{1}{18}$

But $P(A)\,P(B) = \frac{5}{36} \times \frac{3}{4} = \frac{5}{48} \neq P(A \cap B)$. The events A and B are dependent.

TEST YOUR KNOWLEDGE 15.4

1. (*i*) Two events A and B are such that $P(A) = 0.6$, $P(B) = 0.2$ and $P(A \cup B) = 0.8$. Does this imply that A and B are independent ?
   (*ii*) The events A and B are given to be independent. Find P(B) if it is given that $P(A) = 0.38$ and $P(A \cup B) = 0.69$.
   (*iii*) If A and B are independent events such that $P(A \cup B) = 0.5$ and $P(A) = 0.2$, find P(B).
   (*iv*) Events A and B are given to be independent. Find P(B), if it is given that $P(A) = 0.35$, $P(A \cup B) = 0.60$.
2. For two events A and B, let $P(A) = 0.4$ and $P(B) = p$ and $P(A \cup B) = 0.6$
   (*i*) Find p so that A and B are mutually exclusive.
   (*ii*) Find p so that A and B are independent.
3. (*i*) If P(not B) = 0.65, $P(A \cup B) = 0.85$ and A, B are independent events, find P(A).
   (*ii*) If P(not A) = 0.4, $P(A \cup B) = 0.75$ and A, B are given to be independent events, find the value of P(B).
4. (*i*) A coin is tossed twice and all possible outcomes are assumed to be equally likely. E is the event : "at most one head has occurred" and F is the event : "at most one tail has occurred". Show that the events E and F are not independent.
   (*ii*) A coin is tossed twice and all possible outcomes are assumed to be equally likely. A is the event : both head and tail have occurred and B is the event : at least one tail has occurred". Show that A and B are not independent.
5. A coin is tossed three times and all possible outcomes are assumed to be equally likely. E is the event : "both heads and tails have occurred", and F is the event : "at most one tail has occurred". Show that the events E and F are independent.

Answers

1. (*i*) No (*ii*) $\frac{1}{2}$ (*iii*) $\frac{3}{8}$ (*iv*) $\frac{5}{13}$
2. (*i*) $\frac{1}{5}$ (*ii*) $\frac{1}{3}$ **3.** (*i*) $\frac{10}{13}$ (*ii*) $\frac{3}{8}$.

Hint

1. (*ii*) $P(B) = k \Rightarrow 0.69 = 0.38 + k - 0.38\,k$.

INDEPENDENT EXPERIMENTS

15.21. INDEPENDENT EXPERIMENTS

Two random experiments are said to be **independent** if, for every pair of events A and B where A is associated with the first and B with the second experiment, the probability of simultaneous occurrence of the events A and B, when the two experiments are performed, is equal to the product of the probabilities P(A) and P(B) calculated separately on the basis of two experiments.

The event 'A and B' of simultaneous occurrence of events A and B is denoted by $A \cap B$ or more briefly as AB.

Illustration. Let E_1 and E_2 be random experiments of throwing a die and tossing a coin respectively. Let S_1 and S_2 be their respective sample spaces.

$$\therefore \quad S_1 = \{1, 2, 3, 4, 5, 6\} \quad \text{and} \quad S_2 = \{H, T\}.$$

If S represents the sample space of combined experiment of E_1 and E_2, then

$$S = \{1H, 2H, 3H, 4H, 5H, 6H, 1T, 2T, 3T, 4T, 5T, 6T\}.$$

The elementary events in each of E_1, E_2 and their combined experiment are equally likely.

Let A = event of getting number less than 3, and
B = event of getting tail.

$$\therefore \quad P(A) = \frac{n(A)}{n(S_1)} = \frac{2}{6} = \frac{1}{3}, \quad P(B) = \frac{n(B)}{n(S_2)} = \frac{1}{2} \quad \text{and} \quad \text{thus } P(A)\,P(B) = \frac{1}{3} \times \frac{1}{2} = \frac{1}{6}.$$

$$\text{Also,} \quad AB = \{1T, 2T\} \quad \text{and} \quad P(AB) = \frac{n(AB)}{n(S)} = \frac{2}{12} = \frac{1}{6}.$$

$$\therefore \quad P(AB) = P(A)\,P(B).$$

The above equality is not sufficient to infer that the experiments are independent, because by definition, the experiments would be independent if the equality P(AB) = P(A) P(B) holds for all possible events A in E_1 and B in E_2.

Next, we prove a theorem which will lay down a criterion for the independence of experiments.

Theorem. *If the occurrence or non-occurrence of an event in one random experiment does not in any way affect the probability of the occurrence of any event in the other random experiment, then the experiments are independent.*

Proof. Since the occurrence or non-occurrence of an event in the first experiment is not affecting the probability of occurrence of any event in the second experiment, the sample spaces of the experiments are not affected by the events.

Let n_1 and n_2 be the numbers of elementary events in the first and second experiment respectively.

Let A and B be any events associated with first experiment and second experiment respectively.

Let m_1 be the number of cases favourable to the happening to the event A out of n_1 exhaustive, equally likely cases of the first experiment.

$$\therefore \quad P(A) = \frac{m_1}{n_1}$$

Let m_2 be the number of cases favourable to the happening of the event B out of n_2 exhaustive, equally likely cases of the second experiment.

$$\therefore \qquad P(B) = \frac{m_2}{n_2}$$

By the **Fundamental principle of events,** the number of cases favourable to the happening of the event AB in this specified order is $m_1 m_2$. Also the number of elementary events in the combined experiment is $n_1 n_2$.

$$\therefore \qquad P(AB) = \frac{m_1 m_2}{n_1 n_2} = \frac{m_1}{n_1} \cdot \frac{m_2}{n_2} = P(A)\,P(B).$$

$\therefore$ The experiments are independent.

Remark. If A and B are events associated with experiments which are not independent, then the probability of the event 'AB' is found by using the result :

P(AB) = P(A) P(B/A).

This result can also be extended to more than two experiments.

Important observation. If A and B be any two events associated with two different random experiments, then we may use the formula :

P(A in first experiment and B in second experiment)

= P(A in first experiment) . P(B in second experiment),

if on the basis of physical description of the random experiments, the occurrence or non occurrence of an event in one random experiment does not affect the probability of occurrence of an event in the other random experiment.

15.22. WORKING RULES FOR SOLVING PROBLEMS

I. If A and B are mutually exclusive events in a random experiment, then

$$P(A \cup B) = P(A) + P(B).$$

II. If A and B are events in a random experiment, then

$$P(A \cup B) = P(A) + P(B) - P(A \cap B).$$

III. If A and B are independent events in a random experiment then

$$P(A \cap B) = P(A)\,P(B).$$

IV. If A and B are dependent events in a random experiment, then

$$P(A \cap B) = P(A)\,P(B/A).$$

V. If, on the basis of the physical description of two random experiments, the occurrence of an event in one random experiment does not affect the probability of the occurrence of an event in the other random experiment, we conclude that the random experiments are independent and make use of the result :

P(A in first experiment and B in second experiment)

= P(A in first experiment). P(B in second experiment).

ILLUSTRATIVE EXAMPLES

Example 1. *A and B appeared for an interview for two posts. Probability of A's rejection is 2/5 and that of B's selection is 4/7. Find the probability that only one of them is selected.*

Sol. The random experiments 'interview of A' and 'interview of B' are independent.

Let E = event that A is selected

and F = event that B is selected.

$$\therefore \qquad P(\overline{E}) = \frac{2}{5} \text{ and } P(F) = \frac{4}{7}.$$

Also, $\qquad P(E) = 1 - P(\overline{E}) = 1 - \frac{2}{5} = \frac{3}{5}$ and $P(\overline{F}) = 1 - P(F) = 1 - \frac{4}{7} = \frac{3}{7}$.

Required probability $= P(\text{only one is selected})$

$= P(E\overline{F} \cup \overline{E}F) = P(E\overline{F}) + P(\overline{E}F)$ (Using **addition theorem**)

$= P(E)\,P(\overline{F}) + P(\overline{E})\,P(F)$ (Using **multiplication theorem**)

$$= \frac{3}{5} \times \frac{3}{7} + \frac{2}{5} \times \frac{4}{7} = \frac{9+8}{35} = \frac{17}{35}.$$

Example 2. *A husband and a wife appear in an interview for two vacancies for the same post. The probability of husband's selection is 3/5 and that of wife's selection is 1/5. Find the probability that :*

(i) both are selected *(ii) exactly one is selected*

(iii) none is selected. (P.T.U., M.B.A. May 2003)

Sol. The random experiments 'interview of husband' and interview of wife' are independent

Let H = event that 'Husband' is selected

and W = event that 'Wife' is selected.

$$\therefore \qquad P(H) = \frac{3}{5} \quad \text{and} \quad P(W) = \frac{1}{5}.$$

Also, $\qquad P(\overline{H}) = 1 - P(H) = 1 - \frac{3}{5} = \frac{2}{5}$ and $P(\overline{W}) = 1 - P(W) = 1 - \frac{1}{5} = \frac{4}{5}$.

(*i*) P(both are selected) $= P(HW) = P(H)\,P(W)$ (using **multiplication theorem**)

$$= \frac{3}{5} \times \frac{1}{5} = \frac{3}{25}.$$

(*ii*) P(exactly one is selected)$= P(H\overline{W} \cup \overline{H}W)$

$= P(H\overline{W}) + P(\overline{H}W)$ (using **addition theorem**)

$= P(H)P(\overline{W}) + P(\overline{H})P(W)$ (using **multiplication theorem**)

$$= \frac{3}{5} \times \frac{4}{5} + \frac{2}{5} \times \frac{1}{5} = \frac{14}{25}.$$

(*iii*) P(none is selected) $= P(\overline{H}\,\overline{W}) = P(\overline{H})\,P(\overline{W})$ (using **multiplication theorem**)

$$= \frac{2}{5} \times \frac{4}{5} = \frac{8}{25}.$$

Note. In this example, it is worth while to note that $\frac{3}{25} + \frac{14}{25} + \frac{8}{25} = \frac{25}{25} = 1$.

This has happened because the events : both are selected, exactly one is selected and none is selected are *mutually exclusive* and *exhaustive*.

Example 3. *A class consists of 100 students. Out of these 25 are girls and 75 are boys. 10 of them are rich, remaining poor. Out of 100 only 20 students are fair complexioned. What is the probability of selecting a fair complexioned rich girl ?*

Sol. Let A = event that a girl student is selected

B = event that a rich student is selected

C = event that a fair complexioned student is selected.

$$\therefore \qquad P(A) = \frac{25}{100} = \frac{1}{4}, \quad P(B) = \frac{10}{100} = \frac{1}{10} \quad \text{and} \quad P(C) = \frac{20}{100} = \frac{1}{5}.$$

Now, ABC is the event of selecting a rich, fair complexioned girl student. The random experiments of selections are independent.

$$\therefore \qquad P(ABC) = P(A)\,P(B)\,P(C) = \frac{1}{4} \times \frac{1}{10} \times \frac{1}{5} = \frac{1}{200} = 0.005.$$

Example 4. *The odds in favour of one student passing a test are 3 : 7. The odds against another student passing it are 3 : 5. What is the probability that both pass the test ?*

Sol. Let A = event that first pass the test.

$$\therefore \qquad P(A) = \frac{3}{3+7} = \frac{3}{10}$$

Let B = event that second pass the test.

$$\therefore \qquad P(B) = \frac{5}{3+5} = \frac{5}{8}$$

The random experiments of results of students are independent.

$$\therefore \quad P(\text{both pass the test}) = P(AB) = P(A)\,P(B) = \frac{3}{10} \times \frac{5}{8} = \frac{3}{16}.$$

Example 5. *An electric device is made up of three components A, B, C. The probability of failure of the component A is 0.01, that of B is 0.01 and that of C is 0.02 in some fixed period of time. Find the probability that the device will work satisfactory during that period of time, assuming that the three components work independently of one another.*

(P.T.U., M.B.A. May 2004)

Sol. Given P(A) = 0.01, P(B) = 0.01, P(C) = 0.01. The probability that one of the three components A, B, C is defective is given by

$$\begin{aligned}
P(A \text{ or } B \text{ or } C) &= P(A \cup B \cup C) \\
&= P(A) + P(B) + P(C) - P(A \cap B) - P(B \cap C) - P(C \cap A) + P(A \cap B \cap C) \\
&= P(A) + P(B) + P(C) - P(A)\,P(B) - P(B)\,P(C) - P(C)\,P(A) + P(A)\,P(B)\,P(C) \\
& \qquad | \because \text{ the components A, B, C are independent} \\
&= 0.01 + 0.01 + 0.02 - (0.01)(0.01) - (0.01)(0.02) - (0.02)(0.01) + (0.01)(0.01)(0.02) \\
&= 0.04 - 0.0001 - 0.0002 - 0.0002 + 0.000002 \\
&= 0.040002 - 0.0005 = 0.0395
\end{aligned}$$

$$\begin{aligned}
\therefore \qquad \text{Required probability} &= P(\text{None is defective}) \\
&= P(\overline{A} \cap \overline{B} \cap \overline{C}) = P(\overline{A \cup B \cup C}) \\
&= 1 - P(A \cup B \cup C) = 1 - 0.0395 = 0.9604.
\end{aligned}$$

Example 6. *Three group of children contain respectively 3 girls and 1 boy, 2 girls and 2 boys, 1 girl and 3 boys. One child is selected at random from each group. Show that the chance that the group selected consists of 1 girl and 2 boys is* $\frac{13}{32}$. (P.T.U., M.B.A. Dec. 2000)

Sol. There are three possibilities :

(*i*) Boy is selected from group-I and girls from group-II and group-III, or

(*ii*) Boy is selected from group-II and girls from group-I and group-III or

(*iii*) Boy is selected from group-III and girls from group-I and group-II.

I	II	III
1 B, 3 G	2 B, 2 G	3 B, 1 G

$\therefore$ Required probability of selecting a group of 1 boy and 2 girls

$$= \left(\frac{{}^1C_1}{{}^4C_1} \times \frac{{}^2C_1}{{}^4C_1} \times \frac{{}^1C_1}{{}^4C_1}\right) + \left(\frac{{}^2C_1}{{}^4C_1} \times \frac{{}^3C_1}{{}^4C_1} \times \frac{{}^1C_1}{{}^4C_1}\right) + \frac{{}^3C_1}{{}^4C_1} \times \frac{{}^3C_1}{{}^4C_1} \times \frac{{}^2C_1}{{}^4C_1}$$

$$= \frac{2}{3} + \frac{6}{64} + \frac{18}{64} = \frac{26}{64} = \frac{13}{32}.$$

Example 7. *A speaks truth in 60% of the cases and B in 90% of the cases. In what percentage of cases, are they likely to contradict each other in stating the same fact ?*

Sol. The random experiments of speaches of A and B are independent.

Let E = event of A speaking truth and F = event of B speaking truth.

$$\therefore \quad P(E) = \frac{60}{100} = \frac{6}{10} \quad \text{and} \quad P(F) = \frac{90}{100} = \frac{9}{10}.$$

Probability of A and B contradicting each other = $P(E\overline{F} \text{ or } \overline{E}F)$

$= P(E\overline{F}) + P(\overline{E}F) = P(E)\,P(\overline{F}) + P(\overline{E})\,P(F)$

$= P(E)\,(1 - P(F)) + (1 - P(E))\,P(F)$

$$= \frac{6}{10}\left(1 - \frac{9}{10}\right) + \left(1 - \frac{6}{10}\right)\frac{9}{10} = \frac{6}{10} \times \frac{1}{10} + \frac{4}{10} \times \frac{9}{10} = \frac{42}{100}$$

$\therefore$ A and B are likely to contradicts each other in **42%** cases.

Example 8. *A problem in mathematics is given to 3 students whose chances of solving it are* $\frac{1}{2}, \frac{1}{3}, \frac{1}{4}$. *What is the probability that the problem is solved ?*

Sol. The random experiments of trying the problem by the given students are independent.

Let A, B, C be the event of first, second, third student solving the problem.

$$\therefore \quad P(A) = \frac{1}{2}, \quad P(B) = \frac{1}{3}, \quad P(C) = \frac{1}{4}.$$

$\therefore$ P(the problem is solved)

$= P(A \text{ or } B \text{ or } C) = I - P(\overline{A}\,\overline{B}\,\overline{C})$

$= 1 - P(\overline{A})\,P(\overline{B})\,P(\overline{C}) = 1 - (1 - P(A))\,(1 - P(B))\,(1 - P(C))$

$$= 1 - \left(1 - \frac{1}{2}\right)\left(1 - \frac{1}{3}\right)\left(1 - \frac{1}{4}\right) = 1 - \left(\frac{1}{2}\right).\left(\frac{2}{3}\right).\left(\frac{3}{4}\right) = 1 - \frac{1}{4} = 3/4.$$

Example 9. *An investment firm purchases 3 stocks for one week trading purposes. It assesses the probability that the stock will increase in value over the week as 0.9, 0.7 and 0.6 respectively. What is the chance that (i) all three stocks will increase (ii) at least two stocks will increase. Assume that the movement of these stocks are independent.*

(P.T.U., M.B.A. Dec 2003)

Sol. Let A = The event that first stock will increase

B = The event that second stock will increase

C = The event that third stock will increase

Given P(A) = 0.9, P(B) = 0.7, P(C) = 0.6.

(*i*) Required probability $= P(A \cap B \cap C)$

$= P(A)\, P(B)\, P(C)$ | All the stocks are independent

$= (0.9)\,(0.7)\,(0.6) = 0.378$

(*ii*) Probability that at least two stocks will increase

$$= P(A \cap B \cap \overline{C} \quad \text{or} \quad A \cap \overline{B} \cap C \quad \text{or} \quad \overline{A} \cap B \cap C \quad \text{or} \quad A \cap B \cap C)$$

$$= P(A \cap B \cap \overline{C}) + (A \cap \overline{B} \cap C) + P(\overline{A} \cap B \cap C) + P(A \cap B \cap C)$$

$$= P(A)\, P(B)\, P(\overline{C}) + P(A)\, P(\overline{B})\, P(C) + P(\overline{A})\, P(B)\, P(C) + P(A)\, P(B)\, P(C)$$

$$= P(A)\, P(B)\, (1 - P(C)) + P(A)\, (1 - P(B))\, P(C) + (1 - P(A))\, P(B)\, P(C) + P(A)\, P(B)\, P(C)$$

$$= (0.9)\,(0.7)\,(0.4) + (0.9)\,(0.3)\,(0.6) + (0.1)\,(0.7)\,(0.6) + (0.9)\,(0.7)\,(0.6)$$

$$= 0.252 + 0.162 + 0.042 + 0.378 = 0.834.$$

Example 10. *A and B throw alternately with a pair of dice. A wins if he throws 6 before B throws 7 and B wins if he throws 7 before A throws 6. If A begins, find his chances of winning.*

(P.T.U., M.B.A. May 2008)

Sol. Total number of outcomes in a throw of a pair of dice = 36. A can win if he throws 6. Therefore the favourable outcomes are;

(1, 5), (2, 4), (3, 3), (4, 2) and (5, 1).

$$P(A) = \frac{5}{36} \quad \text{and} \quad P(\overline{A}) = 1 - \frac{5}{36} = \frac{31}{36}$$

B can win if he throws 7. Therefore, the favourable outcomes are:

(1, 6), (2, 5), (3, 4), (4, 3), (5, 2), (6, 1).

$$P(B) = \frac{6}{36} \quad \text{and} \quad P(\overline{A}) = 1 - \frac{6}{36} = \frac{30}{36}$$

The Required probability is given by

$P(A \text{ or } \overline{A}\,\overline{B}\,A \text{ or } \overline{A}\,\overline{B}\,\overline{A}\,\overline{B}\,A \text{ or so on})$

$$= P(A) + P(\overline{A}\,\overline{B}\,\overline{A}) + P(\overline{A}\,\overline{B}\,\overline{A}\,\overline{B}\,A) + \ldots\ldots \infty$$

$$= P(A) + P(\overline{A})\, P(\overline{B})\, P(\overline{A}) + P(\overline{A})\, P(\overline{B})\, P(\overline{A})\, P(\overline{B})\, P(A) + \ldots\ldots \infty$$

$$= \frac{5}{36} + \frac{31}{36} \cdot \frac{30}{36} \cdot \frac{5}{36} + \frac{31}{36} \cdot \frac{30}{36} \cdot \frac{31}{36} \cdot \frac{30}{36} \cdot \frac{5}{36} + \ldots\ldots \infty$$

$$= \frac{5}{36}\left(1 + \frac{31.30}{36.36} + \left(\frac{31.30}{36.36}\right)^2 + \ldots\ldots \infty\right)$$

$$= \frac{5}{36} \cdot \frac{1}{1 - \frac{31.30}{36.36}} = \frac{5}{36} \cdot \frac{36.36}{1296 - 930} = \frac{180}{366} = 0.49.$$

TEST YOUR KNOWLEDGE 15.5

1. (*i*) An unbiased die is thrown twice. Find the probability of getting a 4, 5, or 6 in the first throw and a 1, 2, 3 or 4 in the second throw.

   (*ii*) A die is thrown twice. Find the probability of getting an odd number in the first throw and a multiple of 3 in the second throw.

2. (*i*) A and B appeared for an interview for two posts. The probability of A's selection is 1/3 and that of B's selection is 2/5. Find the probability that only one of them is selected.

   (*ii*) The probability that Dimpu gets scholarship is 0.9 and that Pintu gets is 0.8. What is the probability that at least one of them get the scholarship ?

3. (*i*) A husband and a wife appear of an interview for two posts. The probability of the husband's selection is 1/7 and that of wife's selection is 1/5. What is the probability that :

   (*a*) none of them will be selected ? (*b*) both of them will be selected ?

   (*c*) only one of them is selected ?

   (*ii*) The probability of student A passing an examination is $\frac{3}{5}$ and of student B passing is $\frac{4}{5}$. Assuming the two events : "A passes", "B passes", as independent. Find the probability of :

   (*a*) both students passing the examination ;

   (*b*) only A passing the examination ;

   (*c*) only one of them passing the examination ; and

   (*d*) none of them passing the examination.

4. Ganesh appears for an interview for two posts A and B, selection for which are independent. The probability of selection for post A is 1/5 and for post B is 1/8. What is the probability that Ganesh is selected for at least one of the posts ?

5. One ball is drawn from a bag containing 3 red and 2 black balls. Its colour is noted and then it is put back in the bag. A second draw is made and the same procedure is repeated. Find the probability of drawing : (*i*) two red balls (*ii*) one red and one black ball, and (*iii*) two black balls.

6. A box containing 100 tickets each bearing one of the numbers from 1 to 100. If 5 tickets are drawn successively with replacement from the box, find the probability that all the tickets bear numbers divisible by 10.

7. (*i*) A bag contains 7 red, 3 black and 5 white balls. Three balls are drawn one after another without replacement. Find the probability that none is red.

   (*ii*) Two balls are drawn at random from a bag containing 3 white, 3 red, 4 green and 4 black balls, one by one without replacement. Find the probability that both the balls are of different colours.

   (*iii*) Two balls are drawn from an urn containing 2 white, 3 red and 4 black balls, one by one without replacement. What is the probability that :

   (*a*) both the balls are of the same colour ? (*b*) at least one ball is red ?

8. (*i*) Two cards are drawn one by one without replacement from a well shuffled pack of 52 cards. What is the probability that one is a red card and the other is a black card ?

   (*ii*) Find the probability of drawing a 'diamond card in each of two consecutive draws from a well shuffled pack of cards, (*a*) if the card drawn is not replaced after the first draw, (*b*) if the card drawn is replaced after the first draw.

9. A bag has 4 red and 5 black balls, a second bag has 3 red and 7 black balls. One ball is drawn from the first and two from the second. Find the probability of getting (*a*) 3 red balls (*b*) 3 black balls (*c*) 1 red and 2 black balls (*d*) 2 red and 1 black balls.

10. (*i*) The probability of A hitting a target is 4/5 and that of B hitting it is 2/3. They both fire at the target. Find the probability that

(*a*) at least one of them will hit the target

(*b*) only one of them will hit the target.

(*ii*) The probabilities of three students to solve a problem in Mathematics is 1/2, 1/3 and 1/4 respectively. What will be the probabilities in the following cases :

(*a*) All the three solve the problem ? (*b*) None of them solve the problem ?

(*c*) Only one of them solve the problem ?

11. (*i*) 'A' speaks truth in 65% cases and 'B' in 80% cases. In what percentage of cases are they likely to contradict each other in stating the same fact ?

(*ii*) A speaks truth in 75% cases and B in 80% cases. In what percentage of cases are they likely to contradict each other in stating the same fact.

Answers

1. (*i*) $\frac{1}{3}$ (*ii*) $\frac{1}{6}$

2. (*i*) $\frac{7}{15}$ (*ii*) 0.98

3. (*i*) (*a*) $\frac{24}{35}$ (*b*) $\frac{1}{35}$ (*c*) $\frac{2}{7}$ (*ii*) (*a*) $\frac{12}{25}$ (*b*) $\frac{3}{25}$ (*c*) $\frac{11}{25}$ (*d*) $\frac{2}{25}$ **4.** $\frac{3}{10}$

5. (*i*) $\frac{9}{25}$ (*ii*) $\frac{12}{25}$ (*iii*) $\frac{4}{25}$

6. $\left(\frac{1}{10}\right)^5$ **7.** (*i*) $\frac{8}{65}$ (*ii*) $\frac{73}{91}$

(*iii*) (*a*) $\frac{5}{18}$ (*b*) $\frac{7}{12}$ **8.** (*i*) $\frac{26}{51}$ (*ii*) (*a*) $\frac{1}{17}$ (*b*) $\frac{1}{16}$

9. (*a*) $\frac{4}{135}$ (*b*) $\frac{7}{27}$ (*c*) $\frac{7}{15}$ (*d*) $\frac{11}{45}$ **10.** (*i*) (*a*) $\frac{14}{15}$ (*b*) $\frac{2}{5}$

(*ii*) (*a*) $\frac{1}{24}$ (*b*) $\frac{1}{4}$ (*c*) $\frac{11}{24}$ **11.** (*i*) 41% (*ii*) 35%

Hints

3. (*ii*) (*c*) If A itself represents the event of A passing the examination, then the required probability is $P(A\bar{B} \text{ or } \bar{A}B)$.

7. (*iii*) (*a*) Reqd. prob. $= \left(\frac{2}{9}\times\frac{1}{8}\right)+\left(\frac{3}{9}\times\frac{2}{8}\right)+\left(\frac{4}{9}\times\frac{3}{8}\right)=\frac{5}{18}$.

(*b*) Reqd. prob. $= \left(\frac{6}{9}\times\frac{3}{8}\right)+\left(\frac{3}{9}\times\frac{6}{8}\right)+\left(\frac{3}{9}\times\frac{2}{8}\right)=\frac{7}{12}$.

CASE STUDIES

Case 6.1: Tiger Air Express*

Tiger Air Express Company was founded in 1987, primarily to provide charter air services. Soon after, it incorporated tour business and taxi business into its domain and during its first two years of operations, its sales grew by 168 per cent.

Because of its rapid growth, it experienced some difficulties in providing the necessary resources and building proper infrastructure for this growth. These difficulties were due to underestimated requirement of capital for vehicles, maintenance, office facilities, and staff. The Gulf War which resulted in steep increase in fuel costs added more burden on the financially-strapped organization.

The management was having difficulty in exactly-evaluating the financial and operational situation of the company. A well-known accounting firm was hired to develop and install an accounting system that would accurately reflect the company's financial situation at any-given time. As a result of the report, the taxi division was eliminated and the resources were diverted towards the freight and tour divisions of the company, specially the airfreight capabilities.

In order to expand on the airfreight business, further studies were conducted in order to understand the market better. Some insights into the airfreight market were gained through a survey of 44 air freight shippers conducted by an outside agency in 1992. There are two types of services available for forwarding air freight. First, there are integrated carriers. These are the companies which have their own planes. An example is Federal Express. These carriers offer customers pickup and delivery by truck along with airplane shipping. Second, there are freight forwarders. These are the carriers that handle pickup and delivery but use the regular scheduled airlines for air shipment.

A summary of the responses to some of the questions asked in the survey, as noted above, are explained below:

(*i*) 30 per cent of the survey respondents stated that their airfreight expenditures had increased in the past year. 60 per cent indicated no change in these expenditures and 10 per cent reported a drop in expenses.

(*ii*) 50 per cent of the survey respondents used integrated carriers for shipping. However, for small packages, this percentage increased to 75 per cent. Only 19 per cent used freight forwarders. 62 per cent of those who used freight forwarders did so because of their ability to handle international air freight more efficiently and reliably.

(*iii*) 39 per cent of the respondents indicated that they were using more 2-3 days deliveries which was cheaper than one day delivery, than they did 2 years ago.

(*iv*) When the survey asked the customers as to what they looked for in a carrier the responses were as follows:

- On-time delivery : 59 per cent
- Price : 57 per cent
- Customer responsiveness : 43 per cent
- Geographic coverage : 9 per cent
- Single source control : 7 per cent
- Tracing capabilities : 7 per cent.

Questions for Discussion

1. Based on your knowledge of probability theory, what strategy should Tiger Air Express adopt in determining their emphasis on the air freight business, based on the data given?

2. Some of the percentages reported in the survey can be converted into conditional probabilities. Conditional probabilities contain information about the responses in certain categories. Can you describe some of these categories? How would these categories help the management of Tiger Air Express? Explain.

3. If you were a consultant to Tiger Air Express, what recommendations would you give to the management so that they can meet the competition with other companies, offerings based on the type of shippers and shipments that are most probably in demand.

TOTAL PROBABILITY RULE

15.23. THEOREM REGARDING TOTAL PROBABILITY

Statement. *Let $E_1, E_2, ..., E_n$ be n mutually exclusive and exhaustive events, with non-zero probabilities, of a random experiment. If A be any arbitrary event of the sample space of the above random experiment with $P(A) > 0$, then*

$$P(A) = P(E_1) P(A/E_1) + P(E_2) P(A/E_2) + ... + P(E_n) P(A/E_n).$$

Proof. Let S be the sample space of the random experiment.

Since $E_1, E_2 ......, E_n$ are exhaustive, we have

$$S = E_1 \cup E_2 \cup ...... \cup E_n.$$

Now $A = S \cap A = (E_1 \cup E_2 \cup ...... \cup E_n) \cap A$

$$\Rightarrow \quad A = (E_1 \cap A) \cup (E_2 \cap A) \cup ...... \cup (E_n \cap A) \quad ...(1)$$

Since $E_1, E_2, ..., E_n$ are mutually exclusive, we have

$$E_i \cap E_j = \phi \text{ for } i \neq j$$

Now $(E_i \cap A) \cap (E_j \cap A) = (E_i \cap E_j) \cap A = \phi \cap A = \phi$

$\therefore$ $E_1 \cap A, E_2 \cap A, ..., E_n \cap A$ are also mutually exclusive.

By using **addition theorem,** (1) implies

$$P(A) = P(E_1 \cap A) + P(E_2 \cap A) + ... + P(E_n \cap A)$$

$$\Rightarrow \quad \mathbf{P(A) = P(E_1)\, P(A/E_1) + P(E_2)\, P(A/E_2) + ... + P(E_n)\, P(A/E_n).}$$

Remark. In practical problems, it is found convenient to write as follows :

$$P(A) = P(E_1A \text{ or } E_2A \text{ or } ...... \text{ or } E_nA) = P(E_1A) + P(E_2A) + ... + P(E_nA)$$

$$\therefore \quad \mathbf{P(A) = P(E_1)\, P(A/E_1) + P(E_2)\, P(A/E_2) + ... + P(E_n)\, P(A/E_n).}$$

Corollary. In particular if $n = 2$, we have

$$\mathbf{P(A) = P(E_1)\, P(A/E_1) + P(E_2)\, P(A/E_2).}$$

ILLUSTRATIVE EXAMPLES

Example 1. *Two urns contains 2 red, 4 white and 3 red, 7 white balls. One of the urns is chosen at random and a ball is drawn from it. Find the probability that the ball drawn is (i) red (ii) white.*

Sol.

2 Red 4 White	3 Red 7 White
Urn I	Urn II

Let E_1 and E_2 be the events of choosing the first urn and the second urn respectively.

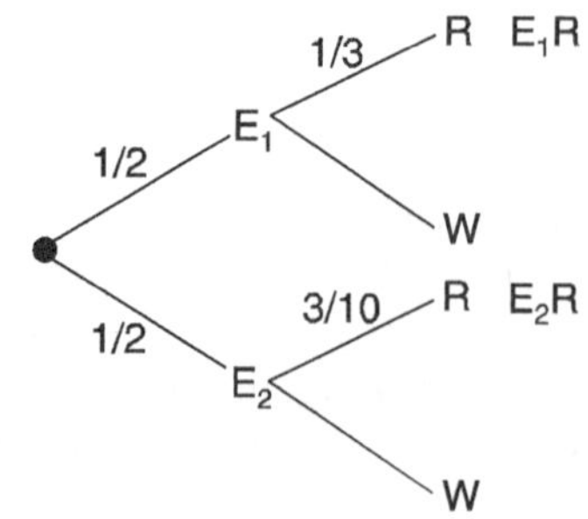

$$\therefore \quad P(E_1) = \frac{1}{2}, \; P(E_2) = \frac{1}{2}$$

(*i*) Let R be the event of drawing a red ball.

$$\therefore \quad P(R/E_1) = \frac{2}{2+4} = \frac{1}{3}, \; P(R/E_2) = \frac{3}{3+7} = \frac{3}{10}$$

Now P(drawing a red ball) = P(R)

$= P(E_1R \text{ or } E_2R) = P(E_1R) + P(E_2R)$

$= P(E_1)\,P(R/E_1) + P(E_2)\,P(R/E_2)$

$$= \frac{1}{2}\times\frac{1}{3}+\frac{1}{2}\times\frac{3}{10} = \frac{19}{60}.$$

(ii) Let W be the event of drawing a white ball.

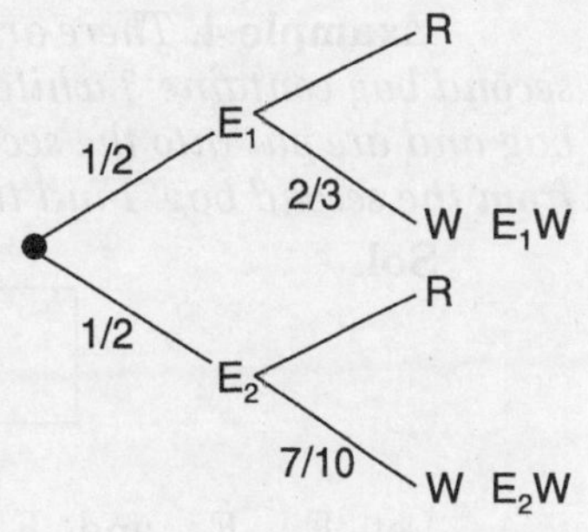

$$\therefore \quad P(W/E_1) = \frac{4}{2+4} = \frac{2}{3},\ P(W/E_2) = \frac{7}{3+7} = \frac{7}{10}$$

Now P(drawing a white ball)

$= P(W) = P(E_1W \text{ or } E_2W)$

$= P(E_1W) + P(E_2W)$

$= P(E_1)\,P(W/E_1) + P(E_2)\,P(W/E_2)$

$$= \frac{1}{2}\times\frac{2}{3}+\frac{1}{2}\times\frac{7}{10} = \frac{41}{60}.$$

Example 2. *One bag contains 5 white and 4 black balls. Another bag contains 7 white and 9 black balls. A ball is transferred from the first bag to the second bag and then a ball is drawn from the second. Find the probability that the ball is white.*

Sol.

5 White 4 Black	7 White 9 Black
Bag I	Bag II

Let W_1 and B_1 be the events of transferring a white ball and a black ball from bag I to bag II respectively.

Let W_2 be the event of drawing a white ball from the bag II after the transfer of one ball.

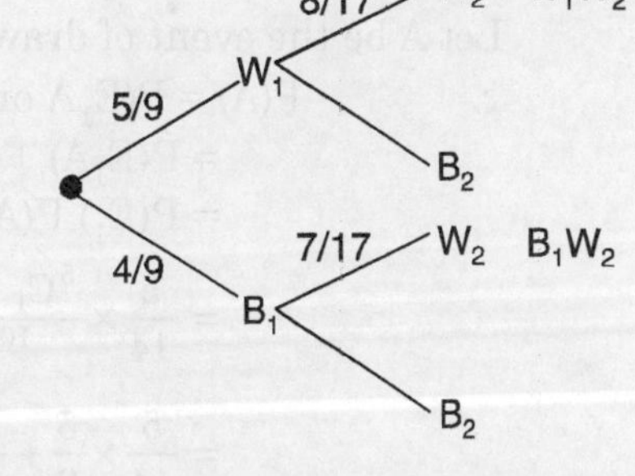

$\therefore$ Required probability $= P(W_2) = P(W_1W_2 \text{ or } B_1W_2)$

$= P(W_1W_2) + P(B_1W_2)$

$= P(W_1)\,P(W_2/W_1) + P(B_1)\,P(W_2/B_1)$

$$= \frac{5}{5+4}\times\frac{7+1}{(7+1)+9}+\frac{4}{5+4}\times\frac{7}{7+(9+1)}$$

$$= \frac{5}{9}\times\frac{8}{17}\times\frac{4}{9}\times\frac{7}{17} = \frac{4}{9}.$$

Example 3. *Suppose that 5 men out of 100 and 25 women out of 1000 are good oretor. Assuming that there are equal number of men and women, find the probability of choosing an oretor.*

Sol. Let E_1 and E_2 be the events of choosing a man and a woman respectively.

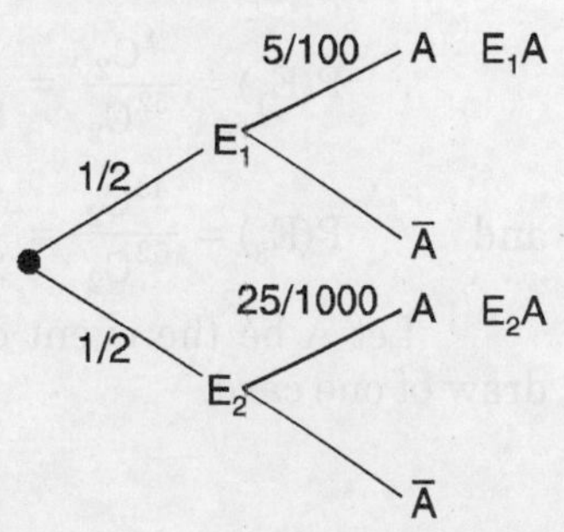

$\therefore \quad P(E_1) = \dfrac{1}{2}$ and $P(E_2) = \dfrac{1}{2}$, because there are equal number of men and women.

Let A be the event of choosing an oretor.

$\therefore \quad P(A/E_1) = $ Probability that a man is an oretor $= \dfrac{5}{100}$

$P(A/E_2) = $ Probability that a woman is an oretor $= \dfrac{25}{1000}$

$\therefore$ P(oretor is chosen) = P(A) = P(E_1A or E_2A)

$$= P(E_1A) + P(E_2A)$$
$$= P(E_1)\,P(A/E_1) + P(E_2)\,P(A/E_2)$$
$$= \frac{1}{2} \times \frac{5}{100} + \frac{1}{2} \times \frac{25}{1000} = \frac{75}{2000} = 0.0375.$$

Example 4. *There are two bags. The first bag contains 5 white and 3 black balls and the second bag contains 3 white and 5 black balls. Two balls are drawn at random from the first bag and are put into the second bag, without nothing their colours. Then two balls are drawn from the second bag. Find the probability that the balls drawn are white and black.*

Sol.

Let E_1, E_2 and E_3 be the events of transferring 2 white, 1 white and 1 black, 2 black balls respectively from the first bag to the second bag.

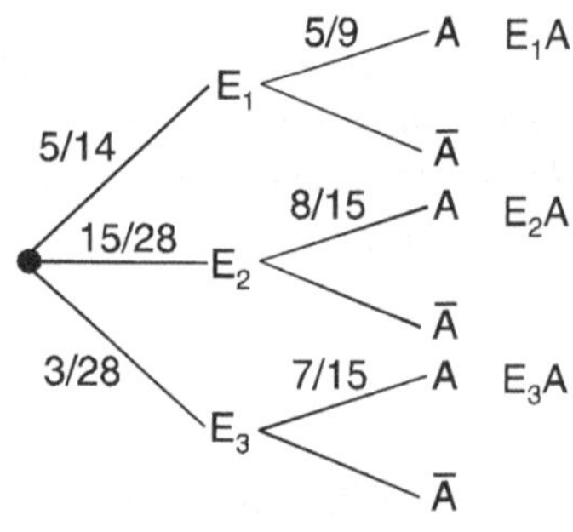

$$\therefore \quad P(E_1) = \frac{^5C_2}{^8C_2} = \frac{10}{28} = \frac{5}{14}$$

$$P(E_2) = \frac{^5C_1 \times {^3C_1}}{^8C_2} = \frac{5 \times 3}{28} = \frac{15}{28}$$

$$P(E_3) = \frac{^3C_2}{^8C_2} = \frac{3}{28}$$

Let A be the event of drawing one white and one black ball from the second bag.

$$\therefore \quad P(A) = P(E_1A \text{ or } E_2A \text{ or } E_3A)$$
$$= P(E_1A) + P(E_2A) + P(E_3A)$$
$$= P(E_1)\,P(A/E_1) + P(E_2)\,P(A/E_2) + P(E_3)\,P(A/E_3)$$
$$= \frac{5}{14} \times \frac{^5C_1 \times {^5C_1}}{^{10}C_2} + \frac{15}{28} \times \frac{^4C_1 \times {^6C_1}}{^{10}C_2} + \frac{3}{28} \times \frac{^3C_1 \times {^7C_1}}{^{10}C_2}$$
$$= \frac{5}{14} \times \frac{5}{9} + \frac{15}{28} \times \frac{8}{15} + \frac{3}{28} \times \frac{7}{15} = \frac{673}{1260}.$$

Example 5. *Two cards are drawn from a pack of 52 cards at random and kept out. Then one card is drawn from the remaining 50 cards. Find the probability that it is an ace.*

Sol. Let E_1, E_2 and E_3 be the events of drawing 2 aces, 1 ace and 1 non ace, 2 non aces in the first draw of 2 cards.

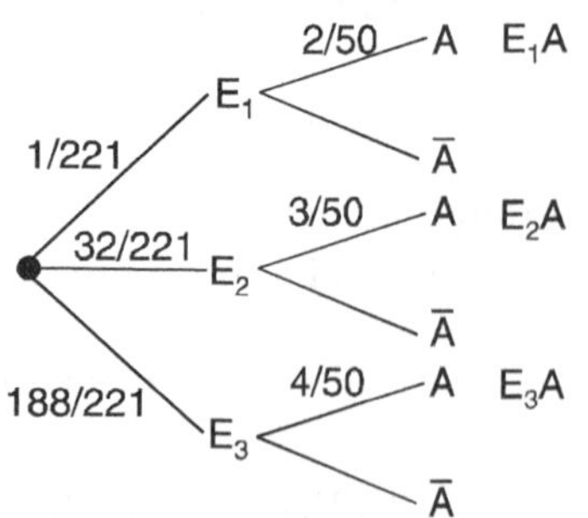

$$\therefore \quad P(E_1) = \frac{^4C_2}{^{52}C_2} = \frac{1}{221}, \quad P(E_2) = \frac{^4C_1 \times {^{48}C_1}}{^{52}C_2} = \frac{32}{221}$$

and $$P(E_3) = \frac{^{48}C_2}{^{52}C_2} = \frac{188}{221}.$$

Let A be the event of drawing an ace in the second draw of one card.

Required probability = $P(A) = P(E_1A \text{ or } E_2A \text{ or } E_3A)$

$$= P(E_1)\ P(A/E_1) + P(E_2)\ P(A/E_2) + P(E_3)\ P(A/E_3)$$

$$= \frac{1}{221} \times \frac{4-2}{52-2} + \frac{32}{221} \times \frac{4-1}{52-2} + \frac{188}{221} \times \frac{4-0}{52-2}$$

$$= \frac{2+96+752}{221 \times 50} = \frac{850}{11050} = \frac{1}{13}.$$

TEST YOUR KNOWLEDGE 15.6

1. A bag contains 2 white and 4 black balls and another bag contains 6 white and 4 black balls. One bag is chosen at random. From the selected bag, one ball is drawn. Find the probability that the ball drawn is white.
2. A purse contains 2 silver and 4 copper coins. A second purse contains 4 silver and 3 copper coins. If a coin is pulled out at random from one of the two purses, what is the probability that it is a silver coin ?
3. A factory has two machines A and B. Past records show that the machine A produced 60% of the items of output and machine B produced 40% of the items. Further 2% of the items produced by machine A were defective and 1% produced by machine B were defective. If an item is drawn at random, what is the probability that it is defective ?
4. (*i*) Find the probability of drawing a one-rupee coin from a purse with two compartments one of which contains 3 fifty-paise coins and 2 one-rupee coins and other contains 2 fifty-paise coins and 3 one-rupee coins.

   (*ii*) A bag contains 3 white and 6 black balls while another bag contains 6 white and 3 black balls. A bag is selected at random and a ball is drawn. Find the probability that the ball drawn is of white colour.
5. Two third of the students in a class are boys and the rest girls. It is known that the probability of a girl getting a first class is 0.25 and that of a boy getting first class is 0.28. Find the probability that a student chosen at random will get first class marks in the examination.
6. In a bolt factory machines A, B and C manufacture 25%, 35% and 40% of the total bolts. Of their outputs 5%, 4% and 2% respectively are defective bolts. A bolt is drawn at random from the output. What is the probability that the bolt drawn is defective ?
7. A bag contains 3 white and 2 red balls and another bag contains 2 white and 4 red balls. A ball is taken from the first bag and without seeing its colour is put in the second bag. A ball is taken from the latter. Find the probability that the ball drawn is red.
8. One bag contains 6 white and 5 black balls. Another bag contains 5 white and 3 black balls. A ball is transferred from the first bag to the second bag and then a ball is drawn from the second bag. Find the probability that ball drawn is white.

Answers

1. $\frac{7}{15}$ **2.** $\frac{19}{42}$ **3.** $\frac{2}{125}$ **4.** (*i*) $\frac{1}{2}$ (*ii*) $\frac{1}{2}$ **5.** 0.27

6. 0.0345 **7.** $\frac{22}{35}$ **8.** $\frac{61}{99}$.

16

Bayes' Theorem and its Applications

16.1. INTRODUCTION

Let there be two or more urns, each containing some white balls and red balls. Suppose an urn is chosen at random and a ball is drawn from that chosen urn. By using *addition theorem* and *multiplication theorem*, we can find out the probability of drawing a white ball (or a red ball) from the urn chosen.

But in case, we are given that the ball drawn is white and we are interested in finding the probability of the event that the ball was drawn from the first urn or the second urn, then the situation is not same as in the previous case. Now the probability of urn drawn will depend upon the colour of the ball drawn.

To tackle this type of problems, **Bayes' theorem** is used. This theorem was enunciated by British mathematician **Thomos Bayes** in 1763.

16.2. BAYES' THEOREM

(P.T.U., M.B.A. DEC., 2009, 2012)

Statement. *Let $E_1, E_2, \ldots\ldots, E_n$ be n mutually exclusive and exhaustive events, with non-zero probabilities, of a random experiment. If A be any arbitrary event of the sample space of the above experiment which occurs with E_1 or E_2 or ...... or E_n and $P(A) > 0$, then*

$$P(E_i/A) = \frac{P(E_i)\,P(A/E_i)}{\sum_{j=1}^{n} P(E_j)\,P(A/E_j)}, \quad 1 \le i \le n.$$

Proof. Let S be the sample space of the random experiment.

$\therefore \quad S = E_1 \cup E_2 \cup \ldots\ldots \cup E_n \qquad (\because\ E_1, E_2, \ldots\ldots, E_n$ are exhaustive)

Now, $\quad A = S \cap A = (E_1 \cup E_2 \cup \ldots\ldots \cup E_n) \cap A$

$\quad = (E_1 \cap A) \cup (E_2 \cap A) \cup \ldots\ldots \cup (E_n \cap A).$

$\therefore \quad P(A) = P(E_1 \cap A) + P(E_2 \cap A) + \ldots\ldots + P(E_n \cap A)$*

$\quad = P(E_1)P(A/E_1) + P(E_2)P(A/E_2) + \ldots\ldots + P(E_n)P(A/E_n)$

$$\therefore \quad P(A) = \sum_{j=1}^{n} P(E_j)\,P(A/E_j). \qquad \ldots(1)$$

***Why this step.** Since $E_1, E_2, \ldots\ldots, E_n$ are mutually exclusive, we have, $E_l \cap E_m = \phi$ for $l \ne m$.

Now, $(E_l \cap A) \cap (E_m \cap A) = (E_l \cap E_m) \cap A = \phi \cap A = \phi$

$\therefore$ $E_1 \cap A, E_2 \cap A, \ldots\ldots, E_n \cap A$ are also mutually exclusive and thus *extended addition theorem* is applicable.

Now, $$P(E_i/A) = \frac{P(E_i \cap A)}{P(A)}, \; 1 \le i \le n.$$

$$\therefore \quad \mathbf{P(E_i/A) = \frac{P(E_i)\,P(A/E_i)}{\sum_{j=1}^{n} P(E_j)\,P(A/E_j)}, \; 1 \le i \le n.} \qquad \text{[Using (1)]}$$

Remark. The probabilities $P(E_1)$, $P(E_2)$, ..., $P(E_n)$ which are known before conducting the experiment are called **prior probabilities.** The conditional probabilities $P(E_1/A)$, $P(E_2/A)$, ..., $P(E_n/A)$ which are calculated after conducting the experiment are called **posterior probabilities.**

Particular cases. (*i*) If $n = 2$, then we have

$$P(E_1/A) = \frac{P(E_1)P(A/E_1)}{P(E_1)P(A/E_1) + P(E_2)P(A/E_2)} \quad \text{and} \quad P(E_2/A) = \frac{P(E_2)P(A/E_2)}{P(E_1)P(A/E_1) + P(E_2)P(A/E_2)}.$$

(*ii*) If $n = 3$, then we have

$$P(E_1/A) = \frac{P(E_1)P(A/E_1)}{P(E_1)P(A/E_1) + P(E_2)P(A/E_2) + P(E_3)P(A/E_3)}$$

$$P(E_2/A) = \frac{P(E_2)P(A/E_2)}{P(E_1)P(A/E_1) + P(E_2)P(A/E_2) + P(E_3)P(A/E_3)}$$

and $$P(E_3/A) = \frac{P(E_3)P(A/E_3)}{P(E_1)P(A/E_1) + P(E_2)P(A/E_2) + P(E_3)P(A/E_3)}.$$

16.3. WORKING RULES FOR SOLVING PROBLEMS

I. Identify mutually exclusive and exhaustive 'priori' events E_1, E_2, ..., E_n (*n* is generally 2 or 3).

II. Find $P(E_1)$, $P(E_2)$, ..., $P(E_n)$ and check that the sum of these probabilities is one.

III. Identify the event A and find $P(A/E_1)$, $P(A/E_2)$, ..., $P(A/E_n)$.

IV. Identify the 'posteriori' event E_i/A whose probability is required. Calculate $P(E_i/A)$ by using Bayes' theorem.

ILLUSTRATIVE EXAMPLES

Example 1. *Assume that a factory has two machines. Past records show that machine I produces 20% of the items of output and machine II produces 80% of the items. Further, 6% of the items produced by machine I were defective and only 1% produced by machine II were defective. If a defective item is drawn at random. What is the probability that it was produced by (i) machine I (ii) machine II ?*

Sol. Let E_1, E_2 be the events of drawing an item produced by machine I and II respectively. Let A be the event of drawing a defective item. Now we have

$$P(E_1) = \frac{20}{100} = \frac{1}{5}, \; P(E_2) = \frac{80}{100} = \frac{4}{5},$$

$$P(A/E_1) = \frac{6}{100}, \; P(A/E_2) = \frac{1}{100}.$$

The events E_1 and E_2 are mutually exclusive and exhaustive.

(*i*) By **Bayes' theorem,** P(machine I produced the defective item)

$$= P(E_1/A) = \frac{P(E_1)\,P(A/E_1)}{P(E_1)\,P(A/E_1) + P(E_2)\,P(A/E_2)} = \frac{\frac{1}{5} \times \frac{6}{100}}{\left(\frac{1}{5} \times \frac{6}{100}\right) + \left(\frac{4}{5} \times \frac{1}{100}\right)} = \frac{6}{6+4} = \frac{3}{5}.$$

(*ii*) P(machine II produced the defective item)

$$= P(E_2/A) = \frac{P(E_2)\,P(A/E_2)}{P(E_1)\,P(A/E_1) + P(E_2)\,P(A/E_2)} = \frac{\frac{4}{5} \times \frac{1}{100}}{\left(\frac{1}{5} \times \frac{6}{100}\right) + \left(\frac{4}{5} \times \frac{1}{100}\right)} = \frac{4}{6+4} = \frac{2}{5}.$$

Example 2. *Suppose that 5 males out of 100 and 25 females out of 1000 are good orators. An orator is chosen at random. Find the probability that a male person is chosen. Assume that there are equal number of males and females.*

Sol. Let E_1 and E_2 be the events of choosing a male and a female respectively.

$$\therefore \quad P(E_1) = \frac{1}{2} = 0.5 \quad \text{and} \quad P(E_2) = \frac{1}{2} = 0.5$$

($\because$ There are equal number of males and females)

Let A be the event of choosing an orator.

$$\therefore \quad P(A/E_1) = \text{Probability that a male is an orator} = \frac{5}{100} = 0.05$$

$$P(A/E_2) = \text{Probability that a female is an orator} = \frac{25}{1000} = 0.025.$$

Required probability = Probability that the chosen orator is a male

= $P(E_1/A)$

By **Bayes' theorem,** we have $P(E_1/A) = \dfrac{P(E_1)\,P(A/E_1)}{P(E_1)\,P(A/E_1) + P(E_2)\,P(A/E_2)}$

$$= \frac{(0.5)(0.05)}{(0.5)(0.05) + (0.5)(0.025)} = \frac{0.025}{0.025 + 0.0125} = \frac{0.025}{0.0375} = \frac{2}{3}.$$

Example 3. *A factory has three machines X, Y and Z producing 1000, 2000, and 3000 bolts per day respectively. The machine X produces 1% defective bolts, Y produces 1.5% and Z produces 2% defective bolts. At the end of a day, a bolt is drawn at random and is found defective. What is the probability that this defective bolt has been produced by the machine X?*

Sol. Let E_1, E_2, E_3, be the events of drawing a bolt produced by machine X, machine Y, machine Z respectively.

$$\therefore \quad P(E_1) = \frac{1000}{6000} = \frac{1}{6}, \quad P(E_2) = \frac{2000}{6000} = \frac{1}{3}, \quad P(E_3) = \frac{3000}{6000} = \frac{1}{2}$$

(Using 1000 + 2000 + 3000 = 6000)

Let A be the event of drawing a defective bolt.

$$P(D/E_1) = 1\% = \frac{1}{100}, \quad P(D/E_2) = 1.5\% = \frac{1.5}{100}, \quad P(D/E_3) = 2\% = \frac{2}{100}$$

The events E_1, E_2, E_3 are mutually exclusive and exhaustive.

By **Bayes' theorem,**

P(defective bolt is produced by machine X)

$$= P(E_1/D) = \frac{P(E_1)\,P(D/E_1)}{P(E_1)\,P(D/E_1) + P(E_2)\,P(D/E_2) + P(E_3)\,P(D/E_3)}$$

$$= \frac{\frac{1}{6} \times \frac{1}{100}}{\left(\frac{1}{6} \times \frac{1}{100}\right) + \left(\frac{1}{3} \times \frac{1.5}{100}\right) + \left(\frac{1}{2} \times \frac{2}{100}\right)} = \frac{1}{1+3+6} = \frac{1}{10}.$$

Example 4. *There are three urns having the following composition of black and white balls :*

Urn I : 7 white and 3 black balls

Urn II : 4 white and 6 black balls

Urn III : 2 white and 8 black balls.

One of these urns is chosen at random with probabilities 0.2, 0.6 and 0.2 respectively. From the chosen urn, two balls are drawn simultaneously at random. Both the balls happens to be white. Calculate the probability that the balls drawn were from urn III.

Sol.

Urn I	Urn II	Urn III
7 White 3 Black	4 White 6 Black	2 White 8 Black

Let E_1, E_2, E_3 be the events of choosing urn I, urn II, urn III respectively.

$\therefore$ $P(E_1) = 0.2$, $P(E_2) = 0.6$, $P(E_3) = 0.2$.

Let A be the event of drawing 2 white balls when 2 balls are drawn from an urn.

$\therefore$ $P(A/E_1)$ = Probability that 2 white balls are drawn, when 2 balls are drawn simultaneously from the urn I,

$$= \frac{{}^7C_2}{{}^{10}C_2} = \frac{21}{45} = \frac{7}{15}$$

Similarly, $P(A/E_2) = \frac{{}^4C_2}{{}^{10}C_2} = \frac{6}{45} = \frac{2}{15}$ and $P(A/E_3) = \frac{{}^2C_2}{{}^{10}C_2} = \frac{1}{45}$.

Required probability = Probability that 2 white balls drawn were from urn III

$= P(E_3/A)$.

By **Bayes' theorem,** we have $P(E_3/A) = \dfrac{P(E_3)\,P(A/E_3)}{P(E_1)\,P(A/E_1) + P(E_2)\,P(A/E_2) + P(E_3)\,P(A/E_3)}$

$$= \frac{(0.2)\frac{1}{45}}{(0.2)\frac{7}{15} + (0.6)\frac{2}{15} + (0.2)\frac{1}{45}} = \frac{\frac{0.2}{45}}{\frac{4.2+3.6+0.2}{45}} = \frac{0.2}{8} = \frac{1}{40}.$$

Note. The events E_1, E_2 and E_3 are exhaustive, because $P(E_1) + P(E_2) + P(E_3) = 0.2 + 0.6 + 0.2 = 1$.

TEST YOUR KNOWLEDGE 16.1

1. Two urns contain 4 white, 6 blue and 4 white, 5 blue balls. One of the urns is selected at random and a ball is drawn. If the ball drawn is white, find the probability that it is drawn from the first urn.
2. There are two bags I and II, containing 3 red and 4 white balls, and 2 red and 3 white balls respectively. A bag is selected at random and a ball is drawn from it. If it is found to be a red ball, find the probability that it is drawn from the first bag.
3. There are two bags I and II. Bag I contains 3 white and 4 black balls and bag II contains 5 white and 6 black balls. One ball is drawn at random from one of the bags and is found to be white. Find the probability that it was drawn from bag I.
4. There are two identical boxes containing respectively 4 white and 3 red balls, 3 white and 7 red balls. A box is chosen at random and a ball is drawn from it. If the ball drawn is white, what is the probability that it is drawn from the first box ?
5. A box contains 4 gold and 3 silver coins. Another box contains 3 gold and 5 silver coins. A box is chosen at random and a coin is drawn from it. If the selected coin is a gold coin, find the probability that it was drawn from the second box.
6. Bag A contains 3 white and 2 red balls. Bag B contains 4 white and 5 red balls. One ball is drawn at random from one of the bags and is found to be red. Find the probability that it was drawn from Bag B.
7. Assume that a factory has two machines. Past records show that machine I produces 60% of the items of output and machine II produces 40% of the items. Further, 2% of the items produced by machine I were defective and only 1% produced by machine II were defective. If a defective item is drawn at random, what is the probability that it was produced by machine I?
8. In a bolt factory, machines A and B manufacture equal number of bolts. Of the total of their output, 1% and 2% are defective. A bolt is drawn at random from the total production and found to be defective. From which machine, the defective bolt is expected to have been produced ?
9. There are 4 boys and 2 girls in Room No. 1 and 5 boys and 3 girls in Room No. 2. A girl from one of the two rooms laughed loudly. What is probability that the girl who laughed loudly was from Room No. 2 ?
10. In a factory, machines A, B and C produces 40%, 40% and 20% respectively. Of the total of their output 1%, 1% and 3% are defective. An item is drawn at random from the total production and found to be defective. Find the probability that this item is produced by the machine C.
11. An insurance company insured 3,000 scooters, 4,000 cars and 5,000 trucks. The probabilities of an accident involving a scooter, a car and a truck are 0.02, 0.03 and 0.04 respectively. One of the insured vehicles meets with an accident. Find the probability that

    (*i*) it is a scooter, (*ii*) it is a car (*iii*) it is a truck.
12. There are three urns containing 2 white and 3 black balls, 3 white and 2 black balls, and 4 white and 1 black balls respectively. There is equal probability of each urn being chosen. A ball is drawn at random from the chosen urn and it is found to be white. Find the probability that the ball drawn was from the second urn.
13. Three bags contain balls as shown in the following table :

Bag	*Number of*		
	White balls	*Black balls*	*Red balls*
I	1	2	3
II	2	1	1
III	4	3	2

A bag is chosen at random and two balls are drawn. They happen to be white and red. What is the probability that they came from the third bag ?

14. (*i*) A man is known to speak truth 4 out of 5 times. He throws a pair of dice and reports that it is a doublet. Find the probability that it is actually a doublet.

(*ii*) A is known to speak truth 3 out of 5 times. He throws a die and reports that it is 1. Find the probability it is actually 1.

15. In a factory, machine A produces 30% of the total output, machine B produces 25% and the machine C produces the remaining output. The defective output of the machines A, B and C are 1%. 1.2%, 2%, respectively. Three machines working together produce 10,000 items in a day. An item is drawn at random from a day's output and found to be defective. Find the probability that it was produced by machine B ?

Answers

1. $\frac{9}{19}$ **2.** $\frac{15}{29}$ **3.** $\frac{33}{68}$ **4.** $\frac{40}{61}$ **5.** $\frac{21}{53}$

6. $\frac{25}{43}$ **7.** $\frac{3}{4}$ **8.** B **9.** $\frac{9}{17}$ **10.** $\frac{3}{7}$

11. (*i*) $\frac{2}{7}$ (*ii*) $\frac{9}{35}$ (*iii*) $\frac{16}{35}$ **12.** $\frac{1}{3}$ **13.** $\frac{5}{17}$

14. (*i*) $\frac{4}{9}$ (*ii*) $\frac{3}{13}$ **15.** $\frac{1}{5}$.

Hint

15. Production of C = 100% – 30% – 25% = 45%

The figure 10,000 is not required for finding the required probability.

PROBABILITY DISTRIBUTION

16.4. INTRODUCTION

We have already studied a lot about frequency distributions. These distributions are based upon observations, *i.e.*, the frequencies for different values of the variable, under consideration, are based on actual observation. For example, if an unbiased coin is tossed 100 times, we may get head 57 times. Here, 57 is the observed frequency but theoretically we shall expect 'head', 50 times. In this section, we shall study ***probability distributions*** and ***frequency distributions*** which are based upon theoretical considerations.

16.5. RANDOM VARIABLE

Let S be the sample space of a given random experiment. A real valued function 'x' defined on the sample space S is called a **random variable.**

Thus, if $s \in S$, then $x(s)$ is a unique real number.

Remark. The values of a random variable are real numbers, connected with the outcomes of the random experiment, under consideration.

In the random experiment of toss of two coins, if we define the random variable (x) as the *number of heads,* then the values of the random variable x are 0, 1, 1, 2 corresponding to the outcomes TT, TH, HT, HH respectively.

We write, $x(\text{TT}) = 0^*$, $x(\text{TH}) = 1$, $x(\text{HT}) = 1$, $x(\text{HH}) = 2$.

In case, there are three coins, then the values of this random variable are 0, 1, 1, 1, 2, 2, 2, 3 corresponding to the outcomes TTT, TTH, THT, HTT, HHT, HTH, THH, HHH respectively.

We can define any number of random variables on the same sample space. If x denotes the random variable, defined as the cube of the number of tails, in the experiment of toss of two coins, then we have

Sample points	HH	HT	TH	TT
x	$(0)^3 = 0$	$(1)^3 = 1$	$(1)^3 = 1$	$(2)^3 = 8$

Random variables are of two types : (*i*) discrete random variable and (*ii*) continuous random variable.

(*i*) A random variable is called a **discrete random variable** if it can take only finitely many values. For example, in the experiment of drawing three cards from a pack of playing cards, the random variable "number of kings drawn" is a discrete random variable taking value either 0 or 1 or 2 or 3.

(*ii*) A random variable is called a **continuous random variable** if it can take any value between certain limits. For example, height, weight of students in a class are continuous random variables.

16.6. PROBABILITY DISTRIBUTION OF A DISCRETE RANDOM VARIABLE

Let x be a discrete random variable assuming values $x_1, x_2, x_3, \ldots\ldots, x_n$ corresponding to the various outcomes of a random experiment. If the probability of occurrence of $x = x_i$ is $P(x_i) = p_i$, $1 \le i \le n$ such that $p_1 + p_2 + p_3 + \ldots\ldots + p_n = 1$, then the function, $P(x_i) = p_i$, $1 \le i \le n$ is called the **probability function** of the random variable x and the set $\{P(x_1), P(x_2), P(x_3), \ldots\ldots, P(x_n)\}$ is called the **probability distribution** of x.

The graph of a probability distribution is also drawn as shown in the diagram. This is also known as a **bar-chart**.

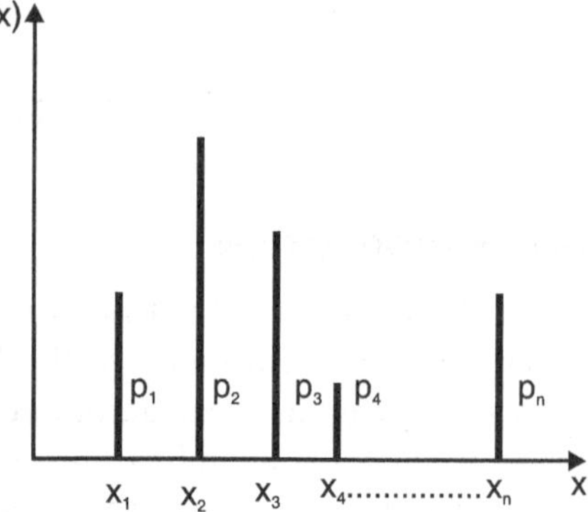

16.7. WORKING RULES FOR FINDING PROBABILITY DISTRIBUTION

I. Identify the random variable and put it as x.

II. Find the possible values of x.

III. Find P(x) for all possible values of x and write P.D. of x.

IV. Check that the sum of all probabilities in the P.D. is one. If this sum is not one, then some mistake is bound to have occurred in the calculation work. Remove the mistake and again verify that the sum of all probabilities is one.

***Why this step.** $x(\text{TT}) = 0$, because the number of heads in the sample point 'TT' is zero.

ILLUSTRATIVE EXAMPLES

Example 1. *A fair die is tossed once. If the random variable x is the "number of even numbers", find the probability distribution of x.*

Sol. Here S = {1, 2, 3, 4, 5, 6}.

Let x denotes the random variable "number of even numbers".

$\therefore$ x can take values 0 and 1, because at most we can get one even number.

$$P(x = 0) = P(\text{no even number})$$

$$= P(1 \text{ or } 3 \text{ or } 5) = \frac{3}{6} = \frac{1}{2}$$

$$P(x = 1) = P(\text{one even number})$$

$$= P(2 \text{ or } 4 \text{ or } 6) = \frac{3}{6} = \frac{1}{2}$$

$\therefore$ The probability distribution of x is

x	0	1
$P(x)$	$\frac{1}{2}$	$\frac{1}{2}$

Example 2. *Find the probability distribution of the random variable "number of heads" when :*

(*i*) *two coins are tossed* (*ii*) *one coin is tossed twice.*

Sol. (*i*) Let S be the sample space.

$\therefore$ S = {HH, HT, TH, TT}

Let x denotes the discrete random variable "*number of heads*".

$\therefore$ The possible values of x are 0, 1, 2.

We have $P(x = 0) = P(\{TT\}) = \frac{1}{4}$

$$P(x = 1) = P(\{HT, TH\}) = \frac{2}{4} = \frac{1}{2}$$

$$P(x = 2) = P(\{HH\}) = \frac{1}{4}.$$

$\therefore$ The required probability distribution (P.D.) is

x	0	1	2
$P(x)$	$\frac{1}{4}$	$\frac{1}{2}$	$\frac{1}{4}$

(*ii*) Let H be the event of getting a head.

Let x denote the discrete random variable "*number of heads*" in two tosses.

$\therefore$ The possible values of x are 0, 1, 2.

We have $P(x = 0) = P(\overline{H}_1\overline{H}_2) = P(\overline{H}_1)\, P(\overline{H}_2) = \frac{1}{2} \times \frac{1}{2} = \frac{1}{4}$

$$P(x = 1) = P(H_1\overline{H}_2 \text{ or } \overline{H}_1H_2) = P(H_1\overline{H}_2) + P(\overline{H}_1H_2)$$

$$= P(H_1)\, P(\overline{H}_2) + P(\overline{H}_1)\, P(H_2) = \frac{1}{2} \times \frac{1}{2} + \frac{1}{2} \times \frac{1}{2} = \frac{1}{4} + \frac{1}{4} = \frac{1}{2}$$

$$P(x = 2) = P(H_1H_2) = P(H_1)\, P(H_2) = \frac{1}{2} \times \frac{1}{2} = \frac{1}{4}.$$

∴ The required probability distribution (P.D.) is

x	0	1	2
$P(x)$	$\frac{1}{4}$	$\frac{1}{2}$	$\frac{1}{4}$

Example 3. *Two cards are drawn successively with replacement from a well shuffled pack of 52 cards. Find the probability distribution of number of queens.*

Sol. Let Q be the event of drawing a queen from the pack of cards.

Let x denotes the discrete random variable "*number of queens*" in two draws.

∴ The possible values of x are 0, 1, 2.

We have $P(x = 0) = P(\overline{Q}_1\overline{Q}_2) = P(\overline{Q}_1)\, P(\overline{Q}_2) = \frac{48}{52} \times \frac{48}{52} = \frac{144}{169}$

$$P(x = 1) = P(Q_1\overline{Q}_2 \text{ or } \overline{Q}_1Q_2) = P(Q_1\overline{Q}_2) + P(\overline{Q}_1Q_2)$$

$$= P(Q_1)\, P(\overline{Q}_2) + P(\overline{Q}_1)\, P(Q_2) = \frac{4}{52} \times \frac{48}{52} + \frac{48}{52} \times \frac{4}{52} = \frac{24}{169}$$

$$P(x = 2) = P(Q_1Q_2) = P(Q_1)\, P(Q_2) = \frac{4}{52} \times \frac{4}{52} = \frac{1}{169}.$$

∴ The required probability distribution (P.D.) is

x	0	1	2
$P(x)$	$\frac{144}{169}$	$\frac{24}{169}$	$\frac{1}{169}$

16.8. MEAN AND VARIANCE OF A RANDOM VARIABLE

We know the method of finding the mean and variance of frequency distributions. In a frequency distribution, we have frequencies corresponding to different values of the variable. Similarly in a probability distribution, we have probabilities corresponding to different admissible values of the discrete random variable.

Now, we shall extend the idea of mean and variance for probability distributions.

Let x be a discrete random variable assuming values $x_1, x_2, \ldots\ldots, x_n$ with respective probabilities $p_1, p_2, \ldots\ldots, p_n$ with $p_1 + p_2 + \ldots\ldots + p_n = 1$.

We define, mean $(\mu) = \dfrac{\sum_{i=1}^{n} p_i x_i}{\sum_{i=1}^{n} p_i} = \sum_{i=1}^{n} p_i x_i \qquad \left(\because \sum_{i=1}^{n} p_i = 1\right)$

and variance $= \dfrac{\sum_{i=1}^{n} p_i (x_i - \mu)^2}{\sum_{i=1}^{n} p_i} = \sum_{i=1}^{n} p_i (x_i - \mu)^2.$

We have $\sum_{i=1}^{n} p_i (x_i - \mu)^2 = \sum_{i=1}^{n} p_i (x_i^2 + \mu^2 + 2\mu x_i) = \sum_{i=1}^{n} p_i x_i^2 + \mu^2 \sum_{i=1}^{n} p_i - 2\mu \sum_{i=1}^{n} p_i x_i$

$$= \sum_{i=1}^{n} p_i x_i^2 + \mu^2.1 - 2\mu.\mu = \sum_{i=1}^{n} p_i x_i^2 - \mu^2.$$

$\therefore$ Mean $(\mu) = \sum_{i=1}^{n} \mathbf{p_i x_i}$ and **variance** $(\sigma^2) = \sum_{i=1}^{n} \mathbf{p_i x_i^2} - \mu^2$.

In short, we write, $\mu = \Sigma \mathbf{px}$ and variance $= \Sigma \mathbf{px^2} - \mu^2$.

The mean of random variable x is called the **expected value** of x and is denoted by E(x). The mean and variance of a random variable are also referred to as the mean and variance of the corresponding P.D.

Remark. S.D. of probability distribution $= \sqrt{\text{variance}} = \sqrt{\Sigma px^2 - \mu^2}$.

16.9. WORKING RULES FOR SOLVING PROBLEMS

I. Identify the random variable (x) and its possible values $x_1, x_2, \ldots\ldots$

II. Find probabilities for all values of the variable x.

III. Draw table and find Σpx and Σpx^2.

IV. Find mean and variance by using the formulae $\mu = \Sigma px$ and variance $= \Sigma px^2 - \mu^2$.

Example 4. *A random variable x has the following probability distribution :*

x	-2	-1	0	1	2	3
$P(x)$	0.1	k	0.2	$2k$	0.3	k

(i) Find the value of k.

(ii) Calculate mean and variance of x.

Sol. **Calculation of mean and variance**

x	p	px	px^2
-2	0.1	-0.2	0.4
-1	k	$-k$	k
0	0.2	0	0
1	$2k$	$2k$	$2k$
2	0.3	0.6	1.2
3	k	$3k$	$9k$
	$\Sigma p = 4k + 0.6$	$\Sigma px = 4k + 0.4$	$\Sigma px^2 = 12k + 1.6$

(*i*) In a P.D., we have $\Sigma p = 1$.

$\therefore \quad 4k + 0.6 = 1 \quad$ or $\quad 4k = 0.4$ or $k = 0.1$.

(*ii*) Mean $(\mu) = \Sigma px = 4k + 0.4 = 4(0.1) + 0.4 = 0.8$.

Variance $= \Sigma px^2 - \mu^2 = (12k + 1.6) - (0.8)^2 = (12(0.1) + 1.6) - 0.64 = 2.16$.

Example 5. *A die is tossed twice. A "success" is "getting an odd number" on a random toss. Find the mean and variance of the number of successes.*

Sol. Let E be the event of getting a success, *i.e.*, of getting an odd number in the toss of a die. On a die, odd numbers are 1, 3, 5.

$\therefore \quad P(E) = \frac{3}{6} = \frac{1}{2}$ and $P(\bar{E}) = 1 - \frac{1}{2} = \frac{1}{2}$.

Let x denotes the random variable "*number of successes*".

$\therefore$ The possible values of x are 0, 1, 2.

$$P(x = 0) = P(\bar{E}_1\bar{E}_2) = P(\bar{E}_1)\, P(\bar{E}_2) = \frac{1}{2} \times \frac{1}{2} = \frac{1}{4}$$

$$P(x = 1) = P(E_1\bar{E}_2 \text{ or } \bar{E}_1E_2) = P(E_1)\, P(\bar{E}_2) + P(\bar{E}_1)\, P(E_2) = \left(\frac{1}{2} \times \frac{1}{2}\right) + \left(\frac{1}{2} \times \frac{1}{2}\right) = \frac{1}{2}$$

$$P(x = 2) = P(E_1E_2) = P(E_1)P(E_2) = \frac{1}{2} \times \frac{1}{2} = \frac{1}{4}.$$

Calculation of mean and variance

x	p	px	px^2
0	$\frac{1}{4}$	0	0
1	$\frac{1}{2}$	$\frac{1}{2}$	$\frac{1}{2}$
2	$\frac{1}{4}$	$\frac{1}{2}$	1
	$\Sigma p = 1$	$\Sigma px = 1$	$\Sigma px^2 = \frac{3}{2}$

Mean (μ) = $\Sigma px = 1$

Variance = $\Sigma px^2 - \mu^2 = \frac{3}{2} - (1)^2 = 0.5.$

Example 6. *Find the mean and variance of the number of heads in the two tosses of a coin.*

Sol. Let x denotes the random variable, "*number of heads*" in the two tosses.

∴ The possible values of x are 0, 1, 2.

We have $P(x = 0) = P(\text{no head}) = P(\overline{H}_1\overline{H}_2) = P(\overline{H}_1)P(\overline{H}_2) = \frac{1}{2} \times \frac{1}{2} = \frac{1}{4}$

where H_i is the event of getting head in the ith toss, $i = 1, 2$.

$$P(x = 1) = P(\text{one head}) = P(H_1 \overline{H}_2 \text{ or } \overline{H}_1 H_2) = P(H_1)P(\overline{H}_2) + P(\overline{H}_1)P(H_2)$$

$$= \left(\frac{1}{2} \times \frac{1}{2}\right) + \left(\frac{1}{2} \times \frac{1}{2}\right) = \frac{1}{2}$$

$$P(x = 2) = P(\text{both heads}) = P(H_1H_2) = P(H_1)P(H_2) = \frac{1}{2} \times \frac{1}{2} = \frac{1}{4}.$$

Calculation of mean and variance

x	p	px	px^2
0	$\frac{1}{4}$	0	0
1	$\frac{1}{2}$	$\frac{1}{2}$	$\frac{1}{2}$
2	$\frac{1}{4}$	$\frac{1}{2}$	1
	$\Sigma p = 1$	$\Sigma px = 1$	$\Sigma px^2 = \frac{3}{2}$

∴ Mean (μ) = $\Sigma px = 1$

Variance = $\Sigma px^2 - \mu^2 = \frac{3}{2} - (1)^2 = 0.5.$

Example 7. *Two cards are drawn successively with replacement from a well shuffled pack of 52 cards. Find the mean and standard deviation for the number of aces.*

Sol. Let A be the event of getting an ace in a draw of one card.

∴ $P(A) = \frac{4}{52} = \frac{1}{13}$ and $P(\overline{A}) = 1 - \frac{1}{13} = \frac{12}{13}$.

Let x denotes the random variable "*no. of aces*".

∴ x can take values 0, 1, 2.

$$P(x = 0) = P(\text{no ace}) = P(\overline{A}_1\,\overline{A}_2) = P(\overline{A}_1)\,P(\overline{A}_2) = \frac{12}{13} \times \frac{12}{13} = \frac{144}{169}$$

$$P(x = 1) = P(\text{one ace}) = P(A_1 \overline{A}_2 \text{ or } \overline{A}_1 A_2) = P(A_1)P(\overline{A}_2) + P(\overline{A}_1)\ P(A_2)$$

$$= \left(\frac{1}{13} \times \frac{12}{13}\right) + \left(\frac{12}{13} \times \frac{1}{13}\right) = \frac{24}{169}$$

$$P(x = 2) = P(\text{both aces}) = P(A_1A_2) = P(A_1)P(A_2) = \frac{1}{13} \times \frac{1}{13} = \frac{1}{169}.$$

Calculation of mean and S.D.

x	p	px	px^2
0	$\frac{144}{169}$	0	0
1	$\frac{24}{169}$	$\frac{24}{169}$	$\frac{24}{169}$
2	$\frac{1}{169}$	$\frac{2}{169}$	$\frac{4}{169}$
	$\Sigma p = 1$	$\Sigma px = \frac{2}{13}$	$\Sigma px^2 = \frac{28}{169}$

$\therefore$ $$\text{Mean} = \Sigma px = \frac{2}{13}$$

$$\text{S.D.} = \sqrt{\Sigma px^2 - \mu^2} = \sqrt{\frac{28}{169} - \left(\frac{2}{13}\right)^2} = \sqrt{\frac{28}{169} - \frac{4}{169}} = \frac{\sqrt{24}}{13} = \frac{2\sqrt{6}}{13}.$$

Example 8. *Two cards are drawn simultaneously (or successively without replacement) from a well shuffled pack of 52 cards. Compute the variance of the number of aces.*

Sol. Let two cards be drawn simultaneously from the well shuffled pack of 52 cards. Let x denotes the random variable "*no. of aces*".

$\therefore$ x can take values 0, 1, 2.

$$P(x = 0) = P(\text{no ace}) = \frac{^{48}C_2}{^{52}C_2} = \frac{188}{221}$$

$$P(x = 1) = P(\text{one ace}) = \frac{^4C_1 \times {^{48}C_1}}{^{52}C_2} = \frac{32}{221}$$

$$P(x = 2) = P(\text{both aces}) = \frac{^4C_2}{^{52}C_2} = \frac{1}{221}.$$

Calculation of variance

x	p	px	px^2
0	$\frac{188}{221}$	0	0
1	$\frac{32}{221}$	$\frac{32}{221}$	$\frac{32}{221}$
2	$\frac{1}{221}$	$\frac{2}{221}$	$\frac{4}{221}$
	$\Sigma p = 1$	$\Sigma px = \frac{34}{221}$	$\Sigma px^2 = \frac{36}{221}$

Variance $= \Sigma px^2 - \mu^2 = \Sigma px^2 - (\Sigma px)^2$

$$= \frac{36}{221} - \left(\frac{34}{221}\right)^2 = \frac{7956 - 1156}{48841} = \frac{6800}{48841} = \frac{400}{2873}.$$

Example 9. *Find the probability distribution of the number of successes in two tosses of a die, where a success is defined as 'a number greater than 4'. Sketch its graph. Also find the mean and variance of the distribution.*

Sol. Let E be the event of getting a success *i.e.,* of getting a number greater than 4 in the toss of a die. On a die, numbers greater than 4 are 5 and 6.

$\therefore \quad P(E) = \frac{2}{6} = \frac{1}{3}$ and $P(\bar{E}) = 1 - \frac{1}{3} = \frac{2}{3}$.

Let x denotes the random variable "*number greater than 4*".

$\therefore$ The possible values of x are 0, 1, 2.

$$P(x = 0) = P(\bar{E}_1\bar{E}_2) = P(\bar{E}_1)P(\bar{E}_2) = \frac{2}{3} \times \frac{2}{3} = \frac{4}{9}$$

$$P(x = 1) = P(E_1\bar{E}_2 \text{ or } \bar{E}_1E_2) = P(E_1)P(\bar{E}_2) + P(\bar{E}_1)P(E_2)$$

$$= \left(\frac{1}{3} \times \frac{2}{3}\right) + \left(\frac{2}{3} \times \frac{1}{3}\right) = \frac{4}{9}$$

$$P(x = 2) = P(E_1E_2) = P(E_1)P(E_2) = \frac{1}{3} \times \frac{1}{3} = \frac{1}{9}.$$

$\therefore$ The P.D. of x is

x	0	1	2
P(x)	$\frac{4}{9}$	$\frac{4}{9}$	$\frac{1}{9}$

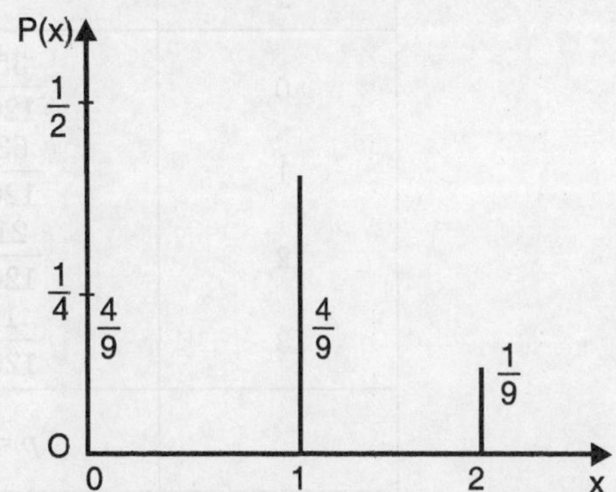

The graph of the P.D. is given in the figure.

Calculation of mean and variance

x	p	px	px^2
0	$\frac{4}{9}$	0	0
1	$\frac{4}{9}$	$\frac{4}{9}$	$\frac{4}{9}$
2	$\frac{1}{9}$	$\frac{2}{9}$	$\frac{4}{9}$
	$\Sigma p = 1$	$\Sigma px = \frac{2}{3}$	$\Sigma px^2 = \frac{8}{9}$

Mean $(\mu) = \Sigma px = \mathbf{\frac{2}{3}}$

Variance $= \Sigma px^2 - \mu^2 = \frac{8}{9} - \left(\frac{2}{3}\right)^2 = \frac{4}{9}$.

Example 10. *Three bad eggs got mixed up with seven good eggs. If three eggs are drawn simultaneously from 10 eggs. Find the mean and variance of the number of bad eggs among them.*

Sol. Let x denotes the discrete random variable "*number of bad eggs*".

$\therefore$ x can take values 0, 1, 2, 3.

$$P(x = 0) = P(\text{No bad egg}) = \frac{{}^7C_3}{{}^{10}C_3} = \frac{35}{120}$$

$$P(x = 1) = P(1 \text{ bad egg}) = \frac{{}^3C_1 \times {}^7C_2}{{}^{10}C_3} = \frac{63}{120}$$

$$P(x = 2) = P(2 \text{ bad eggs}) = \frac{{}^3C_2 \times {}^7C_1}{{}^{10}C_3} = \frac{21}{120}$$

$$P(x = 3) = P(\text{All bad eggs}) = \frac{{}^3C_3}{{}^{10}C_3} = \frac{1}{120}.$$

Calculation of mean and variance

x	p	px	px^2
0	$\frac{35}{120}$	0	0
1	$\frac{63}{120}$	$\frac{63}{120}$	$\frac{63}{120}$
2	$\frac{21}{120}$	$\frac{42}{120}$	$\frac{84}{120}$
3	$\frac{1}{120}$	$\frac{3}{120}$	$\frac{9}{120}$
	$\Sigma p = 1$	$\Sigma px = \frac{108}{120}$	$\Sigma px^2 = \frac{156}{120}$

$$\text{Mean } (\mu) = \Sigma px = \frac{108}{120} = 0.9$$

$$\text{Variance} = \Sigma px^2 - \mu^2 = \frac{156}{120} - (0.9)^2 = 0.49.$$

Example 11. *Five defective articles are mixed with twenty good ones. Four articles are drawn simultaneously at random. Find the mean and S.D. of the defective articles drawn.*

Sol. Let x denotes the discrete random variable *no. of defective articles drawn.*

∴ The possible values of x are 0, 1, 2, 3, 4.

Now, $$P(x=0) = \frac{^{20}C_4}{^{25}C_4} = \frac{4845}{12650}\ ;\ P(x=1) = \frac{^5C_1 \cdot {}^{20}C_3}{^{25}C_4} = \frac{5700}{12650}$$

$$P(x=2) = \frac{^5C_2 \cdot {}^{20}C_2}{^{25}C_4} = \frac{1900}{12650}\ ;\ P(x=3) = \frac{^5C_3 \cdot {}^{20}C_1}{^{25}C_4} = \frac{200}{12650}$$

$$P(x=4) = \frac{^5C_4}{^{25}C_4} = \frac{5}{12650}.$$

Calculation of mean and S.D.

x	p	px	px^2
0	$\frac{4845}{12650}$	0	0
1	$\frac{5700}{12650}$	$\frac{5700}{12650}$	$\frac{5700}{12650}$
2	$\frac{1900}{12650}$	$\frac{3800}{12650}$	$\frac{7600}{12650}$
3	$\frac{200}{12650}$	$\frac{600}{12650}$	$\frac{1800}{12650}$
4	$\frac{5}{12650}$	$\frac{20}{12650}$	$\frac{80}{12650}$
	$\Sigma p = 1$	$\Sigma px = \frac{10120}{12650}$	$\Sigma px^2 = \frac{15180}{12650}$

$$\text{Mean } (\mu) = \Sigma px = \frac{10120}{12650} = 0.8$$

$$\text{S.D. } (\sigma) = \sqrt{\Sigma px^2 - \mu^2} = \sqrt{\frac{15180}{12650} - (0.8)^2} = \sqrt{1.2 - 0.64} = \sqrt{0.56} = 0.75.$$

Example 12. *A balanced coin is tossed 4 times. Find the probability distribution of the number of heads and expectations.* (P.T.U., M.B.A. Dec. 2003)

Sol. Let X denotes the number of heads in the toss of a coin, then X can take the value 0, 1, 2, 3, 4, The sample space S is given by (see figure)

S = { HHHH, HHHT, HHTH, HHTH, HTHH, HTHT, HTTH, HTTT, THHH, THHT, THTH, THTT, TTHH, TTHT, TTTH, TTTT}

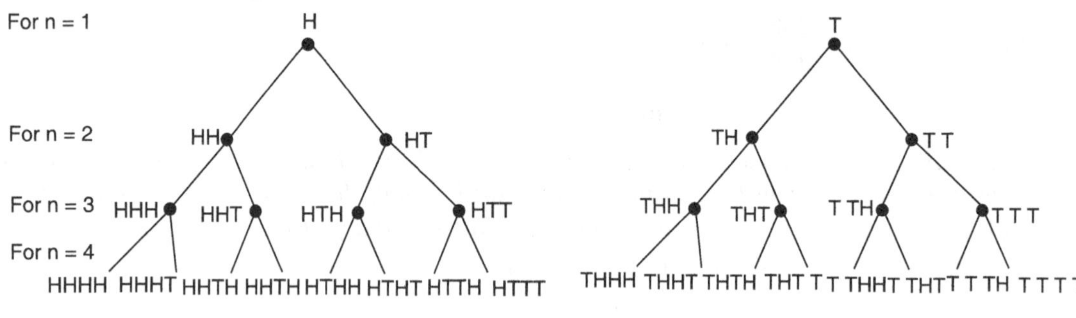

$$P(X = 0) = P \text{ (No heads)} = \frac{1}{16}; \; P(X = 1) = P(\text{One head}) = \frac{4}{16}$$

$$P(X = 2) = P(\text{Two heads}) = \frac{5}{16}; \; P(X = 3) = P(\text{Three heads}) = \frac{5}{16}$$

$$P(X = 4) = P \text{ (Four heads)} = \frac{1}{16}$$

The required probability distribution is given by

X	0	1	2	3	4
P(X)	$\frac{1}{16}$	$\frac{4}{16}$	$\frac{5}{16}$	$\frac{5}{16}$	$\frac{1}{16}$

Also the expectation of X is given by

$$E(X) = \Sigma XP(X) = 0.\frac{1}{16} + 1.\frac{4}{16} + 2.\frac{5}{16} + 3.\frac{5}{16} + 4.\frac{1}{16}$$

$$= \frac{4 + 10 + 15 + 4}{16} = \frac{33}{16}.$$

TEST YOUR KNOWLEDGE 16.2

1. Find the probability distribution of the random variable "no. of sixes" in two tosses of a die.

2. A pair of unbiased dice is tossed. If the random variable x is the sum of two numbers obtained on two dice, find the probability distribution of x.

3. From a well shuffled pack of 52 cards, 3 cards are drawn one-by-one with replacement. Find the probability distribution of number of queens.

4. Find the mean of the following probability distributions :

(*i*)

x	1	2	3
$P(x)$	0.4	0.2	0.4

(*ii*)

x	0	1	2	3	4
$P(x)$	0.1	0.2	0.3	0.2	0.2

5. Find the mean and the variance of the following probability distributions :

(*i*)

x	2	3	4	5
$P(x)$	0	0.4	0.1	0.5

(ii) x	1	2	3	4	5	6
$P(x)$	0.1	0.1	0.2	0.3	0.1	0.2

6. Two urns contain 5 black, 4 white balls and 4 black, 5 white balls. One ball is drawn from each urn. Find the mean and variance of the probability distribution of the random variable "no. of white balls drawn".

7. Find the S.D. of probability distribution of the number of aces drawn, when 2 cards are drawn one by one from a pack of playing cards with replacement.

8. Find the S.D. of probability distribution of the number of aces drawn, when 2 cards are drawn one by one from a pack of playing cards without replacement.

9. Three defective pencils are mixed with ten good ones. Two pencils are drawn simultaneously at random. Find the mean number of defective pencils drawn.

10. A draw of 3 balls in made from an urn containing 7 red and 6 black balls. Find the S.D. of the probability distribution of the discrete random variable "number of black balls drawn".

11. Find the mean and variance of the probability distribution of the random variable "number of tails" when four coins are tossed.

12. A coin is tossed 4 times. Find the mean and variance of the probability distribution of the number of heads. *(P.T.U., M.B.A. Dec. 2003)*

13. A coin is tossed 5 times. 'x' is the number of heads observed. Find the mean and variance of the probability distribution of x.

14. Find the mean and variance of the P.D. of the number of threes in a single throw of three dice.

15. An urn contains 3 white and 4 red balls. 3 balls are drawn one by one with replacement. Find the mean and variance of the probability distribution of the number of red balls.

16. A box contains 16 bulbs out of which 4 bulbs are defective. 3 bulbs are drawn one by one from the box without replacement. Find the mean and variance of the probability distribution of the number of defective bulbs drawn.

Answers

1.

x	0	1	2
$P(x)$	$\frac{25}{36}$	$\frac{5}{18}$	$\frac{1}{36}$

2.

x	2	3	4	5	6	7	8	9	10	11	12
$P(x)$	$\frac{1}{36}$	$\frac{1}{18}$	$\frac{1}{12}$	$\frac{1}{9}$	$\frac{5}{36}$	$\frac{1}{6}$	$\frac{5}{36}$	$\frac{1}{9}$	$\frac{1}{12}$	$\frac{1}{18}$	$\frac{1}{36}$

3.

x	0	1	2	3
$P(x)$	$\frac{1728}{2197}$	$\frac{432}{2197}$	$\frac{36}{2197}$	$\frac{1}{2197}$

4. (i) 2 (ii) 2.2 **5.** (i) 4.1, 0.89 (ii) 3.8, 2.26

6. 1, 0.4938 **7.** 0.3768 **8.** 0.3730 **9.** 0.4616

10. 0.7882. **11.** 2, 1 **12.** 2, 1 **13.** 2.5, 1.25

14. 0.5, 0.416 **15.** 1.714, 0.735 **16.** 0.75, 0.487.

17
Binomial Distribution

17.1. INTRODUCTION

The binomial distribution is a particular type of probability distribution. This was discovered by **James Bernoulli** (1654–1705) in the year 1700. This distribution mainly deals with attributes. An attribute is either present or absent with respect to elements of a population. For example, if a coin is tossed, we get either *head* or *tail*. The workers of a factory may be classified as *skilled* and *unskilled*.

17.2. CONDITIONS FOR APPLICABILITY OF BINOMIAL DISTRIBUTION

The following conditions are essential for the applicability of Binomial Distribution :

(*i*) **The random experiment is performed for a finite and fixed number of trials.** If in an experiment, a coin is tossed repeatedly or a ball is drawn from an urn repeatedly, then each toss or draw is called a **trial.** For example, if a coin is tossed 6 times, then this experiment has 6 trials. The number of trials is an experiment is generally denoted by 'n'.

(*ii*) **The trials are independent.** By this we mean that the result of a particular trial should not affect the result of any other trial. For example, if a coin is tossed or a die is thrown, then the trials would be independent. If from a pack of playing cards, some draws of one card are made without replacing the cards, then the trials would not be independent. But, if the card drawn is replaced before the next draw, the trials would be independent.

(*iii*) **Each trial must result in either "success" or "failure".** In other words, in every trial, there should be only two possible outcomes *i.e., success* or *failure*. For example, if a coin is tossed, then either *head or tail* is observed. Similarly, if an item is examined, it is either *defective* or *non-defective*.

(*iv*) **The probability of success in each trial is same.** In other words, this condition requires that the probability of *success* should not change in different trials. For example, if a sample of two items is drawn, then the probability of exactly one being defective will be constant in different trials provided the items are replaced before the next draw.

17.3. BINOMIAL VARIABLE

A random variable which counts the number of successes in a random experiment with trials satisfying above four conditions is called a **binomial variable.**

For example, if a coin is tossed 5 times and the event of getting head is *success,* then the possible values of the binomial variable are 0, 1, 2, 3, 4, 5. This is so, because, the minimum number of successes is 0 and the maximum number of successes is 5.

17.4. BINOMIAL PROBABILITY FUNCTION

When a fair coin is tossed, we have only two possibilities : head and tail. Let us call the occurrence of head as 'success'. Therefore, the occurrence of tail would be a 'failure'. Let this coin be tossed 5 times. Suppose we are interested in finding the probability of getting 4 heads and 1 tail *i.e.,* of getting 4 successes. If S and F denote 'success' and 'failure' in a trial respectively, then there are ${}^5C_4 = 5$ ways of having 4 successes.

These are : SSSSF, SSSFS, SSFSS, SFSSS, FSSSS.

The probability of getting 4 successes in each case is $\left(\frac{1}{2}\right)^4\left(\frac{1}{2}\right)$, because the trials are independent.

$\therefore$ By using *addition theorem*, the required probability of having 4 successes is ${}^5C_4\left(\frac{1}{2}\right)^4\left(\frac{1}{2}\right)$, which is equal to $\frac{5}{32}$. Now we shall generalise this method of finding the probabilities for different values of a *binomial variable.*

Let a random experiment satisfying the conditions of **binomial distribution** be performed. Let the number of trials in the experiment be n. Let p denotes the probability of *success* in any trial.

$\therefore$ Probability of failure, $q = 1 - p$.

Let x denotes the binomial variable corresponding to this experiment.

$\therefore$ The possible values of x are 0, 1, 2, ..., n.

If there are r successes in n trials, then there would be $n - r$ failures. One of the ways in which r successes may occur is

$$\underbrace{SS.............S}_{r \text{ times}}\ \underbrace{FF.............F}_{n-r \text{ times}}$$

where S and F denote success and failure in the trials.

Now, P(SS .... SFF ..... F) = P(S)P(S) ..... P(S)P(F)P(F) ..... P(F)

($\because$ the trials are independent)

$$= p.p \text{ ...... } p.q.q \text{ ...... } q = p^r q^{n-r}.$$

We know that ${}^nC_r$ is the number of combinations of n things taking r at a time. Therefore, the number of ways in which r successes can occur in n trials is equal to the number of ways of choosing r trials (for successes) out of total n trials *i.e.,* it is ${}^nC_r$. Therefore, there are ${}^nC_r$ ways in which we get r successes and $n - r$ failures and the probability of occurrence of each of these ways is $p^r q^{n-r}$. Hence the probability of r successes in n trials in any order is

$$P(x = r) = p^r q^{n-r} + p^r q^{n-r} + \text{ ...... } {}^nC_r \text{ terms} \qquad \text{(By addition theorem)}$$

or $\quad \mathbf{P(x = r) = {}^nC_r P^r q^{n-r}, 0 \le r \le n.}$

This is called the **binomial probability function.** The corresponding **binomial distribution** is

x	0	1	2 .... n
$P(x)$	${}^nC_0p^0q^n$	${}^nC_1p^1q^{n-1}$	${}^nC_2p^2q^{n-2}$ .... ${}^nC_np^nq^0$

The probabilities of 0 success, 1 success, 2 successes, ..., n successes are respectively the 1st, 2nd, 3rd, ..., $(n + 1)$th terms in binomial expansion of $(q + p)^n$. This is why, it is called **binomial distribution.**

17.5. BINOMIAL FREQUENCY DISTRIBUTION *(P.T.U., M.B.A. Dec. 2003, May 2004)*

If a random experiment, satisfying the requirements of Binomial distribution, is repeated N times, then the expected frequency of getting $r (0 \le r \le n)$ successes is given by

$$\mathbf{N.\ P(x = r) = N.\ ^nC_r\ p^r q^{n-r},\ 0 \le r \le n.}$$

The *frequencies* of getting 0 success, 1 success, 2 successes, ..., n successes are respectively the 1st, 2nd, 3rd, ..., $(n + 1)$th terms in the expansion of $N(q + p)^n$.

17.6. HISTOGRAM OF BINOMIAL DISTRIBUTION

We know the method of drawing histogram of a frequency distribution. The method of drawing histogram of a binomial distribution is analogous to the procedure of drawing histogram of a frequency distribution. In case of a binomial distribution, we mark all the values of the random variable on the horizontal axis and their respective probabilities on the vertical axis. Rectangles of uniform width are constructed with values of the variable at centre and heights equal to their corresponding probabilities.

17.7. WORKING RULES FOR SOLVING PROBLEMS

I. Make sure that the trials in the random experiment are independent and each trial result in either 'success' or 'failure'.

II. Define the binomial variable and find the values of n and p from the given data. Also find q by using : $q = 1 - p$.

III. Put the values of n, p and q in the formula :

$$P(r \text{ successes}) = {}^nC_r\, p^r q^{n-r},\ r = 0, 1, 2, \ldots\ldots, n \qquad \ldots(1)$$

IV. Express the event, whose probability is desired, in terms of values of the binomial variable x. Use (1) to find the required probability.

ILLUSTRATIVE EXAMPLES

Example 1. *An unbiased coin is tossed 10 times. Find, by using binomial distribution, the probability of getting at least 3 heads.*

Sol. Let p be the probability of success, *i.e.*, of getting head in the toss of the coin.

$$\therefore \quad n = 10,\quad p = \frac{1}{2} \quad \text{and} \quad q = 1 - p = 1 - \frac{1}{2} = \frac{1}{2}$$

Let x be the binomial variable, "*no. of successes*".

By **Binomial distribution,** $P(x = r) = {}^nC_r\, p^r q^{n-r},\ 0 \le r \le n.$

$$\therefore \qquad P(x = r) = {}^{10}C_r \left(\frac{1}{2}\right)^r \left(\frac{1}{2}\right)^{10-r} = {}^{10}C_r \left(\frac{1}{2}\right)^{10} = {}^{10}C_r \frac{1}{1024},\ 0 \le r \le 10.$$

Now, $P(\text{at least 3 heads}) = P(x \ge 3) = 1 - P(x < 3)$

$$= 1 - [P(x = 0 \text{ or } x = 1 \text{ or } x = 2)]$$

$$= 1 - [P(x = 0) + P(x = 1) + P(x = 2)]$$

$$= 1 - \left[{}^{10}C_0 \frac{1}{1024} + {}^{10}C_1 \frac{1}{1024} + {}^{10}C_2 \frac{1}{1024}\right]$$

$$= 1 - \frac{1}{1024}\,[{}^{10}C_0 + {}^{10}C_1 + {}^{10}C_2]$$

$$= 1 - \frac{1}{1024}\,[1 + 10 + 45] = \frac{1024 - 56}{1024} = \frac{968}{1024} = \frac{121}{128}.$$

Example 2. *An unbiased coin is tossed six times. Find the probability of obtaining :*

(i) exactly 4 heads *(ii) less than 3 heads*

(iii) more than 4 heads *(iv) more than 4 heads and less than 6 heads*

(v) more than 6 heads *(vi) at least 4 heads*

(vii) at most 4 heads *(viii) 2 heads*

(ix) at least 2 heads.

Sol. Let p be the probability of success, *i.e.*, of getting head in the toss of the coin.

$$\therefore \quad n = 6, \quad p = \frac{1}{2} \quad \text{and} \quad q = 1 - p = 1 - \frac{1}{2} = \frac{1}{2}$$

Let x be the binomial variable, "*no. of successes*".

By **Binomial distribution,** $P(x = r) = {}^nC_r\, p^r q^{n-r},\ 0 \le r \le n.$

$$\therefore \qquad P(x = r) = {}^6C_r \left(\frac{1}{2}\right)^r \left(\frac{1}{2}\right)^{6-r} = {}^6C_r \left(\frac{1}{2}\right)^6 = {}^6C_r\, \frac{1}{64},\ 0 \le r \le 6.$$

(i) P(exactly 4 heads) $= P(x = 4) = {}^6C_4\, \frac{1}{64} = \frac{15}{64}.$

(ii) P(less than 3 heads) $= P(x < 3) = P(x = 0 \text{ or } 1 \text{ or } 2)$

$$= P(x = 0) + P(x = 1) + P(x = 2)$$

$$= {}^6C_0\, \frac{1}{64} + {}^6C_1\, \frac{1}{64} + {}^6C_2\, \frac{1}{64} = (1 + 6 + 15)\, \frac{1}{64} = \frac{22}{64} = \frac{11}{32}.$$

(iii) P(more than 4 heads) $= P(x > 4) = P(x = 5 \text{ or } 6) = P(x = 5) + P(x = 6)$

$$= {}^6C_5\, \frac{1}{64} + {}^6C_6\, \frac{1}{64} = (6 + 1)\, \frac{1}{64} = \frac{7}{64}.$$

(iv) P(more than 4 heads and less than 6 heads)

$$= P\,(4 < x < 6) = P(x = 5) = {}^6C_5\, \frac{1}{64} = \frac{6}{64} = \frac{3}{32}.$$

(v) P(more than 6 heads) $= P(x > 6) = 0.$ ($\because$ The event is impossible)

(vi) P(at least 4 heads) $= P(x \ge 4)$

$$= P(x = 4 \text{ or } 5 \text{ or } 6) = P(x = 4) + P(x = 5) + P(x = 6)$$

$$= {}^6C_4\, \frac{1}{64} + {}^6C_5\, \frac{1}{64} + {}^6C_6\, \frac{1}{64} = (15 + 6 + 1)\, \frac{1}{64} = \frac{22}{64} = \frac{11}{32}.$$

(vii) P(at most 4 heads) $= P(x \le 4)$

$$= P(x = 0 \text{ or } 1 \text{ or } 2 \text{ or } 3 \text{ or } 4)$$

$$= P(x = 0) + P(x = 1) + P(x = 2) + P(x = 3) + P(x = 4)$$

$$= {}^6C_0\, \frac{1}{64} + {}^6C_1\, \frac{1}{64} + {}^6C_2\, \frac{1}{64} + {}^6C_3\, \frac{1}{64} + {}^6C_4\, \frac{1}{64}$$

$$= (1 + 6 + 15 + 20 + 15)\, \frac{1}{64} = \frac{57}{64}.$$

Alternative method

P(at most 4 heads) = $P(x \le 4) = 1 - P(x > 4)$

$$= 1 - P(x = 5 \text{ or } 6) = 1 - [P(x = 5) + P(x = 6)]$$

$$= 1 - \left[{}^6C_5 \frac{1}{64} + {}^6C_6 \frac{1}{64}\right] = 1 - (6 + 1)\frac{1}{64} = 1 - \frac{7}{64} = \frac{57}{64}.$$

(*viii*) P(2 heads) = $P(x = 2) = {}^6C_2 \frac{1}{64} = \frac{15}{64}$.

(*ix*) P(at least 2 heads) = $P(x \ge 2)$

$$= 1 - P(x < 2) = 1 - P(x = 0 \text{ or } 1) = 1 - [P(x = 0) + P(x = 1)]$$

$$= 1 - \left[{}^6C_0 \frac{1}{64} + {}^6C_1 \frac{1}{64}\right] = 1 - \left[\frac{1}{64} + \frac{6}{64}\right] = \frac{57}{64}.$$

Example 3. *A coin is tossed 7 times. What is the probability that head appears an odd number of times.*

Sol. Let p be the probability of success, *i.e.,* of getting a head.

$$\therefore n = 7, \quad p = \frac{1}{2} \quad \text{and} \quad q = 1 - p = 1 - \frac{1}{2} = \frac{1}{2}$$

Let x be the Binomial variable "*no. of successes*".

By **Binomial distribution,** $P(x = r) = {}^nC_r\, p^r q^{n-r}, 0 \le r \le n.$

$$\therefore \quad P(x = r) = {}^7C_r \left(\frac{1}{2}\right)^r \left(\frac{1}{2}\right)^{7-r} = {}^7C_r \left(\frac{1}{2}\right)^7 = {}^7C_r \left(\frac{1}{128}\right), 0 \le r \le 7.$$

Required probability = P(head appearing an odd number of times)

$= P(x = 1 \text{ or } 3 \text{ or } 5 \text{ or } 7) = P(x = 1) + P(x = 3) + P(x = 5) + P(x = 7)$

$$= {}^7C_1\left(\frac{1}{128}\right) + {}^7C_3\left(\frac{1}{128}\right) + {}^7C_5\left(\frac{1}{128}\right) + {}^7C_7\left(\frac{1}{128}\right) = (7 + 35 + 21 + 1)\left(\frac{1}{128}\right) = \frac{64}{128} = \frac{1}{2}.$$

Example 4. *Draw a histogram for the binomial probability distribution of the number of heads in 5 tosses of coin.*

Sol. Let p be the probability of success, *i.e.,* of getting a head.

$$\therefore \quad n = 5, \quad p = \frac{1}{2} \quad \text{and} \quad q = 1 - p = 1 - \frac{1}{2} = \frac{1}{2}.$$

Let x be the Bionomial variable "no. of successes".

$$\therefore \quad x = 0, 1, 2, \ldots\ldots, 5.$$

By **Binomial distribution,**

$$P(x = r) = {}^nC_r\, p^r q^{n-r}, 0 \le r \le n.$$

$$\therefore \quad P(x = r) = {}^5C_r \left(\frac{1}{2}\right)^r \left(\frac{1}{2}\right)^{5-r} = {}^5C_r \left(\frac{1}{2}\right)^5 = {}^5C_r \left(\frac{1}{32}\right), 0 \le r \le 5.$$

$$\therefore \quad P(x = 0) = {}^5C_0 \left(\frac{1}{32}\right) = \frac{1}{32}, \qquad P(x = 1) = {}^5C_1 \left(\frac{1}{32}\right) = \frac{5}{32}$$

$$P(x=2) = {}^5C_2\left(\frac{1}{32}\right) = \frac{10}{32}, \qquad P(x=3) = {}^5C_3\left(\frac{1}{32}\right) = \frac{10}{32}$$

$$P(x=4) = {}^5C_4\left(\frac{1}{32}\right) = \frac{5}{32}, \qquad P(x=5) = {}^5C_5\left(\frac{1}{32}\right) = \frac{1}{32}.$$

∴ The required probability distribution is

x	0	1	2	3	4	5
$P(x)$	$\frac{1}{32}$	$\frac{5}{32}$	$\frac{10}{32}$	$\frac{10}{32}$	$\frac{5}{32}$	$\frac{1}{32}$

The histogram of the Binomial Probability Distribution is shown in the figure :

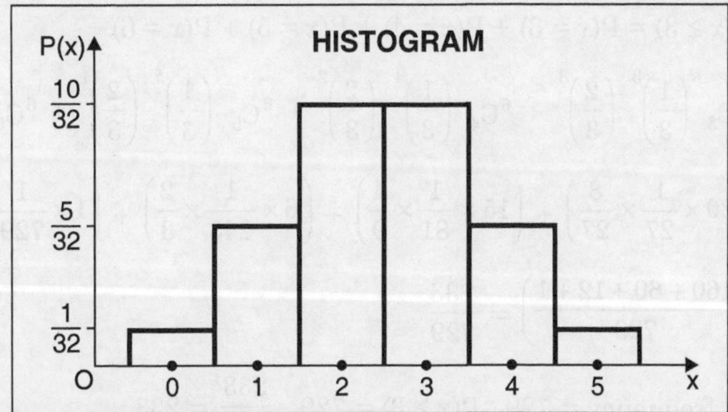

Example 5. *A die is thrown 6 times. If "getting an odd number" is a "success" What is the probability of :*

(i) 5 successes ? *(ii) at least 5 successes ?* *(iii) at most 5 successes ?*

Sol. Let p be the probability of success, *i.e.*, of getting an odd number.

$$\therefore \quad n = 6, \quad p = \frac{n\{1,3,5\}}{n\{1,2,3,4,5,6\}} = \frac{3}{6} = \frac{1}{2} \quad \text{and} \quad q = 1 - p = 1 - \frac{1}{2} = \frac{1}{2}.$$

Let x be the binomial variable "*no. of successes*".

∴ By **Binomial distribution,** $P(x = r) = {}^nC_r\, p^r q^{n-r},\ 0 \le r \le n.$

$$\therefore \quad P(x=r) = {}^6C_r\left(\frac{1}{2}\right)^r\left(\frac{1}{2}\right)^{6-r} = {}^6C_r\left(\frac{1}{2}\right)^6 = {}^6C_r\left(\frac{1}{64}\right),\ 0 \le r \le 6$$

(*i*) $P(\text{5 successes}) = P(x=5) = {}^6C_5\left(\frac{1}{64}\right) = 6 \times \frac{1}{64} = \frac{3}{32}.$

(*ii*) $P(\text{at least 5 successes}) = P(x \ge 5) = P(x=5) + P(x=6)$

$$= {}^6C_5\left(\frac{1}{64}\right) + {}^6C_6\left(\frac{1}{64}\right) = (6+1)\left(\frac{1}{64}\right) = \frac{7}{64}.$$

(*iii*) $P(\text{at most 5 successes}) = P(x \le 5) = 1 - P(x > 5) = 1 - P(x=6)$

$$= 1 - {}^6C_6\left(\frac{1}{64}\right) = 1 - \left(1 \times \frac{1}{64}\right) = \frac{63}{64}.$$

Example 6. *Six dice are thrown 729 times. How many times do you expect at least 3 dice to throw a 5 or 6 ?* (P.T.U., M.B.A. Sept. 1999)

Sol. Let p be the probability of success *i.e.*, of throwing a 5 or 6.

$$\therefore \quad n = 6, \quad p = \frac{2}{6} = \frac{1}{3} \text{ and } q = 1 - p = 1 - \frac{1}{3} = \frac{2}{3}.$$

Let x be the binomial variable "*no. of successes*".

By **Binomial distribution,** $P(x = r) = {}^nC_r\, p^r q^{n-r},\ 0 \le r \le n.$

$$\therefore \qquad P(x = r) = {}^6C_r \left(\frac{1}{3}\right)^r \left(\frac{2}{3}\right)^{6-r},\ 0 \le r \le 6.$$

P(at least 3 dice to throw a 5 or 6)

$$= P(x \ge 3) = P(x = 3) + P(x = 4) + P(x = 5) + P(x = 6)$$

$$= {}^6C_3 \left(\frac{1}{3}\right)^3 \left(\frac{2}{3}\right)^3 + {}^6C_4 \left(\frac{1}{3}\right)^4 \left(\frac{2}{3}\right)^2 + {}^6C_5 \left(\frac{1}{3}\right)^5 \left(\frac{2}{3}\right)^1 + {}^6C_6 \left(\frac{1}{3}\right)^6 \left(\frac{2}{3}\right)^0$$

$$= \left(20 \times \frac{1}{27} \times \frac{8}{27}\right) + \left(15 \times \frac{1}{81} \times \frac{4}{9}\right) + \left(6 \times \frac{1}{243} \times \frac{2}{3}\right) + \left(1 \times \frac{1}{729} \times 1\right)$$

$$= \left(\frac{160 + 60 + 12 + 1}{729}\right) = \frac{233}{729}$$

$$\therefore \quad \text{Required frequency} = 729 \,.\, P(x \ge 3) = 729 \,.\, \frac{233}{729} = 233.$$

Remark. In the above example, the experiment of throwing 6 dice simultaneously is considered as the experiment of throwing a die 6 times successively.

Example 7. *Five men in a group of 20 are graduates. If 3 men are picked out of 20 at random, then what is the probability that (i) all are graduates (ii) at least one is graduate.* (P.T.U. M.B.A. Dec. 2005)

Sol. Let p = The probability that a man is graduate $= \frac{5}{20} = \frac{1}{4}$

$$q = 1 - p = 1 - \frac{1}{4} = \frac{3}{4}. \qquad \text{Also } n = 3$$

Using Binomial distribution,

$$P(X = r) = {}^nC_r\, q^{n-r} p^r,\ 0 \le r \le n$$

(*i*) Required probability = P(all are graduates) = P(X = 3)

$$= {}^3C_3 \left(\frac{3}{4}\right)^{3-3} \left(\frac{1}{4}\right)^3 = 1 \times 1 \times \frac{1}{4^3} = \frac{1}{64}$$

(*ii*) Required probability = P(at least one is graduate) = 1 – P(none is graduate)

$$= 1 - P(X = 0) = 1 - {}^3C_0 \left(\frac{3}{4}\right)^{3-0} \left(\frac{1}{4}\right)^0$$

$$= 1 - \frac{3^3}{4^3} = \frac{64-27}{64} = \frac{37}{64}.$$

Example 8. *In a hurdle race, a player has to cross 10 hurdles. The probability that he will clear each hurdle is 5/6. What is the probability that he will knock down fewer than 2 hurdles ?*

Sol. Let p be the probability of success, *i.e.,* of knocking down a hurdle.

$$\therefore \quad n = 10, \quad p = 1 - \frac{5}{6} = \frac{1}{6} \quad \text{and} \quad q = 1 - p = 1 - \frac{1}{6} = \frac{5}{6}.$$

Let x be the binomial variable "*no. of successes*".

By **Binomial distribution,** $\quad P(x = r) = {}^nC_r\, p^r q^{n-r},\ 0 \le r \le n.$

$$\therefore \qquad P(x = r) = {}^{10}C_r \left(\frac{1}{6}\right)^r \left(\frac{5}{6}\right)^{10-r},\ 0 \le r \le 10.$$

Now, P(knocking down fewer than 2 hurdles)

$$= P(x < 2) = P(x = 0) + P(x = 1) = {}^{10}C_0 \left(\frac{1}{6}\right)^0 \left(\frac{5}{6}\right)^{10} + {}^{10}C_1 \left(\frac{1}{6}\right)^1 \left(\frac{5}{6}\right)^9$$

$$= \left[1 \times 1 \times \left(\frac{5}{6}\right)^{10}\right] + \left[10 \times \frac{1}{6} \times \left(\frac{5}{6}\right)^9\right] = \left(\frac{5}{6}\right)^9 \left[\frac{5}{6} + \frac{10}{6}\right] = \left(\frac{5}{6}\right)^9 \left(\frac{5}{2}\right).$$

Example 9. *The probability of a man hitting a target is 1/4. He fires 7 times. What is the probability of his hitting the target at least twice ?*

Sol. Let p be the probability of success, *i.e.,* of hitting the target.

$$\therefore \quad n = 7, \quad p = \frac{1}{4} \quad \text{and} \quad q = 1 - p = 1 - \frac{1}{4} = \frac{3}{4}.$$

Let x be the binomial variable "*no. of successes*".

By **Binomial distribution,** $P(x = r) = {}^nC_r\, p^r q^{n-r},\ 0 \le r \le n.$

$$\therefore \qquad P(x = r) = {}^7C_r \left(\frac{1}{4}\right)^r \left(\frac{3}{4}\right)^{7-r},\ 0 \le r \le 7.$$

Now, P(hitting at least twice) = $P(x \ge 2)$

$$= 1 - P(x < 2) = 1 - [P(x = 0) + P(x = 1)]$$

$$= 1 - \left[{}^7C_0 \left(\frac{1}{4}\right)^0 \left(\frac{3}{4}\right)^7 + {}^7C_1 \left(\frac{1}{4}\right)^1 \left(\frac{3}{4}\right)^6\right]$$

$$= 1 - \left[1 \times 1 \times \left(\frac{3}{4}\right)^7 + 7 \times \frac{1}{4} \times \left(\frac{3}{4}\right)^6\right] = 1 - \left(\frac{3}{4}\right)^6 \left(\frac{3}{4} + \frac{7}{4}\right) = \frac{4547}{8192}.$$

Example 10. *The probability that a bulb produced by a factory will fuse after 100 days of use is 0.05. Find the probability that out of 5 such bulbs :*

(*i*) *none* (*ii*) *not more than one*

(*iii*) *more than one* (*iv*) *at least one,*

will fuse after 100 days of use.

Sol. Let p be the probability of success, *i.e.*, the bulb being fused after 100 days.

$$\therefore \quad n = 5, \quad p = 0.05 = \frac{5}{100} = \frac{1}{20} \quad \text{and} \quad q = 1 - p = 1 - \frac{1}{20} = \frac{19}{20}.$$

Let x be the binomial variable "*no. of successes*".

By **Binomial distribution,** $\quad P(x = r) = {}^nC_r \, p^r \, q^{n-r}, \; 0 \le r \le n.$

$$\therefore \qquad P(x = r) = {}^5C_r \left(\frac{1}{20}\right)^r \left(\frac{19}{20}\right)^{5-r}, \; 0 \le r \le 5.$$

(*i*) $P(\text{none will fuse}) = P(x = 0) = {}^5C_0 \left(\frac{1}{20}\right)^0 \left(\frac{19}{20}\right)^5 = \left(\frac{19}{20}\right)^5.$

(*ii*) $P(\text{not more than one will fuse}) = P(x \le 1) = P(x = 0) + P(x = 1)$

$$= {}^5C_0 \left(\frac{1}{20}\right)^0 \left(\frac{19}{20}\right)^5 + {}^5C_1 \left(\frac{1}{20}\right)^1 \left(\frac{19}{20}\right)^4 = \left(\frac{19}{20}\right)^4 \left[1 \times 1 \times \frac{19}{20} + 5 \times \frac{1}{20} \times 1\right] = \left(\frac{19}{20}\right)^4 \left(\frac{6}{5}\right).$$

(*iii*) $P(\text{more than one will fuse}) = P(x > 1) = 1 - P(x \le 1) = 1 - \left(\frac{19}{20}\right)^4 \left(\frac{6}{5}\right) = 0.0225$

(Using part (*ii*))

(*iv*) $P(\text{at least one will fuse}) = P(x \ge 1) = 1 - P(x < 1) = 1 - P(x = 0)$

$$= 1 - {}^5C_0 \left(\frac{1}{20}\right)^0 \left(\frac{19}{20}\right)^5 = 1 - \left(\frac{19}{20}\right)^5 = 0.2262.$$

Example 11. *The probability of a man hitting a target is 1/2. How many times must he fire so that the probability of hitting the target at least once is more than 90% ?*

Sol. Let he fires n times. Let p be the probability of success *i.e.*, of hitting the target.

$$\therefore \quad p = \frac{1}{2} \quad \text{and} \quad q = 1 - p = 1 - \frac{1}{2} = \frac{1}{2}.$$

Let x be the binomial variable "*no. of successes*".

$\therefore$ By **Binomial distribution,** $\quad P(x = r) = {}^nC_r \, p^r \, q^{n-r}, \; 0 \le r \le n.$

$$\therefore \qquad P(x = r) = {}^nC_r \left(\frac{1}{2}\right)^r \left(\frac{1}{2}\right)^{n-r} = {}^nC_r \left(\frac{1}{2}\right)^n, \; 0 \le r \le n.$$

$\therefore$ P(hitting target at least once) $= P(x \ge 1)$

$$= 1 - p(x < 1) = 1 - P(x = 0) = 1 - {}^nC_0 \left(\frac{1}{2}\right)^n = 1 - \frac{1}{2^n}.$$

By the given condition, $1 - \frac{1}{2^n} > 90\%$

$$\Rightarrow \quad 1 - \frac{1}{2^n} > \frac{90}{100} \quad \Rightarrow \quad \frac{1}{2^n} < 1 - \frac{9}{10} \quad \Rightarrow \quad \frac{1}{2^n} < \frac{1}{10} \quad \Rightarrow \quad 2^n > 10.$$

Now, $2^1 = 2 \not> 10,\ 2^2 = 4 \not> 10,\ 2^3 = 8 \not> 10,\ 2^4 = 16 > 10.$

$\therefore$ The least value of $n = 4$.

Example 12. *A bag contains 25 items of which 5 are defective. A random sample of two is drawn (without replacement). What is the probability that (i) of both being good (ii) of both being bad (iii) at least one being good.* (P.T.U. M.B.A. May. 2003)

Sol. Let p = The probability of getting a success *i.e.*, the probability of having a defective item.

Given, $$p = \frac{5}{25} = \frac{1}{5} = 0.2$$

$$q = 1 - p = 1 - 0.2 = 0.8$$

Let x be a random variable following the Binomial distribution, then

$$P(X = r) = {}^nC_r\, q^{n-r}\, p^r,\ 0 \le r \le n$$

(*i*) Required probability = P(both items are good)

$= 1 - $ P(None is good) $= 1 - $ P(all items are defective)

$= 1 - P(x = 2) = 1 - {}^2C_2\,(0.8)^0\,(0.2)^2$

$= 1 - 0.04 = 0.96$

(*ii*) Required probability = P(both items are bad)

$= P(X = 2) = {}^2C_2\,(0.8)^0\,(0.2)^2$

$= 0.04$

(*iii*) Required probability = P(at least one item is good)

$= 1 - $ P(at most one item is bad)

$= 1 - P(X \le 1)$

$= 1 - (P(X = 0) + P(X = 1))$

$= 1 - P(X = 0) - P(X = 1)$

$= 1 - {}^2C_0\,(0.8)^2\,(0.2)^0 - {}^2C_1\,(0.8)^1\,(0.2)^1$

$= 1 - 0.64 - 2 \times 0.8 \times 0.2$

$= 1 - 0.64 - 0.32$

$= 1 - 0.96 = 0.04.$

TEST YOUR KNOWLEDGE 17.1

1. An unbiased coin is tossed 32 times. Find the probability of obtaining 2 heads.
2. An unbiased coin is tossed 8 times. Find by using binomial distribution, the probability of getting at least 3 heads.
3. An unbiased coin is tossed 6 times. Find using binomial distribution, the probability of getting at least 5 heads.

4. An unbiased coin is tossed 8 times. Find the probability of obtaining (*i*) exactly 2 heads (*ii*) more than 2 heads (*iii*) all heads (*iv*) more than 5 heads.

5. A pair of dice is thrown 6 times. If getting a total of 7 is considered as a success, what is the probability of getting at least 4 successes ?

6. A pair of dice is thrown 10 times. If getting a doublet is considered a success, find the probability of getting 4 successes.

7. 5 dice are thrown simultaneously. If the occurrence of an even number in a single die is considered a success, find the probability of getting at most 3 successes.

8. A box contains 100 tickets each bearing one of the numbers from 1 to 100. If 5 tickets are drawn successively with replacement from the box, find the probability that all the tickets bear number divisible by 10.

9. If the chance that any of 5 telephone lines is busy at any instance is 0.01, what is the probability that all the lines are busy ? What is the probability that more than 3 lines are busy ?

10. Assume that on an average one telephone number out of 15 called between 2 P.M. and 3 P.M. on week days is busy. What is the probability that if six randomly selected telephone numbers are called, at least three of them will be busy ?

11. A bag contains 10 balls each marked with one of the digits 0 to 9. If four balls are drawn successively with replacement from the bag, what is the probability that none is marked with the digit '0' ?

12. In a box containing 100 bulbs, 10 are defective. What is the probability that out of a sample of 5 bulbs

(*i*) none is defective ? (*ii*) exactly two are defective ?

13. A policeman fires 6 bullets on a dacoit. The probability that the dacoit will be killed by a bullet is 0.6. What is the probability that the dacoit is still alive ?

14. If on an average 1 vessel in every 10 is wrecked, find the probability that out of 5 vessel expected to arrive, at least 4 will arrive safely.

15. The probability that a man hits a target, when he fires is 1/5. If he fires 10 rounds, what is the probability of his hitting the target at least twice ?

16. A student is given a test with 8 items of true-false type. If he gets 6 or more items correct, he is declared pass. Given that he guesses the answer to each item, compute the probability that he will pass in the test.

17. Assume that the probability that a bomb dropped from an aeroplane will strike a certain target is 0.2. If 6 bombs are dropped, find the probability that :

(*i*) exactly 2 will strike the target (*ii*) at least 2 will strike the target.

Answers

1. $\frac{496}{2^{32}}$ **2.** $\frac{219}{256}$ **3.** $\frac{7}{64}$ **4.** (*i*) $\frac{7}{64}$ (*ii*) $\frac{219}{256}$ (*iii*) $\frac{1}{256}$ (*iv*) $\frac{37}{256}$

5. $\frac{203}{23328}$ **6.** $\frac{35}{216}\left(\frac{5}{6}\right)^6$ **7.** $\frac{13}{16}$ **8.** $\left(\frac{1}{10}\right)^5$

9. $\left(\frac{1}{100}\right)^5, 496\left(\frac{1}{100}\right)^5$ **10.** $\frac{57906}{11390625}$ **11.** 0.6561

12. (*i*) 0.59049 (*ii*) 0.0729 **13.** 0.0041 **14.** 0.9185 **15.** 0.6242

16. 37/256 **17.** (*i*) 0.2458 (*ii*) 0.3446.

Hints

9. P(all lines are busy) $= {}^5C_5\left(\frac{1}{100}\right)^5\left(\frac{99}{100}\right)^0$

P(more than 3 lines are busy) $= {}^5C_4\left(\frac{1}{100}\right)^4\left(\frac{99}{100}\right)^1 + {}^5C_5\left(\frac{1}{100}\right)^5\left(\frac{99}{100}\right)^0$

14. P(at least 4 vessels arrive safely) $= {}^5C_4\left(\frac{9}{10}\right)^4\left(\frac{1}{10}\right)^1 + {}^5C_5\left(\frac{9}{10}\right)^5\left(\frac{1}{10}\right)^0$

15. P(hitting the target at least twice) $= 1 - \left[{}^{10}C_0\left(\frac{1}{5}\right)^0\left(\frac{4}{5}\right)^{10} + {}^{10}C_1\left(\frac{1}{5}\right)^1\left(\frac{4}{5}\right)^9\right]$

16. P(student is pass) $= {}^8C_6\left(\frac{1}{2}\right)^6\left(\frac{1}{2}\right)^2 + {}^8C_7\left(\frac{1}{2}\right)^7\left(\frac{1}{2}\right)^1 + {}^8C_8\left(\frac{1}{2}\right)^8\left(\frac{1}{2}\right)^0$

17. (*i*) P(exactly two will strike the target) $= {}^6C_2(0.2)^2\,(0.8)^4$

(*ii*) P(at least two will strike the target) $= P(x \geq 2) = 1 - [P(x = 0) + P(x = 1)]$

$$= 1 - {}^6C_0\,(0.2)^0\,(0.8)^6 - {}^6C_1\,(0.2)^1(0.8)^5.$$

PROPERTIES OF BINOMIAL DISTRIBUTION

17.8. SHAPE OF BINOMIAL DISTRIBUTION

The shape of the binomial distribution depends upon the probability of success (p) and the number of trials in the experiment. If $p = q = \frac{1}{2}$, then the distribution will be symmetrical for every value of n. If $p \neq q$, then the distribution would be asymmetrical, *i.e.*, skewed. The magnitude of skewness varies as the difference between p and q.

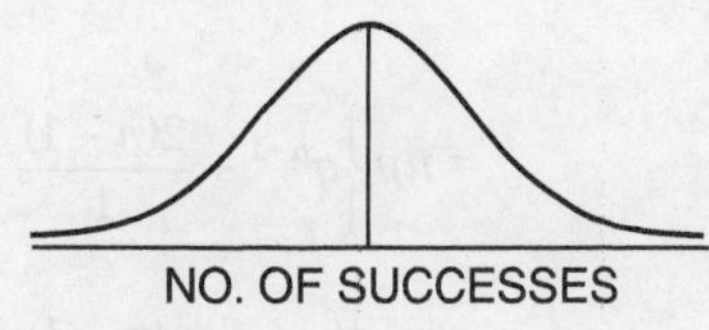

The probabilities in binomial distribution depends upon n and p. These are called the **parameters** of the distribution.

17.9. LIMITING CASE OF BINOMIAL DISTRIBUTION (*P.T.U., M.B.A. May 2002*)

As number of trials (n) in the binomial distribution increases, the number of successes also increases. If neither p nor q is very small, then as n approaches infinity, the skewness in the distribution disappears and it becomes continuous. Such a continuous, bell shaped distribution is called *normal distribution*. Thus, the normal distribution is limiting case of binomial distribution as n approaches infinity.

17.10. MEAN OF BINOMIAL DISTRIBUTION

Let x be a binomial variable and $P(x = r) = {}^nC_r p^r q^{n-r}$, $0 \leq r \leq n$.

Here n is the number of trials and p, the probability of success in a trial.

The *mean* of x is the average number of successes.

$$\therefore \quad \text{Mean,} \quad \mu = \sum_{r=0}^{n} r\,.P(x = r) = \sum_{r=0}^{n} r\,.{}^nC_r p^r q^{n-r}$$

$$= 0\,.\,{}^nC_0 p^0 q^n + 1.{}^nC_1 p^1 q^{n-1} + 2.{}^nC_2 p^2 q^{n-2} + \ldots.. + n.{}^nC_n p^n\,.\,q^0$$

$$= 0 + n \,.\, pq^{n-1} + \frac{n(n-1)}{1.2} p^2 q^{n-2} + \dots\dots + n.1.p^n$$

$$= np \left\{ q^{n-1} + \frac{n-1}{1} pq^{n-2} + \dots\dots + p^{n-1} \right\}$$

$$= np \{ {}^{n-1}C_0 \; p^0 q^{n-1} + {}^{n-1}C_1 \; p^1 q^{n-2} + \dots + {}^{n-1}C_{n-1} \; p^{n-1} q^0 \}$$

$$= np(q+p)^{n-1} = np\,(1)^{n-1} = np.$$

∴ **Mean (μ) of x = np.**

17.11. VARIANCE AND S.D. OF BINOMIAL DISTRIBUTION

Let x be a binomial variable and $P(x = r) = {}^nC_r p^r q^{n-r}, \; 0 \le r \le n$.

Here n is the number of trials and p, the probability of success in a trial.

The variance and standard deviation of x measures the dispersion of the binomial distribution and are given by

$$\text{Variance} = \sum_{r=0}^{n} r^2 . P(x=r) - \mu^2 \quad \text{and} \quad \text{S.D.} = \sqrt{\sum_{r=0}^{n} r^2 . P(x=r) - \mu^2} \, .$$

Now, $\displaystyle\sum_{r=0}^{n} r^2 . P(x=r) = \sum_{r=0}^{n} r^2 . {}^nC_r \, p^r q^{n-r}$

$$= 0.{}^nC_0 \, p^0 q^n + 1^2.{}^nC_1 \, p^1 q^{n-1} + 2^2.{}^nC_2 \, p^2 q^{n-2} + \; 3^2.{}^nC_3 \, p^n q^{n-3} + \dots\dots + n^2 \,.\; {}^nC_n \, p^n q^0$$

$$= 0 + 1 \,.\, \frac{n}{1} pq^{n-1} + 2^2 . \frac{n(n-1)}{1.2} p^2 q^{n-2} + \frac{3^2 . n(n-1)(n-2)}{1.2.3} p^3 q^{n-3} + \dots\dots + n^2 \,.\, 1 \,.\, p^n \,.\, 1$$

$$= np \left\{ q^{n-1} + \frac{2(n-1)}{1} pq^{n-2} + \frac{3(n-1)(n-2)}{1 \times 2} p^2 q^{n-3} + \dots + np^{n-1} \right\}$$

$$= np \left\{ \left(q^{n-1} + \frac{(n-1)}{1} pq^{n-2} + \frac{(n-1)(n-2)}{1 \times 2} p^2 q^{n-3} + \dots + p^{n-1} \right) + \left(\frac{(n-1)}{1} pq^{n-2} + \frac{2(n-1)(n-2)}{1 \times 2} p^2 q^{n-3} + \dots + (n-1)\, p^{n-1} \right) \right\}$$

$$= np \, \{(q+p)^{n-1} + (n-1)\, p(q^{n-2} + (n-2)\, pq^{n-3} + \dots\dots + p^{n-2})\}$$

$$= np \, \{1 + (n-1)\, p(q+p)^{n-2}\} = np \, \{1 + (n-1)\, p.1\}$$

$$= np \, \{1 + np - p\} = np + n^2p^2 - np^2.$$

$$\therefore \quad \text{Variance} = \sum_{r=0}^{n} r^2 . P(x=r) - \mu^2 = (np + n^2p^2 - np^2) - n^2p^2 = np - np^2 = np(1-p) = \mathbf{npq}.$$

Also, $\quad \text{S.D.} = \sqrt{\textbf{Variance}} = \sqrt{\textbf{npq}}$.

17.12. γ_1 AND γ_2 OF BINOMIAL DISTRIBUTION

The values of γ_1 and γ_2 for the binomial probability function

$$P(x = r) = {}^nC_r \, p^r q^{n-r}, \; 0 \le r \le n$$

are given by $\quad \gamma_1 = \dfrac{\mathbf{q - p}}{\sqrt{\mathbf{npq}}} \quad$ and $\quad \gamma_2 = \dfrac{\mathbf{1 - 6pq}}{\mathbf{npq}}$.

17.13. RECURRENCE FORMULA FOR BINOMIAL DISTRIBUTION

Let x be a binomial variable and $P(x = r) = {}^nC_r p^r q^{n-r}$, $0 \le r \le n$.

For $0 \le k < n$, $\qquad P(k) = {}^nC_k \, p^k \, q^{n-k}$

and $\qquad P(k + 1) = {}^nC_{k+1} \, p^{k+1} \, q^{n-(k+1)}$.

Dividing, we get
$$\frac{P(k+1)}{P(k)} = \frac{{}^nC_{k+1}\, p^{k+1}\, q^{n-k-1}}{{}^nC_k p^k q^{n-k}}$$

$$= \frac{n!}{(k+1)!\,(n-(k+1))!} \cdot \frac{k!\,(n-k)!}{n!} \cdot \frac{p}{q} = \frac{n-k}{k+1} \cdot \frac{p}{q}.$$

$$\therefore \qquad \mathbf{P(k+1) = \frac{n-k}{k+1} \cdot \frac{p}{q}\; P(k) \quad for\; 0 \le k < n.}$$

This is the required **recurrence formula**.

17.14. APPLICATIONS OF BINOMIAL DISTRIBUTION

This distribution is applied to problems concerning :

1. The number of defectives items in a sample.
2. The estimation of reliability of systems.
3. Number of rounds fired from a gun hitting a target.
4. Radar detection.

ILLUSTRATIVE EXAMPLES

Example 1. *Find the expectation of the number of heads in 15 tosses of a coin.*

Sol. Here $n = 15$. Let p be the probability of getting a head in a trial, *i.e.*, in a loss. $\therefore p = \frac{1}{2}$.

Let x be the Binomial variable "*no. of heads*".

$\therefore$ Expectation of $x = E(x) = \text{mean} = np = 15 \times \frac{1}{2} = 7.5$.

Example 2. *Obtain the binomial distribution whose mean is 10 and standard deviation is* $2\sqrt{2}$.

Sol. Let number of trials $= n$ and probability of success $= p$.

$\therefore$ P(r successes) $= {}^nC_r \, p^r \, q^{n-r}$, $0 \le r \le n$.

We have mean $= np = 10$ and S.D. $= \sqrt{npq} = 2\sqrt{2}$.

$$\therefore \qquad \sqrt{10q} = \sqrt{8} \;\Rightarrow\; q = \frac{8}{10} = \frac{4}{5}$$

$$\therefore \qquad p = 1 - q = 1 - \frac{4}{5} = \frac{1}{5}$$

$$\therefore \qquad np = 10 \;\Rightarrow\; n\left(\frac{1}{5}\right) = 10 \;\Rightarrow\; n = 50$$

$\therefore$ **P(r successes)** $= {}^{50}\mathrm{C}_r \left(\frac{1}{5}\right)^r \left(\frac{4}{5}\right)^{50-r}$, $0 \le r \le 50.$

Example 3. *A discrete random variable x has mean score equal to '6' and variance equal to '2'. Assuming that the underlying distribution of x is binomial, what is the probability when* $5 \le x \le 6$.

Sol. We have mean $= np = 6$ ...(1)

and variance $= npq = 2$ ...(2)

(1) and (2) $\Rightarrow$ $6 \times q = 2 \Rightarrow q = \frac{2}{6} = \frac{1}{3}.$

$$\therefore \quad p = 1 - q = 1 - \frac{1}{3} = \frac{2}{3}$$

(1) $\Rightarrow$ $n\left(\frac{2}{3}\right) = 6 \Rightarrow n = 9.$

$\therefore$ P(r successes) $= {}^n\mathrm{C}_r\, p^r q^{n-r}$, $0 \le r \le n$

$$= {}^9\mathrm{C}_r \left(\frac{2}{3}\right)^r \left(\frac{1}{3}\right)^{9-r}, \; 0 \le r \le 9.$$

$\therefore$ $\mathrm{P}(5 \le x \le 6) = \mathrm{P}(x = 5 \text{ or } x = 6) = \mathrm{P}(x = 5) + \mathrm{P}(x = 6)$

$$= {}^9\mathrm{C}_5 \left(\frac{2}{3}\right)^5 \left(\frac{1}{3}\right)^4 + {}^9\mathrm{C}_6 \left(\frac{2}{3}\right)^6 \left(\frac{1}{3}\right)^3 = \frac{1}{3^9}\,[126 \times 32 + 84 \times 64] = \frac{9408}{3^9} = 0.4779.$$

Example 4. *If the sum of the mean and the variance of a binomial distribution of 5 trials is 1.8, then find the binomial distribution.*

Sol. Let the binomial distribution be $\mathrm{P}(x = r) = {}^n\mathrm{C}_r\, p^r q^{n-r}$, $0 \le r \le n$.

$\therefore$ Mean $= np$ and variance $= npq$

By the given condition, $np + npq = 1.8$ and $n = 5$.

$$\Rightarrow \quad 5p + 5p(1 - p) = \frac{9}{5} \quad \Rightarrow \quad 25p^2 - 50p + 9 = 0$$

$$\therefore \quad p = \frac{1}{5} \quad \text{and} \quad q = 1 - p = 1 - \frac{1}{5} = \frac{4}{5}$$

$\therefore$ The binomial distribution is $\mathrm{P}(x = r) = {}^5\mathrm{C}_r \left(\frac{1}{5}\right)^r \left(\frac{4}{5}\right)^{5-r}$, $0 \le r \le 5.$

Example 5. *(a) Can the mean of a binomial distribution be less than the variance ? Bring out the fallacy, if any, in the following statement :*

"The mean of a binomial distribution is 15 and its standard deviation is 5".

(P.T.U., M.B.A. Sep. 1999)

(b) Test the validity of the following statement "The mean of the binomial distribution and the standard deviation is 3".

Sol. (*a*) Let n, p, q be the number of trials, probability of success in a trial, probability of failure in a trial respectively.

$\therefore$ Mean $= np$ and variance $= npq$

We have $q < 1$. Multiplying both sides by positive number np, we get $npq < np$.

$\Rightarrow$ variance < mean

$\therefore$ Mean of a B.D. can never be less than the variance.

Second Part. Let mean $= np = 15$ and S.D. $= \sqrt{npq} = 5$.

Putting the values of np, we get, $\sqrt{15q} = 5$.

$$\Rightarrow \quad 15q = 25 \Rightarrow q = \frac{25}{15} = \frac{5}{3} > 1, \text{ which is impossible.}$$

$\therefore$ The given statement is false.

(*b*) Let mean $= np = 3$ ...(1)

and S.D. $= \sqrt{npq} = 3$ ...(2)

Using (1) in (2), we get $\sqrt{3q} = 3$

$$\Rightarrow \quad 3q = 9$$

$$\Rightarrow \quad q = 3 > 1$$

which is impossible.

Hence the given statement is false.

Example 6. *(a) The sum of mean and variance of a binomial variance is 15 and the sum of their squares is 117. Find the distribution.*

(b) The sum and the product of the mean and variance of a binomial distribution are 24 and 128 respectively. Find the distribution.

(c) If the probability of a defective bulb is 0.1, find the mean and the standard deviation of defective bulbs in a total of 900. (P.T.U., M.B.A. May. 2002)

Sol. (*a*) Let the binomial distribution be $P(x = r) = {}^nC_r\, p^r q^{n-r}, 0 \le r \le n$.

We have mean $= np$ and variance $= npq$.

$\therefore \quad np + npq = 15$ ...(1) and $(np)^2 + (npq)^2 = 117$ ...(2)

(1) $\Rightarrow np(1 + q) = 15$ ...(3) (2) $\Rightarrow n^2p^2(1 + q^2) = 117$ ...(4)

$$\Rightarrow \frac{n^2p^2(1+q^2)}{(np(1+q))^2} = \frac{117}{(15)^2} \Rightarrow \frac{1+q^2}{(1+q)^2} = \frac{117}{225} \Rightarrow \frac{1+q^2}{1+q^2+2q} = \frac{13}{25}$$

$$\Rightarrow 25 + 25q^2 = 13 + 13q^2 + 26q \Rightarrow 6q^2 - 13q + 6 = 0$$

$$\Rightarrow 6q^2 - 9q - 4q + 6 = 0 \Rightarrow 3q(2q - 3) - 2(2q - 3) = 0$$

$$\Rightarrow (3q - 2)(2q - 3) = 0 \Rightarrow q = \frac{2}{3}, \frac{3}{2}.$$

$$\therefore \quad q = \frac{2}{3} \text{ because } q = \frac{3}{2} > 1 \text{ is impossible.}$$

$$\therefore \quad p = 1 - q = 1 - \frac{2}{3} = \frac{1}{3}.$$

Putting $p = \frac{1}{3}, q = \frac{2}{3}$ in (3), we get, $n \cdot \frac{1}{3}\left(1 + \frac{1}{3}\right) = 15$.

$$\Rightarrow \qquad n \cdot \frac{5}{9} = 15 \quad \Rightarrow \quad n = 27.$$

$$\therefore \quad P(x = r) = {}^{27}C_r \left(\frac{1}{3}\right)^r \left(\frac{2}{3}\right)^{27-r}, \; 0 \le r \le 27.$$

(*b*) Let the Binomial distribution be

$$P(X = r) = {}^nC_r \, p^r q^{n-r}, \; 0 \le r \le n$$

Here mean $= np$ and variance $= npq$

$\therefore$ Given, $\quad np + npq = 24$ ...(1)

and $\quad np \,.\, npq = 128$ ...(2)

Squaring (1) and dividing it by (2), we have

$$\frac{(np(1+q))^2}{n^2p^2.q} = \frac{576}{128} \quad \text{or} \quad \frac{n^2p^2\,(1+q)^2}{n^2p^2\,.\,q} = \frac{9}{2}$$

$$\Rightarrow \qquad 2(1 + q)^2 = 9q$$

$$\Rightarrow \qquad 2q^2 + 2 + 4q = 9q$$

$$\Rightarrow \qquad 2q^2 - 5q + 2 = 0$$

$$\Rightarrow \qquad 2q^2 - 4q - q + 2 = 0$$

$$\Rightarrow \qquad 2q(q - 2) - (q - 2) = 0$$

$$\Rightarrow \qquad (q - 2)\,(2q - 1) = 0$$

$$\Rightarrow \qquad q = 2, \frac{1}{2}$$

But $q \ne 2$ $\therefore$ We take $q = \frac{1}{2}$ $\therefore$ $p = 1 - \frac{1}{2} = \frac{1}{2}$

Also from (1), $np(1 + q) = 24$

$$\Rightarrow \qquad n \,.\, \frac{1}{2} \cdot \frac{3}{2} = 24$$

$$\Rightarrow \qquad n = 32$$

Hence the required distribution is

$$P(X = r) = {}^{32}C_r \left(\frac{1}{2}\right)^r \left(\frac{1}{2}\right)^{32-r}, \; 0 \le r \le 32.$$

(*c*) Given p = the probability of a bulb being defective = 0.1

$$q = 1 - p = 1 - 0.1 = 0.9, \; n = 900$$

Using Binomial distribution,

$$\text{mean} = np = 900 \times 0.1 = 90$$

$$\text{variance} = npq = 90 \times 0.9 = 81$$

$\therefore$ Standard deviation $= \sqrt{npq} = \sqrt{81} = 9.$

Example 7. *A die is thrown 6 times. What is the probability that there will be (i) no ace (ii) not more than one ace (iii) more than 4 aces ? Find also the mean and the variance of the number of aces (Note that 'ace' means the number 1 (or one dot) on the die).*

Sol. Let p be the probability of success *i.e.*, of getting an ace in the throw of a die.

$$\therefore \quad n = 6, \quad p = \frac{1}{6} \quad \text{and} \quad q = 1 - p = 1 - \frac{1}{6} = \frac{5}{6}.$$

Let x be the Binomial variable "*no. of successes*".

By **Binomial distribution,** $\quad P(x = r) = {}^nC_r\, p^r\, q^{n-r},\ 0 \le r \le n.$

$$\therefore \quad P(x = r) = {}^6C_r \left(\frac{1}{6}\right)^r \left(\frac{5}{6}\right)^{6-r}, \quad 0 \le r \le 6.$$

(*i*) $P(\text{no ace}) = P(x = 0) = {}^6C_0 \left(\frac{1}{6}\right)^0 \left(\frac{5}{6}\right)^6 = 1 \times 1 \times \left(\frac{5}{6}\right)^6 = \left(\frac{5}{6}\right)^6 = 0.3348.$

(*ii*) $P(\text{not more than one ace}) = P(x \le 1) = P(x = 0) + P(x = 1)$

$$= {}^6C_0 \left(\frac{1}{6}\right)^0 \left(\frac{5}{6}\right)^6 + {}^6C_1 \left(\frac{1}{6}\right)^1 \left(\frac{5}{6}\right)^5$$

$$= 1 \times 1 \times \left(\frac{5}{6}\right)^6 + 6 \times \frac{1}{6} \times \left(\frac{5}{6}\right)^5 = \left(\frac{5}{6}\right)^5 \left(\frac{5}{6} + 1\right) = \left(\frac{5}{6}\right)^5 \left(\frac{11}{6}\right) = 0.7367.$$

(*iii*) $P(\text{more than 4 aces}) = P(x > 4) = P(x = 5) + P(x = 6)$

$$= {}^6C_5 \left(\frac{1}{6}\right)^5 \left(\frac{5}{6}\right)^1 + {}^6C_6 \left(\frac{1}{6}\right)^6 \left(\frac{5}{6}\right)^0 = 6 \times \left(\frac{1}{6}\right)^5 \times \frac{5}{6} + 1 \times \left(\frac{1}{6}\right)^6 \times 1$$

$$= \left(\frac{1}{6}\right)^5 \left[5 + \frac{1}{6}\right] = \left(\frac{1}{6}\right)^5 \left(\frac{31}{6}\right) = 31 \left(\frac{1}{6}\right)^6 = 0.0006.$$

Also, mean $= np = 6 \times \frac{1}{6} = \mathbf{1}$ and variance $= npq = 6 \times \frac{1}{6} \times \frac{5}{6} = \frac{5}{6}$.

Example 8. *Calculate P(x successes) for x = 1, 2, 3, 4 and 5, taking n = 5 and p =* $\frac{1}{6}$ *with the help of the recurrence formula of the binomial distribution. Hence, draw a histogram for this distribution.*

Sol. We have $n = 5, \quad p = \frac{1}{6}, \quad q = 1 - p = 1 - \frac{1}{6} = \frac{5}{6}.$

By **Binomial distribution,** $\quad P(x = r) = {}^nC_r\, p^r\, q^{n-r},\ 0 \le r \le n.$

$$\therefore \quad P(x = r) = {}^5C_r \left(\frac{1}{6}\right)^r \left(\frac{5}{6}\right)^{5-r}, \quad 0 \le r \le 5.$$

$$\therefore \quad P(0) = {}^5C_0 \left(\frac{1}{6}\right)^0 \left(\frac{5}{6}\right)^6 = 1 \times 1 \times \left(\frac{5}{6}\right)^5 = \left(\frac{5}{6}\right)^5 = \frac{3125}{7776}.$$

The recurrence formula of binomial distribution is

$$P(k + 1) = \frac{n - k}{k + 1} \cdot \frac{p}{q}\, P(k), \qquad 0 \le k \le n - 1.$$

$\therefore \qquad P(k+1) = \frac{5-k}{k+1} \cdot \frac{(1/6)}{(5/6)} P(k), \qquad 0 \le k \le 5-1$

$\Rightarrow \qquad P(k+1) = \frac{5-k}{k+1} \cdot \frac{1}{5} P(k), \qquad 0 \le k \le 4. \qquad \ldots(1)$

$k = 0$ in (1) implies $P(1) = \frac{5-0}{0+1} \cdot \frac{1}{5} P(0) = P(0) = \frac{3125}{7776} = 0.40.$

$k = 1$ in (1) implies $P(2) = \frac{5-1}{1+1} \cdot \frac{1}{5} P(1) = \frac{2}{5} \times \frac{3125}{7776} = \frac{1250}{7776} = 0.16.$

$k = 2$ in (1) implies $P(3) = \frac{5-2}{2+1} \cdot \frac{1}{5} P(2) = \frac{1}{5} \times \frac{1250}{7776} = \frac{250}{7776} = 0.032.$

$k = 3$ in (1) implies $P(4) = \frac{5-3}{3+1} \cdot \frac{1}{5} P(3) = \frac{1}{10} \times \frac{250}{7776} = \frac{25}{7776} = 0.003.$

$k = 4$ in (1) implies $P(5) = \frac{5-4}{4+1} \cdot \frac{1}{5} P(4) = \frac{1}{25} \times \frac{25}{7776} = \frac{1}{7776} = 0.0001.$

The histogram of the above distribution is shown below :

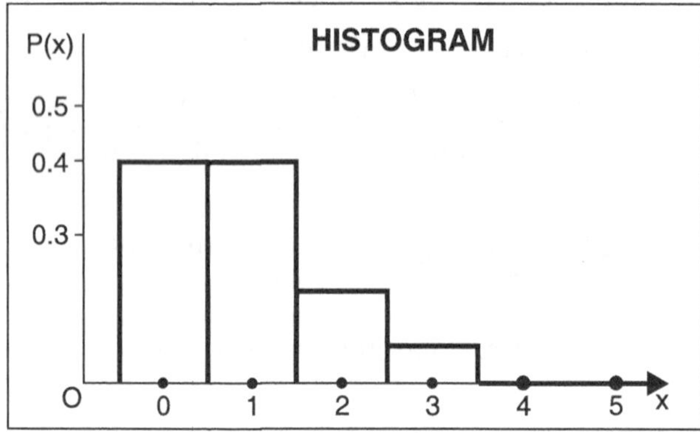

Example 9. *If x follows binomial distribution with mean 4 and variance 2, find :*
$P(|x-4| \le 2)$.

Sol. Let the binomial distribution of x be $P(x = r) = {}^nC_r p^r q^{n-r}, 0 \le r \le n.$

We have mean = 4 and variance = 2.

$\therefore \qquad np = 4 \quad \text{and} \quad npq = 2.$

$\Rightarrow \qquad 4q = 2 \quad \text{or} \quad q = \frac{1}{2}$

$\therefore \qquad p = 1 - q = 1 - \frac{1}{2} = \frac{1}{2}$

Putting $p = \frac{1}{2}$ in $np = 4$, we get, $n\left(\frac{1}{2}\right) = 4$ or $n = 8$.

$\therefore \qquad P(x = r) = {}^8C_r\left(\frac{1}{2}\right)^r\left(\frac{1}{2}\right)^{8-r} = {}^8C_r\left(\frac{1}{2}\right)^8 = {}^8C_r\frac{1}{256}, \quad 0 \le r \le 8.$

Now, $P(|x-4| \le 2) = P(-2 \le x-4 \le 2) = P(-2+4 \le x-4+4 \le 2+4)$

$\because \quad |a| \le b \;\Rightarrow\; -b \le a \le b$

$$= P(2 \le x \le 6) = P(x=2) + P(x=3) + P(x=4) + P(x=5) + P(x=6)$$

$$= {}^8C_2 \frac{1}{256} + {}^8C_3 \frac{1}{256} + {}^8C_4 \frac{1}{256} + {}^8C_5 \frac{1}{256} + {}^8C_6 \frac{1}{256}$$

$$= (28+56+70+56+28)\,\frac{1}{256} = \frac{238}{256} = \frac{119}{128} = 0.929.$$

Example 10. *Evaluate*

(i) $\Sigma(x-\mu)^2 f(x)$

(ii) $\Sigma(x-\mu)^4 f(x)$, *for the binomial distribution.*

Sol. For Binomial distribution

$$f(x) = {}^nC_x\, P^x q^{n-x} \qquad \ldots(1)$$

and

$$\mu = np$$

$$x = 0, 1, 2, \ldots n,\; q = 1-p$$

Consider

$$\mu_r = \sum_{x=0}^{n} (x-\mu)^r f(x) = \sum_{x=0}^{n} (x-np)^r\, {}^nC_x\, p^x q^{n-x} \qquad \ldots(2)$$

Differentiating (1) w.r.t. p, we get

$$\frac{d}{dp}(\mu_r) = \sum_{x=0}^{n} {}^nC_x \left(\frac{d}{dp}(x-np)^r\, p^x (1-p)^{n-x} \right)$$

$$= \sum_{x=0}^{n} {}^nC_x \Big[(x-np)^r \left\{ xp^{x-1}(1-p)^{n-x} - (n-x)(1-p)^{n-x-1}\, p^x \right\}$$

$$+ p^x (1-p)^{n-x}\, r(x-np)^{r-1}(-n) \Big]$$

$$= \sum_{x=0}^{n} {}^nC_x (x-np)^r p^x q^{n-x} \left(\frac{x}{p} - \frac{n-x}{q} \right)$$

$$- nr \sum_{x=0}^{n} {}^nC_x (x-np)^{r-1} p^x q^{n-x} \quad 1p + q = 1$$

$$= \sum_{x=0}^{n} (x-np)^r . f(x) . \frac{(x-np)}{pq} - nr \sum_{x=0}^{n} (x-np)^{r-1} . f(x)$$

| Using (1) and $p + q = 1$

$$= \frac{1}{pq} \sum_{x=0}^{n} (x-np)^{r+1} f(x) - nr \sum_{x=0}^{n} (x-np)^{r-1} f(x)$$

$\Rightarrow \quad \dfrac{d}{dp}(\mu_r) = \dfrac{1}{pq}\mu_{r+1} - nr\,\mu_{r-1}$ | Using (2)

$\Rightarrow \quad \dfrac{1}{pq}\mu_{r+1} = nr\,\mu_{r-1} + \dfrac{d}{dp}\mu_r$

$\Rightarrow \quad \mu_{r+1} = pq\left(nr\,\mu_{r-1} + \dfrac{d}{dp}\mu_r\right)$ ...(3)

(*i*) **Calculation** of $\Sigma(x-\mu)^2 f(x)$

Here $\Sigma(x-\mu)^2 f(x) = \Sigma(x-np)^2 \,.\, {}^nC_x\, p^x q^{n-x} = \mu_2$ | Using (2)

$= pq\left(n\mu_0 + \dfrac{d}{dp}\mu_1\right)$ | Put $r = 1$ in (3)

$= npq$ | $\mu_0 = 1,\ \mu_1 = 0$

(*ii*) **Calculation** of $\Sigma(x-\mu)^4 f(x)$

Here $\Sigma(x-\mu)^4 f(x) = \Sigma(x-np)^4 \,.\, {}^nC_x\, p^x q^{n-x}$

$= \mu_4$ | Using (2)

$= pq\left(3n\,\mu_2 + \dfrac{d}{dp}\mu_3\right)$ ...(4) | Put $r = 3$ in (3)

But from (3), $\mu_3 = pq\left(2n\mu_1 + \dfrac{d}{dp}\mu_2\right)$

$= pq\left(\dfrac{d}{dp}npq\right)$ | $u_1 = 0$

$= pq\dfrac{d}{dp}(np(1-p)) = pqn(p(-1) + 1 - p) = pqn\,(-p + 1 - p)$

$= npq\,(q - p)$ ...(5) | $p + q = 1$

$\therefore$ Using (5) in (4), we have

$\Sigma(x-\mu)^4 f(x) = pq\left(3n\,(npq) + \dfrac{d}{dp}npq\,(q-p)\right)$ | $\mu_2 = npq$

$= pq\left(3n^2\, pq + n\dfrac{d}{dp}[p(1-p)(1-2p)]\right)$

$= pq\left(3n^2\, pq + n\dfrac{d}{dp}(p - 3p^2 + 2p^3)\right)$

$= pq(3n^2\, pq + n(1 - 6p + 6p^2)) = pq(3n^2\, pq + n(1 - 6p(1-p))$

$= pq(3n^2pq + n(1 - 6pq) = npq(3npq + 1 - 6pq)$

$= npq(1 + 3pq(n - 2)$.

Example 11. *The following data are the number of seeds germinating out of 10 on damp filter paper for 80 sets of seeds. Fit a binomial distribution to these data.*

x	*0*	*1*	*2*	*3*	*4*	*5*	*6*	*7*	*8*	*9*	*10*
f	*6*	*20*	*28*	*12*	*8*	*6*	*0*	*0*	*0*	*0*	*0*

Sol. Given $n = 10$, $\mathrm{N} = \sum_{i=0}^{10} f_i = 6 + 20 + 28 + 12 + 8 + 6 = 80$

Also mean $= \dfrac{\sum_{i=0}^{10} f_i x_i}{\sum_{i=0}^{10} f_i} = \dfrac{0 + 20 + 56 + 36 + 32 + 30}{80} = \dfrac{174}{80} = 2.175$

But mean of the binomial distribution $= np = 2.175 \Rightarrow p = \dfrac{2.175}{10} = 0.2175$

$$q = 1 - p = 1 - 0.2175 = 0.7825$$

Hence the binomial distribution to be fitted is

$$= \mathrm{N}\,(q + p)^n = 80\,(0.7825 + 0.2175)^{10}$$
$$= 80.{}^{10}\mathrm{C}_0\,(0.7825)^{10} + 80.{}^{10}\mathrm{C}_1(0.7825)^9(0.2175)^1$$
$$+ 80.{}^{10}\mathrm{C}_2(0.7825)^8(0.2175)^2 + \ldots\ldots + 80.{}^{10}\mathrm{C}_9(0.7825)^1\,(0.2175)^9$$
$$+ 80.{}^{10}\mathrm{C}_{10}(0.2175)^{10}$$
$$= 6.885 + 19.13 + 23.94 + \ldots\ldots + 0.0007 + 0.00002$$

The successive terms in the above expansion give the expected or theoretical frequencies, which are

x	0	1	2	3	4	5	6	7	8	9	10
f	6.9	19.1	24	17.8	8.6	2.9	0.7	0.1	0	0	0

Example 12. *Suppose that a radio tube inserted into a certain type of set has a probability 0.2 of functioning more than 500 hours. If we test 4 tubes, what is the probability that exactly k of these function for more than 500 hours, where k = 0, 1, 2, 3 and 4 ? Also draw a histogram for this distribution.*

Sol. Let p be the probability of success, *i.e.*, a tube will function more than 500 hours.

$\therefore\ n = 4,\ \ p = 0.2 = \dfrac{1}{5}$ and $q = 1 - p = 1 - \dfrac{1}{5} = \dfrac{4}{5}$.

Let x be the binomial variable *"no. of successes"*.

$\therefore$ By **Binomial distribution,** $\mathrm{P}(x = r) = {}^n\mathrm{C}_r\, p^r\, q^{n-r},\ 0 \le r \le n.$

$$\therefore \qquad \mathrm{P}(x = r) = {}^4\mathrm{C}_r \left(\frac{1}{5}\right)^r \left(\frac{4}{5}\right)^{4-r},\ 0 \le r \le 4.$$

$$\therefore \qquad \mathrm{P}(x = 0) = {}^4\mathrm{C}_0 \left(\frac{1}{5}\right)^0 \left(\frac{4}{5}\right)^4 = \left(\frac{4}{5}\right)^4 = 0.4096$$

$$P(x = 1) = {}^4C_1 \left(\frac{1}{5}\right)^1 \left(\frac{4}{5}\right)^3 = 4 \times \frac{1}{5} \times \left(\frac{4}{5}\right)^3 = 0.4096$$

$$P(x = 2) = {}^4C_2 \left(\frac{1}{5}\right)^2 \left(\frac{4}{5}\right)^2 = 6 \times \frac{1}{25} \times \frac{16}{25} = 0.1536$$

$$P(x = 3) = {}^4C_3 \left(\frac{1}{5}\right)^3 \left(\frac{4}{5}\right)^1 = 4 \times \frac{1}{125} \times \frac{4}{5} = 0.0256$$

$$P(x = 4) = {}^4C_4 \left(\frac{1}{5}\right)^4 \left(\frac{4}{5}\right)^0 = 1 \times \frac{1}{625} = 0.0016.$$

The histogram for the probability distribution is shown in the figure :

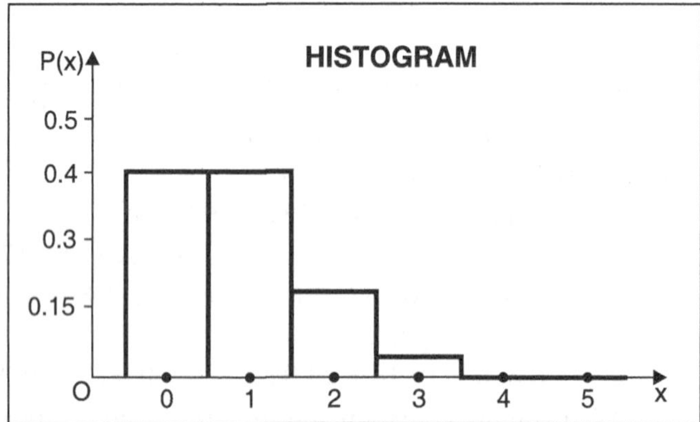

Example 13. *There are 20% chances for a worker of an industry to suffer from an occupational disease. 50 workers were selected at random and examined for the occupational disease. Find the probability that (i) only one worker is found suffering from the disease ; (ii) more than 3 are suffering from the disease ; (iii) none is suffering from the disease.*

Sol. Let p be the probability of success, *i.e.*, a worker is suffering from disease.

$$\therefore\ n = 50,\quad p = \frac{20}{100} = \frac{1}{5} \quad \text{and} \quad q = 1 - p = 1 - \frac{1}{5} = \frac{1}{4}.$$

Let x be the binomial variable, "*no. of successes*".

By **Binomial distribution,** $P(x = r) = {}^nC_r\, p^r q^{n-r},\ 0 \le r \le n.$

$$\therefore \qquad P(x = r) = {}^{50}C_r \left(\frac{1}{5}\right)^r \left(\frac{4}{5}\right)^{50-r},\ 0 \le r \le 50.$$

(*i*) P(one is suffering) $= P(x = 1) = {}^{50}C_1 \left(\frac{1}{5}\right)^1 \left(\frac{4}{5}\right)^{49} = 50 \times \frac{1}{5} \times \left(\frac{4}{5}\right)^{49} = 10\left(\frac{4}{5}\right)^{49}.$

(*ii*) P(more than 3 are suffering) $= P(x > 3) = 1 - P(x \le 3) = 1 - P(x = 0 \text{ or } x = 1 \text{ or } x = 2 \text{ or } x = 3)$

$= 1 - \{P(x = 0) + P(x = 1) + P(x = 2) + P(x = 3)\}$

$$= 1 - \left\{ {}^{50}C_0 \left(\frac{1}{5}\right)^0 \left(\frac{4}{5}\right)^{50} + {}^{50}C_1 \left(\frac{1}{5}\right)^1 \left(\frac{4}{5}\right)^{49} + {}^{50}C_2 \left(\frac{1}{5}\right)^2 \left(\frac{4}{5}\right)^{48} + {}^{50}C_3 \left(\frac{1}{5}\right)^3 \left(\frac{4}{5}\right)^{47} \right\}$$

$$= 1 - \left\{ 1 \times 1 \times \left(\frac{4}{5}\right)^{50} + 50 \times \frac{1}{5} \times \left(\frac{4}{5}\right)^{49} + \frac{50.49}{1.2} \times \frac{1}{5^2} \times \left(\frac{4}{5}\right)^{48} + \frac{50.49.48}{1.2.3} \times \frac{1}{5^3} \times \left(\frac{4}{5}\right)^{47} \right\}$$

$$= 1 - \frac{4^{47}}{5^{50}} \{64 + 50 \times 16 + 1225 \times 4 + 19600 \times 1\} = 1 - \left(\frac{4^{47}}{5^{50}}\right)(25364).$$

(*iii*) $P(\text{None is suffering}) = P(x = 0) = {}^{50}C_0 \left(\frac{1}{4}\right)^0 \left(\frac{4}{5}\right)^{50} = 1 \times 1 \times \left(\frac{4}{5}\right)^{50} = \left(\frac{4}{5}\right)^{50}.$

Example 14. *Assuming that half the population is vegetarian so that the chance of an individual being vegetarian is $\frac{1}{2}$ and assuming that 100 investigators can take samples of 10 individuals to see whether they are vegetarian, how many investigators would you expect to report that three people or less were vegetarian.*

Sol. Let p be the probability of success *i.e.*, an individual being vegetarian.

$\therefore \quad n = 10, \quad p = \frac{1}{2} \quad$ and $\quad q = 1 - p = 1 - \frac{1}{2} = \frac{1}{2}.$

Let x be the Binomial variable "*no. of successes*".

By **Binomial distribution,** $\quad P(x = r) = {}^nC_r\, p^r\, q^{n-r},\ 0 \le r \le n.$

$$\therefore \quad P(x = r) = {}^{10}C_r \left(\frac{1}{2}\right)^r \left(\frac{1}{2}\right)^{10-r} = {}^{10}C_r \left(\frac{1}{2}\right)^{10} = {}^{10}C_r \left(\frac{1}{1024}\right),\ 0 \le r \le 10.$$

$\therefore \quad P(\text{at most 3 vegetarian}) = P(x \le 3) = P(x = 0) + P(x = 1) + P(x = 2) + P(x = 3)$

$$= {}^{10}C_0 \left(\frac{1}{1024}\right) + {}^{10}C_1 \left(\frac{1}{1024}\right) + {}^{10}C_2 \left(\frac{1}{1024}\right) + {}^{10}C_3 \left(\frac{1}{1024}\right)$$

$$= (1 + 10 + 45 + 120)\left(\frac{1}{1024}\right) = \frac{176}{1024}$$

Number of samples, N = 100.

$\therefore$ No. of investigators expected to report at most three vegetarians in their samples

$$= N \,.\, P(x \le 3) = 100 \times \frac{176}{1024} = 17 \text{ (nearly)}.$$

Example 15. *Out of 800 families with 3 children each, how many would you expect to have*

(*i*) *all boy* (P.T.U., M.B.A. May 2001)

(*ii*) *all girls* (P.T.U., M.B.A. May 2001)

(*iii*) *2 boys and 1 girls*

(*iv*) *at least one boy*

(*v*) *at the most 2 girls*

Assume equal probabilities for boys and girls.

Sol. Let p = The probability of getting a boy = $\frac{1}{2}$

q = The probability of getting a girl = $\frac{1}{2}$

$n = 3$

Using Binomial distribution,

$$P(X = r) = {}^nC_r\, q^{n-r} p^r,\ 0 \le r \le n$$

(*i*) Probability of getting all boys

$$= \text{Probability of getting no girls}$$

$$= P(X = 0) = {}^3C_0\, q^3 p^0$$

$$= {}^3C_0 \left(\frac{1}{2}\right)^3 \left(\frac{1}{2}\right)^0 = \frac{1}{8}$$

(*ii*) Probability of getting all girls

$$= P(X = 3) = {}^3C_3\, q^{3-3} p^3 = \left(\frac{1}{2}\right)^3 = \frac{1}{8}$$

(*iii*) Probability of getting 2 boys and 1 girl

$$= {}^3C_2\, q^1 p^2 = 3 \times \frac{1}{2} \times \left(\frac{1}{2}\right)^2 = \frac{3}{8}$$

(*iv*) Probability of getting at least one boy

$$= P(X \ge 1)$$

$$= P(X = 1) + P(X = 2) + P(X = 3)$$

$$= {}^3C_1\, q^2 p + {}^3C_2\, q p^2 + {}^3C_3\, p^3$$

$$= 3 \times \left(\frac{1}{2}\right)^2 \times \left(\frac{1}{2}\right) + 3 \times \left(\frac{1}{2}\right) \times \left(\frac{1}{2}\right)^2 + 1 \times \left(\frac{1}{2}\right)^3$$

$$= \frac{3}{8} + \frac{3}{8} + \frac{1}{8} = \frac{7}{8}$$

(*v*) Probability of getting atmost 2 girls = $P(x \le 2)$

$$= P(X = 0) + P(X = 1) + P(X = 2)$$

$$= {}^3C_0 \left(\frac{1}{2}\right)^3 + {}^3C_1 \left(\frac{1}{2}\right)^2 \left(\frac{1}{2}\right)^1 + {}^3C_2 \left(\frac{1}{2}\right)^1 \left(\frac{1}{2}\right)^2$$

$$= \frac{1}{8} + \frac{3}{8} + \frac{3}{8} = \frac{7}{8}.$$

TEST YOUR KNOWLEDGE 17.2

1. For a binomial distribution with $p = \frac{1}{4}$ and $n = 10$, find mean and variance.
2. The mean and S.D. of a binomial distribution are 20 and 4 respectively, calculate n, p and q.
3. Show that mean of a binomial distribution is always greater than its variance.

4. Find the expected number of boys in a family with 4 children, assuming the sex determination to be equally probable.

5. If the probability of getting a defective bolt is 0.1, find the mean and standard deviation for the distribution of defective bolts in a total of 500 bolts.

6. (*i*) Determine the binomial distribution whose mean is 5 and S.D. is $\sqrt{2.5}$.

(*ii*) The mean and variance of a binomial distribution are 12 and 3 respectively. Find the probability distribution.

(*iii*) Test the validity of the following statement "The mean of the binomial distribution and the standard deviation is 3".

(*iv*) Examine the validity of the following statement "The mean of the binomial distribution is 10 and variance is 16".

(*v*) Is there any fallacy in the statement "the mean of a Binomial distribution is 4 and its variance is 6". *(P.T.U., M.B.A. Sep. 1999)*

7. Determine the probability of 3 successes in a binomial distribution whose mean and variance are respectively 2 and 1.5.

8. For a binomial distribution, the mean is 6 and the standard deviation is $\sqrt{2}$. Find the probability of getting 7 successes.

9. If x follows binomial distribution with mean 4 and variance 2, find $P(x \geq 5)$.

10. If x follows binomial distribution with mean 3 and variance 3/2, find $P(x \leq 5)$.

11. (*i*) Find the binomial distribution when the sum of its mean and variance for five trials is 4.8.

(*ii*) If the sum of the mean and variance of a binomial distribution for 6 trials be $\frac{10}{3}$, find the distribution.

12. (*i*) The mean and variance of a binomial distribution are $\frac{4}{3}$ and $\frac{8}{9}$ respectively. Find $P(X \geq 1)$.

(*ii*) The mean and variance of a binomial distribution are 10 and 5/3. Find $P(x \geq 1)$.

13. About 70% of a certain kind of seeds sold in the retail market germenate when planted under normal conditions. Suppose one package contains 10 seeds. If these are planted, what is the probability of 2 of them germinating ?

14. Past experience show that 80% of the operations performed by a doctor are successful. If he perform 4 operations in a day, what is the probability that at least three operations will be successful ?

15. The probability that a certain kind of component will survive a given shock test is $\frac{3}{4}$. Find the probability that among 5 components tested :

(*i*) exactly 2 will survive (*ii*) at most 3 will survive.

16. It is known that 60% of mice inoculated with a serum are protected from a certain disease. If 5 mice are inoculated, find the probability that :

(*i*) none contact the disease (*ii*) more than 3 contact the disease.

17. Give properties of Binomial distribution. *(P.T.U., M.B.A. May 2004, Dec. 2005)*

Answers

1. 2.5, 1.875 **2.** 20, $\frac{1}{5}$, $\frac{4}{5}$ **4.** 2 **5.** 50, 6.71

6. (*i*) $P(x = r) = {}^{10}C_r \left(\frac{1}{2}\right)^r \left(\frac{1}{2}\right)^{10-r}$, $0 \leq r \leq 10$ (*ii*) $P(x = r) = {}^{16}C_r \left(\frac{3}{4}\right)^r \left(\frac{1}{4}\right)^{16-r}$, $0 \leq r \leq 16$

(*iii*) False. (*iv*) False (*v*) False

7. 0.21 **8.** 0.23 **9.** $\frac{93}{256}$ **10.** $\frac{63}{64}$

11. (*i*) $P(r \text{ successes}) = {}^5C_r \left(\frac{4}{5}\right)^r \left(\frac{1}{5}\right)^{5-r}, 0 \le r \le 5$ (*ii*) $P(x = r) = {}^6C_r \left(\frac{1}{3}\right)^r \left(\frac{2}{3}\right)^{6-r}, 0 \le r \le 6$

12. (*i*) $\frac{65}{81}$ (*ii*) $1 - \left(\frac{1}{6}\right)^{12}$ **13.** $45(0.7)^2 (0.3)^8$ **14.** 0.8192

15. (*i*) 0.0879 (*ii*) 0.3672 **16.** (*i*) 0.0778 (*ii*) 0.087.

Hints

3. Mean – variance $= np - npq = np(1 - q) = np \cdot p = np^2 > 0$.

4. Expected number of boys = mean $= np = 4\left(\frac{1}{2}\right) = 2$.

15. (*i*) P (exactly two will survive) $= {}^5C_2 \left(\frac{3}{4}\right)^2 \left(\frac{1}{4}\right)^{5-2}$

(*ii*) P(at most three will survive) $= P(x \le 3) = 1 - P(x = 4 \text{ or } x = 5)$

$$= 1 - \left[{}^5C_4 \left(\frac{3}{4}\right)^4 \left(\frac{1}{4}\right)^1 + {}^5C_5 \left(\frac{3}{4}\right)^5 \left(\frac{1}{4}\right)^0\right]$$

16. (*i*) P(none contact the disease) $= P(x = 0) = {}^5C_0 \left(\frac{40}{100}\right)^0 \left(\frac{60}{100}\right)^5$

(*ii*) P(more than three contact the disease)

$$= P(x > 3) = {}^5C_4 \left(\frac{40}{100}\right)^4 \left(\frac{60}{100}\right)^1 + {}^5C_5 \left(\frac{40}{100}\right)^5 \left(\frac{60}{100}\right)^0.$$

18

Poisson Distribution

18.1. INTRODUCTION

The Poisson distribution is also a discrete probability distribution. This was discovered by French mathematician **Simon Denis Poisson** (1781–1840) in the year 1837. This distribution deals with the evaluation of probabilities of *rare* events such as "number of car accidents on road", "number of earthquakes in a year", "number of misprints in a book" etc.

18.2. CONDITIONS FOR APPLICABILITY OF POISSON DISTRIBUTION

The Poisson distribution is derived as a limiting case of the binomial distribution. So, the conditions for the applicability of the Poisson distribution are same as those for the applicability of Binomial distribution. Here the additional requirement is that the probability of 'success' is quite near to zero.

18.3. POISSON VARIABLE

A random variable which counts the number of successes in a random experiment with trials satisfying above conditions is called a **Poisson variable.** If the probability of an article being defective is 1/500 and the event of getting a defective article is *success* and samples of 10 articles are checked for defective articles, then the possible values of Poisson variable are 0, 1, 2, ..., 10.

18.4. POISSON PROBABILITY FUNCTION

Let a random experiment satisfying the conditions for Poisson Distribution be performed. Let the number of trials in the experiment be n, which is indefinitely large. Let p denotes the probability of *success* in any trial. We assume that p is indefinitely small, *i.e.*, we are dealing with a rare event. Let x denotes the Poisson variable corresponding to this random experiment.

$\therefore$ The possible values of x are 0, 1, 2, ..., n.

The Poisson distribution is obtained as a limiting case of the corresponding binomial distribution of the experiment under the conditions :

(*i*) n, the number of trials is indefinitely large, *i.e.*, $n \to \infty$.

(*ii*) p, the probability of success in a trial is indefinitely small, *i.e.*, $p \to 0$.

(*iii*) The product np of n and p is constant.

By **Binomial distribution**, $P(x = r) = {}^nC_r\, p^r q^{n-r}$, $0 \le r \le n$, where $q = 1 - p$.

Let $np = m$. $\therefore$ $p = \dfrac{m}{n}$ and $q = 1 - p = 1 - \dfrac{m}{n}$.

$$\therefore \quad P(x = r) = \frac{n!}{r!\,(n-r)!}\left(\frac{m}{n}\right)^r\left(1 - \frac{m}{n}\right)^{n-r}$$

$$= \frac{n(n-1)(n-2)\ldots\ldots(n-(r-1))(n-r)!}{r!\,(n-r)!} \cdot \frac{m^r}{n^r}\left(1-\frac{m}{n}\right)^{n-r}$$

$$= \frac{m^r}{r!}\cdot\frac{n}{n}\cdot\frac{n-1}{n}\cdot\frac{n-2}{n}\ \ldots\ldots\ \frac{n-(r-1)}{n}\cdot\left(1-\frac{m}{n}\right)^n\left(1-\frac{m}{n}\right)^{-r}$$

$$= \frac{m^r}{r!}\left(1-\frac{1}{n}\right)\left(1-\frac{2}{n}\right)\ \ldots\ldots\ \left(1-\frac{r-1}{n}\right)\left(1-\frac{m}{n}\right)^n\left(1-\frac{m}{n}\right)^{-r}$$

$$\therefore \lim_{n\to\infty} P(x=r) = \frac{m^r}{r!}\lim_{n\to\infty}\left(1-\frac{1}{n}\right)\lim_{n\to\infty}\left(1-\frac{2}{n}\right)\ldots\ldots\lim_{n\to\infty}\left(1-\frac{r-1}{n}\right)$$

$$\times \lim_{n\to\infty}\left(1-\frac{m}{n}\right)^n \lim_{n\to\infty}\left(1-\frac{m}{n}\right)^{-r}$$

$$= \frac{m^r}{r!}(1-0)(1-0)\ \ldots\ldots\ (1-0)e^{-m}(1-0)^{-r} \quad \left[\because \lim_{n\to\infty}\left(1-\frac{m}{n}\right)^n = e^{-m}\right]$$

$$= \frac{m^r}{r!}\cdot e^{-m}\cdot 1 = \frac{e^{-m}\,m^r}{r!}.$$

$\therefore$ When n is indefinitely large, we have $\mathbf{P(x = r) = \dfrac{e^{-m}\,m^r}{r!}}$, **r = 0, 1, 2, ...**

This is called the **Poisson probability function.** The corresponding **Poisson distribution** is

x	0	1	2	3 ......
$P(x)$	$\frac{e^{-m}m^0}{0!}$	$\frac{e^{-m}m^1}{1!}$	$\frac{e^{-m}m^2}{2!}$	$\frac{e^{-m}m^3}{3!}$ ....

The constant m is the product of n and p and is called the **parameter** of the Poisson distribution.

18.5. POISSON FREQUENCY DISTRIBUTION

(P.T.U., M.B.A. Dec. 2002, May 2001)

If a random experiment, satisfying the requirements of Poisson distribution, is repeated N times, then the expected frequency of getting $r (0 \le r \le n)$ successes is given by

$$\mathbf{N \cdot P(x = r) = N\,\frac{e^{-m}rm^r}{r!}}, \quad \mathbf{r = 0, 1, 2, \ldots\ldots}$$

18.6. WORKING RULES FOR SOLVING PROBLEMS

I. Make sure that the trials in the random experiment are independent and the success is a rare event and each trial result in either success or failure.

II. Define the Poisson variable and find the value of n and p from the given data. Find $m = np$. Sometimes, the value of m is directly given.

III. Put the value of m in the formula :

$$P(r \text{ successes}) = \frac{e^{-m}\,m^r}{r!},\ r = 0, 1, 2, \ldots\ldots, n. \qquad \ldots(1)$$

IV. Express the event, whose probability is desired in terms of values of the Poisson variable x. Use (1) to find the required probability.

Remark 1. The distribution to be used in solving a problem is generally given is the problem. If it is not given, then the student should make use of Poisson distribution only when the event in the problem is of rare nature, *i.e.,* the probability of happening of event is quite near to zero.

Remark 2. The value of e^{-m} required in any particular problem is generally given with the problem itself. Otherwise, the value of e^{-m} can be found out by using the table given in this chapter. In the examination hall, generally the table of e^{-m} is available for students. If at all the value of e^{-m} is neither given with the problem nor the table of e^{-m} is supplied in the examination hall, then the students are advised to retain their final result in terms of e^{-m}.

ILLUSTRATIVE EXAMPLES

Example 1. *Out of 100 bulbs sample, the probability of a bulb to be defective is 0.03. Using Poisson distribution, obtain the Probability that in a sample of 100 bulbs, none is defective.*
[Given $e^{-3} = 0.04979$]

Sol. Let x be the Poisson variable, "*no. of defective bulbs in a sample of 100 bulbs*".

By **Poisson distribution,** $\quad P(x = r) = \dfrac{e^{-m}\, m^r}{r\,!}$, $r = 0, 1, 2, \ldots\ldots$

Here $n = 100$, $p = 0.03$. $\quad \therefore \quad m = np = 100 \times 0.03 = 3.$

$$\therefore \quad P(x = r) = \frac{e^{-3}\,(3)^r}{r\,!}, \; r = 0, 1, 2, \ldots\ldots, 100.$$

$$\therefore \quad P(\text{none is defective}) = P(x = 0) = \frac{e^{-3}\,(3)^0}{0\,!} = \frac{0.04979 \times 1}{1} = 0.04979.$$

Example 2. *2% of the bolts manufactured by a factory are found to defective. Find the probability that in a packet of 200 bolts not more than 3 bolts will come out to be defective.*
[Take $e^{-4} = 0.0183$]

Sol. Let x be the Poisson variable, "*no. of defective bolts in a packet of 200 bolts*".
By **Poisson distribution,**

$$P(x = r) = \frac{e^{-m}\, m^r}{r\,!}, \; r = 0, 1, 2, \ldots\ldots$$

Here $n = 2000$, $p = 2\% = \dfrac{2}{100}$ $\quad \therefore \quad m = np = 200 \times \dfrac{2}{100} = 4.$

$$\therefore \qquad P(x = r) = \frac{e^{-4}\,(4)^r}{r\,!}, \; r = 0, 1, 2, \ldots\ldots, 200.$$

$$\begin{aligned}
\therefore \quad P(\text{not more than 3 defective}) &= P(x \le 3) \\
&= P(x = 0 \text{ or } x = 2 \text{ or } x = 3) \\
&= P(x = 0) + P(x = 1) + P(x = 2) + P\,(x = 3) \\
&= \frac{e^{-4}\,(4)^0}{0\,!} + \frac{e^{-4}\,(4)^1}{1\,!} + \frac{e^{-4}\,(4)^2}{2\,!} + \frac{e^{-4}\,(4)^3}{3\,!} \\
&= e^{-4}\left[1 + 4 + \frac{16}{2} + \frac{64}{6}\right] = 0.0183\left(\frac{71}{3}\right) = 0.4331.
\end{aligned}$$

Example 3. *There are 50 telephone lines in an exchange. The probability that any one of them will be busy is 0.1. What is the probability that all the lines are busy ?*

Sol. Let x be the Poisson variable, *"no of busy lines in the exchange"*.

By **Poisson distribution,** $P(x = r) = \dfrac{e^{-m}\, m^r}{r\,!}$, $r = 0, 1, 2, \ldots\ldots$

Here $n = 50, p = 0.1. \quad \therefore \quad m = np = 50 \times 0.1 = 5.$

$$\therefore \quad P(x = r) = \frac{e^{-5}\,(5)^r}{r\,!}, \; r = 0, 1, 2, \ldots\ldots, 50.$$

$$\therefore \quad P(\text{all lines are busy}) = P(x = 50) = \frac{e^{-5}\,(5)^{50}}{50\,!}.$$

Example 4. *Eight per cent of the bolts produced in a certain factory turns out to be defective. Find the probability, using Poisson distribution, that in a sample of 25 bolts chosen at random, (i) exactly 3 (ii) more than 3, will be defective. [Take $e^{-2} = 0.135$]*

Sol. Let x be the Poisson variable, *"no. of defective bolts in a sample of 25 bolts"*.

By **Poisson distribution,** $P(x = r) = \dfrac{e^{-m}\, m^r}{r\,!}$, $r = 0, 1, 2, \ldots\ldots$

Here $n = 25,\; p = \dfrac{8}{100} = \dfrac{2}{25}. \quad \therefore \quad m = np = 25 \times \dfrac{2}{25} = 2.$

$$\therefore \qquad P(x = r) = \frac{e^{-2}\,(2)^r}{r\,!}, \; r = 0, 1, 2, \ldots\ldots, 25.$$

(*i*) P(exactly 3 defectives)

$$= \frac{e^{-2}\,(2)^3}{3\,!} = \frac{0.135 \times 8}{6} = 0.18. \qquad \text{(Using } e^{-2} = 0.135)$$

(*ii*) P(more than 3 defectives) $= P(x > 3) = 1 - P(x \le 3)$

$$= 1 - P(x = 0 \;\text{ or }\; x = 1 \;\text{ or }\; x = 2 \;\text{ or }\; x = 3)$$

$$= 1 - [P(x = 0) + P(x = 1) + P(x = 2) + P(x = 3)]$$

$$= 1 - \left[\frac{e^{-2}(2)^0}{0\,!} + \frac{e^{-2}(2)^1}{1!} + \frac{e^{-2}(2)^2}{2\,!} + \frac{e^{-2}(2)^3}{3\,!}\right]$$

$$= 1 - e^{-2}\left[1 + 2 + \frac{4}{2} + \frac{8}{6}\right] = 1 - 0.135\left(1 + 2 + 2 + \frac{4}{3}\right)$$

$$= 1 - 0.135 \times \frac{19}{3} = 0.145.$$

Example 5. *If x is a Poisson distribution such that $3P(x = 2) = 2P(x = 1)$.*
Find (i) $P(x = 0)$ (ii) $P(x = 3)$. *[Given $e^{-4/3} = 0.264$]*

Sol. Let $\quad P(x = r) = \dfrac{e^{-m}\, m^r}{r\,!}, \; r = 0, 1, 2, \ldots\ldots$

We have $\quad 3P(x = 2) = 2P(x = 1).$

$$\therefore \quad 3 \cdot \frac{e^{-m}\, m^2}{2!} = 2 \cdot \frac{e^{-m}\, m^1}{1!}$$

$$\Rightarrow \quad \frac{3m^2}{2} = 2m \quad \Rightarrow \quad 3m^2 - 4m = 0 \quad \Rightarrow \quad m(3m-4) = 0 \quad \Rightarrow \quad m = 0, \frac{4}{3}.$$

$\therefore$ **$m = 4/3$, because $m = 0$ is impossible,**

$$\therefore \quad P(x = r) = \frac{e^{-4/3}\,(4/3)^r}{r!},\ r = 0, 1, 2, \ldots\ldots$$

$$\therefore \quad (i) \quad P(x = 0) = \frac{e^{-4/3}\,(4/3)^0}{0!} = \frac{0.264 \times 1}{1} = 0.264$$

and $\quad (ii) \quad P(x = 3) = \dfrac{e^{-4/3}\,(4/3)^3}{3!} = \dfrac{0.264 \times 64}{6 \times 27} = 0.1043.$

Example 6. *Assuming that the chance of a traffic accident in a day in a street of Delhi is 0.001. On how many days out of a total of 500 days can we expect (i) accident in no street (ii) accident in more than 3 streets, if there are 1000 such streets in the whole city. [Use $e^{-1} = 0.3679$]*

Sol. Let x be the Poisson variable, "no. of streets in which accident occur".

By **Poisson distribution,**

$$P(x = r) = \frac{e^{-m}\, m^r}{r!},\ r = 0, 1, 2, \ldots\ldots$$

Here $n = 1000$, $p = 0.001$. $\therefore$ $m = np = 1000 \times 0.001 = 1$.

$$\therefore \quad P(x = r) = \frac{e^{-1}\,(1)^r}{r!},\ r = 0, 1, 2, \ldots\ldots, 1000$$

$$\Rightarrow \quad P(x = r) = \frac{e^{-1}}{r!},\ r = 0, 1, 2, \ldots\ldots, 1000.$$

(*i*) P(accident in no street)

$$= P(x = 0) = \frac{e^{-1}}{0!} = \frac{0.3679}{1} = 0.3679$$

$\therefore$ No. of days expecting accident is no street

$= N \times P(x = 0) = 500 \times 0.3679 = 184$ days (nearly).

(*ii*) P(accidents in more than 3 streets)

$$= P(x > 3) = 1 - P(x \le 3)$$

$$= 1 - [P(x = 0) + P(x = 1) + P(x = 2) + P(x = 3)]$$

$$= 1 - \left[\frac{e^{-1}}{0!} + \frac{e^{-1}}{1!} + \frac{e^{-1}}{2!} + \frac{e^{-1}}{3!}\right] = 1 - e^{-1}\left[\frac{1}{1} + \frac{1}{1} + \frac{1}{2} + \frac{1}{6}\right]$$

$$= 1 - \left(0.3679 \times \frac{8}{3}\right) = 0.0189$$

$\therefore$ No. of days expecting accidents in more than 3 streets

$= N \times P(x > 3) = 500 \times 0.0189 = 9$ days (nearly).

Example 7. *A box contains 200 tickets each bearing one of the numbers from 1 to 200. 20 tickets are drawn successively with replacement from the box. Find the probability that at most 4 tickets bear numbers divisible by 20.*

Sol. Let x be the Poisson variable, "*no. of tickets bearing number divisible by 20*".

By **Poisson distribution,** $P(x = r) = \frac{e^{-m}\, m^r}{r\,!}$, $r = 0, 1, 2, ...$

The numbers from 1 to 200 and divisible by 20 are 20, 40, 60, 80, 100, 120, 140, 160, 180, 200.

Let p be the probability of getting a ticket with number divisible by 20.

$\therefore \quad p = \frac{10}{200} = \frac{1}{20}.$

Also n = number of trials = 20.

$\therefore \quad m = np = 20 \times \frac{1}{20} = 1$

$$\therefore \qquad P(x = r) = \frac{e^{-1}\,(1)^r}{r\,!} = \frac{e^{-1}}{r\,!},\ r = 0, 1, 2, ..., 20$$

$\therefore$ P(at most 4 tickets bear number divisible by 20) $= P(x \le 4)$

$$= P(x = 0) + P(x = 1) + P(x = 2) + P(x = 3) + P(x = 4)$$

$$= \frac{e^{-1}}{0!} + \frac{e^{-1}}{1!} + \frac{e^{-1}}{2!} + \frac{e^{-1}}{3!} + \frac{e^{-1}}{4!} = \frac{1}{e}\left[1 + 1 + \frac{1}{2} + \frac{1}{6} + \frac{1}{24}\right] = \frac{65}{24e}.$$

Example 8. *A bag contains 30 balls numbers from 1 to 30. One ball is drawn at random, find the probability that the number of balls drawn is multiple of 5 or 6.*

Sol. Let x be the Poisson variable "number of balls drawn is a multiple of 5 or 6"

Here the numbers from 1 to 30, divisible by 5 or 6 are 5, 6, 10, 12, 15, 18, 20, 24, 25, 30

Let p = The probability of getting a ball with number divisible by 5 or 6 $= \frac{10}{30} = \frac{1}{3}.$

TEST YOUR KNOWLEDGE 18.1

1. A company knows on the basis of its past experience that 3% of its bulbs are defective. Using Poisson's distribution, find the probability that in a sample of 100 bulbs, no bulb is defective. [Given $e^{-3} = 0.04979$]
2. Six per cent of the bolts produced in a certain factory turn out to be defective. Find the probability, using Poisson distribution, that in a sample of 10 bolts chosen at random (*i*) exactly 2 (*ii*) more than 2, will be defective. [Take $e^{-0.6} = 0.549$]
3. Twelve per cent of the bolts produced in a certain factory turn out to be defective. Find the probability that in a sample of 25 bolts chosen at random (*i*) exactly 3, (*ii*) more than 3 bolts will be defective, using Poisson distribution. [Take $e^{-3} = 0.049$]
4. Assuming that the probability of a total accident in a factory during a year is 1/1200, calculate the probability that in a factory employing 300 workers, there will be at least two total accidents in a year. [Take $e^{-0.25} = 0.7788$]

5. (*i*) If x has a Poisson distribution such that $P(x = 1) = P(x = 2)$, find $P(x = 4)$. (*P.T.U., May 2008*)

(*ii*) For a Poisson distribution, $3P(x = 2) = P(x = 4)$. Find $P(x = 3)$. [Take $e^{-6} = 0.00248$]

6. Assume that the probability that a bomb dropped from an aeroplane will strike a certain target is 1/5. If 6 bombs are dropped, find the probability that :

(*i*) exactly 2 will strike the target

(*ii*) at least 2 will strike the target. [Use $e^{-1.2} = 0.3012$]

7. A manufacturer of screws knows that 4% of his product is defective. If he sells the screws in boxes of 50 and guarantees that not more than 2 screws will be defective, what is the probability that a box will fail to meet the guaranteed quality ? [Take $e^{-2} = 0.1353$]

8. A manufacturer of bulbs knows that on an average 5% of his production is defective. He sells bulbs in boxes of 100 pieces and guarantees that not more than 4 bulbs will be defective in a box. What is the probability that a box will meet the guarantee ? [$e^{-5} = 0.0067$]

9. In a certain factory turning out razor blades, there is a small chance 1/500 for any blade to be defective. The blades are in packets of 10. Use Poisson distribution to calculate the approximate number of packets containing :

(*i*) no defective (*ii*) one defective

(*iii*) two defective blades in a consignment of 10000 packets. (*P.T.U., M.B.A. Dec. 2000*)

10. The probability that a man aged 50 years will die within a year is 0.01125. What is the probability that out of 12 such men at least 11 will reach their fifty first birthday ? [Given $e^{-0.135} = 0.87371$]

11. The probability of getting no misprint in a page of a book is e^{-4}. What is the probability that a page contains more than 2 misprints ?

Answers

1. 0.04979 **2.** (*i*) 0.099 (*ii*) 0.023 **3.** (*i*) 0.221 (*ii*) 0.363

4. 0.0265 **5.** (*i*) 0.0902 (*ii*) 0.0893 **6.** (*i*) 0.2169 (*ii*) 0.3374

7. (*i*) 0.3235 (*ii*) 0.0893 **8.** 0.438

9. (*i*) 9802 (*ii*) 196 (*iii*) 2 **10.** 0.9917 **11.** 0.7618.

Hints

7. $P(x > 2) = 1 - P(x \le 2) = 1 - e^{-2}\left[\frac{2^0}{0!} + \frac{2^1}{1!} + \frac{2^2}{2!}\right]$.

10. P(at least 11 will reach their 51th birthday) = P(at most 1 will die within a year)

$$= \frac{e^{-0.135}\,(0.135)^0}{0!} + \frac{e^{-0.135}\,(0.135)^1}{1!}.$$

PROPERTIES OF POISSON DISTRIBUTION

18.7. SHAPE OF POISSON DISTRIBUTION

The shape of the Poisson distribution depends upon the parameter m, the average number of successes per unit. As value of m increases, the graph of Poisson distribution would get closer to a symmetrical continuous curve.

18.8. SPECIAL USEFULNESS OF POISSON DISTRIBUTION

The Poisson distribution is specially used when there are events which do not occur as outcomes of a definite number of trials in an experiment, rather occur randomly in nature. This distribution is used when the event under consideration is rare and casual. In finding probabilities by *Poisson distribution,* we require only the measure of average chance of occurrence (m) based on past experience or a small sample drawn for the purpose.

18.9. MEAN OF POISSON DISTRIBUTION

Let x be a Poisson variable and $P(x = r) = \dfrac{e^{-m}m^r}{r!}$, $r = 0, 1, 2, ...$

The *mean of* x is the average numbers of successes.

$$\therefore \quad \text{Mean,} \quad \mu = \sum_{r=0} r.P(x = r) = \sum_{r=0} r.\frac{e^{-m}m^r}{r!}$$

$$= 0.\frac{e^{-m}m^0}{0!} + 1.\frac{e^{-m}m^1}{1!} + 2.\frac{e^{-m}m^2}{2!} + 3.\frac{e^{-m}m^3}{3!} + ...$$

$$= 0 + me^{-m}\left(\frac{1}{1!} + \frac{2m}{2!} + \frac{3m^2}{3!} + ...\right) = me^{-m}\left(1 + \frac{m}{1!} + \frac{m^2}{2!} + ...\right)$$

$$= me^{-m} . e^m = me^0 = m . 1 = m.$$

$\therefore$ **Mean (μ) of x = m.**

18.10. VARIANCE AND S.D. OF POISSON DISTRIBUTION

Let x be a Poisson variable and $P(x = r) = \dfrac{e^{-m}m^r}{r!}$, $r = 0, 1, 2, ...$

The variance and standard deviation of x measures the dispersion of the Poisson distribution and are given by

$$\text{Variance} = \sum_{r=0} r^2.P(x = r) - \mu^2 \quad \text{and} \quad \text{S.D.} = \sqrt{\sum_{r=0} r^2.P(x = r) - \mu^2}.$$

$$\therefore \quad \sum_{r=0} r^2.P(x = r) = \sum_{r=0} r^2.\frac{e^{-m}m^r}{r!}$$

$$= 0^2.\frac{e^{-m}m^0}{0!} + 1^2\frac{e^{-m}m^1}{1!} + 2^2\frac{e^{-m}m^2}{2!} + 3^2\frac{e^{-m}m^3}{3!} + 4^2\frac{e^{-m}m^4}{4!} + ...$$

$$= 0 + me^{-m}\left(\frac{1}{1!} + \frac{2m}{1!} + \frac{3m^2}{2!} + \frac{4m^3}{3!} + ...\right)$$

$$= me^{-m}\left\{\left(1+\frac{m}{1!}+\frac{m^2}{2!}+\frac{m^3}{3!}+......\right)+\left(\frac{m}{1!}+\frac{2m^2}{2!}+\frac{3m^3}{3!}+......\right)\right\}$$

$$= me^{-m}\left\{e^m+m\left(1+\frac{m}{1!}+\frac{m^2}{2!}+.....\right)\right\}$$

$$= me^{-m}\{e^m+me^m\} = me^{-m}e^m(1+m) = me^0(1+m)$$

$$= m(1+m) = m+m^2.$$

$\therefore$ Variance $= \sum_{r=0} r^2.P(x=r)-\mu^2 = (m+m^2)-m^2 = \mathbf{m}.$

Also, **S.D.** $= \sqrt{\textbf{Variance}} = \sqrt{\mathbf{m}}$ **.**

18.11. γ_1 AND γ_2 OF POISSON DISTRIBUTION

The values of γ_1 and γ_2 for the Poisson probability function

$$P(x=r) = \frac{e^{-m}\, m^r}{r!},\ r = 0, 1, 2, ...$$

are given by $\gamma_1 = \frac{\mathbf{1}}{\sqrt{\mathbf{m}}}$ and $\gamma_2 = \frac{\mathbf{1}}{\mathbf{m}}$.

18.12. RECURRENCE FORMULA FOR POISSON DISTRIBUTION

Let x be a Poisson variable and $P(x=r) = \frac{e^{-m}\, m^r}{r!}$, $r = 0, 1, 2, ...$

For $k \geq 0$, $P(k) = \frac{e^{-m}\, m^k}{k!}$ and $P(k+1) = \frac{e^{-m}\, m^{k+1}}{(k+1)!}$.

Dividing, we get $\frac{P(k+1)}{P(k)} = \frac{e^{-m}\, m^{k+1}}{(k+1)!}\cdot\frac{k!}{e^{-m}\, m^k} = \frac{m}{k+1}$.

$$\therefore\quad \mathbf{P(k+1) = \frac{m}{k+1}\, P(k), \quad k = 0, 1, 2, ...}$$

This is the required **recurrence formula.**

18.13. APPLICATIONS OF POISSON DISTRIBUTION

This distribution is applied to problems concerning.

1. The number of persons born blind per year in a country.
2. The number of deaths by horse kick in an army corps.
3. The number of fragments from a shell hitting a target.
4. Demand pattern for certain spare parts.

ILLUSTRATIVE EXAMPLES

Example 1. *A pair of dice is thrown 200 times. If getting a sum of 9 is considered as success, using Poisson distribution, find the mean and variance of the number of successes.*

Sol. Let p be the probability of getting sum 9 in a throw of pair of dice. Out of total 36 outcomes, the favourable outcomes are (3, 6), (4, 5), (5, 4) and (6, 3).

$$\therefore \qquad p = \frac{4}{36} = \frac{1}{9}.$$

Also, $\qquad n = 200.$

$$\therefore \qquad m = np = 200 \times \frac{1}{9} = \frac{200}{9} = 22.22 \qquad | \because \text{ Mean} = \text{Variance}$$

$\therefore$ Mean $= m = 22.22$ and variance $= m = 22.22$.

Example 2. *If a Poisson variate x is such that P(x = 1) = 2. P(x = 2), find the mean and variance of the distribution.*

Sol. Let $\qquad P(x = r) = \dfrac{e^{-m}\, m^r}{r\,!}, \; r = 0, 1, 2, ...$

where m is the average number of successes.

We have $\qquad P(x = 1) = 2 .\ P(x = 2)$

$$\Rightarrow \qquad \frac{e^{-m}\, m^1}{1!} = 2 . \frac{e^{-m}\, m^2}{2!}$$

$$\Rightarrow \qquad m = m^2 \;\Rightarrow\; m = 1 \qquad (\because \;\; m \neq 0)$$

$\therefore$ Mean $= m = 1$ and variance $= m = 1$.

Example 3. (*i*) *For a Poisson distribution, it is given that, P(X = 1) = P(X = 2). Find the value of mean of the distribution. Hence find P (X = 0) and P(X = 4).*

(*ii*) *A random variable X follows a Poisson distribution with Parameter 4. Find the Probability that X assumes the values less than 2.*

Sol. (*i*) Let $\qquad P(X = r) = \dfrac{e^{-m}\, m^r}{r\,!}, \; r = 0, 1, 2, ... \qquad ...(1)$

where m is the average number of successes.

We have P(X = 1) = P(X = 2)

$$\Rightarrow \qquad \frac{e^{-m}\, m^1}{1!} = \frac{e^{-m}\, m^2}{2!}$$

$$\Rightarrow \qquad m = \frac{m^2}{2} \;\Rightarrow\; m = 2 \qquad (\because \;\; m \neq 0)$$

$\therefore$ Mean of the distribution, $m = 2$.

Using (1), we have $\; P(X = 0) = \dfrac{e^{-m}\, m^0}{0\,!} = e^{-2} = \dfrac{1}{e^2} = \dfrac{1}{7.3890} = 0.1353$

and $$P(X = 4) = \frac{e^{-m}\ m^4}{4\,!} = \frac{e^{-2}(2)^4}{24} = \frac{2}{3}e^{-2} = \frac{2}{3} \times 0.1353 = 0.0902.$$

(*ii*) Here $m = 4$. By using Poisson distribution we know

$$P(X = r) = \frac{e^{-m}\ m^r}{r\,!},\ r = 0, 1, 2, ... \qquad ...(1)$$

Required Probability $= P(X < 2) = P(X \le 1)$

$= P(X = 0) + P(X = 1) = e^{-m} + e^{-m}\ .\ m$ | Using (1)

$= e^{-4}\ (1 + 4) = 5e^{-4} = 5 \times 0.0183 = 0.09157.$

Example 4. *A telephone exchange receives on an average 4 calls per minute. Find the probabilities on the basis of Poisson distribution (m = 4), of :*

(i) 2 or less calls per minute *(ii) upto 4 calls per minute*

(iii) more than 4 calls per minute.

Sol. Let x be the Poisson variable "*no. of calls per minute*".

By **Poisson distribution,** $P(x = r) = \dfrac{e^{-m}\ m^r}{r\,!}$, $r = 0, 1, 2, ...$

Here m = Average number of successes *i.e.*, calls per minute = 4

$$\therefore \qquad P(x = r) = \frac{e^{-4}(4)^r}{r\,!},\ r = 0, 1, 2, ...$$

(*i*) P(2 or less calls per minute) $= P(x \le 2) = P(x = 0) + P(x = 1) + P(x = 2)$

$$= \frac{e^{-4}\ .\ 4^0}{0\,!} + \frac{e^{-4}\ .\ 4^1}{1!} + \frac{e^{-4}\ .\ 4^2}{2\,!} = e^{-4}\ \{1 + 4 + 8\} = 0.01832 \times 13 = 0.2382.$$

(*ii*) P(upto 4 calls per minute) $= P(x \le 4) = P(x = 0) + P(x = 1) + P(x = 2) + P(x = 3) + P(x = 4)$

$$= \frac{e^{-4}\ .\ 4^0}{0\,!} + \frac{e^{-4}\ .\ 4^1}{1\,!} + \frac{e^{-4}\ .\ 4^2}{2\,!} + \frac{e^{-4}\ .\ 4^3}{3\,!} + \frac{e^{-4}\ .\ 4^4}{4\,!}$$

$$= e^{-4}\left\{1 + 4 + 8 + \frac{64}{6} + \frac{256}{24}\right\} = 0.01832 \times 34.3333 = 0.6289.$$

(*iii*) P(more than 4 calls per minute) $= P(x > 4) = 1 - P(x \le 4) = 1 - 0.6289 = 0.3711.$

Example 5. *A manufacturer of pins knows that on average 5% of his product is defective. He sells pins in boxes of 100, and guarantees that not more than 4 pins will be defective. What is the probability that a box will meet the guaranteed quality ? ($e^{-5} = 0.0067$)*

(P.T.U., M.B.A. Dec. 2003)

Sol. Let p = The probability that a pin is defective = 5% = 0.05

Also $n = 100$

$\therefore$ $\lambda = np = 100 \times (0.05) = 5$

Using Poisson distribution, we have

$$P(X = r) = \frac{e^{-\lambda}\ \lambda^r}{r!},\ r = 0, 1, 2, ...$$

The box will meet the guarantee if it contains at the most 4 pins defective.

$\therefore$ Required probability = P(X ≤ 4)

$$= P(X = 0) + P(X = 1) + P(X = 2) + P(X = 3) + P(X = 4)$$

$$= e^{-\lambda} + e^{-\lambda}.\lambda + e^{-\lambda}.\frac{\lambda^2}{2!} + e^{-\lambda}.\frac{\lambda^3}{6} + e^{-\lambda}.\frac{\lambda^4}{24}$$

$$= e^{-5}\left(1 + 5 + \frac{25}{2} + \frac{125}{6} + \frac{625}{24}\right)$$

$$= e^{-5}(6 + 12.5 + 20.83 + 26.04)$$

$$= e^{-5}(65.37) = 0.0067 \times 65.37$$

$$= 0.44.$$

Example 6. *If the probability of a bad reaction from a certain injection is 0.001. Determine the chance that out of 2000 individuals, more than two will get a bad reaction.*

Sol. Given p = the probability of a bad reaction = 0.001, (Very small)

$n = 2000$

$\therefore$ $\lambda = np = (2000) \times (0.001) = 2$

Required probability

$$= P(x > 2) = 1 - P(x \le 2)$$

$$= 1 - [(P(x = 0) + P(x = 1) + P(x = 2)]$$

$$= 1 - \left(\frac{e^{-2}2^0}{0!} + \frac{e^{-2}.2^1}{1!} + \frac{e^{-2}.2^2}{2!}\right)$$

| Using Poisson distribution, $P(x = r) = \frac{e^{-\lambda}\lambda^r}{r!}$

$$= 1 - e^{-2}(1 + 2 + 2) = 1 - 5e^{-2} = 1 - 5(0.1353)$$

$$= 1 - 0.6765 = 0.3235.$$

Example 7. *The incidence of occupational disease in an industry is such that the workmen have a 10% chance of suffering from it. What is the probability that in a group of 7, five or more will suffer from it.*

Sol. Let p = The probability of suffering from the occupational disease.

$$= 10\% = \frac{10}{100} = \frac{1}{10} \quad \text{(Very small)}, \quad \text{Also,} \quad n = 7$$

$\therefore$ $\lambda = np = 7.\frac{1}{10} = 0.7$

$\therefore$ Using Poisson distribution, we know

$$P(X = r) = \frac{e^{-\lambda}\lambda^r}{r!}, \; r = 0, 1, 2, \ldots$$

$\therefore$ Required probability = P(x ≥ 5)

$$= P(X = 5) + P(X = 6) + P(X = 7)$$

$$= \frac{e^{-0.7}(0.7)^5}{5!} + \frac{e^{-0.7}(0.7)^6}{6!} + \frac{e^{-0.7}(0.7)^7}{7!}$$

$$= e^{-0.7}\left[\left(\frac{7}{10}\right)^5 \frac{1}{5!} + \left(\frac{7}{10}\right)^6 \cdot \frac{1}{6!} + \left(\frac{7}{10}\right)^7 \frac{1}{7!}\right]$$

$$= e^{-0.7}\left(\frac{7}{10}\right)^5 \frac{1}{5!}\left(1 + \frac{7}{60} + \frac{49}{4200}\right)$$

$$= e^{-0.7}\frac{16807}{10^5} \cdot \frac{1}{120} \cdot \frac{4200 + 490 + 49}{4200}$$

$$= e^{-0.7} \cdot \frac{16807}{10^5} \cdot \frac{1}{120} \cdot \frac{4739}{4200} = e^{-0.7} \cdot \frac{79648373}{10^5 \times 504000} = \frac{15.80 \times e^{-0.7}}{10^5}$$

$$= 0.000784 = 0.0008.$$

Example 8. *The side effect's of a certain drug cause discomfort to only a few patients. The probability that any individual will suffer from these side effects is 0.002. If the drug is given to 3000 patients, what is the probability that (i) exactly 3 (ii) 5 or more than 5 will suffer side effects.*

Sol. Let p = The probability that an individual suffers from side effects
= 0.002 (Very small)

Also $n = 3000$

$\therefore$ $\lambda = np = 300\ (.002) = 6$

Using Poisson distribution,

$$P(X = r) = \frac{e^{-\lambda}\lambda^r}{r!},\ r = 0, 1, 2, \ldots\ldots$$

(*i*) Required probability

$$= P(X = 3) = \frac{e^{-6} \cdot 6^3}{3!} = e^{-6} \cdot \frac{216}{3}$$

$$= 72e^{-6} = 72\ (0.002478) = 0.1784.$$

(*ii*) Required probability $= P(X \geq 5)$

$$= 1 - P(X < 5) = 1 - P\ (X \leq 4)$$

$$= 1 - P(X = 0) + P(X = 1) + P(X = 2) + P(X = 3) + P(X = 4)$$

$$= 1 - \left(\frac{e^{-6}.6^0}{0!} + \frac{e^{-6}.6^1}{1!} + \frac{e^{-6}.6^2}{2!} + \frac{e^{-6}.6^3}{3!} + \frac{e^{-6}.6^4}{4!}\right)$$

$$= 1 - e^{-6}\left(1 + 6 + 18 + \frac{216}{6} + \frac{1296}{24}\right)$$

$$= 1 - e^{-6}\ (1 + 6 + 18 + 36 + 54) = 1 - e^{-6}\ (115)$$

$$= 1 - (115) \times (0.002478) = 1 - 0.2849 = 0.71503.$$

Example 9. *The probability that a man aged 50 years will die within a year is 0.01125. What is the probability that out of 12 such men, at least 11 will reach their fifty first birthday (Given $e^{-0.135} = 0.87371$)*

Sol. Here p = The probability of death = 0.01125 (Very small)

Also $n = 12$

$\therefore$ $\lambda = np = 12\ (0.01125) = 0.135$

Using Poisson distribution, we know $P(X = r) = \dfrac{e^{-\lambda}\lambda^r}{r!}$, $r = 0, 1, 2, \ldots\ldots$

Here required probability

= Probability that at least 11 men reach their 51th birthday

= Probability that at most one dies within a year.

$= P(X = 1) = P(X = 0) + P(X = 1)$

$$= \frac{e^{-\lambda}.\lambda^0}{0!} + \frac{e^{-\lambda}.\lambda^1}{1!} = e^{-\lambda}(1 + \lambda) = e^{-0.135}\ (1 + 0.135)$$

$$= 1.135\ e^{-0.135} = 1.135 \times 0.87371 = 0.99166$$

Remarks. When n is very large and p is very small, we apply Poisson distribution.

Example 10. *Assume that the chance of an individual coal miner being killed in a mine accident during a year is* $\frac{1}{1400}$. *Use the Poisson distribution to calculate the probability that in a mine employing 350 miners, there will be at least one fatal accident in a year. [Use* $e^{-0.25} = 0.78$*]*

Sol. Let x be the Poisson variable "*no. of fatal accidents in a year*".

By **Poisson distribution,** $P(x = r) = \dfrac{e^{-m}\ m^r}{r!}$, $r = 0, 1, 2, \ldots\ldots$

Here $n = 350,\ p = \dfrac{1}{1400}$. $\therefore$ $m = np = 350 \times \dfrac{1}{1400} = 0.25.$

$\therefore$ $P(x = r) = \dfrac{e^{-0.25}\ (0.25)^r}{r!}$, $r = 0, 1, 2, \ldots\ldots$

$\therefore$ P(at least one fatal accident) $= P(x \geq 1) = 1 - P(x < 1) = 1 - P(x = 0)$

$$= 1 - \frac{e^{-0.25}\ (0.25)^0}{0!} = 1 - e^{-0.25} = 1 - 0.78 = 0.22.$$

Example 11. *Red blood cells (R.B.C.) deficiency may be determined by examining a specimen of blood under a microscope. Suppose a certain small fixed volume contains on an average 20 red cells for normal persons. Using Poisson distribution, obtain the probability that a specimen from a normal person will contain less than 15 red cells.*

Sol. Let x be the Poisson variable, "*no. of red blood cells in the specimen*".

By **Poisson distribution,** $P(x = r) = \dfrac{e^{-m}\ m^r}{r!}$, $r = 0, 1, 2, \ldots\ldots$

Here m = average number of R.B.C. in the specimen = 20

$\therefore$ $P(x = r) = \dfrac{e^{-20}(20)^r}{r!}$, $r = 0, 1, 2, \ldots\ldots$

$\therefore$ P(less than 15 R.B.C. in the specimen)

$$= P(x < 15) = P(x = 0) + P(x = 1) + ... + P(x = 14)$$

$$= \frac{e^{-20}(20)^0}{0\,!} + \frac{e^{-20}(20)^1}{1!} + ... + \frac{e^{-20}(20)^{14}}{14\,!} = e^{-20} \sum_{k=0}^{14} \frac{(20)^k}{k\,!}$$

Example 12. *An electric bulb manufacturer finds that 4% of the bulbs are defective. What is the probability that a random sample of 50 bulbs does not have a defective bulb. ?*

(P.T.U., M.B.A. Dec. 2000)

Sol. Let p = The probability that a bulb is defective

$$= 4\% = \frac{4}{100} = 0.04 \text{ (very small)}$$

Also $n = 50$

$\therefore$ $\lambda = np = 50 \times 0.04 = 2$

By Poisson distribution,

$$P(X = r) = \frac{e^{-\lambda}\lambda^r}{r!}, \; r = 0, 1, 2, ...$$

$$\text{Required probability} = P(X = 0) = \frac{e^{-\lambda}\lambda^0}{0!} = e^{-\lambda} = e^{-2} = 0.1353.$$

TEST YOUR KNOWLEDGE 18.2

1. Comment on the following statement : "The mean and variance of a Poisson distribution are equal only if the average occurrence of the Poisson variance is ≤ 4".
2. The standard deviation of a Poisson distribution is 3. Find the probability of getting 3 successes.
3. A telephone exchange receives on an average 3 calls per minute. Find the probability on the basis of the Poisson distribution ($m = 3$), of ;

   (*i*) exactly 1 call per minute (*ii*) exactly 3 calls per minute

   (*iii*) less than 3 calls per minute (*iv*) more than 1 call per minute.
4. If a random variable x follows Poisson distribution such that $P(x = 2) = 9P(x = 4) + 90P(x = 6)$. Find the mean and variance of x.
5. Suppose that a manufactured product has 2 defects per unit of product inspected. Using Poisson distribution, calculate the probabilities of finding a product without any defect, 3 defects and 4 defects. (Given $e^{-2} = 0.135$)
6. A car-hire firm has two cars, which it hires out day by day. The number of demands for a car on each day is distributed as a Poisson distribution with mean 1.5. Calculate the proportion of days on which neither car is used and the proportion of days on which some demand is refused. ($e^{-1.5} = 0.2231$)
7. The number of accidents in a year attributed to taxi drivers in a city follows Poisson distribution with mean 3. Out of 1,000 taxi drivers, find approximately the number of drivers with (*i*) no accident in a year (*ii*) more than 3 accidents in a year.

   (Given $e^{-1} = 0.3679$, $e^{-2} = 0.1353$, $e^{-3} = 0.0498$)
8. If the probability that an individual suffers from reaction by an injection is $\frac{1}{1000}$, find the probability that out of 5000 individuals given the injection (*i*) exactly 5 will suffer from reaction, (*ii*) no one will suffer from reaction. Given that $e^{-5} = 0.00672$.

9. An insurance company has discovered that only about 0.1% of the population is involved in a certain type of accident each year. If its 1000 policy holders are randomly selected from the population, what is the probability that not more than 5 of its clients are involved in such an accident next year ?

10. In a hospital, there are 20 kidney dialysis machines and that the chance of any one of them to be out of service during a day is 0.02. Determine the probability that exactly 3 machines will be out of service on the same day.

11. Suppose that a radio tube inserted into a certain type of a set has probability 0.2 of functioning more than 500 hours. If we test 4 tubes at random, what is the probability that exactly 3 of these tubes function for more than 500 hours ?

12. Write a short note on poisson distribution. *(P.U.T., M.B.A. Dec. 2004)*

Answers

2. 0.0149 **3.** (*i*) 0.1494 (*ii*) 0.2241 (*iii*) 0.4232 (*iv*) 0.8008

4. 1, 1 **5.** 0.135, 0.18, 0.09 **6.** 0.2231, 0.1913 **7.** (*i*) 50 (*ii*) 353

8. (*i*) 0.175 (*ii*) 0.00672 **9.** 0.9994 **10.** 0.0071 **11.** 0.0383.

TABLE VALUES OF e^{-m}

(0 < m < 1)

m	0	1	2	3	4	5	6	7	8	9
0.0	1.0000	0.9900	0.9802	0.9704	0.9608	0.9512	0.9418	0.9324	0.9231	0.9139
0.1	0.9048	0.8958	0.8869	0.8781	0.8694	0.8607	0.8521	0.8437	0.8353	0.8270
0.2	0.8187	0.8106	0.8025	0.7945	0.7866	0.7788	0.7711	0.7634	0.7558	0.7483
0.3	0.7408	0.7334	0.7261	0.7189	0.7118	0.7047	0.6977	0.6907	0.6839	0.6771
0.4	0.6703	0.6636	0.6570	0.6505	0.6440	0.6376	0.6313	0.6250	0.6188	0.6126
0.5	0.6065	0.6005	0.5945	0.5886	0.5827	0.5770	0.5712	0.5655	0.5599	0.5543
0.6	0.5488	0.5434	0.5379	0.5326	0.5273	0.5220	0.5169	0.5117	0.5066	0.5016
0.7	0.4966	0.4916	0.4868	0.4819	0.4771	0.4724	0.4677	0.4630	0.4584	0.4538
0.8	0.4493	0.4449	0.4404	0.4360	0.4317	0.4274	0.4332	0.4190	0.4148	0.4107
0.9	0.4066	0.4025	0.3985	0.3946	0.3906	0.3867	0.3829	0.3791	0.3753	0.3716

(m = 1, 2, 3, ..., 10)

m	1	2	3	4	5	6	7	8	9	10
e^{-m}	0.36788	0.13534	0.04979	0.01832	0.006738	0.002479	0.000912	0.000335	0.000123	0.000045

Illustrations :

1. $e^{-4.37} = e^{-4} \cdot e^{-.37} = (0.01832)(0.6907) = 0.012654$

2. $e^{-6.05} = e^{-6} \cdot e^{-.05} = (0.002479)(0.9512) = 0.002358.$

19

Normal Distribution

19.1. INTRODUCTION

The normal distribution is a limiting case of the Binomial distribution under the following conditions :

(1) When n, the number of trials is very large and

(2) p, the probability of a success, is close to $\frac{1}{2}$.

Remark : (*i*) The normal distribution was first discovered by De'Moivre, in 1733, a French mathematician.

(*ii*) The normal distribution is a continuous distribution.

19.2. NORMAL DISTRIBUTION

(P.T.U., M.B.A. March 1998, Dec. 2001, May 2002, Dec. 2003, May 2003)

The general equation of the Normal distribution is given by

$$f(x) = \frac{1}{\sigma\sqrt{2\pi}}\, e^{\frac{1}{2}\left(\frac{x-\mu}{\sigma}\right)^2}, \; -\infty < x < \infty \;, -\infty < \mu < \infty, \sigma > 0 \;;$$

where $\sqrt{2\pi} = 2.5066, \; e = 2.7183$

The parameters μ and σ are respectively mean and standard deviation of the distribution.

19.3. NORMAL VARIATE

A random variable X is called a normal variate if it follows a normal distribution. If the random variable X follows a normal distribution with mean μ and S.D. σ , then we write $X \sim N(\mu, \sigma^2)$.

19.4. NORMAL CURVE AND ITS PROPERTIES

The graph of the normal distribution is called the **normal curve.**

Properties

(*a*) The graph of the normal distribution is bell-shaped and symmetrical about the line $x = u$. (*i.e.,* If we fold the normal curve about the line $x = \mu$, the two halves coincide).

(*b*) The normal curve is unimodal.

(*c*) The line $x = \mu$ divides the area under the normal curves above x-axis into two equal Parts (see fig.).

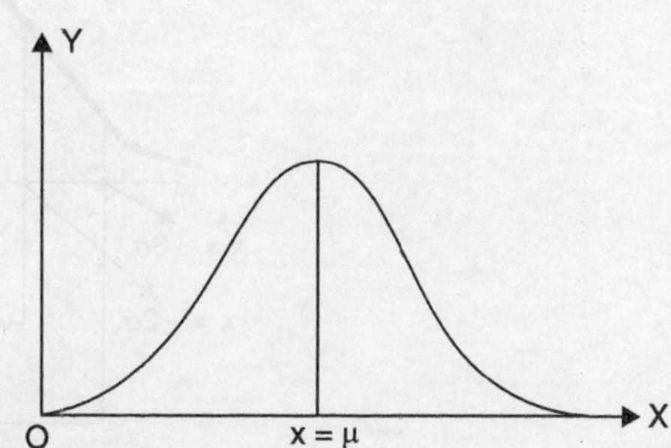

(*d*) The area under the normal curve between any two given ordinates $x = x_1$ and $x = x_2$, represents the probability of values falling into the given interval.

(*e*) The total area under the normal curve above the *x*-axis is 1.

19.5. BASIC PROPERTIES OF THE NORMAL DISTRIBUTION

(*P.T.U., M.B.A. Dec. 2004, 2003*)

The probability density function (p.d.f) of the normal variate X is given by

$$f(x) = \frac{1}{\sigma\sqrt{2\pi}} e^{-\frac{1}{2}\left(\frac{x-\mu}{\sigma}\right)^2}, \qquad -\infty < x < \infty, -\infty < \mu < \infty, \sigma > 0$$

Then the curve $y = f(x)$, known as normal probability curve and satisfies the following properties.

(*a*) The Normal distribution is symmetrical about the line $x = \mu$

(*b*) It is unimodal

(*c*) For a Normal distribution, mean = median = mode

(*d*) The area bounded by the curve $y = f(x)$, and *x*-axis is 1 unit, *i.e.*,

$$\int_{-\infty}^{\infty} f(x)\, dx = 1. \text{ Also } f(x) \geq 0$$

(*e*) The points of inflexion of the Normal curve (can be obtained by putting $\frac{d^2y}{dx^2} = 0$ and verifying that at these points, $\frac{d^3y}{dx^3} \neq 0$) are given by $x = \mu \pm \sigma$.

i.e., these points are equidistant from the mean on either side.

19.6. AREA PROPERTY OF NORMAL DISTRIBUTION

(1) The area under the normal curve between the ordinates $x = \mu - \sigma$ and $x = \mu + \sigma$, is 68.26%.

(2) The area under the normal curve between the ordinates $x = \mu - 2\sigma$ and $x = \mu + 2\sigma$ is 95.44%.

(3) The area under the normal curves between the ordinates $x = \mu - 3\sigma$ and $x = \mu + 3\sigma$ is 99.73%.

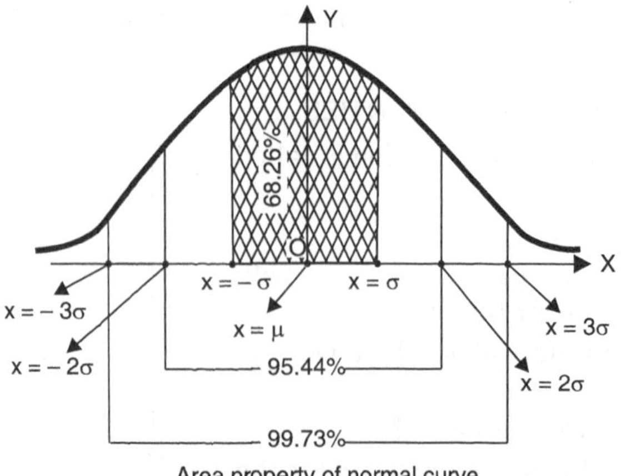

Area property of normal curve

Theorem. *For a normal distribution, the mean deviation about mean is* $\frac{4}{5}\sigma$.

Proof. We know that mean deviation about the mean μ is given by

$$\text{M.D.} = \int_{-\infty}^{\infty} |x-\mu|\, f(x)\, dx$$

$$= \int_{-\infty}^{\infty} |x-\mu| . \frac{1}{\sigma\sqrt{2\pi}} e^{-\frac{1}{2}\left(\frac{x-\mu}{\sigma}\right)^2} dx \qquad \Big| \text{ Put } \frac{x-\mu}{\sigma} = z \Rightarrow dx = \sigma\, dz$$

$$= \int_{-\infty}^{\infty} |z\sigma| . \frac{1}{\sigma\sqrt{2\pi}} e^{-\frac{z^2}{2}} \sigma\, dz$$

$$= \frac{\sigma}{\sqrt{2\pi}} \int_{-\infty}^{\infty} |z| e^{-\frac{z^2}{2}} dz \qquad | \ \sigma > 0$$

$$= \frac{2\sigma}{\sqrt{2\pi}} \int_{0}^{\infty} |z| e^{-\frac{z^2}{2}} dz \qquad \Big| \ |z| e^{-\frac{z^2}{2}} \text{ is an even function}$$

$$= \frac{\sqrt{2}}{\pi} \sigma \int_{0}^{\infty} z e^{-\frac{z}{2}} dz$$

$$= \frac{\sqrt{2}}{\pi} \sigma \int_{0}^{\infty} e^{-t} dt = \sqrt{\frac{2}{\pi}}\, \sigma \left| \frac{e^{-t}}{(-1)} \right|_0^{\infty}$$

$$= \sqrt{\frac{2}{\pi}}\, \sigma (0+1) \qquad \Big| \text{ Put } \frac{z^2}{2} = t \Rightarrow z\, dz = dt$$

$$= \sqrt{\frac{2}{\pi}}\, \sigma = 0.7979 \text{ s} \cong \frac{4}{5} \sigma.$$

19.7. MOMENTS OF NORMAL DISTRIBUTION

Consider

$$\mu_{2n+1} = \int_{-\infty}^{\infty} (x-\mu)^{2n+1} . f(x)\, dx$$

$$= \int_{-\infty}^{\infty} (x-\mu)^{2n+1} . \frac{1}{\sigma\sqrt{2\pi}} e^{-\frac{1}{2}\left(\frac{x-\mu}{\sigma}\right)^2} dx$$

$$= \int_{-\infty}^{\infty} (z\sigma)^{2n+1} . \frac{1}{\sigma\sqrt{2\pi}} e^{-\frac{z^2}{2}} \sigma\, dz$$

$$\Big| \text{ Put } z = \frac{x-\mu}{\sigma} \Rightarrow dz = \frac{1}{\sigma} dx$$

$$= \sigma^{2n+1} \int_{-\infty}^{\infty} z^{2n+1} e^{-\frac{z^2}{2}} dz$$

$$= 0, \text{ since } z^{2n+1} e^{-\frac{z^2}{2}} \text{ is an odd function.}$$

i.e., **all odd order moments about the mean vanish.**

Further, $$\mu_{2n} = \int_{-\infty}^{\infty} (x-\mu)^{2n} \cdot f(x)\, dx$$

$$= \int_{-\infty}^{\infty} (x-\mu)^{2n} \cdot \frac{1}{\sigma\sqrt{2\pi}} \cdot e^{-\frac{1}{2}\left(\frac{x-\mu}{\sigma}\right)^2} dx$$

$$= \frac{\sigma^{2n}}{\sqrt{2\pi}} \int_{-\infty}^{\infty} z^{2n} \cdot e^{-\frac{z^2}{2}} dz \qquad \Big|\ \text{Put } \frac{x-\mu}{\sigma} = z \Rightarrow dx = \sigma\, dz$$

$$= \frac{\sigma^{2n}}{\sqrt{2\pi}} \int_{-\infty}^{\infty} z^{2n-1} \left(e^{-\frac{z^2}{2}} z\right) dz, \text{ Integrating by parts,}$$

$$= \frac{\sigma^{2n}}{\sqrt{2\pi}} \left[\left| z^{2n-1} \left(-e^{-\frac{z^2}{2}}\right) \right|_{-\infty}^{\infty} + \int_{-\infty}^{\infty} (2n-1)\, z^{2n-2}\, e^{-\frac{z^2}{2}} dz \right]$$

$$= \frac{\sigma^{2n}}{\sqrt{2\pi}} \left[(0-0) + (2n-1) \int_{-\infty}^{\infty} z^{2n-2}\, e^{-\frac{z^2}{2}} dz \right]$$

$$= \frac{(2n-1)\cdot\sigma^{2n}}{\sqrt{2\pi}} \int_{-\infty}^{\infty} z^{2n-2}\, e^{-\frac{z^2}{2}} dz$$

Let $I = \int e^{-\frac{z^2}{2}} . z\, dz$,

Put $\frac{z^2}{2} = t \Rightarrow z\, dz = dt$

$\therefore$ $I = \int e^{-t}\, dt = -e^{-t} = -e^{-\frac{z^2}{2}}$

$\therefore$

$$= (2n-1)\,\sigma^2 \cdot \frac{\sigma^{2n-2}}{\sqrt{2\pi}} \int_{-\infty}^{\infty} z^{2n-2} \cdot e^{-\frac{z^2}{2}} dz$$

Hence $$\mu_{2n} = (2n-1)\,\sigma^2 \cdot \mu_{2n-2} \qquad ...(1)$$

Changing n to $n-1$ in (1), we get

$$\mu_{2n-2} = (2n-3)\,\sigma^2\, \mu_{2n-4} \qquad ...(2)$$

Using (2) in (1), we get

$$\mu_{2n} = (2n-1)(2n-3)\,\sigma^4 .\ \mu_{2n-4}$$

....

$$= (2n-1)(2n-3) \ldots\ldots 3.1 .\ \sigma^{2n}\, \mu_{2n-2n}$$

$$= (2n-1)(2n-3) \ldots\ldots 3.1 .\ \sigma^{2n} \qquad |\ \mu_0 = 1$$

Cor. If we put $n = 1, 2,$ in above, we get

$$\mu_2 = \sigma^2,\ \mu_4 = 3.1 .\ \sigma^4 = 3\,\sigma^4$$

$$\therefore \qquad \beta_1 = \frac{\mu_3^{\,2}}{\mu_2^{\,3}} = 0$$

| As odd order moments about the mean vanish

$$\beta_2 = \frac{\mu_4}{\mu_2^{\,2}} = \frac{3\,\sigma^4}{\sigma^4} = 3$$

19.8. PROBABILITY INTEGRAL OR ERROR FUNCTION

The integral $P(z) = \frac{1}{\sqrt{2\pi}} \int_0^z e^{-\frac{z^2}{2}}\, dz$, is known as probability integral or error function.

19.9. PROBABLE ERROR (λ)

It is defined as the deviation on either side of the arithmetic mean, the probability of occurrence of which is equal to 0.5

i.e., It is the value of λ, satisfying,

$$\frac{1}{\sigma\sqrt{2\pi}} \int_{\mu-\lambda}^{\mu+\lambda} e^{-\frac{(x-\mu)^2}{2\sigma^2}}\, dx = 0.5$$

$$\Rightarrow \qquad \frac{1}{\sigma\sqrt{2\pi}} \int_{-\frac{\lambda}{\sigma}}^{\frac{\lambda}{\sigma}} e^{-\frac{z^2}{2}} \,.\, \sigma\, dz = 0.5$$

| Put $\frac{x-\mu}{\sigma} = z \;\Rightarrow\; dx = \sigma\, dz$

| When $x = \mu + \lambda,\ z = \frac{\lambda}{\sigma}$, When $x = \mu - \lambda,\ z = \frac{-\lambda}{\sigma}$

$$\Rightarrow \qquad \frac{2}{\sqrt{2\pi}} \int_0^{\frac{\lambda}{\sigma}} e^{-\frac{z^2}{2}}\, dz = 0.5$$

| $e^{-\frac{z^2}{2}}$ is an even function

$$\Rightarrow \qquad \frac{1}{\sqrt{2\pi}} \int_0^{\frac{\lambda}{\sigma}} e^{-\frac{z^2}{2}}\, dz = 0.25$$

Using the table, $\frac{\lambda}{\sigma} = 0.67 \;\Rightarrow\; \lambda = 0.67\,\sigma \cong \frac{2}{3}\sigma$

Hence the Probable error $\lambda \cong \frac{2}{3}\,\sigma$.

19.10. APPLICATIONS OF NORMAL DISTRIBUTION

This distribution is applied to problems concerning :

(1) calculation of hit probability of a shot.

(2) statistical inference in most branches of science.

(3) calculation of errors made by chance in experimental measurements.

19.11. STANDARD FORM OF THE NORMAL DISTRIBUTION

If x is a normal random variable with mean μ and standard deviation σ, then the random variable defined by

$$z = \frac{x - \mu}{\sigma},$$

is said to be a standard normal variate with mean 0 and standard deviation 1, *i.e.*, $z \sim N(0, 1)$.

The probability density function for the standard normal variate is given by

$$f(z) = \frac{1}{\sqrt{2\pi}} e^{-\frac{z^2}{2}}, \; -\infty < z < \infty.$$

The integral $\int_0^z f(z)\, dz$, cannot be evaluated analytically. The values of this integral for various positive values of z have been given in the table.

ILLUSTRATIVE EXAMPLES

Example 1. *Let z be a standard normal variate, then find*

(*i*) $P(0 \le z \le 1.42)$ (*ii*) $P(z \ge -1.28)$

(*iii*) $P(|z| \le 0.5)$ (*iv*) $P(-0.73 \le z \le 0)$

(*v*) $P(0.81 \le z \le 1.94)$ (*vi*) $P(|z| \ge 10.5)$

(*vii*) $P(-.75 \le z \le 0)$.

Sol. (*i*) We know that

$P(0 \le z \le 1.42)$ = Area under the standard normal curve between the ordinates $z = 0$ and $z = 1.42$

$= 0.4222$

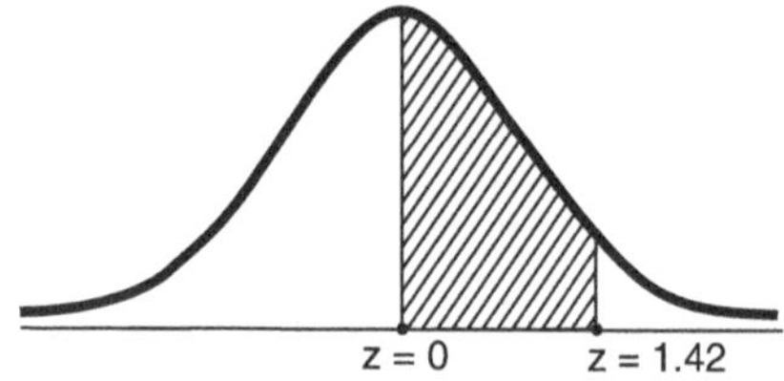

(In the table given in the end, move down the column marked z until we get the entry 1.42 and then move right to column marked 2. The required entry is 0.4222.)

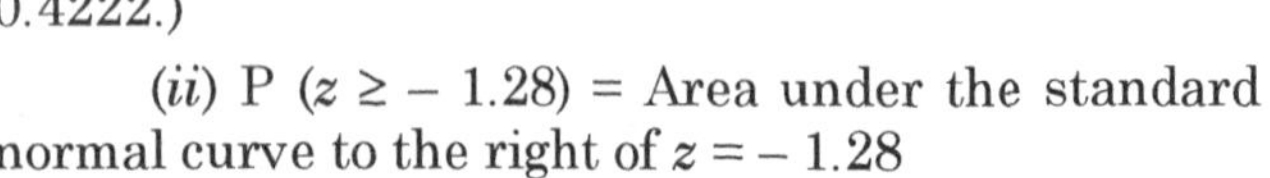

(*ii*) $P(z \ge -1.28)$ = Area under the standard normal curve to the right of $z = -1.28$

$= (\text{Area between } z = -1.28 \text{ and } z = 0) + (\text{Area to the right of } z = 0)$

$= P(-1.128 \le z \le 0) + P(z \ge 0)$

$= P(0 \le z \le 1.28) + P(z \ge 0)$

(due to Symmetry.)

$= 0.3997 + 0.5$ | From normal table | $P(z \ge 0) = 0.5$

$= 0.89997$

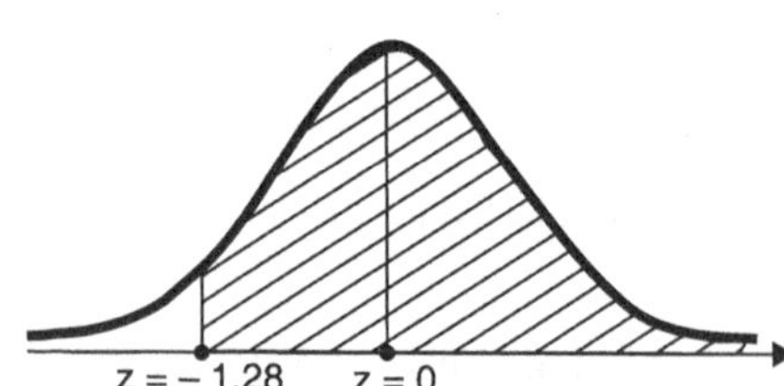

(*iii*) $P(|z| \le 0.5) = P(0.5 \le z \le 0.5)$

= Area between $z = -0.5$ and $z = 0.5$

= 2 (Area between $z = 0$ and $z = 0.5$)

$= 2P(0 \le z \le 0.5)$

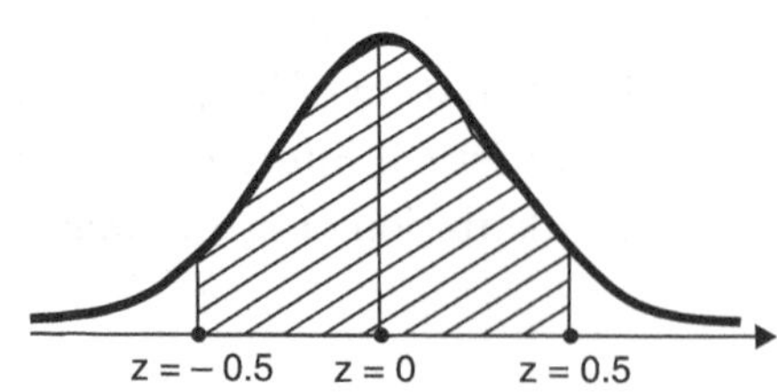

$= 2(0.1915) = 0.3830.$ | From normal table

(*iv*) $P(-0.73 \le z \le 0)$

$= P(0 \le z \le 0.73)$ | By Symmetry

$= 0.2673$ | From normal table

(*v*) $P(0.81 \le z \le 1.94)$

= Area under the normal variate between $z = 0.81$ and $z = 1.94$

= (Area between $z = 0$ and $z = 1.94$) – (Area between $z = 0$ and $z = 0.81$)

$= P(0 \le z \le 1.94) - P(0 \le z \le 0.81)$

$= 0.4738 - 0.2910$ | From normal table

$= 0.1828.$

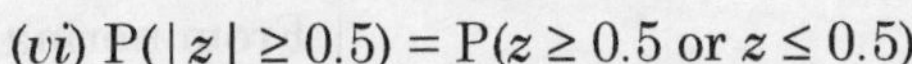

(*vi*) $P(|z| \ge 0.5) = P(z \ge 0.5 \text{ or } z \le 0.5)$

| $|a| \ge b \Rightarrow a \ge b$ or $a \le -b$

$= P(z \ge 0.5) + P(z \le -0.5)$

= (Area to the right of $z = 0.5$) + (Area to the left of $z = -0.5$)

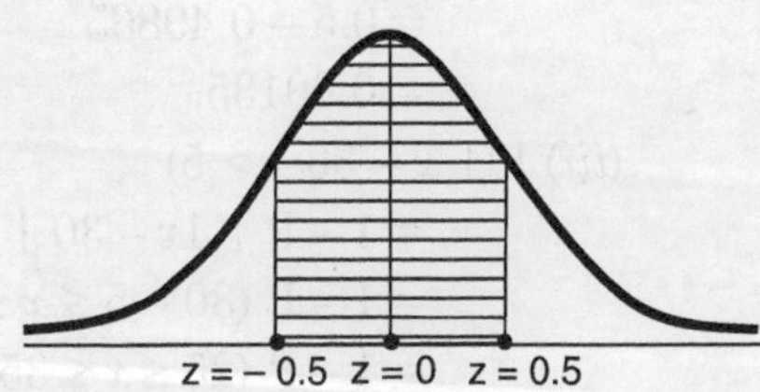

= 2(Area to the right of $z = 0.5$)

= 2 [(Area to the right of $z = 0$) – (Area between $z = 0$ and $z = 0.5$)]

$= 2[0.5 - P(0 \le z \le 0.5)$

$= 2(0.5 - 0.1915) = 2\ (0.3085)$ | From normal table

$= 0.6170.$

(*vii*) $P(-.75 \le z \le 0) = P(0 \le z \le 0.75) = 0.2734.$ | due to symmetry

Example 2. *If x is a normal variate with mean 30 and S.D 5. find*

(i) P(26 ≤ x ≤ 40) *(ii) P (x ≥ 45)* *(iii) P(| x – 30 | > 5)*

(iv) If X is normally distributed with mean 5 and standard deviation 2, find P(X > 8).

Sol. Given x is a normal variate with mean $\mu = 30$ and S.D. $\sigma = 5$.

Let z be the standard normal variate,

then $$z = \frac{x - \mu}{\sigma} = \frac{x - 30}{5}$$

(*i*) When $x = 26$, $z = \frac{26 - 30}{5} = -\frac{4}{5} = -0.8$

When $x = 40$, $z = \frac{40 - 30}{5} = \frac{10}{5} = 2$

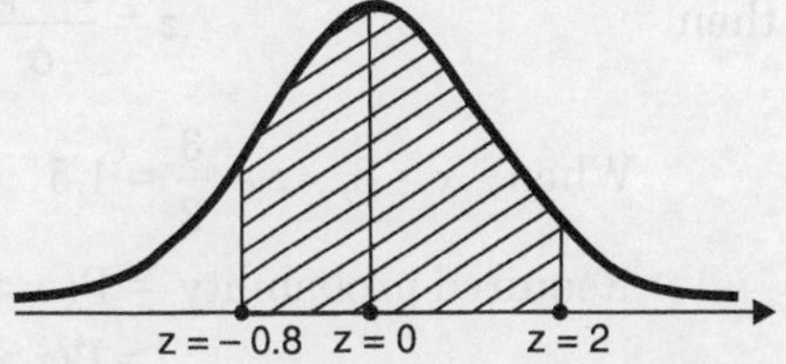

$\therefore \quad P(26 \le x \le 40) = P(-0.8 \le z \le 2)$

= Area under the normal variate between $z = -0.8$ and $z = 2$

= (Area between $z = -0.8$ and $z = 0$) + (Area between $z = 0$ and $z = 2$)

$= P(-0.8 \le z \le 0) + P(0 \le z \le 2)$

$= P(0 \le z \le 0.8) + P(0 \le z \le 2)$

$= 0.2881 + 0.4772$ | Due to symmetry, see table

$= 0.7563.$

(*ii*) When $x = 45$, $z = \dfrac{45 - 30}{5} = 3$

$\therefore$ $P(x \ge 45) = P(z \ge 3)$

= Area under standard normal variate to the right of $z = 3$

= (Area to the right of $z = 0$) – (Area between $z = 0$ and $z = 3$)

$= P(z \ge 0) - P(0 \le z \le 3)$

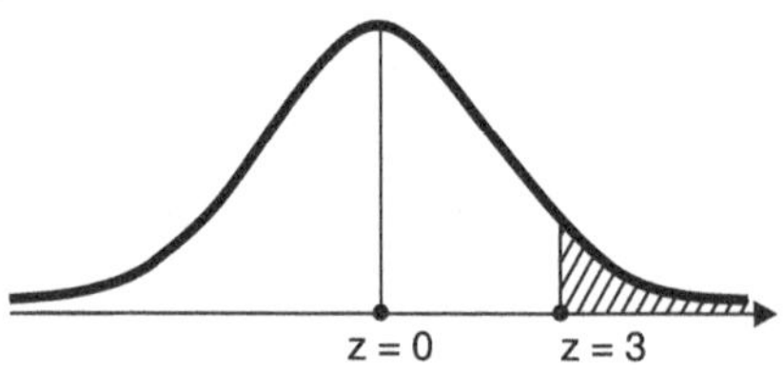

$= 0.5 - 0.49865$ | From normal table

$= 0.00135.$

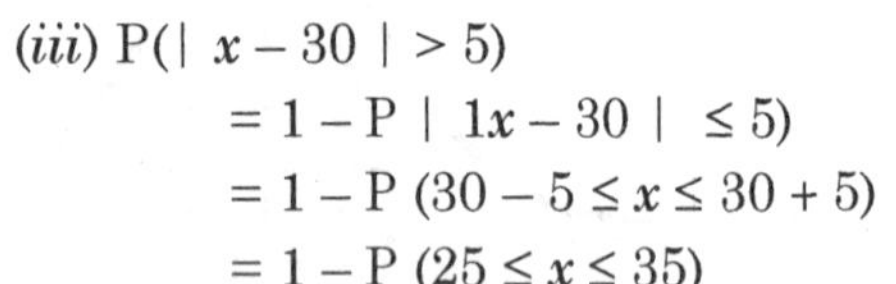

(*iii*) $P(|x - 30| > 5)$

$= 1 - P\ |\ 1x - 30\ |\ \le 5)$ | Note

$= 1 - P(30 - 5 \le x \le 30 + 5)$

$= 1 - P(25 \le x \le 35)$

$|a - b| \le c \Rightarrow b - c \le a \le b + c$

When $x = 25$, $z = \dfrac{25 - 30}{5} = -1$

When $x = 35$, $z = \dfrac{35 - 30}{5} = 1$

$P(|x - 30| > 5) = 1 - P(-1 \le z \le 1)$

$= 1 - 2\,P(0 \le z \le 1)$

$= 1 - 2\,(0.3413)$

$= 1 - 0.6826 = 0.3174.$

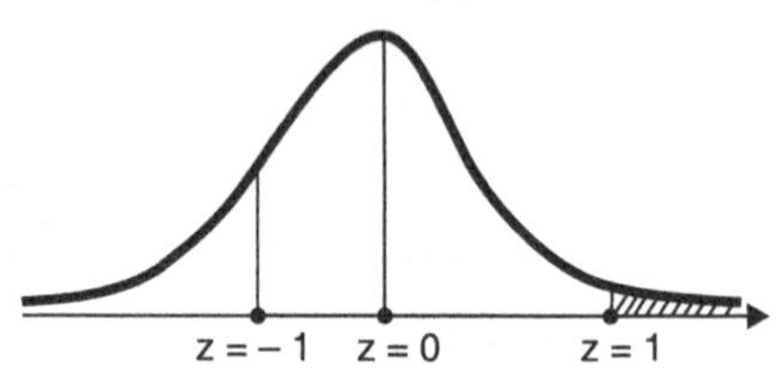

(*iv*) Given x is a normal variate with mean $= \mu = 5$,

S.D. $= \sigma = 2$

Let z be the standard normal variate,

then $z = \dfrac{x - \mu}{\sigma} = \dfrac{x - 5}{2}$

When $x = 8$, $z = \dfrac{3}{2} = 1.5$

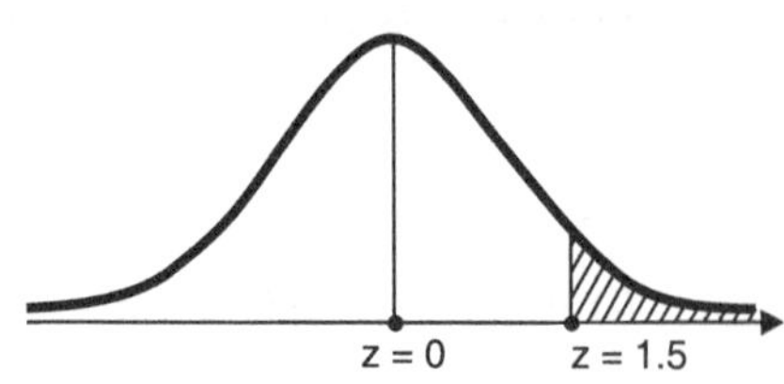

Required probability $= P(x > 8)$

$= P(z > 1.5)$

= Area under standard normal variate to the right of $z = 1.5$

$= P(z \ge 0) - P(0 < z < 1.5)$

$= 0.5 - 0.4332$

$= 0.0668.$

Example 3. *The income of a group of 10,000 persons was found to be normally distributed with mean = ₹ 750 p.m. and standard deviation = ₹ 50. Show that of this group about 95% had income exceeding ₹ 668 and only 5% had income exceeding ₹ 832. What was the lowest income among the richest ?*

Sol. Let x denote the income then, given, x is a normal variate with mean $\mu = 750$ and S.D $\sigma = 50$. Let z be the standard normal variate, then

$$z = \frac{x - \mu}{\sigma} = \frac{x - 750}{50}$$

z = – 1.64   z = 0

(*i*) When $x = 668$, $z = \frac{668 - 750}{50} = \frac{-82}{50} = -1.64$

$$P(x > 668) = P(z > -1.64)$$
$$= \text{Area to the right of } z = -1.64$$
$$= (\text{Area between } z = -1.64 \text{ and } z = 0) + (\text{Area to the right of } z = 0)$$
$$= P(-1.64 \le z \le 0) + P(z \ge 0)$$
$$= P(0 \le z \le 1.64) + P(z \ge 0)$$
$$= 0.4495 + 0.5 = 0.9495$$ | see normal table

Hence required % of persons having income greater than ₹ 668

$$= 94.95\% \cong 95\%$$

(*ii*) When $x = 832$, $z = \frac{832 - 750}{50} = 1.64$

$$\therefore \quad P(x > 832) = P(z > 1.64)$$
$$= \text{Area to the right of } z = 1.64$$
$$= (\text{Area to the right of } z = 0) - (\text{Area between } z = 0 \text{ and } z = 1.64)$$
$$= P(z \ge 0) - P(0 \le z \le 1.64)$$
$$= 0.5 - 0.4495 = 0.0505$$

Hence required % of Persons having income greater than ₹ 832 = 5.

Lastly, to find the lowest income among the richest 100, we need to find the value of r such that $P(x \ge r) = 0.01$

when $x = r$, $\quad z = \frac{x - \mu}{\sigma} = \frac{r - 750}{50} = z_1$, say

z = 0   z = 1.64

Now $\quad P(x \ge r) = 0.01$

$\Rightarrow \quad P(z \ge z_1) = 0.01$

$\Rightarrow \quad 0.5 - P(0 \le z \le z_1) = 0.01$

$\Rightarrow \quad P(0 \le z \le z_1) = 0.5 - 0.01 = 0.49$

$\Rightarrow \quad z_1 = 2.33$ | see normal table

$\Rightarrow \quad \frac{r - 750}{50} = 2.33 = r = 750 + 50\,(2.33) = 866.5$

Hence the lowest income among the richest 100 = ₹ 866.50.

Example 4. *If the salary of workers in a factory is assumed to follow a normal distribution with a mean of ₹ 500 and a S.D. of ₹ 100. Find the number of workers whose salary vary between ₹ 400 and ₹ 650, given the number of workers in the factory is 15000.*

(P.T.U., M.B.A. Dec. 2006)

Sol. Let x be the random variable denoting the salary of workers.

Here mean $\mu = 500$, standard deviation $\sigma = 100$

Let $z = \dfrac{x - \mu}{\sigma}$ be the standard normal variate

When $x = 400$, $z = \dfrac{400 - 500}{100} = -1$

When $x = 650$, $z = \dfrac{650 - 500}{100} = 1.5$

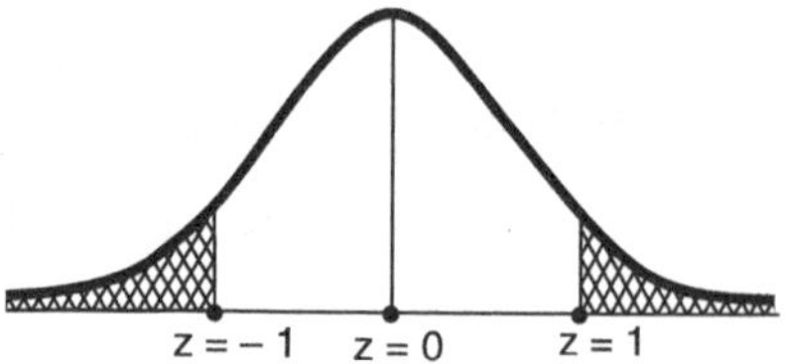

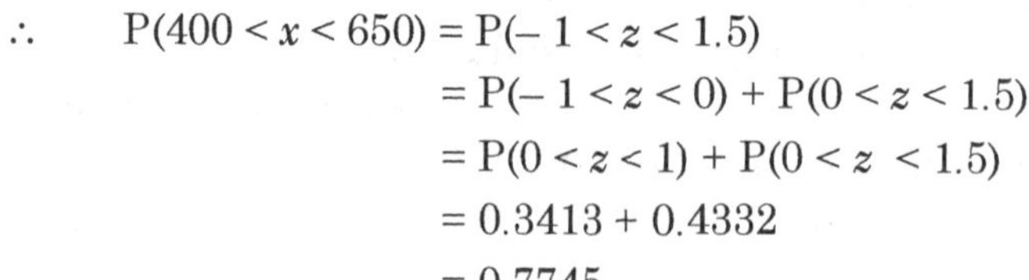

$\therefore \quad P(400 < x < 650) = P(-1 < z < 1.5)$

$= P(-1 < z < 0) + P(0 < z < 1.5)$

$= P(0 < z < 1) + P(0 < z < 1.5)$ | due to symmetry

$= 0.3413 + 0.4332$ | see normal table

$= 0.7745$

$\therefore$ Required number of workers

$= (0.7745) \times 15000$

$= 11617.5 \cong 11618.$

Example 5. *The weekly wages of 1,000 workmen are normally distributed with a mean of ₹ 70 and a standard deviation of ₹ 5. Estimate the number of workers whose weekly wages will be between ₹ 69 and 72.* (P.T.U., M.B.A. Dec. 2000)

Sol. Let X be a random variable following normal distribution.

Given $\mu = 70$, $\sigma = 5$

Let $Z = \dfrac{X - \mu}{\sigma}$ be the standard normal variate

When $X = 69$, $Z = \dfrac{69 - 70}{5} = -0.2$

When $X = 72$, $Z = \dfrac{72 - 70}{5} = 0.4$

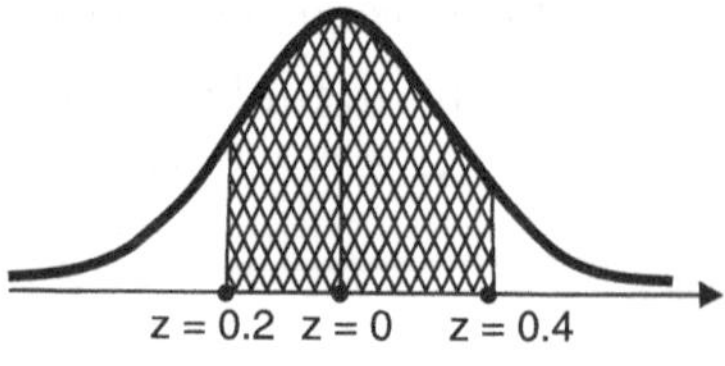

$\therefore \quad P(69 < X < 72) = P(-0.2 < Z < 0.4)$

$= P(-0.2 < Z < 0) + P(0 < Z < 0.4)$

$= P(0 < Z < 0.2) + P(0 < Z < 0.4)$ | due to symmetry

$= 0.0793 + .1554 = 0.2347$ | using normal table

Hence, number of workers getting wages between ₹ 69 and 72

$= (0.2347) \times 1000 = 234.7$

$\cong 234.$

Example 6. *A sample of 100 dry battery cells tested to find the length of life produced the following results*

$\bar{x} = 12$ *hours*, $\sigma = 3$ *hours.*

Assuming the data to be normally distributed, what percentage of battery cells are expected to have

(*i*) *more than 15 hours* (*ii*) *less than 6 hours*

(*iii*) *between 10 and 14 hours ?*

Sol. Here x denoted the length of life of dry battery cells.

Also $z = \frac{x - \bar{x}}{\sigma} = \frac{x - 12}{3}$.

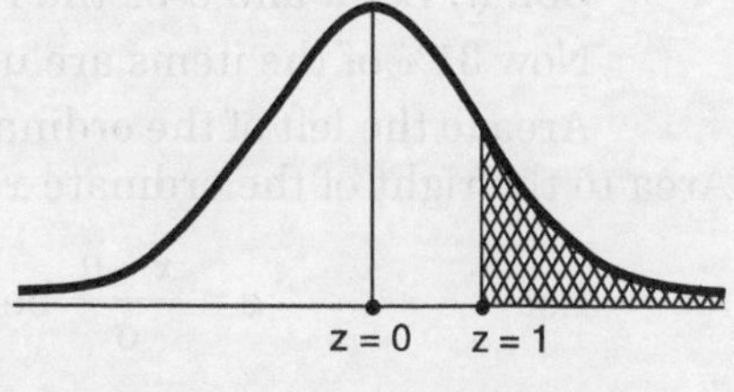

(*i*) When $x = 15$, $z = 1$

$\therefore$ $P(x > 15) = P(z > 1)$
$= P(0 < z < \infty) - P(0 < z < 1)$
$= 0.5 - 0.3413 = 0.1587$
$= 15.87\%$.

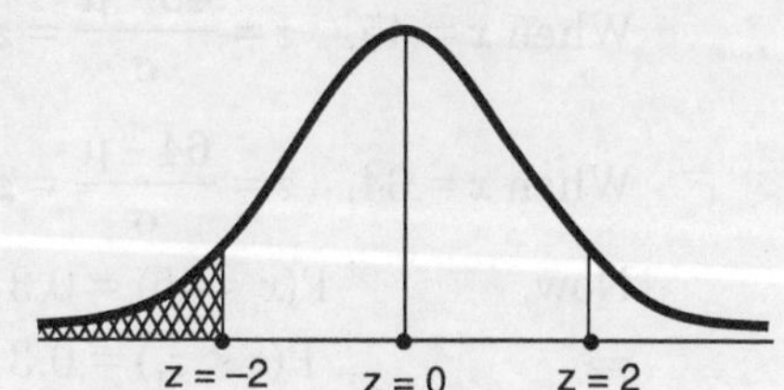

(*ii*) When $x = 6$, $z = -2$

$\therefore$ $P(x < b) = P(z < -2)$
$= P(z > 2)$
$= P(0 < z < \infty) - P(0 < z < 2)$
$= 0.5 - 0.4772 = 0.0228$
$= 2.28\%$.

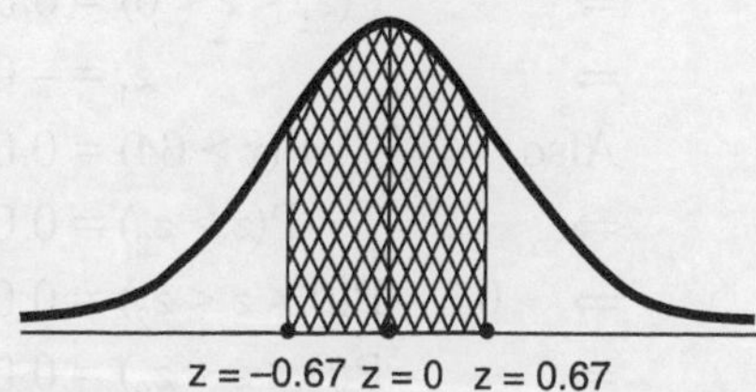

(*iii*) When $x = 10$, $z = -\frac{2}{3} = -0.67$

When $x = 14$, $z = \frac{2}{3} = 0.67$

$P(10 < x < 14) = P(-0.67 < z < 0.67)$
$= 2P(0 < z < 0.67) = 2 \times 0.2487$
$= 0.4974 = 49.74\%$.

Example 7. *Assume the mean height of soldiers to be 68.22 inches with a variance of 10.8 sq. inches. How many soldiers in a regiment of 1000 would you expect to be over 6 feet tall ?*

(P.T.U., M.B.A. Dec. 2000)

Sol. Let X denotes the height of soldiers, following the normal distribution.

Given $\mu = 68.22$, $\sigma^2 = 10.8$

Let $Z = \frac{X - \mu}{\sigma}$ be the standard normal variate

When X = 6 ft = 6 × 12 inches = 72 inches,

$$Z = \frac{72 - 68.22}{3.2} = 1.18$$

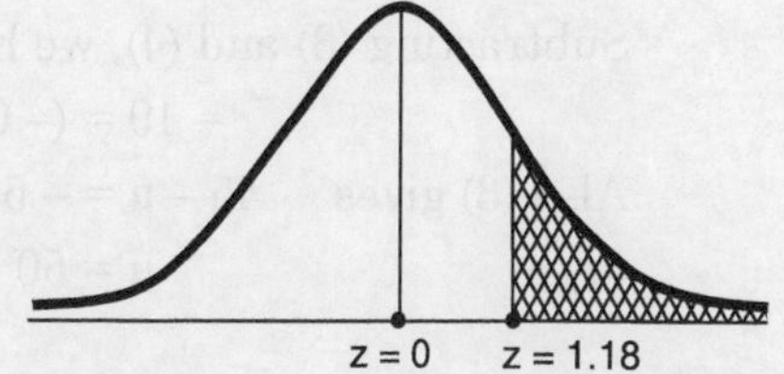

$P(X > 6 \text{ ft}) = P(X > 72 \text{ inches})$
$= P(Z > 1.18)$

$= 0.5 - P(0 < Z < 1.18)$

$= 0.5 - 0.3810$ | using normal table

$= 0.119$

$\therefore$ Required number of soldiers = (0.119) × 1000 = 119

Example 8. (*i*) *In a normal distribution, 31% of the items are under 45 and 8% are over 64. Find the mean and standard deviation of the distribution.*

(*ii*) *In a distribution, exactly normal, 9.85% of the items are under 40 and 89.97% are under 60. What are the mean and standard deviation of the distribution.*

Sol. (*i*) Let u and σ be the required mean and standard deviation.

Now 31% of the items are under 45. It means

Area to the left of the ordinate $x = 45$ is 0.31. Also 8% of the items are over 64. It means. Area to the right of the ordinate $x = 64$ is 0.08

Let $z = \dfrac{x - \mu}{\sigma}$ be the standard normal variate.

When $x = 45$, $z = \dfrac{45 - \mu}{\sigma} = z_1$, (say)

When $x = 64$, $z = \dfrac{64 - \mu}{\sigma} = z_2$ | say

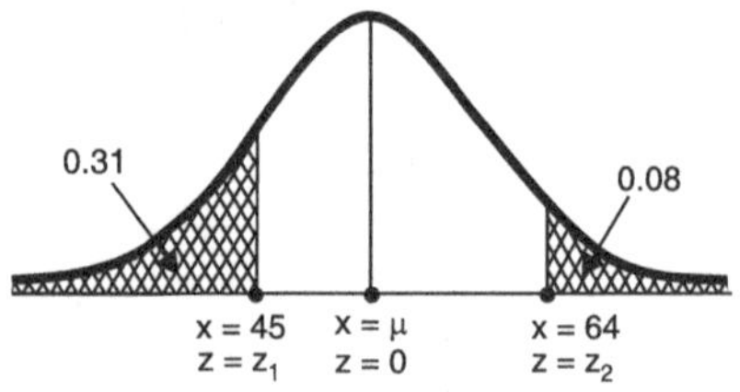

0.31
0.08
x = 45 z = z1
x = μ z = 0
x = 64 z = z2

Now, $P(x < 45) = 0.31$

$\Rightarrow$ $P(z < z_1) = 0.31$

$\Rightarrow$ $0.5 - P(z_1 < z < 0) = 0.31$

$\Rightarrow$ $P(z_1 < z < 0) = 0.5 - 0.31 = 0.19$

$\Rightarrow$ $z_1 = -0.5$ ...(1) $(z_1 < 0)$ | Using normal table

Also, $P(x > 64) = 0.08$

$\Rightarrow$ $P(z > z_2) = 0.08$

$\Rightarrow$ $0.5 - P(0 < z < z_2) = 0.08$

$\Rightarrow$ $P(0 < z < z_2) = 0.5 - 0.08 = 0.42$

$\Rightarrow$ $z_2 = 1.4$ ...(2) | Using Normal table

From (1), $z_1 = -0.5$

$\Rightarrow$ $\dfrac{45 - \mu}{\sigma} = -0.5$

$\Rightarrow$ $45 - \mu = -(0.5)\sigma$ ...(3)

From (2) $z_2 = 1.4 = \dfrac{64 - \mu}{\sigma} = 1.4$

$= 64 - \mu = (1.4)\sigma$ ...(4)

Subtracting (3) and (4), we have

$$-19 = (-0.5 - 1.4)\sigma \Rightarrow 19 = 0.9\sigma \Rightarrow \sigma = 10$$

Also (3) gives $45 - \mu = -5$

$\Rightarrow$ $\mu = 50$

(*ii*) Let μ and σ be the required mean and standard deviation.

Now 9.85% of the items are under 40. It means area to the left of the ordinate $x = 40$ is 0.985.

Also 89.97% of the items are under 60. It means area to the left of the ordinate $x = 60$ is 0.8997

Let $z = \frac{x - \mu}{\sigma}$ be the standard normal variate.

When $x = 40$, $z = \frac{40 - \mu}{\sigma} = z_1$, (say)

When $x = 60$, $z = \frac{60 - \mu}{\sigma} = z_2$, (say)

Now, $P(x < 40) = 0.985 \Rightarrow P(z < z_1) = 0.985$

$\Rightarrow 1 - P(z > z_1) = 0.985 \Rightarrow P(z > z_1) = 0.015$

$\Rightarrow 0.5 - P(0 < z < z_1) = 0.015 \Rightarrow P(0 < z < z_1) = 0.485$

$\Rightarrow z_1 = 2.17$ | Using normal table

Also $P(x < 60) = 0.8997 \Rightarrow P(z < z_2) = 0.8997$

$\Rightarrow 1 - P(z > z_2) = 0.8997 \Rightarrow P(z > z_2) = 0.1003$

$\Rightarrow 0.5 - P(0 < z < z_2) = 0.1003 \Rightarrow P(0 < z < z_2) = 0.3997$

$\Rightarrow z_2 = 1.8$

Here the values of the ordinate $z = z_1$ and $z = z_2$ must be negative.

i.e., $z_1 = -2.17, z_2 = -1.8$

When $z_1 = -2.17$, then $\frac{40 - \mu}{\sigma} = -2.17 \Rightarrow 40 - \mu = -2.17\sigma$ ...(1)

When $z_2 = -1.8$, then $\frac{60 - \mu}{\sigma} = -1.8 \Rightarrow 60 - \mu = -1.8\sigma$ ...(2)

Subtracting (1) and (2), we get

$$-20 = -0.37\sigma \Rightarrow \sigma = \frac{20}{0.37} = 54.05$$

Also (1) gives $40 - \mu = (-2.17)(54.05) = -117.29$

$\Rightarrow \mu = 40 + 117.29 = 157.29.$

Example 9. (*a*) *The marks obtained in a certain examination are found to be normally distributed. If 12.5% of the candidates obtain 60% or more marks, 39% obtain less than 30 marks, find the mean number of marks obtained by candidates.* (P.T.U. M.B.A. May 2008)

(b) Given that the probability of committing an error of magnitude x is $y = \frac{h}{\sqrt{\pi}} e^{-h^2 x^2}$, *show that the probable error is 0.4769/h.*

Sol. (*a*) Let μ be the required mean and x denotes the marks obtained in the certain examination.

Let $z = \frac{x - \mu}{\sigma}$

12.5% of the candidates obtained 60 or more marks. It means

The value of z corresonding to 0.375 (37.5% area) by using the normal table is

$$z = 1.15 \quad \text{or} \quad \frac{60 - \mu}{\sigma} = 1.15 \qquad \ldots(1)$$

39% of the candidates obtained less than 30 marks. It means

The value of z corresponding to 0.11 (11% area) by using the normal table is

$$z = -0.28 \quad \text{or} \quad \frac{30 - \mu}{\sigma} = -0.28 \qquad \ldots(2)$$

From (1) and (2), $60 - \mu = 1.15\sigma, \quad 30 - \mu = -0.28\sigma$

Subtracting, $30 = (1.15 + 0.28)\,\sigma = 1.43\sigma$

$$\Rightarrow \qquad \sigma = \frac{30}{1.43} = 20.97$$

From (1) $60 - \mu = 1.15\,(20.97) = 24.11$

$$\Rightarrow \qquad \mu = 60 - 24.11 = 35.89 \text{ is the required marks}$$

(*b*) Using Normal distribution, we know

$$y = f(x) = \frac{1}{\sigma\sqrt{2\pi}}\, e^{-\frac{1}{2}\left(\frac{x-\mu}{\sigma}\right)^2} \qquad \ldots(1)$$

Also given probability of committing an error is

$$y = \frac{h}{\sqrt{\pi}}\, e^{-h^2 x^2} \qquad \ldots(2)$$

From (1) and (2),

$$\frac{1}{\sigma\sqrt{2\pi}}\, e^{-\frac{1}{2}\left(\frac{x-\mu}{\sigma}\right)^2} = \frac{h}{\sqrt{\pi}}\, e^{-h^2 x^2} \;\Rightarrow\; \frac{1}{\sigma\sqrt{2\pi}} = \frac{h}{\sqrt{\pi}} \;\Rightarrow\; h = \frac{1}{\sigma\sqrt{2}} \;\Rightarrow\; \sigma = \frac{1}{\sqrt{2}h}$$

$\therefore$ Required probable error

$$= \frac{2}{3}\sigma = \frac{2}{3} \cdot \frac{1}{\sqrt{2}h} = \frac{\sqrt{2}}{3h} = \frac{0.4769}{h}.$$

Example 10. *Assume that 4 per cent of the population over 65 years old has Alzheimer's disease. Suppose a random sample of 3500 people over 65 is taken. Find the probability that fewer than 150 of them have the disease.*

Sol. Here $n = 3500$, $p = 4\% = 0.04$

$$q = 1 - p = 1 - 0.04 = 0.96$$

Here $\qquad \mu = \text{mean} = np = 3500 \,.\, \frac{4}{100} = 140$

$$\text{Standard deviation} = \sigma = \sqrt{npq} = \sqrt{3500 \,.\, \frac{4}{100} \cdot \frac{96}{100}}$$

$$= \sqrt{134.4} = 11.6$$

Let x denote the number of people with Alzheimer's disease, then we required to find $P(x < 150)$

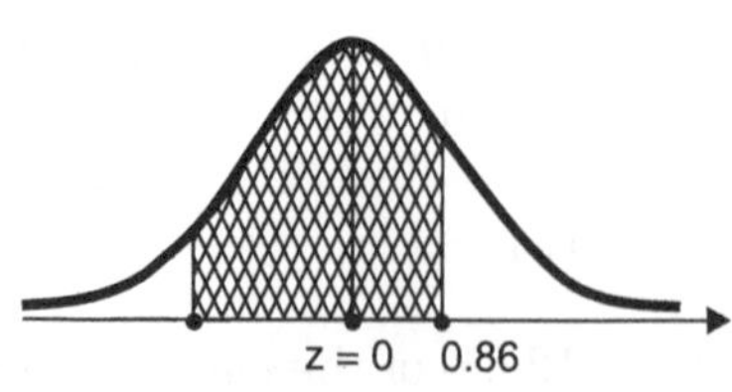

When $x = 150$, $\quad z = \dfrac{x-\mu}{\sigma} = \dfrac{150-140}{11.6} = \dfrac{10}{11.6} = \dfrac{100}{116} = 0.86$

$\therefore \quad P(x < 150) = P(z < 0.86)$

= Area under standard normal variate to the left of $z = 0.86$

= (Area to the left of $z = 0$) + (Area between $z = 0$ and $z = 0.86$)

$= 0.5 + P(0 \le z \le 0.86)$

$= 0.5 + 0.3051 = 0.8051.$

Example 11. *The mean yield for 1 acre plot is 662 kilos with S.D. of 32 kilos. Assuming normal distribution, how many 1 acre plots in a batch of 1000 plots would you expect to have yield (i) over 700 kilos (ii) below 650 kilos (iii) what is the lowest yield of best 100 plots.*

Sol. Given : mean $\mu = 662$. Standard deviation $\sigma = 32$. Let x be the normal variate. Also $N = 100$.

(*i*) When $x = 700$, $z = \dfrac{x-\mu}{\sigma} = \dfrac{700-662}{32} = \dfrac{38}{32} = \dfrac{19}{16} = 1.1875$

$\therefore$ Required Probability $= N.P\ (x > 700)$

$= 1000\ .\ P(z > 1.1875)$

$= 1000$ (Area to the right of $z = 1.1875$)

$= 1000$ [(Area to the right of $z = 0$)

– (Area between $z = 0$ and $z = 1.1875$)]

$= 1000\ [(P(z \ge 0) - P(0 \le z \le 1.1875)]$

$= 1000\ (0.5 - 0.3810] = 1000\ .\ (.1190) = 119$

(*ii*) When $x = 650$, $z = \dfrac{650-662}{32} = \dfrac{-12}{32} = \dfrac{-3}{8} = -0.375$

Required probability

$= N\ P(x < 650)$

$= 1000\ .\ P\ (z < -0.375)$

$= 1000$ (Area to the right of $z = 0.375$)

$= 1000\ [(P\ (z \ge 0) - P(0 \le z \le 0.375)]$

$= 1000\ (0.5 - 0.1443)$

$= 1000 \times (0.3557) = 355.7$

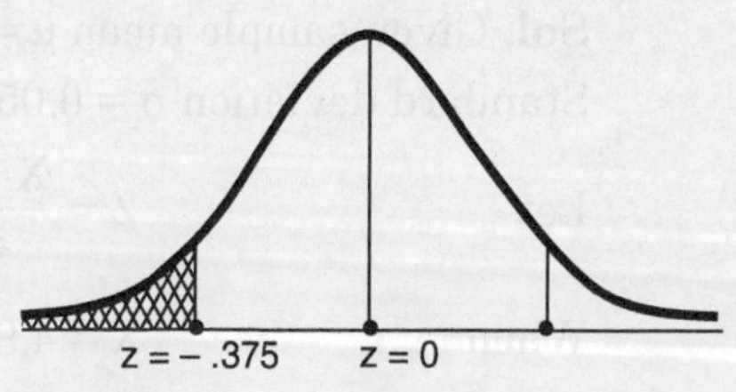

(*iii*) We now find the lowest yield of best 100 plots, we need to find the value of r such that

$$P\ (x \ge r) = 0.01$$

When $x = r$, $\quad z = \dfrac{x-\mu}{\sigma} = \dfrac{r-662}{32} = z_1$, say

Now $\quad P(x \ge r) = 0.01 \Rightarrow P(z \ge z_1) = 0.01$

$\Rightarrow \quad 0.5 - P(0 \le z \le z_1) = 0.01$

$\Rightarrow \quad P(0 \le z \le z_1) = 0.5 - 0.01 = 0.49$

$\Rightarrow \quad z_1 = 2.33$ | See table

$$\Rightarrow \qquad \frac{r - 662}{32} = 2.33$$

$$\Rightarrow \qquad r = 662 + 32\,(2.33) = 662 + 74.56 = 736.$$

Example 12. *The income distribution of workers in a certain factory was found to be normal with mean of ₹ 500 and standard deviation of ₹ 50. There were 228 persons getting above ₹ 600. How many persons were there in all ?*

Sol. Let X denote the income of the workers. Given $\mu = 500$, $\sigma = 50$

Let $Z = \dfrac{X - \mu}{\sigma}$ be a standard normal variate.

When X = 600, $\quad Z = \dfrac{600 - 500}{50} = 2$

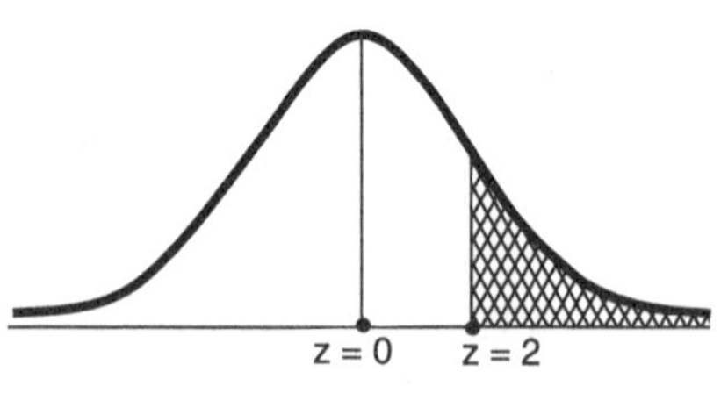

The probability of the persons getting above ₹ 600

$= P(X > 600) = P(Z > 2)$

$= 0.5 - P(0 < Z < 2)$

$= 0.5 - 0.4772$ | Using normal table

$= 0.0228$

Now, there are 228 persons getting salary above ₹ 600. Therefore total number of persons

$$= \frac{228}{0.0228} = 10{,}000.$$

Example 13. *The mean inside diameter of a sample of 500 washers produced by a machine is 5.02 mm. and the standard deviation is 0.05 mm. The purpose for which these washers are intended allows a maximum tolerance in the diameter of 4.96 to 5.08 mm, otherwise the washers are considered defective. Determine the percentage of defective washers produced by the machine, assuming the diameters are normally distributed.*

Sol. Given sample mean $\mu = 5.02$ mm

Standard deviation $\sigma = 0.05$ mm

Let $\quad Z = \dfrac{X - \mu}{\sigma}$ be a standard normal variate.

When $\quad X = 4.96,\ Z = \dfrac{4.96 - 5.02}{0.05} = -1.2$

When $\quad X = 5.08,\ Z = \dfrac{5.08 - 5.02}{0.05} = 1.2$

Probability of non-defective washers

$= P(4.96 < X < 5.08)$

$= P(-1.2 < Z < 1.2)$

$= P(-1.2 < Z < 0) + P(0 < Z < 1.2)$

$= P(0 < Z < 1.2) + P(0 < Z < 1.2)$ | Due to symmetry

$= 2P(0 < Z < 1.2)$

$= 2(0.3849) = 0.7699 \cong 0.77$ | Using Normal Table)

$\therefore$ Percentage of non-defective washers = 77%

$\therefore$ Required percentage of defective washers

$= 100 - 77 = 23.$

TEST YOUR KNOWLEDGE

1. The mean height of 500 male students in a certain college is 151 cm and the standard deviation is 15 cm. Assuming the heights are normally distributed, find how many students have heights between 120 and 155 cm ?
2. An aptitude test from selecting officers in a bank is conducted on 1000 candidates. The average score is 42 and the standard deviation of score is 24. Assuming normal distribution for the scores, find
   (*i*) the number of candidates whose scores exceed 60
   (*ii*) the number of candidates whose scores lie between 30 and 60.
3. In a normal distribution, 7% of the items are under 35 and 89% are under 36. What are the mean and standard deviation of the distribution ?
4. Let X denote the number of scores on a test. If X is normally distributed with mean 100 and standard deviation 15, find the probability that X does not exceed 130.
5. It is known from the past experience that the number of telephone calls made daily in a certain community between 3 p.m. and 4 p.m. have a mean of 352 and a standard deviation of 31. What percentage of the time will there be more than 400 telephone calls made in this community between 3 p.m. and 4 p.m. ?
6. Students of a class were given a mechanical aptitude test. This marks were found to be normally distributed with mean 60 and standard deviation 5. What per cent of students scored
   (*i*) more than 60 marks ? (*ii*) less than 56 marks ?
   (*iii*) between 45 and 65 marks ?
7. In an examination taken by 500 candidates, the average and the standard deviation of marks obtained (normally distributed) are 40% and 10%. Find approximately
   (*i*) how many will pass, if 50% is fixed as a minimum ?
   (*ii*) what should be the minimum if 350 candidates are to pass ?
   (*iii*) how many have scored marks above 60% ?
8. In a certain examination, the percentage of passes and distinction were 46 and 9 respectively. Estimate the average marks obtained by the candidate, the minimum pass and distinction marks, being 40 and 75 respectively. (Assume the distribution of marks to be normal).
9. Suppose the waist measurements X of 800 girls are normally distributed with mean 66 cm and standard deviation 5 cm. Find the number of girls with waist
   (*i*) between 65 cm and 70 cm.
   (*ii*) greater than or equal to 72 cm.
10. Write a short note on Normal distribution. (*P.T.U., M.B.A. May 2004*)
11. Distinguish between Binomial and Normal distribution (*P.T.U., M.B.A. Dec. 2002*)
12. Distinguish between Poisson and Normal distribution (*P.T.U., M.B.A. May 2002*)

Answers

1. 300 2. (*i*) 252 (*ii*) 533 3. $\bar{x}$ = 50.3 σ = 10.33
4. 0.9772 5. 6.06% 6. (*i*) 50% (*ii*) 21.2%
(*iii*) 84% 7. (*i*) 79 (*ii*) 35% (*iii*) 11
8. 37 9. (*i*) 294 (*ii*) 92.

I APPENDIX

Tables

Table I : Inverse Quantities, Powers, Roots, Logarithms

x	$1/x$	x^2	x^3	$\sqrt{x}$	$\sqrt[3]{x}$	$\log x$	x	$1/x$	x^2	x^3	$\sqrt{x}$	$\sqrt[3]{x}$	$\log x$
1.0	1.000	1.000	1.000	1.000	1.000	0.0000	5.5	0.182	30.25	166.4	2.345	1.765	1.7047
1.1	0.909	1.210	1.331	1.049	1.032	0.0953	5.6	0.179	31.36	175.6	2.366	1.776	1. 7228
1.2	0.833	1.440	1.728	1.095	1.063	0.1823	5.7	0.175	32.49	185.2	2.387	1.786	1.7405
1.3	0.769	1.690	2.197	1.140	1.091	0.2624	5.8	0.172	33.64	195.1	2.408	1.797	1.7579
1.4	0.714	1.960	2.744	1.183	1.119	0.3365	5.9	0.169	34.81	205.4	2.429	1.807	1.7750
1.5	0.667	2.250	3.375	1.225	1.145	0.4055	6.0	0.167	36.00	216.0	2.449	1.817	1.7918
1.6	0.625	2.560	4.096	1.265	1.170	0.4700	6.1	0.164	37.21	227.0	2.470	1.827	1.8083
1.7	0.588	2.890	4.913	1.304	1.193	0.5306	6.2	0.161	38.44	238.3	2.490	1.837	1.8245
1.8	0.556	3.240	5.832	1.342	1.216	0.5878	6.3	0.159	39.69	250.0	2.510	1.847	1.8405
1.9	0.526	3.610	6.859	1.378	1.239	0.6419	6.4	0.156	40.96	262.1	2.530	1.857	1.8563
2.0	0.500	4.000	8.000	1.414	1.260	0.6931	6.5	0.154	42.25	274.6	2.550	1.866	1.8718
2.1	0.476	4.410	9.261	1.449	1.281	0.7419	6.6	0.151	43.56	287.5	2.569	1.876	1.8871
2.2	0.454	4.840	10.65	1.483	1.301	0.7885	6.7	0.149	44.89	300.8	2.588	1.885	1.9021
2.3	0.435	5.290	12.17	1.517	1.320	0.8329	6.8	0.147	46.24	314.4	2.608	1.895	1.9169
2.4	0.417	5.760	13.82	1.549	1.339	0.8755	6.9	0.145	47.61	328.5	2.627	1.904	1.9315
2.5	0.400	6.250	15.62	1.581	1.357	0.9163	7.0	0.143	49.00	343.0	2.646	1.913	1.9459
2.6	0.385	6.760	17.58	1.612	1.375	0.9555	7.1	0.141	50.41	357.9	2.665	1.922	1.9601
2.7	0.370	7.290	19.68	1.643	1.392	0.9933	7.2	0.139	51.84	373.2	2.683	1.931	1.9741
2.8	0.357	7.840	21.95	1.673	1.409	1.0296	7.3	0.137	53.29	389.0	2.702	1.940	1.9879
2.9	0.345	8.410	24.39	1.703	1.426	1.0647	7.4	0.135	54.76	405.2	2.720	1.949	2.0015
3.0	0.333	9.000	27.00	1.732	1.442	1.0986	7.5	0.133	56.25	421.9	2.739	1.957	2.0149
3.1	0.323	9.610	29.79	1.761	1.458	1.1314	7.6	0.132	57.76	439.0	2.757	1.966	2.0281
3.2	0.312	10.24	32.77	1.789	1.474	1.1632	7.7	0.130	59.29	456.5	2.775	1.975	2.0412
3.3	0.303	10.89	35.94	1.817	1.489	1.1939	7.8	0.128	60.84	474.6	2.793	1.983	2.0541
3.4	0.294	11.56	39.30	1.844	1.504	1.2238	7.9	0.127	62.41	493.0	2.811	1.992	2.0669
3.5	0.286	12.25	42.88	1.871	1.518	1.2528	8.0	0.125	64.00	512.0	2.828	2.000	2.0794
3.6	0.278	12.96	46.66	1.897	1.533	1.2809	8.1	0.123	65.61	531.4	2.846	2.008	2.0919
3.7	0.270	13.69	50.65	1.924	1.547	1.3083	8.2	0.122	67.24	551.4	2.864	2.017	2.1041
3.8	0.263	14.44	54.87	1.949	1.560	1.3350	8.3	0.120	68.89	571.8	2.881	2.025	2.1163
3.9	0.256	15.21	59.32	1.975	1.574	1.3610	8.4	0.119	70.56	592.7	2.898	2.033	2.1282
4.0	0.250	16.00	64.00	2.000	1.587	1.3863	8.5	0.118	72.25	614.1	2.915	2.041	2.1401
4.1	0.244	16.81	68.92	2.025	1.601	1.4110	8.6	0.116	73.96	636.1	2.933	2.049	2.1518
4.2	0.238	17.64	74.09	2.049	1.613	1.4351	8.7	0.115	75.69	658.5	2.950	2.057	2.1633
4.3	0.233	18.49	79.51	2.074	1.626	1.4586	8.8	0.114	77.44	681.5	2.966	2.065	2.1748
4.4	0.227	19.36	85.18	2.098	1.639	1.4816	8.9	0.112	79.21	705.0	2.983	2.072	2.1861
4.5	0.222	20.25	91.12	2.121	1.651	1.5041	9.0	0.111	81.00	729.0	3.000	2.080	2.1972
4.6	0.217	21.16	97.34	2.145	1.663	1.5261	9.1	0.110	82.81	753.6	3.017	2.088	2.2083
4.7	0.213	22.09	103.8	2.168	1.675	1.5476	9.2	0.109	84.64	778.7	3.033	2.095	2.2192
4.8	0.208	23.04	110.6	2.191	1.687	1.5686	9.3	0.108	86.49	804.4	3.050	2.103	2.2300
4.9	0.204	24.01	117.6	2.214	1.698	1.5892	9.4	0.106	88.36	830.6	3.066	2.110	2.2107
5.0	0.200	25.00	125.0	2.236	1.710	1.6094	9.5	0.105	90.25	857.4	3.082	2.118	2.2513
5.1	0.196	26.01	132.7	2.258	1.721	1.6292	9.6	0.104	92.16	884.7	3.098	2.125	2.2618
5.2	0.192	27.04	140.6	2.280	1.732	1.6487	9.7	0.103	94.09	912.7	3.114	2.133	2.2721
5.3	0.189	28.09	148.9	2.302	1.744	1.6677	9.8	0.102	96.04	941.2	3.130	2.140	2.2824
5.4	0.185	29.16	157.5	2.324	1.754	1.6864	9.9	0.101	98.01	970.3	3.146	2.147	2.2925
							10.0	0.100	100.00	1000.0	3.162	2.154	2.3026

Table II : Trigonometric Functions

x^0	*x (radians)*	sin *x*	tan *x*	cot *x*	cos *x*		
0	0.0000	0.0000	0.0000	∞	1.0000	1.5708	90
1	0.0175	0.0175	0.0175	57.29	0.9998	1.5533	89
2	0.0349	0.0349	0.0349	28.64	0.9994	1.5359	88
3	0.0524	0.0523	0.0524	19.08	0.9986	1.5184	87
4	0.0698	0.0698	0.0699	14.30	0.9976	1.5010	86
5	0.0873	0.0872	0.0875	11.43	0.9962	1.4835	85
6	0.1047	0.1045	0.1051	9.514	0.9945	1.4661	84
7	0.1222	0.1219	0.1228	8.144	0.9925	1.4486	83
8	0.1396	0.1392	0.1405	7.115	0.9903	1.4312	82
9	0.1571	0.1564	0.1584	6.314	0.9877	1.4137	81
10	0.1745	0.1736	0.1763	5.671	0.9848	1.3963	80
11	0.1920	0.1908	0.1944	5.145	0.9816	1.3788	79
12	0.2094	0.2079	0.2126	4.705	0.9781	1.3614	78
13	0.2269	0.2250	0.2309	4.331	0.9744	1.3439	77
14	0.2443	0.2419	0.2493	4.011	0.9703	1.3265	76
15	0.2618	0.2588	0.2679	3.732	0.9659	1.3090	75
16	0.2793	0.2756	0.2867	3.487	0.9613	1.2915	74
17	0.2967	0.2924	0.3057	3.271	0.9563	1.2741	73
18	0.3142	0.3090	0.3249	3.078	0.9511	1.2566	72
19	0.3316	0.3256	0.3443	2.904	0.9455	1.2392	71
20	0.3491	0.3420	0.3640	2.747	0.9397	1.2217	70
21	0.3665	0.3584	0.3839	2.605	0.9336	1.2043	69
22	0.3840	0.3746	0.4040	2.475	0.9272	1.1868	68
23	0.4014	0.3907	0.4245	2.356	0.9205	1.1694	67
24	0.4189	0.4067	0.4452	2.246	0.9135	1.1519	66
25	0.4363	0.4226	0.4663	2.145	0.9063	1.1345	65
26	0.4538	0.4384	0.4877	2.050	0.8988	1.1170	64
27	0.4712	0.4540	0.5095	1.963	0.8910	1.0996	63
28	0.4887	0.4695	0.5317	1.881	0.8829	1.0821	62
29	0.5061	0.4848	0.5543	1.804	0.8746	1.0647	61
30	0.5236	0.5000	0.5774	1.732	0.8660	1.0472	60
31	0.5411	0.5150	0.6009	1.6643	0.8572	1.0297	59
32	0.5585	0.5299	0.6249	1.6003	0.8480	1.0123	58
33	0.5760	0.5446	0.6494	1.5399	0.8387	0.9948	57
34	0.5934	0.5592	0.6745	1.4826	0.8290	0.9774	56
35	0.6109	0.5736	0.7002	1.4281	0.8192	0.9599	55
36	0.6283	0.5878	0.7265	1.3764	0.8090	0.9425	54
37	0.6458	0.6018	0.7536	1.3270	0.7986	0.9250	53
38	0.6632	0.6157	0.7813	1.2799	0.7880	0.9076	52
39	0.6807	0.6293	0.8098	1.2349	0.7771	0.8901	51
40	0.6981	0.6428	0.8391	1.1918	0.7660	0.8727	50
41	0.7156	0.6561	0.8693	1.1504	0.7547	0.8552	49
42	0.7330	0.6691	0.9004	1.1106	0.7431	0.8378	48
43	0.7505	0.6820	0.9325	1.0724	0.7314	0.8203	47
44	0.7679	0.6947	0.9657	1.0355	0.7193	0.8029	46
45	0.7854	0.7071	1.0000	1.0000	0.7071	0.7854	45
		cos *x*	cot *x*	tan *x*	sin *x*	*x (radians)*	x^0

Table III : Exponential, Hyperbolic and Trigonometric Functions

x	e^x	e^{-x}	sinh x	cosh x	tanh x	sin x	cos x
0.0	1.0000	1.0000	0.0000	1.0000	0.0000	0.0000	1.0000
0.1	1.1052	0.9048	0.1002	1.0050	0.0997	0.0998	0.9950
0.2	1.2214	0.8187	0.2013	1.0201	0.1974	0.1987	0.9801
0.3	1.3499	0.7408	0.3045	1.0453	0.2913	0.2955	0.9553
0.4	1.4918	0.6703	0.4108	1.0811	0.3799	0.3894	0.9211
0.5	1.6487	0.6065	0.5211	1.1276	0.4621	0.4794	0.8776
0.6	1.8221	0.5488	0.6367	1.1855	0.5370	0.5646	0.8253
0.7	2.0138	0.4966	0.7586	1.2552	0.6044	0.6442	0.7648
0.8	2.2255	0.4493	0.8881	1.3374	0.6640	0.7174	0.6967
0.9	2.4596	0.4066	1.0265	1.4331	0.7163	0.7833	0.6216
1.0	2.7183	0.3679	1.1752	1.5431	0.7616	0.8415	0.5403
1.1	3.0042	0.3329	1.3356	1.6685	0.8005	0.8912	0.4536
1.2	3.3201	0.3012	1.5095	1.8107	0.8337	0.9320	0.3624
1.3	3.6603	0.2725	1.6984	1.9709	0.8617	0.9636	0.2675
1.4	4.0552	0.2466	1.9043	2.1509	0.8854	0.9854	0.1700
1.5	4.4817	0.2231	2.1293	2.3524	0.9051	0.9975	0.0707
1.6	4.9530	0.2019	2.3756	2.5775	0.9217	0.9996	– 0.0292
1.7	5.4739	0.1827	2.6456	2.8283	0.9354	0.9917	– 0.1288
1.8	6.0496	0.1653	2.9422	3.1075	0.9468	0.9738	– 0.2272
1.9	6.6859	0.1496	3.2682	3.4177	0.9562	0.9463	– 0.3233
2.0	7.3891	0.1353	3.6269	3.7622	0.9640	0.9093	– 0.4161
2.1	8.1662	0.1225	4.0219	4.1443	0.9704	0.8632	– 0.5048
2.2	9.0250	0.1108	4.4571	4.5679	0.9757	0.8085	– 0.5885
2.3	9.9742	0.1003	4.9370	5.0372	0.9801	0.7457	– 0.6663
2.4	11.0232	0.0907	5.4662	5.5569	0.9837	0.6755	– 0.7374
2.5	12.1825	0.0821	6.0502	6.1323	0.9866	0.5985	– 0.8011
2.6	13.4637	0.0743	6.6947	6.7690	0.9890	0.5155	– 0.8569
2.7	14.8797	0.0672	7.4063	7.4735	0.9910	0.4274	– 0.9041
2.8	16.4446	0.0608	8.1919	8.2527	0.9926	0.3350	– 0.9422
2.9	18.1741	0.0550	9.0596	9.1146	0.9940	0.2392	– 0.9710
3.0	20.0855	0.0498	10.0179	10.0677	0.9950	0.1411	– 0.9900
3.1	22.1979	0.0450	11.0764	11.1215	0.9959	0.0416	– 0.9991
3.2	24.5325	0.0408	12.2459	12.2366	0.9967	– 0.0584	– 0.9983
3.3	27.1126	0.0369	13.5379	13.5748	0.9973	– 0.1577	– 0.9875
3.4	29.9641	0.0334	14.9654	14.9987	0.9978	– 0.2555	– 0.9668
3.5	33.1154	0.0302	16.5426	16.5728	0.9982	– 0.3508	– 0.9365

APPENDIX

Table 1 : NORMAL TABLE
AREAS UNDER THE STANDARD NORMAL

$$\text{CURVE} = \frac{1}{\sqrt{2\pi}} \int_0^z e^{-\frac{z^2}{2}} dz$$

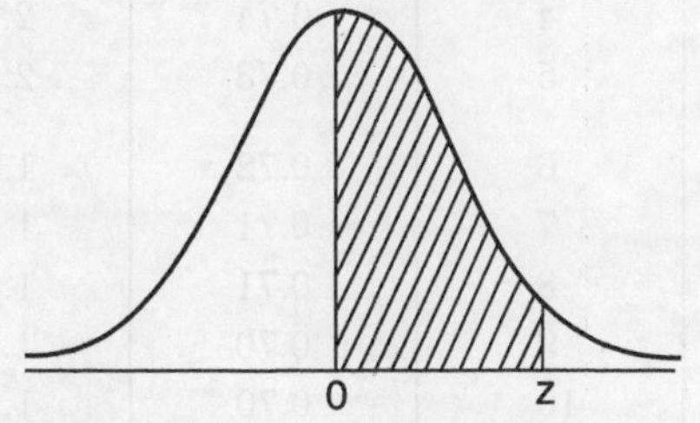

z	.00	.01	.02	.03	.04	.05	.06	.07	.08	.09
0.0	.0000	.0040	.0080	.0120	.0160	.0199	.0239	.0279	.0319	.0359
0.1	.0398	.0438	.0478	.0517	.0557	.0596	.0636	.0675	.0714	.0754
0.2	.0793	.0832	.0871	.0910	.0948	.0987	.1026	.1064	.1103	.1141
0.3	.1179	.1217	.1255	.1293	.1331	.1368	.1406	.1443	.1480	.1517
0.4	.1554	.1591	.1628	.1664	.1700	.1736	.1772	.1808	.1844	.1879
0.5	.1915	.1950	.1985	.2019	.2054	.2088	.2123	.2157	.2190	.2224
0.6	.2257	.2291	.2324	.2357	.2389	.2422	.2454	.2485	.2517	.2549
0.7	.2580	.2611	.2642	.2673	.2704	.2734	.2764	.2794	.2823	.2852
0.8	.2881	.2910	.2939	.2967	.2995	.3023	.3051	.3078	.3106	.3133
0.9	.3159	3186	.3212	.3238	.3264	.3289	.3315	.3340	.3365	.3389
1.0	.3413	.3438	.3461	.3485	.3508	.3531	.3554	.3577	.3599	.3621
1.1	.3643	3665	.3686	.3708	.8729	.3749	.3770	.3790	.3810	.3830
1.2	.3849	.3869	.3888	.3907	.3925	.3944	.3962	.3980	.3997	.4015
1.3	.4032	.4049	.4066	.4082	.4099	.4115	.4131	.4147	.4162	.4177
1.4	.4192	.4207	.4222	4236	.4251	.4265	.4279	.4292	.4306	.4319
1.5	.4332	.4345	.4357	.4370	.4382	.4394	.4406	.4418	.4429	.4441
1.6	.4452	.4463	.4474	.4484	.4495	.4505	.4515	.4525	.4535	.4545
1.7	.4554	.4564	.4573	.4582	.4591	.4599	.4608	.4616	.4625	.4633
1.8	.4641	.4649	.4656	.4664	.4671	.4678	.4686	.4693	.4699	.4706
1.9	.4713	.4719	.4726	.4732	.4738	.4744	.4750	.4756	.4761	.4767
2.0	.4772	.4778	.4783	.4788	.4793	.4798	.4803	.4808	.4812	.4817
2.1	.4821	.4826	.4830	.4834	.4838	.4842	.4846	.4850	.4854	.4857
2.2	.4861	.4864	.4868	.4871	.4875	.4878	.4881	.4884	.4887	.4890
2.3	.4893	.4896	.4898	.4901	4904	.4906	.4909	.4911	.4913	.4916
2.4	.4918	.4920	.4922	.4925	.4927	.4929	.4931	.4932	.4934	.4936
2.5	.4938	.4940	.4941	.4943	.4245	.4946	.4948	.4949	.4951	.4952
2.6	.4953	.4955	.4956	.4957	.4959	.4930	.4961	.4962	.4963	.4964
2.7	.4965	.4966	.4967	.4968	.4969	.4970	.4971	.4972	.4973	.4974
2.8	.4974	.4975	.4976	.4977	.4977	.4978	.4979	.4979	.4980	.4981
2.9	.4981	.4982	.4982	.4983	.4984	.4984	.4985	.4985	.4986	.4986
3.0	.4987	.4987	.4987	.4988	.4988	.4989	.4999	.4989	.4990	.4990
3.1	.4990	.4991	.4991	.4991	.4992	.4992	.4992	.4992	.4993	.4993

Table 2 : Significant values t_v (α) of t-Distribution (Two Tall Areas) [| t | > t_v(α)] = α

d.f.	*Probability (Level of Significance)*					
(v)	*0.50*	*0.10*	*0.05*	*0.02*	*0.01*	*0.001*
1	1.00	6.31	12.71	31.82	63.66	636.62
2	0.82	0.92	4.30	6.97	6.93	31.60
3	0.77	2.32	3.18	4.54	5.84	12.94
4	0.74	2.13	2.78	3.75	4.60	8.61
5	0.73	2.02	2.57	3.37	4.03	6.86
6	0.72	1.94	2.45	3.14	3.71	5.96
7	0.71	1.90	2.37	3.00	3.50	5.41
8	0.71	1.80	2.31	2.90	3.36	5.04
9	0.70	1.83	2.26	2.82	3.25	4.78
10	0.70	1.81	2.23	2.76	3.17	4.59
11	0.70	1.80	2.20	2.72	3.11	4.44
12	0.70	1.78	2.18	2.68	3.06	4.32
13	0.69	1.77	2.16	2.05	3.01	4.22
14	0.69	1.76	2.15	2.62	2.98	4.14
15	0.69	1.75	2.13	2.60	2.95	4.07
16	0.69	1.75	2.12	2.58	2.92	4.02
17	0.69	1.74	2.11	2.57	2.90	3.97
18	0.69	1.73	2.10	2.55	2.88	3.92
19	0.69	1.73	2.09	2.54	2.86	3.88
20	0.69	1.73	2.09	2.53	2.85	3.85
21	0.69	1.72	2.08	2.52	2.83	3.83
22	0.69	1.72	2.07	2.51	2.42	3.79
23	0.69	1.71	2.07	2.50	2.81	3.77
24	0.69	1.71	2.06	2.49	2.80	3.75
25	0.68	1.71	2.06	2.49	2.79	3.73
26	0.68	1.71	2.06	2.48	2.78	3.71
27	0.68	1.70	2.05	2.47	2.77	3.69
28	0.68	1.70	2.05	2.47	2.76	3.67
29	0.68	1.70	2.05	2.46	2.76	3.66
30	0.68	1.70	2.04	2.46	2.75	3.65
∞	0.67	1.65	1.96	2.33	2.58	3.29

Table 3 : F-Distribution

Values of F for F-Distributions with 0.05 of the Area in the Right Tall*

Degrees of freedom for numerator ⟶ (columns); ⟵ *Degrees of freedom for denominator* (rows)

	1	2	3	4	5	6	7	8	9	10	12	15	20	24	20	40	60	120	∞
1	161	200	216	225	230	234	237	239	241	242	244	246	248	249	250	251	252	253	254
2	18.5	19.0	19.2	19.2	19.3	19.3	19.4	19.4	19.4	19.4	19.4	19.4	19.4	19.5	19.5	19.5	19.5	19.5	19.5
3	10.1	9.55	9.28	9.12	9.01	9.94	8.89	8.85	8.81	8.79	8.74	8.70	8.66	8.64	8.62	8.59	8.57	8.55	8.53
4	7.71	6.94	6.59	6.39	6.26	6.16	6.09	6.04	6.00	5.96	5.91	5.86	5.80	5.77	5.75	5.72	5.69	6.66	5.63
5	6.61	5.79	5.41	5.19	5.05	4.95	4.88	4.82	4.77	4.74	4.68	4.62	4.56	4.53	4.50	4.46	4.43	4.40	4.37
6	5.99	5.14	4.76	4.53	4.39	4.28	4.21	4.15	4.10	4.06	4.00	3.94	3.87	3.84	3.81	3.77	3.74	3.70	3.67
7	5.59	4.74	4.35	4.12	3.97	3.87	3.79	3.73	3.68	3.64	3.57	3.51	3.44	3.41	3.38	3.34	3.30	3.27	3.23
8	5.32	4.46	4.07	3.84	3.69	3.58	3.50	3.44	3.39	3.35	3.28	3.22	3.15	3.12	3.08	3.04	3.01	2.97	2.93
9	5.12	4.26	3.86	3.63	3.48	3.37	3.29	3.23	3.18	3.14	3.07	3.01	2.94	2.90	2.86	2.83	2.79	2.75	2.71
10	4.96	4.10	3.71	3.48	3.33	3.22	3.14	3.07	3.02	2.98	2.91	2.85	2.77	2.74	2.70	2.66	2.62	2.58	2.54
11	4.84	3.98	3.59	3.36	3.20	3.09	3.01	2.95	2.90	2.85	2.79	2.72	2.65	2.61	2.57	2.53	2.49	2.45	2.40
12	4.75	3.89	3.49	3.26	3.11	3.00	2.91	2.85	2.80	2.75	2.69	2.62	2.54	2.51	2.47	2.43	2.38	2.34	2.30
13	4.67	3.81	3.41	3.18	3.03	2.92	2.83	2.77	2.71	2.67	2.60	2.53	2.46	2.42	2.38	2.34	2.30	2.25	2.21
14	4.60	3.74	3.34	3.11	3.96	2.85	2.76	2.70	2.65	2.60	2.53	2.46	2.39	2.35	2.31	2.27	2.22	2.18	2.13
15	4.54	3.68	3.29	3.06	3.90	2.79	2.71	2.64	2.59	2.54	2.48	2.40	2.33	2.29	2.25	2.20	2.16	2.11	2.07
16	4.49	3.63	3.24	3.01	2.85	2.74	2.66	2.59	2.54	2.49	2.42	2.35	2.28	2.24	2.19	2.15	2.11	2.06	2.01
17	4.45	3.59	3.20	2.96	2.81	2.70	2.61	2.55	2.49	2.45	2.38	2.31	2.23	2.19	2.15	2.10	2.06	2.01	1.96
18	4.41	3.55	3.16	2.93	2.77	2.66	2.58	2.51	2.46	2.41	2.34	2.27	2.19	2.15	2.11	2.06	2.02	1.97	1.92
19	4.38	3.52	3.13	2.90	2.74	2.63	2.54	2.48	2.42	2.38	2.31	2.23	2.16	2.11	2.07	2.03	1.98	1.93	1.88
20	4.35	3.49	3.10	2.87	2.17	2.60	2.51	2.45	2.39	2.35	2.28	2.20	2.12	2.08	2.04	1.99	1.95	1.90	1.84
21	4.32	3.47	3.07	2.84	2.68	2.57	2.49	2.42	2.37	2.32	2.25	2.18	2.10	2.05	2.01	1.96	1.92	1.87	1.81
22	4.30	3.44	3.05	2.82	2.66	2.55	2.46	2.40	2.34	2.30	2.23	2.15	2.07	2.03	1.98	1.94	1.89	1.84	1.78
23	4.28	3.42	3.03	2.80	2.64	2.53	2.44	2.37	2.32	2.27	2.20	2.13	2.05	2.01	1.96	1.91	1.86	1.81	1.76
24	4.26	3.40	3.01	2.78	2.62	2.51	2.42	2.36	2.30	2.25	2.18	2.11	2.03	1.98	1.94	1.98	1.84	1.79	1.73
25	4.24	3.39	2.99	2.76	2.60	2.94	2.40	2.34	2.28	2.24	2.16	2.29	2.01	1.96	1.92	1.87	1.82	1.77	1.71
30	4.17	3.32	2.92	2.69	2.53	2.42	2.33	2.27	2.21	2.16	2.09	2.01	1.93	1.89	1.84	1.79	1.74	1.64	1.62
40	4.08	3.23	2.84	2.61	2.45	2.34	2.25	2.18	2.12	2.08	2.00	1.92	1.84	1.79	1.74	1.69	1.64	1.58	1.51
60	4.00	3.15	2.76	2.53	2.37	2.25	2.17	2.10	2.04	1.99	1.92	1.84	1.75	1.70	1.65	1.59	1.53	1.47	1.39
120	3.92	3.07	2.68	2.45	2.29	2.18	2.09	2.02	1.96	1.91	1.83	1.75	1.66	1.61	1.55	1.50	1.43	1.35	1.25
∞	3.84	3.00	2.60	2.37	2.21	2.10	2.01	1.94	1.88	1.83	1.75	1.67	1.57	1.52	1.46	1.39	1.32	1.22	1.00

Table 4 : Chi-Square
Significant Values χ^2 (α) of Chi-Square Distribution Right Tail Areas for Given Probability α,
$P = P_r (\chi^2 > \chi^2 (\alpha)) = \alpha$
And is Degrees of Freedom (d.f.)

Degree of freedom (ν)	*Probability (Level of Significance)*						
	0.99	*0.95*	*0.50*	*0.10*	*0.05*	*0.02*	*0.01*
1	.000157	.00393	.455	2.706	3.841	5.214	6.635
2	.0201	.103	1.386	4.605	5.991	7.824	9.210
3	.115	.352	2.366	6.251	7.815	9.837	11.341
4	.297	.711	3.357	7.779	9.488	11.668	13.277
5	.554	1.145	4.351	9.236	11.070	13.388	15.086
6	.872	2.635	5.348	10.645	12.592	15.033	16.812
7	1.239	2.167	6.346	12.017	14.067	16.622	18.475
8	1.646	2.733	7.344	13.362	15.507	18.168	20.090
9	2.088	3.325	8.343	14.684	16.919	19.679	21.669
10	2.558	3.940	9.340	15.987	18.307	21.161	23.209
11	3.053	4.575	10.341	17.275	19.675	22.618	24.725
12	3.571	5.226	11.340	18.549	21.026	24.054	26.217
13	4.107	5.892	12.340	19.812	22.362	25.472	27.688
14	4.660	6.571	13.339	21.064	23.685	26.873	29.141
15	4.229	7.261	14.339	22.307	24.996	28.259	30.578
16	5.812	7.962	15.338	23.542	26.296	29.633	32.000
17	6.408	8.672	15.338	24.769	27.587	30.995	33.409
18	7.015	9.390	17.338	25.989	28.869	32.346	34.805
19	7.633	10.117	18.338	27.204	30.144	33.687	36.191
20	8.260	10.851	19.337	28.412	31.410	35.020	37.566
21	8.897	11.591	20.337	29.615	32.671	36.343	38.932
22	9.542	12.338	21.337	30.813	33.924	37.659	40.289
23	10.196	13.091	22.337	32.007	35.172	38.968	41.638
24	10.856	13.848	23.337	32.196	36.415	40.270	42.980
25	11.524	14.611	24.337	34.382	37.65	41.566	44.314
26	12.198	15.379	25.336	35.363	38.885	41.856	45.642
27	12.879	16.151	26.336	36.741	40.113	41.140	46.963
28	13.565	16.928	27.336	37.916	41.337	45.419	48.278
29	14.256	17.708	28.336	39.087	42.557	46.693	49.588
30	14.933	18.493	29.336	40.256	43.773	47.962	50.892

Note. For degrees of freedom (v) greater than 30, the quantity $\sqrt{2\chi^2} - \sqrt{2\nu - 1}$ may be used as a normal variate with unit variance.

INDEX